The Best Training-Ground for Archaeologists

Francis Haverfield and the Invention of Romano-British Archaeology

P. W. M. Freeman

Oxbow Books

Published by

Oxbow Books, Oxford, Great Britain

© P.W.M. Freeman 2007

ISBN 978-1-84217-280-3

A CIP record for this book is available from the British Library

Typeset in 9pt New Baskerville by M.C. Bishop at The Armatura Press

This book is available direct from
Oxbow Books, Oxford, Great Britain
(Phone: 01865-241249; Fax: 01865-794449)

and

The David Brown Book Company
PO Box 511, Oakville, CT 06779, USA
(Phone: 860-945-9329; Fax: 860-945-9468)

or from our website

www.oxbowbooks.com

Printed in Great Britain by
Short Run Press, Exeter

CONTENTS

ABBREVIATIONS

Am J Archaeol	American Journal of Archaeology
Annual Brit School Athens	Annual of the British School at Athens
Antiqs J	Antiquaries Journal
Archaeol Aeliana	Archaeologia Aeliana
Archaeol Cambrensis	Archaeologia Cambrensis
Archaeol J	Archaeological Journal
Archaeol Rev	Archaeological Review
Biog Jb Alterthumskde	Biographisches Jahrbuch für Alterthumskunde
Brit Museum Quart	British Museum Quarterly
Bull Am Schools Oriental Res	Bulletin of the American Schools of Oriental Research
Bull Am Soc Papyrologists	Bulletin of the American Society of Papyrologists
Bull Inst Archaeol	Bulletin of the Institute of Archaeology
Bull Yorkshire Archaeol Soc Roman Antiq Sect	Bulletin of the Yorkshire Archaeological Society Roman Antiquities Section
Cartog J	Cartographic Journal
CIL	Corpus Inscriptionum Latinarum
Class Assoc Proc	Classical Association Proceedings
Class Rev	Classical Review
Collingwood Stud	Collingwood Studies
Current Archaeol	Current Archaeology
English Hist Rev	English Historical Review
Essex Archaeol Hist	Essex Archaeology & History
Geog J	Geographical Journal
Geog Rev	Geographical Review
Hist Archaeol Rev	History & Archaeology Review
Hist J	Historical Journal
J Architect Archaeol Hist Soc Chester North Wales	Journal of the Architectural, Archaeological & Historical Society of Chester & North Wales
J Brit Archaeol Assoc	Journal of the British Archaeological Association
J Brit Assoc	Journal of British Association
J Chester Archaeol Soc	Journal of the Chester (& North Wales) Archaeological (& Historical) Society
J Egyptian Archaeol	Journal of Egyptian Archaeology
J Hellenic Stud	Journal of Hellenic Studies
J Philol	Journal of Philology
J Roman Archaeol	Journal of Roman Archaeology
J Roman Stud	Journal of Roman Studies
Liverpool Annals Archaeol Anthropol	Liverpool Annals of Archaeology & Anthropology
Liverpool Class Monthly	Liverpool Classical Monthly
NC	Numismatic Chronicle
Norwegian Archaeol Rev	Norwegian Archaeological Review
ODNB	The Oxford Dictionary of National Biography

Palestine Explor Quart	*Palestine Exploration Quarterly*
Oxford J Archaeol	*Oxford Journal of Archaeology*
Pap Brit School Rome	*Papers of the British School at Rome*
Philosoph Quart	*The Philosophical Quarterly*
Proc Brit Acad	*Proceedings of the British Academy*
Proc Cambridge Antiq Soc	*Proceedings of the Cambridge Antiquarian Society*
Proc Prehist Soc	*Proceedings of the Prehistoric Society*
Proc Soc Antiqs London/PSAL	*Proceedings of the Society of Antiquaries (of London)*
Proc Soc Antiqs Newcastle/PSAN	*Proceedings of the Society of Antiquaries of Newcastle*
Proc Soc Antiqs Scotland	*Proceedings of the Society of Antiquaries of Scotland*
Proc Somerset Archaeol Natural Hist Soc	*Proceedings of the Somersetshire Archaeological & Natural History Society*
Quart Rev	*The Quarterly Review*
RIB	*The Roman Inscriptions of Britain*
Scottish Archaeol Rev	*Scottish Archaeological Review*
Sussex Archaeol Colls	*Sussex Archaeological Collections*
Trans Bristol Gloucester Archaeol Soc	*Transactions of the Bristol & Gloucestershire Archaeological Society*
Trans Cambridge Huntingdon Archaeol Soc	*Transactions of the Cambridgeshire & Huntingdonshire Archaeological Society*
Trans Carmarthen Antiqs Soc	*Transactions of the Carmarthenshire Antiquaries Society*
Trans Cumberland Westmorland Antiq Archaeol Soc/TCWAAS	*Transactions of the Cumberland & Westmorland Antiquarian & Archaeological Society*
Trans Essex Archaeol Soc	*Transactions of the Essex Archaeological Society*
Trans Hist Soc Lancs Cheshire	*Transactions of the Historical Society of Lancashire & Cheshire*
Trans Hon Soc Cymmodorion	*Transactions of the Honourable Society of Cymmodorion*
Trans Thoroton Soc	*Transactions of the Thoroton Society*
Trans Woolhope Natural Field Club	*Transactions of the Woolhope Naturalists' Field Club*
Victorian Stud	*Victorian Studies*
Yorkshire Archaeol J	*Yorkshire Archaeological Journal*

PREFACE AND
ACKNOWLEDGEMENTS[1]

Not so long ago, I had dinner with a colleague from the ancient history section of SACE in the University of Liverpool. The conversation ranged wide, from news concerning the School through to less important but more enjoyable gossip. We discussed on-going work, during which I tried to explain the difficulties I was experiencing trying to write an already overdue review on a recently published monograph exploring the relationship of archaeology to ancient history. My problem was that as I read (and re-read) said text I found myself retreating back to opinions first formed when I was starting out as a postgraduate nearly 25 years ago. In short I was becoming dissatisfied again with the argument that (classical) archaeology was but a facet, albeit an equal partner, with mainstream ancient history. It was a surprise when my colleague argued the counter position, and went on to wax lyrical about how the two disciplines complement and enhance each other. To illustrate his argument he cited how closely epigraphy could work in tandem with archaeological evidence. His positivism was surprising. There was me the 'archaeologist' defending the sort of ancient history our monograph was attacking, while he, an ancient historian according to our university, was advancing the case for a rapprochement. He could justify his optimism with the simple statement, and here I have

---

1. The title ('The best training-ground for archaeologists') is from a lecture delivered by Sheppard Frere in 1987, although a case might be made for saying it was first coined by Mortimer Wheeler in 1955 (cf. Chap. 11 and App. 5 below). The full sentence is '...Roman Britain – as Wheeler stated 40 years ago – is still the best training-ground for archaeologists planning to work anywhere in the world' (Frere 1988: 6). In the lecture Frere offered a retrospective on progress in Romano-British archaeology since Haverfield. It seems appropriate to use it here as it expresses a sentiment with which Haverfield would have been in sympathy. To be sure Frere's opinions on the strength of Romano-British studies are the result of Haverfield and his work. A similar perspective was offered by Percy Gardner in an assessment of 50 years progress in classical archaeology written in 1926: 'Though the civilization of and art of (Roman) Britain were at a lower level than those of Gaul' yet they repay investigation. Their remains lie at our doors and their influence lies at the source of our national life. Moreover archaeological work in Britain is a good preparation for such work in Greece, or India or Egypt' (Gardner 1926: 25).

to paraphrase his response, that of course he could argue this because he was trained in the Oxford tradition where epigraphic material and archaeological facts were 'hammered' home together. Whether or not his characterization of his training is accurate, it didn't take long for its implications to sink in. It explained how and why Francis Haverfield, who worked at Oxford over 100 years ago, worked in the way he did. It also explained the real nature of his legacy. In short, Haverfield was an Oxford ancient historian working in a way which was, and is still, largely unique in how epigraphy can inform the past. This statement might seem so obvious that it hardly merits mention. But in the context of this study it is significant in so much that it explains a corrective to the opinion that Haverfield was the first Romano-British scholar. It is undeniable that he was so, but it puts into context how he worked and what he thought was the purpose of Romano-British studies. This interpretation, developed in the following chapters, runs counter to the received version of Haverfield and his work.

I first became aware of Haverfield in the mid-1980s when I worked in the now defunct Dept of Ancient History and Classical Archaeology at the University of Sheffield's excavations at the Roman fort at Brough-on-Noe. This was a site originally excavated by a Haverfield contact, John Garstang in 1903. As was his practice, Haverfield visited the excavations. In the intervening years Haverfield's name cropped up, usually incidentally in other matters that were then preoccupying me. The most important of these was completing a PhD thesis. The subject of that study was an examination of how provinces were organized in the Roman empire with particular attention to those of the late Republic and early Principate. This was to include analysis of post-bellum settlements, the expression *redacta in formam provinciae* and what was believed to be associated with it, along with the various imperial policies connected with the development of the provinces. One aspect of the last element was the introduction of policies of 'romanization'. As the research developed, however, I realized the evidence that I had expected to illustrate the processes could not be found. What I began to appreciate was that the original question reflected the assumption that there was indeed a formal process of annexation. In fact, the assumption owed more to how modern historians believed it to be than what occurred in antiquity. The thesis then became an exercise in explaining how the assumption had arisen and why it was flawed. But it also necessitated decisions to restrict the range of topics that I planned to include in the thesis. One of the casualties was consideration of the archaeological evidence for integration and assimilation. In the years since the thesis (Freeman 1989), I developed a number of themes related to the process of annexation, using case examples, relative to the model I advanced in the thesis (e.g. Freeman 1994; 1996b; 1998). The unifying theme in these studies is that it is difficult to speak of a specific, systematic process of annexation but that the emergence of provinces was the product of a much more gradual sequence of events. One of the implications of this explanation was that it distanced the part of archaeological evidence as an indicator of provincial organizations.

After completing the thesis I returned to the relevance of the archaeological evidence for the evolution of provincial entities. With hindsight what I began to discover was that everything that had been said about the (cultural) integration of the province of Britannia into the Roman empire seemed to go back to Haverfield. His name was usually found in association with statements that he *was* Romano-British studies. In precisely what capacity was normally left unexplained but the frequency of the accolade was intriguing. The more one read around the publications of Romano-British archaeology in the first quarter of the twentieth century, the more the context of his work seemed clearer. The range of activities in which he was involved became increasingly surprising and yet their significance seems to have been lost in the intervening years. This then led to more than a passing interest in the developing debate about where Romano-British studies was leading. For it was at this time that there started to appear a number of publications which challenged what the discipline had become. By implication, the arguments were not positive, but tended to call for a fresh impetus to the study of Britain under Roman rule. It was in particular the publication of Martin Millett's *The Romanization of Britain* in 1990 which led me back to thinking about what I thought was Haverfield's legacy. At the same time the writings of John Barrett, Richard Hingley, Eleanor Scott, Jane Webster and others helped to clarify ideas I was starting to form. What struck me was what was required was a historiographical appreciation of the study of Roman Britain. What surprised me was that I was unaware that this sort of study had not previously been attempted. The nearest was Rick Jones' (1987) study of the archaeologists of Roman Britain. In the intervening years, there have appeared various types of assessments of the form and structure of Romano-British studies but they tend either to be in the form of research agendas which make little more than passing reference to the backdrop to the subject (e.g. James and Millett 2001) or else rather one-dimensional wish-lists (e.g. Hingley 1999). In short, there is still the need for a more critical overview of why Romano-British studies have become the way they are.

While my original interest in the work of Francis Haverfield lay with his work on the subject of 'romanization', as a natural corollary to this I began to take an interest in the career and then the life of the man. As that work proceeded and it become apparent that he was an elusive figure to research, my curiosity developed as I tried to add to what seemed to be a pool of primary source material which was disappointingly slight in comparison to the declared influence of the man. That search became increasingly difficult as I found it harder and harder to identify, let along gain access to, decent archive collections of Haverfield material. This then forced me back to a much closer reading of his extant works.

The reason for a study of the career of Francis Haverfield is simple to explain. The past decade has seen the publication of a number of monographs, and articles exploring the lives and influences of individuals with archaeological interest and who flourished at the end of the nineteenth and the early years of the twentieth centuries. Notable examples include reappraisals of David Hogarth (Lock 1990), Thomas Ashby (Hodges 2000), and Donald Atkinson (Wallace 1994). Jane Harrison (Beard 2000) and now Eugénie Strong (Dyson 2004) are the most recent additions. Complementing this phenomenon has been the appearance of a number of studies which explore the condition of archaeology and classics as academic and social disciplines at the same time (e.g. Stray 1998; Hingley 2000, 2001a, 2001b), along with histories of some of the organizations intended to advance the cause of each (Wallace Hadrill 2001; Todd 2003). A common feature in virtually all the scholarship cited here is Francis Haverfield and the way he impinged on the work of others. Not only was he an intimate of many of these individuals, he was at the same time a leading player in the work of such organizations and his influence played out on the standing of the discipline of archaeology at the time. To be sure he is frequently cited as such in these works. The references, however, are made more in passing rather than being based on a sound assessment of his contribution. Closer examination shows that the acknowledgements are more usually based on repeating received wisdom, wisdom manufactured by others, largely at the time of his death, and repeated almost verbatim in the succeeding decades. Therefore a fresh appraisal of Haverfield's career is desirable, if not necessary. Not only would it link him with the world described by others, more importantly a study is necessary because re-examination of the received version of his career reveals a slightly different impression of the man, a fresh impression which in turn has implications for the development and status of Romano-British studies in this country.

With hindsight there is one article in particular, a relatively short piece, which has influenced me in a way that I have not really appreciated until recently. Over fifteen years ago Rick Jones wrote a piece which attempted '...to understand those peoples who have contributed to the study of Roman Britain and to identify something of what has influenced their views.' Jones established a prosopographial sequence of connections and inferences but acknowledged that he could only scratch the surface and that a fuller study '...involving interviewing people would be instructive, but a rather larger enterprise than (his) can be' (Jones 1987: 84). I am not aware that I consciously decided to take up Jones' challenge but I find what is offered here does address, at least in part, his call. The undertone of his argument was the insularity of Romano-British studies, and more generally, Roman provincial studies. Jones argued that Roman Britain '...has always been a small academic field where most of the main figures have been personally well-known to each other. This means that it is not always easy to disentangle who influenced whom and who was friendly with whom' (p. 84). I would now doubt that it is difficult to disentangle such connections but this monograph endeavours to examine the relationship of at least three of the most important individuals on Romano-British studies. In doing so it has uncovered a series of connections and influence which have been missed in modern appraisals of the same three individuals. Jones further observed the:

> ... enclosed nature of the study of Roman Britain is reinforced by the rarity of contributions from specialists from other periods or countries ...The reluctance of foreign scholars to comment on Roman Britain contrast with the British tradition of being prepared to set off to enter uncharted archaeological territory anywhere in the world. This hangover of Imperial confidence can cause some bemusement among local archaeologists and among those of other countries who do not share the same foreign ambitions. The lack of interchange of ideas within Roman provincial archaeology is remarkable, when it would seem that there was so much in common. Only in the study of Frontiers has there been much common ground established; yet even the Limeskongresses are dominated by the particular and the descriptive, rather than broader analytical discussions. This is partly a function of the particularist nature of much archaeology, where so many problems can seem specific to the material handled. Yet what this has meant is that archaeology is made up of much more strongly national traditions of research than is common in other subjects (p. 84).

The study presented in the chapters below endeavours to explain why some of the characteristics highlighted by Jones have come about. Most, if not all of them, can be attributed to the work and influence of Haverfield. It is for this reason that if there is any merit in the following chapters then it is because they place the history of Romano-British studies in their contemporary European context.

There is one other factor, which has helped to condition this study. There has in the past decade or so been some discussion about whether or not Romano-British studies as a subject taught at university level is experiencing a sort of crisis. The backdrop to this debate is set out in Chapter 1. While some would maintain that there is no real problem, and others argue to the contrary, the debate is predicated on accepting the presumption that Roman archaeology is, and should remain, a major component of a university degree in the discipline. In this respect, Haverfield is presented as the pivotal position in the standing of the subject. For those who believe there is no crisis in Roman studies, it was his work, as 'the father of Romano-British studies', which put in place the basic structure of the subject as it is now understood. Not only did he start the definition of the categories of evidence which are now studied, in creating the historical framework for the subject, he established the interpretative framework for the assessment of the consequences of the Roman occupation of these islands. As such we continue to work within the confines of his legacy. On the other hand, those who argue that 'RB studies' is experiencing problems would have us believe that it is because of that legacy that the subject has tended to ossify into the rather self-fulfilling, uncontentious repetition of the achievements of Roman civilization. In this respect Haverfield, again acknowledging his central position in the creation of the intellectual framework of the subject, has been blamed to the point where some have dismissed his conclusions as anachronistic if not unpalatable. When I commenced work on Haverfield I tended to accept uncritically the reputation of the man. My opinions shifted in the mid-1990s in response to a number of publications which seemed to me to be unfairly critical of him and his work. Rather than dismiss him simply as a product of a time which produced attitudes and interpretation which some today regard as unacceptable, I now argue that a more nuanced understanding of the man is necessary if one is to appreciate why and how he wrote as he did. Likewise it was evident that his opinions were much more subtle in their evolution and exposition than the rather generalised and crude accusation that he was a defender of western (British) colonial imperialism. The main criticism in this respect of the man was his work on 'romanization'. At the same time, however, I was becoming increasingly disenchanted with the way that the romanization debate was developing. Although there was evolving a more sensitive appreciation of how degrees of romanization had been identified, the debate seemed to be following along two broadly parallel lines: between those who continued to argue for a form of positive romanization, perhaps managed explicitly or else implicitly by the imperial authorities, but one which brought benefits for those who wished to romanize for whatever reasons they did, and those on the distaff side who argued for the more negative reaction to it and in particular what was becoming known as post-colonial resistance on the part of elements of provincial populations. In either case the phenomenon of romanization remained central: the belief was one either participated for whatever reasons or one resisted. The overarching omission in this debate is what is Roman material culture? The very building blocks on which all theories of the phenomenon of romanization are based have never been assessed. But make such objects 'Roman'? I had hinted at some of these inconsistencies in a couple of publications, but I always intended that a study of Haverfield should include a detailed reappraisal of his work on the subject which was then intended to complete the shunting of the romanization debate into the intellectual cul-de-sac where it deserved to be placed. As it has transpired, although I still believe the romanization debate remains a red herring, I have decided to omit from this study a detailed exposition of why Haverfield's theory of romanization is no longer relevant to Romano-British studies in the twenty-first century. While I hope to develop this opinion elsewhere, I can justify the decision to exclude the issue from this study for two reasons. The practicalities of size mean that something has had to be dropped from an already over-long manuscript. Secondly, it became apparent as research on Haverfield's career and work developed that what was perhaps more important was what his contemporaries thought of his work and how they, in continuing it, have come to influence how Romano-British studies are perceived today. As will become evident, although the outline of Haverfield's career is reasonably clear, the way that the major events of it as well as the statements he authored are now regarded is the consequence of a particular group of his associates. What also became evident was, despite the central position he is afforded in the pantheon of Romano-British scholarship, the condition of the subject at the time of his death was far from rosy. Indeed I conclude that if the discipline is experiencing some sort of crisis today, it is reminiscent to that it experienced in the years between 1920 and 1945. Rather than spend time trying to explain why Haverfield's opinion on romanization were in fact more a minor component of his work, I think it more urgent to explain why the subject went into decline after his death and yet some still regard him as the great figure.

It is for all these reasons that this is not the work on Haverfield that some might expect. It is not a biography in the conventional sense, in that I have chosen not to construct it as a simple chronological narrative of his career, topped and tailed with passages on the context of his work or career. At the same time, if I had elected to follow a thematic base, then it would make it difficult to follow one of the features that becomes apparent in Haverfield's career: the way his thinking and opinion on certain issues evolved with time. The compromise is to adopt a halfway position, where the text follows a loose chronological structure imposed on an examination of a number of facets of his work.

Whatever Haverfield might have attempted, and irrespective of how successfully it was accomplished, there remains the fact that his reputation post-1919 underwent a degree of modification and redefinition on the part of his main (intellectual and institutional) heirs. In other words, Haverfield's reputation, as reported today, owes as much to those who wrote of him at the time of death as the enduring quality of his own work. During the research for this monograph Mary Beard's (2000) study of the life of Jane Harrison was published. I was keen to read what was in effect a double biography, of Harrison and her Cambridge contemporary Eugénie Strong (née Sellars), not least because the pair had connections with Haverfield. Both reviewed for the fledgling *Journal of Roman Studies* and knew a number of Haverfield associates. I have to admit, however, I approached Beard's work merely as a biography. As this study neared completion and I began to contemplate how to present Haverfield, his life and legacy, I went back to Beard along with some other recent biographies – Hodges on Thomas Ashby (Hodges 2000) and other works of archaeological biography and historiography (e.g. Baldon 1998; Kuklick 1996). What surprised, and worried, me was the way I was presenting my version of Haverfield's life in a manner displayed by Beard for Harrison, where Beard:

> ...raises the question of who wins (and how) in the competition for academic fame. Mary Beard captures Harrison's ability to create her own image. And she contrasts her story with that of Eugenie Sellers Strong, a younger contemporary and one time intimate ...but who lost the race for renown. The setting for the story is Harrison's career in Classical scholarship in this period – its internal arguments and allegiances and especially the influence of the anthropological strain ...Questioning the common criteria for identifying intellectual 'influence' and 'movements', Beard exposes the mythology that is embedded in the history of Classics (Publisher's blurb).

It is true there are many similarities in how Harrison and Haverfield's lives have been written by others. As the following discussion will show, the same considerations and paradoxes underpin assessments of Haverfield's life and in particular how others have used his reputation and the memory created of him. I am not aware of consciously imitating Beard's approach, in fact I know I did not, not least because I found some of her conclusions about Harrison (and Strong) slight and ephemeral, being derived from some questionable evidence, as others have noted. Stephen Dyson has been especially critical of this form of analysis.[2] As will be argued in the following chapters, however, I hope to be able to demonstrate that there is better evidence for arguing that there has been a degree of reinterpretation and re-invention of who Haverfield was and what he has stood for which in turn has resulted in misrepresentation of what he tried to argue for in the nature of Roman Britain and the future development of its study.

I am the first to admit that the text offered here has enjoyed too long a gestation. If I had known it would have taken as long as it has, I would probably never have embarked on it. The research for and the writing of it has been spread over a number of years of short periods of intense activity interspersed by runs of inactivity caused in part by what became cul-de-sacs; involvement in other things; at other times lethargy and otherwise periodic losses of interest. Sitting back and reflecting on what has been produced, the exercise has been at various times a pleasure, at other times an ordeal. The pleasure is from the exercise of reading and appreciating the relationship of seemingly unconnected facts; the pain having to go through the exercise of committing to paper why those facts were, to me at least, significant. But there is another dimension to the self-inflicted pain. Because of the difficulties of tracking down Haverfield material, and therefore the interruptions caused by integrating that which had come to light in the intervening years, and because the preparation of this monograph has been so protracted, there is the corollary that no matter how good I thought was the reading at the time, still one's increasing age, new publications and a waning memory mean that I know that my remembrance of things I know I have read is flawed. I also know that over the years, my changing opinions have been subconsciously influenced by publications, usually short articles but all the more important for their brevity, which I may have

2. For example, Beard '...works from the postmodern concept of archives as the creation of people with agendas and that frees her to shape material to suit her purposes' (Dyson 2001b: 715).

not given all the credit they are due. Re-reading some of these pieces now emphasises my debts and deficiencies yet more. One other consequence of the passage of time is that, unavoidably, I have found my opinions of Haverfield's career and his own opinions have evolved. Some of these changes were easy to introduce to this text, but others are subtler as I have found my own outlook has changed and I have been imperceptibly influenced by the opinions of others.

Throughout the research there has been one abiding worry that, in a small way, has contributed to the delay in this work appearing. Many of the works I have cited have had the advantage on being able to call on sizable archives of material related to their subjects. Perhaps naïvely I believed the same had to exist for Haverfield. But as will become evident, but for one exception, I have failed to track down anything of substance. In some instances I find this hard to believe and remain convinced that in certain places there is some material, perhaps unrecognized, or otherwise unavailable. My abiding fear is that as soon as this work is published more material will come to light which will shatter much of what follows here.

Fifteen years on, my attitudes to Haverfield remain ambivalent. What results is not necessarily a rosy picture. Indeed I have to admit that I do not find him to be an especially likable individual. Many of his contemporaries reported the same experience, although to be fair closer friends testified to a different character close up. But there again, some of his friends do not come over as especially likable souls. I am the first to admit, however, the problems with the source material means that he is an extremely difficult character to pin down to the point that although I believe I have a reasonable control over his published output, I am no closer to the person.

Acknowledgments

It remains to acknowledge those who, in a variety of ways, have shaped or facilitated the work presented here. I have elected to publish this monograph in the format that it appears here simply because I have become disillusioned with the current state of academic publishing. I have lost track of the number of publishers who expressed an interest in taking on this text, only to see them change their minds either because of changes in their publishing policy (at least one stating that they were now only interested in text books) or because the feeling was there was no market for a study of this sort. At the same time I have wanted to retain a degree of control over the final version of the text. The result is perhaps too long and perhaps more discursive than some would like, but so what? It is for these reasons that I am grateful to Mike Bishop and his willingness to edit it and taken on the arrangements for its publication.

Grants and awards for periods of research or for visits to consult archives were made by the Macdonald Bequest at the University of Glasgow, the Research Development Fund of the University of Liverpool, and the Research Fund of what was then the School of Archaeology, Classical and Oriental Studies at the Liverpool University (now the School of Classics, Archaeology and Egyptology). The penultimate push towards completing this text was facilitated by the award of funding for two semesters research leave from the (then) Arts and Humanities Research Board. I am grateful for the support provided by these awards and for references and letters of the support from Christopher Morris of the University of Glasgow, Elizabeth Slater of Liverpool University, John Drinkwater of the University of Nottingham, John Barrett of the University of Sheffield and Richard Hingley of Durham University. I have been fortunate to have received over the years the assistance of a number of librarians and museum curators. To my shame I am sure that some of them have since moved on or even retired since I first consulted them. But for the record, I am particularly indebted to Simon Bailey, University Archivist at Oxford and the staff of the Bodleian Library; to Graham Piddick for his help with the Haverfield Archive in the Ashmolean Museum at the University of Oxford; to Stephen Lion of Carlisle Public Library; to Sheila Noble, Librarian to the Special Collections at Edinburgh University Library; and to Andrew Martin, Librarian of National Library in the National Museums of Scotland. The staff at Manchester Public Library was also of assistance. Tony Wilmott kindly shared opinions and offered critical comments on at least one chapter. At Liverpool, my friends and colleagues, in particular Graham Oliver, Doug Baird, Antony Sinclair, Carmel Malone and Jonathan Trigg, have read and commented on drafts of papers and have generally humoured me as I have 'droned on for Britain' about Haverfield and his connections. Over the years, a number of audiences at conferences and invited lectures at Bristol, Cambridge, Glasgow, Leicester, London, Maryport, Melrose, Oxford, Sheffield and elsewhere have kindly endured various versions of what is argued here.

I am pleased to acknowledge the permission offered by a number of persons and institutions for access to unpublished material. I have used a number of items from the Haverfield Archive by permission of the Administrators of the Haverfield Bequest, University of Oxford. I am grateful to the Council of the Chester Archaeological Society for permission to reproduce the portrait of Haverfield, which was originally included with Margerie Taylor's (1920) Haverfield obituary. John Mawdsley kindly granted permission to use his unpublished BA dissertation on Haverfield's work at Corbridge. Jim Crow, Richard Reece, Richard Hodges and Donald Gordon of the Trimontium Trust have kindly shared Haverfield letters they have in their possession.

I owe debts to a number of individuals whose work and opinions as well as their support have greatly assisted me. In this respect, I am happy to acknowledge Mike Bishop, Greg Wolf, Chris Stray, Tony Wilmott and David Kennedy. Ray Laurence kindly provided a copy of something that was proving difficult to access. I remember with pleasure a long conversation I had with the late Charles Daniels during a midnight walk around Oxford in the early 1990s. His recollections about Ian Richmond were a revelation. But I regret too that I was unable to pursue some of things he mentioned. Likewise Anthony Birley provided a number of insights about his late father's memories. Mike Bishop has provided some invaluable recollections about Haverfield and Corbridge, as has Lawrence Keppie on the work of George Macdonald. Of overseas contacts Dr Brian Croke of Macquarie University has generously shared his work on Mommsen and Britain. In Germany, Professor A. Demandt and Dr Schlange-Solingen provided names and contacts, which have proved to be invaluable. Lea Meistrup-Larsen was a great help in translating some of Mommsen's letters. Closer to home, I am indebted to Jane Webster for sharing publications and in particular to Richard Hingley. It was their work, which originally inspired me to look more closely at Haverfield's work. Richard in particular will disagree with many of the conclusions I have drawn, but he has remained a consistent supporter. During one of the many periods when I wondered if there was any merit in continuing with Haverfield, John Wilkes and Richard Reece kindly agreed to look over a rough early draft of this text. I am embarrassed now to recollect just how crude was that version. Their responses, however, proved to be a salvation. I am especially grateful to Richard for his enthusiastic comments. I know that he too disagrees with some of my opinions but there again: *Quot homines tot sententiae: suo quoque mos* (Terence *Phormio* 203).

My last debt is to Colin Wallace. I first became aware of his interest and work relatively late on the research on Haverfield. Since then, however, he has been an unstinting font of advice. Not only has he read the text here, and shared his work, he has been an invaluable source of information about various Haverfield contemporaries. In many respects he is better qualified to write the definitive study of the evolution of Romano-British studies in the twentieth century, to which this text is merely a first contribution. I hope that the following chapters will stimulate him to complete that work.

CHAPTER 1

From Haverfield to Romanization to Haverfield

It is difficult, even in an autobiography, for an antiquary to give a just presentment of himself: much more difficult is it when the life has to be written by another (Payne *J Brit Archaeol Assoc* LXVI (1890): 237)

Introduction: Why Haverfield?

In an age with a more positive perspective on the potential of archaeology, Francis Haverfield wrote:

There can be little question that more has already been won and more is to be hoped in the future, from the discovery of new facts than from any process of reinterpretation. Nevertheless, reinterpretation will go on. It is necessary if succeeding generations are to adjust the literature or history of the past to themselves. It is also easy: the interpreter has only to sit in his chair and interpret ...Here and there luck or unusual skill may light on items which earlier search has missed; once in a decade a nugget emerges. But, in general, he who sets out in this twentieth century to reinterpret the classics out of themselves is committed beforehand to one or other of two courses. He may be sober and cautious, and his discoveries will be true but tiny: he may interpret freely, and he – or his critics – will find that he has written a novel (1912b: 328).

Haverfield would not sympathize with this study, for it is indeed partly a work of reinterpretation. His was a criticism of contemporary attempts to make something new out of established facts, a process he believed could stretch the limits of credulity. That he could make such a statement is a reflection of just how much he dominated the study of Roman Britain at the start of the twentieth century, a fact which has been accepted with such lack of demur that it is now almost a cliché to repeat the mantra that came into common usage at the time of his death; he 'had set the agenda for the subject'. And it is true. Haverfield dominates the discipline in a manner that nobody has managed to repeat. His influence and opinions still permeate most aspects of the subject as it is now understood. Today, perhaps the best-known facet of this legacy is the issue of its degree of cultural assimilation, otherwise its romanization. But his influence goes deeper. It ranges from refining, if not establishing, the chronological framework for the island's Roman period to defining the topics thought to be relevant to understanding its history. It is for these reasons he might be described as the first scholar, as opposed to an antiquarian, of Roman Britain. This was achieved through a reconciliation of historical and epigraphic evidence with the burgeoning volume of archaeological evidence. Not only was he central to the way that the subject has come to be taught and how it is still executed, he was instrumental in the creation of a number of institutions, which are still central to the study of the Roman past, both in the United Kingdom and overseas.

To his contemporaries Francis John Haverfield was the 'father of Romano-British studies'. His death, on 30 September 1919, was the occasion for widespread lamentation. R.H. Blair, Secretary of the Newcastle Society of Antiquaries, spoke of his demise as 'a very great loss to Roman archaeology and it will be a very difficult matter to replace him.' At the Society's monthly meeting on 29 October a motion to send Mrs Haverfield condolences '...was carried in silence, members rising in their places' (Blair 1919: 117, 125). In the minutes of its annual meeting in January 1920 he was described as 'the leading specialist on subjects connected with the Roman occupation of Britain' (Oswald 1920: 138). W.G. Collingwood wrote that 'he was known everywhere as the chief authority on the most important department of antiquarian study' (1920: 255). The Council of the Society of Antiquaries of Scotland resolved '...to place on record their sense of the grievous loss which learning has sustained through the death of Professor Haverfield ...His removal creates a blank that will be long and keenly felt, alike by those who only knew him as a scholar and by those who were privileged to count him as a friend' (Macdonald 1919–20b: 5). The editor of the RCHM Essex volume reported that his 'wide learning was invaluable to the Commission and whose special knowledge of Roman Britain it will be very difficult to replace' (RCHM Essex (Central and South-West) 1921: xix), while G.H. Jack noted he was '...a leading figure in the realm of ancient history and specially in Roman history' where he was '...considered the chief authority of Roman inscriptions in Britain" (1918–20: 267). Such was his reputation, his opinions could be repeated in the leader columns of the national press (e.g. *The Manchester Guardian*, 29 December 1906). All these acclamations were a result of Haverfield's seminal part in the evolution of Roman studies including Romano-British archaeology. As Macdonald expressed it:

When Haverfield first approached it, the subject of Roman Britain was, to use his own phrase 'the playground of the amateur'. Before his death he could claim that 'our knowledge of the island, however liable to future correction and addition, stands by itself among the studies of the Roman Empire'. He might truthfully have added that this was his own achievement. And it was accomplished almost single-handed, such good work as was done by others was done largely through his inspiration and example ...he penetrated into every nook and corner of his subject bringing to bear upon its problems, not only a vast knowledge and miscellaneous details, but a breadth of outlook, a sureness of touch and surety of judgement (1927: 245; in part repeating Macdonald 1918: 185).[1]

1. To the tributes might be added: '...Our foremost Roman scholar, Mr. Haverfield, then not yet Professor (e.g. pre-1907), but already recognised as the academic master in the field' (Neilson 1912: 40); 'Surely no man ever identified himself more completely with his chosen subject; we may say, in fact, that it was he who raised the study of Roman Britain to its present level. For many years hardly a site has been opened that he had not visited; hardly a Report has appeared that did not acknowledge his generous help ...the memory of his care, his method, and his ripe scholarship is the heritage of those who remain' (Bruton 1920: 73–4). Haverfield was '...well known for his unchallenged position as the leading authority on the history and antiquities of Roman Britain, and as friend, inspirer and adviser of all serious students of these subjects' (Woodward 1920: 7). W.G. Collingwood added; '...he gave us at all times most generous assistance from his unrivalled store of learning and industry in the explanation of Roman sites and in exposition of local Roman history. As the greatest living authority on his subject he did us distinguished honour by identifying himself with our work and by his continual care for all details relating to the Society's welfare. His loss, especially at a time when the prospects of research seemed to be hopefully reviving, is a severe blow not only to his personal friends but to all throughout the world who have at heart the interests of antiquarian study' (frontispiece, *Trans Cumberland Westmorland Antiq Archaeol Soc* XIX: 1919; cf. Oman 1941: 66, 82; Bonarkis Webster 1991: 119). Even in his obituary of Haverfield's friend and co-worker, George Macdonald who died twenty years later, James Curle noted of Haverfield: 'No one in his day had done more to encourage the study of Roman Britain and to gather together the details of the latest discoveries' (1939–40: 127). There is also a short notice in *The Annual Register: A Review of Public Events at Home and Abroad 1919* (London 1920) where it is noted 'His gifts in the art of lecturing brought him great popularity as well as the respect due to his learning' (p. 208). In the *Proceedings of the Cambridge Antiquarian Society* (XXII (1917–20): 18), it was recorded: 'The Society ...sustained a loss in the death of Professor F.J. Haverfield of Oxford ...whose eminence in the study of Roman and Romano-British Antiquities is universally acknowledged.' Such was his name, there is a reference to Haverfield in John Buchan's short story *The Wind in the Portico* (published March 1928 as part of *The Runagates Club* collection). The story concerns another Buchan hero, Henry Nightingale, visiting a reclusive

In the decades immediately after his death, Haverfield's reputation survived largely undiminished. Other than some muted criticism with respect to the way he conducted his fieldwork, the one substantial negative assessment of the man was made by Wheeler, who observed that 'Haverfield's work was not merely a monument, it was a tombstone' (1961: 159), where, with Haverfield's death that phase of Romano-British studies had reached its end, even if subsequent generations of workers did not realize or heed it. Indeed it is striking how much his reputation has remained largely intact in the decades since his demise even if many of his judgments have had to be reassessed. Thirty-five years after his death, Richmond was to eulogize of:

> ...the palmary virtue which inspire those [Haverfield] works are a passion for exact and significant detail, a principle which was at the very root of archaeological study, and the precious gift of sober judgment. Both powers led Haverfield to the truth in matters upon which an accumulating mass of evidence later proved him abundantly right. Since his day the field has been much extended and its crops become sometimes embarrassingly thick; but on the broad and unchanging questions his opinions are no less valuable today when they were formulated with that restraint and wisdom peculiarly his (1957: 3).

Elsewhere, Boon described him as '...greatest of all Romano-British scholars' (1974: 28), Frere 'the real founder of the study of Roman Britain in its full sense as an academic discipline' (1988: 1), Wilkes as 'the pioneer of the study of Roman Britain' (1989: 245) and Todd '...the father of modern Roman-Britain studies' and '...the acknowledged master of modern study of Roman Britain' (1989: xi and 2003: 35). Elsewhere it has been said that '...Haverfield effectively set the agenda for Romano-British studies for more than sixty years ...[His] analytical approach set a style that was followed later by Collingwood ... and Rivet' (Jones 1987: 87) and there '...is little doubt that (his) work set the overall tone, if not the detail, of Romano-British studies for most of the twentieth century' (Manley 2002: 31). With shades of Mommsen's influence on Roman history, if one wants to learn anything concerning Roman Britain, the advice is still to see what Haverfield had to say. As Sheppard Frere expressed it: '...it remains a

---

estate owner who dabbled in the occult following the excavation of a Romano-British temple on his land (cf. J. Buchan *The Complete Short Stories* Vol. 3 edit. by A. Lownie (1997): 178–98).

fact that one reads Haverfield because what he wrote is still true: one reads Collingwood for historiographical reasons' (1988: 2).

These, and there are other, positive assessments explain why Haverfield is regarded as so important in the history of (Romano-)British archaeology. Although a product of the late nineteenth century, he stands at a pivotal point between traditional English antiquarianism and a more rigorous scholarly approach to the island's Roman antiquities. It is curious then that, for all his importance, Haverfield's life and work have not been subject to closer analysis. While his seminal position in Romano-British archaeology is recognized, but for the influence of German methods on his work on Hadrian's Wall (Browning 1989; 1995) and his opinions concerning ancient town planning (Laurence 1994b), there has been surprisingly little detailed re-assessment of his work. Instead most assessments of it tend to emphasize two facets, one that flows in to the other. The first, and the one emphasized in the decades after his death, is his part as the great synthesizer of the increasing amount of information that was becoming available in the early part of the twentieth century, an increase to which he in part contributed. The range of these interests in turn contributed to his other major contribution to Roman studies in this country: the way he was the first (British) scholar to consider systematically the cultural consequences, through archaeological evidence, of the Roman period. This was an effect he called its 'romanization'. It is the 'romanization' of Britain and what he said of it is where Haverfield's opinions continue to generate debate rather than just acceptance of his conclusions as a basis for on-going work. To be sure, judging from the quantity, if not quality, of the output one could be forgiven for believing that this was his only contribution to Romano-British studies. That the 'romanization' is still being debated implies it remains the primary purpose of Romano-British archaeology.

That Haverfield's view of the 'romanization' of Britain became such a widely accepted phenomenon in Roman archaeology it meant, paradoxically, it failed to draw consideration. Instead, what he said held sway for nearly a century. Or least until recently. Its general acceptance was in part due to the strength of his reputation. Furthermore, as an innovation, because it made so much sense, it did not occasion critical appraisal. With time, as will be argued below, the criteria identified by Haverfield for the 'romanization' of Britain were adapted, largely uncritically, by his successors. Those criteria are still used today to identify, explain and justify this particular form of acculturation. It will be contended here, however, that while Haverfield established the archaeology of Roman Britain as a subject for academic study, the parameters he set have not significantly shifted in the ensuing century. Today it is possible to identify two strands to how 'romanization' theory is used. The older tradition, one that goes back to Haverfield, is the positive perspective. In this there is some debate to what extent change was the intention of the outcome of Roman imperial government and how and why native societies might have acquiesced to it. In this sense, where there has been progress in writing about the process of change, it has been with respect to the types of evidence collected, usually in forms unimaginable to Haverfield and his immediate successors, rather than how they are deployed. In other words, continued accumulation of data in the first instance has not changed acceptance of the idea that contact with the Roman empire brought about, to varying degrees, the 'romanizing' of Britain. A second, more recently articulated, counter-position to the positive version of 'romanization' is to emphasize its negative consequences or to look for alternative perspectives. Here the emphasis has been to seek out instances of the rejection or else resistance to 'Roman culture' in the archaeological record. But in working this point, the proponents of this line of attack are in many respects merely contradicting the positivists view. In short those who might criticize or reject Haverfield's opinions on the subject are merely contradicting Haverfield's legacy rather than offering an alternative (or 'theoretically more rigorous') interpretation. What is common to both schools of thought is acceptance of a process of cultural transformation. The juxtaposition of the two schools of thought explains why the debate about what is 'romanization', based as it is on an uncritical reflection of what is Roman material culture, continues. For either school of thought, Haverfield's model of romanization – and more recently, evidence of its 'rejection' – has been attributed to the colonial experience. But this is too simplistic an analogy. Most, if not all summaries of Haverfield's understanding of the phenomenon of 'romanization' tend to be over-generalised, to the point where he has been accused of all manner of crimes ranging from naïvety and ignorance through to snobbery, intellectual élitism and even racism. For some, this aspect of his work represents much that is unacceptable in late Victorian scholarship. If this is so, then the implications are that the issue of the cultural consequences of the Roman occupation of Britain (and indeed of virtually all of Europe) has not developed in a significant manner in the past 100+ years. Indeed one might suggest that the debate has ended up an intellectual cul-de-sac with little or no chance of developing the question 'what is Romano-British archaeology really about?' Does the 'romanization' explanation, whether it is Haverfield's or those models expounded subsequently, continue to be a useful way to interpret the Roman period in Britain? If it was a product of its time, is it useful to continue employing it? Do the conditions which allowed Haverfield to formulate his opinions pertain today?

Some would argue they do: after all, romanization is romanization is romanization. Its acculturation and it happened. What is required is not contemplation about how a phenomenon of transformation which still has a bearing today might be measured, but rather how it facilitated Haverfield's appreciation of what the archaeological remains of the Roman provinces could tell him about the life and aspirations of the provincial population under a particular form of imperial rule. In other words, what is required is a contextual analysis of Haverfield's work. His mode of explanation was the consequence of a process of training and evolution as well as more mundane factors such as career, ambition and niche-making, rather than the identification of an incontrovertible process of cultural change. This point was, and continues to be, missed by his 'successors'. Instead of looking at why he wrote in the way he did, his opinions were largely accepted as the basis for future work. Therefore this study has to examine how those individuals who followed Haverfield worked very much with the same concepts and categories of data in their assessments of the cultural consequences of the Roman occupation. What is required is an analysis of why Haverfield's intellectual 'bequest' was manipulated by those who succeeded him as the leading Romano-British scholars. The nature of these contacts is important because it explains Collingwood's influence on subsequent generations. Establishing the form of the continuity also permits evaluation of romanization studies as they are posited today and in particular their principle weaknesses (cf. Meltzer 1989: 11).

There is another paradox in working with – or criticizing – Haverfield's views on romanization. It remains an explanatory concept that still defies satisfactory quantification. Haverfield may have had, unwittingly, a similar problem. His opinions on the subject were articulated in two major monographs (e.g. 1905; 1912a/1915/1923; 1924: 173) as well as numerous articles, the majority of which have not been used to best effect by those who have written about him. Not surprisingly, he frequently used the term and we can trace from where he might have derived it, but I am not aware of his having examined the nature of the phenomenon that he believed he could see in the archaeology of Roman Britain. Whilst he hinted at its constituent elements, he never actually defined it. Such vagueness ties in with another feature of Haverfield's work: how he has been regarded by subsequent generations. In the absence of definitive statements on his part, his legacy has been variously interpreted in many subtle but still significant ways.

It is almost facile to state that Haverfield's exposure to the form of acculturation for which he is now best remembered was as much a consequence of his time and the prevailing (intellectual) climate as well as his experience as any innovative thinking on his part. And yet, these factors are frequently overlooked. What has not drawn appreciation is how his views were shaped by a number of interrelated themes. There are a number of factors in his life that have a bearing in this respect. They include his family background as well as his education. There was at this time a revolution in teaching methods introduced at Oxford when he was an undergraduate and where his original interests in philology and ancient history started. His introduction to Theodor Mommsen and consequent shift to Latin epigraphy were crucial in his move into Roman archaeology. Then there was the wider social and intellectual climate that not only conditioned him but also the institutions in which he came to work. The concepts and perceptions with which he worked, notably in the categorizing of the data, were very much those of the late nineteenth century. In a similar fashion, neither his contacts with the Continent nor what he saw as his task have previously been fully considered. Little attention has been given to his own position with respect to Roman studies in the broader university curriculum. This, according to received wisdom, was to be achieved not so much by championing the introduction of archaeology as a degree subject at Oxford, as by the appointment of a network of 'students', itself an innovation, and his patronage of (university) training excavations coupled to his attempts to lift the antiquarian tradition and the regional archaeological societies to higher standards. Rather than considering the significance of these sort of factors, where there has been consideration of why Haverfield wrote of the romanization of Britain in the way he did, it tends to emphasize the prevailing contemporary climate of British imperial expansion coupled to the tradition of training Britain's colonial administrators in the accomplishments of classical civilization which determined how Haverfield's opinions of the Roman empire and its civilizing mission. In this characterization, Haverfield is supposed to have use the present to explain the past. In reality the picture is much simpler. Contrary to what some might claim, there is little evidence to prove Haverfield was ever this sort of dyed-in-the-wool apologist for British colonialist policies. Indeed there is enough to argue the contrary. As already noted, while it was widely lamented that he did not produce a definitive work of synthesis (Collingwood 1919: 118; Bosanquet 1920: 141; Bruton 1920: 73; Craster 1920: 69; Rhys Roberts 1920: 349), Haverfield's opinions on the subject were set out in two substantial statements, *The Roman Occupation of Britain* (1924) and in particular *The Romanisation of Roman Britain*, which went to four editions (1905; 1912a; 1915; 1923). Central to both works was the conviction that '...Roman Britain was but a province of a world empire, to be studied in its relation to imperial Rome' and that '...the things he was studying [were] a manifestation of the life and civilization of a great empire. He regarded Roman Britain not as a stage of English History but as an outlying province of Rome' (Craster 1920: 63 and 69). J.B. Bury picked up on this fact in a review of the first edition of *The Romanisation* where: 'Mr. Haverfield ...proceeds to show that the evidence goes to bring Britain into general line with the other provinces ...Britain was no exception to the rule that in the provinces of western Europe the distinction between Roman and provincial disappeared' (1906: 759). In his opinions on 'romanization', instead of linking it as intimately as some believe with the civilizing mission of the British and other European colonial empires, Haverfield looked for other explanatory models to elucidate the process. In fact most recent summaries of his work perpetuate a misconception that Haverfield was eager to counter; the temptation to emphasize the insularity of the subject with which he is usually linked – archaeology. None of these appraisals mentions the influence of contemporary advances in the study of Roman history, of which archaeology was still then an adjunct. Yet this is a point that which recurs in all the obituaries written about him: his belief that the history and archaeology of Britain in the Roman empire could not be understood unless it was placed in its European context, both in antiquity and in the modern era. In this case, Haverfield's work was in accord with developments that were taking place on the Continent. It was this conviction which led Haverfield to emphasize what he saw as the points of similarity between (Roman) Britain and the empire rather than looking to or using the British experience to make sense of the past. This is but one example of how modern treatments often misrepresent Haverfield and his work. In the current debate on whether 'romanization' remains a relevant mode of explanation, these factors have been largely missed. Others will be explored in the subsequent chapters. But for the moment it makes the point that what is desirable is a more considered examination of the factors that conditioned Haverfield and in turn shaped his work.

Haverfield and his work deserve detailed analysis for another reason. As 'the father of Roman Britain', the implication of the accolade are that Romano-British studies represent a distinct and therefore important facet of the (archaeological) history of these islands. One issue which has arisen in looking at Haverfields' work is how others took up his ideas. This is as much in the years immediately following his death as the ways subsequent generations of scholars have used them. The implication of the Haverfield 'father' accolade (and indeed the tone of the previous paragraphs) is an impression of the strength of Romano-British studies. Assisting in this impression is the tradition, one going back to the moment of Haverfield's death, of writing about the development of Romano-British studies as a sequence of 'great' figures, all usually university-based and who, in various ways, used Haverfield's work as the basis for taking the subject further. The relevance of this apostolistic approach, one which tends to emphasize the Oxford connection by linking Oxford-based academics such as Collingwood and Richmond as well as graduates of the same university, requires consideration. There are, however, a number of issues which do not necessarily rest easy with this tradition. For instance, while the tradition emphasizes a link between Romano-British studies and Oxford and the country's other universities, examination of the institutions post-1919 shows that in fact the subject had not established any place in them. There were few, if any, academics in position, which in turn must have implications for the range and quality of instruction in the subject that was on offer. Indeed despite the often optimistic assessments of the progress of the subject in the 1920s and 1930s – progress attributed to Haverfield's initiative in the preceding decades – what is clear is that the bulk of the progress was being made by non-university field-workers. This leads one to question then what did happen in the aftermath of Haverfield's death and why the misapprehension has arisen. For a corollary to the rather over-positive assessments of Romano-British studies in the decades after the First World War, is perpetuation of the impression that the work of Collingwood, Richmond and the 'northern school' marked a 'golden age' of Roman archaeology in this country. That sense of progress in knowledge about the Roman period has been repeated in recent assessments of the accomplishments of those individuals. But if the conclusions about the parlous condition of Romano-British studies in the universities in the 1920s and 1930s are valid, then again a reappraisal of those decades is even more necessary.

I am not aware of anybody who would dispute that the current form of Romano-British studies was a consequence of Haverfield's work. Nowadays the archaeology and history of Roman Britain is recognized as one of the most popular aspects of the discipline 'archaeology'. Just as there is a vibrant lay enthusiasm for it, one might reasonably assume that courses on aspects of the Roman province feature strongly in most university archaeology departments' portfolios of teaching. As a consequence of this interest there is available a multitude of 'textbooks', each a product of their time, looking at all manner of aspects of the Roman occupation of the island. If this impression is true, then logic dictates that Haverfield, as the 'father', played a critical part in the rise of the subject. For some, however, the impression of Roman Britain being an essential component of training in archaeological theory, practice and interpretation offered by Britain's universities has turned out to be something of a chimera. Although comparable reservations were being articulated as far back as the early 1960s, in recent years they have become increasingly frequent and vociferous. In 1999, in a valedictory editorial in the journal *Britannia*, Michael Fulford assessed the current condition of Romano-British studies. In this fin-de-siècle appraisal Fulford characterized the first half of the twentieth century as large-scale town site excavations such as those at Silchester and Caerwent as well as at military sites such as Corbridge and Newstead; and where the research imperative was preoccupied with political and military history and the efforts to reconcile the poor literary sources. In contrast, the second half of the same century saw the introduction of new methods and the influences of fresh attitudes assisted by the rise of rescue/salvage excavation all of which had created a more rarefied approach to the accumulation of data. Irrespective of its evolution, Fulford suggested that Romano-British studies in the university sector were in decline just as there was a fresh impetus of research money (from developer sources as well as the Heritage Lottery Fund). In explaining why Romano-British archaeology appeared relatively weak in the universities, Fulford cited such factors as the rise of 'prehistory' at the expense of historical archaeology, and the pernicious influence of the government's quinquennial Research Assessment Exercises, with their emphasis on the output of 'international' quality research which seems to mean working overseas, the engagement with foreign scholars, regions and periods and the relative cheapness of working abroad. Following Fulford's pessimistic conclusions, in the same year the Archaeology Committee of the Society for the Promotion of Roman Studies (SPRS) circulated a questionnaire among the UK departments of archaeology, soliciting information on the range of teaching in Roman archaeology they offered. I do not know if Fulford's observations about the decline of Romano-British studies in the universities was the catalyst for the Roman Society's survey, but it did strike a chord with his successor as the editor of *Britannia* who spoke of 'the seeming recent decline in the number of university-based Romano-British specialist teachers' (*Britannia* 30 (2000): vii). The SPRS survey was concerned that it was now possible for students reading for degrees in archaeology to experience the discipline without any contact with Roman aspects. This was regarded as a potentially worrying development in the light of the fact that Roman archaeology constituted a major element in the nation's heritage. The responses to its questionnaire were digested and the results circulated in 2000. The impression which had occasioned the original survey were confirmed and the implications serious.[2] In the aftermath, the committee asked for responses and observations as to how this situation had arisen and how it might be redressed.

At the time the SPRS questionnaire was being circulated I had reached the conclusion of the first phase of the research which constitutes the core of this text. My original interest was in Haverfield's work on romanization and in particular a feeling that the point of his work in this respect was being misrepresented by some. Independent of the SPRS survey, I had become increasingly dissatisfied with the way the evolution of Romano-British archaeology has commonly been described. For some time I had harboured the impression the root problem the SPRS survey came to highlight lay not so much in the present, as the society's response seemed to imply, but that it was more to do with problems which went back to the early decades of the twentieth century. It was an easy, but ultimately lazy, assumption that if this was the case then the blame could be laid at Haverfield's door. It is a view which has often been repeated by others. He is, after all, the 'father' of the subject. It was therefore largely Haverfield's fault that Romano-British studies were stagnant and unexciting. Fieldwork and its interpretation were now merely accommodated into the agenda and framework that he had created. With time, however, it became apparent that to blame Haverfield for the on-going malaise in Romano-British

---

2. The results of the survey were not widely distributed although a report was circulated within the society. It did, however, occasion a meeting organized by the SPRS in November 2002 ('*Whither Roman Archaeology*'; cf. James 2003). But the meeting was more a combination of celebrating of what was going on in the subject, suggesting where developments might occur and how funding could be obtained rather than exploring the trends the original survey seem to have indicated (viz. the teaching of Romano-British archaeology). Noteworthy in James' rather optimistic review of the meeting is the omission of a number of critical comments raised on the day. Instead we are informed 'Roman archaeology has come an enormous distance in the last decade, becoming an innovative and reflexive subdiscipline. More vibrant than it has been for a century, it can now stand on equal terms with its peers. It may have been in crisis 20 years ago, but is not now; however it faces institutional and operational challenges shared with the rest of archaeology. Its biggest special challenge remains learning how to communicate better, not least, how to encourage other archaeologists to become involved, to everyone's enrichment' (p. 183).

studies was not entirely fair. Work since the SPRS's survey suggested the problems lay more in the period immediately after Haverfield's death, in the years between the two world wars. At best he seems to have been an unwitting witness rather than the culprit. Instead, as will be discussed below, the cause appears to lie with the years when R.G. Collingwood was active, the man universally regarded as the next 'great' in the pantheon of Romano-British scholarship. At the same time this was also the period when Eric Birley and Ian Richmond were establishing careers at Durham and Newcastle, when they were running excavation programmes with precise research objectives; refining the parameters and chronology for the subject; interpreting the subject as one based on the military history of the province into which the 'civil' facet of the island is fitted; and introducing courses in aspects of the archaeology of Roman Britain with the concomitant creation of 'schools' of students to develop those themes in a way that Haverfield had been unable to achieve.

It is for these reasons then that the text offered here represents the coming together of a number of strands and other observations about what Romano-British studies have become. If this study requires further justification in the light of Haverfield's belief of the positive progress of data collection and the negative results of reinterpretation, then it lies with how a number of misrepresentations concerning him and about the subject have come to the fore. What exactly was Haverfield's work and therefore his legacy?

The sources for Haverfield

Before we examine the nature of Haverfield's work, some comment about the quality of the evidence is required. It transpires that the material for constructing an appreciation of him is both diverse and yet limited. An assessment of their relative qualities as well as their strengths and deficiencies is thus necessary. On the one hand there is what I shall call the primary data, that is a corpus of unpublished or private material in the form of drafts and letters and, on the other hand, his published work, including monographs, articles and other essays. To describe the latter group as secondary may read as perverse, but I have done so for two reasons. What is evident is that, over a relatively long career, not surprisingly Haverfield's ideas evolved. Nor was he averse to changing his opinions in the light of new discoveries. There are therefore occasionally some contradictions in his published work. In contrast it is in the primary group that we can often see how his opinions were formed or reviewed. There is, however, a substantial problem in using this material. As will become apparent, the quantity of material that survives is severely

compromised. This means that one is heavily dependent on his published statements combined with the opinions of those who worked with
or were affected by him. For a third category of evidence is the large collection of obituaries and other reminisces of his life and work.

Haverfield left no substantial memoir of his life. What he did occasionally provide were semi-autobiographical anecdotes, most notably
those in his Presidential Address to the Somerset Antiquarian Society
(Haverfield 1919a). Many of the same sorts of snippets from the numerous obituaries, national and regional, and other notices can be
combined to construct a narrative for, as we have seen, his demise was
the occasion for numerous obituaries and other notices.[3] One of the
striking features of the obituaries is how Haverfield and his accomplishments meant different things to different writers. The longest and most
substantial of the notices was provided for the *Proceedings of the British
Academy*, of which Haverfield was a fellow (Macdonald 1919–20a). That
notice was republished in the 1924 introduction to Haverfield's Ford lectures (*The Roman Occupation of Britain* and edited by Macdonald).
Macdonald's accounts have since become the canonical version of
Haverfield's life and work. Close reading of the two memoirs, however,
shows that the 1924 version contains some small but potentially significant alterations to the original entry which may have a bearing on how
the memory of Haverfield and his reputation was shaped in the decade
after his death.[4] The notices can be supplemented with a number of
later opinions and anecdotes which offer general rather than specific assessments of his work.

One stage removed from the 'published' version of his life, on a more
intimate level Haverfield's personal papers are disappointing. At the
outset, based on the strength of his reputation, I naïvely believed there

---

3. The list includes *The Times* 2 October 1919; Anderson 1919; Blair 1920;
   Bosanquet 1920; Bruton 1919; R.G. Collingwood 1919; W.G. Collingwood
   1920; Craster 1920; Jack 1918–20; Anon. 1919; Anon. 1919–20; Rhys Roberts 1920; Taylor 1920; Woodward 1920. There is the possibility of another
   obituary or notice in the *Transactions of the Essex Archaeological Society* (XV
   (1920): 244). Macdonald's 1919–20a Biographical note for the British Academy was also published separately and then lavishly reviewed by W. Page, the
   editor of the *VCH*, in the *Archaeological Journal* (I (1922): 249–51). For all the
   obituaries, a curious feature is the omission of any notices contributed by foreign and particularly German scholars. The reason must lie with the fact
   that most of the generation he knew was dead by the time he died.
4. Macdonald provided at least two other assessments of Haverfield' life (Macdonald 1918 and 1927). For our purposes it is the 1924 version, because of
   the way that others have used it, which is here the primary account.

had to exist a substantial Haverfield *Nachlaß*. Under the terms of his will Haverfield left his papers and library to the University of Oxford. They were transferred shortly after his death to the Ashmolean Museum where they formed the core of a reference collection of Romano-British studies (hereafter the Haverfield Archive). Naturally there must have been a degree of clearing out of his papers, but still the archive holds what must be a tiny fraction of his original papers and correspondence.[5] Contained in the collection is a small cache of letters from James Curle, the excavator of Newstead, to Haverfield. They span the period August 1905 to February 1909. The letters have been recently edited by Donald Gordon (2005), although without a detailed commentary of their contents. Other than the material retained in the archive, I have not, as of yet, tracked down any other substantial corpus of Haverfield correspondence in the United Kingdom. The Institute of Archaeology at Oxford holds some of his lantern slides and a postcard photo album. There are a dozen or so personal letters and a few papers pertinent to Haverfield in the archives of the Bodleian Library, but nothing in his colleges (New, Christ Church and Brasenose) and effectively nothing with the Society of Antiquaries of London, the Society for the Promotion of Roman Studies, nor the British Academy. The Local History and Archives Collection of Manchester Public Library holds ten Haverfield letters written to Charles Roeder along with a copy of the latter's *Roman Manchester* (1906) into which are pasted a number of letters, press-cuttings and notes in Roeder's hand.[6] In Scotland there are two small collections of Haverfield letters. The Special Collection in Edinburgh University Library holds at least six pieces of correspondence. A slightly more problematic collection is in the archives of the Society of Antiquaries of Scotland, currently stored in the library in the National Museums of Scotland. The Society's Minutes Books record at least six items of correspondence between Haverfield and its Council. Unfortunately a search of the Society's letter files failed to find any of them. This is a pity as one or two of the letters look to be significant in terms of Haverfield's plans in the late 1890s. The search did recover one otherwise non-minuted letter.[7] For elsewhere

---

5. I know of two instances where Haverfield letters were – or are still – pasted into the back of his books when they were transferred to the Ashmolean Library, and later in to the Sackler Library.

6. Roeder's book and therefore the letters are curated in the city's library as file *MR 277* and span the period October 1899 to October 1906.

7. The references to the unlocated letters are to be found in the Council Minutes for 2 and 16 December 1899, 30 October 1900, 3 November 1903, 20 March 1906 and 5 May 1914.

I am told there is little or no material in the archives of the various regional archaeological societies (e.g. Chester, Newport and the National Museums of Wales). Nor is there anything concerning the Silchester excavations now stored in Reading Museum.[8] For Haverfield's work on Hadrian's Wall on behalf of the Cumberland Excavation Committee there are odd papers in Carlisle Public Library but the principle records are said to have been destroyed in the 1930s. With respect to his involvement with the Northumberland Excavation Committee at Corbridge, few documents of the 1906–14 excavations survive but for some notebooks and at least one plan (Bishop 1994: 16).[9] Photographs of the period commissioned by the Corbridge Excavation Fund are variously held at the Corbridge Site Museum, the English Heritage Historic Plan Room at Keysign House, the Society of Antiquaries of Newcastle and the Northumberland Record Office. Again, I have not been able to check this material. Haverfield was a frequent writer to *The Times* (and less so to *The Manchester Guardian* and *The Observer*). The newspapers also published résumés of many of his public lectures. The letters and articles are usually about archaeology, new discoveries and reports on his lectures. Usually concerning professional matters (such as complaints about the work of others), very occasionally the letters discuss other issues. The earliest letter dates to August 1900 which seems surprisingly late when one considers how much he published later on. There are also some of his reviews in *The Times Literary Supplement*. Finally, a number of individuals hold copies of Haverfield letters, all of whom have kindly let me see them, while the odd Haverfield letter appears in the sale catalogues of manuscript and letter dealers. In contrast to the poverty of Haverfield material in Britain, there is a large collection of correspondence with Mommsen, concerned mainly with matters philological and epigraphical, preserved in the Staatsbibliothek in Berlin. These letters

---

8. I had no response to my enquiries about possible papers in the archives of the *Victoria County History* based at the Institute for Historical Research at UC London. There are other private collections which I suspect contain Haverfield letters. Despite a number of requests, however, it has not been possible to gain sight of their contents.

9. Since the publication of his study of the Corbridge excavations, Mike Bishop informs me that the 'plans in the archive at Corbridge now include actual excavation plans on graph paper, carefully coloured in for phasing, and distinct from the pen-and-wash plan by Knowles I mentioned in the 1994 book, which was not an excavation plan as such.' There are evidently some photographs in the Richmond collection in the Ashmolean Museum. Bishop believes that these particular photos 'might be Haverfield's album which Richmond "inherited."'

are being worked on by Brian Croke.[10] In the same Berlin archive are letters between Haverfield and other leading German scholars, including Otto Hirschfeld, Emil Hübner and Ludwig Darmstädter.

While the primary sources for Haverfield's life might be deficient, it is fortunate that he was such a prolific writer. Originally started as a catalogue prepared for the *Journal of Roman Studies* (Macdonald 1918), attached to Macdonald's 1924 memoir is a bibliographical summary of Haverfield's output which lists nearly 500 publications. In addition to Macdonald's catalogue, at about the same time, A.M. Woodward compiled a much shorter list for Rhys Roberts' (1920) obituary for Haverfield in the *Yorkshire Archaeological Journal*. Macdonald's catalogue is a curious amalgam. It is neither comprehensive nor exhaustive. He acknowledged that it did not include the majority of Haverfield's reviews, although it does list occasional examples, ones which '...appeared to have a permanent significance as embodying definite pronouncements upon special points' (Macdonald 1924: 39).[11] This statement is questionable. For Macdonald omitted many contributions

---

10. Given the lack of a larger Haverfield archive, the survival of this collection is all the more remarkable in the light of Mommsen's request concerning the disposal of his own papers (Anon. Theodor Mommsen's last wishes. *Past & Present* 1 (1952): 71). Because of the complexity of the accession numbers/referencing system used in the Berlin collection, for my purposes I have used, with his permission, the sequence of numbers devised by Croke for each of the letters. A concordance of his system relative to the Berlin numbers is to be found in Appendix 1.

11. Macdonald does not explain how the bibliography was put together. In the 1918 version, however, it is reported it was compiled mainly by Margerie Taylor with the assistance of James Curle and G.F. Hill. Craster's 1920 obituary acknowledges that Taylor provided him with 'a manuscript bibliography of Professor Haverfield's articles.' Macdonald conceded that both versions of his list were not exhaustive. Some items of importance may have been accidentally overlooked. It deliberately omitted, however, the anonymous articles as well as most of his signed and unsigned book reviews. His letters to the press were likewise regarded as ephemeral. The 1924 Macdonald list does include some trifling material (e.g. a letter to *The Athenaeum* July 23 (1892): 138; a paragraph in E. Strong's 'A note on two Roman sepulchers reliefs' (*J Roman Stud* IV (1914): 147–56, at p. 148). Items omitted from the list include the circumstances behind the discovery of a Roman milestone from Castleford in the early 1880s (Haverfield 1897d), an important summary of a lecture Haverfield delivered to the RAI in 1904 (Haverfield 1903f), his contribution on Inchtuthil in Sir Alexander Muir Mackenzie's *Memoirs of Delvine* (1904; cf. Pitts and St. Joseph 1985: 38–9 and n. 23); and squeezes in the *Chester Journal* V (1895).

that provide information and insights that are valuable in understanding the evolution of Haverfield's thinking and his attitudes. I have not attempted an exhaustive search but have limited myself to his 'preferred' journals (the *Classical Review*, the *Journal of Roman Studies*, the *English Historical Review*, the *Archaeological Journal* etc.). I suspect, however, that many unnamed reviews I have seen in this research are also Haverfield's. That said, even from the 'preferred' periodicals it is clear that Haverfield had the opportunity to peruse most if not all the major publications of the period. And like any good reviewer, he used such opportunities to commence the process of articulating ideas and lines of research. In addition to using his reviews as markers, they often reveal other aspects of the man; his favourites and his biases; the way that they become more and more impatient in tone to the point where they are often quite brutal, if not rude; his dislike of non-academic writers and his irritation at others' failures to keep up to date and, by implication, to ignore his opinions. In many of his publications Haverfield was not averse to stating facts and expressing opinions which have a wider resonance and that might say something about his inner thoughts. They are also instructive in illuminating how his thinking on a number of fronts developed. As Macdonald put it, when Haverfield '…wrote with serious intent, his writing was so extraordinarily relevant that it will be unsafe for future writers to neglect what he had said' (1918: 185).

The reliance on published material renders Haverfield something of an anonymous character, an impression not helped by a somewhat insular and difficult personality. Yet when one considers his work and connections, the opposite impression is as strong. Haverfield's career flourished at a time when there were major intellectual debates advanced by important figures, many of whom he knew personally. Indeed he contributed in a number of small ways to those discussions. On the one hand there were his British connections, in terms of local archaeologists and with university bodies. On the other, he was also an intimate of many of the leading European scholars of the day. The sum of the correspondence in Britain and abroad is evidence of just how many of the leading figures in historical and archaeological research that Haverfield knew, and these on more than passing terms. Taken together these links show that Haverfield was a major figure, albeit one not to advertise the fact, in the teaching and researching of the humanities in Britain. There is one other general point to be noted here which might be regarded as an advantage when writing about Haverfield. What is surprising in looking at many of his publications is the degree of recycling the same material in different publications with small but often significant additions. He was not averse to reusing the same material time and again and publishing verbatim many articles in different formats.[12] Two inadvertent advantages in the propensity to recycle is that it permits us to see by their repetition what particular themes especially interested him, while at the same time providing an insight to how his thinking on such issues evolved as the passages were adapted and modified for different purposes. It should also be noted here that Haverfield's propensity to reuse extracts of his work elsewhere was a practice not restricted just to him. His principle obituarist, George Macdonald, did exactly the same – republishing the same obituaries in different places.

One more step removed from the primary and secondary sources, there is always the chance of material residing in the personal papers of some of his contacts (e.g. M.V. Taylor and Donald Atkinson), but again I have been unable to locate any such collections. What would be extremely interesting to find are the collected papers of other informants (notably Macdonald), as well as Haverfield's widow or her family's possessions.[13] There is the diary kept by G.L. Cheesman in the Bodleian Library along with a memoir about the same individual. Then there are autobiographies and published memories of other Haverfield associates and in turn biographical studies of them (e.g. Thomas Ashby (Hodges 1994; 2000); F.G. Simpson (Simpson 1976); Donald Atkinson (Wallace 1994) as well as the numerous studies of R.G. Collingwood)). A surprising 'discovery' was Carl Schuchhardt's (1944: 230–54) reminiscences of his meeting with Haverfield in Oxford in the early 1900s. Elsewhere I have drawn extensively on the memories of Haverfield and Oxford penned by his contemporaries. Among these is the autobiography of Percy Gardner (1933), as well as those of Charles Oman (1941), George Beardoe Grundy (1945) and O.G.S. Crawford (1953). Others who wrote of Oxford in Haverfield's time include William Warde Fowler (Coon 1934), Lewis Farnell (1934) and slightly later in time Maurice Bowra (1966) and William Hayter (1974). That said, there is another

---

12. In the early part of his career, with the repetition of themes and points in the likes of *The Academy*, *The Antiquary* and the *Classical Review*; compare Haverfield 1911c and 1912c: his published lectures, his reviews of Traill's *Social England*, his same introductions and observations in the contributions to the various volumes of the *Victoria County History*, his other major works of synthesis, especially *The Roman Occupation of Britain* and his Pelham and Cheesman obituaries.

13. In desperation I tried contacting the known Breakwells. At the time of her death her address was 28 Milverton Crescent, Leamington Spa. The enquiries drew a blank. Coincidentally the authoress Frances Mabel Robinson (1858–1956) was also born in Milverton Crescent.

striking feature of Haverfield's career. Whatever his reputation and prominent position at Oxford, it is surprising just how little evidence there is of him interacting with his colleagues there, some of whom were major national figures. He must have known most if not all the teachers at Oxford concerned with instruction in aspects of the classical world. And yet, as has already been noted, his name is a curious omission in the autobiographies and other memoirs of a number of individuals of that time. For example, one of the other leading academics of the time was Gilbert Murray and was a close friend of some Haverfield acquaintances, notably G.L. Cheesman. Haverfield shared certain opinions on contemporary politics similar to those of the Professor of Greek. And yet there is no mention of him in accounts of Murray's life.[14]

Because the amount of primary evidence concerning Haverfield is limited, this work does not pretend to be a biographical study in the conventional sense. I have deliberately eschewed a conventional chronological, year-by-year structure. Nor is it intended to be a history of the archaeological study of Roman Britain although there is need for one. Rather it is more a study of the early years of modern Romano-British studies relative to what was going on in the universities. It cannot be denied that Haverfield operated at an exciting time in British archaeology. This was the time of a number of 'significant' archaeological discoveries: in the Near and Middle East, in Egypt, the continuing work at Pompeii, the Germans in Greece and Asia Minor, Schliemann at Troy and Mycenae and John Evans' work in the eastern Mediterranean which in turn trickled down in the public perception of archaeology as well as inspiring similar work in this country. At about the time he became active in northern England there commenced a series of epoch-making excavations on Roman military and civilian sites in Britain as well as on the Roman frontier in Germany. Then there were the beginnings of a revolution in the teaching of the subject in Britain's older universities, a change occasioned by government intervention and the rise of their newer metropolitan counterparts. Changes in teaching methods and the concomitant improvement in the standards of research led to better-quality publications and a more focused research agenda. It was facilitated too in part by the rise of national or-

---

14. In spite the fact he must have known them, Haverfield does not feature in contemporary accounts of Oxford life: e.g. in Jackson's 1917 study of the life of Ingram Bywater; in Coon's account of Warde Fowler's life; Percy Gardner's reminiscences; in Farnell's or Fisher's autobiographies; nor in Charles Oman's daughter Carola's memoirs of her Oxford childhood (e.g. 1892–1914; cf. Oman 1976).

ganizations – the British Academy, the (British) overseas Schools of Archaeology and a shift in attitude of the Society of Antiquaries of London. To these facts should be added the rise of regional (archaeological) societies that improved more generally standards at grass root level. At the same time as these changes, the general air of confidence and prosperity of the late Victorian/Edwardian era created a broader public appreciation of the subject and in turn a demand, one met in part by the national and regional societies and the mass publication broadcast of their results. At governmental level, we see the beginnings of state intervention and supervision of the 'nation's heritage'. For instance, there were parliamentary acts between 1892 and 1913 as well as the establishing of the Royal Commissions of Ancient and Historical Monuments in Scotland and Wales and of the Royal Commission of Historical Monuments in England in 1908. At the same time, however, many of these advances were disjointed. What was needed was to bring them together in a more formulated scheme of interpretation and articulation of the results. As will be demonstrated, Haverfield was in many respects at the forefront of these developments and was regarded by some as something of the 'fixer', bringing these strands together.

There is one other issue concerning Haverfield and how his legacy is regarded today. There is the matter of the transmission of the legacy. Haverfield's reputation owes as much to those who wrote about him immediately after his death as his publication. However the more one looks at Haverfield's work, the more one finds that the assessments of others, normally preserved in the obituaries, are often selective in their recollection. The major culprit in this sense is George Macdonald's descriptions of Haverfield's life. In the subsequent chapters much time is spent trying to identify and explain why this and other distortions may have occurred. For the moment it will suffice to say that, with the benefit of hindsight, there appears to have been created a number of misrepresentations about his work that have served to distort his significance. For want of a better term, I have called this 'the Haverfield myth'. There are a number of facets to the 'myth', some of which will be examined presently. Perhaps the most influential – or most frequently repeated – of them is Haverfield, being so badly affected by the losses amongst his band of 'students' during the First World War, he went into what became a terminal decline. While there is something in this assessment, the strength of the argument is weakened by the fact that it is extremely difficult to identify the members of the group. Another good example of the same sort of fudging apparent in assessments of Haverfield's life and work can be found in Macdonald's admittedly short description of Haverfield and his antecedents (Macdonald 1924).

Although this is not intended to be a biography of Haverfield, at least not in the conventional sense, a summary of his ancestry and family connections is desirable, not least because the primary authority for this sort of material Macdonald's principal memorial is sufficiently vague and selective to engender, if not suspicion, then curiosity. Close examination of it reveals some interesting facts – and omissions – about Haverfield and his family. Macdonald presumably received much of his information from his subject but closer readings shows not only are the summaries of some of the lives therein short but the detail is selective and/or obtuse. That it is written in such an obscure fashion always struck me as curious, if not suspicious. In fact it seems that some members of the family enjoyed a number of important and influential connections, which deserved lengthier description.

The origins of the family are indisputable. It was in Somerset from at least the 1500s, a tradition continued in the way the Haverfields are found in that county and its neighbours in the next three centuries and the way some of the London branch of the family later retired there. It is once we start to read of the 'later' Haverfields, however, that the story becomes interesting. The relevant passage is as follows:

> John Haverfield …soon after the middle of the eighteenth century, was appointed Superintendent of Kew Gardens by the Princess Dowager of Wales on the recommendation of Lord Bute …John Haverfield *primus* died …in 1784, leaving as his successor in office a son of the same name. A daughter of John Haverfield *secundus* survives in a Gainsborough portrait. His eldest son, likewise a John, held commissions in the 43rd and 48th Foot and served as Assistant-Quartermaster-General in Spain and Portugal in the year of Talavera. Lieutenant-Colonel Haverfield died in 1830. He had been twice married. His first family continued the name of John Haverfield for one generation and the tradition of soldiering for three; two of his great-grandsons fell in action in 1915. His second wife was Isabella Frances Meyer, … William Robert, the only issue of John Haverfield *tertius* and Frances Meyer, was ordained in 1850 (Macdonald 1924: 15).

There is much here which is glossed over. How and why a member of a Somerset family should end up in London, evidently through the patronage of Lord Bute, a well-known floriculturist (cf. Schweizer 2004) can not now be disentangled but the Royal appointment brought John Haverfield into intimate contact with the household of George III and with it status and social connections to the point that he, and the next two generations of Haverfields, occupied an eponymous house which still stands on Kew Green. Equally as significant, and emphasizing their social standing, is the fact that Haverfield *primus*, *secundus* and *tertius*, with members of their immediate families along with other court favourites, are buried in the grounds of the church of St Anne's on Kew Green that was patronized by the Royal family. Contrary to what Macdonald might imply, Haverfield *primus* fathered three sons, two who became Royal gardeners: John (*c*.1741–1820) and Thomas, along with William (*c*.1750–1828), who, after being the first Haverfield to go up to university, became a church minister. Thomas was to die in mysterious circumstances.[15] It is probably the three sons of *primus* who sat for the favourite court artist, Johann Zoffany.[16] Haverfield *primus'* first son, Haverfield *secundus*, was to marry the Housekeeper at Kew, Elizabeth Tunstall, after which her family name was frequently used in the subsequent generations of Haverfields. It was Haverfield *secundus'* daughter, Elizabeth (*c*.1776–1817), who was painted by Thomas Gainsborough in *c*.1782.[17] Although Haverfield *secundus* left the Royal employ ('retired') after 1795, when he was replaced by William Aiton as Superintendent following a revision of the terms of employment for those working in the Royal Household, he remained very much a local worthy with solid social connections – a JP and trustee of at least one local school – and appears to have made something of a living as a

---

15. The second son of Haverfield *primus* at the time of his death was, or was close to being, removed from his post as 'His Majesty's gardener at Hampton Court.' In a letter from Sir Henry Strachey (Master of the King's Household) to George III (6 December 1804), it is reported Thomas Haverfield was undergoing a criminal prosecution for fraud. Strachey did not know the full details of the case but adds Haverfield's '...affairs have been for some time in a deranged state, and his health so bad that his life has been almost daily in danger.' Strachey then discussed when and how to dismiss him. The terms of Haverfield's contract at Hampton were originally drawn up in 1785 (e.g. a year after his father's death). There is no response from the King. However, a footnote adds that *The Times* (Tuesday 11 December) reports the death 'on Sunday last' of Thomas Haverfield of Hampton Court (cf. A. Aspinall (*The Later Correspondence of George III. Vol. IV (January 1802–December 1807)*, (1968): 253–4; #2975)). It is not clear if he died of natural causes or otherwise. I can find no record of the prosecution or a coroner's report in *The Times*.

16. The Zoffany picture, in the archives at Kew Gardens, is undated. If it is not the three sons, then it is the father and two sons. There is also in Kew an unattributed portrait of Haverfield *primus*.

17. The subject, *Miss Haverfield*, married, in November 1794, James Wyld of Speen, Bucks., later rector of Blunsdon St Andrew's, Wilts. (Ingamells 1985: 99). The portrait was displayed in an exhibition at Burlington House in 1893, which Haverfield must have attended (*The Times* 30 December 1893). Both Gainsborough and Zoffany are buried in the same St Anne's cemetery as the Haverfields.

landscape designer-gardener, working for instance with the architect Sir John Soane.[18]

Haverfield *secundus* fathered two boys, one of them mentioned by Macdonald (= Haverfield *tertius*), although the reality of his status is somewhat distorted. He did serve in the Peninsular campaign but perhaps not with such an illustrious record as Macdonald implies. According to Ward (1957: 185) Lt-Col John Haverfield (1780–1830) was educated at Rugby and the Royal Military College (1804–6). Previously a Captain in the 48th (Northamptonshire) Regiment), he was made Assistant Quarter Master General in Portugal and Spain (a fact partially repeated on his gravestone at St Anne's as Assistant Quartermaster of the Forces), in April 1809. Following the completion of the Vimeiro campaign, however, he disappears from the army returns from June 1809 when presumably he retired. Ward attributes his removal as part of a general purge of incompetence and lethargy in the army in the Peninsula undertaken by Wellington. In contrast to Haverfield *tertius*, his brother, Thomas Tunstall Haverfield (*c.*1785/88–1866) enjoyed a much longer and potentially more influential career as a cleric to the establishment. Yet he is anonymous in Macdonald's account. Educated at Corpus Christi (Oxford), he was Rector of Goddington (Oxford) from 1826 until his death.[19] He too is buried at St Anne's, where he was once the curate (1812–18). Perhaps his most important appointment was as the Chaplain to HRH Duke of Sussex (1773–1843), Queen Victoria's favourite uncle and a Royal who once provoked a constitutional crisis when he eloped to marry in Rome. This Haverfield was the author of ecclesiastical and other works including *Notes on Kew and Kew Gardens* (1862) in which he recounted a number of anecdotes of the Kew Haverfields.[20] He was also a prominent freemason (cf. *The Times* 6 July 1842). It is strange then that Macdonald missed Thomas Tunstall, not least because as a prominent clerical, he was probably more of a 'High Church' than 'Low Church' persuasion.[21]

---

19. BA in 1807, MA in 1810, a BD in 1818 and college fellow in 1812–27 as well as Senior Dean for 1826.
20. These included *Almighty God to Whom All Hearts Open*; *The Church Catechism and Rite of Confirmation* (1818); *12 Sermons on Doctrine and Practice* (1835) as well as *The Fugitive of the Cevennes Mountains* (1860), a novel set during The Terror and adapted from the original French edition by M.J. Porchat.
21. There are other indications of T.T. Haverfield's social outlook. In January 1811 he delivered the sermon at the funeral of the noted Anglican social reformer and educationalist, Sarah Trimmer (1741–1810). It was an oration so well received it was subsequently published as *A Sermon Occasioned by the Death of Mrs. Trimmer, Preached at New Brentford, January 6th 1811; cf.* B. Brandon

The other Haverfields of this generation are largely anonymous. The Lieutenant-Colonel married twice. Out of his first marriage came (Major) John Haverfield (1811–1881) who served some of his time in Ireland and where he married. He was the step-brother to another Haverfield *tertius* son, one from the second marriage to Isabella Frances Meyer. This was the infirmed William Robert Haverfield (*c*.1828–1882), father of Francis John Haverfield. Major Haverfield too had one son, Major Henry Wykeham Brook Tunstall Haverfield (1847–1895), and so Francis' step-cousin. H.W.B.T. Haverfield was to marry in 1887, Evelina Scarlett (1867–1920), daughter of William Frederick Scarlett, 3rd Baron Abinger. As Evelina Haverfield, although she remarried after her first husband's death, she became a prominent, if not notorious, suffragette in the years before the First World War, after which she was a noted champion for Serbian relief. This is another family association completely ignored by Macdonald. It is difficult to understand why he failed to make more of these various linkages.[21]

These are associations on the male line of the Haverfield's family.[22] Just as curious is Macdonald's failure to follow through Francis' mother's lineage, although it also clear from looking at whom he visited and where he went on holiday etc., Haverfield retained closer links with that side than his father's. Francis' mother was Emily Druse Poynter

---

Schnorrenberg (Sarah Trimmer) *ODNB* 55 *(Tomson–Usher)*: 2004: 381–3.

21. There are other Haverfields of which Macdonald might have made more. For example, Robert Ross Haverfield (1819–1889), in a notice in *The Times* (5 June 1889) is described as having emigrated to Australia in *c*.1838 where he established a career first as a journalist and then as an explorer of the interior. Slightly later, there is the cousin Eleanor Louisa Haverfield (b.1870) who was to become a prolific authoress, mainly of stories for girls with such unforgettable titles as *Nancy's Fancies* (1899) – 'A graceful little study of children's thought and ways'); (with E. Velvin) *A Terrible Feud and Other Stories for Children* (1900); *Meriel's Choice* (n.d.); *The Discovery of Kate* (n.d.); *Our Vow, a Story for Children* (1899); *Queensland Cousins* (n.d.); *Rhoda; A Tale for Girls* (1905); *The Contest* (1906; 'A striking New Novel portraying a struggle between Capital, Labour and Love'); *Bobby's Surprise: A Story for Children* (1907); *The Girls of St Olaves* (1919); and *The Girl from the Bush* (n.d.) along with contributions to various girls annuals and collected stories.

22. This summary allows us to make sense of Macdonald's statement about the generations of soldiering Haverfields: The son is John Haverfield (1811–1881), the grandson H.W.B.T. Haverfield and the two great grandsons who died in 1915, John C. Haverfield of the 24th Punjab Regiment and Oliver John Calley (1893–1915) of the Wiltshire Regiment and a nephew of H.W.B.T. Haverfield.

Mackarness (1831–1862), a daughter of John Fielder Mackarness (1820–1889), Bishop of Oxford and Alethea Buchanan Coleridge (1826–1909), younger daughter of Sir John Taylor Coleridge and ultimately descended from the family of the poet, Samuel Taylor Coleridge. In addition to Emily, the Mackarness-Coleridge union produced a number of sons, some who went on to prominent ecclesiastical office. In time, a daughter (so a cousin) of one of Francis's uncles, Charles Coleridge Mackarness (1850–1918), FA Cup winner (1874) and one time Bishop of Scarborough, was to conduct the marriage of the Eton schoolmaster R.P.L. Booker, who most obituarists agree was Francis Haverfield's closest friend.

While Macdonald ignored virtually all this history, there are elements that may have had a bearing on Francis Haverfield's career. In this respect there are three distinct strands: the family's links with the Establishment, whether it be the Court, the Church or the Army (and there are other members of the family not described here who followed these routes); its strong (Anglican) religious commitment; and thirdly, an outlook coupled to a sympathy for what might be regarded as liberal social issues. It is striking how prominently the church featured at least in Haverfield's early life. Although there is no other conclusive proof of his religious commitment in general, there is good incidental evidence that he was exposed to what might be described as 'High Church' influences from an early age which seem to have continued into at least his early twenties. Not only was his father a cleric of a known doctrinal persuasion, there was tradition of other members of his parents families, going up to colleges with known connections with the 'High Church', Oxford or Tractarian Movement (cf. Chapter 3) before taking holy orders.[23]

---

23. Bruton (1919) called Haverfield 'the Pope of Roman Britain.' As he was certainly not a Catholic, I am at a loss to explain the derivation of this accolade, unless Bruton uses the word 'Pope' to describe Haverfield's tendency to, or to be credited with, infallibility. Bruton's language suggests a familiarity with Haverfield. Obviously more than an acquaintance (cf. Ch.8), I cannot judge how close. What is apparent is that Haverfield retained a degree of closeness with the Church. In addition to his father's connections with it, other members of Haverfield's family enjoyed long and successful careers as clerics. His father went up to Exeter College, then known for its close association with the Tractarian movement (cf. Ch.3). His maternal grandfather, John Fielder Mackarness had already attended Exeter. After a fellowship there (1844–6) and a church preferment in Worcestershire (1846–55) Mackerness moved in 1855 to Devon until Gladstone nominated him Bishop of Oxford (1870–88).

Given the eulogistic tone of the memoir, it is surprising Macdonald elected not to make anything of these facts but rather to praise exactly the same characteristics in Haverfield as if they were unique. Instead Macdonald's story really only starts with the birth of Haverfield *tertius'* son, William Robert and the father of Francis, and who continued one of the family's tradition, that of entering the Church.[24] The outline of Francis' career can be swiftly sketched (cf. Taylor 1920; Macdonald 1924: 15–38).

The father of three sons and four daughters, Mackarness had something of a reputation as a 'liberal'. But this was liberalism of a relative sort. In *c.*1873 he attacked W.H. Pater's *Studies in the History of the Renaissance*, which '...advocated the claim of aesthetic enjoyment to be the sole end of human life and activity'. In a sermon delivered at the Cathedral of Christ Church, Mackarness '...dwelt on what he conceived to be an imminent danger, viz. that the Oxford tutors, when free from clerical restrictions would instill the principles (of Pater's book) into the minds of their pupils' (Jackson 1917: 77). On the other hand, Mackarness was involved in the 'celebrated' prosecution of the Rev. T.T. Carter, vicar of St Andrew's, Clewer. On a number of occasions, Carter was charged and prosecuted by members of his congregation who claimed he held or enjoyed 'ritualistic' practices. Mackarness, as Carter's Bishop, was asked to adjudicate on these accusations, usually finding in favour of his rector, but more on the grounds of defending his 'legal' powers against external interference than out of any sympathy for Carter's beliefs, of which he did not necessarily approve (Bonham 2001). One of Mackarness' sons, the Venerable Charles Coleridge Mackarness (a graduate of Exeter in 1873 and 'a dedicated Tractarian', cf. *The Times* 2 March 1918; Crouch 2000), went onto become vicar of Scarborough and Archdeacon of the East Riding, retiring 1917. Various letters show Haverfield visited Scarborough at least in 1889, where his sister was a resident from at least 1901. C.C.M. was also a pupil and close friend of Ingram Bywater. Another son, F.M.C. Mackarness, acted as Haverfield's solicitor for his will of 1912 while one of its executors was C.M. Blagden, an Oxford cleric who went to become the Bishop of Peterborough. When John Mackarness married Alethea Buchanan Coleridge, he joined a family with known 'Tractarian' sympathies, not least John Taylor Coleridge (1790–1876), friend and biographer of John Keble as well as John Newman. Coleridge's son, John Duke (1820–1894), the first Baron Coleridge whose first son, Bernard John Seymour (1851–1927) married Mary Alethea Buchanan Mackarness in 1876. She was Haverfield's ?aunt. In 1883, Haverfield obtained an appointment at Lancing College, a school thought to be overly influenced by 'High Church' rituals (cf. Ch.4). Two Haverfield Winchester and Oxford contemporaries had even stronger church affiliations. According to Reynolds (1975: 20; 54–5; 56 etc), David Margoliouth and Charles Oman were to become leading figures in the evangelical movement at Oxford. Reynolds also cites other Haverfield-Oxford connections who were Oxford evangelicals, including Archibald Sayce and more surprisingly William Ramsay.

Born in Shipston-on-Stour, the first of two siblings, both of Francis' parents died when he was relatively young. His mother as a result of childbirth in 1862, his father, because of the long bouts of illness, as

---

24. One might speculate that the name Francis, otherwise not attested in the family, was a reference to Haverfield's paternal grandmother. The course of W.R. Haverfield's career is not entirely clear (cf. *Crockford's Clerical Directory* 1860; Macdonald 1924). Born in *c*.1828, he entered Exeter College (in April 1845, aged 17 years), and was an exhibitor at Corpus Christi (1846–9), where he took his BA and an MA (1852). He was ordained in 1850, became a Deacon and Priest in 1852, held two curacies in Somerset, one at St John's the Baptist at Batheaston (1852), followed by one at Shipston-on-Stour (where Francis was born). Married in 1859, he became Perpetual Curate of Headington Quarry, Oxford (1864, at The Holy Trinity Church; cf. de Villiers 1957). Dogged by ill health he retired to Bath, according to Macdonald (1924: 15–16), in *c*.1866, where he lived in seclusion until his death on 7 September 1882. He is buried at St John's the Baptist, Bathwick. The 1881 census has him residing (as a 'clergyman without care of souls') at 2 Alma Villas, Charlcombe (Somerset), with his two children and four female servants. The Oxford don A.H. Sayce (1845–1933) was to recollect that when he was 16 years old (= *c*.1861/2): 'Bath was beginning to be stirred by the controversies of Ritualism. The Abbey Church was in the hands of the Simeonite Trustees, and its rector, Mr Kemble, was a shining light of the Evangelical party. But a little church dedicated to St John the Baptist, was built in the parish of Bathwick, to accommodate the overflow congregation of the parish church, and it was at once captured by representatives of what, by comparison with the Abbey sect, was supposed to be a Ritualistic party. The first incumbent was the father of Professor Haverfield, lame and crippled in the spine, and all those of us who had "High Church" leanings made a point of attending his ministrations whenever it was possible. Judging from the size of the congregation the number must have been few' (Sayce 1923: 20–1). Sayce's recollection of the dates is probably at fault. The Simeonites were followers of Charles Simeon (1759–1836), a leader in the Evangelical Revival of the early nineteenth century. One of the features of the Trust was that it attempted to bring a degree of reality to contemporary religion at a time when it believed that the Church had become detached and too worldly. Towards this end it endeavored to purchase church livings. The 'Ritualistic' party was a 'high church' movement which tended to emphasize the importance of ritual, in the form of wearing the Eucharistic vestments, the use of incense and lighting, lectionary and the correct prayer book, in the practice of Christian ceremony. Accused of harbouring sympathies too close to the Catholic Church, the 'Ritualists' were increasing acted against by their opponents through a combination of church and legal petitions and ultimately court cases. It would seem that William Haverfield was of a 'High Church' persuasion. By coincidence, in 1841 the antiquarian Rev. H.M. Scarth assumed the curacy of Bathwick and, in turn came to exert an indirect influence on the young Haverfield's interest in the region's antiquities.

well as his handicapped condition, appears to have been exceptionally remote.[25] In the Macdonald version the schematic course of Haverfield's life can be divided into three distinct phases. The accuracy of this periodization is examined below. For the moment, the first includes his childhood and schooling, before going up to Oxford in 1879 and then his time as a schoolmaster at Lancing College. Haverfield junior was educated at a preparatory school at Clifton, then Winchester, and went up to New College, on the back of the Goddard scholarship, where he matriculated on 16 October 1879, aged 18 years. The signs are his time at Winchester and Oxford was not happy. In fact the impression is that Haverfield's childhood was a largely solitary and unhappy time. The effects of the premature bereavements and his schooling were to affect adversely his personality, rendering him shy, awkward and introverted. With no proficiency at sports and therefore no interest in them, at Winchester 'he had a predictably rough time' where it is clear he was bullied (Bonarkis Webster 1991: 119). Instead, much of his work at school was self-driven.[26] The spirit

25. It is surprising that, other than a passing reference to the circumstances of her birth, Macdonald has nothing to say about Haverfield's sister, Katherine Emily. Indeed in all of the Haverfield correspondence I have seen, she is completely absent. Macdonald (1924: 16) reports that Haverfield's mother died while giving birth to her. There is some fudging here. In fact, she was born at Hampstead on 13 May 1862 and christened on 11 June, the day after her mother passed away. Katherine died on 11 November 1908, aged 45 years in Scarborough, where in the 1901 census she is recorded as the deputy superintendent of a home. Haverfield is known to have visited his cousin C.C. Mackarness in Scarborough on a number of occasions but there is no indication if he met with her. It is tempting to link Ms Haverfield's position with an institution associated with Mackarness' church, St Martin's, where his sister (Julia, otherwise unknown) was, from 1882, superintendent of St Martin's Lodge in Scarborough (for ladies, created in 1875).

26. Bonarkis Webster is presumably elaborating on statements in Macdonald 1924 and Oman 1941. It is also clear, however, via Christopher Hawkes, she had access to unpublished memories of some of Haverfield's school contemporaries. The principal was Cuthbert Hamilton Turner (1860–1930), a fellow student at Winchester and New, along with (Sir) Charles William Chadwick Oman (1860–1946) and David Samuel Margoliouth (1858–1940). Like Haverfield, after gaining a similarly disappointing degree at Oxford, Turner went onto a career in that university. He was Lecturer in Theology at St John's (1885), assistant to the Regius Professor of Ecclesiastical History (1888), fellow of Magdalen (1889–1930) and ultimately Dean Ireland's Professor of Exegesis of the Holy Scriptures (1920–30: cf. Bate 1937). Oman was to become Chichele Professor of Modern History (Robertson 1946) and Margoliouth Professor of Arabic in the same university (cf. Murray 1940b;

of individuality continued at Oxford. Although awarded a First in Classical Moderations (1880), for Greats he took only a Second in 1883, a consequence of a lack of interest in philosophy and anything else which did not stimulate him. Unable to obtain a college fellowship, in 1884 he accepted a Sixth Form tutorship at Lancing College, taking his MA in 1886. Other significant events of this time were his introduction to Theodor Mommsen and an invitation to assist in the updating of the *Corpus Inscriptionum Latinarum* volume VII (hereafter *CIL* VII). Out of this invitation came Haverfield's almost frenetic work in the archaeology of Roman Britain, which in turn created a momentum that was eventually to get him back to Oxford. In 1892, after winning the Conington Memorial Prize in 1891 (cf. *The Times* 7 July 1911), he returned as senior student and tutor at Christ Church.

The return marks the start of the second phase of Haverfield's career. It is in this period that he embarked on what might be called a 'mission' for (Roman) archaeology in this country. That 'mission' had been shaped by his exposure to the work of Mommsen as well as his growing dissatisfaction with what had been achieved by British antiquarians up to that time. The major features of this period are the enthusiasm he threw in to a variety of mutually complimentary schemes: in his involvement in a number of exca-

---

1949). Oman, like Haverfield, disliking the Winchester emphasis on sport, was also bullied there. Bosanquet (1920: 137) records other Winchester contemporaries were David Hogarth, Sir Cecil Smith and A.H. Smith. With Haverfield's lack of interest in sporting activities, it is curious that he contributed a chapter on the athletic records of Christ Church to F.E. Robinson's *Two Oxford Colleges* (1900), where an anonymous reviewer commented 'Indeed we could find it in our hearts to wish that more space had been found for this subject (viz. famous Christ Church men) at the cost of the omission of a jejune chapter on the athletic records of Christ Church by Mr F.J. Haverfield' (*The Times* 16 August 1900). The headmaster at Winchester during Haverfield's time there (*c*.1874–9) was the Rt Rev. George Ridding (headmaster 1867–84). The Winchester historian J. D'E. Firth (1954: 40) along with a later headmaster, Montague Rendall held the earlier part of Ridding's period of office in high regard. Whatever his experiences at Winchester, they did not prevent Haverfield revisiting the college in later years to speak to the school nor to contribute an article to *The Manchester Guardian* on its 500th anniversary (30 March, 1887). Rendall, when he became second master at Winchester in 1899 received a letter of congratulation from Haverfield: '[a]n even more distinguished and reserved Wykehamist, F J Haverfield, wrote: "The news of your appointment gave much pleasure to everyone. It is a good place to have, better than Headmasterships, and you will do it well"' (quoted in D'E. Firth 1954: 62).

vations, programmes designed to address specific issues while at the same time having a training component; his efforts to involve the universities in such work along with their more traditional ways of teaching; by his trying to reduce the importance and influence of the regional archaeological societies; and by his attempt to foster a cadre of 'students' who were to disseminate the message more widely. In addition to these initiatives, Haverfield was also at the centre of the reporting of the discoveries and progress that he and others were making, not least, his pains to improve the quality of the publication of the results of the same. The success of the work undertaken at this time served to strengthen his reputation such that it contributed to his elevation to the pre-eminent academic post in history and antiquarian archaeology in this country. The close of the second phase of his career came not with his elevation to the Camden chair in 1907, but rather with the outbreak of the First World War. Not only did the war interrupt, possibly fatally, the momentum that had been developing before its declaration, it severely affected his health in 1915, a breakdown which is widely reported was a consequence of the disruption brought to the group of 'students' with which he was associated.

While it is true that some of Haverfield's vitality returned after 1916, one can still detect a significant change in the focus of his work in the third and final phase of his career. For instance, his involvement in fieldwork seems to have petered out. The range of his publications also seems to shift towards more synthesizing overviews than the sort of site-specific discussions which characterized much of his pre-1914 output. The change in emphasis was in part obviously a consequence of the fact that archaeological excavation in Britain in the aftermath of the war did not resume on anywhere near the scale that had existed before it. A general loss of enthusiasm coupled with the loss of contact with continental (i.e. German) scholarship was a contributory factor. This phase of his career ended with his premature death, aged 58, in 1919.

Among a number of distinguished awards, Haverfield was made a FSA in 1891, and elected to the British Academy in 1904 (joining its Council in 1908). According to Macdonald (1924: 26), he was an active member of a small number of archaeological and antiquarian societies, including the Newcastle Society of Antiquaries from 1889 (and a Vice-President in 1906), the Cumberland and Westmorland since 1890 (a Vice-President in 1899 and its President from 1915), and the Somerset Antiquarian and Natural History Society (from 1916 and its President for 1918).[27] He also served in various capacities on excavation

---

27. Macdonald fails to mention Haverfield's membership of the Royal Archaeological Institute (since 1885 and as a Life Compounder, 1890). Among the

committees (e.g. Chester, Silchester and Wroxeter) and was intimate, directly or indirectly, with others.[28] He was a member of the Royal Commission on the Historical Monuments of England from 1909 and the first President of the Society for the Promotion of Roman Studies in 1910, an organization he was central in creating, and marginally less so with the British School of Archaeology at Rome. Honorary degrees were conferred by the universities at Aberdeen (1905) and Leeds (1910) and he was a corresponding member of the Imperial German Archaeological Institute (the Deutsche Archäologische Institut).

It is by combining these various sources of information that we can compensate in part for the deficiencies in the primary source material. Although we can create a framework for Haverfield's career, in spite of the large number of obituaries and memoirs of his life, it has to be said he comes over as a rather lonely individual. Undoubtedly as much a consequence of a lack of evidence and his difficult childhood, his circle of friends seems to have been small. His acknowledged closest associates were G.L. Cheesman, George Macdonald, Charles Oman and R.P.L. Booker.[29] Clearly familiar with a great number of other persons,

---

numerous local societies of which he was a member there was the Essex Archaeological and Chester societies. He was also an honorary member of the Woolhope Naturalists' Field Club (a member from 1895) and a member of the Earthworks Committee of the Congress of Archaeological Societies from 1903 to 1919 (when it was minuted that the '...gap left by the death ...of ...Professor Haverfield will not be easily filled – *Report of the Committee in Ancient Earthworks and Fortified Enclosures*. Congress of Archaeological Societies 1919: 6). Macdonald also omits that Haverfield was President of the Oxford Architectural and Historical Society between June 1908 and November 1919 (cf. Pantin 1939). Nor is there any mention of his contributions to its volumes. He was a founder member of the Northumberland and Durham Classical Association. In 1903–4 he is listed as a donor to the Graeco-Roman branch of the Egyptian Exploration Fund. Macdonald also notes Haverfield serving on the board of governors of a couple of schools but misses that he had served since 1912 as one of Oxford's representatives on the Joint Committee of the Universities and Head Masters' Conference.

28. E.g. with the work of the Manchester branch of the Classical Association and its excavations at Manchester and Castleshaws and in south Wales at Gellygaer. An undated and unlocated press clipping in the Liverpool Institute of Archaeology scrapbooks (in the Museum collection, SACE in the University of Liverpool), reporting on two years of excavation by John Garstang at Ribchester, noted the creation of a joint-committee which included Sir Henry Hornby, the Rev. Evan Hames, H. Openshaw, P. Gruebner and Haverfield.

29.

such acquaintances were more at the professional rather than the personal level. At the same time, his difficult personality cannot but have contributed to the smallness of his inner circle.[30] We have seen that Haverfield seems to have been detached from at least the paternal side of his family and where he seems to have compensated for it with a closeness with some distant relatives, in particular the Mackarnesses and, more strangely, the Coleridges, a family with which he was associated through the marriage of his maternal grandfather. This link would explain why Haverfield appears to have occasionally based himself at Ottery St Mary in Devon, the Coleridge family seat although it is not evident with whom he associated there.

It is a commonplace in biographical studies to attribute events and influences in childhood to the subsequent development of the subject under review. In Haverfield's case, however, I am uncertain if any of these family connections ever influenced him in a direct or explicit manner. Of his opinions of religion in general, he was to later to say that given his time again, he would have concentrated on the late Roman to post-Roman period. It might be pushing the evidence to suggest this was a period characterized in contemporary scholarship with the rise of Christianity in Britain. For the moment, therefore, I am reluctant to say much more than that Haverfield's character, his shyness but intellectual aggressiveness, might have been married to a driving self-motivation which grew into ambition in the first part of his career and as a unchallengeable self-confidence verging on arrogance and infallibility in the latest phases might be traced back to his unhappy early years.

After Haverfield

In the manner the historiography of Romano-British studies is written, Haverfield is regularly attributed the creation and definition of the subject. His achievement was on a number of levels, most of which were accepted and expanded upon by the subsequent generation of workers, of which the most significant are supposed to have been R.G. Collingwood, Ian Richmond and to a lesser degree Eric Birley and even less so R.E.M. Wheeler. But just as serious as the creation of the

---

Macdonald's memoir of Haverfield claims that in '…writing the …sketch I have received help from practically all of Professor Haverfield's surviving friends whom I have had occasion to mention by name' (1924: 38). A check reveals Macdonald cites three named individuals (Oman, Mackenzie, and Anderson) and one unnamed source from his Lancing days. He surely used more, not least Margerie Taylor.

30. Charles Oman was to write that Haverfield '...was angular, untidy and reti-
cent, sometimes morose, a man of few friends, but full of interest, if you
could draw him out on one of the subjects in which he was interested' (Oman
1941: 66). While at New College, Haverfield was '...already keen on all
branches of archaeology, and set on explanation. To the ordinary athletic or
apolaustic undergraduates he was unapproachable – they did not take any
notice of one whom they regarded as odd and untidy, nor was he ready to
"suffer fools gladly"'. Collingwood wrote of 'his energetic temperament and
forcible tongue have won him the name of a dangerous critic and a difficult
colleague' (1919: 118: cf. Macdonald 1924: 26). Macdonald noted on a
number of occasions, often on the testimony of others, how Haverfield could
be 'difficult' (p. 18–19), possessing a 'forceful personality (that) did not always adjust automatically to the views and customs of older or more
conservative colleagues' (p. 21–2). 'He was also inflexible and prone to
brusqueness' (p. 36–7). Macdonald was no angel in this respect. But there
again there is Collingwood's observation, as reported by Graham (1981:
214), '...that strife among learned men was a sure sign of vigorous forward
movement in whatever discipline was concerned.' Page too wrote of
Haverfield's biting tongue and impatience, but paid homage to the fact that
his '...ever ready help to a good cause and encouragement for every deserv-
ing endeavour brought him numerous friends. The pleasure it was to him to
draw together those who were likely to be helpful to each other in their work
will be in the memory of many. "Whom would you like to meet?" was his in-
variable question, as Dr. Macdonald reminds us, when a weekend invitation
was accepted' (Page 1920: 250). Wheeler (1961: 157) too recorded the way
Haverfield could intimidate even his most distinguished colleagues. 'He was
quick to take up a challenge and could hit hard, but he could also admit that
he had been mistaken' (Bosanquet 1920: 140; cf. Craster 1920: 65).
Bosanquet also noted his difficult character and his uncompromising utterances 'free from intellectual timidity' (p. 138). His transfer to Brasenose in
1907 was not easy; '...He came to us from Christ Church, and at first with the
instinctive loyalty of his nature he undoubtedly felt keenly the severance
from his colleagues, pupils and institutions to whom he had become bound
by twenty-six years of service. In his first years here his love for C[hrist]
C[hurch] made him perhaps a little difficult as a colleague at Brasenose' (*The
Brazen Nose* 1919: 5). Something of a disciplinarian, as college censor he
brought, '...order to a turbulent college' (Bosanquet 1920: 138). O.G.S.
Crawford, in a passage meant to emphasize the importance of the stratified
location of archaeological finds reminisced; 'There were some ...who recognised it; Haverfield was one, and I well remember an occasion when he
exhibited a single potsherd of Arretine Ware at a meeting of the Society of
Antiquaries of London. The Society was then dominated by dilettanti and
collectors, and I am sure Haverfield did it to provoke them into reaction'
(1953: 31). Nor was Haverfield averse to criticizing directly opinions with
which he disagreed or disapproved (e.g. Haverfield 1903d; 1904c: 249). On
occasion he made belligerent statements concerning differences of opinion

Haverfield 'myths' was, many of them have been repeated by subsequent writers which has in turn perpetuated an impression of the man which is not strictly accurate. For instance there is the way that contemporary assessments of Haverfield's influence suppose an almost seamless continuity with his 'successors', notably Collingwood. In the received version, Collingwood is supposed to have taken on the baton from Haverfield and to have carried Romano-British studies into the 1930s, and with it the emergence of Eric Birley and Ian Richmond and so in to the post-Second World War period. Elsewhere this continuity has been called 'the Oxford (Durham) School', an impression some have been happy to repeat into the 1980s (Frere 1988) or else as a parallel 'northern school'. In either case, the corollary is the future of Romano-British studies lay with the universities. But there are a number of issues, if not problems, in this sort of description. In the first place the contribution of the non-Oxford, and indeed non-university based R.E.M. Wheeler is completely ignored despite the fact that the first part of his archaeological career was firmly rooted in Romano-British archaeology. Birley too tends to be marginalized in the Oxford perspective of the subject. Second, a closer examination of Collingwood and his relationship with Haverfield indeed suggests a different perspective. Again Haverfield's legacy and how Collingwood reacted to it will form a substantial portion of the latter part of this monograph. Finally there is the question, already hinted at, of the relative strength of the subject in the 1920s and 1930s and in particular within the country's universities. Therefore we cannot avoid discussion of the significance of Haverfield's 'descendants'. It also means that we need to look again at what was going on in the university sector post-1919.

In the conventional (university-focused) explanation of the progress of Romano-British studies, after Haverfield the next major figures are R.G. Collingwood and I.A. Richmond. Robin George Collingwood was born in 1889, the son of the noted and well-regarded Cumbrian antiquarian, William Collingwood, and through whom he was introduced to the leading archaeologists and antiquarians of the time, including Haverfield. Collingwood went up to University College, Oxford with a

---

with regard to the reporting of the progress of the Silchester excavations. While to a limited number of his contemporaries 'he was a perennial source of knowledge and debate' (Oman 1941: 82–3), even his associates were not immune (e.g. Charles Roeder of Manchester, Newbold, Atkinson and Garstang; cf. Haverfield 1902b). But to end on a positive, Macdonald claims Haverfield mellowed after the War! (1924: 37; cf. *The Times* 2 October 1919).

scholarship. After taking a First in *Literae Humaniores*, he was elected to a tutorship in philosophy at Pembroke in 1912. During this time he continued in his father's footsteps and was heavily involved in the archaeology of north-west England. As an undergraduate he participated, with Haverfield, on the Corbridge excavations in 1911 and 1912, and under Haverfield's patronage directed at Ambleside in 1913. At Oxford, after Haverfield's death in 1919, he combined teaching in philosophy with offering courses in aspects of Roman Britain. He also continued to undertake fieldwork in the north during the summer months throughout the 1920s. In 1934 he became Waynflete Professor of Metaphysical Philosophy (and so a fellow of Magdalen College). With declining health, he resigned his chair and returned to his father's house at Coniston. He died in January 1943.

In contrast to Haverfield, Collingwood has been the subject of more detailed academic study, although it has been claimed he was never been the subject of a biography (Levine 2004: 253).[31] He has long been claimed as one of the 'great' Romano-British scholars. Nor has his reputation suffered because of the exceptional range of his intellectual interests and because he published an autobiography (Collingwood 1939; Simpson 1996). In the aftermath of his death Collingwood was the subject of a large number of obituaries and others assessments, a situation assisted by the fact that the potential pool of source material is far greater than for Haverfield. His personal papers, saved for posterity, were transferred to the Bodleian Library at Oxford in 1978. Unfortunately the indications are that this archive, as with most of the subsequent scholarly research on Collingwood and his methodology, concerns his philosophical and historiographical work rather than his archaeological. Collingwood's career has been characterized, like Haverfield's, as going through three distinct phases (1912–25, 1925–33 and 1933–43). It is the first two of these periods, which are of principal interest here. A renaissance in Collingwood studies began in the 1960s, which means that there are available a good number of recent semi-biographical studies. In turn this has been followed more recently by his 'discovery' by some archaeological theoreticians who have occasioned a reappraisal of his archaeological writings. So much so, that he has been held up as a model for how the study of Roman Britain and archaeology in general might be read (e.g. Scott 1990; Bradley 1994; Hodder 1995;

---

31. Other than entries in biographical dictionaries and others encyclopedia, the situation might be about to change: it is reported F. Inglis is preparing such a study (*The Independent* 27 May 2005). I am grateful to J.K. Davies for this notice.

Hingley 2000). The irony of this re-discovery is that, as was noted at the time of his death, Collingwood's '...work in archaeology, as Collingwood himself always maintained, was a side-line or hobby. Although in it he was to make a reputation which many academic men might covet for their one and only activity, he was and remained purely a philosopher' (McCallum in McCallum *et al.* 1943: 464). There is still however, scope for re-assessment of his Romano-British work relative to his philosophical publications. Virtually all the available studies normally work from the 'wrong' perspective, relating his philosophy of history to his archaeological studies. The following text attempts to do the opposite: to assess his archaeological work relative to his philosophical. This observation and its implications are frequently forgotten in assessments of the progress of Romano-British studies after Haverfield. Nor is this fact helped, as will be argued below (cf. Chapter 11), by Collingwood's waning interest in Romano-British studies from the late 1920s, when the emphasis of his output was more concerned with works of synthesis rather than investigation, a development usually ignored in most assessments of his career. That said, the existence of the papers as well as the *Autobiography* means that we do not have to look at his archaeological publications so closely as we have to do for Haverfield.

The next in line in the pantheon of 'greats' in Romano-British archaeology is said to be Ian Archibald Richmond, although it could be argued that he was not a scholar of the same stature as Haverfield or Collingwood. Nor has his reputation survived as well, although he has had a significant influence on certain aspects of Romano-British studies. Born in 1902, Richmond developed at an early age a passion for archaeology and in particular that of Roman Britain. In 1919 he went up to Corpus Christi (Oxford) and where still an undergraduate, he published his first article in 1922. He claimed that his inspiration in reading about Roman Britain was Haverfield, in teaching R.G. Collingwood, and in the techniques of excavation R.E.M. Wheeler (for whom he worked at *Segontium* in 1921–2). Graduating with a disappointing degree, Richmond went on to the British School at Rome (as Gilchrist Scholar, Craven Fellow and Goldsmith's Senior Student) where he came to know another Haverfield associate, Thomas Ashby. In 1927 Richmond was appointed Lecturer in Classical Archaeology and Ancient History at Queen's University, Belfast and remained there for the next four years. In 1930 he replaced Ashby as director of the school in Rome but had to resign in the same year citing health problems. Rendered unemployed, a chance meeting with Eric Birley at Birdoswald in 1934 resulted in the latter suggesting to his employers (Durham University and Armstrong College at Newcastle) that his post might be split. The outcome was that Richmond was appointed to Newcastle in 1935 where he was to remain until 1956 when he translated to the newly created chair of Roman archaeology at Oxford. He died, in post, in 1965. Published memories and other anecdotes about Richmond emphasize his great enthusiasm and energy especially in the field rather than his intellectual interests compared to those of the former pair. Assessing his 'position' in the archaeological firmament is hampered by the fact he was not the subject of the same number of obituaries as either Haverfield or Collingwood. The 'problem' is that he did not develop the sort of broader range of scholarly interests that his two predecessors enjoyed. Haverfield, superficially at least, appears to have operated in a far greater range of archaeological disciplines than did Richmond, while Collingwood's reputation is double-edged: archaeologist and philosopher at one and the same time. In contrast, in spite of his many monographs, Richmond comes over as a limited specialist – perhaps the natural consequence, one generation removed, of the process that Haverfield set in motion with the first steps to creating a group of material or subject experts to develop Romano-British archaeology. In this respect Richmond's expertise lay in the archaeology of the Roman army. His monographs come almost as a consequence of his elevated position: as a senior academic he was expected to perform rather than wanting to put over a particular line of interpretation. Any assessment of Richmond has to fall back on the relatively restricted corpus of obituary notices as well as the general themes which appear in his major works. The conditions, however, for a study of Richmond are as complicated as those for Haverfield. The problem in this respect is that the consequences of Richmond's career continue to exert an influence on the current structure of Romano-British studies which makes it difficult to come to a realistic appraisal of his work. To put it bluntly, there are still too many Richmond 'students' occupying academic positions who do not welcome critical comment about him. For this reason the section on Richmond is necessarily briefer than I would wish. But what it does demonstrate, I hope, is the form of continuity from Haverfield and down to the present.

Organization and structure

Following this introductory chapter, Chapter 2 sets out the contextual background to Haverfield's career, and in particular the strengths and especially the weaknesses in British archaeology at about the time he became active coupled with comment on the evolution of Romano-British studies. As a facet of the 'archaeology' of these islands, they have traditionally lain in an anomalous position. Although strictly speaking a period/subject defined by a political event (the annexation of Britain to an imperial system), it is clearly not part of later prehistoric archaeology. As such it has tended to be lumped, albeit to nobody's satisfaction, as part of classical archaeology, not least because it seems to stray into aspects it shares with its Mediterranean version; i.e. in epigraphy, numismatics, pottery and art. This situation was squarely a consequence of the way that archaeology developed in the late nineteenth century. As is well known, the origins lie in Europe in the late seventeenth century although the consequences of the advances in 'Roman archaeology' did not reach Britain until some 150 years later. It was only late in that century that the archaeology of Roman Britain, rather than being an adjunct of classics or epigraphy or numismatics etc., came to be accepted as a respectable intellectual, if not academic, discipline. The lack of such awareness was due to a combination of the deficiencies in the British university system and its reluctance to absorb developments occurring in mainland Europe. It thus requires an assessment of the position of Romano-British studies in the universities, as well as the structure of British (regional) archaeology that Haverfield used to his advantage. Haverfield's intellectual development at Oxford was profoundly influenced by the introduction of new ('German') teaching methods and what was called even then 'the new ancient history' which was to have consequences for his scholarly training. To appreciate this fact, one has to examine the academic tradition from out of which Haverfield emerged. Chapter 3 examines in more detail how Theodor Mommsen influenced Haverfield's outlook and created a template for his career. There was also the influence of Mommsen's way of writing about the provinces of the empire.

Although Haverfield graduated in 1883 with what was seen as a disappointing degree before going into schoolmastering, this should be seen as the formative period in his career and is examined in Chapter 4. After making contact with Mommsen he moved into epigraphy as an editor for the *CIL* which in turn led to a familiarization crash course into the Roman archaeology of Britain. Such was the quality of his output in the period 1884–92, Haverfield was able to return to Oxford. This in turn put him in the position to replace his mentor Henry Pelham as the Camden Professor in 1907. In time, Haverfield's work led to a redefinition of the remit of the chair. Haverfield also developed close contacts with most of the leading Roman archaeologists in Europe of the time. His ability to report the results of work on the continent served to reinforce his reputation and influence in this country. It also conditioned the way he saw Britain as part of Roman Europe rather than as an island entity. By the analysis of this aspect of his career we might be able to assess the widely accepted belief that Haverfield was a Romano-British archaeologist, when in fact he might be better described as a mainstream Oxford historian with multifarious interests in Roman history but who also happened to write much about the Roman province of Britain.

From this position we move on to look at what can be called Haverfield's 'mission' with respect to the development of Roman studies in this island (Chapter 5). One of Mommsen's many achievements was the way he transferred scholarship to national institutions. In the same way Haverfield looked to the precedent and attempted to do in his own way the same in Britain. Whilst the results of Haverfield's 'mission' were not on the grand, international scale of Mommsen and in the long term much of it failed or else was subsumed by other developments, what is striking is how far his work extended. The 'mission' was to be accomplished in a variety of ways. The first theme is how Haverfield attempted to institutionalize Roman studies in Britain. This was to be accomplished by a variety of media used through the 1890s, 1900s and 1910s. Although not an excavator of any talent, he was closely involved in a number of high-profile excavations, which gave him access to results and an overview on progress (cf. Chapter 6). It included those at Chester, Silchester and Caerwent, and slightly later Hadrian's Wall and Corbridge. In turn he came to monopolize the scene by establishing himself as the national broadcaster of recent progress by becoming the correspondent for at least two major periodicals. He was similarly associated with other high-profile publications such as the nascent *Victoria County History* (*VCH*) and the Royal Commission on the Historic Monuments (RCHME) series. Nor was he detached from key state organizations and certain regional societies. His tentacles also extended to the provincial museums. Furthermore, he occupied a central position in the creation of institutions meant to facilitate Roman studies (the British School at Rome and the Society for the Promotion of Roman Studies as well as the Classical Association). Finally there was his relationship with the teaching of (Roman) archaeology in the fledgling provincial universities of England. While Chapter 7 looks at some of the larger schemes of research with which Haverfield was involved, along with other aspects of his work after he returned to Oxford, and in particular the way he integrated geography with an understanding of how it affected the development of Roman Britain.

The outbreak of the First World War was a personal disaster for Haverfield. It halted, if not destroyed, much of the momentum which had been building up since the late 1890s. It effectively severed many European contacts. It interrupted excavation work, disrupted Oxford and saw a number of his 'students' enlist, some not to return. Haverfield is supposed to have employed an increasingly refined system of talent-spotting promising undergraduates at Oxford for fieldwork. Some 'students', or better expressed associates, participated on his excavations and were then encouraged to specialize in the writing of site reports and/or to gain field experience on other sites. Some went on to university appointments. Outside of academia, Haverfield relied on a network of informants and well-placed individuals. He was a member (and office bearer) in a number of the more important regional archaeological and antiquarian societies. In turn this network of informants and contacts gave him an (overbearing) influence on how Roman Britain was presented. Chapter 8 is a detailed examination of who might have made up what transpires to be an elusive group. What this chapter demonstrates is that the belief that Haverfield's health and vitality collapsed because of the losses of the First World War is true. But to attribute Haverfield's decline to the demise of so many of his 'students' is wrong, for, with three or four tenuous exceptions, it is extremely difficult to identify who was lost.

Although in many respects Haverfield's plans and projects did not come to fruition, for reasons largely beyond his control, Chapter 9 explores just how successful was the work he completed between 1892 and 1919. Such were the successes that his influence had a defining effect on the major figures to follow him, including Robin Collingwood and later Ian Richmond. Although Haverfield was to use archaeological data in a way that had not been done previously, he still saw the discipline as an adjunct of ancient history, one to flesh out aspects of the past where literary (and epigraphic) sources were deficient. In turn his writings expounded a number of themes. These views were expressed in a small number of seminal publications which will be analysed for what they reveal about Haverfield's 'mission'. In recent times there has been some debate as to whether Haverfield's perception of the Roman world was overly influenced by his conception of the 'mission' of the British empire. Chapter 10 examines the validity of this hypothesis, where it will be argued that, contrary to what some would maintain, Haverfield was not overtly influenced as such and that where he might appear to have been, then the impression was unintentional. The conclusions will be bolstered by the pan-European outlook already noted. The most enduring of Haverfield's opinions was the effect of the Roman occupation of the island – its 'romanization'. In turn his conclusions continue to effect how the process is interpreted today and the depth of its penetration.

The best known of Haverfield's 'students' is R.G. Collingwood, who is the subject of the first part of Chapter 11. While some claimed he went on 'to carry the Haverfield torch' an impression Collingwood was happy to repeat, closer analysis of the facts shows his work was offered more as correctives to Haverfield's views. For Collingwood frequently articulated their differences in a very explicit manner. Compared to Haverfield, Collingwood wrote a greater number of more influential or enduring works, many of which went through a number of editions. What has not been appreciated is that it is possible to see Collingwood's thinking evolving in these works, not least his increasing sense of detachment from Romano-British studies. In turn his opinions have had significant consequences on what developed in the subject after his own death. Collingwood's successor in Romano-British scholarship is supposed to have been Ian Richmond, although the sense of continuity is somewhat forced. There was also the part played by R.E.M. Wheeler and Eric Birley. Although 'taught' by Collingwood, Richmond's most important work was undertaken first in Italy, at the British School in Rome and later, with his appointment at Armstrong College/Newcastle University before his translation to a newly created professorship at Oxford. Despite the rather tenuous link between Collingwood and Richmond, the latter's career will be examined in the same chapter. It will explore how Haverfield's conclusions largely underwrote the work of the two as well as other scholars and in turn lay the basis for the thesis that there has been no real progress in Romano-British studies since Haverfield. Chapter 12 will bring together the conclusions of the preceding chapters to offer an overview of how Romano-British archaeology evolved in the years after Haverfield's death.

CHAPTER 2

Roman Britain in the mid-nineteenth century

So-called histories of archaeology almost invariably, despite their titles, devote themselves exclusively to prehistoric archaeology. This is indefensible: for the restricted area of Britain, for instance, a history of archaeology, after prehistory, must engage in the archaeological evidence for the Roman occupation, with the increased complexity of not only military and civil field monuments and material culture in the technology of artefacts, but of numismatics and epigraphy and the specialised archaeology that constitutes art history (Piggott 1989: 8).

Introduction

Before looking at Haverfield's contribution to Romano-British studies it is necessary to establish the condition of the subject up to the time he became active in the late nineteenth century. At least three themes come to mind. On the one hand there is what had been accomplished in the subject up until then. Although the subject of British antiquarianism has been treated by a number of modern authorities, there is an imbalance in the scope of such appreciations. Historians of the development of archaeology have usually been at pains to emphasize how one of the accomplishments of medieval and post-medieval writers was that they gradually came to understand the longevity of man's antiquity. The emphasis, however, has been on the appreciation of man's technological development in the prehistoric era and explains why, generally speaking, antiquarianism has been studied by those whom we might characterize as prehistorians or archaeological theorists. Out of such realizations came appreciation of his technological and cultural attainments. In contrast, antiquarianism relative to the Roman period has been until relatively recently largely neglected by modern writers. In a similar fashion, while credit is often accorded for the improving methods of recording that many antiquarians devised, what is frequently missed is their sensitivity to what they observed. The subsequent interpretations of that data may have been flawed but, in the long term, it is the recognition of it which is relevant here.

The second question is when did Roman Britain come to be recognized as a discrete topic of research in this country? The usual way of writing about British antiquarianism is to treat it as a largely undifferentiated mass of explorers and writers, some better than others, who happened to tour and draw and map that which they came across. Some of them were more systematic in their approach but as a whole, and in a largely negative fashion, antiquarianism is regarded as being indiscriminate in what it discussed. So how and when were the Roman antiquities of this island appreciated as being separate from the mass?

The third and final issue about Roman archaeology in Britain up to the middle of the nineteenth century is who executed the research, both at the regional and national levels. As will become evident, up to the start of the twentieth century the universities (meaning Oxford and Cambridge) were not contributors to any extent in research into the island's Roman past. While this deficiency will be explored in more detail below, what even Haverfield appreciated was how it was the local antiquarian, archaeological, architectural and natural history societies who were responsible for setting the momentum for research. The impetus for this burst of activity went back to the first half of that century, although this is not to ignore the work of the preceding three centuries. Part of the reason why Haverfield came to dominate the scene lies with his dissatisfaction with how and what the regional societies had achieved and continued to do. In time, it was part of his and his generation's achievement to usurp the dominant position of the amateur and regional archaeologist. But it was not until the early twentieth century that there developed what approximated to organized programmes for study and research, some of it executed indirectly through the leading universities. It is therefore necessary to understand why Haverfield felt that the power and influence of the amateur and his society had to be moderated. Understanding this will then allow us to appreciate whom he believed should be setting the agenda and why.

Romano-British studies in the nineteenth century

In defining Romano-British archaeology we are presented with the problem of what exactly it is. Because it encompasses types of material not found in its prehistoric counterpart but more common in its Mediterranean form, in at least the nineteenth and early twentieth centuries it tended to be a subsidiary branch of classical archaeology. It is a widely acknowledged fact that there has yet to be written, in English at least, a satisfactory study of the origins and development of classical archaeology. With the exception of the work of Stephen Dyson, what is available is either dated (e.g. Gardner 1926) or one-dimensional studies (e.g. Boardman 1985 on the teaching of classical archaeology at Oxford) or else the discipline is included in various entries in encyclopaedias and dictionaries of archaeology (e.g. Thomson de Grummond 1996). Despite a resurgence in the historiography of archaeology and ancient history, prehistory continues to monopolize the history of ideas relative to archaeology, which explains why the literature on the evolution of archaeology as prehistory (and anthropology) is much larger. The same bias applies equally to textbooks on archaeological method. For example, the various works of Glyn Daniel (1950; 1967; 1981) and repeated by others (e.g. Trigger 1989; Malina and Vasicek 1990) in discussing the European context of archaeology would attribute most, if not all, of the methodological and theoretical advances in archaeological practice to prehistorians (e.g. Clark 1989; Hodges 1990: 83). Where there is consideration of the classical counterpart then it has been treated in a scant or cursory fashion. When it does discuss the subject it is either in the context of (pre-mid-nineteenth century) antiquarianism or with respect to certain individuals and their excavations (e.g. Curtius at Olympia, Evans' Knossos, Schliemann at Troy and Mycenae and the discoveries of the nineteenth century in Egypt and the Middle East) or their work on creating definitive corpora of data, of which Greek pottery is a good example. In this respect the criteria for the selection of such excavations lies as much with the publicity that the discoveries generated as their scholarly significance. This uneven impression is all the more disappointing given the fact the achievements of classical archaeology long outstripped those of the investigation of European prehistory (Trigger 1989: 40; Snodgrass 1999: 107).

Hodges (1990: 89, citing Dyson 1989a; cf. 1993) attributed the failure to appreciate why classical archaeology was the way it was to a lack of self-reflection and analysis among its practitioners. Indeed, drawing on previous work by Childe, Renfrew and Snodgrass, Dyson produced an admirable summary of the development of classical archaeology from the late seventeenth century (Dyson 1993: esp.195–8; see also 1989b). Some of the salient points he emphasized have a bearing on what is argued in the subsequent chapters. Dyson's main points are:

1:     'the strong influence of German scholarship with its emphasis on the systematic collection of facts as a precursor to any real knowledge, and to the increasingly dominant position of science in the intellectual life of the period. Scholars in most humanistic fields, including Classical archaeology, argued that their generalizations had to be based on solid, systematically organized bodies of data. This collection of facts increasingly replaced the use of Classical material in general cultural debates. Catalogues and compendia came to dominate scholarly production.'

2: Classical archaeology gradually separated from such disciplines as anthropology, art history and history to be aligned more with classical philology. With '...the subordination of material culture research to the study of elite texts ...[this] separat[ed] Classical archaeologists from those in other disciplines concerned with the understanding of the relation between objects and culture, while burdening them with the time-consuming mastery of philological skills that were only marginal to their core rôle as archaeologists.'

3: The result of this shift was the rise of a timid empirical research model, one based on the 'big dig mentality' coupled to the development of specialization and fragmentation in the processing of the results of such excavations. Such work did not require the formulation of overarching models of cultural change. 'Research on museum collections fostered similar attitudes. Most effort there went into the cataloguing and ordering of decontextualized material. What passed for theory was often aesthetic connoisseurship.' In its self-confident isolation, classical archaeology was inured to the developments underway in other subjects, including archaeology.

4: The importance of hierarchy. Whereas the newer discipline of the 'new archaeology' was fresher and (more) attractive to a younger generation of students and therefore less referential in its attitude to its elders, 'modern Classical archaeology had been built on an almost ancient Chinese sense of hierarchy and ancestor worship. It had neither the structures nor the will to foster iconoclastic debate.'

One of the reasons for the recent growth in historiographical treatments of archaeology lies with the introduction of new conceptual approaches to the understanding of archaeological material. Again this form of analysis commenced in the archaeology of prehistory; and where some of the effects of the theoretical debate, if not in practice, have percolated down to interpretation of classical antiquity and classical archaeology, albeit some time after it affected its prehistoric counterparts. Even then, there has been some resistance (cf. Renfrew 1980; Dyson 1981; Snodgrass 1985; 1987; Courbin 1988 etc.). Classics and its variants in the guise of the 'classical reception' have, however, profited, where there has been something of a boom in appraisals of what 'Rome' is supposed to have meant to later European writers, historians and politicians. Increasingly modern historians have contributed to the debate, onto which some archaeologists are now grafting their opinions (e.g. Jenkyns 1980; the Demandts in Mommsen 1996; Edwards 1996; 1999; Stray 1998; Hingley 2001a etc.). In the realm of archaeology, Roman archaeology – and by association Romano-British archaeology – has generally been badly served but for certain (European) Roman sites, (notably Pompeii and Herculaneum; Parslow 1998a and b; Cooley 2003: in general Johnson 1989). In contrast, that of ancient Greece has been better treated in recent years (Stiebing 1993; Marchand 1996; Shanks 1996).

If classics and ancient history are undergoing something of a reflexive renaissance, and by association classical archaeology too, other than generally negative comments about the moribund state of the discipline, the archaeology of Roman Britain has until recently been poorly served. Snodgrass (1999) in this respect is a short but honourable exception. Where the evolution of Romano-British studies has impinged on the historiography of Roman studies then it has been in respect to modern receptions, interpretations and adaptations of the image of Rome. In such studies, the part of Roman Britain has rarely merited much discussion in the rather broad sweeping analyses of what Rome came to mean to the inheritors of her legacy.

The study of the achievements of late medieval British antiquarian tradition over the last ten years has also enjoyed something of a renaissance with the analysis of the work of some of the individuals who wrote about aspects of what they thought was the Roman period (e.g. Hepple 1999; 2002: Keppie 2003 etc.), and where the treatment has largely been as appreciation of contemporary images of the past (e.g. Smiles 1994) or as part of the social context of archaeology (Kendrick 1950; Evans 1956; Hudson 1981; Levine 1986; Chapman 1989a and b; Brand 1998; cf. Sweet 2004 for a recent bibliography). But still the conclusions of such work have not been related to how Romano-British studies developed in the late nineteenth century. Instead, the likes of national figures such as Camden, Leland and Stukeley have been placed in relation to European scholarship or British national history or the history of ideas. In the same way there is still no substantial or satisfactory treatment, which examines why the discipline of Romano-British studies is presented in a manner that has remained essentially unchanged since the turn of the nineteenth century. Much overdue, there has been in recent years something of a boom in the critical analysis and therefore the historiography of Romano-British studies whether as a discipline or of the work of individual workers (Bradley 1990; 1994; Cunliffe 1984; Jones 1987; Potter 1986; 1987;

Frere 1988; Browning 1989; 1995; Scott 1990; Hingley 1991; 1993; 1994; 1996a; 1997; 2000; 2001a; Freeman 1991; 1993; 1996a; 1997; Simpson 1996; Wallace 1994; 2002; Henig 2004). Before this, the last substantial statements on the history of the subject were those produced by Haverfield himself and to a lesser degree by Eric Birley (1959; 1961), whose assessments were limited to the work of some of the more distant antiquarians.

It is difficult to explain why contemplation of Romano-British stud-ies has commenced. What are now regarded as similar controversial points were being made as far back as the early 1960s (Wheeler 1961), although it must lie in part with the 'theoretical' revolution of the 'New Archaeology' of the 1960s and 1970s in British archaeology along with its offspring of the 1980s and into the 1990s. Jones (1987) discussed some of the other factors, which might have a bearing on the issue. One of those he highlighted was the way the authors of certain influential works on Roman Britain almost rejoice in parading an absence of theo-retical grounding or methodological approaches or intellectualizing in their approaches to the subject. Instead, in Jones' opinion, writers such as Frere and Salway, as authors of '...descriptive narratives', preferred to let the evidence speak for itself. Jones regards the repetition of such a tradition as a sub-conscious lack of confidence in the strength of the ar-chaeological evidence that could be used to supplement the historical and other literary sources, which have traditionally underpinned the framework for understanding the Roman period in British history. However, with the explosion in excavation works and the concomitant influences in other aspects of archaeological thought and periods since the late 1980s, there have been signs of an intellectual revolution in Romano-British studies.

Romano-British studies from the Middle Ages to the nineteenth century

Conventional wisdom has the origins of Romano-British archaeology, and indeed British archaeology in general, lying with the work of the 'antiquaries' of the sixteenth, seventeenth and eighteenth centuries of which the same 'major' names invariably recur (Kendrick 1950; Daniel 1950; 1967; 1981; Crawford 1953: 21–35: Evans 1956; Piggott 1976; 1989; Ashbee 1972; Marsden 1983; Schnapp 1993; Smiles 1994; Parry 1995; Hicks 1996). But such emphasis has produced a skewed sense of the past, where 'great' individuals predominate. This fact was appreci-ated by Mendyk who wrote that: '...there is no general account of the English antiquaries, certainly none that is comprehensive and treats the subject in depth. This is doubly true of the regional writers, who comprised a major segment of the antiquarian school of thought in seventeenth Britain' (1989: 37). Rosemary Sweet's *Antiquaries* (2004) now fills that gap.

As in Romano-British historiography, there has been in recent years a revival of interest in the work of the medieval and post-medieval writers of British history, and in particular to trace the way the shifting political and intellectual climates, particularly of the seventeenth and eighteenth centuries, influenced their work. It goes without saying that the acceptability of such opinions was as much a reflection of the fluctuating fortunes of the Catholic and Protestant churches in this island (Smiles 1994: 124). In turn the study of (ancient) Britain underwent a significant change between 1750 and 1850, '...from a peripheral antiquarian pursuit to recognition as a central concern for antiquarianism and for the increasingly professional academic discipline of archaeology' (Smiles 1994: 8). Generally speaking the work of the earlier antiquarians was indiscriminate in what they choose to record even if they were often working to preconceptions or particular sub-agendas (Piggott 1976: 1f.). Their works were a combination of multi-period descriptions of antiquities, usually without a connecting narrative. Descriptions of what are now known to be prehistoric monuments were mixed with historical sites. In these accounts Roman-period sites (and so Roman history) received cursory treatment. Instead they were subsumed into one of two general themes that preoccupied such writers: one that emphasized the uniqueness or insularity of English history or else that which maintained the island's proximity to Europe. The second was the matter of the origins of English history and so society. In this case there was again a divide: the earlier, going back in part to the earlier antiquarian movement, maintained it was derived from the Celts, the survivors of pre- and Roman times. In this elements which were emphasized were the Druids and the resistance of some notable Britons to Rome, both of which extensively permeated contemporary descriptions and art of the past. The second school, one which developed later on and came to dominate academic circles and in particular the later nineteenth century, was that which emphasized British links to the Anglo-Saxons.

> It is well known that the nineteenth century witnessed the emergence in England of a strong Anglo-Saxon bias to its history, powerful enough to construct an image of English nationality and British destiny in almost exclusively Anglo-Saxon terms. The recognition of the dominance of England within the United Kingdom and the celebration of the English way of life as a superior form of civilization was not necessarily an exclusive preoccupation of the English, nor was it universally believed

> ...Nevertheless, as a generalization it needs little qualification: the Victorians fashioned themselves as Anglo-Saxons first and foremost. Such an emphatic racial identity offered a reductive reading of English civilization based on the ethnic attributes of Celt or Saxon and ignored the finely nuanced texture of cultural development over thousands of years (Smiles 1994: 113).

This explanation meant playing down the Celtic contribution and was in part a reaction to the nascent Celtic identity-nationalism. It was one that emphasized their failings and savagery. Rather than in their antiquities, the Anglo-Saxon version traced the legacy through a number of contemporary values and institutions (e.g. in their attitudes to democracy and law, in their martial characteristics, it their adherence to Christianity etc.), to the point that racial stereotypes were deployed ('...by the 1840s the centrality of race to any discussion of human culture was not in doubt and the triumph of Anglo-Saxon culture could be sought in biological rather than cultural explanation' (Smiles 1994: 121).

One of the achievements of the Renaissance was an appreciation of the fact that ancient texts demonstrated a connection between Britain (and Gaul) and the Roman empire. The question became the longevity of that link. 'The (English) Reformation created a sense of natural destiny and so the desire to understand the origins of the native from its earliest (historical) times. Likewise there was the ecclesiastical imperative when the search was on for the early English church' (Parry 1995: 2). The quality of the work at this time (the later Middle Ages) tended to emphasize the insularity of Britain's past (Piggott 1989: 19), even if the models for studying the past were derived from European examples: '...Roman archaeology ...had highly respectable roots in the Italian Renaissance ... and even the remains of the remote British province of the empire long continued to share something of the esteem attributed to classical studies of literature and art' (Piggott 1989: 27). An equally important legacy of the 'antiquarian' movement was that it created the basis for the first attempts to identity an archaic (English) history and society. Significant contributors in this sort of approach were John Leland (1503–1552 – 'the Pausanias of Tudor England' – Schnapp 1993: 139), William Lambarde (1534–1601), William Camden (1551–1623) and John Aubrey (1626–1697). Lambarde's *A Topographical and Historical Dictionary of England* (*c*.1577), a part of Tudor England's break from the papacy and the creation of the Anglican church, was more concerned to set out '...the English antecedents, which he found in "Saxon" monuments, language and social institutions than in the Roman' (Mendyk 1989: 20). Leland's pioneering interest in topographic work still owed more to the medieval tradition than the 'new learning' of the sixteenth century. That said he did make observations about Roman antiquities in England and Wales in his *Itinerary* (1549) and *Collectanea* (1715). His lasting contribution to English antiquarian studies lies in the fact he was '...the first in England to put forward a method which combined the study of sources with a "peregrination" something which was a defining characteristic of British archaeology' (Schnapp 1993: 140; cf. Balme 2001 on Aubrey's riding). Schnapp is especially enthusiastic about Leland's contribution to antiquarian studies as a discipline, with his emphasis on the 'careful observation of landscape, the earth and objects ...Never has an antiquary written so emphatically that knowledge of the past demanded ... application of observation and imagination which alone led to archaeological reconstruction ...To this was Leland's invention of the 'typological-chronological method which consisted of systematically classifying ...archaeological categories' (1993: 191). In fact Schnapp rather optimistically claims Leland might be regarded as the inventor of 'theoretical archaeology' (p. 194). Although unpublished, John Aubrey's *Monumenta Britannica* was widely read and appreciated in his lifetime (Hunter 1975; Balme 2001: 5–11). Divided into three sections, Part I was a study of Druidism, Part II was devoted to what was regarded as architecture, included descriptions of Roman camps, forts and settlements while Part III looked at more archaeological structures, 'barrows, urn burials tombs, earthworks and so on' (Schnapp 1993: 190). Here were described, among other items, Roman pavements and coins. Aubrey's achievement was that his material was set out for its own sake and not to establish a semi-historical pedigree. The logic was that once the evidence had been adequately catalogued only then could it be interpreted and its significance assessed. It is for these reasons that Ashbee described Aubrey as the first man '...to associate positively the men and the field monuments' and as '...undoubtedly the founder of British field archaeology, and is the first to whom the appellation 'archaeologist' can be given' (Ashbee 1972: 46–7). By far and away, however, the most significant of the later medieval antiquaries was William Camden whose *Britannia* was first published in 1586 (Kendrick 1950: 143ff.; Piggott 1976; 1989: Schnapp 1993: 139–40). Drawing his inspiration from the likes of Flavio Bondio (1388–1463) and his topographical histories of Rome (*Italia Illustrata* (1453), *Roma Triumphans* (1459) and *Roma Instaurata* (1466)), Camden was, unlike some of his successors, especially interested in the Roman period, its remains and its documents. Schnapp (1993: 122) placed Camden's work in its European context although he fails to acknowledge his interest in Roman inscriptions and indeed the Roman period as a whole. For instance, his was the first important description of Hadrian's Wall. He travelled along its length (except for the central portion) in 1599. The magnitude of Camden's task, his achievements along with the purpose to the *Britannia,* was summarized by Piggott as:

> I do not think we can escape from the conclusion that the *Britannia* was originally planned to elucidate the topography of Roman Britain, and to present a picture of the Province, with reference to its development through Saxon and mediaeval times, which would enable Britain to take her natural place at one within the world of antiquity and that of international Renaissance scholarship. Language and title alike declared its purpose, it was to have a European appeal and ...was to establish Britain as a member of the fellowship of nations who drew their strength from roots struck deep in the Roman Empire ...To the Roman skeleton, Camden added English flesh and blood (1976: 43).[1]

Schnapp is especially good at dissecting Camden's methodology.

> His [Camden's] method was topographical ...using Roman geography ...as his starting point ...[and] constructing a local history for each English city ...Precision as to time and presence as to space were Camden's two imperatives; and to this end he inverted the rules of historical cartography; the linguistic study of place-names to determine their Gallic, Saxon and Roman origins, the reconstruction of territorial traditions from tradition and the study of coinage ...he emphasized the Anglo-Saxon nature of the origins of the British people. Camden ...not only made the study of antiquity into a science, any more than he had approached the history of the pre-Roman population of Great Britain in a radically new way, but he gave British archaeology a framework of reference (regional history) a method of observation (the combination of literary information with description of the landscape) and a technique

---

1. Camden '...created an organic whole out of a vague incoherent, ill-understood material. The scholar who does this creates an epoch in historical writing as surely as a Vergil or a Tennyson creates an epoch in literary style ...Haverfield himself performed the same task for Roman Britain' (Crawford 1953: 22). 'The Britannia, by presenting to the world the Roman antiquities of Britain, was designed to entrench the author's native land among those European nations that claimed the mighty Roman Empire as their origin' (Mendyk 1989: 50); Camden aimed, in part, 'to demonstrate the importance of Britain in the Roman Empire, partly, to show foreign scholars that antiquarian scholarship in England could match continental achievements. As an international showpiece for English antiquities, the Britannia succeeded, at the same time as Camden compatriots were failing to meet the continental challenge to produce neo-classical historical narratives' (Hicks 1996: 32).

of exploration (the close study of topynomic and numismatic sources) which dominated archaeology from the seventeenth century to the start of the eighteenth century (1993: 140–1).

In time, the *Britannia* '...transformed the state of antiquarian studies and gave all future research a starting point and a base of reference' (Parry 1995: 3). It had revealed an abundance of material remains to be explored, described, explained and interpreted. A reflection of its significance is the fact that after his death it went through a number of editions which necessitated updates and additions. The most important of these were Philemon Holland's 1610 revision (the first English translation), the 1695/1722 editions produced by Edmund Gibson and finally Richard Gough's 1789 version. Each of these revisions included the addition of new sections. 'To begin with, the work was addressed to the European world of scholarship. Successive editions catered for a new class of reader anxious to read antiquarian literature' (Ashbee 1972: 42; cf. Schnapp 1993). In his own lifetime, in 1607, Camden added sections on Roman coins and inscriptions, the latter of which particularly interested him. Hepple described the 1586 *Britannia* as 'the foundation of Roman epigraphy in Britain' (Hepple 2002: 177) and has shown how the twelve inscriptions in the first edition became the 110 in the 1607 version. Another noteworthy feature of antiquarianism of this time was its collaborative nature (Parry 1995: 6; Mendyk 1989: 50; Balme 2001). Camden was able to make the improvements to the *Britannia* because he was assisted by a number of regional correspondents. Indeed Camden owed much to John Dee who, from 1574 '...deserves recognition for (making the earliest post-medieval recording of Roman inscriptions in Britain) and his name should properly appear in the foundation history of Roman epigraphy in Britain' (Hepple 2002: 181). Another source was Reginald Bainbrigg who helped seek out and record inscriptions in north-west England (Crawford 1953: 23; Haverfield 1911b). In fact Hepple (1999) has shown how in 1599 Camden and Richard Cotton toured the western end of Hadrian's Wall looking for Roman remains and inscriptions, an account of which was contained in the ?1600 *Britannia*, a trip which has 'been recognized as the starting point for the systematic Roman Wall studies.' Camden's and Cotton's tour however was anticipated by Bainbrigg who toured earlier in the same year and passed on his information to Camden. This intelligence evidently did not make it into the 1600 edition, but following another tour in 1601, Camden did include Bainbrigg in the 1607 version.

Conventional histories of British antiquarianism emphasize 'big names'. Over-shadowed by the 'national' figures were the regional counterparts of the time, men who often worked at 'county' level (Mendyk 1989; Parry 1995). Simmons (in Lysons 1806: v) divided English approaches to topographical and local history since the sixteenth century in one of two ways: either as part of 'the history of England as a whole ...; the other, that of a single tract of the country, a county or one town or parish, should be considered as an end in itself. The first may be called the "extensive" approach; the second the "intensive".' Indeed the regional format had been in part established by Camden who in turn might have drawn inspiration from earlier examples (Kendrick 1950: 144–5). The first 'county' history of Britain was published in 1576 by William Lambarde, and his *A Perambulation of Kent*, 'the first book of county antiquities' (Parry 1995: 241).[2] Although he did not refer to topographical features, Lambarde expressed the hope that others would imitate his 'model' for other counties. There soon followed a range of regional and county-based descriptions which established a format that was to be followed for the next 400 years (Kendrick 1950: 157ff.; Mendyk 1989: 24ff.). Whatever the strengths and merits of such writers, ancient literary sources informed their appreciation of topography (Piggott 1989: 21). The apogee of this approach was during the late eighteenth and early nineteenth centuries when:

> ... authors of these works were as a rule not professional scholars. Sometimes they were hack-writers who wrote history of any county which seemed to require it: but the best of them were residents (landowners, clergy &c.), educated men whose interests were centred in their own counties and whose appetite for information connected with their home-district was omnivorous. Hence the local knowledge contained in these works is almost always of an extremely high order: it is accurate, critical, and intelligent. But the general equipment of historical and archaeological learning in the light of which the local facts are interpreted is often defective, so that the authors observe their facts correctly but are apt to misunderstand their significance (Collingwood in Collingwood and Myres 1936: 468–9).

Despite the achievements up to the early eighteenth century the impetus and reputation of antiquarian-archaeological research was

---

2. Simmons (in Lysons 1806: vi) suggests that Camden may have been influenced by Richard Carew's *Survey of Cornwall* (1602) and Sir William Dugdale's *Antiquities of Warwickshire* (1656).

beginning to show signs of decline.[3] This fact, with one or two exceptions, is reflected in the absence of the sort of great names of the
preceding century in the standard histories of British antiquarianism
in the mid- to late eighteenth century. The one exception is William
Stukeley (1687–1765), author of the *Itinerarium Curiosum Centuria I*
(1725), the result of fifteen years of touring English counties. The
planned sequel, *Centuria II* was never published although it survives in
draft form (Ashbee 1972: 49). Again with the emphasis on upstanding
monuments, much effort was expended on prehistoric sites such as
Avebury and Stonehenge and in turn the Druids. Stukeley did, however, describe Hadrian's Wall. Interestingly he was secretary in 1745 of
a Society of Roman Knights, a group which broke from the London Society of Antiquaries, disenchanted by its inertia and which was
concerned with protecting what it perceived to be Roman antiquities
(Piggott 1950: 55–6; 1989: 143; Ashbee 1972: 51).

Stukeley exemplified that for late medieval and early modern antiquarian writing, the starting point for British history – and therefore for
the description of what are now regarded as archaeological monuments
– lay with the Druids, not least because they were the earliest 'Britons' to
appear in Roman sources (Smiles 1994: 75ff.). It was only from the
mid-eighteenth century that there were the beginnings of a degree of
specialism in the work of some antiquarians. Types of sites (military, urban etc.), specific sites and categories of objects were appreciated for
what they were. There also developed a more specialized description of
classes of sites, for instance hillforts, standing circles, barrows etc., significantly all vestiges of prehistoric activity (Ashbee 1972: 46). In this
trend are found the beginnings of a better appreciation of the identification of the 'Ancient Briton'. Previously, descriptions of these types of
sites had been incorporated in the description of 'historic' monuments.
Now, informed by the likes of the European discovery of North America
and 'primitive' societies there and elsewhere, it was appreciated that
some 'primitive' sites in Britain might be connected with the island's
primeval ancestors. With regard to Roman remains, Alexander

---

3. Mendyk (1989: 24 and 54) linked the change to a shift in the focus of
   antiquarianism, from a preoccupation with monuments, and so landscapes,
   to the natural and pseudo-sciences (e.g. geology to paleontology in its most
   basic sense); or otherwise an empathy with more contemporary surround-
   ings than the more distant past. It also meant that the study of the past
   tended to begin with the Saxons (Parry 1995: 3). There was in addition to
   this the rise of heraldric studies.

Gordon's *Itinerarium Septentrionale* (1726) described such antiquities in north Britain, and for the first time, Scotland. John Horsley (1684–1732), author of the *Britannia Romana* of 1732 (but written between 1727–29, and in part to correct Gordon), was a real field archaeologist: he explored the (English) countryside in search of antiquities. His '...may be regarded as the first and in many ways still the best book on Roman Britain as a whole' (Collingwood in Collingwood and Myres 1936: 466; cf. Birley 1958b; Ashbee 1972: 48). In preparing the 1789 edition of Camden's *Britannia,* Gough was assisted by (General) Robert Melville (1723–1809) whose fieldwork first revealed the existence of Roman military remains north of the River Tay. In turn, Melville inspired General William Roy (1726–1790) to compile his *Military Antiquities of the Romans in Northern Britain* (Piggott 1976: 51, 145). Roy was originally commissioned in 1745 to map Scotland in the aftermath of the Jacobite rebellion. His survey was not published until 1793. The delay, however, has not stopped him being described as the 'inventor of modern field archaeology' (Crawford 1953: 36). One of the consequences of his work was the greater use of maps to illustrate patterns of distribution and location. According to Piggott, Horsley's (and later Gordon's) work emphasized fieldwork research and '...a single minded attention to a limited archaeological objective' (1989: 27). They were the:

> ...first archaeologically minded antiquaries ...who deliberately rejected much of their traditional subject-matter to concentrate on the actual objects of antiquity, and particularly, since from the days of Camden topography formed an integral part of antiquarian studies, to monuments in the countryside. What with hindsight we conceive of as the beginnings of real archaeology in Britain was inseparably bound up with fieldwork, not with studies in museums (p. 26).

Stukeley and his generation represented the last gasp of traditional English antiquarianism. Its subsequent decline is more accurately reflected in the organizations of the time which had been created to foster and disseminate the appreciation of such researches. At about the time of the later medieval antiquarians there were the first hesitant moves towards forming (learned) societies for the *literati* and *dilettanti*, drawing members from the aristocracy and upper professional classes. Such societies nurtured an interest in the distant past and antiquities as well as language, customs, art, literature and philosophy (Smiles 1994: 16). Of the more archaeologically orientated of these groups, the oldest (surviving) is the Society of Antiquaries of London (SoAL), formed in 1707 (Evans 1956), while in Scotland the interests of the like-minded were represented from 1780 by the Society of Antiquaries of Scotland in Edinburgh (Bell 1981). It published from 1792 the *Archaeologia Scotica*, which was later merged, in 1890, with the society's *Proceedings*. These and other societies, representing those with an interest in antiquities in its loosest sense, having flourished in the seventeenth and eighteenth centuries experienced declines in membership in the nineteenth. The drop was due to a number of factors. Antiquarianism had become unfashionable and even a topic of ridicule, a situation not helped by a series of well publicised hoaxes, notably those associated with Stukeley (Piggott 1976; 1989: 33). It was increasingly believed that antiquarianism could not offer anything to historical researches, especially when the island's history only really commenced sometime later in the Roman period (Smiles 1994: 10). In addition to these factors, the momentum that helped antiquarianism in the seventeenth and eighteenth centuries was largely self-generated, owing little or nothing to the country's universities. The lack of university engagement was in part due to the emphasis placed on the study of the classics in their curricula, while the relative lack of fashion attached to Roman studies, itself a consequences of external political and religious reasons, was also relevant. With the rise of the Anglo-Saxon origins for British antiquity, there was no stimulus for the detailed study of the islands Roman remains as there had once been for those of the Ancient Britons when the Celtic origins was once fashionable. The Roman was, in effect, squeezed out in the dialogue about British origins. In contrast, the political and social climate of the time made Greek history and culture more attractive. As evidence of the stagnation that characterized late Regency antiquarianism we can see that in the subsequent decades there were published no works of significant synthesis on the island, a situation reflected in part by the relative decline in Roman history elsewhere in the island at the expense of Hellenic studies (Jenkyns 1980: Turner 1986; 1989).

The popular retreat from antiquarianism was exemplified by the failure of Gough's edition of Camden: '...It was undertaken too late, when the usefulness of Camden's great pioneer work was diminishing with the appearance of detailed county or regional histories, and it was undertaken at a time when historical and archaeological studies were at a noticeably low ebb' (Piggott 1976: 52). But if antiquarianism was in reverse in the popular sense, this is not to under-estimate the continuing significance of the likes of Gough's achievements. Besides editing Camden, he was also the author of two major works in the best tradition of (English) antiquarianism – *British Topography* (1768) and *Sepulchral Monuments of Great Britain* (1786). In 1799 he tried to pass on to the British Museum his papers etc. but its dithering resulted in him offering the collection to Bodley's Library at Oxford. As it transpired, the collection came '...to be preserved in the "Antiquaries" Closet erected for keeping Manuscripts, printed Books and other Articles relating to British Topography ...so that all together they may form one uniform body of British antiquities' (Philip 1997: 592). Gough's gift consisted of nearly 4000 volumes. In the longer term '...the Antiquaries Closet became known as Gough's Room and the concept of a specialized-subject collection, new in the Library's history, led to the building-up of a topographical collection in which all items are still classified as additions to the original Gough collection, a lasting tribute to the importance of Gough's work' (Philip 1997: 592). In time, as we will see, Haverfield was to exploit his works and the collection.

With respect to the relative decline of antiquarianism, the problem was that it was not advancing but standing still. It was limited to the description of monuments, artefacts and/or with fanciful interpretation. It has been suggested that many of the problems were based on the absence of a more sophisticated understanding of the past, not least because studying the Roman past had to work from the extant literary sources.. While there were advances in other disciplines (e.g. in geology, history etc.) they had not yet filtered through to the study of the (material) human past. The culminative effect of all this was that there was supposed to be a decline in the range and quality of archaeological research in Britain for what has been said to be the next 150 years (Piggott 1976: 49; 1989: 33). This impression is in part explained by the rise of the archaeology of prehistory (from *c*.1860 onwards), as emphasized in histories of British archaeology with the corollary that (Roman) antiquarianism stood still. This judgment, however, may not be entirely fair. The fortunes of Roman archaeology were rejuvenated at the start of the nineteenth century with the commencement of a number of major excavations, admittedly on the Continent. Then there was the creation of the German Archaeological Institute in Rome (cf. Chapter 3) and improved standards of excavations in Rome and at Pompeii and Herculaneum exerted a profound influence on the popular perception of Roman history. Riding in parallel with these projects was the appearance of a number of antiquarians and archaeologists who were to effect a lasting influence on the subject. These innovations were complimented by the publication of a number of seminal monographs. For example, between 1801 and 1807 Samuel Lysons published his *Reliquae Britannico-Romanae (Containing Figures of Roman Antiquities Discovered in England)*, a work

Haverfield went as far as to describe as 'perhaps the most magnificent volumes ever published on the Roman antiquities of this country' (1924: 81).[4]

Hudson (1981: 38) has commented on the expanding range and improving quality of the work of British antiquarians from the mid-nineteenth century onwards. It is true on a 'national' scale that there are no 'names' but this may be a consequence of the prejudices of modern writers, mainly 'prehistorians', when there were the likes of William Cunnington, William Borlasse, Richard Colt Hoare etc. pioneering in England's middle prehistoric past (Ashbee 1972: 54ff.; Marsden 1983; Schnapp 1993: 277ff; Dyer 1975). But there were what were recognized as significant Roman specialists. The one individual of the period most frequently noted in the development of the subject in Britain is the London pharmacist and antiquarian Charles Roach Smith (1807–1870; Haverfield 1911c). Not only did he amass an impressive collection of artefacts accumulated as the city grew at that time, Roach Smith also recorded the location of his (major) finds. The material was published in his *Collectanea Antiqua* (seven vols, 1848–80). Roach Smith was also involved in the creation of a number of archaeological and antiquarian societies (e.g. the British Archaeological Association (1843) and the Historical Society of Lancashire and Cheshire (1848)). Although his work in archaeology effectively ended by 1854, Roach Smith had established the archaeology of the city. He was the first to classify samian/arretine pottery in Britain, the results of which he published in his *Illustrations of Roman London* (1859). This innovation was not matched until Haverfield and his contemporaries' efforts 50 years later. In addition to Roach Smith, however, there were others who developed interests or specialisms in what is now appreciated as Romano-British archaeology. There is, for instance, the Hon. Richard Cornwallis Neville (1820–1861), a friend of Roach Smith, whose contribution to Roman and British antiquities is beginning to be appreciated (Martin in prep.; Ebbatson (1994: 58) has even gone as far as to suggest that Neville '...coined, or at least brought into common usage, *c*.1850, the term "Romano-British" as opposed to "Roman",

---

4. Coincidentally, Lyson's brother Daniel, another noted antiquarian, in his *Environs of London (Volume the First. County of Surrey* (1792: 210) praised Haverfield's great-great-grandfather John Haverfield, the first of the Haverfield Royal gardeners (cf. Ch.1) for being '...well known for his taste and skill as an ornamental gardener...' I am grateful to Colin Wallace for confirming this reference.

Anglo-Roman", "Britannico-Roman" or "Pre-Saxon".'[5] Neville was indicative of an improving perception of the Roman antiquities of theses islands. According to Ebbatson, this fact is reflected in the way that up to 1861, 'Romano-British remains accounted for 64% of below-ground investigations recorded in the *Archaeological Journal*.'

Indicative of a revival in Roman antiquities, at about the same time, elsewhere other site-specific descriptions started to appear (Collingwood in Collingwood and Myres 1936: 474). This was another feature of the period, the emergence of a more skilled type of local antiquarian. Some of the leading contributors in this respect will be discussed in more detail below, but, as a generalization, most of them remain relatively unknown except in their locality. For example, there was the publication of a number of studies of Hadrian's Wall throughout this and the next century (Richmond in Collingwood Bruce 1957). For Birley a sea-change in approaches to the study of the Wall was initiated in 1813 with the creation of the Newcastle Society of Antiquaries, a foundation which '...marks the end of merely antiquarian interest and the beginning of methodological study which had lain dormant since Horsley's death' (1961: 22; Jobey 1990). Birley owed the identification of this phase of research on the Wall to a paper by R.G. Collingwood (1921c), in which it was argued that a third phase in the study of the Wall is visible from the second quarter down to the end of the third quarter of the eighteenth century. A major event of this period was the publication of Rev. John Hodgson's contribution on the Wall to the *History of Northumberland* (Vol. III; Pt II – 1840). Elsewhere, Breeze (2003) in summarizing the state of mural studies up to the 1850s, has described the circumstances of John Collingwood Bruce's interest in the Wall and his being the first description of it (*Handbook of the Roman Wall*), published in 1851. The third edition, published in 1863, has been described as valuable because it summarized the results of excavations by a third important figure of this time, John Clayton of Chesters (cf. Johnson 1989: 17–19). Another significant development of this time was between 1857 and 1858 when Henry MacLauchlan produced the first accurate survey of the Wall (*A Survey of the Roman Wall* and his *Memoir*). The reason why these sorts of studies worked was because the raw data had some sort of contextual location, where it was related to a known event: Hadrian's

---

5. Neville, the 4th Lord Braybrooke, established at Audley End a museum of the finds from the Roman site at Great Chesterford and its environs. Elected an FSA in 1847, he published extensively in the *Archaeologia* and the *Journal of the British Archaeological Association* (cf. Smail 2004; Martin in prep.).

Wall. In other words, the components of the monument could be related to one another and to the landscape in which they lay. Elsewhere, other parts of the country were not so well served at this time. As with Hadrian's Wall, the earliest attention on the Antonine Wall in Scotland was in pursuit of its inscriptions (Keppie 1998a). With respect to its description, in September 1825 the Rev. John Skinner kept a detailed record of his perambulation along its length (Keppie 2003). Randall (1946: 80), citing Haverfield (1910b), noted that the Roman period in Wales was especially neglected down until the end of the century, when the situation began to change with the commencement of a series of Roman fort and villa sites in the Principality. Prior to this there was not much produced that was worthy of merit.

It is now appreciated that in some respects what some antiquaries of the early nineteenth century were beginning to acknowledge was the significance of relating monuments to landscapes in order to reconstruct the past. Crawford, echoing a line of interpretation typified by Daniel, expressed it as '...field archaeology of the eighteenth and early nineteenth centuries belonged to what may be called the "county gentlemen school", whose outstanding merit was that they rode about the country and saw things for themselves' (Crawford 1953: 24). A good example of this realization was articulated by the Cambridgeshire cleric and antiquarian, C.H. Evelyn White. When attempting to explain the significance of some earthworks at Cottenham, he justified his approach by noting:

> The lamented John Richard Green, to whose singularly erudite investigations in the field of history, we owe so much, has, in his admirable preface to the *Making of England*, thus forcibly borne testimony to the extreme value of what I may perhaps be allowed to refer as *territorial evidence*, in the endeavour to arrive at something like an intelligent appreciation of the conditions under which the ancient Britons became subject to Roman rule (1902: 93).

In other words, Evelyn White was articulating the principles of landscape archaeology to supplement and even inform the available ancient literary sources. By any criterion Evelyn White is not a major figure in the history of Romano-British antiquarianism. Nor are his opinions necessarily original. Others were making comparable observations, but there is a tendency to minimize the point they were making. It is a matter of debate who formalized the various strands of previous practice into a discipline recognized as 'landscape archaeology'. We have seen that Crawford believed that John Aubrey was the first British field archaeologist but still wanted to see the invention of the subject as a relatively late phenomenon. Barker and Darvill felt confident enough to claim that landscape archaeology 'is a relatively new field of enquiry. It initially grew from a number of academic traditions, perhaps most particularly the field of geography' (1997: 1). The validation for this assertion was Aston and Rowley's 1974 seminal introduction to the discipline. Acknowledging that some antiquarians had made a useful contribution to the subject, it was Beresford's *History on the Ground* (1957) and, to a lesser extent, Hoskins' *Making of the English Landscape* (1957) which were crucial. They could cite the work of Paul Ashbee (1972) as a summary to what had been accomplished before this date. Even later, in a volume of essays presented to Christopher Taylor, it was stated of the discipline 'landscape archaeology', it '...is hard to give a precise date for the subject's genesis', although the author plumped for Hoskin's as the 'seminal text' (Williamson 1998: 1). In the same volume, Fleming selected Crawford's *Archaeology in the Field* (1953), while even later Bowden (2001: 29), in acknowledging Hoskin's contribution 'as the single most influential book for landscape studies in Britain', still credited Crawford's *Archaeology in the Field* as important. Whatever opinions one prefers, the general conclusion is that landscape archaeologists seem to want to play down the part of late medieval and early modern antiquarianism as landscape archaeologists (e.g. and as repeated in the works of Hoskins, Beresford and Taylor).

Haverfield was guilty of the same misapprehension or seems not to have been aware of it in at least his earlier publications. It also partly explains why, for the period up to the mid-nineteenth century, in recounting the evolution of Roman antiquarianism the writing of the progress of the country's Roman-period archaeology has not been well-served. Because the negative aspects of the antiquarianism were highlighted by the likes of Haverfield and because the study of the phenomenon of antiquarianism was traditionally the preserve of medieval historians and prehistorians, the longer term significance of antiquarian-archaeological research in to the Roman period has been dismissed, if not ignored. Instead, analysis of the work achieved as a whole had tended towards grouping in multi-period descriptions of the antiquities of the island. This approach meant that there was the lack of a satisfactory historical framework in which to place the monuments and objects thus described. But out of the negative, there is a positive which is perhaps even more important. The treatment of monuments as monuments, admittedly forced in the absence of an historical framework into which to place them, meant that there was concomitant emphasis on sites as features in landscapes and that, if sense and meaning was to be made of sites, they had to be read against one another and their locality, supplemented where possible by whatever documentary material was thought to be of utility. Likewise monuments, frequently without the support of any other material were naturally studied as another facet of the trend towards typological analysis of the classification of monuments. Antiquarianism remained essentially data collection, a tradition of which Haverfield was critical. Until 1800, work had involved the identification, recording and description of classes of object, whether they be coins, pottery and inscriptions, as well as Roman forts. The same tendency continued into the next century when antiquarian and therefore archaeological research in Britain enjoyed a revival. A work typical of the nineteenth century taste for the study of antiquities, but omitted by Haverfield, was the Rev. J.Y. Akerman's *An Archaeological Index to the Remains of Antiquity of the Celtic, Romano-British and Saxon Periods* (1847). Akerman admitted that his main evidence was 'sepulchral' but he also included descriptions of other monuments (viz. amphitheatres, 'stations', camps and roads), villas, potters' stamps, pavements, walls milestones, coins, silver plate and lead pigs. A slightly broader canvas is evident in Godwin's *The English Archaeologist's Handbook* (1867). In this, 50 pages were devoted to Roman Britain, with information drawn from various antiquarian sources. That said there were the beginnings of a shift towards describing certain types of Roman monuments in the preceding century which gathered pace in the next, one which on occasion tended to emphasize a sensitivity towards the appreciation of what sites and landscape represented. The shift to the more comprehensive and critical appraisal of the Roman remains of Britain at the regional level is a feature of the latter half of the nineteenth century. But it is a trend that Haverfield, and others, have tended to under-estimate, if not ignore. In the Editorial to the first issue of the *Archaeological Review* (March–August 1888), G.L. Gomme praised the strength and range of regional archaeological and antiquarian research in this country.[6] But he posed, and answered, an important question: '...there is considerable activity in Great Britain in matters of archaeological interest. The question – is it well directed and concentrated? ...To this question there can be but one answer and that a very humiliating one – absolutely nothing is done to bring all this excellent machinery into full working order' (p. 1–2). Gomme argued that the national organizations (such as the Society of Antiquaries of Lon-

---

6. (Sir) Lawrence Gomme (1853–1916) was Clerk to the London County Council and a noted authority on the history and antiquities of the city.

don) were best placed to at least organize work, but interestingly added that there had been in at least 1790 plans for it to compile a plan of Roman Britain. Nothing was achieved. Some regional societies, or their members, might initiate programmes of research, but it was usually not matched by their neighbours or to the same standard. One of Gomme's solution to the problem was to promise that the *Review* would publish an occasional series of indices of the archaeological remains (and in particular the Roman) of the counties of England, in which would be reported sites and finds derived from searches of earlier publications as well as the outcome of recent research. Haverfield was to provide one such inventory – for Sussex (Haverfield 1888e).[7]

Another demonstration of the trend towards specialist descriptions is the emphasis that antiquarians of all ages have placed on the study of Roman roads; a class of monument that is invariably undatable but which, as far as the students of them are concerned, manipulate and change the countryside that they traverse. In turn the identification and 'chasing of roads' required a degree of sympathy when exploring the countryside as well as Saxon charters and other medieval documents. We can see this sort of interest in the likes of Camden and his ilk, as well as in W. Long's *Observations on Roman Roads in the South of Britain* (1836). Honourable but far from exhaustive mention might be made here of the series of handbooks designed to aid the fieldworker (e.g. Codrington 1903; Forbes and Burmester 1904), as well as the work of G.B. Grundy and ultimately Ivan Margary (1962; 1973; cf. Crawford 1953: 51–86).

For our purposes the achievements of British antiquarianism up to the later nineteenth century were its shift to regional studies and the emphasis placed on the appreciation of topography and landscape. This is a point frequently ignored in assessments the accomplishments of English antiquarianism. Haverfield certainly did so. In truth Haverfield enjoyed an ambivalent relationship with British

---

7. Because the *Archaeological Review* (*AR*) lasted only four issues before it amalgamated with the *Journal of Folklore*, the number of counties catalogued is small. Under the banner 'Roman remains in ...', listed here are those that appeared as well as who, where it is recorded, compiled the entry: *Archaeological Review* 1 (1888): Wiltshire, Gloucestershire, London (north of the Thames), London, (south of the Thames – J.E. Price), Sussex – (Haverfield); *AR* II (1889) – Essex, Yorkshire (both J.E. Price); *AR* III (1889) – Lincolnshire (J.E. Price); *AR* IV (1890) – Dorsetshire (sic – J.J. Foster). Foster remains anonymous but John Edward Price worked at Brading villa and at Colchester. I owe these details to Colin Wallace.

antiquarianism. Much of his work can be characterized as antiquarian rather than archaeological in tone, especially when he published reappraisals and corrections of the work of earlier researchers. So on the one hand he worked closely with it, used it as a basis for his own work and in doing so often praised some of its achievements. For example, he turned *Cotton Iulius F. vi Notes on Reginald Bainbrigg of Appleby* into a description of 63 Roman inscriptions in Westmorland and Cumbria compiled by Camden (cf. Haverfield 1911b). But still he was frequently critical, often highly so, of what antiquarianism had accomplished. Whilst he reserved some of his most trenchant opinions for more recent work, few were exempt. For instance, in a discussion on the antiquity of (pre-Norman) place names, he wrote:

> Nothing has been a greater source of confusion in the study of Romano-British topography than the attempts, made first – and worst – by Camden – to identify apparently similar names without having their history. It is absolutely necessary in all cases to research, and I believe that no better work could be done by local archaeologists than a detailed examination of the significance, the origin and the various forms and proper use of their local place names (1896c: 37).

In this example, Haverfield chose to emphasize that the importance of the contribution to the understanding of the Roman legacy lay in the study of toponyms and place names, which naturally enough often referred back to Roman antecedents. Nor was this a one-off. Throughout his career similar sentiments were repeated, occasionally verbatim, where he was highly critical of what he considered to be the disproportionate amount of effort put into identifying the origins of certain place names. Typical of this is his review of Gomme's *Roman Remains II*, where Haverfield wrote of the entry on Chester-Deva:

> ...the article in which Deva is placed at Fordsham on the Weaver, 'because Deva sounds like Weaver', illustrates the erudition and ability of the average contributor too admirably to be spared. This writer is hardly outdone even by the antiquary who once identified Camerton with Camulodunum and the neighbouring villa of 'Temple Cloud' with the Templum Claudii (*Classical Review* II 1888: 147).[8]

8. The antiquary was the Rev. John Skinner of Camerton (cf. Haverfield *VCH* Somerset I (1906): 290, 367), the Antonine Wall walker. Elsewhere he was a dismissive of a Mr Bellows and his theories concerning the street plan of Roman and modern Gloucester (Haverfield 1913c: 119 n. 1).

Elsewhere, Haverfield corrected earlier descriptions of the circumstances of the discovery, '...the carelessness which is characteristic of many English antiquarians' (1902c: 342). Similar corrections are to be found in a discussion of earlier ideas of the derivation of the Cornish place name Liskeard (Haverfield 1903d). Elsewhere, when opining on the reliability of antiquarian accounts used by Ordnance Survey surveyors, Haverfield cited the example of incorrect identifications in Somerset: 'Taunton shall give a typical instance. The city possessed at one time a local enthusiast by way of an antiquary and a medieval bridge. The antiquary rechristened the bridge Roman and so it stands to this day in the Ordnance maps, with two or three imaginary Roman roads inscribed on the same authority close to it' (1906b: 169).[9] Another issue related to the use of maps was the possible survival of evidence of centuriation in England. In 1889 Haverfield was attacking J.E. Price for his uncritical acceptance of H.C. Coote's views on the subject (Haverfield 1889b). The matter of Roman land divisions arose again twenty years later when Haverfield examined the evidence for Essex (1918d).[10]

If in the Haverfield version of things there were problems with the way fieldworkers worked along with reservations about the context within which archaeological research took place in the nineteenth century, the attempts to synthesize the results of the work of the seventeenth and eighteenth centuries into what we might describe as 'histories' of the (Roman) province was another relatively late phenomenon. Other than wider-ranging histories of Rome and her empire which might refer to affairs in Britain, 'significant' works, but still largely ignored by Haverfield, were Scarth's *Roman Britain*

9. The Taunton antiquarian was either C.G. Webb or, more likely, J.H. Pring, '...an enthusiastic believer in a Roman Taunton, but his arguments are largely worthless' (Haverfield *VCH* Somerset I (1906): 367).

10. On 3 October 1935 a C.E. Low wrote to *The Times* recounting how Haverfield in a letter to the *English Historical Review* in *c.*1912 speculated on the possibility of centuriation in Essex: '...the eminent writer was not very tolerant of attempts to see traces of centuriation in our English maps, so that one wondered how far this letter should be regarded as ground bait for the incautious; that in its main purpose the statement was to be taken seriously goes without saying. Anyhow, through the gate thus opened many sheep flocked with all sorts of wild surmises ...Your correspondent waited for the Professor to start his slaughter of the foolish innocents. But alas! came instead the news that Haverfield was dead.' Low's reference is partially incorrect. It was published in 1918 = Haverfield 1918d.

(1883)[11], commended by Collingwood (Collingwood and Myres 1936: 465), Rhys' *Celtic Britain* (1884 with later editions), and G.L. Gomme's *Romano-British Remains I and II* (1887), two volumes of excerpts on archaeological finds compiled from *The Gentleman's Magazine Library* but damned in review by Haverfield in *The Academy* (22 October and 1 November 1884, and more substantially in the *Classical Review*, see below Chapter 5). Other publications Haverfield effectively ignored were H.C. Coote's *The Romans in Britain* (1878 with later editions)[12] and

11. H(enry) M. Scarth (1814–1890) was born in Durham and educated at Edinburgh before going up to Christ's College, Cambridge (BA 1837 and MA 1841). Ordained in 1837, he became Deacon at Lichfield and Priest in 1838. He was curate of Eaton Constantine (Salop) between 1837 and 1841, was Rector of Kely (1841), and that of Bathwick 1841–71, after which he was Rector of Wrington (1871–90). He was also Prebendary of Wells between 1848 and 1890 and Rural Dean of Portishead from 1880. He died in Tangiers, aged 76. The Haverfields' links with Bathwick were noted in Ch. 1. Haverfield seems to have known Scarth personally (cf. Haverfield 1919a: xxiv). Scarth published a number of books and articles on antiquarian themes, especially on Roman Bath. He '...ranked among the best English authorities on Roman antiquities and specially the relics of the Roman occupation of Britain, but was inclined to believe the influence of the occupation was more permanent than is generally admitted by historians' (W. Hunt in S. Lee (ed.) *DNB vol. 50 (Russen–Scobell)* (1897): 405–6 (revised for the *ODNB* vol. 49 (p. 192) by E. Baigent) citing a review in *The Saturday Review* (15 December 1883 lvi: 769: obit. – *Proc Soc Antiqs London* 13: (1889–91): 141). Sir John Rhŷs (1840–1915), Jesus College and Fellow of Merton, was from 1877 first (Jesus) Professor of Celtic at Oxford. His especial interest was Ogam. He was a correspondent with Haverfield, and was cited as an authority by the latter on a number of occasions (e.g. Haverfield 1892c). Haverfield mentions Rhŷs and his advice in a number of letters to Mommsen, described him as 'my friend' (*The Antiquary* XXVIII (1893) and generally respected his opinions (e.g. *The Academy* 7 November 1891 where he offered a correction to Rhŷs' reading of some inscribed lead pigs). Elsewhere it was said of Rhŷs; 'As a scholar (he) combined with great industry and learning a singularly active reconstructive imagination' (Fraser 1927: 457–8; cf. obit. *Proc Brit Acad* 1925; *Archaeol Cambrensis* 71 (1916): 98–100).

12. Henry Charles Coote (1815–1885) between 1840 and 1857 worked in and wrote about the legal profession. He was also heavily into the study of English history and folklore. According to one of his obituarists, his name was chiefly associated with his attempts to prove that Roman settlers in Britain were not exterminated in the post-Roman Germanic invasions and that the laws and customs of the Anglo-Saxon period went back to the Roman period. His arguments were developed in *A Neglected Fact....* (1864) but drew little attention until Freeman savaged them in *Macmillian's Magazine* in

even later, F. Sagot's *La Bretagne Romaine* (1911). These and the others works repeated two persistent problems. Few, if any, had yet appreciated that one could write an account of Roman Britain based to any substantial degree on its archaeological remains and discoveries. There was a strong tradition of (antiquarian) description but no recognition of the fact that such descriptions could be included in a narrative history. Most of them tended to share the same methodological structure, one which was still based on literary and epigraphic evidence but with little reference to other forms of archaeological evidence. At the same time, another problem which compounded the chances of writing such works was access, or rather the inaccessibility, to the data. Conybeare complained, 'Much of the most valuable material, indeed, has never been published in book form, and must be sought out in the articles of the Antiquary, Hermes etc. and the reports of the many local Archaeological Societies' (Conybeare 1903: v).

With respect to writing about Roman Britain, according to Randall (1946) the quality of the output can be split into two phases. The former was typified by Scarth's *Roman Britain* (1883), which '...might almost as well as have been written in the eighteenth (century) under the influence of Horsley and Camden', and came to a close with Conybeare's 1903 monograph of the same title (Randall 1946: 80)[13], and replacing

---

1870. Coote reviewed and reiterated his opinions in *The Roman in Britain*, with a thesis which was widely accepted, if not by Freeman and his group (cf. L. Stephens (ed.) *DNB XII Conder-Craigie* (1887): 162–3 – revised by N. Banerji for the *ODNB* vol. 13 p. 303).

13. Rev. John William Edward Conybeare (1843–1931), the son of W.J. Conybeare, the first Principal of the Liverpool Collegiate Institute (1842–8), was educated at Trinity College, Cambridge, (BA 1866, MA 1869). Ordained in 1868, there then followed a series of church appointments before he converted to Catholicism in 1910. Throughout his life Conybeare retained strong antiquarian interests, not least of Cambridgeshire. Haverfield certainly knew him: sometime between 1903 and 1915 he was writing to him about samian found near Barrington (cf. Haverfield Arretine fragments in Cambridge. *Proc Cambridge Antiq Soc* XX (1915–16): 53–9). Conybeare's acknowledgements to his 'sources' are instructive. He provides a list of 'later' (= modern) authorities with the caveat '...modern books on Roman Britain tend to become obsolete, sometimes with startlingly rapidity'. He cites as his chief authorities the *Monumenta Historica Britannica* (1848), *CIL* VII (1873) and Elton's *Origins of English history* (1890): '... and yet more to Mr Haverfield's invaluable publications in the "Antiquary" and elsewhere, without which to keep abreast of the incessant development of my subject by the

Scarth in the series published by the Society for Promoting Christian Knowledge's Early Britain series. Also in the series was Codrington's *Roman Roads in Britain* (1903). Randall's second phase commenced with Haverfield, not least because his work represented a much higher standard of research, one which involved a more critical appreciation of the 'facts' and ideas repeated by earlier researchers. Indeed a major part of Haverfield's career was devoted to improving the results of earlier research. For nearly twenty years, from 1890 onwards, in offering corrections of the opinions of any number of local antiquaries, Haverfield published a series of short studies on such subjects making comments, mostly negative, not least pointing out their mistakes, about such work. Likewise his extant unpublished writings contain similar negative observations about the level of competence and methodological rigour that most earlier writers demonstrated. Haverfield's work culminated in his bringing together his opinions on the strengths and more importantly the weaknesses of British antiquarianism in the first of his Ford lectures (*The Study of Roman Britain: A Retrospect*: Haverfield 1924: 59–88), where he sketched the progress of the subject from William Malmesbury (*c*.1090–1143) down to the early nineteenth century. As we will see, his conclusions were not wholly positive. To assess their veracity, his assessments can be set against those made by Collingwood in his (critical) bibliography of earlier work in *Roman Britain and the English Settlements* (Collingwood and Myres 1936: 462–78).

If in Randall's scheme Haverfield and his writings initiated a second period in the writing about Roman Britain, his characterization may have been overly influenced by latter day attitudes to antiquarianism. But it is noteworthy that as far as the (general) historians of archaeology are concerned judging by their failure to mention

---

antiquarian spade work now going on all over the land would be an almost hopeless task' (Conybeare 1903: iv). Conybeare said that he was writing 'to give a readable sketch of the historical growth and decay of Roman influence in Britain, illustrated by the archaeology of the period, rather than a mainly archaeological treatise with a bare outline of the history.' One reviewer complimented this 'admirable little book', noting that there '...is, indeed there could not be, any attempt at literary style; but, in spite of this, the book is more than a mere chronicle of events. The facts are put together in a readable and attractive manner, and their value is enhanced by footnotes and references to authorities, while frequent references to archaeology and kindred subjects by way of illustrations greatly add to the book's interest and utility' (cf. *Man* IV (1904): 196).

anything other than the works of Camden *et al.*, there was nothing noteworthy to report. Even in the 1930s Collingwood could claim that modern '...books wholly dealing with Roman Britain are not very numerous' (Collingwood in Collingwood and Myres 1936: 465).[14] Indeed his list starts with Mommsen's 1883 *Provinces of the Roman Empire*. This does not ignore the fact that there had been histories of Britain published in the Middle Ages. These derived the origins of the British people from literary and other spurious documentary sources and were composed relative to the author's position to the relationship of England/Britain to Europe that had affected earlier antiquarian writers. There had also been overview histories of the island. Smiles (1994) has examined the course of historical and antiquarian studies from the sixteenth through to the mid-nineteenth centuries and brought out how such works became subsumed in the debate about the origins of the British. Published at this time were the likes of William Harrison's (1534–1593) *Description of Britaine* and *Description of England* and John Clapham's *Historie of England* (1602) and *Historie of Great Britaine* (1606), both of them narratives of Roman Britain and Saxon England (Kendrick 1950: 180). Slightly later was David Hume's *History of England* (1754–62) which traced the beginnings of English history to the Roman invasion, although it elected to cover its Roman history in a brief statement, not least because of a suspicion of antiquarian evidence (Smiles 1994: 10). As it was, the evidence cited was derived entirely from literary sources rather than from archaeology. Hume's account was later republished in a number of updated editions. Slightly different in format was Francis Grose's *The Antiquities of England and Wales* (6 vols., 1773–87), a compilation for public consumption and those who wished to learn the skill of the antiquar-

14. The failure of antiquarian-type writers to do so was due to conceptual inadequacies. Another feature of the Renaissance was the rediscovery of ancient writers and texts, works which in turn could be studied for moral lessons and, for instance, in statecraft. It was also the start of the process of text analysis and the creation of definitive *editio princeps* of the authors being rediscovered. But Renaissance scholars did not dare '...to write the history of Greece and Rome because they believed the ancient historians had written these narratives once and for all. Thucydides and Livy might be imitated but not replaced' (Hicks 1996: 310). Scholarly effort was put into understanding such writers, not analysing them. The same attitude pervaded the accounts of British antiquarians. Monuments might be used to supplement non-literary evidence but if there was not so much literature to work with, then their efforts were bound to remain puny.

ian, but at the expense of Roman remains (Sweet 2004: 318–19). In 1845 the first edition of Robert Stuart's *Caledonia Romana* appeared (with a second, revised edition prepared by R. Thompson in 1852). The Roman occupation of Wales received a similarly late treatment, with the publication of J.E. Lee's *Isca Silurum* in 1862 (Lloyd 1946).

We have seen that one of the most significant factors in shaping writing of ancient British history was the relationship of the island to the continent: between the pan-European and the insular perceptions. Reflective of the preoccupation of assessing Britain's relations with early medieval Europe, other publications of the time which treated Roman Britain were more concerned with the better-documented post-Roman/early medieval period. In these accounts, Roman Britain is usually treated in a summary fashion, almost exclusively from its (defective) historical sources; differences in opinion were played out over the degree of the Roman legacy on post-fifth-century society. Naturally enough, Haverfield had occasion to summarize what he thought to be the *communis opinio* with regard to the Roman presence in Britain at the time that he flourished. In the mid- to late nineteenth century, British antiquarian scholarship typically tended to reject the Renaissance tradition of the island's European link. The new model, drawing on the precedent set by William Lambarde, emphasized Britain's isolation and the eradication of the evidence of the Roman presence by the Saxons. The practice continued over the next two centuries. G.L. Gomme highlighted the difficulties in identifying clearly Roman period sites (by which he meant 'stations' and 'roads'), a fact which he believed '...clearly point(s) to the almost complete eradication of Roman civilisation from British and English history' and that '...if the stamp of an implacable antagonism is shown in other ways to have been heavily laid upon Roman monuments in Great Britain, there needs some very powerful arguments to prove that institutions, law, culture, and art survived around the wreck of the more indestructible physical evidence of Roman greatness' (1887 (ii): vi–vii). Towards the end of the same century there was a reaction to this sort of conclusion. In his *Romans of Britain*, a reply to E.A. Freeman's attack on his earlier *A Neglected Fact in English History* (1864), Coote continued to argue for the survival of Roman law and practice into Anglo-Saxon times (which later influenced such works as M. Sharpe's *Middlesex in Roman and Saxon Times* – 1919). Coote '...took a very decided view of the influence of the Romans in Britain, and his work is the great authority upon the subject, and a monument of lifelong devotion of a study of which few Englishmen realize either the importance or the fascination' (Gomme 1887 (ii): vii). In this view of the past, the Anglo-Saxons took on and developed certain aspects of the Roman presence in Britain. Freeman had argued, however, for homogeneity of the English race, that Roman civilization had minimal effect and equally minimal consequences for the future evolution of British society. One of the problems, therefore, of this trend was to isolate the earliest history of Britain from the rest of Europe and which meant the Roman presence in the island was neglected. Judging by his failure ever to cite Coote as an authority but the occasional negative comment about his opinions, Haverfield did not rate his contribution to Romano-British scholarship.[15]

Another drawback to much of the literature concerning Roman Britain available even at the time that Haverfield appeared on the scene was that the archaeological component continued to remain so poorly understood. Anticipating Collingwood's comments in the 1930s (in Collingwood and Myres 1936: 465), in recommending the strengths of the literature available *c.*1912, John Ward (1911a) could point to few not entirely satisfactory general introductions.[16] Other texts he mentions are qualified with the judgment that they are too historical (and not sufficiently archaeological) in content.[17] Ward was emphasizing indirectly that the list was all in all pretty poor. Specialists and lay readers

---

15. For instance, he once wrote of Mr Coote '…in a treatise of which ingenuity and ignorance are about equally characteristic' (Haverfield 1918d: 292; cf. 1889b).

16. Ward cites Horsley (1732), Wright's *The Celts, the Romans and the Saxons* (1852), Scarth (1883), Conybeare (1903), the relevant sections of Traill's *Social England* (1902–04), Gough's edition of Camden, King's *Munimenta Antiqua* (1799–1806) and *The Gentleman's Magazine*.

17. This included Elton's *Origins of English History* (1889), H.C. Coote's *Romans of Britain* (1878), Mommsen's *Provinces of the Roman Empire* (1886), Babcock's *Two Last Centuries of Roman Britain* (1891), Bury's *Gibbon's Decline and Fall of the Roman Empire* (1896), John Rhŷs' *Celtic Britain* (1884/1908), Hogarth's *Authority and Archaeology* (1899) and Charles Oman's *England Before the Conquest* (1910). Rhŷs' *Celtic Britain*, written 'in the days of little books' (Preface to the 1st edition, 1884: iii) covers 'Britain in the time of Julius Caesar', 'Britain down to the Claudian conquest' and 'the Romans in Britain and how they left it'. Down to the 1908 edition, he continued to draw on Hübner and so the *CIL* as well as Mommsen but no other (archaeological) authorities. See also, A. del Mar's *Ancient Britain in the Light of Modern Discoveries* (1900), which manages to omit any reference to its archaeology, ignores Haverfield's updates on the island's epigraphy and other archaeological work and cites Scarth's *Roman Britain* of 1883 as 'an able and interesting work, drawn from antiquarian sources' along with G.F. Scott Elliot's *The Romance of Early British Life, from the Earliest Times to the Coming of the Danes* (1909).

alike had no satisfactory general history of Roman Britain written with due regard to the archaeological evidence. But there was better quality work of the area in and around Hadrian's Wall (notably with Bruce's *Roman Wall*) and in a number of specialist themes (e.g. epigraphy and the updates of recent finds, mosaics, and roads, including monographs by Codrington (1903) and Forbes and Burmester (1904)). With respect to the literature of other regions and special sites, Ward was able to recommend little, other than rather dated antiquarian accounts (25 to 50 years old) and the interim reports of the likes of the Silchester, Manchester and Gellygaer excavations. Implicit in Ward's summary was that his *The Roman Era in Britain* (1911) was in many respects the first systematic attempt to bring together the evidence to construct a narrative history of the archaeology of Roman Britain, a fact recognized in the favourable review in the *Archaeologia Cambrensis* for 1912.

Ward's opinions about the poor state of knowledge was not unique. At about the same time as he was complaining, Haverfield made his own attempt to assess the progress of British antiquarianism including what he considered to be the more important studies on Romano-British archaeology compiled in the nineteenth century. Among these were John Carter's *Architecture* (two folios, 1795–1816), the eighteen volumes of Britton and Brayley's *Beauties of England and Wales* (1801), the four quartos of Samuel Lyson's *Reliquae Britannico-Romanae* (1801–07) and with his brother, Daniel, the six-volume *Magna Britannia* (1806–22), intended to cover the entire country but ultimately limited to six of them. He was also to note, however, that such works were little heeded in scholarly circles of the time (Haverfield 1919a: xxvi n. 4). In contrast, Haverfield was dismissive of A.W. Whatmore's *Insulae Britannicae …Down to the Close of the Roman Period* (1913; cf. Haverfield 1914a). In fact there was not much else of the later nineteenth century he could commend.

The organization and execution of archaeological research

The impression of the period of late-medieval to eighteenth-century Britain is one of archaeological research being undertaken by a largely unorganized band of dedicated antiquarians and other members of the educated minor nobility. Such individuals tended to work alone although often sharing their results. In contrast, in the nineteenth century a more critical appreciation of British antiquity emerged, a realization which was to re-energize research and is reflected in the quality of publications in that century. That this occurred was in part due to improvements in the education, and therefore the critical appreciation, of those who had traditionally devoted themselves to antiquarian research. We have seen that the late medieval period saw the first attempts to create antiquarian societies, although most of these organizations ultimately failed. They were prone to fashions in taste and had a limited membership which was based on (social) class and grand dilettantism. On the other hand the nineteenth century has been characterized as a period when archaeology in Britain, like university education, became professionalized. It is a curious phenomenon of the late 1830s and early 1840s that there occurred the almost overnight appearance of numerous regional archaeological (often linked with antiquarian, architectural and natural history as well as historical) societies.[18] The earliest of the regional archaeological, rather than antiquarian, societies was the Warwickshire Natural History and Archaeological Society of 1836. The oldest surviving is the Sussex Archaeological Society (1846), with its journal, the *Collections*. The phenomenon was appreciated by Haverfield and was examined in greater detail by Piggott (1976: 171ff.). Previously, study had been at the county-regional level or in the form of histories of 'national' organizations. It was at this time that the Society of Antiquaries in London patronized a series of county studies, first under its authority and later its auspices. At various times it proposed to coordinate the compilation of regional lists of Roman sites (cf. Chapter 5) while Gomme had initiated something similar in the *Archaeological Review*. The emphasis on the county level continued with the pioneering studies of George Fox (1833–1907) and his work on Roman Norfolk, Shropshire and Suffolk (Fox 1889; 1897; 1900), which developed from an earlier lecture on Roman Norfolk offered to the RAI AGM in Norwich in 1889. Fox represented a new type of better-qualified antiquarian. A native of Norwich, he was an artist and architect to the well-to-do, interested in medieval antiquities. In addition to the three studies already noted, he also wrote of the Roman remains of Leicester, and Wroxeter as well, the Roman coastal defences of Kent. In 1889 he joined St John Hope in working at Silchester, the results of which he wrote about (Fox and Hope 1889–91). Awarded an honorary MA by Oxford University in 1894, he became the honorary curator of the Silchester collection in Reading Museum (*obit.*, probably by Mill Stephenson *Archaeol J* 65 (1908): 338–9; Hudson 1981: 31).

The reasons for this explosion in archaeological work lie with a combination of factors. In the early nineteenth century, again principally

18. For examples of the English societies and their journals: Collingwood and Myres 1936: 472–3: Hudson 1981: 15–42; Levine 1986; Westherall 1998.

due to political developments, Roman history revived as a subject of study and which had implications for the Roman history of this island. The revival in antiquarian-archaeological studies was helped by better topographic studies at this time and by the explosion in individual county and parish histories, written by local officer holders and clerics, as well as archaeological monographs as well as the rise of printing clubs (Westherall 1998: 24ff.). Piggott has also emphasized the part played by contemporary developments in the study of geology. Haverfield (1924) attributed other factors to the nineteenth-century renaissance: the reform of the franchise and the Poor Laws, the development in churchmanship, and changes in elementary education. Such processes were helped by the Evangelical Revival religious movement – the Tractarians (or 'Oxford Movement') of the 1830s and 1840s. Their relationship with archaeology has been explored by Piggott (1976). The growing sense of unity among dissenting religious groups strengthened their hold in the English lower and middle-classes in the first half of the nineteenth century, especially in the commercial and industrial parts of the country. In reaction to this the Anglican High Church, shaken out of its lethargy by a group of theological students at Oxford and Cambridge, developed a degree of self-consciousness which included (better) appreciation of its past. This attitude eventually filtered down to churches and parishes. One consequence was an interest in the (medieval) architecture of buildings (and so their archaeology), or as it came to be known, the science of ecclesiology. The refurbishment of church buildings that had fallen into decay and ruin from the Middle Ages also stimulated an interest in ancient buildings. According to Piggott, it was not entirely coincidental that the earliest archaeological societies tended to be concentrated in those parts of England dominated by the Anglican church, with an agricultural and squirearchical backdrop, and not in the newer industrial areas like the Midlands and the North where non-conformity was prevalent and where antique churches were relatively absent.

The 'Oxford Movement' then might be seen as a significant catalyst in the explosion of archaeological interest that followed in England. The situation was even more marked in Scotland where few archaeological societies emerged. This phenomenon was attributed to the strength of the church there, but in fact it was neither the Anglican Church nor the local gentry but the Society of Antiquaries of Scotland which repressed local structures. The society dominated the scene in a way that the London and Newcastle societies never had. Clarke (1981) attributes the situation in Scotland to the comparatively small local rural population in comparison to England. The successful societies in Scotland happened to be located in the southern parts of the country where there was a larger population and closer proximity to active societies in northern England. But the church was not the only factor in the rise of (middle-class) archaeology. There was also the intellectual climate, and the emergence of a capitalized, propertied and leisured class. European colonialism made it easier to travel and work in the eastern Mediterranean. Discoveries from there stimulated work in the United Kingdom. Complementing these secular trends, were the effects of the late eighteenth-century Romantic movement which had emphasized local culture, an interest in ballads and songs, local traditions, churches, abbeys and castles. These interests fostered a changing perception of history, one which tied in with the preoccupation of the late medieval and regency periods in local antiquarianism. Out of all these trends came an appreciation of (medieval) art, buildings and so other more ancient monuments. It is these facts which occasioned the creation of the early architectural and archaeological societies and explains the emphasis on ecclesiastical history in the journals of these societies as well as in parish histories of the time. The success of the regional societies was also facilitated by their willingness to publish the results of work of their members, often on an annual basis. Developments in printing technology and the improved ability to circulate journals through the fledgling Post Office facilitated publication and distribution. With the increase in publishable material, and the societies willingness to exchange journals, yet more positive consequences occurred. Nevertheless, Haverfield complained (for instance, in *The Athenaeum*) that the societies were far too prepared to publish weak material at the expense of undertaking decent excavation projects.

The growth of the archaeological societies was also facilitated by changes at Oxford and Cambridge universities. One of the consequences of the reforms of the universities from the mid-nineteenth century (cf. Chapter 3) was an increase in the number of graduates produced by the two institutions. The rises and falls in student admissions at Oxford have been studied by Lawrence Stone (1975: 59–70). In the nineteenth century he has identified two periods of expansion in student recruitment, 1805–24, and particularly 1860–1909. These increases, especially in the first period, were due to the rise of the middle-class, prospering under the industrial and commercial revolution, and in turn the growth of the public schools. While these factors also influenced Stone's second sub-period, reform in the teaching and examination processes at the university also made their contributions. University education became relatively cheaper at this time. While many graduates continued to go into the church and so preserve the traditional strength of British antiquarian research by clerics, the real rise was in the numbers going into professions thereby creating a growing educated proto-middle class.

Finally there were the more relaxed social conventions which came with the regional societies. The larger membership permitted a degree of social intermixing which was not known in the late-medieval antiquarian societies. For instance, the new societies often tended to open their membership to women. In addition to organizing series of evening lectures (often in the winter), improvements in the national and regional road network and the development of the railway system made the countryside more accessible and facilitated summer tours and excursions by the societies (Hudson 1981: 43). Not only did the rise of the railways facilitate travel and the dissemination of information but, in their construction, they also wrought destruction which attracted archaeologists. It was not long before many societies started to consider organizing and funding their own fieldwork, especially as there was an increase in the rate of discoveries with the advance of the country's industrialization. This invariably meant excavation.

With the emergence of an educated middle class coupled to the other factors already rehearsed, the mid-nineteenth century also saw the initiation of a number of ambitiously large, well-publicised, relatively well-funded and, in certain terms, highly successful excavations.[19] Many of these programmes were on Roman period sites which reflected a renewed interest in the Roman period of British history. Towards the end of the century, Haverfield was closely linked with some of them and in turn was to report much of the work on Roman sites in a series of statements of progress in a variety of journals from the 1890s onwards. This included such initiatives as Chester, Silchester and later Wroxeter. Browning's statement, however, that 'the turn-of-the-century excavations at Silchester and the Roman Wall both inaugurated a new era in how excavations were executed' is misleading (1989: 354). To say that '...whereas previous

---

19. There was, for instance, James Buckland (1814–1884), Professor of Geology at the Royal Agricultural College at Cirencester and his excavations at and analysis of the material from Cirencester in the early 1850s (Ebbatson 1994: 58), which built on Samuel Lyson's work on the Great Pavement from Woodchester, Gloucestershire. In the words of one commentator, 'A modern reappraisal of Lyson's and Buckman's work would be of great interest, and it is perhaps a fitting reminder of today's specialization that this has not been attempted' (Torrens in Wacher and McWhirr 1982: 78).

ventures had been undertaken by individuals these two excavations were sponsored by antiquarian societies' (Silchester by the Society of Antiquaries of London, the Roman Wall by the Cumberland and Westmorland Society) misses the work that they – and other regional societies – had initiated before the 1890s. Thomas Wright excavated at Wroxeter between 1859 and 1867 on the back of public subscriptions and private benefactions. He was also the author of *The Celts, the Romans and the Saxons*, a work emphasizing the failings of the Celts under Roman rule (1852; cf. Smiles 1994: 126; White and Barker 1998: 17). As we will see, Silchester too had been subject to excavation in the 1860s under the patronage of the landowner, the Duke of Wellington. Such excavations were well-run for the time and equally well-published. At about the same time Hadrian's Wall was being subjected, especially by the Cumberland and Westmorland Society, to a series of small scale yet still significant excavations and other projects under the guise of its various Hadrian's Wall committees. The Scottish Antiquaries had co-ordinated their first excavations at Inveresk in 1783, but it was not until late in the next century, in 1890, that it started its own systematic and substantial series of excavations. In 1892 the Glasgow Archaeological Society (with Haverfield as '...close adviser and financial helper': Stevenson 1981: 177) began a series of soundings along the Antonine Wall and, in 1895, at Birrens, before moving to Birrenswark (also known as Burnswark), Lyne, Camelon, Inchtuthil, Castlecary and, in 1902–3, Rough Castle. From 1905 to 1910, the Society supported James Curle's excavations at Newstead. At the same time the Scottish societies were also increasingly supporting the exploration of non-Roman period sites. That said, such large scale, multi-year projects to which the sponsoring societies provided funding for excavation as well as a medium for publishing reports did in turn encourage other less ambitious research schemes, though still significant at a regional level. These included excavation of urban sites and in time a number of villa sites as well as forts and along Hadrian's Wall. In Wales at the end of the century there commenced two major projects: at the Roman fort at Gellygaer (1899), the first large-scale excavation of a fort in Wales and undertaken by the Cardiff Naturalists Society, and in the same year under the auspices of the (London) Society of Antiquaries, at Caerwent. Significantly, Haverfield's name invariably appears in the lists of subscribers, committee members, or as advisor on many, if not all, of these projects.

Along with the proceedings of the national and regional societies, there was another medium where antiquarian and archaeological notices could be placed which must have had a far greater impact on the public's perception of archaeology. These were journals which appealed to the interests of the educated gentleman, as for instance, from 1665, the *Philosophical Transactions* of the Royal Society and the *Archaeologia* (from 1770). Necessarily wide-ranging in their scope, journals such as *The Athenaeum* (from 1828, a 'Journal of English and Foreign Literature, Sciences, the Fine Arts, Music and Drama') and *The Edinburgh Review* frequently accepted reports on recent discoveries as well as points of interpretation and reviews of new publications. Another periodical was *The Gentleman's Magazine* 'which stood first among antiquarian publications from 1731 to 1868, maintaining its reputation also for general literature, under its editors, John Gough Nicols, succeeded by Mr. J.H. Parker and Mr. Walford' (T. Morgan *J Brit Archaeol Assoc* XLVI: 1890): 239). As we will see, the magazine played a pivotal rôle in Haverfield's career as an archaeologist of Roman Britain. *The Reliquary (and Illustrated Archaeologist)* was '...devoted to the study of the early pagan and church antiquities of Great Britain; Medieval architecture and ecclesiology; the development of the arts and industries of man in the past ages; and the survivals of ancient usages and applications in the present'.[20] First published in 1860, it eventually ceased to appear after 1909. Aimed at a slightly more specialized readership was *The Antiquary* of 1890 which included archaeological and antiquarian reports.[21] It stopped publishing in 1915.

---

20. *The Reliquary* (and *Illustrated Archaeologist* – 1860–84: 1886–94 and 1903–09 cf. Riden 1979), *The Illustrated Archaeologist* 1893–4; the pair combined 1895–1909.
21. *The Antiquary*, started in May–June 1871 as *The Antiquarian*, becoming *The Antiquary* (in July down to December 1873) and then merged with *Long Ago* (1873–94), was '...a fortnightly medium of intercommunication for archaeologists, antiquarians, numismatists, the virtuosi and collectors of articles of virtu' (as quoted in Hudson 1981: 100). It should not be confused with *The Antiquary* ('...a magazine devoted to the study of the past' – cf. Appendix 2). Relaunched, with a new format and reduced cover price in 1895, 'The Antiquary will also endeavour not only to retain the position it has earned as the leading English Archaeological magazine of the day, but if possible, to become of even more service to the study of Archaeology in the future as time goes on' (*The Athenaeum* 15 December 1894: 815). *The Archaeologist and Journal of Antiquarian Science* (edited by Halliwell Philips) from 1841, after ten issues, lasted less than one year (cf. Evans 1949: 1; Westherall 1998: 23). Other representative journals include *Blackwood's (Edinburgh) Magazine* (cf. Finkelstein 2002), *The Academy* (1869), *The Antiquarian Magazine and Bibliog-*

There was also the national (and regional) press which frequently carried letters and shorter articles. In national terms, *The Times*, *The (Manchester) Guardian* and *The Observer* were the most prominent.[22] The multiplicity of these publications and willingness to publish reflected the growing popularity of archaeology in Britain from the middle of the century with what was a lay, or semi-informed readership. Of course, as with the public dissemination of archaeology today, the problem with the media was that it tended to deal only with the immediate, reporting sensational or unusual finds rather than the results of the fuller consideration of the data or with overviews. In turn the language employed to describe them and the conceptual frameworks into which they were to be located were still hindered by the broader limitations of Romano-British history that Haverfield was at pains to highlight.[23] That said he had to use the likes of *The Antiquary* and later *The Athenaeum* before he moved on to academically more weighty vehicles such as the *Proceedings of the British Academy* and ultimately, from 1910, the *Journal of Roman Studies*.

Despite the proliferation of periodicals, the drawbacks with the (major) journals, regional and national, were many. The national journals were too much of a mish-mash of antiquarianism. Roman archaeology was often submerged in them, not that it had much of a voice in the first instance (as shown by the absence of major overviews for the public). Instead such bodies were dominated on editorial boards by medievalists and ecclesiasticals and the absence of Romanists hindered the wider

rapher (1882–7), *Walford's Antiquarian Magazine*, *The Western Antiquary* (1881–93), *The Archaeological Review* (1888–90) which merged with *The Folklore Journal* to create *Folklore* along with *Countrylife* and *The Illustrated London News*; (cf. Collingwood in Collingwood and Myres 1936: 472).

22. I have yet to find a satisfactory discussion of the rôle of the press, especially the popular national and regional, nor of periodicals in the reporting and dissemination of archaeological and antiquarian discoveries. It no doubt played a part but it is impossible, at present, to quantify how much so. The study of the wider social significance of popular periodicals in the nineteenth century is evidently still a fledgling discipline (cf. the essays in Blake *et al.* 1990). At best the subject is a side theme for the likes of Hudson (1981), Levine (1986) and Musty (1986).

23. For example, Haverfield wrote to *The Athenaeum*: 'May I utter a protest against the article on Roman roads in Britain published in the current number of the Nineteenth Century? It is not credible to English scholarship that such an article should find a place in one of the leading monthlies' (*The Athenaeum* 12 November 1898: 683).

perception of what the Roman period was about, as Haverfield noted indirectly (e.g. 1911a: xi). Haverfield's attack on what he regarded as the
moribund position in the national scale of things was assisted by his willingness to speak out and to address the national societies (e.g. his
numerous utterances to the London Society of Antiquaries).[24] At the regional level, the societies were too parochial and their publications and
readership limited in size and their interests. But until there was created
a more appropriate platform from which Roman archaeology could be
broadcasted, Haverfield was forced to use what there was available then.

By the mid-nineteenth century there were four 'national' or su-
pra-regional bodies concerned in one way or another with aspects of
antiquarian and archaeological study: the British Archaeological Association (BAA, with its *Journal*), the Royal Archaeological Institute (RAI,
and the *Archaeological Journal*), The Irish Archaeological Society and the
Cambrian Archaeological Association. With the proliferation of regional societies and a growing awareness of what archaeology in the
United Kingdom could achieve, it is not surprising that there soon occurred moves to unite the various local organizations under a national
body with broader goals designed to raise standards and broadcast
better antiquarian studies. The first real challenge to the established organizations like the three major (British) antiquaries societies came in
1836. In that year the London Society of Antiquaries failed to cater adequately to those of its members with numismatic interests and who in
turn broke away to form the Numismatic Society of London. The foundation of the BAA, modelled on the British Association for the
Advancement of Science (BAAS), was justified on the grounds that the
established (English) societies were outmoded, inadequate and, in the
case of the London society, distinctly not provincial. According to
Westherall, the BAA was the consequence of the 'unwillingness on the
part of the Antiquaries to sanction the creation of active subsidiary bodies such as a numismatic committee, ...repeated in 1843 when the
Council refused to sponsor directly the creation of a committee of its active antiquaries to promote the preservation of national antiquities'
(1998: 27). The leading figures behind the BAA were Charles Roach

---

24. The Society's *Proceedings* note the following contributions per year; 1891 – 1;
    1892 – 2; 1893 – 1; 1894 – 3; 1895 – 2; 1896 – 2; 1897 – 2; 1899 – 3; 1900 – 1;
    1903 – 1; 1905 – 2; 1906 – 1; 1907 – 1; 1908 – 3; 1909 – 3; 1910 – 5; 1911 – 2;
    1912 – 2; 1913 – 2; 1914 – 2; 1915 – 1; 1917 – 1. All these utterances were on
    aspects of the archaeology of Roman Britain including those field projects
    with which he was directly involved.

Smith and Thomas Wright, who in turn created a 'central board' to which the likes of Albert Way, Director of the Society of Antiquaries and nineteen others were adlected (*J Brit Archaeol Assoc* I (1846): i–xv). The new organization's mission was to be '...the encouragement and prosecution of researches into the arts and monuments of the early and middle ages' (cf. Westherall 1994). Again in imitation of the BAAS, the BAA held the first of a series of (archaeological) congresses at Canterbury in 1844. T.J. Pettigrew in his address to the BAA in 1850 claimed that its formation was the catalyst in the establishing of other national and regional antiquarian societies. It had also engendered higher standards in reporting and the interpretation of the evidence. From 1849 it published its *Notes and Queries*. That this had occurred was, in Pettigrew's opinion, because of the relative failure of the London Society, in spite of all the preferential treatment it had received in the past 150 years (Pettigrew 1851). Indeed such treatment was perceived as elitist in both attitudes and membership.

Internal arguments in the BAA resulted in the creation in 1846 of the breakaway Archaeological Institute of Great Britain and Ireland which was to become the Royal Archaeological Institute in 1866. The RAI's mouthpiece was the *Archaeological Journal*. The BAA relaunched its *Journal* (and for a short time for 1862 the *Collectanea Archaeologia*, but which ceased with its second volume in 1871). The reasons for the split between the organizations now seem trivial although they ultimately went back to clashes of personalities among the leading members of the original BAA (Evans 1949; Westherall 1994). The schism and the failure of the two groups to reconcile their differences were blamed on each other (e.g. Pettigrew 1851; Chapman 1989a and b). Despite their professed more general, populist outlooks, the two organizations were still relatively socially elitist in membership and attitudes, with the Archaeological Institute being regarded as slightly more patrician.[25] In terms of their activities, both organizations shifted to the study of 'primeval' subjects, with their energies directed towards the study of antiquity as a science. A reviewer in the *Archaeological Journal* of 1850 defined archaeology as 'the accumulation of facts (and) their classification'. These efforts naturally led to the creation of schemes of classification of artefacts and site types, as well as the rise of a jargon and technical language (Chapman 1989b). In the long term, the existence of two national associations was largely counter-

---

25. In contrast, the BAA was at the time just after the split denounced for attracting its membership from the trades and from 'professionals'.

productive.[26] Both organizations remained financially weak and under-strength. There were a number of attempts to reconcile the two organizations in the hundred years after the split but the discussions came to nothing. The two bodies continued to organize their separate annual congresses and visits, and to host a bewildering range of papers and subjects. Such eclecticism is apparent in the list of papers presented to the Congress of Archaeological Societies (4th held in 1892: cf. *The Athenaeum* 23 July (1892): 138). But their memberships declined from the 1860s, in part as a consequence of the rise of the regional and local archaeological societies (Chapman 1989b: 28ff.). A reconciliation of sorts was effected in 1889 when the Congress of Archaeological Societies met. This was the first of a series that continued down until 1945 (when it was replaced by the Council for British Archaeology), and was made up of various sub-committees that were meant to report work and to co-ordinate field research (e.g. its Earthworks Committee).[27]

It goes without saying that the leading archaeologists of the mid-nineteenth century were not academics but members of the professional middle class with a strong interest in antiquarian issues. They in turn dominated their societies, national and regional. In the BAA this meant characters such as T.J. Pettigrew (1791–1865), Thomas Wright (1810–1877), James Parker and Joseph Mayer (1803–1886) along with Albert Way (1806–1874) of the rival Archaeological Institute. What is striking in this group is their background, and the esteem in which they were held. Pettigrew was a surgeon by profession, Wright recognized as a historian, linguist and antiquarian, and Mayer, a Liverpool goldsmith and jeweller who used part of his wealth not only to create a noted collection of antiquities but also to fund Wright's work at Wroxeter (as well to embellish his home city: Gibson 1988; White 1988). In turn they exerted their influences and played out their rivalries through the national and regional archaeological societies (e.g. Evans 1949; 1956; Hudson 1981). Standing proud above all these figures was Roach Smith. Haverfield's London 'druggist', Roach Smith was the subject of

26. Although the (R)AI could claim a larger and perhaps more influential membership in at least its early decades (for a survey of the membership of the RAI 1845–1942, see Ebbatson 1994). Still that membership contained few university persons and no 'real' academics (and so no 'archaeologists') although it did tend to draw on staff based in the British Museum (Westherall 1994: 19).

27. At the time of the BAA/RAI fissure, the London Antiquaries supplemented their *Archaeologia* with the *Proceedings*, which from 1920 onwards, was replaced by the *Antiquaries Journal*.

two lengthy death notices in the same volume of the *Journal of the British Archaeological Association*, in one of which was written:

> He may be said to have been almost the founder of the new school of Romano-British archaeology. The reactionary spirits since the days of Camden, Horsley and Lysons, had much dampened new researches into Roman history, as connected with Britain; but Mr. Smith …marked out for himself a plan of further discoveries in this line by collecting Roman remains, by personally examining walls, and walking over Roman roads, camps and dykes, while he paid special attention to the Roman coins discovered.[28]

There is no explicit evidence of Haverfield's attitudes to either the BAA or the RAI. Curiously, Macdonald (1924) failed to advertise that he had been a member of the RAI since 1885. Irrespective of the claims of the BAA and the consequences of its split with the RAI, and despite the improvements in fieldwork and the reporting of it, Haverfield remained highly critical of the general quality of work undertaken in the second half of the nineteenth and the early twentieth centuries.[29] Despite the relative improvement in archaeological research in the nineteenth century, Haverfield was still as dismissive of what was being achieved by the societies: there was much effort but little quality. His criticisms in this respect are numerous, some of which are discussed more fully below. As an example of how acidic his (public) pronouncements could be, in the preamble to a published version of a lecture delivered to the Classical Association in 1912 on the history of Roman London, he claimed:

---

28. The obituary was probably written by Thomas Morgan, VP and Hon. Treasurer of the BAA: cf. *J Brit Archaeol Assoc* XLVI (1890): 237–43, at p. 237. The other obituary was by G. Payne, (pp. 318–30). Roach Smith's memories of the time can be found in his *Retrospections, Social and Archaeological* (1886). For obituaries of the other individuals mentioned here: Wright cf. *J Brit Archaeol Assoc* XXXIV (1878): 262–4, 496–8; Way cf. *J Brit Archaeol Assoc* XXX (1874): 198–9; Meyer cf. *J Brit Archaeol Assoc* XLII (1886): 107–8. The only connection I have found between Haverfield and Roach Smith is the former dropping his name in an article on the location of the Portus Adurni (cf. *The Academy* 20 April 1889).

29. To make the point, in *The Athenaeum* (22 October (1892): 559) he commented on the way the Cumberland and Westmorland Society was undertaking work in their province in a way which should be a model for other regional societies and their archaeologists.

Roman London .... illustrates in more than one way the worst features of English archaeological study. There has been no want of interest in the subject. In England, indeed, Roman archaeology has throughout received a fuller share of general public interest than in any other country. Thanks to our classical system, nearly everyone has read a little Caesar and, it may be, some Tacitus, and though he has forgotten nine-tenths of it, he generally deems himself fitted to enquire into the history of the Roman empire. ...Unfortunately, it has also been thought needless to do more than be interested. I will not enquire whether this result too is due to our classical education: the fact is plain that our astonishing crowd of *θυρσοφόροι* is balanced by a woefully small band of *βάκχοι*, and scientific work is rarer here than in lands where general interest is far less frequent. Like most Englishmen, our students have had plenty of native ability; like most Englishmen, they have firmly declined to improve their native ability by special training. The British archaeologists, like the British soldier, has been deemed able to go anywhere and to do anything – and he has done it freely. The pages of our antiquarian journals are crammed with notes of Roman remains found in London and exhibited to this or that society. But the notes record the exhibitors more often than the exhibits; they tell us who brought an object up for inspection; they do not tell us what precisely the object was, or where exactly it was found, or whether anything definite was found with it. This is the case not only with small objects, but with big things ...we have the difference between the trained archaeologist and the Englishman whose 'ability' is his all. Meanwhile, those who have special knowledge, those who know Latin or even Greek, who have read a little Roman history and understand a few Roman technical terms, the teachers in our universities and classical schools, have turned their backs. A university is scattered all over London. Classical schools abound in it. But, until 1909, the best book, and indeed the only good book, on Roman London was written by a druggist (Haverfield 1912c and republished as Haverfield 1911c: 141–2, from where the extract here is derived).

Many of the issues raised in this lecture – the uncritical use of Latin sources, the pre-eminence of the classics in the school and university curricula, the poor record keeping of finds and excavations, the under-funding and amateur execution of fieldwork and research – are to be found repeated elsewhere. In the bibliography to his contribution on Roman Britain to the *Cambridge Medieval History*, Haverfield wrote that:

> ...the literature of Roman Britain contains a larger proportion than the literature of any other historical subject, of unsound and unscholarly work. Much of all this is valuable as a record of finds but the interpretation of the finds and the theories based on them are often worthless, even when they seem to be authoritative (1911d: 367).

This was a theme Haverfield raised in numerous publications where he was critical to the point of damning of the work of local antiquaries and their archaeological societies. Typical of his opinions is a lecture to the Research Department of the Royal Geographical Society (RGS) in December 1905. Throughout his presentation are a series of trenchant comments. For example:

> Local inquiries of the best local archaeologists are good in their way. But they are, themselves, wholly inadequate. In many districts there does not exist a competent local authority, whose opinion can safely be accepted about each of the various groups of antiquities which have to be included (on OS maps). A man may know much of Roman remains, without having any real acquaintance with medieval abbeys or neolithic [sic] flints. Indeed the case is worse than this. For, in the existing condition of English archaeological studies, there are few competent local authorities on any branch of knowledge, and in many districts there are none at all (1906b: 172).

Haverfield's solution was for existing, or newly created national, organizations to take on responsibility for the 'standardization', but with caution. In the same presentation he praised the work of the *VCH* and the Earthworks Committee of the London society and their attempts to record, and so to filter out spurious examples of monuments of Britain. In this respect he noted:

> It may not be easy to arrange collaboration between these and other attempts now in progress to catalogue and plan minutely our local antiquities. But it is obviously absurd, though it is not at all unEnglish, that independent efforts should proceed simultaneously towards the completion, several times over, of the same task (p. 172).

Still the local societies were not the best mechanism ('which, with all due deference to the work they do, contain a considerable proportion of visionaries' – p. 175). Haverfield preferred developing links with the London society and the RGS.

There was one other institution which should have had a significant part to play in the practice of (archaeological) research in general in Britain at this time: the British Museum. The early history of the museum has been rehearsed elsewhere, but some developments were very significant (Miller 1973). In many ways the museum's tortuous acceptance of British antiquities, and in turn Romano-British archaeology, mirrors the general history of Roman archaeology in this country. The 1753 Act of Parliament which created the museum meant it to be the nation's centre for national history, fine arts, books and manuscripts, organized into three sections: manuscripts with (medals and coins), natural and artificial products and printed books (Miller 1973: 60; Clark 1989: 5). The acquisition in the early nineteenth century of Egyptian antiquities and other marbles, terracottas, bronzes and gems led, in 1814, to the creation a fourth department, Antiquities and art which included prints, drawings, medals and coins. A fifth department, that of Botany, was established in 1827. Ten years later Prints and drawings was separated from Antiquities as a department while Natural History was split into Geology (with Paleontology and Mineralogy) and Zoology. Mineralogy became a separate department in 1857 (Murray 1904: 127–44). Irrespective of the fine words of its enabling act, by the mid-nineteenth century the museum was under attack for being little more than a receptacle for costly antiquities derived mainly from overseas at the expense of a national collection (Ebbatson 1994: 44; Miller 1973: 191ff.; MacGregor 1998: 127ff.). This was in addition to the generally acrimonious atmosphere that characterized the museum in the first half of the nineteenth century. From 1845 Thomas Pettigrew of the BAA criticized the museum's trustees and petitioned for the creation of a more formal collection of national antiquities. At about the same time, the Duke of Northumberland, through the RAI was championing the cause for a British collection, based in the first instance from his own collection of artifacts displayed as in his own British Museum at Alnwick Castle, but to be absorbed in to the British Museum (Ebbatson 1994: 44–5). The reluctance on the part of the trustees and the government to do little but accept private donations culminated in the case of the disposal and ultimate relocation of the Faussett collection of late Roman and Anglo-Saxon antiquities. The main players in this controversy were Roach Smith and Joseph Meyer who at Roach Smith's instigation not only purchased the collection when the BM declined to do so, but then placed it (along with other material) in his own Museum of National and Foreign Antiquities in his home city of Liverpool (White 1988). The 'scandal' evidently shamed the BM into a more proactive policy with respect to creating a national collection (MacGregor 1998: 129ff.; Miller 1973: 210), especially when Northumberland was made a museum trustee in 1861 and (Sir) A. Woollaston Franks (1826–1896), another leading member of the RAI, became the curator for the museum's British and Medieval collections. When faced with his own personal and commercial difficulties Roach Smith's Romano-British collection, assembled over twenty years, was purchased by the museum in 1856 for the princely sum of £2000. Roach Smith declined a higher offer in order to ensure that his collection remained intact. Part of the problem was that the museum's principal officers were not committed – in fact not interested – in antiquities and archaeology in general. This was certainly so of objects from non-classical contexts. If the acquisition and display of Egyptian and Assyrian objects remained problematic when the likes of Antonio Panizzi, the museum's Principal Librarian (= Director, 1856–66) was content to argue for limiting its holdings to classical and pagan art and to lose the rest of the collection (Miller 1973: 190–1), then there was little or no prospect for British antiquities. No wonder then, that in 1849 the original Romano-British antiquities room (acquired in 1837) was required for other purposes meaning that in subsequent years only part of the museum's holdings were shown (Dalton 1922: I; cf. Miller 1973: 210). Miller reports

> A description of the Museum published as late as 1850 recounts that all the antiquities of ancient Britain and Gaul were contained in four cases in one room, whilst a further thirteen cases displayed 'various British and Medieval Antiquities temporarily deposited in this room.' The writer regrets that the collection was not yet rich enough to fill an apartment of its own (p. 211).

But the situation was to change. In spite of the reluctance on the part of some to the museum developing its non-classical holdings, they were fighting against the tide. Government pressure through a Royal Commission made the recommendation that something should be done to improve the situation, a fact recognized by some within the museum (Miller 1973: 211). Elsewhere, just as the mid-nineteenth century saw a series of developments that shaped the future course of archaeological research in this country, the same factors played out on the museum. A general decline in interest in classical antiquity at the start of the century and a concomitant rise in non-classical archaeology, itself a consequence of the Gothic revival and the development of biblical studies and in the Near East, was a major factor. The beginnings of a more scientific and systematic appreciation of prehistoric antiquity, notably with its classification into the Three Age System also contributed and started to influence how collectors assembled their own collections, which from about this time were being increasingly absorbed in to the museums' own collection. At the same time the recruitment through more rigorous procedures of examination and so a greater degree of competence amongst its staff was significant, especially when there were appointed at this time a number of assistants etc who with better training and a far greater exposure to developments in academia as well as in subjects kindred to their 'specialisms', were to be major figures in the institution in the latter half of the century (Miller

1973: 191–5; 209–11). And still the antiquities collection as a whole – Egyptian, Near Eastern, British, Medieval, as well as Ethnographic – continued to expand.

Indicative of the expansion of the museum's 'antiquities' collection, in 1860, Panizzi proposed to rearrange the Dept of Antiquities into a Dept of Greek and Roman Antiquities, a Dept of Oriental Antiquities (meaning Egyptian and Assyrian), and a Dept of Coins and Medals with perhaps a fourth department, that of Ethnography and British and Medieval Antiquities which might otherwise be notionally attached to Greek and Roman Antiquities. In the end, Medieval Antiquities and Ethnography was appended to the Oriental department but with Franks taking responsibility for it (Miller 1973: 299–300). The first Keeper of Greek and Roman Antiquities was Charles Newton (between 1861 and 1870 and 1886), whose period of office was marked by the continuing growth of its holdings. His successor was A.S. Murray (Keeper 1870–1909), and his in turn A.S. Smith (1909–25). It has been said that the creation of the Departments of British and Medieval Antiquities and Ethnography in 1866 '...originated in the efforts of the Trustees [of the museum] about 1850 to meet the demand for a Museum of National Antiquities by the creation of a department which was to function as such a museum within the framework of the British Museum' (Hill 1945: 367; cf. Miller 1973: 313; MacGregor 1998: 135). Between 1880 and 1883 the Natural History collection was transferred to its own museum building and through the course of the century there opened a number of London-based galleries and other museums along with the British Library which meant that the BM became a focus for antiquities (Clark 1989: 5). At the museum, the new British collection was placed under the keepership of Franks who was succeeded by C.H. Read[30] and later by Ormonde Dalton (1921–8). Franks, 'the virtual creator of the collections from which the Department of British and Medieval Antiquities eventually grew' (Miller 1973: 194), originally joined the museum in 1851 to help with presenting the pre-Roman British coins (Miller 1973: 212) and had advanced in the reorganization of the Dept of Antiquities in 1860–1. In 1886 he was appointed, after petitioning Panizzi and demonstrating to him how the rate of acquisitions of British antiquities was outstripping Egyptian, as keeper of

---

30. (Sir) Charles Hercules Read (1857–1929) was Keeper of the Dept of British and Medieval Antiquities at the BM 1896–1921. A stalwart of the London Antiquaries, he was their secretary (1892–1908) and its Chairman (1908–14 and 1919–24; cf. Dalton 1922).

a new British and Medieval Antiquities department. His tenure of this post was marked by the acquisition of a number of private collections, some of them with significant prehistoric assemblages (Miller 1973: 314–15). In 1915 the removal of the museum's medieval collection to a new gallery made available a room large enough to display most, if not all, of the Romano-British collection. The transfer to the new room was completed with a formal opening in December 1918 and commemorated by the publication of the museum's *A Guide to the Antiquities of Roman Britain in the Dept of British and Medieval Antiquities* in 1922 (cf. Dalton 1922). It was not until 1921, however, on his retirement, that Read's Dept of British and Medieval Antiquities was further divided into a new Dept of Oriental Antiquities, Ceramics and Ethnography (which, in turn, was split into Oriental and Ethnography in 1938). The British department was now under the keepership of R.A. Smith who worked on its prehistoric, Romano-British and Anglo-Saxon acquisitions. As late as 1969 the museums' trustees decided to create a separate Dept of Prehistoric and Romano-British Antiquities (along with a Dept of Medieval and Later Antiquities) out of the old British and Medieval department (cf. Kendrick 1971; Bruce-Mitford 1971).

The fractured evolution of a distinct Dept of Romano-British antiquities in the museum is a fair reflection of the standing of the subject in terms of academic study at the time. However, whilst other departments developed from the mid-century international reputations on the basis of the work they undertook, notably in the Dept of Coins and Medals and on the antiquities of the classical period (Miller 1973: 304; Gardner 1933: 25ff.), the list of those who worked on Romano-British (and prehistoric) material was not especially distinguished until R.A. Smith. According to Miller, it was Read's achievement that he was responsible for the fact, 'that the public were aware of the abundant material available within his Department, and he organized an impressive series of guides and catalogues to inform them of what it now contained. This work was mostly carried out by his able assistants, one of whom O.M. Dalton …remarked "This work had many elements of adventure: they were novices called upon to write as authorities"' (1973: 316). What this shift in staff activities reflected was an evolution of the museum for the purposes of curating, to that of scholarship and study. Under Read the collection continued to grow with yet more acquisitions. Furthermore, while the museum sponsored some archaeological expeditions overseas, up to the late nineteenth century the systematic exploration for antiquities in these islands was poorly served. However the museum and its keepers increasingly, through the later part of that and the next century, became the experts on the archaeology of the country and in many respects came to shape how the archaeology of the Roman period in Britain, not least in its guides to the antiquities of the period, was interpreted.

The most obvious omission in this summary of British archaeology in the second half of the nineteenth century is the country's universities. None of the antiquarians discussed so far held university appointments. At best they were minor royal appointments, perhaps with a degree, or else they were members of the lesser nobility or soldiery. Later on they were clerics enjoying a country living tied to a particular Oxbridge college or else leisured members of the upper middle classes. The failings were lamented by Haverfield on a number of occasions. His comments on the ancient universities and British antiquarianism became increasingly critical (cf. Chapters 7 and 9). Interestingly, his objections were not so much that academics had not written sufficiently but rather that they had failed to get involved and undertake fieldwork. Instead, when it did occur to them to work, they invariably elected to work overseas. Haverfield did, however, recognize that there was a dearth of competent excavators, both in the universities and in the regional societies. Therefore he argued that the universities' duty was, in the first instance, to train fieldworkers rather than to teach Romano-British history or archaeology.

Conclusion

On 11 August 1891, Sir John Evans delivered to the Royal Archaeological Institute a lecture which summarized progress in archaeology in Britain over the past 35 years. Of the study of Roman Britain he could point to the fact that 'numerous villas have been unearthed' and exploration had been undertaken and/or was continuing at Richborough, Reculver and Pevensey (by Roach Smith), as well as at Wroxeter, Silchester, Cranborne Chase and along Hadrian's Wall (by John Clayton and Dr Bruce). Of the *CIL*, he observed that it 'has concentrated our knowledge ...Mommsen is still labouring in the same department, and so far as Britain is concerned, is fortunate in having secured the aid of Mr Haverfield, who is now investigating the walls of Roman Britain' (Evans 1891: 259). In spite of the progress that Evans reported, by the end of that century we still find something of a paradox in the state of British archaeology. The standards of exploration and the reporting of it had revived after a period of some decline. Indeed there was a general air of optimism in the fact that the quality of work was thought to have improved and was continuing to do so. And yet Haverfield, while acknowledging this progress, was still critical of what had been achieved. In one sense he may have been too critical, and in his denigrating of the achievements of the more recent two hundred years of experience failed to appreciate how antiquarianism had developed. While many of its practioners continued to make the kinds of mistake Haverfield took an almost triumphalist pleasure in ridiculing, what many of them had shown was that a history of the Roman period could be identified and read with the minimum of reference to the historical sources. Another unfortunate consequence of Haverfield's belittling of the regional antiquarians and other enthusiasts was effectively to guarantee that they were written out of subsequent histories of Romano-British, and indeed British, archaeology. But of course, by setting out 'to improve' the quality of antiquarian research in this country, Haverfield could not fail to set himself as better and above those whom he made a career out of criticizing.

It has been said that in: '...the early nineteenth century, interest in the remote past was an antiquarian hobby practiced largely by rural clergy: by 1900 archaeology was a science, a component in the sweeping Victorian reassessment of the age and nature of the past, a university subject and a profession' (Novo in Mitchell 1988: 32). By tradition, histories of (British) archaeology have tended to present the evolution of the subject as a set of progressive, positive stages of transition, from antiquarianism based in the humanities through to the development of a science, whether it be in the form of 'systematic' techniques of excavation or the application of 'scientific' approaches to the analysis of data. The same distortion is evident when the development of British antiquarian research is characterized as a line of succession from Aubrey ('the effective founder of British field archaeology' – to Stukeley, Colt Hoare and the Cunningtons (Crawford 1953: 24). In the main, the advances in the study of man's (pre-)history are regarded as the achievement of the 'prehistorians'. Meanwhile classical archaeology, for the reasons offered by Dyson (1993), disappeared down its own cul-de-sac, to become the almost mechanical excavation of the known events and achievements of the better understood world of classical antiquity. In this characterization, antiquarianism in Britain came to represent, if not a term of derision, then one imbued with a sense of amateurism and uncritical or indiscriminate acceptance of a past which could not be corroborated. It is what Haverfield certainly believed.[31] If

---

31. Typical of his attitudes is the way Haverfield characterized the work of other fieldworkers. It was a compliment to be described as 'competent' or an 'archaeologist'. For example, in the *VCH* Somerset. I (1906), Governor Thomas Pownall was a 'competent archaeologist' (p. 227 n. 1) while J. Douglas 'a most competent archaeologist' (p. 308 n. 3).

this summary is valid then it does a disservice to those 'antiquarians' who continued to work through the nineteenth century and who worked to a higher standard than their predecessors.

The reasons for the negative attitude to antiquarian study of this time lies with the way the subject continued, according to twentieth century tastes, to remain largely indiscriminate in what it described. Prehistoric, Roman, Dark Age and medieval frequently continued to be mixed up. But this was in part a product of the pre-determined framework for presentation (e.g. by conceptual limitations and by writing by region/county rather than by the sort of historic periods more commonly used today). Glyn Daniel (1950: 13–14) drew attention to the fact that, at the 1844 Congress of the BAA, the sessions were divided into four sections: primeval, historical, medieval and architectural antiquities, with the primeval relating to British, Roman and Saxon, down to the conversion to Christianity. While it is not certain for how long the association retained this structure, for some it indicates the unsystematic, uncritical and uninformed understanding of the past. Yet despite the largely negative light in which antiquarians and antiquarianism of this time is held today, it was not so much of a problem for contemporaries. The term 'antiquarian' as an epithet remained in use as a term of status and competence well into the twentieth century. Haverfield frequently, but not always in a complimentary sense, used the expressions antiquary and antiquarian for other fieldworkers, as he himself was described (and in a more positive context). In his case he seems to have used the term as a word for those he did not approve or otherwise respect. That said the continued acceptability and efficacy of the discipline into the modern era can be seen reflected in the continued success of the journals, some of them the 'mouthpieces' of what started off as (and remain) antiquarian societies (the *Journal of the British Archaeological Association*, the *Archaeological Journal*, the *Antiquaries Journal* and more lately *Antiquity*, as well as some of the more-enduring regional and county journals). It was only a relatively later development that saw the emergence of period specialist journals: the *Journal of Roman Studies* (1911) and, more appositely, its Romano-British studies daughter, *Britannia* (1970), and the *Proceedings of the Prehistoric Society* (itself a consequence of the creation of the Prehistoric Society in the 1930s) and *Medieval Archaeology* (for the Society for Medieval Archaeology, founded in 1957, created to facilitate study of the period from the fifth century to the sixteenth, and '...to further the study of unwritten evidence of British history since the Roman period'). The fact is that antiquarianism, for all its weaknesses that many, including Haverfield, were happy to highlight, remained a significant aspect of the study of

Britain's past. Rather than worry about why this was so, it would be better to appreciate the strength of its contribution to the history of British archaeology. By the end of the nineteenth century medieval antiquarianism had through a process of trial and error and the influences of kindred disciplines become a more rigorous discipline, one better able to identify the function and date the monuments that attracted it. As important, if not more so, was the fact the subject, with some exceptions, continued to treat its material as part of the continuum of British history, where the prehistoric merged almost seamlessly into the Roman and it into the post-Roman. Period distinctions were not so evident or important. In certain instances, some categories of evidence and monuments attracted a more detached approach (e.g. Roman roads, where the early literature about them shows their study to be 'chancy and haphazard' and yet extensive in its range: Margary 1962: 95; cf. 1973). But these were the exception rather than the rule. With one or two notable exceptions, the Roman period continued to be treated as a part of British-English history.

Another feature of British archaeology at this time was that in terms of the execution of work the situation was now driven by individuals, most of whom worked through the burgeoning regional societies, dominated as they frequently were by cabals. At the same time national organizations such as the British Archaeological Association and the Royal Archaeological Institute were not involved in any significant fashion in the execution of this work. What was being undertaken was either in the traditional manner of wealthy antiquarians, such as the London Society of Antiquities, or else their poorer brethren supported by sympathetic patrons or the improving finances of regional antiquarian, architectural and archaeological societies. As such there was no overall or co-ordinated (national or regional) research strategies in terms of Roman or any other period of archaeology. While the educated classes were demonstrating an increasing interest in what archaeology was being exposed throughout the Industrial Revolution, conversely there was no formal instruction in the subject in Britain's universities which meant that, as Haverfield prophesied, the subject would remain largely the preserve of the antiquarian and the ill-informed curious. A reflection of the lack of engagement from the universities and academics in general can be gauged in the relative poverty of any substantial contemporary literature on the archaeology of the island. What there were still the same sort of fanciful musings and other outpourings of clerics, antiquarians and semi-professional excavators. Finally, this 'improved' condition of British archaeology had been reached largely by a process of insular development, one without reference to what had been happening on the Continent.

Hudson, when summarizing the state of British archaeology at the end of the nineteenth century, drew pride in the unique combination of the professional and the amateur, with his emphasis on the latter group. For:

...the national and local societies devoted to archaeology (have) been of the greatest benefit to the experts and the merely interested alike. It has kept the subject alive and, incidentally, made it much easier to survive economic and political changes. The truth is, and one might as well say this bluntly, that the people who appear to be so anxious to achieve what they call professional status are nearly always people who feel in one way or another insecure. Without the professional label, they are never sure about their niche in society and they are always liable to feel that their work is not receiving adequate public recognition. This craving for status is much more likely to occur among people who, as a result of their intelligence, education and possibly good fortune, have been able to rise socially and to achieve something barred to their parents, a skilled middle-class occupation. They require some form of public acknowledgement that the job is important – income alone is not sufficient for this – and, equally essential, a guarantee that funds will continue to be available to finance it. A job is socially expendable, a professional is clearly something that society needs. This yearning to be considered professional is not, of course, peculiar to archaeologists. It is very marked among, for example, teachers and museum staffs and always for the same reasons. Paradoxically, the confirmed 'amateurs' – the word is very inadequate and misleading – seem to feel much more secure than the would-be professionals (1981: 13).

Haverfield, as we have seen was especially critical, of the same sense of amateurism that Hudson regarded as a virtue. If this is so, then as we shall see, according to some, the change to 'professional' standards if not professionalization, was due in no small measure to Haverfield. But what was required was a number of substantial developments that no one individual could initiate. The series of developments in the second half of the nineteenth century came at a convenient moment for Haverfield, developments which he was able to exploit and take a stage further. The subject was ripe for a fresh initiative. By the last quarter of the nineteenth century there existed the beginnings of the various corpora of explorations by national and regional antiquarians. The early Victorian period was also marked by an increase in the activities of organized archaeological societies as well as the labours of independent excavators. But much of this work was disjointed and uncritical. At least the outlook and institutions were in position to allow a more rigorous approach to the study of British antiquity in general and Roman Britain in particular. The raw data for the composition of a critical overview of Roman Britain was to hand too. The publication of that data was being continuously improved. But still by the middle of the nineteenth century few, if any, had attempted to produce a definitive overview of the island in the Roman period. In many ways Haverfield's interest in Roman Britain came at an opportune moment. In time he, along with the likes of W.G. Collingwood were to become '...the destructive agents of an age of "scepticism". Haverfield pruned rigorously, then proceeded to enrich the roots of his subject and presently trained the quickened tree of knowledge to bear better fruit' (Richmond 1941: 178).

CHAPTER 3

Oxford, Mommsen and the 'new Ancient History'

> English scholarship, as it existed in 1914, had grown from nine-
> teenth century German roots: in philosophy, in classics, in theology,
> in philology, in science and medicine, in psychology. Germany was
> the place to which English scholars went for their training if they
> could, and from which they learned their methods and academic
> standards (Hynes 1990: 68).

Introduction

The previous chapter examined the intellectual and (non-university) institutional backdrop to the condition of Roman studies in Britain up to
the latter half of the nineteenth century. The emphasis was less on Roman history and so 'Roman archaeology' as such, not least because the
latter was still not appreciated as a facet of Roman history. Indeed, according to some, the alleged weakness in the execution of fieldwork and
the dissemination of its results was a direct reflection of the way the nation's (ancient) universities had failed to engage with the subject. We now
move to why the universities were so remiss, why they had to reform and
how change was effected. For it was in large part a shift in how teaching
and research were perceived in late-nineteenth-century Oxford and
Cambridge which facilitated the development of archaeology as a recognized discipline. This will then allow us to comprehend the environment
in which Haverfield was to operate. With respect to ancient history and
ultimately Romano-British studies the situation changed as a consequence of developments on the continent, in particular Germany. One of
the mechanisms by which many of these changes were introduced to Britain was through the many different works of the greatest scholar of the
day, Theodor Mommsen.

Oxford academia in the nineteenth century

With one or two exceptions, blessed with hindsight the general opinion among historians is that eighteenth-century Oxford was not a

distinguished time in terms of its scholarship and teaching (cf. Stone 1975: 37; *contra* Mitchell 1988: 7–8; a middle position is followed by Midgley 1996: 3; Harrison 1994b; Brock and Curthoys 2000). This negative impression owes much to the published memoirs of the likes of Edward Gibbon and slightly later Mark Pattison. And yet by the end of the nineteenth century it has been said that there had been effected, as with many other institutions of the time, the professionalizing of Britain's universities, with the concomitant effect of breaking down the relationship between scholarship and gentlemanly amateurism (Engel 1975; 1983; Stray 1998: 5; Levine 1986). As to what caused this change, the answer is to be found in a variety of issues which were discussed in both Oxford and Cambridge, issues raised by dons, the alumni and later by state intervention. The complexities of the multifarious discussions of the period are largely beyond the scope of this study but it is necessary to summarize the situation by the later nineteenth century, in order to explain the form of university that Haverfield was to work in. It will also help to explain what had shaped his mentors, men who were a product of the controversies of the mid-century. It was these controversies which in turn determined what kind of instruction best suited students, and in turn Haverfield's scholarship and ultimately how Romano-British studies developed.

Two of the more pressing questions debated in nineteenth-century Oxford were the relationship of the university to the (Anglican) secular establishment and the issue what was the purpose of a university education and how it be best executed. A movement for reform of what was perceived to be an undemanding educational system in Britain, itself a consequence of the low reputation of Oxford in the eighteenth century, had begun to crystallize early in the following century. It led to discussion about how both might be improved (e.g. Grundy 1945: 61: cf. Croke 1991). In retrospect, it is possible to identify two facets to this debate, both of which created their own controversies. There was that controversy, with a wider social resonance, that concentrated on the influence of the Church in the training and maintenance of Christian values. One way that this debate was manifested in the first half of the century was in the 'Oxford Movement' or the Tractarians and where the issue was how and what to educate society's élite, whether their position be based on birth, wealth or piety (but not academic potential). On the other hand there was the debate, which concerned should and if so how the university might reform itself. The impetus for such changes came as much from the various factional positions and attitudes within the University as from outside of it. But reforms while trying to solve the problems which occasioned the 'reforms, also generated consequences which in turn that had to be worked out. Although a number of individuals contributed to both these and other debates in Oxford, it is difficult to accommodate comfortably both these issues in one account however. It is for this reason that I propose to treat them separately and will try to draw together the implications of either as and where appropriate.

At the start of the nineteenth century the (Anglican) church dominated all aspects of Oxford and its colleges. College studentships and fellowships were normally closed to founders' kin or particular localities or schools but where academic qualifications or potential were certainly not criteria in awarding them. For some it was this tradition of patronage and other archaic practices which determined the poor repute of the university. In turn it engendered debate within the university and its alumni as to how the situation might be improved. By general consent the preferred *modus operandi* was by internal mechanisms rather than by the imposition of an external (viz. government) authority. The problem was that because of the weakness of the university relative to its colleges, reforms could only come from the latter, which meant that change (and resistance), where it occurred, was not uniform or consistent. Whatever the merits and strengths of the different opinions, the inability to change the situation, and so to improve the university's standing, was due in large measure to the power of independence of its colleges. While they could, if they so wished, have reformed themselves and ultimately the university, the process was never uniform or consistent or made in the name of the institution.

There were a number of weaknesses, which stopped the university evolving as an institution for the transmission of learning. The first of these was its reliance on college tutors and later, increasingly on private tutors (Bill 1973; Engel 1983). At the start of the eighteenth century tutors were originally 'guardians' of students but who increasingly came to function as 'teachers' at the expense of university professors and college lecturers. While the duties of tutors were not defined, they were essentially schoolmasters to students who went up to university at an age earlier than their modern counterparts. This relationship also determined how the tutors tended to teach – as schoolmasters – a situation worsened by the fact there were relatively few of them. Those that there were, were either overworked, expected to teach everything that the college offered in an undemanding curriculum, or else preferred lethargy and inactivity. For those who did 'teach' in large classes undifferentiated by ability, the instruction usually involved the reading and interpretation of a limited range of Greek and Latin authors with little instruction and the minimum of work on the part of the tutor or the student. The system '...was not designed to impart knowledge but to infuse Christian

principles and to train the mind through the mental discipline necessary for construing Greek and Latin authors' (Bill 1973: 75). Either way,
the teaching by tutors tended towards the unoriginal and unimagina-
tive. More positively, it was the combination of the tutor as moral
guardian, teacher and, because of the nature of their appointment, clergyman which created the tradition of the liberal education at Oxford.

The first real attempt to change the situation came from Oriel. At
the start of the eighteenth century the college introduced competitive
examinations for degrees, with the corollary of rewarding of academic
potential and attainment which in turn meant an improvement in the
quality of potential fellows and tutors. These changes meant that the tutors increasingly dealt with more and better candidates. The colleges'
initial response to the crisis was to try and accommodate and then sub-
ordinate the reforms to the religious basis of the tuition. This is what
J.H. Newman *et al.* were to attempt in the college in the 1820s and
1830s, where they '...sought to achieve these ends by introducing private classes and the study of particular books and by strengthening the
pastoral relationship between tutor and pupil' (Bill 1973: 76). In 1821
Oriel was the first college to render its fellowships to open competition
and to elect fellows from outwith its precinct. Under its Provost Edward
Copleston (1776–1849), building on the work of his predecessor John
Eveleigh, the college continued to initiate reforms which affected the
college's fellowships.[1] In Mark Pattison's opinion the reforms were
flawed. The introduction of competitive examinations produced the
major features of mid-Victorian Oxford – a weak professoriate, the high
degree of college authority and reliance on an extensive network of private teaching. Another problem Pattison highlighted was that the new
arrangement, in its willingness to draw on the best men available, went
beyond the confines of Oriel, and in doing so, the '...men thus picked
out as men of original minds were apt to have too little respect for the
past because they were ignorant of it. A man who does not know what
has been thought by those who have gone before him is sure to set an
undue value upon his own ideas – ideas which have perhaps been tried
and found wanting' (Pattison 1988: 50–1). Widely recognized at that
time as one of the two or three best colleges in Oxford in terms of intellectual life (the others were Balliol and Christ Church), the benefits of
this change were felt almost immediately with the election of what came
to be a number of notable fellows, including John Keble, Richard

---

1. This included reforming the way college revenues were collected and dispersed among its fellows.

Whately, Thomas Arnold, John Henry Newman, Richard Hurrell Froude and Robert Wilberforce (cf. Bill 1973: 25; Rothblatt 1997).[2] Unfortunately the successes of this change were to have corrosive implications. For instance, the introduction of 'new blood' led to the rise of the Oriel school known as the Noetics,[3] based around Whately, Edward Copleston and Edward Hawkins, a group:

> ...who knew nothing of the philosophical movement which was taking place on the continent, they were imbued neither with Kant nor with Rousseau, yet this knot of Oriel men was distinctly the product of the French Revolution. They called everything in question; they appealed to first principles, and disallowed authority as a judge in intellectual matters. There was a wholesome intellectual fervent constantly maintained in the Oriel common-room, of that kind which was so dreaded by the authorities of the German States in the days of the Terror (1851) (Pattison 1988: 51).

A second problematic consequence of the innovations at Oriel was that some of the new fellows tried to change the college's teaching. The attempts of Newman, Hurrell Froude and Wilberforce to alter the college curriculum to the advantage of its better undergraduates in anticipation of preparing them as candidates for university examinations were opposed by the college provost, and the leading Noetic, Edward Hawkins, who was alarmed that the changes meant the weakening of the college's (or his) authority. There were also reservations about Newman's views on the relationship between tutor and pupil, where he believed pastoral responsibilities for all the undergraduates should be divided between the three tutors. Hawkins proposed a liberalizing of the previous arrangement and entering all undergraduates under a common name and particular tutors. Newman refused to compromise, leading Hawkins to remove the recalcitrants from their tutorships in 1831. One of the longer-term consequences of this devel-

---

2. Keble (1792–1866) – elected 1812, Professor of Poetry 1831–41, Vicar of Hursley, Hants 1836–66); Whately (1787–1863) – elected 1811, Archbishop of Dublin 1831–64; Arnold (1795–1842) – elected 1815, Headmaster of Rugby School 1828–42; Newman (1801–1890) – elected 1822; Hurrell Froude (1803–1836) and Wilberforce (1802–1857) – Archdeacon of the East Riding), both elected 1826.

3. 'The Noetics, from the Greek word meaning "pertaining to the mind or intellect," were a group of fellows of Oriel ...mainly Whigs in politics, who believed in the comprehensiveness of the Church of England and were critical of the Tractarians' (Green in Pattison 1988: 178, n. 77).

opment was that Oriel's standing began to decline, to be replaced by Balliol. Then there was for the future Newman's alleged partisanship in the election of Oriel fellowships. 'Newman did not lose sight of the old Oriel principle of electing for promise rather than for performance: only, instead of looking for promise of originality, he now looked for promise of congeniality' (Pattison 1988: 60).

This, however, is to get ahead of ourselves. Unlike Oriel, and to a lesser degree Balliol, few colleges were able to generate enough tutors to handle the increased expectations. But even if the colleges did open up their fellowships, it would not have had instant or major effects. Tutors tended to be drawn from the college fellows (Bill 1973: 109). Unfortunately, many fellows opted for non-Oxford residency. Under the conditions of their fellowships, most of them were expected to take holy orders which, in turn, led to a college living. Nor did the low status of a tutorship help the situation, where many fellows used their position as a stepping-stone to a career outside the university rather than to double up as teachers. Therefore the number of permanent fellows was small and the turnover great. Unsurprisingly, most colleges had difficulty in finding enough tutors. The situation was not helped by the weakness of the university professoriate which was not respected by the colleges. The shortfall in college tutors was increasingly met by private tutors. In time this group became increasingly important. In response to their market, such individuals tended to offer smaller and more specialized classes than the colleges. In the short term the private tutors kept the university functioning. However, their '...specialised knowledge was a corrosive force on the traditional liberal education of the university' (Bill 1973: 79).

In the short term the opening-up of fellowships at Oriel had minimal consequences for the rest of the university. It was not evenly matched in other colleges which left a problem not addressed until the 1850 Royal Commission. Indeed it has been said the main purpose of the great reforms of 1850–80 was to correct these deficiencies and to restore the damage of the inflicted in the first half of the century (Rothblatt 1975: 303). What the changes at Oriel did do however, was to precipitate another debate which in turn was to have reverberations for Oxford and in particular what teaching was meant to do, what it should represent and how it might be executed. Discussion and debate, along with pamphleteering and controversy about what the university should be continued after 1830s Oriel. One of the more important caucuses of those who preferred to retain and strengthen the university's links with the Church was the Tractarian Movement which gathered around Newman, Keble, Edward Pusey, and Mark Pattison before his 'defection' (Bill 1973).

The Oxford Movement and University reform

In Chapter 2 it was noted that the 'Oxford Movement' of the 1830s played an important part in the development of a more appreciative study of Britain's archaeological past. The Tractarians were an ultra-High Church movement with its emphasis on the rôle of tradition, the sacraments and authority (cf. Nockles 1997; Ward 1997). Its origins lie in the consequences of developments in eighteenth-century philosophy and the French Revolution and the way they seemed to be undermining the pillars of contemporary faith by questioning society's very foundations, including the Church and the State. 'The men of the Oxford Movement were convinced of a great truth, namely that the English Church was a living part of one Holy Catholic Church: it was no state created body, but part of a society founded by the Lord Himself with supernatural powers and supernatural claims. That truth had been very largely forgotten or slurred over during the preceding centuries, though not entirely. It was the work of the Oxford Movement to revive it, with all that it implied; morally, theologically, socially' (Ollard 1940: 146). While it claimed to '...revitalise the university's religious life ...the movement opposed any attempt to alter the Anglican character of the university' (Seiler in Mitchell 1988: 567; cf. Mozley 1882). '...For a time it seemed as if they (the Tractarians) would succeed in the regeneration of the Church of England. They were not ritualists: their whole claim was that the English Church was one with the medieval church whose shrines it had inherited' (Hobhouse 1939: 87). Many of the leading figures in the movement were those who were to benefit from the opening up of the Oriel fellowships. The 'Movement' is said to have begun with a sermon on the theme of 'National Apostasy' delivered by John Keble in July 1833. The Movement, or Tractarians, was also known as the 'Puseyites' after Edward Bouverie Pusey (1800–1882; another Oriel Fellow (1822) and Regius Professor of Hebrew and Canon of Christ Church 1828) because of the series of tracts he wrote. A number of individuals associated with the Tractarians also contributed to the debate concerning the future of teaching and research at Oxford and how the system might be reformed.

The influence of the Movement was two-fold. It is possible to trace the evolution of a more rigorous expectation of university education back to it, with its emphasis on the careful and studious analysis of the works of the Early Church Fathers. The Movement's doctrine was set out in the 90 *Tracts for the Times*, edited by Newman between 1833 and 1841. It was the publication of the Nineteenth Tract, in which Newman sought to reconcile the 39 Articles with Catholic doctrine, which was to result in his marginalization from mainstream Anglican society. Newman and Pusey were also indirectly instrumental in setting in train a set of important innovations that may have had a longer-term effect. The two established first a house for disciple-scholars in Oxford and shortly later one at Littlemore (known as 'The Monastery') for the purpose of Newman publishing his series of the lives of the Church Fathers. Mark Pattison, who was to be an important catalyst for change in the future, was one such researcher. The significance of the group of young 'scholars' assembled was its emphasis on detailed and systematic analysis of the original sources. This initiated a new type of research that went in tandem with the 'movements' general revitalizing of interest in the study and presentation of its church buildings.

The second facet of Tractarianism which was to have, albeit indirect, implications was its interest in church architecture (and music). Theirs was a concern with it as a means to embellish the act of worship and was a consequence of the (Neo-)Gothic Revival, which was to cause a revival in, but inflicting much damage on, (Oxford) college buildings. The result of the association of the leading Tractarians such as Hurrell Froude and his interest in medieval architecture (Ollard 1940: 148), with antique ecclesiastical architecture was the creation in 1839 of the Oxford Society for the Study of Gothic Architecture. It is unsurprising then that the society's committee was heavily laden with known Tractarians (eleven out of the sixteen committee members were 'adherents'). One of its early secretaries was J.H. Parker, the Oxford publisher (including Newman's tracts) and later keeper of the Ashmolean Museum (cf. Chapter 4). Although the society was not driven by dogmatism – it remained one of the few places where the pro- and anti-doctrinaires could meet in friendly association – still its main business was inevitably heavily ecclesiastical in tone (Ollard 1940: 156). From the 1860s the society, in the aftermath of the decline of Tractarianism, dropped its emphasis on ecclesiology (Pantin 1939: 185). In its place the tendency was towards subjects more generally local historical and archaeological in tone.[4] In 1860 the transformation was confirmed when the society formally added 'Historical' to its title to become the Oxford Architectural and Historical Society (Prout 1898). Under Parker, the society was:

> …chiefly educational and local. It has indeed included in its …'Proceedings' not a few valuable papers; but its main work, its characteristic work,

---

4. Another organization concerned with the protection of England's antique buildings was the Society for the Preservation of Ancient Buildings in which William Morris and Ingram Bywater were leading members (Jackson 1917: 41–2).

has been and still is, to arrange each terms excursions in Oxford, and its neighbourhood, for successive generations of undergraduates ...the rudiments of archaeology as taught from examples on the spot (Burrows 1890: 352).

Between the Tractarians and its opponents in the 'Low Church' (with their preference for evangelical conversions and spiritual transformation), was the 'Broad Church' which tried to play down the sort of doctrinal and ecclesiastical issues that separated the extremes of the other two. Instead it emphasized the national and inclusive nature of the church. It also championed the case for the critical and historical study of the Bible in such publications as *Essays and Reviews* (1860), to which Mark Pattison (1813–1884), Benjamin Jowett and Frederick Temple (1821–1902) contributed. Many of the same opinions were set out in Pattison's *Suggestions on Academical Organization* (1868), *Essays on the Endowment of Research* (1876) in which it was argued that universities had other functions than educating young men and in his *Memoirs of an Oxford Don* (1884).

In one sense the Oxford Movement was doomed to fail. It was, after all, trying to defend the status quo, but the nature of the end could not have been anticipated. Newman's conversion to Catholicism in late 1845 effectively killed it, even if many of its adherents continued to operate in Oxford. In the long term, the rejection of the Tractarians had the effect of weakening the significance of the Church in Oxford. After his conversion, Newman continued to express similar views as Rector-elect to the new Catholic University in Dublin, opinions that were developed in his *The Idea of a University* (1852). While the Church's position was to be further eroded by the Royal Commission of 1850, what the earlier controversy accomplished was to stimulate debate about what education at Oxford should be about. In the short term, according to Pattison, the Movement's demise was due to a general loss of interest and fatigue with secular controversies. In their place, a new interest in research arose:

By the secessions of 1845 ...dates the regeneration of the University. Our thoughts reverted to their proper channel, that of the work we had to do. As soon as we set about doing it in earnest we became aware how incompetent we were for it, and how narrow and inadequate was the character of the instruction with which we had hitherto satisfied. We were startled when we came to reflect that the vast domain of physical science had been hitherto wholly excluded from our programme. The great discoveries of the last half century in chemistry, physiology etc., were not even known by report to any of us. Science was placed under a ban by the theologians, who instinctively felt that it was fatal to their speculations. Newman had laid it down that revealed truth was absolute, while all other truth was relative – a proposition which will not stand analysis, but which sufficiently conveys the feeling of the theologians towards science. More than this, the abject deference fostered by the theological discussion for authority, whether the Fathers, or the Church, or the Primitive Ages, was incompatible with the free play of intellect which enlarges knowledge, creates science, and makes progress possible. In a word, the period of Tractarianism had been a period of obscurantism, which had cut us off from the general movement; an eclipse which had shut out the light of the sun in heaven. Whereas other reactions accomplished themselves by imperceptible degrees, in 1845 the darkness was dissipated, and the light was let in in an instant, as by the opening of the shutters in the chamber of a sick man who has slept till mid-day. Hence the flood of reform, which broke over Oxford in the next few years following 1845, which did not spend itself till it had produced two Government commissions, until we had ourselves enlarged and remodeled all our institutions (Pattison 1988: 122–4).

The controversies circulating at Oxford at this time did not exist in a vacuum. Elsewhere in the country there had been disquiet expressed about the quality of its teaching and indeed the relevance of an institution which was so heavily connected with the ecclesiastical establishment. Opposing the Tractarians, Bill (1973) described the opponents as a radical group of two distinct elements; the educationalists who wished to see improved standards of teaching and examination and a small but highly articulate group of anti-clerics, inspired by the scientific and intellectual climate of the time which opposed the Tractarians. It wanted to see a secular institution led by a strengthened professoriate. A leading figure in this group was Halford Vaughan (1811–1885), Regius Professor of Modern History (1848–57). While this group ultimately failed in its desires, Vaughan was an influential witness to the Royal Commission of 1850. Benjamin Jowett was a lukewarm member of the radicals.

In the light of the dissatisfaction of the conditions at Oxford in 1850 a Royal Commission was '...set up by the government to investigate the state of (Oxford and Cambridge) universities with a view to recommending much-needed reforms in their constitutions and teaching' (Green in Pattison 1988: 8; Engel 1983). The commission was to inquire into the state of the university, its discipline and studies (Bill 1973: 88–116). Plans to examine its revenues were, however, thwarted. Opinions differ as to why the commission was initiated. Some attribute it to the problems with the tutorship, others link it to the 'scandal' associated with Pattison's failure to obtain the mastership of Oriel in 1851 (the events of which are summarized by Green in Pattison 1988; Appdx 1).

Whatever the reasons for its creation, the commission was loaded with 'reformers'. The recommendations made in its report of 1852, incorporated in the Oxford Act two years later, are commonly summarized as opening up the college fellowships to selection and competition. Not only would these changes create more and better tutors but in the longer term would generate more reforms. However a slightly different perspective on the purpose and results of the commission is offered by Bill (1973). In his opinion, the work of the commission, and therefore its conclusions, inevitably determined by the prospect of the university's own Examination Statute of the same year, was not going to work. The problem was that the reforms did not create enough fellows and tutors to teach the consequences of the new statute. The solution would have been to ease the conditions for the creation of more of the kind. To this end there were a number of suggestions: (i) curbing the non-residency of fellows; (ii) by improving conditions so as to encourage fellows and tutors to stay at Oxford (e.g. by the relaxation of obligations to take holy orders); and (iii) by offering fellows better prospects of advancement within the university (e.g. by reviving the professoriate). But such suggestions, especially the last one, were opposed by the conservatives in the colleges. The debate centered on what rôle professors should have in a reformed university. Should they be for the pursuit of learning, or to teach in the capacity of superior tutors? For the fact was that, whatever the status was of professors, they would, because of the shortage of tutors, have to teach. The conservatives were against the introduction of 'teaching' professors because they argued that education was an issue of moral instruction. Professors were there to create knowledge and to acquire information. This argument was influenced by the rise of new subjects, especially in the sciences. By definition, then, professors were not educationalists and were therefore regarded as unsuitable to teach. Indeed they were a potentially dangerous influence on young minds.

The submissions made to the commission were incorporated in its final report, and published in 1852 (the so-called *Blue Book*: Bill 1973: 117–27). Its recommendations were not universally welcomed. The university's response was presented in two documents; one by the moderate Tutors Association, the other from the Heads of College. These two responses generated a reply on behalf of the radicals for reform led by Vaughan (*Oxford Reform and Oxford Professors*: Bill 1973: 128ff.). A significant objection made by the moderates to the Commission's report and the radicals was that it was too heavily influenced by German universities and methods. After digesting the positions advanced in the three replies, Gladstone presented the Oxford Bill to Parliament in

1854 which was slanted more to the moderates than the spirit of the Commission or the radical reformers. It endeavoured to preserve the collegiate and Anglican character of the university. From this position it would accommodate any means to strength the professoriate within the system. The Bill's passage was not easy and involved a number of amendments. By the time that it was passed the principle components of the act were to unfreeze the curriculum, to open the way for the foundation of new 'schools' and the renewal of the college tutorial system by increasing the proportion of residential teaching fellows to non-resident prize-fellows. They also meant an increase in student numbers attending the university. The consequence of these reforms was the rise of the professional college tutor as a career option. The range of studies was also diversified to include science, law and history (Stone 1975).

Depending on one's outlook, the events of 1850–4 were at best only a partial success or at worst a complete failure. On the one hand, Vaughan and the radicals had failed and the 'reformers' were still not satisfied. Reforms were still needed. The issues raised by the 'reformers' were not dead. This was a recurring problem with reform at Oxford in the nineteenth century. The various commissions, investigations, pamphlets and statements produced throughout the century frequently introduced changes to the Oxford degree, but in the medium and long term they all invariably failed because they failed to address the original problem: how to teach the changes. Their longer-term influence was on another Royal Commission in 1870 with a remit to look at the issue of college finances which had been sidestepped in 1850.

A consequence of the debate and concomitant factionalism of the first half of the nineteenth century was that it served to crystallize opinions about what should be a university education. The contribution of the ecclesiastics to the debate was concerned with maintaining their traditional, pre-eminent, position so to consolidate their stranglehold on the university. The second half of the century was to see the rise of the less strongly committed secular groups of academics, people who argued about how a university and its college, detached from the influence of the Church, might function. Leading figures among this group of 'reformers' included Mark Pattison now at Lincoln College, Jowett, Ingram Bywater and later Henry Nettleship, influenced as they were by developments in some German universities (Christie 1895; Green 1957; Sparrow 1967: 62–149; Bywater 1894a). Other dons, again mainly fellows at Oriel, along with William Ramsay (of St John's), William Warde Fowler (Lincoln) and Henry Pelham (Exeter), shared an outlook which went '...beyond the needs of one's College to those of the whole University and beyond the needs of teaching to those of learning of research. They desired that Oxford should not overly popularise knowledge and conduct the necessary round of examinations, but should definitely encourage scientific inquiry and advance true learning' (Green in Pattison 1988: 4–5).[5] Pattison, Jowett and their like felt that the colleges were too strong at the expense of the university but that at the same time the institution was a closed shop based on birth, religion and wealth in which natural ability was stifled and the power and influence of the Church remained excessive.

But this group was not necessarily united. Instead of the ideals articulated by the likes of Pattison, there was another more utilitarian approach to the rôle of education, one which shared, in part, comparable objectives to those of the 'researchers'. The focus of the group was the Common Room at Exeter College where there were among others a number of distinguished scholars, including Ingram Bywater, Henry Tozer, William Ramsay, Ray Lankester and ultimately Henry Pelham (Haverfield in Pelham 1911: x). Theirs was an outlook which saw the purpose of the University to produce men to work in the public service, of which the administration of a colonial empire was a major part. Credit for the transition has been accorded to Benjamin Jowett (1817–1893), first as Master of Balliol (elected 1870) and then as university Vice-Chancellor (1882–6), who saw to the '...transition of Oxford University from an Anglican institution into one to prepare the elite (through the College tutorial system) for offices of responsibility in lay society' (Symonds 1986: 10). In time Jowett's influence on his own college was to affect Magdalen when (Sir Thomas) Herbert Warren (1853–1930) moved there as President from Balliol in 1885 (Magnus 1932; cf. Bailey (1927). Jowett was a biblical and classical scholar as well as an educationalist. Author of *The Dialogues of Plato* (1871) and *Thucydides' History* (1881), more controversially he adopted a critical but practical position on the reading of the Bible (e.g. *Commentary of St Paul's Epistles* (1855)). His *On the Interpretation of the Scriptures* in *Essays and Reviews* of 1860 argued that the Bible should be read like any other book. The hostile reaction to these opinions led him to abandon biblical studies and to concentrate on the translation of classical texts and the production of editions. He became Regius Professor of Greek in 1855. His energies were also transferred to working towards university

---

5. Coon (1934: 19) includes in this rather disjointed group of 'innovators' '...Stubbs, Conington, Pattison, W.L. Newman, Henry Smith ...and among the juniors of that day Bywater, H. Nettleship, Monro of Oriel and Robinson Ellis' (cf. Clark 1913–14).

reform. 'In brief Jowett encouraged the recruitment, not only from the aristocracy but from the middle class of Imperial administrators who would govern the Empire in a humanist rather than a religious spirit and would concern themselves meticulously with the details of administration' (Symonds 1986: 29).

In 1872 the second Royal Commission reported. Its recommendations were wide-ranging but in the light of what happened twenty years later, were again not entirely successful. It recommended making the working of the university more democratic. This was to be achieved by reducing the powers of the heads of colleges and by breaking the traditional links between certain colleges and families, schools and other places. There was to be the creation of faculties while the professorial system was to be overhauled. Fellowships and scholarships were to be opened to free competition with the abolition of life fellowships, the establishing of prize fellowships with stipends etc. to be standardized, while fellows were now allowed to marry. With respect to the power of the Church, non-conformist students were to be allowed to read for the BA degree while fellows no longer had to take holy orders. Despite the scope of these reforms: 'When we consider the work of this commission, we are struck by one significant feature in it; it did much for education, very little for learning by which I mean the investigation of truth for its own sake in any department of knowledge' (Warde Fowler in Coon 1934: 18). What the 1870 commission, its report and the Oxford and Cambridge Act (1877) did do was to clarify further the position of the various groups who held opinions on what and how the university should be teaching. Again, two broad groups can be identified. While they might not necessarily be regarded as 'radical' by today standards, they represented something of a challenge to the old Oxford establishment. The groups might for convenience be defined as: (i) conservative-traditionalists with a liberal approach (as exemplified by Charles Oman (1941) and George Grundy (1945); and (ii) the practical approach – (of which Jowett is the best remembered example) within which there was a 'research' group typified by Bywater, Pelham *et al.* (Coon 1934: 239–46).

Sayce in his *Reminiscences* summed up the differences between the Pattison and Jowett:

> Mark Pattison was the recognised leader of a small but increasing number of students who maintained that the primary function of a University as opposed to a school or college was to encourage research rather than success in examinations or in political or professional life. Knowledge was to be cultivated for its own sake; not for that of the honours and emoluments it might buy. It was a new doctrine to a world that

was priding itself upon having swept away all abuses of the past by the simple expedient of competitive examinations and by substituting the commercial system of the bourgeoisie for patronage and the claims of inheritance.

While Pattison tended to influence via his writings, in action Sayce believed he was little better than useless. In this respect he was the antithesis of Jowett:

...the representative and leader of the opposite party in University politics. For Jowett, the University ..was a sort of finishing school, or rather the nursery and stepping off ground for a career of social and political distinction. Knowledge was desirable only in so far as it enabled a man 'to get on in the world' ...By that time the movement for the endowment of research was beginning to make some way in the University as well as in the world of letters generally, and at Oxford it became the fashion to classify our friends as either 'Researchers' or 'Educationalists' (1923: 85–8).

Jowett's vision of university education recoiled, or so it was widely believed, from the sort of research ideology championed by Bywater, William Warde Fowler and, slightly later, Pelham. Percy Gardner, Lincoln Professor of Classical Archaeology, summarized the two opposing schools and how they viewed the purpose of a university as:

the first consider(ed) it as a national institution and a place for the training of young men for service in Church and State, the second regarding it as primarily a place of learning and science. Everyone would allow that both ends are to be aimed at; but naturally some of the teachers would place education in the best sense in the first place, others would be more concerned with the advancement of learning. Speaking roughly, one would say that these two tendencies lead respectively to the College and the University points of view, which need not always clash, but yet so shew a dividing of the ways (1933: 70–1).

Whilst the records show that the practical approach to university education prevailed – as judged by the number of Oxford (and Cambridge) graduates who went into government service – the spirit of Pattison *et al.* was not completely extinguished.

The seventies were years of hope and even of measurable progress in the University ...A few Oxford men at that time had acquired methods of modern research in Germany. They were discontented with Oxonian indifference to learning as well as with the narrowness of its educational system. This feeling was expressed in an unofficial association of younger dons which met two or three times a term in 1876 and 1877 and formulated a liberal programme. The experiences of several of its members in foreign institutions, and Pattison's *Suggestions on Academical Organization* are keys to its activities. Its goal was inspired rather by the Rector of Lincoln than by the Master of Balliol. The spirit of reform, which had been in the air for some years and was now exemplified by this group, led to the appointment of the Second University in 1877, a body which brought its achievements to a successful conclusion (Coon 1934: 45).

Thirty years on was published William Warde Fowler's *An Oxford Correspondence* (1903), an allegorical debate presented as a fictitious correspondence between a 'new' thinking don and a recent graduate '...which suggests that the Oxford tutorial system needs enrichment by some element of German "research" methods, and it was enforced by his practice as tutor, which was to question his pupils and set them thinking and searching and not to hand them ready made opinions' (Matheson 1927: 195; cf. Coon 1934: 210, 217–33). The *Correspondence* was a response to Gardner's *Oxford at the Crossroads* (1903) criticism of the Oxford curriculum which Fowler '...thought too astringent' (Green 1979: 521). Warde Fowler was later to balance this opinion in a short critique of the strengths and, above all, weaknesses of German scholarship and training (1916: 72–7). Furthermore the younger generation of dons who were attracted to Pattison came to fill positions of influence and authority. One sympathetic supporter of reform was Henry Pelham who was to occupy the Camden professorship (1889–1907). That he was receptive to the developments that were occurring on the Continent at this time can be seen in his appreciation of the work of Theodor Mommsen as well as his reporting on the most recent results of work on the German *limes* (Pelham 1906). According to Haverfield, Pelham believed that Oxford had to evolve in three areas; to strengthen itself as a home of scientific and learned research in all subjects; to widen and increase its range of studies; and to open its doors to all forms of students including women. Typical of the time, for Percy Gardner German methods meant 'encyclopedic knowledge and scientific method' (Gardner 1933: 49), combined with (over-) organization. Elsewhere Gardner was to be slightly more critical of German scholarship and in particular its tendency to create 'schools'; of interpretation and the pursuit of 'new theories, pp. 82–7).[6]

---

6. As an example of his opinions: '...the various schools in Germany, always flowing and ebbing, always turning in fresh directions, always at war one with another, are so various in their theories that to say that a man follows the Germans is to say nothing distinctive. Moreover the tendencies of the Ger-

Commissions and reforms continued to sit and make changes throughout the subsequent decades. In 1877, another commission on the University of Oxford recommended the creation of new professorships at university level for subjects not then covered by college teaching in order to cover the fullest range of scholarship and teaching to rival Europe. That it occurred was in due to the decision to revive the position of the professoriate in the 'new' university. The acceleration in the creation of new professorships – for instance the chair of Latin was first established in 1878 – and by implication the official recognition that this meant, must also have been assisted by the creation of similar posts in a number of the newer provincial universities which in the first instance were often modelled on the Oxbridge example, especially in the range of subjects they offered. Furthermore in the 1870s and 1880s there was the repeal of the Test Acts which had barred teaching posts at the (ancient) universities to non-conformists, while all degrees (expect for Divinity) were made open to dissenters. Celibacy restrictions on college fellows too were also removed. All this led to the accelerated growth of a professional scholarly community: 'As the rate of graduate ordination declined, the comfortable belief of the learned clergyman in permanent truths which were necessary harmonious aspects of a

---

man intellect have become in the course of the evolution of thought in the two countries so different from our English ways that a literal adoption of the views of any great German writer by an English contemporary is almost out of the question ...The tone of the German mind is philosophic and abstract; it tends above all things to the arrangement of a system. It seems to us tainted with the vice of megalomania. This is largely the result of the organization of the great German universities. A savant will commonly owe his promotion to a Professorship to some striking new theory or collocation of facts, which nearly always contains some fresh light, but hardly ever, it ever contains nothing but truth. And when a Professor has found his circle of pupils, he at once tries to form a school, to collect around him promising young men and to imbue them with his particular views. All this puts a premium on originality, on the development of certain ways of thinking and working, and the more a teacher extends his personal influence, the more highly he is regarded. In England we have nothing to correspond to what may be called the professorial system of Germany. Indeed, we are so far from it that many of our most influential thinkers are what would be called in Germany amateurs, men who have by diligence and ability worked their way to striking views in some department of history or research, but do not teach ...men who have had no pupils, and have influenced their contemporaries mainly by their writings' (pp.82–3).

greater Truth gave way to the don's moralised quest for a truth which was not permanent but progressive, and thus open to discussion and revision. For some men, caught between a faith to which they could no longer subscribe and a scientific naturalism which seemed empty of moral value, the pursuit of truth in the humanities offered a substitute' (Stray 1992: 6).

One reason for looking in detail as far back as the Tractarians and the influence of the likes of Mark Pattison is because it draws out the connection between how Oxford was evolving in the first 75 years of the nineteenth century and how those developments impinged on Ingram Bywater, Henry Nettleship and Henry Pelham, each of whom were regarded as mentors in Haverfield's academic career. It is easy to construct a link back to Pattison and his group, who was at one time closely associated with Newman and his other disciples. Indeed Pattison's *Memoirs* are replete with allusions to what an Oxford education up to the 1840s meant and what it should be. From Pattison, with his contacts along with his public utterances, even notoriety, this prosopographical line establishes a link between what Newman expounded through the common rooms at Oriel and Exeter and thence to Pelham to Haverfield and then on. The emphasis, to varying degrees was on research and '...contact with the most recent work of foreign research' as the dynamic for good teaching (Haverfield in Pelham 1911: iv). How far that research should be passed on to students was a moot point. It is not coincidental that a widely noted concomitant of the 're-form' movement, whose frequency merely emphasizes contemporary practices or lack of them, is the way that certain dons corresponded with and even visited foreign (viz. German and French) scholars and their institutions (Haverfield in Pelham 1911: xi; Croke 1991; 1994; Coon 1934: 19; e.g. Pattison (Christie 1895), Nettleship (Bywater 1894a: 237). In time it was something for which Haverfield was later widely praised (Macdonald 1919–20a: 485; 1924: 29–30; 1927: 245).

There is also another reason for emphasizing the significance of the Tractarians and their approach to research. Although his obituaries do not refer to any great sense of religiosity in Haverfield's life, there are indications that the High Church might have featured prominently in at least his early life. Not only was he born of a family which served the Church, but his father was a graduate of Exeter College, then closely associated with the 'Movement'. As we have seen too, he preached at a church at Bathwick again then known for its Anglican connection (cf. Chapter 1 n. 25). It is not possible to assess how much his father influenced Haverfield, but in the year of his death, Haverfield obtained his first professional appointment, as a master at the new public school at Lancing, an institution then charged by some with practising High Church rituals. It seems implausible that Haverfield could have accepted the appointment without an appreciation of what the school and its founder stood for. If so, it again suggests that at this time he may have retained a degree of religious enthusiasm which is not evident in later life. In this context we might remember Bruton's otherwise curious comment that Haverfield was 'the Pope of Roman Britain.'

We have looked so far at the condition of the University of Oxford by the time of the later nineteenth century. How did archaeology feature in the university and its teaching? It goes without saying that the origins of British archaeology as a discipline of instruction owed its origins to the introduction to classical archaeology and ultimately to the strength of the classics at the country's two most ancient institutions. At Oxford the prominence of classics lay with its position in the degree of *Literae Humaniores*. By the time of the 1870 Act, the principal school, established for over two hundred years for a first degree in Arts at Oxford was that of *Literae Humaniores*. In a degree involving four years, undergraduate students worked for Classical Moderations (or Mods) which meant five terms' study of the Greek and Latin languages. For the next seven terms candidates entered on Greats (with a combination of ancient history and philosophy, ancient and modern). Most opinions of the time approved of the general range of instruction in a variety of subjects. Haverfield's professional colleague Percy Gardner, a graduate of Christ's Cambridge, lamented how his undergraduate years would have been better spent at Oxford. 'The bent of my mind was towards philosophy, literature and history rather than towards mathematics or exact scholarship. The Oxford course of Literae Humaniores would have exactly suited me' (Gardner 1933: 13). Gardner believed it the ideal framework for instruction in advanced subjects such as archaeology. 'It would be tedious to relate the course of my struggles, for thirty-eight years, to secure some due recognition for archaeology in the course of *Literae Humaniores* at Oxford, in my opinion, in spite of some weaknesses, the best existing school of education in the world' (p. 59). His beliefs were based on the opinion:

...that Oxford preserves in her school of *Literae Humaniores* more completely than any other university the tradition of the Renaissance, while by no means neglecting the modern studies which claim recognition. While not rivalling the German universities in learning, she has maintained even more than they the unbroken tradition of humanist culture, which to some extent has influenced even the most modern developments of knowledge' (p. 63).

Paradoxically while it was the lack of interest in philosophy at the expense of lexicography that explains in part Haverfield's First in Mods it was the same indifference which led to his subsequent failure to get no more than a Second in Greats, which in turn thwarted his efforts to obtain a college fellowship in 1883. And yet, by the time he had become part of the Oxford establishment, he was extolling the unique merits of *Lit. Hum.* (Haverfield 1912d). The same kind of sentiments, and therefore indicative of the reluctance to change the system, were still being trumpeted well into the same century:

> ...It is an education in the study of classical antiquity in a full sense with an important extension into today. The whole course requires a good preparation before anyone can start it. He must have enough command of the ancient languages to be able to read them in bulk and to know what the text means. If he can do this, he will, when he finishes have had a training which exercises his mind in three quite different directions, first in ancient literature, which introduces him to a world unlike his own, second in ancient history, which is a stiff discipline in the use of evidence and the assessment of historical facts, and third in abstract thinking, both in interpreting the works of philosophers and in forming some kind of philosophy for himself (Bowra 1966: 243–4).

The (Jowett) sort of utilitarian approach to a university education had a consequence on another issue which concerned some dons at this time; the question of compulsory classics for undergraduates. The conservative view was that change was not necessary, indeed would be detrimental to the purpose of education. The '...teaching of Classics had an important place. The lessons of the history of the Greek city states were often applied to relations between British and the old Dominions, whilst in the government of dependent territories comparison was frequently made with Rome' (Symonds 1986: i). The study of the Greek philosophers was thought to shape and inspire standards of personal conduct whilst that of the Athenian Empire provided lessons on policy and 'democracy gone mad.' The argument was that the study of Greats was the best possible preparation for a political or administrative career because it taught good judgement, a view that persisted when George Stevenson (1922) questioned the relevancy of teaching Roman history in the twentieth century. The strength of this argument can be detected in the Macaulay Committee of 1854 which was to inquire in to the examination of Indian Civil Service (ICS) candidates; '...its recommendations defined the policy guidelines for the examination, training, and selection of ICS candidates.' What is more:

...Macaulay's Committee defined its priority as the recruitment for the East India Company's service of young Englishmen who would have 're-ceived the best, the most liberal, the most finished education that [their] native country affords'. In practice this meant changing the qualifica-tions of age so as to ensure that 'considerable number of the civil servants of the Company should be men who have taken the first degree in arts at Oxford or Cambridge'. In accordance with this general aim, the syllabus of the examinations was to be 'confined to those branches of knowledge to which it is desirable that English gentlemen who mean to remain at home should pay some attention'. As one might expect, the Committee argued that in Greek and Latin the examination should be 'not less severe than those examinations by which the highest classical distinctions are awarded at Oxford and Cambridge'. But the examina-tion had to be flexible enough in this area so as not to exclude any part of Britain or any class of its schools. Skill in Greek and Latin versification must have 'a considerable share' in determining the issue of the compe-tition, especially as the fact that great figures such as Fox, Canning, Grenville, Wellesley et al surpassed in this accomplishment, indicated how 'powers of mind ...properly trained and directed, may do great ser-vice to the State' (Majeed 1999: 92–3: cf. Dewey 1973).

For the moment the teaching of (compulsory) classics remained central to the *Literae Humaniores* degree but, in the longer term, if other disciplines were to be introduced to the degree then it was inevitable that classics would have to compromise. As long as the study of classics then was a cen-tral component of the Oxford degree and any proposals to remove it from its prominent position were bound to arouse the opposition of the traditionalists and conservatives within the university. The privileged sta-tus of classics first came under attack in the mid-nineteenth century The origins of the issue of compulsory classics at Oxford at least can be traced back to the University Examination Statute of 1850. A leading voice in this was Halford Vaughan who, in his proposal for overhauling under-graduate degrees, through the Statute championed the case for introducing new subjects through the schools, notably by the creation of a School of Jurisprudence and History (the so-called 'Fourth School': Bill 1973: 68–87). At the heart of the issue was whether the subjects of the new school (essentially Modern History) were suitable to the 'liberal educa-tion' that the university prided itself in providing. Vaughan '...denied that the study of classics was the only or the best way of training the mind or that it was the only basis of a truly liberal education. "I cannot ...assign that very great practical effect to the actual study of languages, as a means of giving a discipline to the mind, which many claim for them". He as-serted instead that the justification of the new studies lay precisely in their educational value, and strongly discounted the view that the university ought to provide professional training' (quoted in Bill 1973: 86–8). These reservations also explain his antipathy to theology. The counter-argument, expounded by Edward Freeman, was that they were not. New subjects such as modern history were not sufficiently intellectually rigorous – whereas classics was – but were likely to tend towards superficiality and controversy. They would also lead to a degree of specialism which would be followed by superficiality and erroneous interpretations of the past. Whereas the 'traditional' system of construction provided a solid basis for 'true' historical scholarship, for all periods and issues. Freeman was also concerned that the new subjects would draw students away from the more exacting classes. Opening up the more recent past (e.g. the sixteenth and seventeenth centuries) also ran the risk of reawakening old political and religious controversies.

It was for these sorts of reasons that compulsory classics remained central in the Oxford degree up until the First World War and was essential in the university's entrance examinations. But the situation had, by force of necessity, to change (Currie 1994: 128). It is said that it was the arrival at Oxford in 1902 of the scholars, and in particular those from North America, on the back of the Rhodes Bequest in the early years of the twentieth century which contributed most to the erosion of compulsory Greek at Oxford (Engel 1983: 265 and n. 37: cf. Allen 1955).[7] Under normal circumstances candidates for a first degree had to submit to a qualifying examination at the end of their first year of study, Responsions (or 'Smalls'). At the start of the new century the impending arrival of scholars, especially Americans, alarmed the classics traditionalists who were skeptical of candidates being up sufficient quality. At the expense of accepting the Rhodes Bequest, the fear was that this would bring the Greek question to a crisis, with the threat of ending the compulsory instruction in the language. This, it was argued, was only the thin of the wedge. The alarmists saw the logical end of the process as the end of Latin and ultimately an assault on Christian civilization. The short-term solution to the problem devised by the Rhodes Trustees was for its scholars to take a qualifying examination before entering Oxford. This was later modified to the Rhodes Qualifying Examination in Latin and Mathematics with successful candidates being permitted to mug-up on Greek and to be examined in

---

7. This was a development for which Haverfield seems to have had much sympathy (Croke 97; cf. Elton 1955; Symonds 1986: 167; Grundy 1945: 95–6). It was the Rhodes scheme too which indirectly led to the introduction of the degree of DPhil at Oxford in 1917; cf. Ch.4.

it later in their (Oxford) career. This arrangement continued until late 1918 when the qualifying examination and indeed compulsory Greek was abolished. The war had demonstrated the weakness of Britain's industrial base and the provision of teaching in the sciences and technical subjects. Indeed the issue of Greek had been raised in the mid-nineteenth century, with the rise of the more pragmatic Natural Scientists and changes in opinions as to what learning was about. In the debate concerning education at Oxford at this time, a 'liberal' education was regarded as the means to develop the mental faculties for the purpose of dealing with all aspects of life. However the new scientists saw science as a means to developing the mind beyond utilitarian considerations. Natural scientists now tended to see education as a means '...to their conclusions by the light of the facts and to be content with no knowledge unless it was as thorough as circumstances permitted' (Jackson 1917: 178). While the classicists still maintained that Greek sharpened the faculties of the mind, and argued that it imbued and affected all aspects of Western civilization, in terms of language, history and the arts in general, they had to admit it had minimal influence on certain topics (e.g. the sciences). This relative irrelevancy meant that certain classes of students were forced to waste their time learning a language which they would rarely, if ever, have to use. Content to argue that it was sufficient to learn its rudiments at school, some were prepared not to force it at university level. This was, for instance, the position adopted by Ingram Bywater who expressed his opinions towards the end of his life (Jackson 1917: 177, 197–8). Recognition of these facts led to various initiatives for educational reform (e.g. the Board of Education's Committee on Classics in 1919 which reported in 1921). The Teacher's Guild set up an Education Reform Council which published a pamphlet which proposed that knowledge of Greek and Latin should not be a condition for entry to Oxford and Cambridge. The strength of the argument for compulsory classics was not helped by a split between the Greekists and Latinists. The latter were prepared to jettison the former as a compulsory requirement, because they argued their discipline had a greater importance to 'Western civilization', whereas the relevance of Greek was to an understanding of philosophy and so for training for *Literae Humaniores* (Currie 1994: 111). The situation was made all the more worse by the fact that not all Greekists supported the idea of compulsion. Opposition to compulsory Greek was led by a (minority) group at Oxford, centred on Gilbert Murray (Stray 1998: 224) but in the end Murray dropped his opposition, to the chagrin of many of his colleagues, and there followed the abolition of the requirement of a pass in Greek for entry to an ordinary degree (Thomson 1957: 252).

Haverfield's contributions to the debate about the teaching of classics and in particular the relevance of Greek tuition are not clear. They were made in a number of public utterances. On the one hand, he was critical of them. His line of attack was not so much the issue of the classics and the conditioning of young minds as that the emphasis on classics was at the expense of other forms of evidence that could illuminate the ancient world. In this he was of similar opinion with Percy Gardner. What was important was that archaeology was where progress might be made. Such views were expressed in the inaugural lecture to the Roman Society in 1910 where he declared: 'the field of non-literary evidence offers a still wider and more fertile area of virgin soil. That is, indeed, the chief work now to be done in Roman history, to wring life and blood out of stone …The more I study the ordinary written materials, the harder I find it to learn the truth from them, the more often I feel that the story which they tell is not the story which is worth telling …It is no doubt hard to construct a "story" out of archaeological evidence, but it is certainly possible to construct history' (Haverfield 1911a: xv–xvi). Similar opinions were expressed in an address to the Cambridge Antiquarian Society, also in 1910 (cf. Appendix 3) and repeated in his opening comments in another public lecture, this time about Roman London delivered in January 1912 at the end of the AGM of the Classical Association (Haverfield 1912c and also published as Haverfield 1911c). It is difficult to link the opinions articulated in the lecture with the on-going tensions within the association (Stray 1992), but taken at face value, they tie in quite comfortably with Haverfield's interest in breaking the over-particularization in the study of literature. That said he did allude to the current debate about the teaching of Greek (at Oxford). Before addressing the audience on his advertised subject, Haverfield opened with a series of observations which were critical of the '…busy days devoted to Greek and to Grammar' and that the Association had '…at last found time when its life is nearly over and most of its members have departed, to turn and remember ancient history and the Roman Empire and English national antiquities. It has not …wholly fulfilled the professions of interest in these subjects when it asked me to lecture. The Greek, it seems, has once more ousted the Roman and I feel that I am here on a false pretence' (1912c: 103). In this respect the teaching of Greek had turned students away from the subject and therefore from appreciating the ancient world. 'No doubt both Greek and Grammar are important. But I have in my time taught both Greek and Grammar and History and I believe it is possible to hold the balance between them. I believe, too, that it is not only possible but necessary'. The comment 'Few things have so powerfully helped the recent revolts against Greek and against Grammar ... as the tendency to over-emphasize these subjects' (p. 104) confirms where his sympathies lay. He then went on to argue how he believed that the teaching of languages involved in the first instance the use of abstract concepts while archaeology could illustrate with greater effect the ancient society than the rather mechanical inculcation of the ancient languages. And yet we also have seen Haverfield's spirited defence of the way Oxford *Literae Humaniores*, with its emphasis on philosophy, ancient history and classics was such an ideal training for young minds (Haverfield 1912d).

The preceding paragraphs have concentrated on the sort of climate for the execution of research and learning that was being created in Oxford in the latter half of the nineteenth century. Its significance lies with the fact that this was the climate Haverfield entered when he went up to New College in 1879. It was also the environment that would shape his approach to learning and to foreign scholarship in the next twenty years. This still leaves open, however, the topic of the relevance of archaeology to what was being debated in Oxford. We have seen that archaeological research in Britain had developed since the Middle Ages largely independent of the country's two most ancient universities. By the middle of the nineteenth century, the situation had begun slowly to change. Some of the reasons for this change have already been discussed, where most of them can be attributed to changes in society and the rise of a professional educated middle class. Almost as important was the impetus given to the study of its past by the Tractarians. The middle-term consequence of these developments was the rise of an element in society with a much acuter perception of the past and appreciation that it could be studied systematically. In short there was the beginning of a demand for more formal instruction in the nature of Britain's past. At the same time as there was general discussion of the purpose of a university education, the place of the classics and so archaeology was raised. The late nineteenth century was the time of a number of significant discoveries in classical archaeology, much of it driven by German government initiatives coupled to scholarship (see below). Parallel to these, the disciplines of Egyptology and papyrology were also producing significant progress. Not surprisingly some of these consequences trickled into Oxford. The future Minister of Education, H.A.L. Fisher[8], then a student at New, experienced at first hand

---

8. Herbert Albert Laurens Fisher (1865–1940), educated at Winchester, tutor in modern history at New College; Vice-Chancellor of the University of Sheffield (1915) and President of Board of Education with ministerial status

the change in emphasis in the late-nineteenth-century university curriculum and commented in particular on how it affected the study of classical antiquity.

> This particular type of Oxford Don (typified by Canon Spooner) is now not so common as it was in the eighties. Examinations have become more specialized, teaching and lecturing more erudite. When I was an undergraduate a First Class man in the School of Lit Hum was expected to reach a first-class level both in philosophy and history. Now excellence in one of these branches is thought to be sufficient. The prodigious inrush of new knowledge on the side of Greek and Roman antiquities has led to a great deal of work which is really post-graduate being undertaken at the undergraduate stage. The exact distribution of proto-Corinthian pottery engages the mind yet virgin of political knowledge. The Greats man passes from specialist to specialist. Able and enthusiastic tutors pour into him the results of their independent researches (1940: 48–9).

The implications of these discoveries had a number of consequences. They stimulated research and brought about the introduction of new courses into the curriculum. The natural conclusion to this process would have been the introduction of a School of Archaeology at Oxford in recognition of the specializing teaching then being developed. That it did not was not assisted by Haverfield's opposition to it (cf. Chapter 4).

We can see that there occurred in the nineteenth century a shift in what a university education meant. This in turn affected how it effected its task. For Romano-British studies, whether it be as history or archaeology, to emerge as something more from the long-established tradition of antiquarianism, it could only progress at university level. Antiquarianism could otherwise survive as informed but essentially lay reading. Even then, such change could only emanate from external sources. By the time that Haverfield returned to Oxford, those influences were beginning to take effect there. They came in the form of the idea of a research ethos which was being promulgated and was being established by certain dons. This process started with academics pursuing research for themselves. The inspiration for these developments in Britain was from the Continent, and in particular from Germany, and a fresh and innovative appreciation of the potential for the study of classi-

---

(1916). He remained in Cabinet until the fall of the Lloyd George government in 1922 and was an MP until 1926 (cf. Murray 1940a).

cal antiquity. It was only a matter of time before these 'foreign' influences started to influence some of the Oxford dons and more significantly their 'students' which in turn was going to lead to the formalizing of the process and the rise of bands of students based on particular academics.

Europe and the development of Roman studies: Theodor Mommsen

We have seen how some of the late-nineteenth-century Oxford 'reformers' advocated German innovations for the instruction of students. We now come to examine the process by which some of those innovations came to permeate contemporary Oxford, and in particular the study of the classical past through its archaeological remains. It has to be repeated that the same inadequate treatment of classical archaeology is evident in histories of classical scholarship, where the emphasis is on philology, textual criticism and later, ancient history. Discussion of the development and function of archaeology in this context tends to be reduced to the analysis of art and architecture, fine pottery and topography. What can be said is that in its initial phases at least, in classics and in the other humanities, the developments in early nineteenth-century Germany had little immediate effect in British academic circles. For as far as classical scholarship is concerned the growth of (classical) archaeology is to be attributed to developments in the phenomenon of *Altenwissenschaft*, otherwise the 'science of antiquity', which was the culmination of fourteenth-century humanism and the seventeenth-century preoccupation with textual criticism. The 'invention' of *Altenwissenschaft* has been variously credited which serves to reflect the fact that it is impossible to see it as a coherent discipline but rather a unity of direction. Credit for the development of classical archaeology is normally accorded to Johann Joachim Winckelmann (1717–1768), 'the first great creative and critical scholar in the field of Classical Archaeology' (Peck 1911: 402). This, however, was archaeology in the sense of the appreciation of ancient art. For Wilamowitz-Mollendorff it was Friedrich G. Welcker (1784–1868) aided and abetted by August Boeckh (1786–1867) and Karl Otfried Muller (1797–1840) who created the same science '...from a fusion between the school of Boeckh and the school of Welcker and Muller came the concept of "*Altenwissenschaft*"' (Wilamowitz-Mollendorff 1982: xi). But despite the confidence of this attribution, others have been equally lauded. Peck referred to Friedrich Wolf's (1759–1824) teaching being marked '...by great breadth since he held that classical study dealt with every phase of the life and thought of antiquity' (p. 404).

Likewise Pfeiffer, pointing to Wilamowitz-Mollendorff deliberately underplaying Wolf's part, believed that '...all Wolf's achievements in particular areas of classical studies were subordinated to his general conception of these studies, for which he invented the comparative *"Altenwissenschaft"'* (1976: 175).

The problem is that the evolution of *Altenwissenschaft* involved the coming together of a number of previously independent scholarly strands, each with their own methodological developments. Irrespective of who did or who did not devise the discipline, what is important for our purposes is what it came to represent and how it proposed to address its subject matter. By the mid-nineteenth century most of the 'tools' for the study of antiquity which are now commonly applied had been identified, even if some practitioners preferred to give preference to certain types of evidence over others. The previous centuries had been concerned with establishing *editiones princeps* of the ancient authors (Reynolds and Wilson 1974). From this evolved a more critical use of such writers. Barthold Georg Niebuhr's (1776–1831) *History of Rome* revolutionised the study of early Roman history by his willingness to assess critically the extant sources for the early history of the city, a body of information which had long been dismissed as unreliable, if not worthless ('...[in] 1810–1811, in an extraordinary concentration of thought, he virtually created the modern study of Roman history' (Momigliano 1982: 8). Niebuhr's *History* was translated into English by Julius Hare and Cannop Thirwall between 1826 and 1842 which in turn inspired Macaulay's *Lays of Ancient Rome* (1842). From the critical study of the literature of antiquity, another characteristic of the later nineteenth century in the context of archaeology was '...the compilation of corpora to each of the classic languages' (Peck 1911: 441) and then inscriptions. To this was added numismatics, sculpture and architecture as well as fine pottery and metalwork. Whilst he was by far not the first to exemplify this, one has only to look at the range and breadth of projects executed or initiated at about this time in which Theodor Mommsen was involved. What makes Mommsen so important were his attempts to integrate the various categories of evidence in to the broader picture. Complimenting the more scientific approach to the study of the past was the concentration on marshalling the raw data for its study. But still, in this scheme of things, the development of archaeology was limited. Its potential, as appreciated today had not yet been realised. A passage from Wilamowitz-Mollendorff's *History of Classical Scholarship* makes the point and in doing so says much about how contemporaries perceived what the subject was about:

> Archaeology was still a poor relation among university departments. It was almost completely unrepresented at headquarters (Berlin!) and Bonn was the only place that possessed a museum of plaster casts devoted to teaching. It had been augmented by Welcker, the curator was now Otto Jahn (1813–1869), who was in charge of the classical teaching and quite capable of running both (1982: 150).

According to at least one historian of the subject, by the end of the nineteenth century *Altenwissenschaft* was running out of steam. The situation was retrieved when '...the amazing energy of Welcker and his contemporaries, inspired by the aged Mommsen, checked the incipient decline and inaugurated an age of even greater triumphs than the first of the century had seen' (Wilamowitz-Mollendorff 1982: xiii). And indeed as far as contemporary opinion is concerned, the most brilliant culmination of the development of *Altenwissenschaft* was Mommsen. 'In the second half of the nineteenth century Mommsen had decided, by the sheer weight of his scholarly production, the old German battle between classicism and *Altenwissenschaft* in favour of the latter. Classicism, defined as the study of classical texts belonging to the traditional canon had given way, by the end of the nineteenth century at least, to *Altenwissenschaft* defined as the study of ancient cultures and embracing all that remains of these cultures: literature, artefacts and ...documents' (van Minnen 1993: 5–6).

For our purposes these developments were not immediately realised in Britain and where their effect was minimal. That they were followed was initially amongst teachers and educationalists, men such as Thomas Arnold, then headmaster of Rugby School and later Regius Professor of Modern History at Oxford (1841; cf. Bamford 1960 and 1975), Connop Thirwall (1797–1875) and Sir George Cornewall Lewis (1806-1863) and his *Inquiry into the Credibility of the Early Roman History* (1855) which was an attack on Niebuhr. He was also the editor of the *Edinburgh Review* (1852–5) which became a medium for attacks on the quality of teaching and research at Oxford.[9] Thirwall was later expelled from Trinity College, Cambridge 'for attacking the institution of compulsory chapel [which] ...dramatically highlights the powerful rôle of

---

9. '...It is the stimulating force and not the achievements of Niebuhr's studies that Fowler emphasises, and he clashes that Niebuhr is the grandfather of the Oxford School of Modern History, with Thomas Arnold and Cornewall Lewis as his historical children. Arnold he regards as the immediate paramount influence in bringing the study of history into high respect in his University' (Coon 1934: 248).

Anglicanism at the ancient universities' (Stray 1998: 61; cf. Winstanley 1940: 73–8; Engel 1983). However the adherents of what was occurring on the continent were not fully taken in. They retained critical comment. For example, Arnold was lukewarm to the new German historiography represented by Niebuhr and later Mommsen. He still preferred to see historical sources used to construct what has been called providentialist history – in this case Rome – with history for moral purposes (Dowling 1985: 584). It was for these reasons that despite their obvious importance for the future development of historical research, the developments on the continent were not immediately appreciated in Britain or in the universities. This was a time in Britain when there was a reaction to the study of Roman history. The reasons for this retraction are numerous. The authority of Gibbon's *Decline and Fall* at the end of the eighteenth century temporarily killed innovation. Roman history was seen as a template for practical Republicanism while Greek history became fashionable for its idealism (Turner 1986; 1989).

The preceding paragraphs have implied that the catalyst for a revolution in writing about Roman ancient history in this country and throughout Europe came through the work of Theodor Mommsen (1817–1903). With his undoubted scholastic and political importance to mid-nineteenth-century Germany, Mommsen has been the subject of much appraisal (cf. the bibliography in Demandt and Demandt in Mommsen 1996: 1–62; Weidemann 1997).[10] The significance of the variety of his interests was that he broke with the tradition of German scholarship's concentration on Hellenic culture and in doing so established Roman history as an independent entity in the study of antiquity. 'The version of *Altenwissenschaft* embodied by Mommsen and accepted by many of his contemporaneous classicists and ancient historians, was a product of nineteenth century historicism. It aimed at encompassing all there was to know about the ancient world and then to reconstruct ancient culture as a whole from the bottom up, so to

10. The major events in Mommsen's career include: 1838 enters Kiel University: 1843 passes State examinations with a dissertation on Roman guilds and goes on to practice law: 1844 Danish government scholarship to study antiquities of Italy (especially those of Borghesi); 1848 Professor in Roman Law at the University of Leipzig: 1851 dismissed for ('liberal') political agitation; 1852 Professor of Roman Law at University of Zurich; 1854 Professor of Roman Law at Breslau in Prussia (having assumed control of the *CIL* project in Berlin in 1858); 1861 Professor at Berlin University; 1863–95 while also holding the Permanent Secretaryship of the Berlin Academy of Sciences.

speak' (van Minnen 1993: 9). For the purposes of studying the development of Haverfield's career, there are two Mommsen publications which stand out: the *Corpus Inscriptionum Latinarum* (*CIL*) and his study of the history of the Roman state (the *Römische Geschichte* in five volumes, although the fourth was never published – I 1854; II 1855; III 1856; V 1885). The link between the two publications is significant. As part of his work as the great organiser-administrator of the time, it was Mommsen who was instrumental in finally seeing the *CIL*, the consolidated corpus of the inscriptions of the Roman empire, into life. Furthermore, at the time of his death he had managed to edit five of the fifteen volumes that had been published. These volumes, in Haverfield's eyes, not only set a new standard for the treatment and discussion of ancient evidence they also highlighted new themes in Roman history. In turn Mommsen marshalled the evidence presented by the *CIL* to especial effect in the *Geschichte*.

In explaining how Haverfield's career came to follow the course it did, the fifth volume of the *Geschichte* is pivotal. For it demonstrated how it was possible to write of the impact of the Roman empire without reference to the primary literary sources which tended to be Rome-centric in their reporting (Freeman 1997). The context of this volume was in turn conditioned by what should have been the fourth but never published volume. In theory it should have covered the history of Rome under the emperors down to the late Roman period. The reasons why the fourth volume never appeared have preoccupied historians and various explanations offered (Demandt in Mommsen 1996: 1–30; Freeman 1997). The reasons advanced to explain the 'failure' include Mommsen's disinterest in the 'tittle-tattle' and corruption of the imperial court and a lack of coherency coupled to potential themes in the period. A loss of enthusiasm, vitality and a more general lack of interest have also been cited. That he had discussed some of the events and institutions in earlier publications may have taken away the urgency to complete it. There may have been ideological and political reservations relative to his time which inhibited him. Finally the 'failure' may lie as much with a combination of external factors, including Mommsen's evolving plans and priorities, his preoccupation with the *CIL*, as with any major intellectual problem. Some of the explanations adduced by other writers to explain the situation can be refuted. Mommsen had previously written about the period and had the material prepared. So the failure was not necessarily due to a lack of evidence or ideas, as the recent publication of the notes made by the Hensels of Mommsen's lectures on the history of the Roman empire under the emperors delivered in 1882/3 and

1885/6 show (Mommsen 1996).[11] Looking at these and other extant lecture notes made up to 1886 by others, much of the same material appears in the fifth volume of the *Geschichte*, *The Roman Province* (and which was later translated as *The Provinces of the Roman Empire*). Whatever the reasons, the failure to publish volume IV had implications for what was included in its fifth counterpart.

One of the themes common to both the Hensel 'lectures' and the *Provinces* was the civilizing of the Roman empire, a phenomenon Mommsen called 'romanization'. But the criteria by which he defined the process were discussed indirectly rather than explicitly. It is difficult to say which of the accounts were formulated first although the balance favours the lecture version over the monograph. In the Hensel lectures, a section significantly entitled '*Domestic Policies I*' (Mommsen 1996: 207–57; 265ff. etc.), presented lines of thinking which reappear in the work of later writers on Roman Britain. For instance, one measure of 'romanization' was language which '...is a critical vehicle for national integration – the spread of Latin signifies Romanization' (p. 207). It was also reflected in grants of (Roman) citizenship, which Mommsen asserted were not merely a symbolic gesture. What went with such grants was the obligation '...to be able to express oneself in the language of the Roman citizen. The granting of citizenship to men of standing was thus a prelude to national integration' (p. 208 and 105; 163; 174). Another mechanism for the dissemination of romanization was the army (p. 208; 258). Mommsen also gave a special place to coinage: coins circulated in the provinces, were invariably inscribed in Latin and were minted to a universal, consistent standard (p. 216ff.). The common strand in these criteria is that they were manifested as language or more accurately, in its physical expression: in writing.

---

11. Not included in Demandt's discussion (in Mommsen 1996) of the missing fourth volume of the *Geschichte*, G.B. Grundy recounted a conversation with Eduard Meyer from just before the First World War; '...he told me a very interesting thing about Mommsen ...He said that Mommsen had in his account of Julius Caesar attributed to that great man so much that formed a part of the organization of the empire under Augustus that when he came to look into the evidence of what Augustus did he could not give a true account of his organization without stultifying what he had already published on the work of Julius; and that he was not disposed to do. His history of the Roman provinces under the empire was compiled from what he had collected for the comprehensive work of the empire which he had originally designed' (Grundy 1945: 153).

It should be self-evident how crucial to Mommsen's general methodology was the part played by his involvement in Latin epigraphy. Not only did he treat this as a discipline in itself, but he attempted to use for other purposes the information collected in the process of ordering the raw data into definitive corpora. For his interests lay as equally with the history of Rome and her empire and with aspects of its culture. Mommsen also afforded inscriptions and coins a new primacy in writing Roman history. In short, he identified new categories of evidence and made them available to ancient historians and archaeologists which meant that the treatment of the past and issues to be assessed had to change. Along with the creation of new themes, the ability to assess the reliability of the source material improved. In the spirit of the age, the purpose of ancient history was 'historical objectivity'. These innovations 'removed the issue of Roman decadence from the debate for contemporary moral and political lessons' (Dowling 1985: 581). The production of neither narrative nor biographical history could now suffice. The weakness in Mommsen's (lecture) version of the 'romanization' of the empire is that none of the provinces, not least Britain, were covered in any systematic fashion. Detailed discussion was limited to military affairs (e.g. Mommsen 1996: 161–2, 258–62). As to why romanization should have occurred, it was attributed to the aspirations of individual Romans:

> ... Caesar's idea – global in scale, like all his ideas – was to Romanize the entire Empire from the Atlantic Ocean to the Euphrates. This idea was never abandoned: it was maintained throughout the entire imperial age. Caesar's ideas were far more of a legacy to posterity than those of Napoleon, for example. But they flagged in the implementation. Augustus was already more hesitant in its execution than Caesar had been, and his successors were even more so. Persistent as it was, the idea ground to a halt in the execution, which compels us to regard it as a failure. As so often in history, the possible was achieved by wanting the impossible (p. 209).

The sentiments aired in the (Hensel) lectures can be found in Mommsen's *Provinces* where the *raison d'être* to volume V of the *Geschichte* were set out. Dismissing the corruption and degradation which infected Rome in the Christian era, Mommsen wrote that the achievements of the Roman mission were to be found in the provinces:

> The carrying out of the Greek-Latin civilising process in the form of perfecting the constitution of the urban community, and the gradual bringing of the barbarian or at any rate alien elements into this circle, were tasks, which from their very nature, required centuries of steady ac-

tivity and calm self-development; and it constitutes the very grandeur of these centuries that the work once planned and initiated found this long period of time, and this prevalence of peace by land and sea, to facilitate its progress. Old age has not the power to develop new thoughts and display creative activity, nor has the government of the Roman empire done so; but its sphere, which those who belonged to it were not far wrong in regarding as the world, it fostered the peace and prosperity of the many nations united under its sway longer and more completely than any other leading powers has ever succeeded in doing. It is in the agricultural towns of Africa, in the homes of the vine-dressers on the Moselle, in the flourishing townships of the Lycian mountains, and on the margin of the Syrian desert that the work of the imperial period is to be sought and found (Mommsen 1886: 4–5).

The format of the *Provinces* allowed for a more systematic treatment of the issue of the romanization of the provinces than had the Hensel lectures. Each of the provincial chapters is broadly consistent in organization: starting with a run through of the (military) history of each of them. There follows a consideration of the criteria that Mommsen thought indicative of the provinces becoming 'romanized'. The basis for the assessments remained epigraphy and numismatics which provided evidence of law, language, literature, political and social institutions as well as religion. Not surprisingly, evidence of each was found to varying degrees where there were inscriptions and because Mommsen read the evidence at face value. In this respect, his assessment of the degree of the penetration of what he called Italian culture is not significantly any different to that found in modern accounts of the same provinces. In one case he could even speak of the Germanisation of the Romans rather than the other way round. The one form of evidence in his account conspicuous by its absence is any reference to the results of excavation. In Mommsen's vocabulary archaeology was epigraphy and, to a lesser degree, numismatics. The only references to fieldwork are some brief footnotes to the *limes* in Lower Germany and Raetia and along the Danube. Excavations in Greece and Asia Minor as well as North Africa are there, but with regard to life in Spain, the Gauls, non-frontier Germany and Britain, there is nothing. The failure to cite work in these regions was probably due in part to his access to recent publications. It may not have been helped, in the case of Britain, by the dearth of on-going work. Above all, it is a reflection of Mommsen's attitude to archaeological evidence, although his significance was that he mapped out a course for the development of Roman studies and in doing so defined a range of evidence with which the mission of the empire might be assessed.

Archaeology as 'Big Business' – the German model

There was another dimension to Mommsen's academic output, which albeit indirectly, might be relevant to Haverfield. Not only did Mommsen publish extensively, he was central to the creation of a number of state-funded or centrally run programmes designed to catalogue or else investigate further what was already known of classical antiquity. At the same time, in the spirit of the age such projects would explore and emphasize Germany's relationship to that antiquity. This was a time, to paraphrase Mommsen's description of it, when 'big scholarship' (*Großwissenschaft*) was invented and when archaeology became 'big business'. In turn, it is hard not to see Haverfield's efforts in the institutionalizing of British (Roman) archaeology being influenced by what happened in Germany in the latter half of the nineteenth century. The significance of these developments was twofold. Not only did they provide a model for demonstrating how the study of the past might be organized and set to agendas but it also fostered a climate of emulation, personal (Haverfield and Mommsen) and national (British versus German).

As part of the process to forge a German nation, the second half of the nineteenth century witnessed an explosion in state-funded scholarship in Germany (Stürmer 2000). One eye-witness could eulogize on the fact that the:

> ...Academies of Germany have given to the world or are in the course of giving us, in great part owing to the influence of Professor Mommsen, an astounding series of collective works, in each of which some class of remains of the civilisation of Greece or of Rome is put together in the most complete way by the combined efforts of many scholars. There is the Corpus of Greek Inscriptions, the Corpus of Latin Inscriptions, the Corpus of Byzantine Historians, the Corpus of Sarcophagi, of Attic Sepulchral Monuments, of Greek Coins, of Greek Terra-Cottas, and several others. Great works like these can only be carried out under two conditions, when scholars are organized, and when the State provide funds ...But we have not exhausted the list of historical works produced by the Berlin Academy. There is the edition of Aristotle, and of Greek Commentaries on Aristotle, the Prussian State records of the eighteenth century, monumental editions of the works of Ibn Saad, Kant, Humboldt. Due to the support of same institutions is the new edition of Greek Christian writers of the first three centuries (Gardner 1902b: 105–6).

It was no wonder that there were calls at the end of the century and the start of the next for the creation of comparable centralized organizations in Britain. In Mommsen's conception of the Roman provincial world, inscriptions were the primary source of information. His involvement in the systematic cataloguing and description of the (Latin) inscriptions of the Roman provinces facilitated this interest. Central to this was *CIL*, the genesis of which went back to the late 1840s, when it was proposed to create a series of volumes that would bring together all the known Latin inscriptions of the Roman world. The inspiration for the programme derived from the work on the cataloguing of Latin inscriptions in Italy in the previous century. Such was the size of the project, it was recognised early on that it would have to be co-ordinated, and more importantly funded by a state institution. The early discussions about the project were hindered by arguments about who would control it. By dint of his proposal submitted in 1847 and the number and range of his publications on the Latin language, inscriptions and culture in the 1840s and 1850s, Mommsen established his academic credentials and ability to run the scheme funded through the Prussian Academy of Sciences. By 1856 he had gained control of the programme and volume editors were appointed, largely on his advice.

The original scheme of publication for *CIL* envisaged fifteen volumes divided among the Roman provinces. The format for the volumes was to be consistent. Each was to be published in Latin, to the same dimensions – 39cm × 29cm ('folio' size). Inscriptions were to be grouped by the (ancient) towns/territories in which they were discovered. In presenting the texts, there were no line illustrations and very few photographic plates (Keppie 1991: 371). The first volume appeared in 1862 (Gordon 1983: 9). By the time the fifth volume of the *Geschichte* was published in 1885, Mommsen had to hand versions, parts and supplements of *CIL* I, II (Spain), III I (including Egypt, Asia, the Greek provinces and Illyricum), IV (Pompeii) V (Gaul), VI (Rome), VII (Britain), VIII Africa and IX and X (Italy), not that this was necessarily significant given his control over the unpublished material (see Gordon 1983: 50–3 for a detailed breakdown of the various fascicles).

The *CIL* was but one 'nationalized' project with which Mommsen was intimately associated. With regard to the evolution of systematic archaeological research in Prussia/Germany the complex sequence of events and politics which went with these developments have been discussed at length by Marchand (1996). By the second half of the nineteenth century there were in Germany three 'national' organizations devoted to *Altertumskunde*. The oldest was the Institut für Archäologische Korrespondenz/Deutsches Archäologisches Institut (IfAK/DAI). The IfAK was founded in 1829 and had come out of the private association of dilettante who had formed the Hyperboreisch-Römische Gesellschaft (HRG) of 1823. The HRG was concerned '...to see and catalog [sic] as many ancient artworks – Roman, Etruscan and Egyptian, as well as Greek – as possible' (Marchand 1996: 54). In 1829 it broadened its horizons to metamorphise into the IfAK which '...planned to make Rome the collecting point for all European work on monuments ...the institute's main purpose was the collection and publication of drawings and information conveyed to it by scholar, antiquarians, and collectors' (Marchand 1996: 54 and 58). In this mission it limited its scope to Greece and Rome and did not envisage excavation to acquire material. With royal support, if not yet state financial assistance, the IfAK developed a bureaucratic structure with a Directorate and subsections. In time it was increasingly funded by annual subsidies from the state, becoming an organization which emphasized as an organ of state its German-ness with an interest in excavation not only overseas but at home (Marchand 1996: 60). By the 1870s, and following German unification, the IfAK became the DAI, a state organization and received a regular budget derived from the Foreign Ministry. At this time the DAI was primarily concerned with excavations overseas, and prestigious projects at that. Under its auspices the great excavations began, most notably at Pergamum while at the same time it retained a physical presence in Rome and Athens.

Somewhat different to the IfAK/DAI was the Reichs-Limeskommission (RLK). The origins of this organization date to 1852 following a conference of the Union of German Historical and Antiquarian Societies and the creation of the Römisch-Germanisches Zentralmuseum in Mainz and the Deutsches Museum in Nuremberg. The former museum was to be the dominant institution. The undertone in creating these two institutions was to stimulate scientific research into the past while acting as *foci* for nationalist sentiments. The belief was that by collecting '...all the relevant material in one place ...[it] would allow for comparative study of artifacts, an essential step towards determination of the boundaries of Germandom, Slavdom and Celtdom ...local groups would benefit from the scientific insights generated by co-ordination, and the public would learn to appreciate the cultural achievements of its ancestors' (Marchand 1996: 169).

The RLK, originally proposed by Mommsen in the 1870s, was a confederation of local archaeological and antiquarian societies (the *Vereine*) interested in exploring the evidence of the Roman military frontier (the *limes*) along the Rhine. In Mommsen's proposal the RLK '...called for the joint direction of excavations and publications by civil and military officials' under a centralized control (Marchand 1996: 173; cf. Birley 1991: 10). In other words, replacing their direction by local archaeologists with officials in Berlin. Initially thwarted by Bismarck, the RLK became a reality in the 1890s, following the intervention of the Prussian

Education Minister, Gustav von Großler whose proposal called for the division of the *limes* zone among fifteen *Streckenkommissionen* each responsible for a number of *castella*. With guaranteed Reichstag funding, via the Ministry of the Interior, work commenced in 1892 under Friedrich Schmidt-Ott, with a short season at Unterböbingen. Subsequent years witnessed financial crises as the results of excavations and improvements in excavation techniques made exploration more and more costly. By 1901 34 *castella* etc. had been excavated, but still less than 50% of the known sites had been studied. In 1903 excavation ceased and the resources were directed towards clearing the considerable excavation backlog. This was overseen by Ernst Fabricius, director of the RLK from 1898. Not surprisingly, with its highly structured organization and its pre-occupation with the Roman army, directors of the Kommission tended to be drawn from the military working with archaeologists in a collaborative fashion reminiscent of the *CIL*. In many respects the work of the RLK was highly successful with the recovery of a massive amount of data. Publication, however, was slow and the programme was bedevilled by dissension and resentment from the (southern) regional archaeological societies to what was seen as Prussian control even after unification.

The third German archaeological organization which featured at this time was the less important Berliner Gesellschaft für Archäologie, Ethnologie und Urgeschichte (BGAEU: Marchand 1996: 174–6). This organization had been founded in 1869 and came to be concerned with ethnographic and by implication, prehistoric studies. In time the DAI, came to assume responsibility for the RLK which was to become the Römisch-Germanische Kommission (RGK), '...the central state institution dedicated to national archaeology' (Marchand 1996: 176). The reason for the change lies with the diminishing scope of the DAI's original brief. Towards the end of Bismarck's chancellorship in 1890, the DAI was increasingly concerned at the prospect of losing opportunities to work in Italy. To compensate for this loss it began to cast its attention back to Germany, at a time when the accomplishments of antique Germanic society were beginning to be appreciated by professional historians and archaeologists. Both the more classically oriented DAI and the more German-looking BGAEU coveted control of the 'German-centric' RLK. Mommsen opposed the DAI/RLK link-up, arguing that the DAI should serve scholarly archaeology internationally while the RLK would '...inevitably have to serve national interests and organize local amateurs' (Marchand 1996: 177). Following a protracted battle, the DAI emerged with control of the RLK which then became the RGK. The DAI had effectively acquired a German branch to compliment its overseas offices in Rome and Athens. In Marchand's opinion the argument about who was to control the RGK led to a series of dislocations which were to haunt German archaeology in the future. The most serious of these was the effective division of research into German (later) prehistory, between those who studied *Germania Romana* – as agreed by the RGK and the northern museums – and those concentrated on *Germania Libera*, in museums in eastern Prussia and Saxony. Another consequence, one with implications for what was to occur in Britain, was that the regional societies were displaced even more by professional archaeologists and state organs, both of which were critical if not dismissive of the work of the amateurs. Instead of co-operation and co-ordination, regional excavators were excluded from the formulation of research strategies and their execution, despite the promises of national leaders (Marchand 1996: 176–9).

Why was Mommsen so interested in collaborative projects such as the *CIL* and the RLK/RGK? An obvious answer lies with nationalism, where the nascent German state was eager to parade its classical credentials by offering to take the lead in the study of the ancient world. More prosaic is the fact there must have been a degree of reality, where it was appreciated that such tasks were just too large for one or two individuals. But whatever the objective, as it has been said: '...through comparative linguistics, numismatics and epigraphy, Mommsen was trying to create a body of material which had the status of archival evidence and which would serve as a control on the narratives of historical writers' (Weidemann in Mommsen 1996: 174). Above all, Mommsen's work put him in a position not only to be familiar with on-going work in ancient history (in Germany) but it also permitted him to control its direction and progress:

> The full story of how Mommsen exercised his patronage as the Secretary of the (Berlin) Academy of Sciences remains to be told, but it is clear that he gave his support to a wide range of historical projects ...In the case of the MGH (*Monumenta Germaniae Historiae*) and CIL, the speed of production (and sometimes the use of inexperienced graduate assistants) resulted in misunderstandings and errors of transcription: unfortunately the authority enjoyed by both projects means that some of these errors remain unquestioned even today. Another project which Mommsen supported, or more precisely seized control of ...was the study of the Roman limes in south-western German... Mommsen effectively took the study of the limes out of the hands of local South German archaeologists and transferred it to Berlin. He was also in a position to control appointments in ancient history at Prussian universities ...As other parts of Germany increasingly came under Prussian influence,

> Mommsen could arrange for his own pupils to be given university appointments (Weidemann in Mommsen 1996: 45).

A number of features of the German experience of institutionalizing the acquisition and dissemination of knowledge are reminiscent of what was to occur in Britain and with Haverfield. Firstly these large projects and organizations were dominated by professional administrators and academics at the expense of local, regional societies and antiquarians. Indeed, this saw contention develop between the professional and the local. The reputation of the antiquarian contribution to the study of Germany's (Roman) past was increasingly downplayed by Mommsen. 'Mommsen's praise for local research, in fact, ...proved in practice to be rather backhanded. His assessment of the sluggish progress made by the *Vereine* seems to have been based on a knowledge of "professional" publications only' (Marchand 1996: 174). At the local level this brought hostility to interference from those perceived as outsiders. As we will see, Haverfield's attempts to construct a similar, centralized authority for developing Roman archaeology in Britain met with similar opposition, where the criticisms offered made direct reference to the German experience.

As has already been indicated, and will be demonstrated more fully in Chapter 5, Mommsen was to exert a profound influence both on British ancient historians and in particular on Haverfield, in terms of intellectual outlook and in how Roman archaeology might develop. Haverfield's first exposure to Mommsen must have come during his time as an undergraduate at Oxford rather than in his time at Winchester. Indeed it is no coincidence that all those dons linked with Haverfield were friendly with Mommsen. Contemporary accounts emphasize just how affected Haverfield was by his publications. In the first instance, the effect would have been the first three volumes of the *Geschichte* and the earlier volumes of the *Staatsrecht*. In 1885, two years after Haverfield's graduation, Mommsen published the delayed fifth volume of the *Römische Geschichte, The Roman Provinces*, '...a work which produced an immediate and lasting effect' upon Haverfield (Craster 1920: 63–4), and one he was later to translate (Haverfield 1909a). Haverfield admired Mommsen's reconciliation of the literary-historical sources with the archaeological evidence to construct a coherent narrative of the empire's provinces. Indeed he wrote that Mommsen '...did more than any scholar living or dead to extend the range of historical enquiry to archaeological regions' (1904a: 86; cf. 1924: 81; 88).

The developments in Roman studies on the continent had a far-reaching effect in Britain. With the benefit of hindsight, Haverfield attributed the introduction to Oxford of what he called 'new Ancient History' to three dons: Henry Pelham, William Warde Fowler and James Strachan Davidson.[12] Haverfield believed that each of them had been influenced as undergraduates and then tutors by the publication of Mommsen's *Römische Geschichte,* the early volumes of the *CIL* and the *Staatsrecht* (Haverfield in Pelham 1911: xvi; cf. Haverfield 1907a; Coon 1934: 247; Macdonald 1919–20a: 480–1; Haverfield 1924: 34–5). Of Pelham and Strachan Davidson, Marett (1941: 84) was to write '...all I can say is that Oxford was lucky to have such stars shining in its firmament at the same time.' Similarly William Ramsay (1895: xvii) acknowledged a debt to Pelham and Mommsen. In reality what Haverfield and others were acknowledging was the culmination of a process of development that had been gathering momentum as far back as the start of the eighteenth century. What is more, these developments were occurring in subjects other than ancient history. In addition to these names, a number of classicists and philologists had appreciated even earlier the significance of Mommsen's work. Fisher was to claim that it was York Powell who was, as far back as 1888, the first to appreciate the strengths of German learning (*The Times* 4 February 1932), while others link it with the likes of Ingram Bywater and Henry Nettleship.

What exactly was the 'new ancient history' to which Haverfield alluded? In its execution, perhaps the best – certainly the most concise – exposition of what it meant is to be found in a lecture Pelham delivered in Liverpool in December 1899 (Pelham 1899). Here the emphasis was on the critical appraisal of the data available to the historian. There were perhaps three elements to the discipline: (i) Mommsen's published works which turned on (ii) his methodology and use of new categories of material (epigraphic and numismatic) and a more rigorous use of existing forms, and (iii) German teaching methods, with the greater use of the tutorial system. In each of these aspects Strachan Davidson, Warde Fowler and Bywater were lauded. Nettleship's teaching too was singled out by Haverfield: 'The pupil may not suitably criticize the master, but for myself, I do not hesitate to call him a great scholar. He was not perhaps – at least in manner – an effective lecturer for undergraduate audiences – when he had three or four pupils by himself in his own rooms, the inspiration was unmistakable and unforgettable' (Haverfield 1893a: 370). It is the idea of the personal tutorial derived from the German practice of the seminar which was crucial in

---

12. James Strachan Davidson (1843–1916) undergraduate Balliol College 1862–6; fellow at Balliol 1866–1916 and Senior Dean 1875–1916; cf. Davis 1927.

this respect. Either of these means of discourse was the vehicle for the exploration and dissection of knowledge and opinions. Typical of the recognition of the importance of the media, Bywater frequently visited Germany and France in order 'to make personal acquaintance of leading continental scholars, as well as to attend gatherings of scholars (Philologen-Sammlungen) in order to take stock of progress of knowledge in various departments' (Jackson 1917: 47–8).

So far we have considered Haverfield connections and those familiar with and sympathetic to Mommsen's work. In turn we have begun to see how Mommsen's work and methods may have influenced Haverfield. However the situation is not necessarily so clear-cut. There were those who expressed reservations about Mommsen's work, either because of the way he used the source material or because of his conclusions. Good examples of these sorts of reservations can be found in the work of E.A. Freeman and G.B. Grundy.[13] Part of Freeman's problem was that he prided himself as a writer of narrative histories. He had little time for the philosophy of the discipline or approaches which, he believed, made facts fit theories (Bratchell 1969). In this outlook he was not alone. For instance, according to Dowling (1985: 580), Thomas Arnold's failure to produce much of substance was a consequence of his rejection of 'new' German approaches to history: where Arnold represented a providentialist interpretation based upon the literature, and a newer ostensibly objective interpretation based upon the methods of empirical

---

13. Freeman (1823–1892: undergraduate Trinity College, Oxford 1841. Fellow 1845. Regius Professor of Modern History 1884–1892), published on a wide range of subjects, including *History of the Norman Conquest* (six vols; 1867–79), *The Growth of the English Constitution from the Earliest Times* (1872), *The Methods of Historical Study* (1886) and *History of Roman Sicily* (1891–4; cf. Cronne 1943). He was well known for his views on the positive influences of German/Aryan civilization on its modern European counterpart (and at the expense of the Celtic influence). He also retained a pan-European rather than (British) imperialist attitude to world history. However, his opinions gradually declined, from an intellectualized position to the point where they are now decried as racist or racialist in tone. His early influences were High Church Oxford and which also explains his strong and continuing interest in ecclesiastical architecture. He was friend of the likes of Bryce, Stubbs, Green, Cox as well as Sayce and Müller (cf. Parker 1981; Burrow 1981; Momigliano 1994). Grundy's career and connections with Haverfield are discussed below in Chs. 6 and 8. It would be interesting to know more of Haverfield's contacts with Freeman. Haverfield, at one time complimenting him of his skills as a historian, was to write he was '...too cold to the charms of archaeology' (Haverfield 1912d: 17).

science, typified by Niebuhr and Mommsen. Slightly later, Grundy (1945: 151; 64, 152) was to articulate similar reservations. Nor were the criticisms restricted to the academic fraternity. Mommsen's opinions could impinge on the preserve of the antiquarian. With respect to his writing about Roman Britain, the publication of *The Provinces* elicited at least one detailed critique, that by the noted English antiquarian and writer, Henry Scarth (1887). Scarth's criticisms of Mommsen's picture of Roman Britain covered a number of themes. He rightly berated Mommsen's occasional lapses of knowledge of the geography of the island. He also pointed out his opinions about the light penetration of Roman influences in Wales were contrary to the evidence. This theme was followed up by Haverfield a few years later who received the acclaim for making the point. But in other respects, Scarth's reaction to Mommsen was in part the response of the 'Little Englander' incorporating unfamiliarity with developments in scholarship on the continent with a failure to appreciate the strength of Mommsen's ability to reinterpret the evidence to hand. In other instances, many of Mommsen's statements or predictions have since, despite what Scarth might have said, turned out to be accurate if not valid.

Irrespective of the criticisms raised by contemporaries, the influence of Mommsen was established and remained dominant until the late 1930s. This was in contrast to his declining reputation elsewhere in Europe (Croke 1991: 51). As already indicated, notable early British Mommsen adherents included James Strachan Davidson, William Warde Fowler, Henry Pelham and William Ramsay. Their point of difference was on how far each was prepared to accept his conclusions. For instance, the publication of the *History of Rome*, the early volumes of *CIL* and the *Criminal and Civil Law* and his reception of them put Warde Fowler '...in the vanguard among historians in his University' (Coon 1934: 249). His opinions were most explicitly expressed in a 1909 lecture he delivered on Mommsen and subsequently published in 1920. Strachan Davidson (1901) too was not entirely convinced. That Mommsen did influence his writings on late Republican history was noted by Coon:

> ...In a review of his Julius Caesar, W.T. Arnold says that Fowler has written a very good book (viz. *Julius Caesar and the foundations of the Roman imperial system* – 1899) and adds that it would have been, in his opinion, still better if he had never read a line of Mommsen. The only considerable disagreement between Fowler and his friend, Professor Conway, seems to have been on the issue of Mommsen and Caesar. Conway would have vol. IV of Mommsen's History burned in the playground of every English school that possessed it. And so he finds it difficult to acquiesce

in that view expressed in a sketch of the life and work of Mommsen
(p. 266).

If the implications of the 'new ancient history' were slow to permeate
through Oxford, their effects on antiquarian and archaeological research in Britain were even more slowly appreciated and therefore
took even longer to take affect. Naturally enough their implications
were even more obscure for historians, antiquarians and archaeologists beyond the universities. There were signs, however, that they
were taking affect at the end of the century.

Mommsen and Oxford: Henry Nettleship, Ingram Bywater and William Warde Fowler

The nature of Mommsen's relationship with English scholarship is the
subject of on-going work by Brian Croke (1991; manusc.). His study
commences with Ingram Bywater before passing, indirectly via Henry
Pelham, to Haverfield. The basis for this framework lies in Jackson's
Ingram Bywater: The Memoir of an Oxford Scholar, where Bywater,
Nettleship and Pelham were all linked by a respect for and intimacy with
Mark Pattison (Jackson 1917: 43). Ingram Bywater (1840–1914) was
Regius Professor of Greek (1893–1908) who, along with Haverfield, was
to become 'Mommsen's chief British disciple' (Croke manus.; cf. Jackson
1915–16; 1917; Cannan and Allen 1918). Bywater was a 'student' of
Robinson Ellis, Corpus Professor of Latin, as well as a friend, yet critical
pupil, of Benjamin Jowett. As a Fellow at Exeter he became a close friend
of Pattison. Bywater's association with Mommsen appears to date back
to at least *c*.1872 when he was delegated in to ask Mommsen if he was
able to receive an honorary DCL from Oxford, an offer Mommsen had to
decline (Jackson 1917: 53). In 1880 Bywater was co-ordinating the sending of replacement volumes for the library Mommsen had lost in a fire at
his house in Charlottenburg in that year. The two shared mutual acquaintances as well. Bywater was on friendly terms with two Mommsen
associates, Hermann Usener (1834–1905, Professor at Bonn University)
and Jacob Bernays (1824–1881, 'Professor extraordinary' in the Faculty
of Philosophy and Librarian also at Bonn; cf. Sandys 1908: 176 and
184). In time Bywater came to act as a literary contact for Mommsen at
Oxford, using the collection there to advise on textual problems and arranging for collators to work for him (Croke manusc.). According to
Croke, Bywater's contact with Mommsen began to wane after 1885 and
was lost by 1890, by which time Haverfield filled the rôle. For some,
Bywater was a significant influence on the (young) Haverfield's career.
Other than in his teaching, it may have extended to his first publica-

tions. He was editor of the *Journal of Philology* (1879–1914), where many of Haverfield's earliest utterances were placed.

One Haverfield connection overlooked by Croke is Henry Nettleship (1839–1893), another member of the Pattison's circle, who was friendly with John Conington[14] and had come under the influence of Moritz Haupt, of Berlin University (Nettleship 1885: 1–22). Nettleship knew another German scholar who came to feature prominently in Haverfield's later career, Emil Hübner. Nettleship had in turn been introduced to Hübner via Mark Pattison (Stearn in Bywater 1894a). It was from Nettleship that Haverfield's earliest (scholarly) interests in Roman Britain, through Tacitus, evolved (Craster 1920: 63). In later life Haverfield was to write: 'Thirty years ago, …I was an undergraduate far more concerned with philology than with the Roman Empire' (Haverfield 1913b: 146), sentiments repeated in the preface to Haverfield's new edition of Conington and Nettleship's *Works of Virgil* (1899):

> I am unwilling to close this preface without bearing witness to the heavy loss which Latin scholarship sustained by Mr Nettleship's death. I have tried elsewhere to estimate his worth – and Professor Bywater has done it far better in the Dictionary of National Biography. My own debt to him, as pupil and as a friend, has been very great in Latin scholarship (p. x).[15]

It was Nettleship's 'pushing' him towards Latin lexicography which started Haverfield's subsequent interest in epigraphy (Macdonald 1924: 18).[16] Indeed Haverfield went as far as to describe himself as a

---

14. John Conington (1825–1869), variously student, scholar and fellow of Magdalen and UC, in 1854 became the (first) Corpus Professor of Latin. Conington was a champion of opening-up of fellowships, having suffered under their restrictions in his early years. Unsurprisingly he worked closely with the Oxford University Commission. Initially a liberal, and an agitating proponent of reform in the university, after his translation to the Latin chair, his opinions went through a sea change. According to Pattison he became an ultra-conservative in Oxford politics, a committed adherent to 'High Church' values which in turn he used to shape his opinions of others. Pattison also claims the quality of his work declined (1988: 127–30; cf. Bywater 1894b). Connington's *Vergil* (1863–71) was savaged in review. A new edition was prepared by Nettleship and that later by Haverfield.

15. H.A.L. Fisher (1940: 54) rated R.W. Macan and Pelham the best lecturers in his time at the university, and thought as highly of Nettleship and W.W. Fowler, even if he never managed to hear them.

16. Nettleship – Lincoln and Corpus Christi colleges and later Professor of Latin (1878–93), author of *Satires English and Latin* (1893). Obit. Haverfield 1893a

'student of Nettleship', a claim echoed by Bosanquet (1920: 137). Elsewhere Haverfield, when reviewing what was essentially a 'failed' project (Nettleship's attempt to compile a Latin-English lexicon which had got no further than the letter A), still managed to provide an effusive account of what had been accomplished (*The Academy* 7 December 1889). After Nettleship's death in 1893, Haverfield edited his *Collected Essays*, a copy of which he sent to Mommsen who too was clearly familiar with Nettleship's work.

Despite the credit Haverfield accorded him in his contribution to revolutionizing the teaching of Roman history in Oxford, Haverfield is conspicuous by his absence in Coon's biography of William Warde Fowler.[17] This is surprising for their careers overlapped. It is true that the two were members of different colleges, but it is likely that under the sort of arrangement between Warde Fowler's Lincoln, Oriel and later Corpus Christi colleges (which must have come through Nettleship), Haverfield could have sat in on Warde Fowler's lectures on Roman history.[18] Warde Fowler was at this time recognised as one of, if not the best,

---

and a contribution to the *Biograph. Jahrbucher* XXII (1898): 79–81. Nettleship was educated at Lancing College where Haverfield was to teach between 1883 and 1892. Was he in some way instrumental in Haverfield obtaining the post?

17. Warde Fowler (1847–1921) – undergraduate New and Lincoln colleges 1866–72; fellow at Lincoln 1872–1921; college tutor 1873–1910; sub-rector 1881–1906. He retired in 1910. The only direct connection I have found between Warde Fowler and Haverfield is a footnote in the former's account of the life and work of Mommsen, where Haverfield's updating of *CIL* VII is noted; '...since this lecture was written (in 1909) the work of preparing a new edition of vol. VII of the Corpus has been in the hands of Prof. Haverfield of Oxford, whose recent death is an irreparable loss to British scholarship' (1920: 261). Another leading academic of the time who does not appear to have influenced Haverfield to any recorded degree was Archibald Henry Sayce (1845–1933), (extraordinary) Professor of Assyriology (Gunn 1949; cf. Garstang 1933). But there are links. Sayce (1923: 20–1) recollected that as a youth he attended the Bath church at which Haverfield's father preached (cf. Ch.1, n. 25). Sayce also crops up in one of Haverfield's letters to Mommsen (Croke 12). Correspondence between Haverfield and Sayce is preserved in the Bodleian Library, Oxford, dated 1888 and 1914, with Haverfield responding to antiquarian and epigraphic questions.

18. This would have been under what became known as the 'Combination System', where tutors from different colleges could agree, initially informally, to pool lectures in order to avoid unnecessary repetition of themes as well as to encourage a degree of specialist teaching. Jackson (1917: 65–6) maintained

lecturers on the subject in Oxford (Murray 2000: 341). Again, both claimed to have been profoundly shaped by Nettleship (Coon 1934: 24–5, 223). In addition to these connections, Warde Fowler is said to have been instrumental in getting Pelham his readership in Ancient History in 1887. Perhaps the relative lack of contact with Haverfield can be explained by Warde Fowler's professed ignorance of archaeology and his well-known preoccupation with his college (Coon 1934: 73). What Coon's memoir does emphasize is the outlook the two shared in many subjects. There was, for instance, their admiration for Mommsen's (published) work, although Warde Fowler's opinions were more tempered (Coon 1934: 265), as well as their appreciation of the poor standing of Oxford scholarship in the first half of the nineteenth century (Coon 1934: 17; 247). Not surprisingly there was a mutual respect for continental contacts and in particular German scholarship and its (teaching) methods, although again Warde Fowler was to modify subsequently his opinions (1916; cf. Coon 1934: 119–21, 197–9, 260).[19] The two also shared similar views on the purpose of (higher) education, with an emphasis on the need for the proper training of future specialists.[20] Warde Fowler's outlook in this respect can be traced back directly

---

its introduction was the result of the poor quality lectures and facilities for their delivery. Originally devised by lecturers in the School of Law and Modern History in the mid-1860s, the practice gradually spread (e.g. to Divinity, Mathematics and parts of *Lit. Hum.* as well as to certain colleges). H.A.L. Fisher claimed Alfred Robinson (1844–1895), former Warden of New College, 'was one of the makers of the inter-collegiate lecture system' (1940: 46; cf. F. Boase *Modern English Biography* III: 221–2). The arrangement, however, was deemed not to be so successful for *Literae Humaniores* (Engel 1983: 89–93; Jackson 1917: 66), even if Pelham was '...one of the first of those inter-collegiate lecturers, whose pupils are limited to no one College, and who attract so large a body of learners and deliver such authoritative and commanding lectures that, in this respect, they are the untitled equals - or even superiors – of the Professors' (Haverfield in Pelham 1911: xi).

19. 'Bywater respected German scholarship, especially for its organization and successful prosecution of study and research, but disliked its competiveness and tendency to personal controversy' (Jackson 1917: 54–5).

20. On the conviction that good teaching was indispensable in higher education, (Warde Fowler) '...often expressed the view that a university could not realize its true meaning without great enthusiasm for learning. *An Oxford Correspondence* – was met with warm approval by many who had the University's interest at heart. In simple language it suggested that the real student's mind would be active with first hand-work. Oxford men had been content to

to Pattison, Rector of Lincoln where Warde Fowler, after completing his BA there, was offered a fellowship in 1872.

Henry Pelham and William Ramsay

Along with Nettleship and Bywater, the one person with whom Haverfield is most usually associated is Henry Francis Pelham (1846–1907).[21] Indeed it was Haverfield who was to be his principle obituarist (Haverfield 1907a; 1907–08; 1911a; 1912b), joined only by Davidson (1958). As the Camden Professor, Pelham enjoyed a great reputation within the university, although his name was apparently not so well known abroad. Indeed it has been said that following William Camden instituting the chair in 1622, the list of occupants had not been distinguished until the appointment of first Henry Rawlinson, then Pelham and then Haverfield (Piggott 1976: 41; Haverfield in Pelham 1911: xvii). When looking at Pelham's career one is struck by the number of generous assessments of it (e.g. Matheson 1911; Coon 1934: 73; Evans 1943: 283; Grundy 1945; Engel 1983: 170–2; Murray 2000: 339ff.). H.A.L. Fisher felt that a ' ...few hours with (R.W.) Macan or Pelham opened out the vi-

---

retail the wares of German workers, often without even marking them as "Made In Germany". To be sure, the successful performance of first hand work in classical subjects requires a wide knowledge of ancient life and history and literature, and ought not to be encouraged to "do it off his own bat" until he is a thoroughly qualified scholar' (Coon 1934: 80). In contrast to Warde Fowler, and perhaps more typical of the time, for Percy Gardner, German methods meant 'encyclopaedic knowledge and scientific method' (1933: 49) combined with (over-) organization, sentiments developed elsewhere (e.g. p. 82–7). Perhaps indicative of how far the influence of German techniques had penetrated Oxford at the time, H.A.L. Fisher (1940: 59) claimed that after Oxford, he deliberately eschewed the chance to study in Germany, but decided to go and study in Paris: 'To the best of my belief no Oxford man had preceded me in that quest. I was the first of a long series, the first to break with the established tradition that post-graduate study in historical science could only be profitably be carried on among the Germans.'

21. In his Haverfield obituary, Bruton (1919) suggested that the professor '...was always proud to acknowledge that his interest in his subject had been largely fostered by two men – Prebendary Scarth and professor Pelham.' Scarth's influence was noted in Ch.1 n. 25. Pelham: undergraduate Trinity College 1865–9; fellow at Exeter 1869–73/1882–9; college tutor 1869–89; Reader in Ancient History 1887–9 (cf. Davidson 1958: 43–6); President of Trinity College 1897–1907; Camden Professor of Ancient History and fellow of Brasenose College 1889–1907.

sion of a new discipline: that of critically handling the original sources for the history of ancient times. To be taken over the text of Herodotus by Pelham was fine introduction to the intelligent study of history. We were allowed to catch the secrets of the workshop and shared in the delight of the chase. ...Though we did not then know it, we stood on the brink of a brilliant era of archaeological discovery which changed the whole landscape of early Greek history' (1940: 55). John Myres, a student and later a colleague of Pelham's, believed him to be the best lecturer he ever heard (Dunbabin 1955: 350). Because of his administrative duties, Pelham was never a productive scholar. As Master of Exeter, he carried heavy college and university administrative loads combined with an extensive involvement in university politics, where he was known as an organizer and facilitator. 'Pelham had great practical ability and was an admirable speaker. No one carried more weight in the counsels of the University, whether as a member of the Hebdomadal Council or of Congregation' (Jackson 1917: 43). His loyalty to his college and teaching duties, notably tutorial work, at the expense of other matters was not uncommon for the time (Engel 1983: 127–8). 'Pelham, unlike Bywater, was not a genuine student but a man of affairs' (Jackson 1915–16: 524). In this capacity Jackson (1917: 47) has Pelham as the front man for Bywater, the influence in the background (Cannan and Allen 1918: 5). Descended from staunchly Whig stock, his father was once Bishop of Norwich, Pelham's relatively liberal opinions meant he was satirized by Oxford 'conservatives' such as Charles Oman (1941: 144). Within the university he was a member of the group of reformers known as 'The Club' (Murray 2000: 340). Not only was he influential in '...help[ing] to introduce Geography and Archaeology' to Oxford (Haverfield in Pelham 1911: xvii), along with the schools of geography and anthropology, Pelham was instrumental in the development of the Bodleian Library and the Ashmolean Museum. He was also involved in creating the Society for the Promotion of Hellenic Studies (1879), and in establishing the British schools of archaeology in both Athens (1886) and Rome (1902) as well as in the foundation of the British Academy (1902). A champion of women's education in Oxford, Pelham was a committee member and later President of Somerville College. In addition to these interests he was '...a tireless promoter of the study of Roman Britain' (Murray 2000: 340). Murray also reports that Pelham went out of his way to support 'vulnerable' young scholars, noting his patronage of A.H.M. Greenidge and George Grundy. Under the circumstances Haverfield might be added to this list. It is because of his other commitments that Pelham's views are few, caused by his failure to publish much of substance (Haverfield 1907–08: 366 and in Pelham 1911: xiv, xxi). His scholarly output effectively ceased from 1890, in part a consequence of a double cataract he developed in that year. It is therefore disappointing to have so little material with which to work, not least because he was a correspondent with, and ultimately a 'friend' of, Mommsen (cf. Appendix 1). In truth, he published little other than the odd article disputing points of interpretation with Mommsen, and where an indirect influence can be detected in Pelham's reports on work on the Roman frontier in Germany (Pelham 1897; 1906), work which as already noted, went back to Mommsen, and culminated in Pelham and others petitioning for a co-ordinated scheme of research along the Hadrianic frontier (cf. Chapter 6). There was also his *Outlines of Roman History* (1890) intended as a prolegomenon to a history of the Roman empire.

According to Oswyn Murray, by the late nineteenth century, Oxford was arguably the most significant centre in the world for teaching, research and publication in ancient history. This 'golden age' (1872–1914) of ancient history at Oxford was all down to Henry Pelham, 'the architect of ...change in ancient history' and who '...provided for the first time the leadership that the discipline had lacked' (Murray 2000: 339). As evidence for the depth of his contribution, in 1907, at the time of his death whilst still Camden Professor, and complemented by the work of the Professor of Archaeology (P. Gardner) and two lecturers in archaeology (L.R. Farnell of Exeter and J.L. Myres of New)[22], Murray says that under Pelham there were 25 other individuals teaching ancient history in the university in a 78 lecture series (Murray 2000: 341). It is debatable just how much Pelham was able to shape the discipline at the university but it is undeniable that he played a considerable part in many of the changes that affected the university in his lifetime.

The foundations for Oxford's pre-eminence were the consequence of the reforms of the structure of the university and its teaching conducted over the previous 30 years. The emphasis now was on tutorial type instruction, a mode that particularly suited ancient history, undertaken by professional college tutors aided by inter-collegiate lectures arrangement. The momentum was maintained by the way that the ancient historians

---

22. Lewis Richard Farnell (1856–1934): 1874, Open scholarship in classics with a First in *Lit. Hum.* and in 1880 a Fellow at Exeter College. His mentors were Tozer, Jackson, Pelham and Bywater. In 1883 he was sub-rector of his college and in 1913 its rector. Between 1920 and 1923 he was university Vice-Chancellor. Farnell was noted for his philo-German sympathies, at least until the First World War, complimented by extensive travels in Germany (cf. Farnell 1934; Marett 1934). (Sir) John Linton Myres is discussed in more detail in Ch.8.

started, in late 1903, their own talking – or dining – club, where naturally enough, by 1905 the members discussed the business of teaching and the assessment of their subject. This arrangement of meetings was formalized in 1914 with the formation of the Sub-Faculty of Ancient History.

In this group of Haverfield's academic connections, although not mentors in his career but contemporaries of Pelham's and so in some respects another set of influences on Haverfield, were William Mitchell Ramsay (1851–1939), the first Professor of Classical Archaeology at Oxford and later Professor of Humanities at the University of Aberdeen and Percy Gardner, Ramsay's successor to the Oxford professorship. Ramsay and Haverfield shared a number of mutual acquaintances, not least that with Mommsen. Born in Glasgow, Ramsay was educated at Aberdeen University before moving to St John's, Oxford (1872) where he became a fellow (1876) following a brief interlude at Göttingen (1874). He became professor at Oxford in 1885, only to resign his position the following year because of what he perceived to be a lack of support from the University. Knighted in 1906, he returned to Aberdeen where he remained until he retired in 1911. Ramsay is an extremely interesting and yet elusive character. His career has recently been examined again by Brian Croke who describes him as a '…sensitive soul, perhaps too sensitive (even paranoid)' and somebody (too) heavily dependent on Mommsen's help and encouragement, to the point that Mommsen was asked to support Ramsay's application for the Lincoln chair (Croke 1994; cf. Headlam in Hogarth 1899). In his (surviving) letters to Mommsen, Ramsay comes over as a self-possessed individual. He described himself as a socialist, a claim significant for the time. His political outlook coupled with his connections with German scholarship were later to cause him to oppose Britain's position in the Boer War as well, with others, the declaration of war with Germany. He was a signatory to a letter from a group of dons addressed to *The Times* which objected to the possibility of the war between Britain and Germany.[23] Ramsay is now best remembered for his work on late Roman

23. The letter, from the group writing to put on record the friendship and co-operation of German colleagues, is: '…We regard Germany as a nation leading the way in the Arts and Sciences and we have all learnt and are learning from German scholars. War against her …will be a sin against civilisation. If by reason of honourable obligations we are unhappily involved in war patriotism, might still over months, but at this juncture we consider ourselves justified in protesting against being drawn into the struggle with a nation so near akin to our own, and with whom we have so much in common' (*The Times* 1 August 1914 and followed up on 15 August). Later on Sir William Ramsay KCB was to write to the same newspaper (27 August 1914) saying he was often mis-

and early Christian Anatolia, which he visited for the first time in 1880 and where he combined an extensive knowledge of the literary sources with field explorations. His particular interests were the geography and topography of the region relative to early Christian literary sources. Throughout his publications, he constantly acknowledged his debts to Mommsen. Like Pelham he was a regular correspondent with the German. The two first met in either 1882 or 1883, Ramsay being drawn to him through an interest in Roman epigraphy.

How close the relationship between Haverfield and Ramsay was is difficult to gauge. They certainly knew one another, not least when Mommsen visited Oxford. The two were travelling companions when v. Sarwey toured northern Britain in 1893 (cf. Chapter 6). Because Haverfield was awarded an honorary doctorate by Ramsay's university in 1905, it is tempting to see the offer coming in some way through Ramsay.[24] Elsewhere Ramsay made acknowledgements to Haverfield in some of his works.

Mommsen at Oxford

Taylor records that before '...he had taken his degree he [Haverfield, i.e. 1883] was writing to Mommsen about an inscription recently discovered in Oxford' (Taylor 1920: 65). Although she did not provide a precise date reference for this, the earliest (surviving) Haverfield contact with Mommsen is a letter he wrote him asking for an opinion on an inscription from Broussa (*sic*: Prussa in Turkey, 1 May 1883). Correspondence with Mommsen about this particular inscription survives in

---

taken for Ramsay. In the light of the professor's recent public utterances, Ramsay KCB wanted it noted he was not to be associated with them.

24. Haverfield was one of nine individuals honoured. The others included Thomas Hardy, the Cambridge ancient historian J.B. Bury, the Right Honourable David James Mackay, (the Lord Reay and the first President of the British Academy), Edward Robinson (Director of the Museum of Fine Art at Boston) and John Struthers (Secretary of the Scottish Education Department). The graduands travelled to Aberdeen on a specially chartered train ('the first wholly sleeper between London and Aberdeen') on 5 April. A snowstorm delayed their arrival to two hours before the occasion. It was this ceremony, which was the occasion for Bury and Hardy's subsequent friendship (cf. <http://www.abdn.ac.uk/English/Aberdeen.htm>). Haverfield also received, in 1910, an honorary degree from the University of Leeds and where there was Professor William Rhys Roberts (1858–1929), Professor of Classics (1904–23) and another admirer of Haverfield and his work.

Berlin (Croke 1: cf. *The Academy* 12 and 19 May 1883).[25] In fact he was also writing to him about another inscription, one from Nicopolis (but which had been moved to West Park, Fordingbridge. He returned to this inscription in *The Academy* 29 August 1891). Haverfield wrote to Mommsen because of the latter's authority as the Latin epigraphist *par excellence*. According to Croke, Haverfield, if not introduced to Mommsen by Bywater, certainly benefited from a letter of recommendation from him. 'In 1883 Bywater wrote to the Berlin professor, who was pleased with the quality of work done by Haverfield on some inscriptions, that Haverfield was only a novice but was zealous and painstaking'. Bywater had evidently been introduced to Haverfield via Pelham. That said, the 1 May letter in Berlin, from Haverfield to Mommsen concerning the Broussa inscription, implies that it was Nettleship who made the original suggestion that he should write to Germany. Indeed as noted above, Nettleship had better connections with German epigraphy, through his contacts with Hübner. Whatever, with Mommsen's reply there followed a stream of letters from Haverfield to the end of the year and which subsequently developed into a long friendship (Macdonald 1919–20a: 479; cf. 1924: 20).[26]

With his reputation in England steadily improving among a small group of classicists and ancient historians, Mommsen visited Oxford twice, both relatively late in life (cf. Croke 1991). The first occasion was in September 1885, a visit that William Ramsay was anticipating and for which he was the conduit (Mommsen resided at Exeter), although he was away from Oxford for part of the time. The pair seem, however, to have been able to leave calling cards at Sanday's and Nettleship's residences. This would have been the occasion when Mommsen met Warde Fowler in Lincoln College (Warde Fowler 1920: 251) and made the acquaintance of Pelham. The Oxford element of the trip, as with his

---

25. In the latter letter, Haverfield reports Mommsen had written to him about his reading and had offered some corrections.

26. Mommsen died on 1 November 1903, after which his son, Wolfgang, wrote to Haverfield: '...You have known (Mommsen) personally and been able to render him many services, of which he often spoke thankfully to me; only a few days before his death I heard him mention your name and he was telling me to remind him in a few days to write to you. Now I can only thank you for all your kindness to him and ask you to keep him in good memory' (Letter, 9 November, Haverfield Archive); '...I can assure you that he (Mommsen) always considered you as one of his best friends ...You used to travel through Germany formerly in your holiday time ...it would give us great pleasure to make you welcome in our house' (31 January 1904, Haverfield Archive).

second visit, was undertaken in part to consult original manuscripts held in the university. Mommsen also spent part of the time in London from where Mommsen wrote to Bywater, the other host, trying to arrange his time in Oxford (Jackson 1917: 53) and to where Mrs Ramsay was forwarding his mail and Ramsay himself was advising on theatres and second-hand booksellers. During the same visit, Haverfield wrote to Mommsen's son, also in London, asking if father and son would care to dine with him. Mommsen's second visit to Oxford in March 1889 was hosted by ?Ramsay, Pelham and perhaps Haverfield, although at least one of them (Pelham) appears not to have been around. Pelham learnt from Ramsay that Mommsen was in London and proceeded to invite him as his guest to Exeter. Mommsen accepted the invitation but Pelham was to write and regret that he first had to break an appointment and later to apologize that he was unable to see Mommsen for longer. It seems that on this occasion Ramsay did not manage to meet the German scholar. Furthermore, for both visits there is no record of Haverfield, by then at Lancing, meeting Mommsen. But this must be coincidence for from 1890 Haverfield became Mommsen's main contact in Britain.[27]

Conclusion

Addressing the historical section of the Royal Archaeological Institute at its AGM at Dorchester on 4 August 1897, H.H. Howorth lavished generous praise on recent developments in German historical methodology. Highlighting a number of virtues in this, one facet he commended was in the form of a rhetorical question; 'Where have we the young men who have gathered around Mommsen, Sybel and Curtius and others in Germany, and have learnt their profession by working in the workshops of real masters – doing the hodman's work for the practical builder and brick setter?' (Howorth 1898: 130). Moving to the intellectual quality of published work he noted: 'It would be impossible for a German student to publish the ridiculous and uncritical crudities which sometimes pass for history among us' (p. 131). The solutions, to Howorth's mind, were new standards and training in the universities. He also pointed to recent German work

---

27. In 1932 the Warden of New College (H.A.L. Fisher) reminisced about one of Mommsen's Oxford visits. On one occasion he sat next to him (when he was working on Cassidorus) in the Bodleian and could report of Mommsen's high opinion of Haverfield and Pelham but his general disregard for the rest of the university and the town (*The Times* 4 February 1932).

opening up new sources of information. For instance, it '...is true that the Corpus Inscriptionum &c. &c., has so largely displaced the ancient professed writers of Greek and Roman history in the pages of Mommsen.' At the same time, archaeological research was the most important new source of information (p. 139ff.). He also appreciated, however, the amount of damage that had been inflicted by earlier un-qualified excavators. His solution came way as a request: 'May I again express the hope from this chair that those who have the custody of what remain [e.g. the likes of the Chief Inspector of Ancient Monu-ments, Pitt-Rivers?] will refuse to allow amateur and people without the requisite training, knowledge, or resources to tamper with these invaluable documents' (= sites: p. 141). To his contemporaries it was Haverfield's achievement to bridge the gap between Mommsen's methodology and its practical execution in the United Kingdom. This he achieved both in his university and among the archaeological fra-ternity. The next chapter will explore some of the ways Haverfield managed to effect this transformation.

Haverfield went up to Oxford at an interesting time in the univer-sity's history. There had been major changes in the nature of teaching, in its process of examination and in the ethos that underpinned re-search. During his time as an undergraduate, he was exposed to a group of academics who were at the forefront of innovations in both teaching and research. Not only did these individuals condition his attitude to study, they also afforded him access to the leading figures on the conti-nent who were driving the developments that so influenced Bywater, Nettleship and Pelham. On current evidence there is nothing to show that Haverfield was regarded as an exceptional student or that he ulti-mately gained intimate entry to this circle. Although he took a First in Classical Moderations, he had ultimately to be satisfied with a Second in *Literae Humaniores*. His 'failure' was widely attributed to the fact that he allowed himself to be distracted by reading off the prescribed 'cur-riculum' rather than concentrating on philosophy (W.G. Collingwood 1920: 255; Macdonald 1924: 17–18; Oman 1941: 66; Croke manus.). As we will see in the next chapter, the influence of his teachers contin-ued, however, after he graduated in 1883 when he went into school mastering, during when he remained in contact with at least some of his Oxford mentors (notably Bywater and Pelham).

As important, however, were the implications of a series of develop-ments and discoveries which were being made in the study of antiquity. As H.A.L. Fisher expressed it, while he was an undergraduate in the 1880s, from '...that moment onwards archaeological discoveries have descended on us in a cataract which shows no signs of diminishing in a volume. Oxford men have taken a prominent, perhaps a leading, part in the great movements of human curiosity, as the names of [F.G.] Kenyon and [Arthur] Evans, of [David] Hogarth, [Bernard Pyne] Grenfell [1869–1926] and [Arthur Surridge] Hunt [1871–1934], of J.L. Myres, Leonard Woolley, J.D. Beazley suffice to remind us' (1940: 56). In turn Haverfield's return to Oxford in 1892 saw him come back to a university where the implications of the changes of the mid-century were starting to take effect. He was now part of a group of academics and researchers, all sympathetic to the 'research' ethic. His return came at a time when the potential for archaeology (along with other subjects, e.g. geography) as a discipline distinct from classics was becoming all the more apparent. The next chapter will look more closely at how some of these implications worked themselves out.

CHAPTER 4

Lancing College, the *CIL* and the return to Oxford

Introduction

From examining the methodological and institutional structure of Roman archaeological research in Britain by the late nineteenth century, we now move to how Haverfield fitted into the discipline when he returned to Oxford in 1892. Following an enforced exile, some of his obituarists regarded his return as almost inevitable. The years up to 1892 can be described as the formative period in Haverfield's career. It was on the basis of the work undertaken up to this time that he received a Senior Studentship at Christ Church, perhaps with Pelham's support. In turn, his return opened up a number of opportunities, where the information and in particular, the lessons learnt in that earlier period were applied.

Haverfield post-1883

There is no information about what Haverfield planned to do when he graduated in 1883. Although there is nothing to prove he desired to remain at Oxford, given that he was already publishing articles in *The Academy*, it is likely. Under normal circumstances he should have expected to go through the run of competitive examinations for the college fellowships available in that year but his Second in Greats would have been an insurmountable hindrance. The death of his father in September 1882 would have severed the financial support he had previously enjoyed. Therefore it is no surprise that in 1884 he accepted the offer of a position at Lancing College. Again it would be useful to know more about the circumstances behind the decision to enter school mastering, not least because of his and the school's association with the 'High Church', and the fact that some of his Oxford patrons had links to it. That Haverfield's maternal grandfather and later his father were undergraduates of Oxford at the time of the Tractarian controversy there, and that the latter was regarded as a 'High Church' preacher, are equally suggestive of Haverfield retaining, at least at this time, some sympathies with religion and schooling (cf. Chapter 1).

Lancing College was one of a group of schools established by the Rev. Nathaniel Woodard (1811–1891). The Woodard Church of England Schools Society (founded 1847) was intended to create a series of '…institutions on the lines of the older public schools but with greater economy and by such means to foster Tractarianism' (Barnard 1947: 150; cf. Gardner 1973: 173–85).[1] Woodard believed that the developing middle class had become estranged from the Church. His experience in his London parishes had demonstrated that efforts to educate the labouring classes were doomed to fail as long as their (middle class) teachers remained the ill-educated who were opposed to the Church. Therefore he proposed a scheme of (boarding) schools staffed by Oxford graduates '…for the recovery by the Church of its position as the educator of the nation' (Adamson 1930: 273). Because his schools were so closely associated with the 'Evangelical revival', there circulated accusations of them using suspect ceremonies. Another principle common to Woodard's schools was that they kept their fees artificially low to facilitate the spreading of the message. In time the Society came to create three grades of schools to meet the pockets of various tiers of the middle and lower-middle classes. Lancing, effectively founded in 1849, being in the first rank and meant to provide candidates for Oxbridge, was modelled on Winchester. Woodard relied on the zeal of religious types working in a professional (teaching) environment. Theirs has even been described as self-sacrificing devotion but because of the unrealistically low fees, Woodard failed to pay the proper rate and therefore saw a high turnover of staff. In this, the seeds of the limited success of the schools were ensured. Unsurprisingly, all the schools experienced financial crises. A more positive feature of the schools was, as they tended to draw their students from the towns and the region's agricultural hinterland, there was not as much need for the sort of full classical curriculum offered by the more traditional (and expensive) public schools. They were therefore able to innovate to some degree in what they taught. It is not known to what extent Haverfield was in sympathy with Woodard's mission, but given the fact that Woodard was

---

1. Without a formal schooling, Woodard was educated at Magdalen Hall, Oxford (1834) where he was influenced by the Oxford Movement and Tractarianism. After serving in a number of parishes in east London, in 1847 he became the curate of Shoreham (cf. Adamson 1930; Handford 1933; Barnard 1947; Gardner 1973).

active in the work of his schools up to the time of his death, it is reasonable to assume a degree of empathy. Indeed Handford (1933: 1) claims
Haverfield was '...an earnest admirer of Woodard.' The history of
Lancing regards the period 1875 to 1889 as the college's 'Golden Age'
and attributed it to a combination of the headmasters R.E. Sandeson
(1862–86), who was in post at the time of Haverfield's appointment,
and the Revs. H.W. Mackenzie and J.H. Williams (the Senior Classical
Tutor), as well as Haverfield (Handford 1933: 129ff., 155; Gardner
1973: 174). Assessments of Haverfield's abilities as a teacher, are at face
value, positive. The future Lord Chancellor, the Right Hon. Viscount
John Sankey, owed him a particular debt: '...he united the enthusiasm
of the scholar with the inspiration of the teacher, and could make the
driest detail interesting' (Handford 1933: xiv). In a similar fashion,
Handford opined:

> Lancing had indeed been fortunate in keeping as long a scholar of the
> learning and ability of Haverfield. For clever boys he must have supplied
> interest and inspiration such as it falls to the capacities of few to offer.
> And his interests went beyond the narrow limits of the class-room. His
> original investigations into local antiquities, his encouragement of the
> study of natural History and General Science provided for those who de-
> sired it a width of intellectual outlook which was particularly required at
> the time (p. 175).

Reading between the lines, however, it is clear his contemporaries
thought Haverfield was not well-suited to a large class or the
run-of-the-mill instruction of students he considered to be of average
ability.[2] The headmaster at the time when Haverfield left Lancing was

---

2. At Lancing, Haverfield was known as 'The Doodle' (Handford 1933: 175).
   In May 1930 there was established at Lancing the 'Haverfield Archaeological Society' affiliated to the Sussex Archaeological Society (cf. *Sussex Archaeol
   Colls* LXXII (1931): xliv). Coincidentally Max Mallowan (1904–1978), a future Professor and Director of the Institute of Archaeology, attended
   Lancing before going up to New College (cf. Oates 1980). Sheppard Frere,
   later Professor of the Archaeology of the Roman empire at Oxford, was also
   once President of the Society (Frere 1988: 2). Another potential legacy of
   Haverfield's time at Lancing is a long description in Handford's history of the
   school (1933: 358ff.) of the archaeological remains scattered over the college's
   estates. Handford refers to Haverfield's work on sites recorded on the early
   versions of the OS maps of the area, while Haverfield published articles looking at aspects of the archaeology of the vicinity (e.g. Haverfield 1888d; 1888e;
   1889a; 1892e; 1892f). Curiously, none of these are mentioned in Sharpe's

Mackenzie who provided an assessment of his abilities as a schoolmaster for Macdonald's retrospective on Haverfield (cf. Macdonald 1924: 18–19 and reprinted in Handford 1933: 175–7). Mackenzie's 'tribute' is double-edged in its opinion of Haverfield as an educator and contains nuances that, as we will see, reappear in his later career.

Haverfield's time at Lancing undoubtedly influenced some of his earliest published work, most notably in his reviews of editions of classical texts.[3] In turn it is possible to detect strands that were to feature in his later work. For example, of W.C. Compton's *Caesar's Seventh Campaign in Gaul* (1889), he observed: 'This is in several ways a noteworthy schoolbook ...Mr. Compton, has it seems studied the campaign in the country where it was fought – would that more school masters were so energetic ...It is to be hoped, and it is to be expected, that other editions will follow the example of Mr. Compton. It is impossible to have too much 'realism' in our teaching, whether the teaching be done in a school or a university' (*Class Rev* III (1889): 449). Perversely, Haverfield then proceeded to outline some of the drawbacks of the 'realist' approach and its influence on schoolboys. There were other advantages in being at Lancing. The appointment did not inhibit research, for at the same time he acted as a conduit for a number of foreign scholars which in turn generated the odd essay: he claimed that whilst there, Mommsen asked him for a copy of a Greek inscription at West Park (Fordingbridge: Haverfield 1883: 292). He also undertook collations of Oxford manuscripts including the MS Victor in the Bodleian, again for Mommsen, and in 1884 for Theodor Birt on the Claudian *Scholia* (Haverfield 1888b: 271; cf. Croke 8; 10; 11). In addition to his duties, as noted above, he travelled widely through Europe in his vacations (especially in Germany, Austria, Italy and the Balkans), improving his (modern) languages as well as familiarizing himself with archaeological work there (Anderson 1919: 166). Out of these visits came a number of articles, including catalogues of material in continental museums (e.g. Haverfield 1891a).[4] It is for these reasons this was the crucial period in

---

1910 study of east Sussex and the Roman invasion.

3. Haverfield also wrote on aspects of the school's history for the *Lancing College Magazine*; cf. Handford 1933: 1, 50.

4. Haverfield's interest in the Danube-Balkans region dates to 1887 when he published on Roman Dacia which was a consequence of his visit to the Danube area that year (Haverfield 1887). His subsequent visits resulted in: A misread Roman inscription from Hungary (*The Academy* XIII. 1887); Haverfield 1888c; The gold bars of Kraszina (*Classical Review* III. 1889); Ro-

Haverfield's career. 'In his strenuous leisure he pursued various lines of original research but finally concentrated on Roman epigraphy and Roman Britain, under the influence of Mommsen' (Macdonald 1927: 244; 'he had gained a European reputation as the leading authority on Roman Britain while engaged in the work of a schoolmaster at Lancing' – Collingwood 1919: 117). Without doubt, however, the most significant event of this period was a meeting with the German scholar in Berlin in either 1887 or 1888.

Haverfield, Hübner and the *CIL*

In early 1889 the *Archaeological Review* published a short letter.

> I have been asked to prepare a collection of Roman inscriptions found in Britain and either not published, or incorrectly published in the VII vol. of the *Corpus* and in Dr Hübner's three supplements in the *Ephemeris*, the last of which goes down to 1878 (Haverfield 1888a: 267).

For some of his obituarists Haverfield, over all his other talents, was primarily an epigrapher (Craster 1920: 64–5; Curle 1939–40: 128). George Macdonald, believed that amongst his many skills, he was pre-eminent in ancient history, epigraphy and archaeology. Sir Charles Hercules Read, then President of the London Antiquaries wrote of his death 'Roman epigraphy ...lost an exponent who was *facile princeps* in this country' (1919–20: 1; cf. Bruton 1920: 73; Collingwood 1939: 82). The basis for these impressions goes back to Haverfield's involvement in the *CIL*. Received wisdom has, as a salient feature of Haverfield's career, Mommsen's invitation to him to contribute to the *CIL* series when the former was only 28 years old. His obituaries imply that from the start he was to assist with the *CIL* proper. For instance, 'Haverfield ...when he was still quite a young man ...had won the confi-

---

man remains in Carniola (*Archaeological Review* III. 1889 – where Haverfield summarized a report published in an obscure German language journal of finds made from Dernova in Carinthia since 1883. The implications are that Haverfield was familiar with the site); Finds of Roman coins in Roumania (*Numismatics Chronicle* X. 1890); Haverfield 1891b). There are letters which survive where Haverfield notes his visits to the Danube, in the summer of 1887 and in 1888 to Galicia and Romania, during which he met Mommsen's 'student' Alfred v. Domasweski in Pest (Croke 24). Much later, another article resulting from his familiarity with the geography and ethnography of Hungary was his questioning of the German ancestry of the artist Albrecht Dürer (Haverfield 1915c).

dence of Mommsen so completely that the veteran Hübner was asked to make way for him as editor of the British section of the Corpus Inscriptionum' (Macdonald 1918: 185). Closer examination of the evidence, however, suggests that the circumstances of his participation were not so clear-cut and that his initial contribution was to be far less prominent. By a process which will be explained below, Haverfield seems to have engineered a much more intimate involvement. This involved a degree of self-advertisement on his part and him playing up to Mommsen. On the other hand it also resulted in his alienating others involved in the scheme.

The earliest attempts to catalogue the Roman inscriptions of Britain had been made by the antiquarians of the Middle Ages. For instance, Janus Gruter (1560–1627) published in 1602 British examples in his *Inscriptionum Romanorum*, a corpus of ancient inscriptions. Volumes more concerned with the inscriptions of Britain started with the likes of Leland who included sections on this sort of material in their works. In its later editions, Camden's *Britannia* included catalogues of Roman inscriptions. The 1607 edition published 80 examples from northern England: '...this is Camden's principal contribution to the serious study of antiquities in the field' (Kendrick 1950: 147). It involved cataloguing with limited emendations of variable quality. Likewise, Horsley's *Britannia Romana* of 1732 enjoyed a high reputation among epigraphers. Less satisfactory was the Rev. J. McCaul's *Britanno-Roman Inscriptions* (1863). Horsley was superceded in 1873 by the publication of Volume VII of the *Corpus Inscriptionum Latinarum*, edited by Emil Hübner. Educated at Berlin and Bonn, a traveller in Italy, Spain and England, and an 'extra-ordinary' professor (1863) and later a full professor at Berlin, Hübner (1834–1901), was a distinguished historian and archaeologist (where this meant epigraphy) who had previously published on aspects of British Latin epigraphy (Hübner 1857), notably the *Inscriptiones Brittanniae Christianae* (1876) which considered material predominantly from Wales.[5] In the preparation for *CIL* VII, Hübner, who had visited Britain in 1866 and 1867 (Keppie 1998a: 34), was assisted by J. Collingwood Bruce, the first 'student' of the Roman Wall in Britain (Richmond in Collingwood Bruce 1957: viii), who was already working on his *Lapidarium Septentrionale* of the four northern English

---

5. He was also the author of a number of texts, including his series *Outlines of the History of Roman Literature* (1869), *Latin* (1876), and *Greek Grammar* (1883) and was at various times the editor of the journals *Hermes* (1866–81) and the *Archäologische Zeitung* (1868–72).

counties (Birley 1966b: 226). At much the same time, Roman inscriptions were being included in larger corpora of inscribed stones (e.g. J.O. Westwood's *Lapidarium Walliae: The Early Inscribed and Sculptured Stones of Wales* (1876–9)). Compared to its companion volumes, *CIL* VII was not a success. Revisions were necessary because of the numerous factual errors and incorrect readings in the original volume that were a consequence of Hübner's rather hurried visits and his ignorance of British geography, rather than new discoveries. What is certain is that Haverfield never had much of an opinion of his abilities as a commentator on at least the Roman inscriptions of Britain. He was later to complain of the poor quality of editing to Mommsen, and was to repeat the same criticisms in a number of articles. Indeed, he made something of an art highlighting Hübner's 'howlers'.[6] For instance, in one of the few foreign language reviews of any of Haverfield's publications, S. Reinach observed of Haverfield's sniping at Hübner in his 1914 review of Haverfield's *Roman Britain in 1914* (Haverfield 1915a: e.g. Hübner 'with his too frequent carelessness – a carelessness which make the 7th volume of the Corpus far less valuable than the rest of the series'), '…Mais n'oublions pas que c'est ne de plus anciens' (*Revue Archéolique* 3 (1916): 167).

Hübner started to update *CIL* VII in two supplements published as volumes III (1877) and IV (1881) of the *Ephemeris Epigraphica*. In the meantime, elsewhere smaller collections of inscriptions were being published which were distinct from the *CIL*. For example, until his death in March 1887 W. Thompson Watkins edited occasional reports on new inscriptions found in Britain in the *Archaeological Journal* (e.g. XLV 1888: 167–86). In *The Antiquary* (XIX 1899: 135), Haverfield wrote

---

6. From this time, there are numerous examples of Haverfield publishing carping comments of Hübner (e.g. *The Antiquary* XXIV (October 1891). Elsewhere in a letter to Mommsen in the same month, Haverfield was rubbishing other Hübner opinions (Croke 47). In a catalogue of Roman sites in Sussex, Haverfield wrote; 'I have purposely omitted many references, particularly those printed by Hübner' (1888e: 434). Elsewhere, in *The Academy* (8 March 1890) he was criticizing Hübner for republishing in the *Ephemeris* (IV: 698 p. 207) a forged stamped 'Roman' tile first published by W.T. Watkins. At the same time as he was working on his plans and publications, Haverfield was also assisting others to publish (e.g. J. MacDonald's *Tituli Hunteriana* (1897–8). Another article, (On the discovery of a fourth inscribed pig of Roman lead in Derbyshire – Haverfield 1894d), is in fact two separate pieces, one by Haverfield, the other by Hübner. Finally there is the issue of the inscriptions from Chester, cf. Ch. 6).

to the editor announcing he would be continuing the series of epigraphic updates previously submitted to the *Archaeological Journal* by Watkins. We have seen how Haverfield had been in correspondence with Mommsen since at least mid-1883 and when Mommsen would have known of his interests in Latin epigraphy and his associated publications. It is also probable, if not certain, that Haverfield first met Mommsen in 1885 when he tried to see him in London. He certainly saw him in Oxford in March 1889. Before that meeting, however, he must seen Mommsen in Berlin in late 1887 or early 1888 and as a consequence of it (or an otherwise missing letter) was invited to contribute as an editor to the *Additamenta quarta ad Corpus* VII of *CIL*, a fact Haverfield advertised in the *Archaeological Review*. Along with discussions of particular groups of inscriptions, Haverfield pushed home the point by publishing in the *Archaeologia Oxoniensis* (1892) an overview, 'MS. Materials for Romano-British Epigraphy'. In the interim and as preliminaries to the *Ephemeris*, Haverfield published numerous 'periodic' statements and updates of newly discovered inscriptions in Britain and made statements correcting or reinterpreting previously published examples (e.g. *Archaeological Journal* 1890, 1892, 1893; *Classical Review* 1893, 1894). In this he was assisted by a number of friends and contacts.[7] Following on from Mommsen's invitation, Haverfield produced the fourth and fifth fascicles of the *Additamenta* in the *Ephemeris Epigraphica* (vols VII in 1892: 273–354 and IX in 1913: 509–690). The Berlin Mommsen-Haverfield correspondence shows that the process of completing the *Ephemeris* was not plain sailing. In volume VII Haverfield acknowledged debts to Bruce, Hodgkin, R.S. Ferguson, Clayton, (Rev.) J. Raine, A.W. Franks, A.H. Smith and C.R. Smith and Arthur Evans. Interestingly, there is no mention of Hübner. In volume ix, credit is accorded to George Macdonald and the deceased Mommsen with help from a number of Oxford students and others.[8] At a point not presently known, following the ninth volume of the *Ephemeris*, it was decided (perhaps by Haverfield) not to continue with the series nor to produce a revised version of *CIL* VII, leaving the question about what to do with a new edition with British scholars. The

---

7. E.g. in *Romano-British Inscriptions 1892–3* (Haverfield 1893d: 279) assistance was rendered by Hodgkin, Chancellor Ferguson, R. Blair, Pelham, Hogarth, R.H. Smith and Ramsay.

8. Those acknowledged were J.G.C. Anderson, G.L. Cheesman, D. Atkinson, T. Ashby, P. Dodd, A.L. Smith, P. Newbold and M.V. Taylor, as well as Hermann Dessau, Alfred von Domasweski and Emil Ritterling.

decision was to pursue what was to become *The Roman Inscriptions of Britain* (*RIB*), the genesis of which is discussed in Chapter 7.

Much of this summary repeats the received version of Haverfield's involvement in the *CIL*. It has Haverfield almost as a passive participant, one talent-spotted by Mommsen. Since he was so young (aged 27 or 28 years) and a 'mere' schoolmaster, the invitation was regarded by some as remarkable and a reflection of his potential, an impression which persists today: the invitation '...was a sensational compliment that led him in the long term to his (Haverfield's) appointment first to a Fellowship and then to the Professorship at Oxford' (Wilkes 2002: 127). In turn it is supposed to have stimulated further his interest in the context – the archaeology – of the material. The received version of the invitation, however, may not be entirely accurate. The earliest (extant) letters from Haverfield to Hübner start in May 1889 although Haverfield first mentioned him in correspondence with Mommsen in July 1887. Not surprisingly the invitation to Haverfield seems to have caused Hübner problems in which Mommsen had to mediate. Hübner was clearly unhappy about the situation. This leads one to suspect that Haverfield, and in turn his obituarists, might have overstated the significance of Mommsen's invitation. Confirmation of this hypothesis might be preserved in Berlin in a (draft) copy of a letter from Mommsen's Berlin residence, written in English in a second, more elegant, hand. It has no catalogue number but is dated 11/1/1889 and is addressed to Haverfield Esq. at Lancing College. While it is not known if it was sent, the contents are revealing. In it Mommsen writes:

Dear Sir,

You may be aware that the commission you kindly undertook to collect for my Ephemeris epigracal [sic] the Roman inscriptions discovered recently in Britain and not inserted in the former volumes of this periodical has given occasion to misunderstanding. Professor Hübner, the editor of our Vol. VII, believes that we intend to deprive him of his right to publish the Supplementum in the same size which in due time may be required. No such intention subsists or has ever subscribed. We agreed, as you will remember, only about the article for the Ephemeris. As I cannot ?request any publication in the said journal from Mr. Hübner, I have required your good services and I am happy to have obtained them. Please try to leave no doubt about it, that our intention is limited to the Ephemeris, and have nothing in common with the *Corpus* itself and its possible further continuation. This communication is private, if it is possible to keep out the public discussion [sic], in case of necessity you are free to use it as you think fit. Please send me a line, that you have got this letter and that you agree with its contents.

Haverfield was not joining the *CIL* as such but was merely editing a subsidiary publication. Understandably, Hübner reacted to the way a relative unknown seemed to have supplanted him. It is not surprising then that following the 'invitation', Mommsen had to write to Haverfield in January 1889 in order to clarify his duties relative to Hübner. It would then explain Haverfield's letter to the *Archaeological Review* at about the same time which was in effect a public clarification, if not stand-down on Haverfield's part, of the situation. The nature of Hübner's relationship with Mommsen has not yet been assessed and is, for example, largely ignored in Wickert's biography of Mommsen (1959–80). Knowing more about Haverfield's relations with Hübner would also be instructive. In the light of Mommsen's letter, with its undertones of conspiracy (Hübner to be left out of the picture), it cannot be coincidence that the amount of discussion between Haverfield and Mommsen concerning Hübner increased after March 1890, where Haverfield almost seems to be reporting back to Mommsen.[9] There is at least one letter in Berlin, which indicates considerable antagonism on Hübner's part. In this instance, Haverfield writes to Mommsen that even if Hübner wished to continue his work on inscriptions, still he was excluded from the 'Supplement (i.e. the *Ephemeris*?: Croke 36 – 3 April 1890). In short Haverfield profited, perhaps with a connivance, at Hübner's exclusion from the *CIL*.

It is undeniable that Haverfield used his association with the *CIL* as a means to acquiring a familiarity with other aspects of Britain's epigraphic remains. Nor was he slow to continue to advertise or exploit the fact elsewhere. In the collection of letters deposited by Charles Roeder in Manchester Public Library is a note from W.T. Arnold dated 6 March 1889. In it, Arnold writes:

> Mr Haverfield, professor at Lancing College writes to me 'Do you know anything of a lead plate – how thick? – said to be preserved by a Mr Roeder in Manchester' ...On reference to the Archaeological Journal (cf. XLIV: 125) I find the plate was found at Chester, and is mentioned by the late Mr. Thompson Watkin in his list of the Britanno-Romano inscriptions for 1886, as being in your possession. Mr Haverfield has

9. The extant correspondence between Haverfield and Hübner (viz. twelve letters and postcards) commences in May 1889 and goes down to at least November 1897. In the light of the problem created with Haverfield becoming involved in the *Ephemeris*, he seems to have written to Mommsen on a regular basis reporting his work with and, interestingly, what Hübner was up to (e.g. Croke 34, 36, 48, 67, from March 1890 to at least November 1895).

undertaken to bring out the annual list of Britanno-Roman inscriptions in the Arch. Journal which was done for many years by Mr. Watkin. He is a well-known scholar in this department and of course an entirely trustworthy and responsible person. Might I ask you to communicate with him direct …Mr Haverfield has been asked by Mommsen to edit the Britanno-Roman inscriptions found since the appearance of the 7th vol. of the Corpus for the Ephemeris Epigraphica.

This letter is loaded with all manner of questions, not least of them is how and to what extent did Arnold, a well-known (liberal) journalist and respected writer on ancient history, know Haverfield?[10] Haverfield presumably used him as the intermediary because he was a leading figure in Manchester. Whatever the answers, the letter emphasizes a number of points about Haverfield at this time. In a relatively short time, in just over a year, all by his own self-promotion, he had established his name as the conduit for the (Latin) epigraphy of Britain, a reputation which was the foundation for his subsequent career. He was now a philologist who specialized in epigraphy.

Haverfield's participation in the *CIL* had one other equally important consequence. In the conventional explanation of his development as an archaeologist, the commission is supposed to have occasioned his interest in Romano-British archaeology/British antiquarianism. According to Anderson (1919), it was only after

---

10. William Thomas Arnold (1852–1904), grandson of the Arnold of Rugby School fame, nephew of Matthew Arnold and the son of the former J.H. Newham associate, Thomas Arnold. Educated at the Birmingham Oratory and Rugby, he graduated from UC Oxford in 1876. He initially settled there in 1879 as a writer and coach, after winning the Arnold Prize for an essay on Roman provincial administration (which subsequently went into three editions as a monograph). He then joined *The Manchester Guardian* for which he worked as a journalist and reviewer. Forced by ill health to retire in 1898, he moved to London. On the basis of Arnold's later publications, much influenced by his politics ('A Gladstoneian liberal in politics, he fought with courage and consistence through the long home rule controversy of 1885–1895'), he and Haverfield must have shared a similar outlook on the outside world. Arnold retained extensive interests in history, literature and art. 'In spite of the exacting character of his work as a journalist Mr Arnold always remained keenly interested in subjects concerned with Roman history, especially provincial administration' (Shuckburgh in Arnold 1914: cf. G.S.W(ood) 1912; Montague 1907; obits. *The Times* 30 May 1904 and *The Manchester Guardian* 30 May 1904).

Mommsen's invitation that Haverfield's interest in Roman Britain really developed and in particular with its archaeology.

> The impression that the remains of ancient Bath had made on his boyish imagination was still strong (Haverfield had been brought up there as a boy). To his more mature intelligence a much wider vista was now opened up. Here was a definite bit of work to be done and he felt more and more drawn to the doing of it. Thus it came about the scholar and the historian developed into the archaeologist. His study of Roman inscriptions broadened into a study of Roman forts and roads and 'villa', of pottery and fibulae and of the host of 'minor' objects which to him were full of possibilities as links in the chain of evidence (Macdonald 1919–20a: 478–9; cf. 1924: 21; Bosanquet 1920: 138).

This summary again requires qualification. In fact, although his interest at this time was no more than a hobby, Haverfield acknowledged a real interest in antiquities when he was a schoolboy. At that time, a major influence was Henry Scarth, a cleric who had been once based in the area before Haverfield's father preached at Bathwick and who was the author of an influential book about Roman Britain (Bruton 1919; cf. Chapter 1). Later on Haverfield's explorations went further afield (Haverfield 1919a: xxiii; Macdonald 1924: 17).[11]

The return to Oxford

Whatever might have happened between Haverfield and Mommsen and Hübner around 1888–9, it was on the back of his work in the period 1885–91 that Haverfield returned to Oxford in 1892, and to Christ Church as Senior Student (as its fellows were known).[12] His obituarist in

---

11. An anecdote links Haverfield with Roman inscriptions as far back as *c*.1880. According to Houlder (2005), Haverfield was in the vicinity of Castleford in that year when two fragments of a Roman milestone were dug up. He prevented the discoverer from breaking them further by purchasing them and then tried to have them placed in a local museum. When his offer was rebuffed, Haverfield presented them to the Leeds Philosophical Society who displayed them in their own museum until the collection was handed to the Leeds city museum service. Haverfield subsequently reported the milestones, later to become *RIB* 2273/2274. There seems to be some confusion about the publication of this milestone. The entry in *RIB* has at least one notice in the *Proceedings of the Leeds Philosophical Society* 78 (1897) but Bonser (1964) has it as *Roman Milestone found at Castleford* in the *Publications of the Thoresby Society* 9 (1899): 97–8.
12. Ironically, the moment of his return was temporarily delayed. Through 1892 an influenza epidemic swept Britain claiming, among its victims in January

The Times (2 October 1919) reports that prior to this, his Oxford friends were '...always trying to bring him back ...' Winning the Conington Prize in the previous year for a dissertation about classical learning may have assisted the return. The return did not reduce his energetic proselytizing and visits nor did harm to his reputation. In 1897–8 James Macdonald, father of Haverfield's later co-worker and literary executor George Macdonald, oversaw the first attempt to publish an illustrated critical commentary of the inscriptions held by the University of Glasgow in its Hunterian Museum, the *Tituli Hunteriani* (Keppie 1998a). In this work, Macdonald *père* was assisted extensively by Haverfield, so much so that an anonymous reviewer noted how the author '...has had the assistance from the ubiquitous Mr Haverfield (ubiquitous wherever Roman remains occur)' (*Archaeol J* LV (1898): 199–201 at p. 200). At Christ Church, Haverfield's duties included the librarianship and the junior and senior censorships during which he acquired something of a reputation as a disciplinarian. He also produced a series of descriptions of the colleges' architecture, history and paintings.[13] In other words there was not much experience in higher administration or aspects of it which required interaction and a degree of tact and diplomacy. In May 1907, the year of his marriage, on the death of Pelham and while on his honeymoon in Italy, he was elected to the Camden professorship which necessitated a move to Brasenose (*The Times* 22 May 1907).[14]

Prince Albert Victor, the Duke of Clarence. The epidemic plagued the country for the rest of the year and meant that the new academic session at Oxford was postponed for ten days. For reforms of the Christ Church studentships which occurred in the same year that Haverfield returned to Oxford, and when the college chose '...to revise its statutes to permit the election of ordinary fellowships by nomination of independent researchers as well as university professors and readers'; cf. Engel 1983: 265.

13. As College Librarian (1904–08) he was responsible for updating the College's music catalogues (http://www2.chch.ox.ac.uk/library/music/page.html). Continuing the musical link, Haverfield also donated an antique clarinet to the Ashmolean. Paradoxically his college publications started to appear as he was about to leave for Brasenose; *Brief Guide to the Portraits in Christ Church Hall, Oxford* (1904, with subsequent editions): Note on a detail in the architecture of Christ Church and Note on the date of part of the great quadrangle of Christ Church, Oxford. *Proc Soc Antiqs London*[2] XII (1909) and XXIII (1910).

14. Haverfield's marriage is a difficult subject about which to write. He married Winifred Ethel Breakwell, born *c.*1879. She was 'sometime scholar of Somerville College', then the university's only women's college, founded in 1879. Educated at Durham College of Science, she went up to Oxford in

The provision for archaeology at Oxford at the end of the century
Haverfield's return to Oxford in 1892 came at a crucial time in the university's history. We have seen that the consequences of the reforms started in the mid-nineteenth century were starting to generate other effects there towards the end of the century; have explored the provisions for instruction in archaeology there up until the end of the same century; and in particular its general relationship to the structure of the degree of *Literae Humaniores*. One of the implications of these reforms was that archaeology was on the rise and continued to be so. We now move to examine how the discipline evolved from the 1890s onwards, from about the time of Haverfield's return to the university. By the time of his death some thirty years later, the subject was beginning to show signs of taking root. That it had managed to do so was the happy outcome of a number of developments coming together in that period. Looking at the two developments (the general trend in the university and Haverfield's return), it is tempting to link the two, as some have done. In reality the developments that occurred through the 1890s were due to separate issues and the contribution of others rather than Haverfield.

One of these developments was the progressive undermining of the primacy of classics in the undergraduate degree *Literae Humaniores*. With the slowly eroding status of classics and the rise of ancient history as a separate subject late in the century, the discipline one would expect to have profited is archaeology. It is indisputable that archaeology

---

1899 and graduated with a BA, III Class in 1903 where she has specialized in mathematics. In the 1901 census she is recorded as domiciled at Jesmond, Newcastle upon Tyne, where her profession is unrecorded. Judging from the address on a letter written from Leamington Spa and addressed to Charles Roeder, their courtship might have gone back to at least October 1906 and where her parents eventually resided. She and Haverfield married in April 1907. The age difference was Haverfield's 46 to her 28 years. To some, his decision to marry was surprising and there are comments to the fact that it took him some time to adjust to the change (e.g. Macdonald 1924: 24). Then there is also the curious clause in Haverfield's will of 1911 with respect to the disposal of their joint possessions. She was, at the time of her death, described as a tutor at St. Hugh's College, Oxford (cf. Ch.9). It was shortly after his appointment that a Decree of Convocation at Oxford '...prescribed that the Camden Professor should lecture mainly on Roman History while to the newly found Wykeham Chair was assigned the History of Greece and Greek Lands' (22 February 1910; cf. Stuart Jones 1943–4: 190).

benefited from the improvements then being made to the Ashmolean Museum, but these did little for the teaching of the subject. Where change was to be effected, it would have to come from within, by interested parties making the challenge via the Board of Studies of *Literae Humaniores*. It has to be said that this challenge did not come from the fledgling archaeological fraternity or the 'new' ancient historians, although some support was lent from these quarters. Instead the attack emanated from educational reformers, some outside the university, who wanted to make the institution more relevant to the nation's practical needs. This assault was complemented by those who wanted to add to 'newer' disciplines and schools to the curriculum. Part of the failure on the part of 'archaeologists', classicists and historians to advance the cause of archaeology was the relative poverty of understanding what the subject could involve. A lecture delivered in 1890 by Montagu Burrows, (Chichele) Professor of Modern History, summarized recent innovations at Oxford which, in the speaker's opinion, were putting the university on a par with Cambridge and London as the centres for 'archaeological study' (Burrows 1890). The developments were (i) J.H. Parker's reborn Oxford Architectural and Historical Society; (ii) the 'new Oxford Historical Society'; and (iii) the university's recent creation of a readership in Medieval Palaeography. With all these innovations, Burrows connected some form of instruction being provided to undergraduates (and even ladies!) in compensation for what the university had traditionally not offered. It does not require emphasizing here, however, that two of Burrow's 'innovations' were strictly speaking non-university or collegiate, if closely linked, and that his appreciation of archaeology started with architecture and language. Classical archaeology and any other manifestation of the past was ignored, if not excluded.

We saw in Chapter 3 how the reforms of Oxford in the second half of the nineteenth century gave a fresh impetus to the introduction of new subjects and ways of teaching in the university. In the spirit of the age, these included such social sciences as the kindred disciplines, geography, anthropology and archaeology. Each of the three, however, shared the same chequered history in struggling for 'official' recognition. What each of them shared was in one-way or another a long tradition of instruction in the university. There was a momentum to establish them more formally in the late nineteenth century, itself a reflection of the shift towards the social sciences in that century and each was accorded Diploma status at about the same time.

While a Geography department at Oxford was formally constituted as late as 1896, the reasons why the subject managed to establish itself there before the other two subjects have been discussed by Scargill (1976). They lie with the fact that the subject had been taught in some way or another in its colleges since the sixteenth century. Perhaps more important was the fact that agitation and financial support for formalizing the subject came from a powerful external force, the Royal Geographical Society (RGS), which had at various times supported and part-funded posts in the university. The subject could also rely on the support of classicists and their kind who appreciated the importance of an understanding of ancient geography. In 1879 the university responded to yet another approach from the RGS to appoint a new five-year readership. The university initially proposed not to fill the readership in ancient history at Brasenose, created in 1868 but vacant since 1878, and to make the post an appointment in geography. While the university was eventually forced to withdraw its original offer and asked the RGS for assistance, practical support in this respect came from Henry Pelham and John Myres. The outcome was the appointment of H.J. Mackinder as the first Reader in Geography in 1880, a process which was to culminate in the creation of a School of Geography in 1899, in which Pelham again appears as a major supporter (Haverfield in Pelham 1911: xix). For four years, from 1891, the RGS also endowed a studentship (in reality a travel scholarship) whose recipients included George Grundy (1892) and John Beazley (1894). In its early years teaching in the department in ancient geography was offered by Grundy. With regard to anthropology, it was again classicists and historians such as Pelham and Myres who were instrumental in establishing the subject. Teaching in the subject was on offer as early as 1895 when there was an attempt to include the subject as one for examination in the Honours School of Natural Science. The attempt failed, but it did become a subject for a PG Diploma in 1905 when a Committee for its introduction was formed (Read 1906: 56). Interestingly the diploma included a large measure of what is now regarded as 'prehistory' while there was also some provision for instruction in Romano-British subjects (Clark 1989: 11). Formal instruction commenced in 1906, with its first reader E.B. Tylor, and the first examinations conducted in 1909.

In contrast to anthropology and geography, archaeology was in a weaker position. The former pair were relatively new disciplines, innovative to the point of revolutionary with fresh approaches to the study of antiquity. Archaeology, as taught at Oxford, came out of a much more traditional backdrop, that is classics and ancient history. Where archaeology came into this scheme of study was when undergraduates chose from a list of approved 'special subjects'. As a consequence of the reforms of the 1870s, in 1872 the new Board of Studies for *Literae Humaniores* '...took the decisive conceptual leap of establishing ancient history as a discipline separate from the (classical) authors listed for study.' The New Examination Statutes defined the periods for study (with a choice from two periods of Greek history and two from its Roman counterpart). What is more, the structure was still flexible enough to adapt and change. In the 1880s, criticisms of the mechanistic nature of the teaching and the predictability of the essay and examination questions led to a greater emphasis on additional subject and special subjects for outstanding students. Such changes opened the way for the introduction of more archaeological-based subjects, whether it meant classical art, sculpture or numismatics. The lack of formal instruction partly explains how and why it was difficult for 'dons' to develop formal groups or schools of 'students'. While Harrison (1994a: 89) has attributed the failure of Oxford to create archaeology as a stand-alone subject to resistance in the collegiate structure of the University, there were a number of initiatives (Currie 1994). Nor was it for want of some trying to engineer changes. But the tenor of the reforms championed by some was rather for archaeology to have a higher profile in *Literae Humaniores* rather than root and branch innovation. In the years immediately before the outbreak of the Second World War the arrival of European refugees in Oxford gave impetus to such pleas; prior to the First World War the efforts were thwarted. Therefore it was reliant on the support of open-minded scholars, in an institution where the status of classics was starting to come under scrutiny in Jowett's university. Otherwise students constructed a degree in ancient history, classics or, later on, anthropology which had to varying extent archaeological components. In Haverfield's time student engagement with the subject was even less formal. Candidates were left to their own initiative, either derived from their experience before 'going-up' to Oxford, or as part of their course of study which invariably meant classical archaeology and where the range of archaeological subjects was limited initially to aspects of Greek art and architecture.

Something approaching formal instruction in Roman and Greek archaeology filtered only slowly into the Oxford curriculum. That it occurred was through a variety of routes, most notably through the teaching of ancient history in *Literae Humaniores*. Modifications to the structure of Greats and the concomitant increase in the number of archaeological subjects offered to candidates represented a relatively gentle form of revolution. The list of subjects offered only slowly increased to include 'Roman' subjects. Surprisingly Haverfield appears not to have offered such options but they were by H.G. Evelyn White

(1907 – *The General History of Roman Britain, with Special Knowledge of the Saxon Shore and of the Civilisation and Culture of the Non-Military Area*) and G.L. Cheesman (1907 – *The Development of the Roman Frontier Defences in the Western Provinces from 70 to 211*). Haverfield's teaching at this time appears to have remained with epigraphy, assisted where possible by the likes J.G.C. Anderson. A more direct, head-on approach was to demand that archaeology be recognized as a discrete subject in the degree of *Literae Humaniores*. The question would then be what should be dropped or relegated. This was the method Percy Gardner, Professor of Classical Archaeology from 1887, tried but without much success. The reasons for Gardner wanting to change the system were a combination of subject interest coupled to dissatisfaction with the fact that the prevailing teaching arrangement of tutorials was both inefficient and merely repetitive. He was in the anti-Jowett tradition, where Gardner advocated learning for its own sake and not for the training of young minds for future public service. The prevailing system, or so he argued, deflected dons from undertaking proper research as well as excluding students from the results of that work. As part of the seeds of its own decline, the success of teaching at Oxford meant that its students tended to be inward looking in terms of their exploration of the subject. The situation was compounded by the way that from the 1890s the university was increasingly looking to produce candidates for the Indian Civil Service and its examinations. Instead of the traditional round of tutorials which, year in year out, looked at the same old problems in Greek and Roman history[15],

---

15. This tendency was also reflected in the ossification of publications from Oxford dons in this period. Their teaching '...created an academic industry based on the production of books for undergraduate teaching as much as research: the handbook, the epigraphic collection and the historical commentary became the hallmark of Oxford scholarship; a scholarship which was always better at elucidating old problems than finding new ones. It was a tradition based on ancient texts, not on the discoveries of archaeology. Great works of history, narrative or theoretical, were not forthcoming; collections of articles based on the typical conundrums of undergraduate courses were more common ...which left the subject much as before and simply served to adorn a reading list for future students. Success and strength bred parochialism; free at last from German influence, Oxford failed to see that the continental professorial tradition was yet capable of producing greater insight and originality than the conscientious grind of weekly tutorials on central topics' (Murray 2000: 342–3). A notable exception to this tendency, and one written not by an Oxford professor but somebody then at the British Museum, was Gardner's *New Chapters in Greek History* (1892).

Gardner on a number of occasions put forward proposals to introduce new Special Subjects, mainly archaeological and largely Greek in emphasis, at the expense of other Greek elements, to Greats.

According to Boardman, Percy Gardner is a seriously neglected figure in terms of the development of archaeology at Oxford. 'Gardner is not easy to judge. Anecdotes about him ...are generally unkind and they are also unfair' (1985: 46; cf. Hill 1937). The neglect is due to a variety of factors. Gardner (1846–1937) matriculated from Christ Church College, Cambridge, with Firsts in the Classical and Moral Sciences triposes (1869). In 1871 he was appointed as an assistant keeper in the Dept of Coins and Medals at the British Museum, specializing in Greek coins although he was later to drift away from the subject citing his dislike of the increased specialism that had overtaken it. The absence of any prospect resembling 'advanced instruction' (in classical antiquity) at Cambridge and later at Oxford, led Gardner to believe that the best training he received was during his time at the British Museum. At the moment of appointment there he was placed under the supervision of R. Stuart Poole, Keeper of Coins. With little or no previous exposure to 'the memorials of the past' but more concerned with the post 'merely as a means for securing financial independence' and 'hoping for leisure evenings to give to my favourite studies in philosophy and theology', Gardner was set to work on the *Catalogue of Greek Coins* then underway (1933: 26). The appointment evidently introduced him to a more rarified, scholarly atmosphere, one which encouraged original research through a combination of sound familiarity with the evidence, rigorous methods of analysis and the free exchange of ideas and the results among dedicated specialists (who happened in the main to be based in museums). 'After a few months there was no more question of merely performing routine duties, but of an ever growing interest in historical and particular Hellenic studies, an interest which indeed never eclipsed my older passion for philosophy and religious thought, but which worked in harness with it. I went to the British Museum in 1871 wearied, out of health, inclined to despondency. I left it in 1887 keen, full of health and activity, thoroughly fitted to undertake work in historic teaching and writing' (1933: 26–7). It was during his time at the British Museum that Gardner's interest shifted to 'Greek archaeology'. This was a consequence of a life-changing visit to Greece in 1877 accompanied by Charles Newton and where they saw the results of the recent German work at Olympia and Schliemann's excavations at Mycenae. He returned to the UK re-energized and with a fresh outlook on how the past might be informed by the results of archaeological research, even if this meant in the sense of art and architecture. In 1880 while continuing to hold his museum post he became the Disney Professor of Archaeology at Cambridge.

In 1887 Gardner resigned his London and Cambridge posts so that he could take up the new Lincoln Chair of Classical Archaeology at Oxford. Here Gardner was regarded as both a difficult character and something of a maverick. The impact of his mainstream research interests (Greek numismatics and vases) and in general the way archaeology was helping to rewrite Greek history were diminished by his writings on the unpopular subject of evolutionary Christianity, its psychological basis and historic origins (e.g. *Exploratio Evangelica* (1899)). He was, however, seen as an organizer and 'doer'.[16] If he was not regarded as a good teacher, his scholarship had the reputation for being meticulous and methodical (Hill 1937: 464). His appointment to the Lincoln chair was linked with the newly reorganized Ashmolean Museum. He was also a great pamphleteer. In this capacity he petitioned and cajoled the university authorities for more funds so as to add to its collection of sculptural casts and to embellish the museum's library and photograph collection.

One of the reasons why Percy Gardner is such a significant figure in the development of archaeology at Oxford is because his were the most serious attempts to promote it in the curriculum. His efforts, however, were not to come to much. He claimed that on at least three occasions his attempts to integrate his subject into *Literae Humaniores* were thwarted (Gardner 1933: 59). He believed that although the suggestions were supported by senior members of the School's Board, his proposed expansions, submitted in 1890, 1898 and 1900 were vetoed by a group of (junior) academic reactionaries known as 'Young Oxford' and focused on the Non-Placet Society who constituted the majority of the Board. That the opposition could rally its case Gardner believed was due in large part to the structure of the university and its propensity to create (large) committees to '...determine matters, and so diminishing the responsibility and initiative of individuals ...I fancy that a large proportion of Oxford teachers, whatever they might say, rather enjoy attendance at Boards and Committees. The overlapping and the waste of time are beyond dispute; but on the other hand, if the Heads of Departments are languid and inert, Committees may keep those Departments up to their work. Autocracy or Bureaucracy: it is a very old

---

16. For all his liberal interests and politics, in 1896 Gardner opposed the admission of women students to full membership of the university (Gardner 1933: 67–8, 72–3; cf. Hill 1937; Boardman 1985; obit. *The Times* 19 July 1937).

dispute ...It was really a protest against the inertia which I found always one of my most serious foes' (1933: 71–2).

At the moment of his appointment, Gardner had to teach mainly on the history of Greek and Roman monuments and their aesthetic qualities but soon came to concentrate on Greek sculpture. The shift from numismatics to sculpture is reflected in the pattern of his publications. During his time at the British Museum he came to specialize, without any previous instruction, in Greek numismatics and was the principle researcher for a number of catalogues of the museum's collection. The change explains his efforts in the first place to centralize the university's collection and then to improve its collection of casts and other copies of ancient art. The introduction of a paper on Greek mythology in 1890 (what he called 'elementary instruction in archaeology' (Gardner 1933: 60) was the result of a private pamphlet (*Classical Archaeology at Oxford* (1899); Boardman 1985: 47–8). In 1890, in response to his agitation, the university set up a committee 'on Professor Gardner's motion', with Pelham and Lewis Farnell as members. The committee recommended the introduction of a special subject on Greek sculpture in Hons. Mods. and that classical archaeology be made available in Greats as special subjects in the final examinations (e.g. Greek mythology and art) as an alternative to either modern philosophy or Roman history. The former recommendation was passed but what happened to the latter is unknown (Murray 2000: 350). Gardner, following his decision to focus on the teaching of Greek sculpture, later decided to give up the teaching of prehistoric Greek art in preference to his 'friend' and 'student', J.L. Myres, with Gardner concentrating on classical Greece. Later still, in 1914, Guy Dickins was appointed as Lecturer in Classical Archaeology when Gardner was finding it increasingly difficult to keep pace with advances in the subject.

The resistance to the introduction of archaeology at Oxford led Gardner to revise his line of attack and to try and engineer changes from the bottom up. This meant its introduction at school level. In 1900, with his brother Ernst, he spoke to the Headmasters Conference.[17] This outcome of the discussion between university teachers of classical archaeology and a sub-committee of the Headmasters Conference was a pamphlet, the purpose of which was to provide an informed catalogue of teaching aids so to assist in the better instruction of archae-

---

17. Ernst Gardner (1862–1939) Gaius and Gonville College, Cambridge; First student at the British School of Archaeology at Athens, excavating in Egypt, Cyprus and Greece and Yates Professor of Classical Archaeology at UC London (1896).

ology in the nation's (public) schools (Gardner 1902a). Gardner's advocacy of the teaching of the subject at school level was in part a desire to strengthen the movement to have the subject introduced into the universities where more and better instructors might be produced.[18] The argument was presented to the schools because Gardner believed that changes at Oxford would only result, not if Oxford was reformed but by increasing the sense of expectation and competence of students while they were at school. Referring to the way the German education ministry took '..students who show aptitude for archaeological studies (were) furnished with the means of spending 2 or 3 years in the archaeological schools of Rome or Athens, where they pass to appointments at home', he also conceded that while the British Schools in the same cities were functioning '...it is exceedingly difficult to keep up a supply of students for them with adequate preliminary teaching.' The pamphlet also defined the meaning and so explained the merits of studying 'the methodical or scientific knowledge of the outward and visible side of Greek and Roman civilization; and more particularly the light to be gained in regard to that civilization by the study of its extant remains, architectural, artistic and individual' (p. 5).[19]

While Gardner's initial efforts where not entirely successful, one outcome was a number of other public utterances. Another pamphlet was his *Oxford at the Cross-Roads,* a critique on the structure of *Literae Humaniores* (Gardner 1903; Engel 1983: 215). In this Gardner returned to the attack on the practical vision of a university education where he advocated the emphasis should be on learning for learning's sake against the prevailing attitude of training for a career. However he was later to acknowledge '...the book on the whole missed its mark: it did not fit in with any great current of Oxford opinion' (Gardner 1933: 72). Gardner's ideas were not only received coolly at Oxford, but also resulted in an acrimonious public dispute with T.E. Page, schoolmaster of Charterhouse (1873–1910) and a member of the Classical Association from 1904 (Rudd 1981). At the Association's AGM in 1903, Gardner

---

18. I.e. 'It is a misfortune that the rigid examinations system of Oxford and Cambridge oblige them (students) to select certain branches of archaeology, and exclude others from the course' (p. 9); 'the persistent neglect of the subject (Classical Archaeology) in English universities meant a shortage of schoolmasters for the schools' (p. 20).

19. We might note how Gardner's definition of classical archaeology did not mention Roman Britain, an impression reinforced by the emphasis his bibliography places on monographs etc. on work in Greece, Italy (especially Rome) and the Orient.

called for a greater rôle for the study of (classical) art and architecture in secondary education. The acrimony commenced when Gardner was attacked by Page in a letter to *The Times*. The crux of Page's criticisms was that he disliked what he regarded as faddism in education, an abhorrence that went as far as deploring the use of illustrated lectures. In particular he disliked the idea of specialism in teaching which detracted from a broader appreciation of the world of classical antiquity and especially at the cost of its literature (*The Times* 24 December 1903; Stray 1998: 206. Haverfield had been using slides at the Society of Antiquaries since 1892, as well as three-dimensional maps). Gardner's response to Page's complaints was published in the same newspaper five days later and when he insisted that Page should not regard archaeology as a rival to the classics but as an ally. This was followed up with another letter from Gardner (*The Times* 4 January 1904), in which he explained some of the problems he had encountered in trying to teach schoolboys about archaeological research. Later on, in 1914, Gardner proposed to replace Greek prose at Oxford with Greek archaeology, a move opposed by Grundy who put up an argument for a Diploma in Classical Archaeology. The proposal was revived in 1907 by Gardner (with Farnell and Myres, both Greek 'archaeologists') supported by Pelham, Bywater, Grundy, Warde Fowler, How and Tod. Haverfield's support, however, was more lukewarm. Indeed in December 1906, he wrote to Gardner about what he thought of archaeology as a subject for instruction. While we do not have Gardner's initial enquiry or his response to Haverfield's opinions, what Haverfield had to say is informative. It appears Gardner suggested establishing a university School of Archaeology. But Haverfield would have none of it.

> I do not think I should object to you drawing a line between history & archaeology, if only you would draw one also between art & archaeology. To my thinking there are several subjects of great importance which can be ranked side by side, history, art, theology, law etc. each of these (practically speaking) is suited to be the domain of a 'School'. Archaeology is not one of these. It is a group of subjects, some epigraphic, some anepigraphous, some half & half, which find their common element in that they all require a more or less similar method of study – inscriptions, coins, sculpture, vases, artistic & in-artistic – All of these lie outside the ordinary literary (& aesthetic) methods of work in all sorts of ways, in which some other ancillary studies like palaeography do not, and possess (as I said) a sort of unity. They seem to me to be collectively denoted by a bad word, Archaeology. None of them, practically speaking, is fitted to belong to a 'School' – a Final School in Archaeology would not (to my thinking) hop [sic] even with the other 'Schools'. But bits of them may be introduced (conveniently, if illogically) into 'Schools', while the whole

might form the multiplex subject of a more or less Postgraduate course, called Diploma or what you like (16 December 1906: *Bodleian Ms Eng. Lett. c. 55 fols 75–6*).

Evidently forgetting Grundy's earlier suggestion, Gardner was to claim he was instrumental in the creation of the Diploma of Archaeology at Oxford (Gardner 1933: 60), but it took some time. The diploma was formally instituted in 1909 and the first candidates, including V. Gordon Childe and Joan Evans, Arthur Evans' stepsister, examined in 1910. Haverfield's response to Gardner's proposal is surprising given the way he had been trying to advertise the need for a better standard of teaching and training in the study of British antiquity in the 1890s as well as for University reform. For instance, Haverfield's opinions seem inexplicable when, in July 1907, he was a signatory to a letter addressed to the Editor of *The Times* calling for reform at Oxford. Of the sixteen signatories, at least seven might be regarded as ancient historians-archaeologists.[20] The gist of their demands were:

- the constitution and machinery of the university required revision
- that relations between the university and its colleges, constitutionally and financially needed modification
- 'a central direction of our studies required enabling the Faculties to the authority to them in other seats of learning'
- that studies in the university were too narrow 'in scope and that fresh endowments of various branches are necessary, and especially that a greater encouragement should be given to research which at Oxford is probably to a larger extent divorced from teaching than in any other great University'

In short they wanted at least another Royal Commission to look at the structure and workings of the university. Haverfield's relatively negative comments on the independence of archaeology as a subject also sit rather uncomfortably with his (then better known) support of the School of Geography at Oxford. But at least his opinions were consistent. His letter to Gardner was not out of the ordinary. On a number of other occasions he made comments about the unfashionable, difficult limitations of the subject. For example, in a lecture on Roman Yorkshire delivered at the annual general meeting of the RAI in York in July 1904 it was reported:

---

20. That is A.J. Evans, L.R. Farnell, P. Gardner, Haverfield, D. Hogarth, R. Macan and J. Myres.

Mr. Haverfield said the subject of Roman Britain was not very popular, on account of it being difficult and distant. It was difficult because it involved the study of the whole Roman Empire, because during the last fifty years the study of that empire had expanded with amazing rapidity, and was hard to keep up with the development. It was also a distant subject. Do what they would, Roman remains never came home like medieval life. We felt indistinctly that between us and the Romans there was a great gulf fixed, that we could not make a national hero of Caratacus, and unless the question was one of local topography, the consideration of Romano-British life seems a far off alien study. The state of things, he thought, would not last long, because of the growth of Imperial sentiments in England would soon awaken an interest in other Empires (Haverfield 1903f: 382–3).

In contrast Haverfield was more positive about the prospects of Roman archaeology. In a lecture to the Lancashire and Cheshire Antiquaries Society he commented on the rise of Roman frontier studies and attributed it to a drift to the study of the Roman provinces, itself due, in part, to Mommsen 'in his last and perhaps his most astonishing work on the provinces of the Roman Empire' (*The Manchester Guardian* 11 January 1906).

If Gardner should be regarded as an important figure in the introduction of archaeology at Oxford, still – for all his campaigning – he retained reservations concerning its introduction and development in its broadest sense at Oxford. Sharing the same reservations with others, while welcoming the use of archaeological investigation (especially in Greece), he regretted the trend:

> ...to study prehistoric art of the Aegean rather than historic Greek art. It is of course an immeasurably easier task. It avoids the great fields of Greek civilization and religion, and concentrates on an art which has to be explained by itself without literary help. Whereas one can learn in a few months all that has been published as to Aegean art, Classical art and archaeology are the work of a busy lifetime. But the former study leads only to a field hedged in, producing beautiful flowers, but furnishing no view beyond; the latter study works in with the literature of Greece, and shews the foundation of the art of the civilized world (1933: 37).

Gardner also bemoaned the tendency '...especially among the younger archaeologists, ...to extreme specialization, to take up some small plot in the wide field, and to cultivate it rather intensively than extensively. The tendency probably originated in the German universities, where the enormous output of books, and the necessity that any student who takes up a subject should read everything published in regard to it, greatly narrows the outlook of researchers. Men of wide purview ...are now extremely rare' (1933: 65). Gardner's criticism may have been directed at the growing number of 'special subjects' that university dons were offering for instruction. 'I disliked the rise of specialism in archaeological research. Not least because it made it difficult for one man to keep up with the massive progress then underway' (1926: 1). At about the same time that Gardner was reminiscencing, George Hill observed that in the period *c*.1900–10 there arose an interest in Byzantine history and architecture. In his opinion '...[p]artly it was fostered by a suspicion, however, unwarranted, that Classical Archaeology was becoming exhausted: and this combined perhaps with a decline in the study of the classical languages and literature, sent students and amateurs further afield. Young would-be archaeologists were turning increasingly to prehistoric antiquities, a "soft option" which required little knowledge of Greek or Latin, and as to which, at the time, scientific treatment being still in a primitive stage no one could say you were wrong' (Hill 1945: 363).

In his retirement Gardner continued to lament the failure to integrate more fully (classical) archaeology into the curriculum. 'At Oxford, the Board of Literae Humaniores has repeatedly refused to allow Archaeology any place in the Final Schools. At Cambridge the recognition of the study though theoretically more generous has in practice been small' (Gardner 1926: 23). One of the reasons why he was so keen to see classical archaeology introduced more formally was that the ongoing erosion of classics meant the study of antiquity was also likely to be weakened. 'At present, it is to be feared, a day of trial for classical education has come. Modern subjects and the study of the physical sciences are pressing hard for a greater share in education. It is time to call in the reserves, to bring all our knowledge of antiquity, from whatever quarters, to bear on our teaching; to give life to ancient history by bringing its fruits before the eyes as well the minds of the young, to exhibit ancient art as a growth parallel to that of classical literature, and equally with it a guiding star for all time' (Gardner 1926: 25).

Haverfield knew Gardner, but surprisingly did not merit mention in the latter's autobiography. The only acknowledgments are a review of Hogarth's *Archaeology and Authority* (1899) and in Gardner's retrospect on 50 years progress in classical archaeology. In the former Gardner praised Haverfield's contribution on the Roman world, complimenting him on his use of inscriptions and the results of excavations on the Palatine and at Carnuntum and Hadrian's Wall (*Class*

Rev XIII (1899): 369–71). In the second work, when writing about progress in Romano-British archaeology, Gardner observed: 'I could not treat satisfactorily on Roman Britain in a couple of paragraphs; so I prefer merely to mention the great work on Roman Britain by my colleague Professor Haverfield, whose death we so greatly regret' (1926: 25). It is also curious that Haverfield, given his prominent position at Oxford and as the country's leading Roman archaeologist, does not appear to have supported Gardner's proposal, nor to have contributed in any substantial fashion to the argument between Page and Gardner on the rôle of archaeology in the (school's) teaching of classics. We might imagine, however, Haverfield would have been sympathetic to his professorial colleague against the traditionalist, purist views of the Charterhouse schoolmaster. But in truth the evidence is that Haverfield was never a supporter for the introduction of (Romano-British) archaeology at Oxford. Part of the problem was that he continued to see it as a facet of classical archaeology and Roman history and therefore a part of *Literae Humaniores*. It was not worthy of independent study. Indicative of this attitude is a lecture J.L. Myres delivered to an American audience in 1915, *The Provision for Historical Studies at Oxford,* in which he summarized what was offered in his university with regard to archaeology and classical antiquity between 1913 and 1915 (summarized as Appendix 4 below). One of the striking features of the list, compared to the modern era, is the variety of teaching that dons were expected to cover, not least Haverfield who offered courses ranging from ancient (Roman) history to the geography of Britain whereas Roman Britain as a separate subject is correspondingly slight. Curious too is the fact that epigraphy, neither Latin nor that of Britain, did not feature significantly in Haverfield's portfolio.

What Gardner's and Myres' observations demonstrated was that archaeology (least of all its Romano-British form) would never really be established in the Oxford curriculum until the opposition to its wider instruction to undergraduates was overcome. Until this happened, student exposure to the discipline was going to be limited with the effect that there could not be created specialists or those familiar with the discipline, who could in turn teach the subject, and so bring on a new generation. Instead the prevailing arrangements guaranteed the teaching of the same 'old' subjects. As Gardner said and Myres implied, opposition to change, somewhat surprisingly, came from younger dons (from a group one would have thought would have been more sympathetic to innovation). Their opposition was based on the wish to obtain and protect their college positions. Where and when changes came, it was with the rise of disciplines which did not, in the first instance, impinge on the primacy of classics and ancient history in a way that archaeology was being sold to them. This meant that geography and (social) anthropology had a relatively easier acceptance. Nor is it coincidental that those who came to champion the cause of archaeology and its better integration at Oxford, owed their sympathies either to gaining their archaeological training outside of Oxford (and Cambridge: e.g. Ramsay, Evans, and Gardner), and/or through their exposure to the ancillary subjects (Myres, Grundy, Marett, Farnell etc.). One other contributory development to the cause was the inception and establishment of the Craven fellowship and the encouragement it gave to travel and research overseas, and in doing so, broadening the horizons of the holders.

With regard to research degrees at Oxford at this time, the situation was no better for graduate students. Not only was there the absence of formal training at first degree level, but during most of Haverfield's lifetime there was even less provision for advancement at postgraduate level. J.L. Myres summarized the situation in 1915 when he tried to explain the peculiarities (and indirectly the inadequacies) of Oxford's recruitment of postgraduate students and their supervision. In the first place the structure of *Literae Humaniores* did not assist. Secondly there remained the issue of the university's statutes and its relations with the colleges.

> Oxford degrees are conferred solely on the double qualification of residence and profiency. The University keeps no register of attendance at courses, and expects no reports from lecturers. For flagrant misconduct, either the University or the residential college to which a student belongs may suspend his residence, and thereby postpone the completion of his degree course, perhaps indefinitely; and Colleges sometimes suspend for flagrant idleness. In theory ...students have complete freedom to attend what courses they please. If their choice is restricted, it is as a matter of College discipline only (1915: 111–12).

Myres alluded to another, perhaps more relevant, problem with respect to postgraduate research at Oxford. As was becoming tradition there, good graduate students were increasingly retained in college positions as teachers of one form or another. These appointees would be delegated what Myres regarded as an overload of teaching. Because 'teachers' were not given the opportunity to develop research specialisms, their teaching tended to be repetition of what they had been taught as undergraduates. Again the burden of teaching meant they too were not encouraged to innovate.[21] As archaeology at this time comprised such a minor part in the degree of *Literae Humaniores*, with its emphasis on classics, ancient history and philosophy, there was little prospect that the vicious cycle of the same old subjects being taught being broken. 'This deficient organization of antiquarian studies leads directly to overlap and duplication in the favoured subjects. This is conspicuous in Ancient History where our habits of teaching a few limited periods with intimate reference to great historical texts has led us to neglect those periods of history for where the texts are less valuable as literature' (p. 14). To make the point, Myres could cite how, up to 1915, Greek history was oversubscribed with tutors offering courses based on Herodotus and Thucydides against only two courses for all later Greek history. The fact, according to Myres, that Oxford encouraged its students to travel meant that, in many cases, their exposure to the results of foreign research, caused many potentially valuable postgraduates to study elsewhere, exacerbating the problems at Oxford.

Until the First World War, the only 'higher' research degrees open to graduate students were the BLitt/BSc introduced in 1895 (Levine 1986: 157; cf. Woodward 1967: 29). Prior to this, one '...simply "stayed on for future study" in a predominantly undergraduate college, working with a professor or with a senior member whose prime loyalty lay to his undergraduates' (Harrison 1994a: 89). Myres regarded the new degree as commensurate in standing to the PhD degree awarded by foreign universities. A candidate for the Oxford degree did not have to undertake any formal course of instruction but prepared a dissertation under supervision. But the candidate's supervisor (of any rank in the University) was not expected to give formal instruction to his charge. Instead he only had to be satisfied that the candidate was making good use of his time and that he was adequately supported.

---

21. Arnold Toynbee recounted a story where, in 1911, he had tried to 'convert' his slightly older contemporary and mentor G.L. Cheesman, another Haverfield associate, to at least an interest in Byzantine history: 'To his [Toynbee's] surprise and discomfiture, his confident approach was met by his friend [Cheesman] with a vehement refusal that would have been becoming in a conscientious novice bent on qualifying for admission to a rigorous monastic order ...The apprentice tutor's [Cheesman] hostility explained that his manifest duty, now that he had obtained his appointment as a don, was to concentrate on the task of mastering the particular subject for the teaching of which he had made himself responsible to his college. Now that he had found the confines of his intellectual province, "pastures new" were henceforth out of bounds for him' (1954: 30).

There were however relatively few takers. The university introduced another higher degree in 1900. The DLitt, determined by established candidates' published work (or as it was put, 'professional efficiency, based on solid contributions to learning via published and approved work' – Myres 1915: 10), was about as unsuccessful. It was normally awarded ten years after matriculation and by the submission of books and papers. At least in the early years, it was therefore really open to Oxford staff and graduates whose professional advancement did not necessarily require such recognition. It was for these reasons that the degree of DPhil at Oxford was not formally instituted until 1917 and only then as a result of influences from the United States (Elton 1955: 94, 113; Engel 1983: 265; Winter 1994: 15). Pre-First World War most US graduate students were going to Germany for advanced study to obtain the degree of *philosophiae doctor* (or PhD) because Oxford was incapable of understanding or was not prepared to recognize the first degree awarded by most American institutions. They would only come to Britain/Oxford if it offered a degree commensurate with the German/US PhD. As the prospect of a BLitt was not sufficient and because they were excluded from the DLitt, in 1916 the proposal for a doctoral degree was made in order to redirect such students. The suggestion was accepted with the proviso that the title of the degree, in order to distinguish it from its German counterpart, should be the DPhil (Currie 1994: 125). The degree was to be awarded after the submission of a supervised thesis, following a prescribed period of study. But even with the introduction of the new degree still there were some senior academics who rejected the idea of organized post-graduate research (e.g. Grundy in the *Oxford Magazine* 8 December 1916, 26 January and 26 February 1917; Oman 1941; Currie 1994: 125ff.). The 'opposition' justified itself with arguments that 'motivated students' worked for themselves to acquire knowledge and to write about it rather than relying on 'organized' programmes of research (e.g. as typified by Charles Oman; Robertson 1946: 301). Whatever, by the time that these innovations took affect, Haverfield was effectively not in a position to contribute or to benefit.[22]

---

22. Even then he seems not to have been overly impressed with the introduction of a (higher) degree by a specific period of study. Of S. Gsell's *Essai sur le règne de l'Empereur Domitian* (1894), originally a 'thèse de doctorat', he opined: 'The writer of such theses (we have them or something like them in England) seems to me to be liable to one of two errors. They are apt either to aim at the fabrication of epochs and the sonorous disclosure of sweeping novelties, or they painfully concentrate labourious attention on some possibly "corrector" view of insignificant trifle. In either case, in the desire to be original, they reveal their inability to grasp the proportions of things and to master the matter which forms their subject' (*Class Rev* VIII (1894): 373).

Before the shift to establishing postgraduate degrees, there was one other way for dons to develop a cadre of students. By the turn of the century, Haverfield's pre-eminent position as the authority on Roman Britain would have made him the obvious focus for students going up to Oxford who had an interest in a form of archaeology that owed more to the antiquarian tradition than formal instruction. In the first instance, he could cultivate students from his own college (e.g. Thomas Ashby at Christ Church), and later on might cast his net wider. In addition to Haverfield attracting students, there seems to have been an element of him talent-spotting likely students. This was not unusual for the time, as Maurice Bowra was to recount in the years after the First War (Bowra 1966: 120). Into this category came such Haverfield associates as John Garstang. Another important medium by which 'students' made contact with 'mentors' was by the 'old school network', an arrangement reinforced by the fact that certain (English) public schools retained, for historical reasons, close links with specific colleges. Schoolmasters too might recommend students to their college and/or particular dons, while the colleges might also actively canvass the schools, as D'E. Firth (1954) recounts happened with Winchester and New College. Indeed with regard to Haverfield, the most important connection was that between Winchester and New.[23] Through this association Haverfield, as a Wykehamist, was introduced to Thomas Ashby and G.L. Cheesman. And finally there were instances of promising Oxford undergraduates being referred to him, as was, for example, Leonard Woolley.

Outside of formal instruction, there were a number of extra-curricular activities by which students could engage with archaeology. One of the main sources was via the societies that existed within the university. For instance, we have seen that in 1860 the former Society for Promoting the Study of Gothic Architecture was reinvented as the Oxford Architectural and Historical Society. But both these organizations were extra-curricular and were concerned with the medieval and later architectural and literary sources of Oxford (Burrows 1890). In 1870 the Oxford Philological Society was established by D.B. Munro of Oriel, which consciously included ancient history and archaeology in its remit. It published its own transactions (1879–1910) but evidently faded away in the 1900s. Percy Gardner claimed that he, along with Arthur Evans

---

23. This link goes back to the two establishments sharing a mutual founder, William of Wykeham, who established New College in 1369 and Winchester in 1373 (cf. Harvey 1982; D'E. Firth 1954).

and Lewis Farnell (and so post-1895) reconstituted the Society in an attempt to broaden its appeal.

> It was decided that the presidency should be annual, not permanent, that the meetings should be more frequent and that the scope of the papers should be classical philology in the broadest sense. In fact we formed on a small scale, limited to our own University, an institute of classical learning, with three sections, history, philology and archaeology, each of which subjects was to be represented in the papers read each term. We hoped that the classical Professors and tutors would enter warmly into the project, and give the Society the benefit of any discoveries they might make in the course of their reading and lecturing (1933: 45).

While Gardner believed the reinvention of the society was a success, he acknowledged that its reception was impaired by the fact Oxford 'teachers' were too immersed in their own research combined with their tendency to attend only those papers which had a special interest for them. The Oxford Ancient History Society of 1874 was '...to encourage research and to introduce the best undergraduates to it.' It functioned until 1893 (holding 57 meetings). Founded by Pelham, it was largely driven by Charles Oman. It again attempted to integrate ancient history and archaeology. It amalgamated with the Philological Society in 1893. In 1908 Haverfield tried to launch a new set of informal meetings for senior members of staff and the better undergraduates, but it is not known if this initiative ever succeeded (Murray 2000: 345–6). Students could, from 1919, supplement their interest and engagement with practical archaeology with involvement in the university's archaeological society, started by E.T. Leeds, H.H. Sutherland and D. Harden (Frere 1988: 1).

The Ashmolean Museum and Arthur Evans

Gardner's ability to campaign for the cause of archaeology at Oxford was strengthened by the evolution of another non-collegiate institution into a major centre for the study of classical antiquity (Murray 1904; MacGregor 1997a and b; 2001; Ovenell 1986; White 1994; Whiteley 1997; Clark 1989: 6–7). Indeed, he was to be a significant participant in its development. What was to become the Ashmolean Museum of Art and Archaeology at the university owed its origins to the bequest in 1683 of Elias Ashmole's collection of antiquities, itself incorporating the Tradescant's collection of curiosities and rarities. At that time, Ashmole's collection was housed in a specially constructed three-storied building close to the Sheldonian Theatre. In the subsequent centuries the original collection was added to and embellished by further gifts, benefactions and bequests which were curated by a keeper, a position again initiated by Ashmole. Ashmole's intention in making his bequest and the university's plans were that it was to be '...an institution designed for the study of natural philosophy, with a laboratory superbly equipped for experimental research, with a magnificent lecture hall, and with a museum of objects close at hand to aid and illuminate these studies' (Ovenell 1986: 25). In time the duties of the keepers and the organization of the collection along with its management were slowly but progressively more precisely defined. By the mid-nineteenth century the Ashmolean collection represented a large and under-used, if not moribund, resource of disparate material, variously acquired by and scattered throughout the university. At the same time, the collection suffered in comparison to other developments in the Broad Street building where the collection was then housed and where there was also teaching of chemistry and philosophy, as well as the exhibition of specimens for the display in mineralogy, geology and palaeontology (MacGregor 1997a: 598).

The arrangements for the museum were substantially changed in the latter half of the century and were linked with the progress of (classical) archaeology in the university. Up to that time, the collection comprised a pot-pourri of elements; archaeological and antiquarian, artistic, ethnographic, geological and palaeontological, flora and faunal. By then the collection was too large and, with the developments in new academic disciplines, notably the social sciences and anthropology, parts of the Ashmolean were removed to new locations. But the Ashmolean's centrality to these developments was not established. So much so, the Bodleian Library between 1855 and 1866 acquired possession of its books and manuscripts and the coin and medal collection, but declined to take the assemblage of artefacts. Elsewhere, in 1863 what was then considered to be the natural science collection was moved to a new science museum. The next significant step was the creation of a museum with a focus on archaeological objects. This transition was the achievement of the keepers J.H. Parker (1870–84) and his successor Arthur Evans (1884–94), and according to himself, Gardner.

John Parker (1806–1884) was originally an Oxford bookseller with Italian connections who had the time and money to indulge in his passion, medieval architecture. After moving to Rome in 1866 and publishing a number of studies on medieval architecture – which were rubbished in review by the likes of Pelham (Riddell 2004). Parker returned to become a leading figure in the Oxford Architectural and Historical Society (cf. Chapter 3). In time, he managed to arrange for the transfer of the society's possessions and meeting rooms to the

185

Ashmolean. Having established a foot-hold in the building, Parker then wrote to the Dean of Christ Church College, Henry Liddell, about the future of the museum and how it should now be dedicated as an archaeological and historical museum. His proposals struck a chord, so much so that in 1868 Parker applied for the museum's keepership which was about to become vacant with the promise he would make a permanent endowment to the museum (MacGregor 1997a: 604). Equally important, if not more so, Parker promised to bring with him the support of wealthy patrons and supporters. It was these facts which led to Parker's appointment in 1869 and his assumption of the keepership in 1870 along with acceptance of most of his proposals, one of which was that the museum should have a board of management made up of five visitors, including the Camden Professor of Ancient History. As soon as he entered office, Parker began his programme of changes. A series of public controversies, however, concerning the curation of objects, the competence of some of the minor staff and the prospect of major bequests in the future, notably by C.D.E. Fortnum, led to public debate and more changes. In 1878 there was a petition, signed by 132 senior members of the university, to the Hebdomnal Council for the creation of a new Museum of Archaeology and Art to house the university's collection of marbles and casts. The proposal emphasized Greek and Roman antiquities, and where it was suggested 'libraries dedicated to classical epigraphy and to numismatics …should form prominent components' (MacGregor 1997a: 605). Toward this end there was also the prospect that one of Parker's contacts, Fortnum, might deposit his collection of antiquities with the university, as long as it was not in the developing university museum. Parker's proposals were helped in 1881 when the Rev. Greville Chester of the Palestine Exploration Fund, who had been gifting antiquities to the museum since 1865, circulated a pamphlet entitled *Notes on the Present and Future of the Archaeological Collections Belonging to the University of Oxford*. Among his many complaints, Chester criticized the dispersed condition of the university's collection. His statement was followed later in the same year by Fortnum himself, now one of the Ashmolean's leading benefactors, adding to Chester's complaints.

The two attacks led to a university response in December 1881. Written on its behalf by Pelham, presumably in the capacities of Camden Professor and President of Trinity and so automatically one of the museum's Visitors, it was alert to Chester's observations and that changes were imminent. Plans were afoot to create a new professorship in classical archaeology and that the authorities, while recognizing the need for a new museum building, could not then afford it. It proposed, however, to refurbish its existing building. Finally, the university was going to establish a committee to consider the future of the dispersed nature of its collection. Following some minor hitches, by the time of Parker's death in 1884 virtually everything Pelham had promised was in place, with the new Lincoln professorship, tied to the museum, about to be filled. It was Parker's successor in the keepership, Arthur Evans, who in turn pushed through a building programme and other changes, supported at Committee level by Pelham. Evans' importance lies with his part in the rise of a form of archaeology that went beyond Oxford's traditional interest in classical archaeology, and with developments at the Ashmolean Museum. Complementing this was a massive renovation of the collection, one meant to transform it into a resource for archaeological research.

The development of the Ashmolean Museum as the focus for the study of archaeology in the university was linked with the parallel decline of the university's galleries (Whiteley 1997). The independence of the art collection, previously guaranteed by the office of the curator, was diminished in 1884 when the management of the collection was supplemented by the appointment of an additional six curators. The change was occasioned by the rise of classical archaeology within the university and in particular the creation of the new professorship in the subject; held first by William Ramsay and then Percy Gardner. Gardner, again supported by Pelham, wanted to develop the galleries' collection of casts and other copies of representative examples of ancient sculpture, not so much for the purpose of display or the aesthetic appreciation but for the purposes of teaching and instruction (Gardner 1933: 57). It has been said that Gardner regarded this part of the Ashmolean as a facet of ancient history and not so much art history as history through art (*DNB* 1931–40). It was the combination of Gardner and Pelham, aided and abetted by Evans which meant that the 'influence of the archaeologists brought a change of emphasis' in the Ashmolean and art gallery. Pelham was even prepared to suggest that they charge an entrance fee to the gallery in order to reduce access to them. He also proposed to close the collections for certain times so that teaching with reference to the material might occur. Under his pushing, the fledgling Art School was removed from the gallery's basement (Whiteley 1997: 627–8).

The transformation of the Ashmolean from an under-used and under-resourced collection to an internationally renowned institution is usually credited to Parker and in particular his successor as the keeper of the collection, Sir Arthur Evans. But one of the new curators, Henry Pelham was as much a driving force. For instance, it was he who created an archaeological library in the Galleries, which in time absorbed the collection of art books. Evans' life (1851–1941) has been extensively documented, not least by his half-sister (Evans 1943; MacGregor 1997b: 7–8). Before taking a First in History at Brasenose, Evans' had visited eastern Europe and the Balkans in 1871. During this time, following in part the footsteps of his father, Sir John Evans, he developed antiquarian rather than archaeological interests. He also studied at Göttingen and later Trier. It was as a consequence of his Balkan travels that Evans junior '...became a deliberate rebel against 'classical antiquity' and against the Oxford concentration of interest upon the articulate sophisticated civilizations of classical Greece and Rome' (Faber 1957: 386). In *c.*1875 Evans met the Oxford historian Edward Freeman. Rather surprisingly, given their different backgrounds and political outlooks, a lasting friendship developed between the two which resulted in Evans marrying Freeman's daughter. The basis of their friendship appears to have been a mutual hatred of Ottoman rule in Europe. Another consequence of their friendship was that Evans' was to follow Freeman in his opposition to Oxford 'reformers' such as Benjamin Jowett. In 1878 the university considered creating an archaeological travelling studentship but with strings attached. They included knowledge of Greek and Turkish along with a period of residence in Italy, Greece or Turkey for nine months per annum, the rest of the time being based in the British Museum. In 1883, encouraged to apply for the award, Evans was reluctant to commit himself as he did not want to go to London nor wanted to learn Greek at the expense of his interests in the Balkans. Indeed he objected to the way that the studentship seemed to be focused on what he considered to be classical archaeology. His objections were articulated in a letter to Freeman in March 1883.

> ...the only objection to this restriction that can be reasonably urged is that in that case the studentship might not be called a studentship of Archaeology in general. The great characteristic of modern Archaeological progress has been the revelations as to periods and races of men about which history is silent and for prehistoric Archaeology, no European field is perhaps now more important than the unworked Illyrian one, where indeed the prehistoric Period extends in many parts almost to our own days. ...Oxford ...seems to have set itself to ignore every branch of Archaeology out of its own classical beat. To this day almost alone among universities it does not possess an Ethnological museum, nor are there so far as I know any lectures on such subjects (quoted in Evans 1943: 222).

Regarding himself an unrealistic candidate for the studentship, Evans contemplated in 1883 applying for the university's new (Lincoln)

Chair in Classical Archaeology. Again, however, he doubted if he stood much chance, feeling the appointment would be decided by a group who were not favourably disposed to his interests, and indeed to archaeology as a whole. The two most important players in this respect were Charles Newton, (first) Keeper of Greek and Roman antiquities at the British Museum, who Evans maintained had stopped him getting the studentship, and Jowett. Evans believed that the pair thought archaeology ended at the start of the Christian era and was a subject for the orient, not Europe. Faber (1957), however, has shown that Evans was somewhat disingenuous in his portrayal of the situation. In the first place, Evans cannot have been seriously considered for the chair. He had no real archaeological background, in terms of a specialism or general competence. Secondly, although discussion about the chair had commenced as far back as 1883, circumstances dictated that it was not filled until early 1885, by which time Evans had been offered the keepership of the Ashmolean Museum in succession to Parker. The new professorial post eventually went to William Ramsay who soon resigned to be replaced by Percy Gardner, a Newton protégé.

With Parker's death in 1884, Evans' application for the post of Keeper was helped by the fact that his father-in-law had recently been elevated to the Regius Chair of Modern History. Evans saw his primary task to consolidate the collection into one. In the opinion of one recent historian of the museum, he succeeded 'not only in saving the Ashmolean but in transforming it into a revitalized centre of international repute, fitted to the demands of the century to come' (MacGregor 1997a: 606). In this he was assisted by a number of other major figures in the university including Pelham and in particular the new Lincoln Professor, Percy Gardner. Evans' half-sibling was to eulogize on Pelham's support as he attempted to win battles in the university over budgets and the keepership acquiring control of the various university collections. Evans and Pelham had been contemporaries at Harrow. Pelham was to become '...a tower of strength: he had inherited from his Whig ancestors an instinct for statesmanship and the manner of a great gentleman: he had known Arthur (Evans) since their school days, and he could sift the gold from his sometimes fantastic schemes and interpret them in favourable and comprehensible terms to such people as the officers of the University Chest. To find in a man who carried such weight in the University the understanding that comes of long friendship and the sympathy that comes of a shared learning was a stroke of fortune to which Evans owed much' (Evans 1943: 283; cf. Haverfield 1907a).

Evans' work for the future of the Ashmolean commenced within six months of his appointment. In his inaugural lecture (*The Ashmolean Museum and the Archaeological Collection of the University*), he '...explained his plans to make the Ashmolean Museum an archaeological collection of European importance' (Ovenell 1986: 252) and announced a six-part scheme to improve the security of the collection and its building, to refurbish parts of the building and to reunite the collection. The process began when Evans offered to transfer to the Pitt-Rivers anthropological museum the ethnological part of his collection in exchange for the appropriate elements from other parts of the university's holdings (e.g. the coins in the Bodleian etc.). 'Evans pressed strongly his conviction that "...the juxtaposition of the Numismatic Collections with our other antiquities, is of vital importance for the sound study of Archaeology"' (MacGregor 1997a: 607). Other Evans initiatives of about this time included refurbishing the upper gallery of the Broad Street building and the consolidation of the university's collection of paintings in it. Having won these battles and improved the budget for acquisitions to enhance the collection, Evans moved to the next stage of his scheme of development. In a public lecture, *The Ashmolean Museum as a Home of Archaeology in Oxford* (1884), Evans returned to the relatively poor provisions with which he still had to work. Again he pointed out the current situation served to inhibit the possibility of gifts from benefactors and other supporters. MacGregor (1997a: 608) reports that at this time an average 2,000+ accessions per year were being made to the collection and included donations from the fieldwork of Oxford archaeologists such as D.G. Hogarth and J.L. Myres as well as Flinders Petrie in Egypt. More objects and collections were acquired either as permanent additions or as temporary loans of varying duration, including Evans' father's own collection (which the museum finally acquired in 1909 and 1927). Evans' petitioning, chivvying and general energetic proselytizing slowly took effect. By 1889 he was able to complete the creation of archaeological library in the museum, in part to compensate for the removal of borrowing rights from the Bodleian Library. The natural conclusion to this massive expansion was the inevitable petition for a new purpose-built building to house the collection. What this proposal meant was the amalgamation of the Ashmolean and the art galleries into one collection which, in turn, necessitated the construction of a new (Ashmolean) building added to the existing galleries (Whiteley 1997: 629). Again Evans was able to enhance his proposal with the possibility of support from a benefactor. This was, again, Charles Fortnum, who not only promised to put up £10,000 for the building but also the eventual accession of the remainder of his collection and library. The new building was eventually erected at the rear of the University Galleries in Beaumont Street. Not only was it to house all of the Ashmolean Collection but also to accommodate the offices of the Professor of Classical Archaeology, 'thus ensuring a closer involvement of the Museum with teaching faculty' (MacGregor 1997a: 609). The transfer was completed by November 1894 when the new Ashmolean Museum was opened. In the meantime Evans, with Gardner, continued to agitate for more resources to facilitate the growth, presentation and study of the collection. Evans' keepership of the Ashmolean collection:

> ...from moribund cabinet of curiosities to twentieth century museum which the Ashmolean had undergone was as vitally necessary as it was timely. The discipline of archaeology and art history with which it now concerned itself simply had not existed a century earlier and it is difficult to imagine how the Ashmolean could have embraced them without the complete metamorphosis which had been achieved (MacGregor 1997a: 610).

In Joan Evans' biography of her stepbrother, based to a large degree on his private papers, the impression is that, in getting the improvements for the Ashmolean, the issue was a battle of wills between Evans, egged on in part by his father-in-law, against the university's Vice-Chancellor, Benjamin Jowett. The basis for this impression was Jowett's alleged antipathy to archaeology. The facts, however, have again been reassessed by Faber (1957) who has argued that whatever his opinions about the value of archaeology as an academic discipline, Jowett recognized that it was there to stay and that if it was to be practiced properly then it required the best support. This included the new chair in classical archaeology along with better facilities. Furthermore he had appreciated these facts as far back as 1882 when he was about to enter office. Nor does consultation of the records of meetings of the Ashmolean Museum suggest any opposition from Jowett. What Evans (and his father-in-law) perceived as opposition on his part was more to do with Jowett waiting to be persuaded of what precisely required to be done. Therefore, according to Faber, although Evans presented his arguments and machinations against Jowett as his victory, in reality, he was pushing against an open door. What is more, Evans' version of the events plays down the contribution made by others, including Gardner. Indeed Gardner's autobiography implies he saw as his task – and his achievement – upon his appointment to the Lincoln chair, first to amalgamate, consolidate and conserve-repair the university's dispersed collection of classical antiquities. Second, he had to secure a library and lecture room. In this he acknowledged the support of Pelham. It was only then, in 1893, that his plans coincided with Evans' desire to create a new museum of art and antiquities. According to Gardner, the two worked well in tandem: 'I gladly joined in the project and together we reigned, he as Keeper and I as Professor, over the new Museum, without any friction or jealously' (Gardner 1933: 59).

Ovenell's (1986) and MacGregor's (1997a; 2001) histories of the Ashmolean Museum end at 1894, at the apex of Evans' career there. By then the Ashmolean Visitors and the gallery curators were meeting together which, in reality, meant a strengthening of the archaeological component at the expense of the art collection (Whiteley 1997: 629). Following the restructuring of the university's holdings in 1908, when the separate keepership of the Universities Galleries was merged with the collections of antiquities, Evans resigned his keepership, to be replaced in January 1909 by David Hogarth as Keeper of the Antiquarium. Hogarth had been friendly with Evans for some time and is another individual with whom Haverfield must have interacted, even if the records are deficient. Evans and Hogarth travelled together in the Balkans, along with Robert Bosanquet (then known as an excavator on Crete). Hogarth and Evans were later to fall out over their respective outlooks on excavation strategies (Evans 1943: 340–2; Lock 1990). What is more significant is the way that Evans had made the Ashmolean a centre not just for the display of archaeology but also for its teaching. That this was important can be seen in Cheesman's diary of 1913 where he records his and Haverfield's classes were conducted in the museum. The importance of the institution is reflected in the fact that following the reading of his will, Haverfield's library of books and other papers was deposited in the museum (cf. Chapter 9).

The extent of Haverfield's involvement in the Ashmolean remains at present unquantified. Despite the fact that he contributed a memoir,[24] there is nothing to show how Haverfield interacted with Parker. In fact Haverfield was distant from Oxford at this time. Nor does he seem to have been as active in its management as Pelham and Gardner. What there is is much incidental evidence to link Haverfield with Evans. The two were clearly on very friendly terms. They certainly knew one another from the late 1880s, for Haverfield mentioned Evans in letters to Mommsen. Slightly later, Haverfield was describing Evans as 'my friend' (1890: 231). Elsewhere Evans' opinions were frequently sought (e.g. Haverfield 1892b). The pair co-authored an article on recent discoveries in 1893 in Berkshire (*The*

24. Cf. *Biog. Jahrb.* VII (1885): 7.

Athenaeum 26 August 1893).[25] In 1897, with Evans' permission, Haverfield published the results of Evans' (and Prof. Moseley's) excavation, twelve years previously, at the Roman villa at Frilford (cf. Evans 1897). They also dined together (e.g. Schuchhardt 1944). It is these connections which explain how Haverfield, in spite of his own lack of involvement, was able to profit from the development of its facilities and resources. In addition to using the museum's facilities for classes, with the Camden Chair came appointment as one its Visitors.

Conclusion

This chapter and those that preceded it have summarized the beginnings of Haverfield's scholarly career, from his departure from Oxford, his attempts to establish an academic credibility while otherwise employed and finally his return to the university. We have also defined the conditions of the university at that moment and have established who were his mentors and friends at the time he returned. By the end of the century there were signs that archaeology, at least in the guise of classical archaeology (as well as Egyptology and its Near Eastern counterparts), had begun to establish itself within the Oxford curriculum. In contrast, at Cambridge, the emphasis was on prehistoric archaeology as well as classical. The broader context for these developments was set out in Chapters 2 and 3. This chapter has been concerned with more of its detail. If dons involved in the instruction of archaeological teaching were not leaders in the charge for reform, there were still some who wished to advance the cause of their subject. While Haverfield has been put in the group which preferred changes to the advantage of archaeology at Oxford, he was in reality on its margins. The potential was there, but it was on the back of the work of others, whether it be prehistoric (anthropology), classical and/or Roman to develop or related subjects. Haverfield profited from such development by association rather than design. In this respect, there are two significant points to emphasize. The first is that, with regard to his work as an academic and university teacher, Haverfield's position seems contradictory. As we will see, he was largely condemnatory of the way its predominate position at Oxford had inhibited the instruction in archaeology there. Yet it is surprising how Roman Britain did not feature significantly in his teaching. Instead of this, the impression is

---

25. This was also reported in *The Antiquary* (XXVIII 1893: 161) describing the visibility, from the ground surface, of cropmarks at Long Wittenham (Berks.), which Evans and Haverfield visited.

that his main concerns were epigraphy and ancient (Roman) history. He does not appear to have been a champion, or a leading supporter, of reform in favour of the greater presence of either Romano-British studies or archaeology in general at Oxford. What is more, as we have seen, if anything Haverfield was against establishing anything that looked like a separate unit, whether a School or something else, in archaeology. Such battles were fought out by others and took time where the leading characters in this respect were the likes of the Gardner brothers, Percy and Ernest, and Arthur Evans. To be sure the status of Roman archaeology at Oxford was only confirmed with Ian Richmond's translation to the first professorship of the Archaeology of the Roman Empire in 1956, although 'improvements' in other facets of the discipline continued after the First World War. According to Currie (1994: 116), classical art and architecture came to then to feature more prominently in *Literae Humaniores* while Lewis Farnell, as the university's VC, advised classics students take a more realistic approach to the subject and that they take up archaeology. These facts are, as we will see in the next chapter, in contradiction to Haverfield's public condemnations of the failure of England's two ancient universities to advance the cause. The implications of these two features of Haverfield's career at Oxford are that the position of Roman Britain, whatever he might accomplish himself, continued to be fundamentally weak. Despite the expansion in the provision for archaeology in the university, the subject possessed no secure roots there. If things did not change, the chances were his work were going to proceed into an (institutional) cul-de-sac with regard to what he could do with it at Oxford. His work up to *c*.1910 had put his particular form of archaeology in a much stronger position at Oxford. And yet by 1920 the situation was no better, perhaps even worse, as Collingwood was to assert (1939: 120) and as the numerous obituaries about Haverfield show. The one overwhelming factor which destroyed the progress made was the outbreak of the First World War and what came with it. We can now look in greater detail at what was accomplished in the aftermath of his return to Oxford and in the light of his earlier experiences and why, in the end it went wrong. Two themes might be identified here. First, there was the rise of an ethos of graduate students gravitating around an established academic. Later on, these students were to be awarded higher degrees and college or university positions. The second theme was the better utilization of the university's resources for the teaching of classical antiquity.

CHAPTER 5

The 'mission' – on paper

Introduction
The preceding chapters have summarized the condition of (Romano-British) archaeology by the end of the nineteenth century. In this we have considered its relationship with developments in the same discipline in Europe as well as with at least one of Britain's universities and its stronger regional societies. Even before his return to Oxford in 1892, Haverfield had already appreciated the great number of weaknesses in the discipline as well as its potential strengths. Following his return, we can find more emphasis in his publications on calls for changes in the situation. The intellectual basis for the petitioning was the work of Mommsen, but while he appreciated his achievements, still Haverfield was aware of their limitations.

Mommsen and Archaeology
The implication of the preceding chapters is that Mommsen created a framework for the (future) study of the Roman empire. Into this he introduced the contribution of archaeology, with the proviso, as he understood it. There were two fundamental flaws, however, in his redefinition. First there was his comprehension of what constituted archaeological data.[1] In his case it was limited to epigraphic, and to a lesser degree numismatic, evidence. According to Percy Gardner

---

1. Mommsen never professed to be an archaeologist of any competence or necessarily to understand the results of excavation. For instance, in a letter to Haverfield (July 1894 – Croke 63) he admitted 'I sent you today a notice about the limes from a philogical [sic] point of view. I cannot cope with the curious discoveries made by our diggers'. Elsewhere (December 1899 – Croke 88) Mommsen admitted that despite the achievements of the Limeskommission in Germany, '[t]hough they call me "President" I am Limes Ignoramus' first quality.' A few years later Haverfield was to recollect that 'Mommsen, talking of some local archaeologists, once said to me: "Oh yes, we are very grateful to these gentlemen for what they send us, but we do not tell them all we think of them"' (1910b: 57).

(1933: 37), Mommsen's contribution to archaeology was the way he used numismatic evidence to illuminate ancient history. These limitations also meant that the scope of his ability to interpret the consequences of Roman imperial government was severely restricted. His problem was that he was an ancient historian and epigrapher dabbling in a discipline in which he was neither trained nor familiar with the potential of the developments in other aspects of archaeological research. Even if he was not suspicious of what the archaeologists were telling him, there was still the considerable problem that he was unable to comprehend the potential scope of its implications. Weidemann highlighted the fact that by the mid-1880s Mommsen may have reached a point of information overload. Mommsen's 'Hensel' lectures, published in 1996:

> ...consist of analyses of particular problems which are effectively separate digressions – on coinage, tax reforms ...In one respect, these analyses illustrate how much new material had been brought to light in the previous thirty years, largely as a result of Mommsen's own research. But they also show the sheer quality of new material had led to a much greater level of specialization than was necessary in the mid-century. It has been pointed out that Mommsen's view of modern scholarship as highly co-ordinated team-work meant that his pupils were world experts in limited areas, but found it hard to synthesize. The same seems to have applied to Mommsen himself: in the thirty years since he had written volumes I–III of the *History of Rome*, he and his followers had produced so such detailed research that he was no longer in a position to produce a coherent account ...Volume V, on the Roman provinces, appeared in 1885, and here the emphasis on detailed research as opposed to an all-embracing story-line was not much a drawback: but Mommsen was (far) from being able to combine (e.g.) domestic politics and the story of military activity in frontier regions (Weidemann in Mommsen 1996: 46–7).

The deficiency in Mommsen's application of archaeological data was noted by Haverfield who claimed that Pelham had planned to prepare a history of the Roman empire but gave up, not least because Mommsen was incapable of it (in Pelham 1911: xv; although Grundy (1945: 87) doubted Pelham ever had such a work in mind).[2] This point

---

2. In a review of Haverfield's edition of Pelham's *Essays*, which was also in part a memoir, Anderson (1911), while praising the work, noted Haverfield explained why Mommsen and Pelham did not attempt the Roman empire volume. Anderson doubted the reasons but did not offer his opinions why.

was repeated in numerous articles and in at least one of the obituaries that Haverfield wrote of Mommsen (Haverfield 1903a; 1903b; 1904a; 1904b; 1912b; 1924: 81, 86; cf. Freeman 1997). As an example, Haverfield developed these opinions in a critical review of Ferrero's *Grandezza e decadenza di Roma* (1902–07) which also served as a vehicle for praising yet again Mommsen's accomplishments. It also explained why Haverfield believed that the future elucidation of antiquity would lie not with the reinterpretation of what had become overworn literary sources, but with epigraphic and archaeological data.[3] In this respect, Mommsen; '...led the way. He taught his colleagues to collect and edit scientifically the vast masses of Roman inscriptions and to elicit from them that many-sided and copious information about ancient life which ancient writers have omitted wholesale. He added at one stroke a huge body of evidence to the resources of the Roman historian. Now it is becoming possible to advance from inscriptions to the unin-scribed' (1912b: 327). Some of these ideas had already been expressed in an earlier article Haverfield contributed to Hogarth's *Authority and Archaeology: Sacred and Profane* (1899), where the editor was attempting to demonstrate how archaeological evidence could effect understand-ing of the antiquity of civilization. Haverfield's chapter was on the archaeology of the Roman world (pp. 296–331). Again it is worth look-ing in some detail at what he had to say in this piece. The article opened with Haverfield having to demonstrate how poor Roman his-torical-literary sources are: there being none extant for pre-historic Rome, relatively few and universally poor for the Republic and there being not much better in terms of scope and quality for the Empire. For this reason archaeological evidence in the Roman period takes on an even greater importance than for Greek history: 'On the other hand, the archaeological evidence is extensive and indeed extraordi-nary. No state has ever left behind it such abundant and instructive remains as the Roman Empire' (p. 299). That data was categorized as (i) inscriptions, (ii) coins, and then (iii) ruins and roads. After this pre-

---

3. 'Theodor Mommsen ...transformed Roman history in the course of his long life as no scholar or thinker has ever yet transformed any branch of the intellectual life of man ...his work was unique. In every corner of his subject he marked an epoch. His amazing and nearly incredible power of work – he wrote or helped to write nearly 1100 books or papers of various sizes – and his infinite capacity for detail, formed only one side of the man' (1912b: 324–5).

amble, Haverfield moved on to a run through of the main historical periods of Roman history.

> The bulk of what we know about the Roman Empire is supplied by archaeological evidence. That tells us of emperors, of political institutions, of wide-reaching tendencies, of social, religious, commercial phenomena which ancient historians never mention. It transfigures the whole conception ...As presented to us by archaeology, it is a highly organised and coherent state of wheels within wheels, in which the Emperor is often less important than the statesmen round him and the central city less noteworthy than the populations of the provinces (p. 308).

A recurring theme throughout this chapter is the importance of epigraphy (and Mommsen) to the study of ancient history. In Haverfield's opinion, it was from epigraphy that there grew the tendency to the exploration of remoter regions and then (scientific) excavation. The reason why inscriptions are important is because they:

> ...provide a considerable part of this material, provide also the clearest instances of the conditions attending its use. Thanks to Mommsen – for the organizer of the Corpus (the CIL) was also its interpreter – we know how to study the inscriptions of the Empire. Many of them are striking, but the most striking are rarely the most important. The importance of any one of these inscriptions does not, as a rule, depend on its individual merits or interest, but on its place among other inscriptions. Epigraphy is a democratic science. If an inscription can be combined with others like it to prove some fact, it possesses importance; if not, it is unimportant. Among the tens of thousands of Imperial inscriptions known to us, perhaps a hundred may claim an individual value ...But the vast majority of these documents are valueless and uninstructive until they are combined (p. 313).

The result of this work is that epigraphy-archaeology changed the perception of the Roman empire (p. 316). To demonstrate this, Haverfield looked at the administrative institutions of the empire. But the nearest that he got to discussing the cultural implications of archaeological research are with regard to (Roman) towns and colonies (p. 325ff.), where their introduction meant the appearance of a degree of uniformity to the provinces. The same sense of uniformity is visible in provincial art too, with Celtic art being forced for the moment to the fringes of the empire (p. 326). Finally there was a brief assessment of the frontiers and armies of the empire, before Haverfield concluded:

> Such are some general features of the Empire as revealed to us by archaeological research. They are not the only prominent features and

some might say they are not altogether the most prominent, nor are the discoveries which support them the most striking or sensational. Forts and frontiers, sepulchral ornament and Samian ware are not promising subjects. But that is not the whole account of the matter. Interesting and sensational discoveries are not always helpful to the historian ... These things provide pleasures to the imagination which are forbidden to the student of history. Nor, again, do the completest remains always tell the most ... Their proper function is to convince the beholder of the reality of ancient life, quite as much as to increase his knowledge of it ...But in the end it is not the edifice ... but countless inscriptions and sculptures, whole or imperfect, scattered over the whole Empire (p. 330–1).

Haverfield's knowledge of work in Europe was facilitated by a number of personal visits and the publications which resulted from them. We can also see this in his connections with continental scholars, and in particular his association with Mommsen. The Haverfield Archive in the Ashmolean Museum preserves some of his correspondence with Emil Ritterling and Ernst Fabricius. In Berlin, in addition to the letters to Mommsen is preserved correspondence to Ludwig Darmstädter, Otto Hirschfeld (described as 'one of the ablest of German scholars – after Mommsen'; *Class Rev* XIII (1913): 327) and Emil Hübner. He also knew Hans Dragendorff, Felix Hettner (excavation director of the RLK) and Karl Zangemeister of Heidelberg and the *ORL*.[4]

---

4. In a letter to *The Times* (14 April 1919), reporting on the false rumours that bombing had destroyed the museum at Trier, Haverfield wrote of Hettner, 'a most distinguished archaeologist and virtual founder of the museum and ... his successor, a most competent museum administrator, Dr. Kruger.' Evans (1896) acknowledged Haverfield wrote on his behalf to Zangemeister for information. In addition to the names already noted, it is inconceivable that Haverfield was not on more than nodding terms with the leading German (Roman) historians and archaeologists of the day. This would have meant the likes of E. Kruger and K. Schumacher. There was a particular link with Dragendorff (1870–1941). Educated at Berlin and Bonn and after travelling in Italy, Greece and the Near East (as a fellow of the German Archaeological Institute) between 1890 and 1892 Dragendorff was Professor at the University of Basel. With the creation of the RGK in 1902 he became its Director, followed by the General Secretaryship of the DAI. In 1922 he joined Albert-Ludwigs University, Freiburg. His main work was on Thracian graves, and Roman Germany. His seminal work on *terra sigillata* (cf. *Bonner Jahbucher* XCVII; 1895), developed his dissertation *Vasculus Romanorum Rubris*, '...which elevated the study of Roman ceramics from dilettantism to a serious discipline. The influence of this article upon Roman archaeology is beyond estimate' (obit. *Am J Archaeol* 45 (1941): 429). Haverfield's work on

Haverfield's admiration for the accomplishments of German (and Austrian) scholarship and research, or more precisely of certain writers, is well known, not least because of the way scholars in each country took serious notice of what the others were producing. Early on in his career Haverfield was to write: 'A German reviewer said lately that every important German work in classics is at once reviewed and read in France and vice versa. It would be well if this were true of England also' (*The Academy* 15 July 1882). But still he often commented on the failings of Europeans and the failure of writers from there to use the most up-to-date research coming out of Britain.[5] We have already noted his criticisms of German opinions on the date and function of Hadrian Wall. Elsewhere of J. Jung's *Grundriss der Geographie von Italien und dem Orbis Romanus* (1897) he wrote: 'Not to criticize further, it appears unfortunately true that there, as in so many German books, the antiquities of our island are unsatisfactorily treated and imperfectly known to the author' (*Class Rev* XII (1898): 174–5). There is, however, another, perhaps surprising, facet to his interaction with continental scholarship. On a number of occasions Haverfield commended French research and what he called the Gallic practice of archaeology. The vehicles for acknowledging this were the cycle of reviews of particular monographs as well as naming specific individuals in other circumstances (notably Joseph Déchelette, Franz Cumont, Rene Cagnat and Herman Dessau).[6] As far back as 1887 in the *Classical Review* (I (1887): 162) in a favourable review of Cagnat's *Cours elementaire d'epigraphie latins* (1886), Haverfield claimed '...the growth of classical studies in France has been more marked in epigraphy than in anything else and M. Cagnat is not the least known among French epigraphers.' His appreciation, however, went beyond praising individual scholars. In 1893, again in the *Classical Review*, in an otherwise gloomy review of

---

sigillata owed much to Dragendorff, a fact he acknowledged in print (cf. Haverfield 1917: 237).

5. E.g. *Class Rev* XII (1898); Review of L. Joulin *Les establissements gallo-romain de la plaine de Matres-Tolosones. Class Rev* XV (1902): 175; of Dessau and *ILS* III (*Class Rev* XXXII (1918): 192–4); C. Jullian's *Vercingetorix* (1901) *English Hist Rev* XVIII (1903): 332–6); H. D'Arbois de Jubainville's *Les Celtes depius les temps des plus anciens jus'qu'en l'an 100 avant ere* (1904) *English Hist Rev* XIX (1904): 745–6.

6. As with German works, this is not to say that he was not uncritical in his treatment of such works. He slated the British section of L. Le Roux's *L'Armée Romaine de Bretagne* in the *Journal of Roman Studies* (II (1912): 284).

Cagnat's *L'Armée romaine d'Afrique* (1892), still there was praise for French approach to archaeological research and publication. Of Gsell's *Essai sur le règne de l'empereur Domitien* (1894), in another highly favourable review, its '...fault, of course is, its length – rather a common fault in some French books ...were it shorter, it would doubtless be more interesting to read, but it would be less useful' (*Class Rev* VIII. (1894): 373). Similar comments were offered of P. Le Jay's *Inscriptiones antique de la Côte-d'Or* (1899), where the '...chief fault of the book is a certain verbosity which may possibly be justified in a work of this character – as it would be in the local journals of archaeology in England' (*Class Rev* IV (1890): 379). Finally, in a discussion on Roman Cirencester, Haverfield observed that, in trying to write a history of a single site, only the French possessed a tradition of such studies. His belief was that by starting with single site studies one could piece together strands and patterns not apparent in literary sources in order to identify trends and in turn perhaps evidence of imperial policies, or more accurately, their outcome. 'Unfortunately, the historical study of single sites has been undertaken by no scholars in this country, except in France. Even epigraphists, who meet many dates on inscriptions and, whose work leads them to study closely the character and history of single spots have seldom essayed the task...' (p. 161). It is surely for this reason, Haverfield's report also included catalogues of finds from the site (including mosaics, coins and its samian). It goes without saying that many of Haverfield's opinions were in contrast to his frequently exasperated comments about the organization of English archaeology, and in particular the influence of the regional societies, typified by his comments in the presidential address at the inaugural meeting of the Roman Society (Haverfield 1911a).

Of Haverfield's other continental contacts, one would like to know more about his relationship with Mikhail Ivanovitch Rostovtzeff.[7] How and when Haverfield first made his acquaintance is not preserved. While better known in German academic circles, he studied in Europe between 1895 and 1898, Rostovtzeff knew the British epigrapher B.P. Grenfell and numismatist B.V. Head and visited London in 1898. Haverfield was reviewing his work favourably from at least 1911 (e.g. *J Roman Stud* IV: 1914). Haverfield, with Cheesman, dined with him in

---

7. There are a few letters from Rostovtzeff in the Haverfield Archive but all date post-Haverfield and so after Rostovtzeff's departure for the USA. The earliest explicit connection between the two is evidently a 1910 obituary to August Mau.

Oxford in 1913 when the Russian was in the UK presumably to attend that year's Historical Congress in London. This was also the occasion of his visit to the Caerwent excavations (Boon 1989: 10). In early 1918 Rostovtzeff left St Petersburg for a scholarly visit to Sweden and Britain not to return to Russia for reasons discussed by Shaw (1992) and Bongard-Levin (1999). Via Sweden, in August 1918 he ended up in Oxford, obtaining membership of Corpus Christi but renting accommodation in the town. During this visit those with whom he got on with particularly well were R.B. Mowat[8] and J.G.C. Anderson, another Haverfield associate and who assisted Rostovtzeff in a number of ways (Bongard-Levin 1999: 18). At the start of 1919 the university conferred on him an honorary DLitt degree while in May, Haverfield recommended that he be invited to deliver a course of (six) lectures from October on *The Economic History of Hellenism and Rome*. At the same time he was undertaking research, writing and also lecturing elsewhere, notably in Paris. In his time at Oxford, Rostovtzeff assisted Haverfield on epigraphic matters (Last 1953), visited Carlisle (Haverfield 1922) and collaborated with Stevenson and Stuart Jones on (the reliefs) at Cirencester, when he called Haverfield his 'friend' (Haverfield 1920b). Rostovtzeff's time at Oxford, however, soured and he left with not especially fond memories. A variety of reasons for the disillusionment have been offered, ranging from his personality, his, by Oxford standards, range of interests (and opinions), and possibly anti-Russian sentiments within the university. His failure to obtain the Camden chair on Haverfield's death finally caused him to leave for the University of Wisconsin and later Yale (Momigliano 1966: 98; Bowersock 1974: 18; 1986: 391; 1993; Bongard-Levin 1999: 40).[9]

Rostovtzeff's two best-known works on the ancient world, the *Social and Economic History of the Roman Empire* (1926) and the *Social and Economic History of the Hellenistic World* (1941), both appeared after

---

8. This was Robert Balmain Mowat (1883–1941), brother of J.L.G. Mowat, who was one of the co-signatories of the CEC appeal in 1894 (cf. Ch.6). R.B. Mowat, following a long and varied career eventually ended up as Professor of History at the University of Bristol (1928).

9. Wes' 1990 account of Rostovtzeff's period of 'exile' in Britain is virtually silent about his time in Oxford, but it is treated in far greater detail by Bongard-Levin (1999: 40) who drew attention to a negative review that Hugh Last penned of Rostovtzeff's *SEHRE*, one that upset Anderson and Macdonald, two Haverfield acolytes. Last also authored a similarly unsympathetic obituary of Rostovtzeff that set out why he was not suitable for Oxford: cf. *J Roman Stud* XLIII (1953).

Haverfield's death, but there is no doubt that he, like most scholars of the time, would have appreciated the way Rostovtzeff combined archaeology with literary sources to bring the world of classical antiquity to life, even if the interpretation might cause problems. Frere (1988: 2) felt that R.G. Collingwood and Wheeler '...were too greatly influenced in the years before the (Second World) war by the themes of Rostovtzeff.' The conceptual model in both these works owed more to Rostovtzeff's background and experiences, and it is debatable how far Haverfield would have been comfortable with this largely negative verdict of the accomplishments of the Roman empire.

From epigraphy to archaeology

Complementing his European connections was Haverfield's training in philology and continued interest as an epigrapher. His conviction was that Mommsen's major innovation in the study of classical antiquity lay with his mastery of the literary sources and his use of epigraphic evidence. With his background and influences it is unsurprising that Haverfield (1924: 86–8) made extensive use of epigraphic and archaeological evidence, complemented when necessary by his knowledge of continental parallels, but in which he also minimized the importance of other types of literary evidence. This approach was increasingly refined in his chapters in the *Victoria County History* series (*VCH*) and his numerous contributions to national and regional archaeological journals (Macdonald in Haverfield 1924: 40–57 for a list and below). As an epigrapher this brought him to discuss a corpus of data, theoretically consistent in its form throughout the (western) Roman empire. Perhaps the most important aspect of this, other than a familiarity with the evidence, is the epigrapher's preoccupation with a relatively uniform body of information; the Latin language. In turn there are the common institutions and terminology which frequently occur in inscriptions. The very ubiquity of Latin inscriptions, naturally enough, encouraged one to see the empire as a homogeneous entity. That same (cultural) homogeneity of source material had already shaped Mommsen's *Provinces* and conditioned his lectures on the empire under the emperors (Mommsen 1996; cf. Freeman 1997). Not surprisingly then, in wanting to place his British evidence in context, this led Haverfield, unwittingly, to use the indigenous archaeological evidence to confirm the homogeneity of Roman Europe.[10] To be sure,

10. The same logic is evident in a letter of about the same time (November 1895), where R.C. Bosanquet summarised his approach to a recently set (un-

this was one of the criticisms Collingwood levelled in his 1924 review of *The Romanisation of Roman Britain*. Even Macdonald recorded that one of Haverfield's favourite maxims, repeated in his inaugural address to the Roman Society was that '...it is of no use to know about Roman Britain in particular unless you also know about the Roman Empire in general' (p. 27).

The precedent created by Mommsen with its accomplishments (and weaknesses) was appreciated by Haverfield.[11] While Mommsen realized some of the potential of forms of archaeological evidence, other than epigraphic and to a lesser degree numismatic, he never used them. Instead, Haverfield clearly seems to have seen the potential. One might even suggest that it was the weaknesses in Mommsen's work, that Haverfield highlighted, which determined the latter's career. Indeed, the impression is almost of a conscious decision on his

---

dergraduate) essay: '...I began it light heartedly two years ago, when an essay subject was set "The extent and duration of Roman civilisation in Britain". Literature is soon exhausted; then I began collecting facts about roads, inscriptions, finds of coins, bronze vessels, pottery. Certain objects were imported – some could be dated – that went to prove commerce; but what were the criteria of civilisation in a Roman province? I saw that I must study the same points for provinces corresponding to Britain – Gaul, Germany, and Raetia, and for countries north of the frontier, before I could at all tell how archaeology should be read into history. So I worked at the Dutch finds at Leyden' (1938: 42).

11. There is potentially one other aspect of research where Haverfield shadowed Mommsen. It is known that in spite of his considerable scholarly interests and varied output, Mommsen claimed that given his time again he would have preferred to specialize in late antique history rather than Roman law, the magistracies or the history of Rome (Demandt in Mommsen 1996: 10 for references). This interest is reflected in his editions of Jordanes and Cassiodorus as well as co-ordinating the *Monumenta Germaniae Historica* (MGH). A *Monumenta Historica Britannica*, edited by Petrie and Sharpe, appeared in 1848 but was soon out of date in the light of critical study of the sources. Haverfield demonstrated an interest in Britain's late Roman to early Medieval history, although it differed from that of Mommsen in a number of ways. Haverfield's forays came from the direction of critical appraisal of early accounts of the island, like those discussed in the first chapter of *The Roman Occupation of Britain*, before moving on to the antiquarianism of the High Middle Ages (e.g. Haverfield 1889a; 1901a; 1902a; 1910b; 1911d; 1915d). In terms of Roman chronology, there were also many publications on aspects of 'the end' of the Roman province (e.g. 1899h; 1904e; 1905; 1912e; 1916e; 1918c; 1919a).

part to devote his career to this aspect of classical antiquity and where Mommsen's career set a model for his own. Hence the efforts, particularly from the 1880s, to become familiar with the archaeology of Britain which resulted in him becoming the most influential representative of work of his time. In 1918 he was to claim to have read '...nearly all the publications of the many local societies which deal with our national antiquities and to form an opinion of their merits' (Haverfield 1919a: xxiv) and that he possessed over 4000 books and other publications related to Roman Britain.

It was suggested in Chapter 1 that Haverfield's career might be divided into three phases. The first includes his going up to Oxford before moving to Lancing College (1879–92); the second period extends from his return to Oxford down to his translation to the Camden professorship and onto the moment of his collapse in late 1915. The third goes on to his death in 1919. To determine if this phasing is valid and, if so, to assess its significance in the light of there being virtually no primary documents relating to his views, we have two options that are mutually compatible. In the first we can look at the general nature of his publications and see where he was placing to them in order to see what were his interests. This should allow identification of a chronological development. In turn, if there is a pattern, then we can examine in detail the contents of such statements to see if there is anything that might indicate how his thinking about Roman Britain and the evidence for it might have developed.

Patterns in Haverfield's record of publication.

The two tables below summarize where Haverfield placed his publications. Both are compiled from the bibliography of Haverfield's publications produced by Macdonald, assisted by M.V. Taylor and others. The circumstances behind the compilation of the list were discussed in Chapter 1. Macdonald did not describe the criteria by which he put the list together except for including some of his more important reviews. The picture may be distorted by the fact that not only did some journals cease publication but Macdonald omitted a few articles and most of Haverfield's reviews. The tables therefore reflect all the inadequacies of that list. He was also, in a few instances, uncertain of the precise year of publication of a small number of entries. Finally there seems too to be an element of Macdonald (and Taylor) selecting particular publications for a higher position in the list either because of their contents/subject matter or because they appear to be what he, Macdonald, considered to be seminal statements. I have how-

The Best Training-Ground for Archaeologists

1882
Academy 2
JP 1
Other 1

1883
Academy 1
JP 2

1884
Academy 1
German 1

1885
JP 2
HER 1

1886
JP 1
German 1

1887
Academy 4
Others 1

1888
Academy 1
JP 4
AR 2
Suss Coll 1

1889
Academy 2
AR 2
AJ 1
Arch Ael 2
PSAN 4
CR 6
Glouc Trans 1

1890
Academy 2
AJ 1
PSAN 2
CR 1
Athenaeum 1
NC 1
Other 1

1891
Academy 1
AJ 1
PSAN 1
CR 4
Athenaeum 2
Antiquary 6
TCWAAS 1
Arch Cambr 1
German 1

1892
Academy 1
AJ 2
Arch Ael 3
PSAN 2
PSAL 4
CR 1
Athenaeum 3
Antiquary 4
Chester J 1
Arch Oxon 1
Suss Coll 1

1893
Academy 2
AJ 2
Arch Ael 2
PSAN 1
PSAL 1
Athenaeum 1
Antiquary 2
TCWAAS 1

1894
Academy 5
PSAN 3
PSAL 3
CR 2
Athenaeum 2
Antiquary 4
Arch Oxon 1
German 1

1895
Academy 2
EHR 1
PSAN 2
PSAL 1
CR 1
Antiquary 1
TCWAAS 4
Chester J 2
Arch Oxon 1

1896
Academy 1
EHR 2
PSAN 2
PSAL 2
CR 1
Athenaeum 1
Antiquary 1
Chester J 2
German 1

1897
Arch Ael 2
PSAN 1
PSAL 2
CR 2
Antiquary 4
TCWAAS 3

1898
PSAN 3
CR 2
Athenaeum 1
Antiquary 2
TCWAAS 3
Archaeologia 1
Chester J 3
German 1

1899
PSAL 4
CR 2
Antiquary 1
TCWAAS 5
Edin Rev 2
Chester J 1
JAI 1
JTS 2
German 1
Others 1

1900
AJ 2
PSAL 1
CR 3
Athenaeum 1
NC 1
Antiquary 1
TCWAAS 2
PSAS 1
Chester J 1
Edin Rev 1

1901
JP 1
PSAN 1
Athenaeum 3
Antiquary 2
TCWAAS 1
Suss Coll 1
German 1

1902
AJ 1
Arch Ael 2
Athenaeum 1
NC 2
Antiquary 3
TCWAAS 1
German 1

1903
AJ 2
Athenaeum 2
TCWAAS 1
Arch Camb 1
Suss Coll 1
German 2
Other 1

1904
HER 1
Arch Ael 2
Athenaeum 1
TCWAAS 1
PSAS 1
Lancs 1
DAJ 1
German 1
Pearson's 3

1905
AJ 1
PSAL 2
CR 3
Athenaeum 2
German 2

1906
PSAN 1
Archaeologia 1
PBA 1
Pearson's 1
Geog Journ 1

1907
PSAL 1
CR 1
NC 1
Reliquary 1

1908
Arch Ael 1
PSAL 1
Archaeologia 1

1909
Arch Ael 1
PSAL 2
Lincs Notes 1
Carmenth 1
German 1

1910
Arch Ael 1
PSAN 1
PSAL 4
CR 1
PSAS 1
Cymmrod 1

1911
AJ 1
Arch Ael 1
PSAN 1
PSAL 1
TCWAAS 3
JRS 3
Edin Rev 1
German 1

1912
AJ 1
Arch Ael 1
PSAN 2
PSAL 1
Athenaeum 1
TCWAAS 1
JRS 3
PCA 1
JISI 1
Quart Rev 1
German 2

1913
EHR 1
Arch Ael 1
PSAL 1
CR 1
TCWAAS 2
Wilts Mag 1
German 2

1914
Arch Ael 1
PSAL 1
CR 3
Antiquary 1
TCWAAS 1
PBA 1
JRS 2
Bath Soc. 1
German 1

1915
AJ 1
Arch Ael 3
CR 2
TCWAAS 3
PBA 1
JRS 2
YAJ 1
Wilts Mag 1
Burlington 1

1916
Arch Ael 1
TCWAAS 1
JRS 1
Arch Cambr 1

1917
TCWAAS 1
CAS 1

1918
HER 1
AJ 1
Arch Ael 1
TCWAAS 1
PSAS 1
Somers Proc 1

1919
CR 1
TCWAAS 2
Somers Proc 3
Essex Arch 1

1920
TCWAAS 2
Archaeologia 1

Plus contributions to the Pauly-Wissowa (1913, 1914, 1916, 1919 & 1921).

Table 1: Breakdown of publications by year and their location

ever taken the list at face value and assumed that in its organization there is a sense of primacy in the order of the citations.

Table 1: Breakdown of publications by year and their location
For the purposes of tracking the evolution of Haverfield's interests from philology, etymology and epigraphy to more antiquarian and archaeological issues, I have omitted those monographs and works he edited, as well as chapters and other contributions he made to volumes, including the *VCH*, edited by others. Museum and site guides too have been excluded, as are his letters to the national newspapers, contributions to encyclopaedias and obituaries. I have, however, left in articles of an antiquarian interest which were not necessarily related to Romano-British archaeology. The position of each title in this list is determined by the year each of them first appears in Macdonald's list (and include the number of entries per journal).

Table 2: Publications and journals by order of precedence
Derived again from Macdonald's bibliography, this Table provides an indication of Haverfield monographs and contributions to other works as well as his letters to national newspapers but excludes the contributions to German publications. His reviews are also omitted.

In dissecting the Macdonald list there are a number of interesting patterns. With regard to Table 1, *The Academy* was originally a bi-monthly journal published from 1869 edited by C.A. Appleton, a sympathiser of Mark Pattison, and intended '…to record all that was worth chronicling in the works of letters and science, and to contain articles signed by persons who could speak with authority on the subjects on which they wrote' (Jackson 1917: 44). The journal went into something of a decline when it started to publish articles on theological issues by authors denigrated as having no known competence. As such the editor lost the indulgence of his publishers who eventually sold the title on, with the journal 'losing its original character'. As we have already seen, the *Journal of Philology* was edited by one of Haverfield's mentors, Ingram Bywater, from 1879 down to his death in 1914. Founded in Cambridge in 1868, Bywater's editorship was '…fruitful in two directions: first of all in maintaining the high standard of excellence in the articles contributed to the *Journal*, and secondly by bringing him into confidential communication with many of the contributors, especially with those whom his example helped to inspire. He never grudged any time or trouble spent in assisting younger men with aims and ambitions similar to his own' (Jackson 1917: 101–2). Table 2 seems to confirm that Macdonald listed, albeit crudely, Haverfield's publications into an order of precedence. Obviously sole-authored

1882	1883	1884	1885	1886	1887	1888
Academy	Academy	JP	JP	JP	Guardian	JP
	JP	Academy	Obit - German		Academy	Suss Coll
					EHR	AR
						Academy

1889	1890	1891	1892	1893	1894	1895
AJ	Oxf Hist Soc	CR	CR	CR	CR	Antiquary
Arch Ael	CR	AJ	EE	Antiquary	Antiquary	CR
Gloucs Trans	AJ	Antiquary	Antiquary	AJ	PSAL	Archaeologia
AR	PSAN	Athenaeum	AJ	PSAL	PSAN	PSAL
PSAN	Other	Arch Cambr	Arch Ael	TCWAAS	EHR	TCWAAS
CR	NC	TCWAAS	PSAN	Arch Ael	Arch Oxon	Chester J
Academy	Academy	Academy	PSAL	PSAN	Athenaeum	EHR
	Athenaeum	PSAN	Chester J	Athenaeum	Academy	PSAN
			Arch Oxon	Academy		Arch Oxon
			Athenaeum			Guardian
			Academy			Academy
			Suss Coll			Edin Rev

1896	1897	1898	1899	1900	1901	1902
Antiquary	CR	Edited	Monograph	VCH	Athenaeum	Contribution
CR	Antiquary	Contribution	Contribution	Chester J	VCH	Arch Ael
Archaeologia	PSAL	Antiquary	Edinb Rev	Edinb Rev	VCH	Athenaeum
Contribution	TCWAAS	CR	Antiquary	Antiquary	Antiquary	Antiquary
PSAL	Arch Ael	Archaeologia	Contribution	CR	JP	VCH
TCWAAS	PSAN	TCWAAS	CR	PSAL	TCWAAS	TCWAAS
PSAN		PSAN	TCWAAS	AJ	PSAN	AJ
Chester J		Chester J	PSAL	TCWAAS	Suss Coll	NC
EHR		Contribution	Chester J	PSAS		Encycl Brit
Guardian		Athenaeum	JAI	NC		Contribution
Athenaeum		Obit	Thoresby	Athenaeum		
Academy			JTS			
Contribution						

1903	1904	1905	1906	1907	1908	1909
Atheneaeum	Athenaeum	Athenaeum	PBA	Obit - Athenaeum	VCH	Translation
AJ	VCH	VCH	Archaeologia	CR	Archaeologia	Arch Ael
TCWAAS	TCWAAS	CR	PSAN	PSAL	PBA	Lincs Notes
EHR	Arch Ael	AJ	VCH	NC	Year's Work	PSAL
Arch Cambr	PSAS	PSAL	Contribution	Reliquary	PSAL	NCH
Contribution	Lancs Trans		Pearson's	NCH	Arch Ael	Carmen. Soc
Suss Coll	EHR		Geog Journ	Year's Work		
Contribution	DAJ		Monograph	Monograph		
Obit	Monograph					
	Pearson's					
	Contribution					

1910	1911	1912	1913	1914	1915	1916
Cymmond	Contribution	Monograph	Monograph	PBA	PBA	TCWAAS
CR	Contribution	Quart Rev	EE	CR	CR	Arch Ael
PSAL	Edinb Rev	Other	EHR	JRS	AJ	JRS
PSAN	JRS	JRS	CR	TCWAAS	TCWAAS	Year's Work
Arch Ael	CR	VCH	Wilts Mag	Contribution	Arch Ael	Class Assoc
PSAS	Contribution	TCWAAS	PSAL	PSAL	JRS	Arch Cambr
Inv Hist Mon	AJ	PCA	TCWAAS	Arch Ael	CR - obit	Inv Hist Mons
Monograph	TCWAAS	PSAL	Arch Ael	NCH	YAJ	Monograph
Encycl Brit	Year's Work	Contribution	Times	Somers Arch	Wilts Mag	Contribution
	PSAL	AJ	Contribution	Antiquary	Burlington	
	PSAN	JISI	Inv Hist Mons			
	Arch Ael	PSAN				
		Arch Ael				
		Year's Work				
		Athenaeum				
		DNB				
		Inv Hist Mons				

1917	1918	1919	1920
TCWAAS	TCWAAS	CR	Contribution
Year's Work	Arch Ael	TCWAAS	Archaeologia
Camb Antiq Soc	AJ	Somers Proc	TCWAAS
	Year's Work	Essex Arch	
	PSAS		
	EHR		

Table 2: Publications and journals by order of precedence

monographs are listed first. Curiously the contributions to neither the *VCH* nor the Inventories of Historical Monuments – for which Haverfield was and is often still best remembered – feature strongly. Overviews and annual reports likewise do not rate significantly. What is masked in Macdonald's list is the number of reviews, especially in the *Classical Review* which refer to epigraphical and archaeological matters as well as commentaries and philology. Contributions to German publications are invariably listed at the end of the year entry. Elsewhere the magazines (*The Academy, The Athenaeum* and *Pearson's Magazine*) tend to come lower down in the entries. With respect to more 'heavyweight' journals, both tables show how strikingly Haverfield tended to restrict himself to a relatively small number of them, but this may be as much a reflection of the number of specialist journals at the time he was writing. Still it is curious that he did not use the *Archaeological Review, Archaeological Journal* and *Archaeologia* more than he did. His stalwarts in the early years remained *The Academy* and the *Journal of Philology*, the latter unsurprisingly with his interests in the classical languages and literature of the period. From 1891 the *Classical Review* appears in his list, although Haverfield had been submitting reviews to it for a couple of years. The *Review* also included many of his statements on Latin epigraphy, both in Britain and abroad. From 1890 there is an increasing use of the *Proceedings of the Society of Antiquaries of Newcastle*, and slightly later (and therefore significant?), the *Proceedings* of the London Society. *The Antiquary* was important from 1891, unsurprisingly bearing in mind that this journal was devoted among other things, to antiquarian and archaeological subjects (cf. Chapter 2 and Appendix 2).

Of the more antiquarian-archaeological journals, with one exception (1902) the *Transactions of the Cumberland and Westmorland Archaeological and Architectural Society* always rates higher than the *Archaeologia Aeliana*. In his middle years 1893–1910), the *PSAL* comes to feature higher in precedence than the *TCWAAS*, the *Archaeologia Aeliana* and the *PSAN* (even turning up at its meeting before the *PSAL*). The use of the *TCWAAS* and the *Archaeologia Aeliana* is unsurprisingly a reflection of his increased involvement in archaeological work in northern England. First used in 1891, the *TCWAAS* became an important conduit from 1893 as Haverfield was preparing for what became the work of the Cumberland Excavation Committee. At the same time, in reporting projects in which he was involved elsewhere, he used the pertinent regional journals, notably the *Journal of the Architectural, Archaeological and Historical Society of Chester and North Wales* (e.g. in 1892d, 1895, 1896c, 1898, 1899f, 1900 etc.). By 1900 the *Classical Review* had faded as a major site, as had *The Antiquary* by 1902. This must

surely have been because he was no longer providing his regular statements to it. Paradoxically, the less specialized *The Athenaeum* remained
a consistent site down to 1907.

In his later years, one also finds Haverfield contributing to more unusual periodicals, itself a reflection of more specialized publications. In
1898 he submitted a paper about a Roman charm in the Middle Ages to
the *Journal of the Anthropological Institute* as well as in the first volume of
the *Journal of Theological Studies* (1899). Slightly later he was publishing
with the *Geographical Journal* (1906 and concerning antiquities mapped
by the Ordnance Survey) and the *Journal of the Iron and Steel Institute*
(1912, on iron blooms from Corbridge). He even reviewed (an archaeological report) for *Man* in 1916. At the same time, Haverfield in his later
career seems to have shifted even more towards patronizing more re-
gionally based publications (e.g. Wiltshire 1913; Bath and Somerset
1914; Somerset 1918; and Essex 1919).

In summary, the impression of the two tables is that the evidence
supports the general phasing of Haverfield's career already noted. In
the period 1870–87 the preferred journals were more philological than
antiquarian. Following his contact with Mommsen and Haverfield's engagement with British epigraphy from *c*.1888, we start to see the
beginnings of a transition to archaeological periodicals such as the *Archaeological Review* and the *Archaeological Journal*. That shift accelerated
through the 1890s, reinforced as it was with his increasing involvement
in excavation in the latter half of that decade. The impression is of
Haverfield's placement of his articles shifting away from language and
linguistic issues in either general periodicals or specialist publications
(the *Journal of Philology*, the *Classical Review*) in preference for the more
specialized archaeological journals, both national and regional with, in
the case of the former, further refinement to more authoritative periodicals, culminating in the *Journal of Roman Studies*.

The phases in the preference for where he published, complimenting as they do his professional career, are part-paralleled in the course
of Haverfield's other interests. From the time of his first publications in
1882 up to 1892/3, his work was more to do with Greek and Latin philology with a trend towards (Latin) epigraphy. It might also be noted
that the tone of this work was more conciliatory compared to his later
work, which is perhaps a reflection of his junior status. During this time,
his preferred outlets were the *Journal of Philology* and the *Classical Review*. From *c*.1893 down to *c*.1905/6 we see a shift towards more antiquarian-archaeological orientated publications and including works of
synthesis and reportage. Articles on more traditional philological issues
progressively declined although he continued to publish new inscrip-

tions and reinterpret others. This was the period when he contributed the series of Quarterly Notes on Roman Britain to *The Antiquary*, which were more archaeological in tone than the Roman Inscriptions in Britain 1888–90 (*Archaeol J* XLVII (1890). It was also during this time that he was at his most active in terms of fieldwork, including the Chester (1890–2) and Silchester (1890–1909) excavations as well as the CEC programme (1894–1903). It also incorporated the early years of the Corbridge excavations (1906–14), but as we will see, his interest in this particular project waned soon after it started. During this phase the preferred journals included the *TCWAAS*, the *Archaeol Aeliana*, the *Archaeologia*, and the *Proceedings* of the London and Newcastle societies. At about the time of his elevation to the Camden chair, *c.*1907, the tone of his publications seem again to have shifted, this time to larger, broader works of synthesis (e.g. as exemplified by the likes of the various editions of *The Romanization of Roman Britain*, the Ford lectures, his contributions to the *VCH* volumes and his views on ancient town planning and Roman imperialism etc.) along with a contributions to encyclopaedias, other edited works and overseas, notably German, counterparts. In contrast the syntheses to *The Antiquary* ceased in 1902, those to *The Athenaeum* stopped in 1905. The thrust of this phase of his work was more archaeological and epigraphical, with some pieces of antiquarian interest.

The shifts in Haverfield publications might reflect an evolution in his attitude to the study of the history of antiquity and in particular Britain: from a purely linguistic, textual approach to a more artefactual, archaeological outlook. To be sure, a closer examination of his publications – notably his articles and reviews, rather than the monographs – is instructive for tracing the evolution of his thinking on a number of subjects connected with the study of Roman language, history and archaeology. Not surprisingly, his opinions were initially conditioned by his interests in the classical languages and in turn his involvement in epigraphy and in part by his experiences as a schoolmaster. Written towards the end of the first phase of his career, two Haverfield reviews, best read as one piece, which Macdonald omitted from his bibliography of Haverfield's works, are his comments on L.G. Gomme's *The Gentleman's Magazine Library – Romano-British Remains I* and *II* (*Class Rev* I (1887): 298–300 and II (1888): 146–7). The omission is curious in the light of what Haverfield was to say and the implications of his comments. Although he was to express similar opinions in *The Academy* (1887), the two reviews exemplify Haverfield at his destructive best.

In the first review Haverfield set out the background to the *'Remains'*. Between 1731 and 1868 *The Gentleman's Magazine* was one of the chief archaeological journals in England. Up to the moment it ceased printing reports about antiquities, '...its editors included archaeology among the many subjects which interested the cultivated gentleman, and the paper was a recognized organ, as indeed it was the only monthly organ, of those who wished to read or write about matters archaeological' (*Class Rev* December 1897: 298). Because the magazine was such a storehouse of information, there had frequently been plans to put together an index of entries. But this was not achieved until Gomme undertook to prepare in eight volumes a 'classified collection of its principal contents.' In 1887 Haverfield was reviewing the first of a two-part Romano-British section.

The review opened with an assessment of Gomme's introductory essay to the volume in which he had stated that the character of the Roman occupation of the island was military and not social. Roman Britain consisted of the luxurious occupants of the villas, of town merchants and the garrison. Haverfield thought this picture reflected Hübner's opinions in *CIL* VII (with the implication that they were not properly credited and were probably wrong). Gomme, however, was more concerned with attacking some of the conclusions expressed by H. Coote in his *The Romans of Britain* (1878) and the Anglo-Saxon scholar Frederic Seebohm's denial of the alleged continuity between Roman and English history. Coote's *Romans*, 'a recension of my *A Neglected Fact in English History*', was in fact a reply to E.A. Freeman's criticisms of the original *Neglected Fact*. Freeman believed that the barbarians who occupied Britain in the fifth century created a *tabula rasa*, leaving neither Roman nor *coloni*. The implications of this were that the occupiers created a homogeneity of race in England. On the other hand, Coote believed that the Anglo-Saxons in fact found a society of inequality, of slaves, and the dominant and the subservient, with the implications of a society which still owed much to Roman institutions and therefore a degree of continuity. Gomme placed the end of Roman Britain at 410 with the Romans leaving little trace of their presence. Haverfield suggested in this respect Gomme was confusing the continuity between Romans and Britons and Romans and Saxons. Other criticisms raised by Haverfield included Gomme recommending Scarth's *Map of Roman Britain* for more detail, to which the reviewer added: 'That map, which does duty for other books besides Mr Scarth, is the reverse of good, and I do not understand Mr Gomme's mention of it' (p. 299).

These were relatively minor points. Haverfield reserved his main criticisms of the *Remains* for how the volume was set out and what it purported to do. Gomme claimed his book was important because it constituted a representative record of Roman remains in England. Haverfield said it was not. For instance, it reprinted, unchanged, unscholarly original entries. Nor was the index complete: Haverfield counted a number of instances of entries that were omitted. Patently non-Roman remains were retained, the original illustrations were omitted. Gomme also decided to exclude at this stage coin finds (but promised a separate volume on numismatics). All in all Haverfield concluded:

> ...the whole matter is that the book is very unsatisfactory ...The most disappointing feature is the incompleteness. Mr Gomme in his Preface lays great stress on the value of the work as a contribution to an index of all the Roman remains in England, and it is rather trying to find that so far this contribution is worthless ...And yet the work is sorely needed. I suspect, however, that more has been done towards it than Mr Gomme thinks, and that what is really wanted is unity. At present we are all by ourselves doing the same things and wasting labour. Thus that indefatigable antiquarian, Mr Thompson Watkin indexed the *Gentleman's Magazine* for his own use long before. Mr Gomme's book was thought of. With division of labour, a new *Britannia Romana* ought to be possible, only the labour must be thorough and scholarly. Absolute completeness may be unattainable, though Mr Watkin's work on Cheshire and Lancashire, and Hübner's *Corpus*, show that one can come very near it, But an imperfect index is as bad as none: and the contribution before us is decidedly imperfect (p. 300).

Haverfield seems to have expected Gomme to take note of his criticisms before the appearance of Part II of *The Remains*. If so, then he was disappointed and gave vent to his reservations with regard to the format of the next part in a second review. Opening with 'I regret to have now to say that, so far as I can judge, the defects have not been entirely remedied' (p. 147), he complained that Gomme's list of the chief antiquarians was deficient in detail. Likewise pavements (meaning mosaic floors) and inscriptions were badly served. He complained again at the omission of a section on coins. In short he argued the weaknesses and omissions of this volume, as with Part I, forced one to go back to the original issues of the *Gentleman's Magazine*. In the end, although he acknowledged that the volume(s) had certain merits, still:

> ...Mr Gomme and others have claimed more. The work has been styled, in particular, a contribution towards a complete index of Roman remains in Britain, and this claim I cannot let go unchallenged ...If reasonably complete, it is invaluable; if its percentage of omissions be at all high, it is, as an index, almost useless. It may have other uses: this one it cannot have. It is indeed a pity that *Romano-British Remains* were even

set up as an index. Mr Gomme has gained considerable reputation as an archaeologist in subjects of which I confess I know less than I ought; he is editor of an archaeological review, and has written books which are spoken of with praise and respect. It is to be feared that some will take his volumes as confirming all that the *Gentleman's Magazine* has to tell us about Roman remains found in our islands, while others will be led to underrate the value of completeness in such matters. In the present state of English archaeology, neither result is desirable. The study of Roman Britain is already in a sufficient muddle; and it can be extricated only by accurate and scholarly work (p. 147).

Re-reading the two reviews, the impression is that it was the inadequacies of these summaries that set Haverfield on his course in Romano-British archaeology. Significant is the fact that at least the first part of his review to the *Classical Review* was probably written at the time, or just before, he was invited to participate in *CIL* VII.[12] If the chronology is correct, then it is in contrast to the view that it was an invitation to become involved with the *CIL*, as many of his contemporaries believed, which occasioned his interest in the archaeology of Roman Britain. For it cannot be coincidental that the issues highlighted in the two reviews are those that came to figure so prominently in subsequent work.

Haverfield's 1902 contribution to Traill's *History* is another good demonstration of his ability to target the 'right' publication for review, knowing that his comments would have a greater resonance than mere observation. It typifies his often aggressive attitude to the work of others.[13] These views were originally articulated in reviews and letters and

12. In July 1887 Haverfield was warning Mommsen of Gomme's inadequacies (Croke 22). In 1897 it seems that Gomme (and a Mr Nevill) proposed to compile an 'Index to the Publications of Archaeological Societies for the past two hundred years' (*The Antiquary* XXXIII: 104).

13. Macdonald (1924: 23) called him an 'indefatigable reviewer'. Others might have expressed it differently. Some of his reviews read as blunt to the point of rudeness (e.g. his comments on W. de Gray Birch's competence as an epigrapher (*The Academy* 22 June 1889), and H. Williams *Christianity in early Britain* (1912) and L. Le Roux's *L'Armée Romaine de Bretagne* (1911) in the *J Roman Stud* II (1912): 115 and 284). Elsewhere he could display a dry sense of humour. In a letter to *The Times* (4 December 1918) questioning recent reports of the quality of the iron ore deposits at Spitsbergen (sic), Haverfield begged to differ on their quality, adding he had been reading a recent report of the Dept of Scientific and Industrial Research which claimed that while the deposits there were plentiful, they were poor. Moreover he challenged why Spitzbergen had become Spitsbergen, wondering if the former sounded *too* German for current tastes. He noted too the '...latest use of the island is said

to be as a good summer resort for broken down university professors. I commiserate them – and "Spitsbergen".' In summarizing recent publications on Roman history and archaeology in *The Athenaeum* series (18 April 1903), Haverfield wrote of B. Henderson's *The Roman Legions in Britain, AD43–78* (*English Hist Rev* XVIII (1903): 1–23) '...it is not worth the paper on which it is printed', even after Henderson acknowledged Haverfield's assistance. Elsewhere, in an appendix to an interim report on the Cumberland Excavation Committee, Haverfield drew attention to a recent German publication: 'We desire in these Reports to avoid controversy except such as arises directly from our work, we do not therefore propose to discuss here the paper by Dr. Emil Krüger on *Die Limeslagen in nördlichen England* ...Nor do we wish silence to be interpreted as agreement with Dr. Krüger's view. We should like, therefore, to say briefly that we cannot regard his article as contributing any real advance towards the solution of the Mural problem. Dr. Krüger treats his evidence, both ancient and modern, with such arbitrariness, and he commits serious errors in points of fact, which initiate his criticisms and theories alike. These defects neutralise the useful material which is also contained in his paper' (1904c: 249). Of Gomme's *The Making of London*, '...I am afraid that, although it appears under the authority of a University Press, I am unable to accept many of the statements in it. Several of them ...I noted in my article as being in my opinion quite untenable' (1911c: 141 n.1). Haverfield was a master of the put-down. Of McElderry's *Notes on Roman Britain* (*Class Rev* XVIII (1904): 398–9 and 458–61) he wrote the author's views '...are interesting and form a pleasant change from the general style of many English writers on the subject. But I do not think they can all be taken as they stand' (*Class Rev* XIX (1905): 57–8). W. Pfitzer's *Ist Ireland jemals von einem römischen Heere betrieten werden?* (1893) was the product of a controversy with W.T. Watkins, a British epigrapher well-known to Haverfield. Haverfield's opinions of Pfitzer's efforts are summarized as: 'Mr. Watkins was not a scholar' (*Class Rev* VIII (1894): 324–5). He was lukewarm about J.E. Egbert's *Introduction to the Study of Latin Inscriptions* and attacked E.A. Freeman and B. Lupus' rejection of his theories in a review of Lupus' translation of Freeman's *Sicily* (*Class Rev* XI (1897): 67–9 and 362–3). He entered into written argument with T. Rice Holmes (*Class Rev* XXVIII (1914): 45–7 and 82–3). Indeed Rice Holmes had already paid generous tribute to Haverfield in his second major work (*Ancient Britain and the Invasions of Julius Caesar* (1907 – 'Francis Haverfield, scholar, archaeologist and practical excavator, while making himself the foremost authority of the history of Roman Britain' (p. 7) and '...the researches of the eminent scholar who has so greatly enlarged our knowledge of Roman Britain' (p. 254)). In a certain light there seems to be a hint of sarcasm here. It certainly did not inhibit Rice Holmes from including a 30-page digression criticizing Haverfield's (and others') theories on the position of the Cassiterides. Haverfield also reviewed Rice Holmes' *Caesar's Conquest of Gaul* (1899) in the *English Hist Rev* (XVIII (1903): 332–6). Ac-then in fuller articles. It is also an excellent example of how he tended to recycle his opinions as well as material he had published earlier. And of course, it is a fair reflection of his opinions – opinions which, because the *History* went through a number of editions, evolved. Haverfield's first complaints about the work, were expressed in a letter to *The Antiquary*: 'I need only here say that the sketch of Roman Britain contained in the first volume of Traill's Social England is quite untrustworthy: the details I must leave for another occasion' (*The Antiquary* XXIX (1893): 245). This was followed up by a letter to *The Academy* in the following year. In criticizing the contributions made by its six contributors and after highlighting the innumerable mistakes of fact contained in the entries, Haverfield concluded the:

> ...result (of the volume) is most surprising and unsatisfactory. The pages due to Mr. F.T. Richards, of course, contain competent work, even if they hardly reach the best level of this able scholar: the rest is a melancholy .... Dr. Traill ...aims at supplying scholarly summaries of the best results connected with his subject ...The part of which I have been alluding is a striking exception, against which it seems fair to forward a protest and a warning (*The Academy* 24 March 1894: 254).

These two statements, however, were merely him warming to the 'task'. They were followed by a full review of the Roman Britain section which appeared in the *English Historical Review* (Haverfield 1894a). Many of the points made in the earlier statements reappear here, and more could have been made but were not ('It is impossible to deal with these statements without a treatise on Roman Britain' p. 725). One point Haverfield made which seems, at face-value, to be at variance to what he was to say elsewhere, was his criticism that the (cultural) influence of the Roman army in Britain was underplayed in the *History*. His main

---

knowledging that it was an 'excellent' book, he then launched into two pages of criticisms ('it is solid, valuable and often interesting but mole rustica. Its heterogeneous contents do not seem to be collected on any one plan' (p. 333)). Another to feel the warmth of his opinions was A. Gudeman and a possible Agricolan invasion of Ireland (*Class Rev* XIII (1899): 302–3: XIV (1900): 51–3). Some of his private letters too, show Haverfield happy to discourse with some of his 'preferred' colleagues, no matter how distinguished they might be (eg. with Lord Abercromby over the reliability (or unreliability) of the latter using W.C. Borlase's *Nænia Cornubiae, a Descriptive Essay; Illustrative of the Sepulcher and Funeral Customs of the Early Inhabitants of the County of Cornwall* (1872) as an authority on Cornwall).

reservations, however, concerned the question of the 'end of Roman Britain'. Richard's argued the Romans broke Britain, although Haverfield maintained that it offered Rome the longest resistance of all the (European) provinces. Richards also magnified the importance of the Celts, reducing the Roman occupation to a mere interlude before the arrival of the Anglo-Saxons, in an explanation described as typical of the period, one which created a divide between Roman Britain and Anglo-Saxon England. With the arrival of the Saxons, in this explanation, the Romans and their influence vanished without a trace '...leaving an uninfluenced Celtic element to resume its interrupted supremacy' (p. 726). Haverfield argued strongly against this line of interpretation and that the Saxons would have found a British populace influenced to varying degrees by four centuries of exposure to Rome:

> The kind and quality of such survivals varied; they were more marked, perhaps, in agriculture than in matters of town life, of law, or of civic institutions, and they were more marked in certain districts than elsewhere. Our knowledge is too small to allow of a certain verdict, but it may at the present time, be permitted to suppose that while there were both Celtic and Roman survivals in a predominantly English England, the Roman or romanised elements were not the least extensive or unimportant (p. 726).

Three years later, in 1897, in reviewing Maitland's *Doomsday Studies*, Haverfield summarized the prevailing views on the relationship between Roman Britain and 'Saxon-England' (e.g. that civilization of Roman, British and Saxon Britain was continuous, that the Roman and the British was continuous but the Saxon was different or else there was a break when the Romans left):

> ...these three views involve different answers to two questions: first, what was meant by the departure of the Romans; and second, what was meant by the conquest of the Saxons. I have myself always argued that the Romans and Britain were continuous. When the Romans departed, about AD410, their departure I believe, meant much less than (for example) a departure of the British from India or the French from Algiers would mean nowadays; Romans or rather Romano-British civilization survived, and the educated folk at least ...continued to speak Latin. On the other hand, Mr. Freeman seems to me to have been substantially right in arguing that the Saxon conquest meant the extermination, the expulsion from Saxon territory, of the defeated Britons. The character of the conquest probably varied in various parts of England. British chiefs may, in some cases, have joined the invaders and obtained honourable place among them ...But in general I think that probability favours Mr. Freeman; there were, perhaps, Roman and British elements in later England. Professor Maitland's new book tends to prove this

> more fully from the Saxon side than perhaps could have been done by
> any other living man; it is a potent reinforcement to the view that Eng-
> land is mainly English (*The Antiquary* XXXIII (1897): 104–5).

The Gomme and Traill reviews came at a time when Haverfield had
only just established himself at Oxford as an authority on Roman Britain. In the original edition of Traill, the Roman sections were written
by F.T. Richards, fellow and tutor of Trinity College. Haverfield's comments, discussed below, led to his contributions to the second edition
in 1898 and another version in 1901/1902. In the subsequent editions,
Haverfield was specially commissioned to contribute new sections on
the Roman army in Britain, the art and civilization of the province and
the English before England.

Read in tandem, and knowing what was to occur in later years, it
might be said that from these rather inauspicious (insomuch as they were
based on negative criticisms) beginnings, Haverfield's preoccupation
with archaeology might be traced. Prior to this, his previous writings at
best had been concerned with reporting inscriptions and emending passages and words from the classical authors. It is of course true that the
science of epigraphy was at this time regarded as a central part of archaeology. We have also seen how Haverfield's skill in the study of inscriptions
was conditioned by his training as a philologist and linguist, and it would
be foolish to deny how important epigraphy was to his development as
an archaeologist. In 1890 in a review of *CIL* III, as well as two other books
on Latin epigraphy he wrote by way of a preface:

> Of late years English scholars have vigourously prosecuted the study of
> Greek inscriptions. Money has been subscribed, grants made by learned
> bodies expeditions sent to the east, extensive excavations set on foot. Ev-
> ery fragment found has been carefully edited, public lectures have been
> given, handbooks and manuals compiled by experienced authors. All
> this contrasts strangely with the state of Latin epigraphy in England.
> The work done by Mr. A.H. Smith and Professor Ramsay in Asia Minor
> and by Mr A.J. Evans in Illyricum is indeed most admirable, but it stands
> alone. Even the inscriptions found in our own island have been left to
> antiquarian societies, and though one or two of these, like the Newcastle
> Society of Antiquarians, produce good results, they cannot as a whole be
> taken to represent trained English scholarship. Hardly any professional
> scholar in England has troubled himself about the inscriptions recently
> found at Chester: no university has voted money to assist in the comple-
> tion of the excavations there. This is perhaps natural, for the charm of
> Hellenism is apparently infinite. Yet one cannot help regretting that
> classical archaeology should now mean to our scholars nothing more
> than Greek archaeology, and that the fashion should count a Hellenistic
> potsherd of more value than a Roman city ...Fortunately, this view does

not obtain abroad. In Germany, France and Italy, the editing and elucidation of inscriptions goes steadily forward (*Classical Review* IV: 232–3).

We have seen how it looks like Haverfield commenced work on what
was to become the *Ephemeris Epigraphica (VII)*, the addimenta to *CIL* VII
no later than late 1888. In 1891 his mentor Henry Pelham used the occasion of reviewing it to set out an agenda for the future of archaeology
and its further research in England in general:[14]

> It is a good omen for the future that an English scholar, and a scholar
> trained at one of the older Universities, should have been found (by the
> Berlin authorities for CIL) who was able and willing to perform such a
> task efficiently. For it is high time that something should be done in Eng-
> land and by Englishmen to place before the world a critical and
> complete statement of all the extant evidence bearing on the Roman
> conquest and occupation of Britain.

The problem was the work that had been undertaken in the past had
been unsystematic and intermittent while the researchers had been
largely unskilled.

> The consequence is that the records of this period in our history are in a
> frightfully chaotic condition. They are stored in provincial museums
> and private collections or have to be disinterred from innumerable
> newspapers and journals. To remedy this state of things it is necessary
> first of all that the work of exploration and excavation should be system-
> atically carried on under competent direction, and the results critical-
> ly tested, accurately described and carefully registered. In such a work the
> Society of Antiquaries might well take a lead. We want in England unoffi-
> cial counterparts both to the Italian Office of Excavation and to the
> official *Notizie degli scavi*. In the second place, the task of sifting and ar-
> ranging the existing material must be seriously taken in hand. In this
> direction, the labours of the late Mr Watkins, of Mr L. Gomme and oth-
> ers have broken the ground but much more remains to be done. The
> 'organization of understanding' which all this implies is no doubt a diffi-
> cult matter, but one obstacle which exists is at present can and should be
> removed. The responsibility for the existing chaos rests largely upon the
> Universities. Misled by too exclusive a devotion to the literary remains of
> antiquity, they have allowed their students to pass out into the world
> ignorant of or indifferent to monumental records. The discovery and in-

---

14. There is a potential problem here. The *Ephemeris Epigraphica* VII was actually
    published in 1892. Pelham's review appeared in the *Classical Review* V
    (1891): 74–5. The implications are that Pelham saw the completed volume
    before it went to press.

terpretation of these has consequently been left, in the great majority of cases, to untrained hands. We hope that the appearance of Mr. Haverfield's book is a sign of change for the better: and that academic learning will in future be brought into closer and more constant contact with local enthusiasm and experience (*Class Rev* V (1891): 74–5).

I have repeated at length Pelham's opinions because to a very great degree they reflect Haverfield's subsequent preoccupations. This includes criticisms of the poor state of the nation's museums, of the part played by the nation's universities, the over-emphasis on ancient literary *testimonia*, the poor quality of antiquarian research, and the chaotic structure of excavation and it publication. One could conclude that Haverfield set himself to take up the task defined by Pelham only after this review but, in the light of the Gomme reviews, one suspects that Haverfield was party to what Pelham had to say.

Pelham's review had the effect of linking Haverfield with future progress in Romano-British studies. The next stage in the process was the way that Haverfield was to become the conduit for reporting new discoveries, which in turn provided him with the opportunity of becoming central to research. This appears to have been accomplished by a variety of methods. One of the frequently noted features of Haverfield's career was how close were his relations with the English regional and local archaeological and antiquarian societies. Yet he seems to have retained an ambivalent opinion about the worth of the work they undertook. A good demonstration of this is his involvement in a survey that was undertaken in the county of Herefordshire in the early 1890s. The course of the survey is interesting, not least for the light it sheds on Haverfield's mode of action at a time when he was still trying to establish his position in British archaeology. It is also instructive of how the management and course of archaeological research in this island was proceeding. The origins of the survey lies with a proposal made in a paper delivered by J.O. Bevan at the 28 July 1891 meeting at Llanthony of the Woolhope Naturalists Field Club (Bevan 1890–2 and p. 201).[15] As it transpired it was decided to link

15. The Rev. James Oliver Bevan (1863–1930), before his ordination was a civil engineer, although there is no record of his career in the Minutes of the Institute of Civil Engineers. Educated at Emmanuel College, Cambridge in the 1860s and ordained in 1867, he moved onto a series of curacies. He was also temporarily Headmaster of Bromsgrove School. An FSA from 1895, and prior to this Secretary of the Herefordshire branch, and occupying the living of Vowchurch near Hereford, he retired to Eastbourne (Haverfield 1896d: cf. obit. *The Times* 24 February 1930).

the Herefordshire survey with an initiative the Society of Antiquaries of London had proposed in 1888, which in turn was the coming together of two interlinked developments.

The first of these developments was marked in June 1888 when George Payne read to the Fellows of the London society a paper reporting on the creation of an archaeological map prepared on lines '…laid down by a special committee of the society that had been appointed by the Council to confer with Mr Payne.' In the report of the June reading it was hoped Payne's map '…will form the first of a complete series of archaeological county maps to be published in the Archaeologia' (*Proc Soc Antiqs London* 12 1887–9: 228). The second development came in November of the same year. As far back as 1879 the society's president, the Earl of Carnarvon, had been calling for an archaeological survey (of prehistoric monuments) as the best way to preserving them (*Proc Soc Antiqs London* 10 (1883–5): 279; 283). Coincidentally the fledgling British Association for the Advancement of Science (BAAS) had been harbouring similar plans. As the Woolhope Club's representative to the BAAS, in 1890 Bevan reported that following the association's annual meeting in Leeds in ?1888, its Anthropological section had recommended that the prehistoric remains of Britain be tabulated in a series of typological groups. The inspiration for this suggestion, according to Bevan, lay with the recording of ancient remains undertaken by the Birmingham Philosophical Society. The BAAS proposal called for mapping the nation's ancient remains on the one-inch Ordnance Survey map series. Bevan also noted that:

> …the Society of Antiquaries has undertaken an Archaeological Survey of England. They enter not only the prehistoric, but the Roman and Saxon remains and earthworks. Each county would be accompanied by a list which would be classified under different heads and indexed, so as to show the discoveries which had been made. The road along which we should travel is, in this respect more than any others, definitely marked out for us. The Ordnance Survey furnishes a rough catalogue, and all the elements of position. It is not too much to expect that a correspondent … could be found in every district or parish to undertake to classify the information obtainable respecting the monuments of the past within his limit, and to communicate such information to a Committee of the Club, who would sift it and prepare it for publication. I venture to suggest that this work, including the provision of a Map similar to one published by the Kent Archaeological Society is well within the scope of our constitution and our energies (1890–2: 218).

As a consequence of his report, Bevan and James Davies, a local solicitor and another club secretary, were delegated to circulate among the membership a request for information concerning archaeological remains in the county.

Regardless of what might have happened to the BAAS proposal, in the same year, 1888, Sir John Evans, the Antiquaries' next President reported that following the receipt of a memorial presented by a large number of archaeologists and their societies, the London society had decided to organize a congress of archaeological societies. One of the purposes of the conference was '...to discuss the great question of the better organization of archaeological research', including fieldwork and the preservation of ancient monuments and records. Such issues might be addressed by the creation of lists of ancient objects and by a general archaeological survey of England and Wales by counties, along the lines of a '...plan approved by the Society of Antiquaries and begun in Kent' (*Proc Soc Antiqs London* 12 1887–9: 233–4). The congress met on 15 November 1888 when it decided to create a small committee to report in the following spring (cf. President's Address 30 April 1889. *Proc Soc Antiqs London* 12 1887–9: 397; Evans 1956: 329–30). A second congress of archaeological societies was held in July 1890 when resolutions '...were passed in favour of the preparation in duplicate of archaeological maps of each county with the view one of the copies being eventually deposited in our library' (*Proc Soc Antiqs London* 13 1889–91: 142).

Following the delivery of Payne's report, in the subsequent years other county surveys were published, the earliest ones, as promised, in the pages of the *Archaeologia*. These included John Evans' survey of Hertfordshire and Ferguson (and Swainson Cowper) on Cumberland and Westmorland (sic) which acknowledged Payne's survey as its template (Payne 1888; Evans 1892; Ferguson 1893). In the meantime, Bevan and Davies continued with their plans for Herefordshire, but not without problems. In 1892 Davies was lamenting to the club, and at some length, the slow progress that they had by then made (*Trans Woolhope Natural Field Club* 1893–4: 2–3). Nearly 700 letters '...had been forwarded to the clergy, magistrates, county councillors, and principal landowners, with a request that they would kindly note any objects of Archaeological interest in their respective neighbourhoods, but your Secretaries (Davies and Bevan) regret to say that these circulars and returns were not very numerously answered', leaving the two to do most of the primary research themselves, sifting through the club's archives (cf. Haverfield in Bevan *et al.* 1896: 1). Their search identified *c.*500 '... Archaeological objects of varied character, under the several heads of the Pre-Roman, Roman, Anglo-Saxon, and Medieval.' In the subsequent discussions at the meeting, the club's President, H. Cecil Moore, also reported: 'If the map be prepared and the prefatory remarks and index communicated, the Society of Antiquaries would bear the expense of preparing the map and setting the index &c., in type, and the Woolhope Club could have what copies were wanted at the mere expense of print and paper' (*Trans Woolhope Natural Field Club* 1893–4: 2–4).

It was because the London society had taken the Woolhope's proposal under its wing that Davies presented a reading of the survey of Herefordshire to the society in November 1893, and when it was noted that this '...survey, omitting the medieval portion, will be printed in continuation of the series already published by the Society' (*Proc Soc Antiqs London* 14 1893–5: 5). Davies and Bevan were then at work on Volume 2, a two map survey of the county's medieval remains. The published version of the survey, described as Vol. 1, appeared three years later not in the *Archaeologia*, but published independently (Bevan *et al.* 1896; cf. *Trans Woolhope Natural Field Club* 1895–7: 237).

Haverfield's part in the Herefordshire survey appears to have been in the capacity of reader for the London society. For it was reported on 5 April 1895 that Bevan and Davies' map had been completed and that it had been sent to the Society of Antiquaries, '...where it is now undergoing careful scrutiny and revision by Mr. Haverfield' (*Trans Woolhope Natural Field Club* 1895–7: 10). Elsewhere, it was said Bevan and Davies' '...list was revised by another member of the Woolhope Club, Mr. F. Haverfield, Student and Tutor of Christ Church, Oxford, who also compiled the accompanying sketch of ancient Herefordshire' (Haverfield in Bevan *et al.* 1896: 1). Haverfield referred to this episode as being involved '...with two Hertfordshire Archaeologists' on pre-Conquest antiquities in that county (Haverfield 1899f: 281). To be sure, although the report is credited to three authors, in reality the main text and the two accompanying appendices were Haverfield's. His scrutiny must have been extensive and severe. Not surprising, the footnotes to the main text, written in Haverfield's inimitable style, include many correctives to received opinions. The club's presidents' address of 23 April 1897, while complimenting Bevan and Davies, and linking their work with the other London society surveys (viz. Kent, Hertfordshire, Lancashire with Cumberland and Westmoreland (sic) went further. The membership should not forget:

> ...Mr. F. Haverfield who has revised the whole and summarised the mounds and earthworks, and the ancient roads in two appendices. Mr. Haverfield has exhibited himself a wise student and tutor. A deliberate consideration of his calm judgment, based as it is upon an accurate and extensive knowledge of Romano-British history, so far as it has been revealed to us by numerous authorities, has made us more prudent; our

consciences have pricked us that we have been enthusiastic and too rash in accepting the explanations and interpretations of later writers, which have suffered the penalty of getting exaggerated into traditions of earlier inhabitants, and we have been led into the wisdom of retaining an open mind upon many so-called traditions of the ancient history of Herefordshire, until further revelations produced by discoveries, especially by excavation, afford us more safe and sure justification for our opinions (*Trans Woolhope Natural Field Club* 1895–7: 6–7).

The timing of Haverfield involvement in Herefordshire is interesting and cannot have been coincidental. That he was asked to perform as reader of the Bevan and Davies manuscript may have been occasioned because he had previous experience of conducting such county-level surveys. For he had undertaken in 1888 his own survey-catalogue of Roman sites in Sussex but without conducting any corroborative fieldwork to compliment the list he created (Haverfield 1888e). His participation came at a time when he had just returned to Oxford and was attempting to confirm his place there. That he was acting as the Society of Antiquaries' reader for the survey is indicative of his prominent position in the society. Explicitly described as an Oxford don, Haverfield's participation marks yet another demonstration of the beginnings of the slow shift in the study of Roman Britain, from the world of the antiquarians and their societies to the universities. Twenty years after the Herefordshire survey was published, Haverfield was to slate in review Bevan's monograph *Towns of Roman Britain* (1917; see below). In this he was to admit as part of their 1891–3 collaboration he did not really get to know Bevan. The implications of this admission are that Haverfield as the Oxford don offered his services, through the London society, to the Woolhope Club. In the short term the club received the help of an 'expert'. At the same time, by piggy-backing on the work of others, Haverfield spread further his name and influence in regional Romano-British studies. There was one other consequence to Haverfield's involvement in the survey, for he was to publish in the Woolhope Club's transactions a short paper on the survival of Roman place-names, which unsurprisingly concentrated on instances from Herefordshire (Haverfield 1895–7).

Despite the rapid publication of three county surveys soon after the scheme was first proposed, the Society of Antiquaries' initiative seems to have as equally rapidly faltered. Later surveys, ostensibly undertaken under its patronage, while read in London, appear not to have been published. On 13 December 1894 G.F. Beaumont delivered a paper to the society on the archaeological survey of Essex which it was said was to be published in the existing series (*Proc Soc Antiqs London* 14: 1893–5:

269). At another meeting of the society, on 5 April 1900, T.J. George reported a similar survey of Northamptonshire which again was to be published separately (*Proc Soc Antiqs London* 15 1899–1901: 148). There are no signs, however, that these surveys went in to print. It was noted in Chapter 2 that in the 1890s, the society did not have a monopoly on the production of county surveys. Another reason for the failure may be that the society's initiative was superceded by the appearance of rival surveys such as the *Victoria County History* which started to appear in 1900. It may not be coincidence that in 1902 George contributed the section on prehistoric man in the first volume of the *VCH* Northamptonshire while Haverfield, while acknowledging George's help, described the county's Roman remains.

Another device that Haverfield used at this time to establish a position in British archaeology was to ensure that he was the conduit for the dissemination of recent work, both here and on the continent. In the same year as his Gomme reviews (1888), as a consequence of his recent visit to south-eastern Europe in 1887, Haverfield lamented the absence of 'handbooks' for any of the archaeological museums of Europe: 'I venture to think that students would equally welcome a work which should, for example, describe briefly the Roman remains preserved in local museums in Western Germany' (1888c: 274). He then proceeded to describe a number of museums he had seen in southern Austria, Hungary and elsewhere in the Balkans. In the end, although he did not produce any such European handbooks, Haverfield did oversee the production of a number of specialist guides for British museums. One of the reasons the (European) handbooks did not appear is probably because Haverfield was commissioned to produce in a number of different locations a series of regular reports on recent progress in Roman archaeology in Britain. Mirroring the other developments in his career, such reports were published in a variety of increasingly 'significant' publications, from popular magazines to eventually what was supposed to be the pinnacle of academic publishing in this country, the *Proceedings of the British Academy*. Haverfield's résumés of progress over the 25 years are interesting not just for the information they provide about individual projects, but also because they offer an insight into how his thinking was evolving about the importance of the island's archaeology and therefore the history of the province. The first efforts to report ongoing work were in the pages of the *Archaeological Journal* (XLVII: 1890) when he started to publish regular updates on recent discoveries of inscriptions, continuing a series originally overseen by W.T. Watkins (cf. XLV: 1888; cf. *The Antiquary* XIX 1889: 135). The articles are generally optimistic and are noticeably more complimentary and more willing to

acknowledge the contributions of his informants. Unlike the later contributions, there are not so many negative comments, although he did
dismiss Watkins and especially de G. Birch's reading of some inscriptions recently recovered from Chester (p. 243). In 1891, while still at
Lancing, but surely as a consequence of his invitation to contribute to
the *CIL*, Haverfield was asked to submit occasional reports, usually four
per annum, on on going work in Britain while continuing his reports in
the *Archaeological Journal*. In his first submission to *The Antiquary* he reported that as '...an epigraphist, I may be pardoned for laying most
stress on inscriptions' (*The Antiquary* XXIII (1891): 9), but he asked that
his readers forward information to him. Similarly, in 1892 he was requesting that new discoveries be reported to him: 'I shall, at all times,
be very grateful for any account of any new finds. I think it is not wholly
unfair to expect such assistance from other English archaeologists'
(1892b: 176). In the following year, reporting on inscriptions in Britain,
he noted that the task of revising inscriptions in Britain was not helped
by the lack of museums and the fact inscriptions tended to be scattered
among the nation's country houses (1893d: 279).

By the end of the series in 1902, Haverfield had provided 37 reports
on discoveries in Britain to *The Antiquary*. Their format was largely consistent, with him usually making introductory comments before going
on, in the earlier submissions at least, to describe the progress of what
he considered to be the most important projects (usually military and
urban), followed by rural sites (invariably villas) and stray finds by
less-well-known antiquarians. Here, he rarely offered comment on the
work of others, except occasionally to acknowledge his informants. The
sources of information were a combination of what he had been told (or
been written to about), what he had gleamed from the national and regional press and the result of his own visits. But he was aware that he was
not seeing everything of relevance. In *The Antiquary* (XXVI 1892) he
complained: 'I wish ...I could feel confident that all important discoveries were duly reported to some centre for publication in some such list
as that which I attempt. I have during the past two or three years come
accidentally upon really important finds, about which no word seems to
have appeared in any English "Proceedings" or "Transactions" or any
sort of periodical, while full accounts have been published abroad.'
Finally, these reports, again more so in the earliest submissions, were
places where he could highlight any relevant publications, British or
foreign, with comments, positive or negative. In the later years, the format changed slightly, with Haverfield grouping the discoveries by
region rather than topic. The sections on recent publications became
increasingly infrequent. It is clear that Haverfield's commitment to the

series progressively declined. This was in part due to delays caused by ill health, the effects of other unspecified problems and a general lack of material. The seasonal nature of the work he reported also made for some short summaries. Indeed in slack periods he used the articles to make observations about the state of archaeological research in Britain and to offer suggestions about how to remedy it (cf. Appendix 2). Some of these ideas were to reappear elsewhere later. As some examples, as early as 1892 he was calling on the regional societies to divert their energies from annual conferences and excursions for their members and instead to consider undertaking small scale, but detailed, excavations which would not only be informative but instructive in excavation techniques (*The Antiquary* XXVI (1892): 169ff.). In 1895 he was writing that the year was one of promise rather than performance (*The Antiquary* XXXI (1895): 201). Later, in 1897, commenting on the proposal to publish an index of the publications of the archaeological societies, he bemoaned the fact that the plan did not include the work of the non-societies. In this, his criticisms were directed towards the universities (*The Antiquary* XXXIII (1897): 105).

Another reason for Haverfield's declining enthusiasm for *The Antiquary* may have been its restricted readership. At about the same time as his commitment to the magazine was starting to falter he started to make contributions to the *Classical Review* in a series of contributions entitled *Discoveries of Roman Remains in Britain* which covered the years 1893, 1894, 1896 and 1898 (Haverfield 1893c; 1894b; 1896b; 1898c). In comparison to *The Antiquary* reports, these contributions are much slighter. Later still, in 1900 he started to submit annual reports on the same sort of material to the more highbrow *Athenaeum*, summarizing the results of 1899. The series continued down to 1905. Again the format was largely consistent, with the reports opening with general comments on the state of Romano-British archaeology before moving on to summarize on-going 'big' projects (e.g. Silchester and Caerwent) as well as military sites (Hadrian's Wall, and the work of the 'Scotch Society' – the Glasgow Archaeological Society along the Antonine Wall) before looking at other 'lesser' sites and projects. Again, the articles would close with comments on the publications of others. In the 1900 submission, Haverfield was to note the scale of excavation in Britain was outstripping the supply of competent directors with the consequence that more and more unskilled excavations were occurring (*The Athenaeum* 13 January 1900: 56). He was to develop this call in the following year: 'There is still grave danger lest we outrun our supply of men who are competent and willing to direct excavations – indeed, it is more than a danger. Why do not a few of our capable university archaeologists turn their attentions to the antiquities of their own country?' (*The Athenaeum* 5 January 1901: 24). Making such observations also afforded Haverfield opportunity to continue to dominate the agenda in the fashion that had been attempted in the 1880 and early 1890 reports.

Following the last contribution to *The Athenaeum* (reporting on 1904), in its aftermath nothing really replaced these annual articles, although he continued to submit occasional reports. The only other major pieces of archaeological synthesis he was to produce were reports on Roman Britain in 1912, 1913, 1914 and 1915 summarizing the previous year's work for the British Academy with all but the first being published in its *Proceedings*. In a fashion comparable to his experience in Britain, Haverfield made similar reports in German language journals. The process began with reports on Hadrian's Wall in 1896 in the *Korrespondenzblatt der westdeutschen Zeitschrift für Geschichte und Kunst* and was followed up, usually on epigraphic topics, in the same journal in 1898, 1899, 1903 and 1905. In time the reports were published in the *Archäologischer Anzeiger*, the mouthpiece of the Deutsches Archäologische Institut. In the early years these were simply reports but from 1909 onwards look more like overviews.[16] In turn the process came to be reversed, with Haverfield being able to report work in Germany to a British readership.[17] From his contacts with German scholarship also came the invitations to submit various entries to the *Pauly Wissowa Real-Encyclopädie Bände* I (1921), IA (1914), VIII (1913), IX (1916) and X (1919).

In terms of what Haverfield thought of the merits of the archaeological material he increasingly had to summarize and interpret, it is at about this time that we also see a slightly more expansive appreciation of the potential of all forms of inscriptions. In reporting on an inscribed *patera* from Barochan he added: 'I venture to impress on archaeologists the importance of noting all inscriptions on such smaller finds. We know that pelves (mortaria) were manufactured largely in Gallia Narbonensis, and Samian (pseudo-Arretine) largely in central Gaul, and we have learnt this solely from observation of potter's marks. We have seen that other maker's names have enabled us to trace some scattered bronze vessels to their Campanian home. In time, we hope thus to

---

16. *Archäol Anzeiger* XVI (1901); XVII (1902); XVIII (1903); XIX (1904); XX (1905). The change is evident in *Archäol Anzeiger* XXIV (1909); XXVI (1911); XXVII (1912); XVIII (1913) and XXIX (1914).

17. *Proc Soc Antiqs Newcastle*[2] VI (1893); *The Academy* 13 October 1894: *Proc Soc Antiqs Newcastle*[2] VIII (1898).

learn something about the real centres and distribution of Roman man-ufactured objects. Hitherto writers on Roman trade have erred by knowing too little of Roman history and antiquities and archaeologists have neglected the commercial aspects of their discoveries' (1892b: 201). The distinction between traditional literature and epigraphic-ar-chaeological evidence was taken a stage further in the same year, when Haverfield discussed an aspect of religion in northern (Roman Britain). In looking at the cults of the Mother Goddess he introduced his paper with the observation:

> It has often been remarked that the history of the Roman empire is based on two kinds of authorities which are strongly different. The re-cords of most ages confirm or correct one another: the literature and the inscriptions of the empire rarely touch. Facts, even names, mentioned in the one seldom appear in the other, and an inscription ...is all but unique. But the difference is nowhere most startling than in religious matters (*Archaeol Aeliana* XV (1892): 314).

In making these sorts of statements what we see in Haverfield is the emergence of what we would recognize today as an archaeologist in the modern sense of the word. In 1893, in the light of A. Riese's *Das Rheinische Germanien in der antiken Literatur* (1892), Haverfield was sug-gesting what was needed in Britain was a comparable 'source book' for the Roman province: 'It were much to be hoped that others in other parts of what was the Roman Empire would follow his example. For Britain the labour would not be great and I hope that some day I may (in default of abler scholars) try to fill the gap' (*Class Rev* VII (1893): 171). Of H.W. Preston and L. Dodge's *Private Lives* of the Greeks and Romans, he expanded the review to say that: 'It is time, I think that books on the subject of Roman Private life should take fuller account of archaeology', because books such as this tended to be more linguistic than archaeological, become methodical dictionaries of technical terms and had but '...seldom get to the full idea of describing life as generally lived by Romans' (*Class Rev* XVI (1902): 181). To make the point, Haverfield suggested jewellery and burial practices as potential topics, as well as agriculture and trade – 'It might have been worth while to indicate some of the features which distinguish ancient from modern trade.' In short this was a call for a wider outlook and a more profound insight on ancient life. In August of the same year, in an ad-dress to the Cambrian Archaeological Association, after making some general comments about trying to identify the ancient name of the small Roman fort at Gaer near Brecon, he admitted he was not overly concerned with the name. For:

> [o]ur predecessors in the study of Roman Britain have paid far too much attention to the identification of names ...If I can prove, for example that Bravonium is Leintwardine, as a scholar I am of course bound to note the fact, and I may thereby gain an item which combined with other items, will slightly advance knowledge. But I should make more progress if I could dig up and discover (apart from all questions of name) what the place was like in Romano-British days: whether a military post, or a posting station, or a village, whose inhabitants reached such-and-such a degree of wealth, or practised such-and-such an occupation. It is by learning these details, far more than by studying place names, that we may hope to recover some knowledge of the civilisation of Roman Britain. The thing is the important matter, not the name (Roman forts in South Wales. *Archaeol Cambrensis* LVIII (1903): 12–13).

For Haverfield the 'thing' was the fort. The point becomes the fort in its historical context. That progression continued in the next decade. Another example of Haverfield's (public) shift from language (and epigraphy) to archaeology can be seen in the way that he frequently called for a reconciliation between the two disciplines, with the emphasis on practioners of the former listening to the progress in the latter. After hearing a paper at the Society of Antiquaries of London, Haverfield was to write in the *Classical Review* that: 'Classical scholars in England have always been separated by a strange and regrettable gulf from the English archaeological societies and their work. It is therefore possible that readers of the *Classical Review* may have overlooked an interesting contribution to the interpretations of Caesar, recently read ...before the Society of Antiquaries'; *Class Rev* XIX (1905): 206). In the context of the time it was said, even more startling is his summary of what archaeological evidence was about. In his 1912 lecture to Oxford undergraduates, he observed:

> We talk somewhat professionally of archaeological evidence. It is well to remember that, if that evidence had happened to refer to the present, instead of the past, we should call it economic and not archaeological: so much of it refers to just the things which engage the reader of an ordinary social pamphlet (1912d: 25).

As will be discussed more fully in Chapter 6, Haverfield's involvement in a number of major (English) excavation projects also put him in a position to broadcast the achievements of recent research and in some respect control their dissemination. This allowed him to comment on the nature – and so quality – of work then being undertaken. It will be demonstrated that it offered him chances to ask for more and better run excavations, preferably with properly trained university students.

It also provided him the opportunity to complain either about the way that writers, frequently European but not exclusively so, were ignorant of recent publications or to bemoan that not enough space was given to issues of Roman history to which Britain was able to contribute. For example, of E. Ruggerio's *Dizinonaro Epigrafico di Antiochita Romane* (Fasc. 23–39), he noted '...a few other details which show that Mr Ruggerio, or his contributors, are less acquainted with the antiquities of Roman Britain and with the literature of the subject than they are with the corresponding material on the Continent. But in this they are simply imitating other foreign scholars, who rarely avoid extraordinary blunders in dealing with Britain' (*Class Rev* IX (1895): 236, and repeated in the *Class Rev* X (1896): 126). Likewise to a largely positive review of J. Jung's *Grundriss der Geographie von Italien und dem Orbis* (1897), he added that the work was short on Britain, a common trait of German texts, although he did concede that 'Britain was not, in most ways, an important province: the space allotted to it ...is naturally and rightly a small space' (*Class Rev* XII (1898): 175). However fifteen years later, in a review of J.S. Reid's *Municipalities of the Roman Empire*, he could write: 'I cannot help thinking (I may, of course, be hopefully prejudiced) that Roman Britain deserved somewhat more attention. After all, we know more about the towns of Britain than about those of any other Roman province. No place has been so excavated so thoroughly as Silchester. It is in Britain that we learn what the municipal life of the Empire really came to' (*Class Rev* XXVIII (1914): 172). Haverfield's complaint that British research was not being properly used could be an instance of the Little Englander, but in fact it was more to do with the aim of trying to demonstrate just how much Britain was part of the Roman empire, with the same range of institutions and material culture being handled by continental scholars. Likewise, his complaints might be an indirect reference to the still variable quality of publication in Britain. For despite all his attempts to overhaul the discipline and its broadcasting, the progress was not necessarily smooth. For instance, as late as 1917, in a damning review of his former collaborator, J.O. Bevan, and his *Towns of Roman Britain*, he started with:

> I regret to be unable to praise this booklet, all the more because, twenty years ago, I assisted Mr Bevan, then a Herefordshire vicar, in preparing a small archaeological survey of that county, of which I have pleasant recollections, though I have not the honour of his personal acquaintance. Still I am not compelled to say that Mr Bevan has not properly achieved the interesting task which he set himself, and that, I think, largely because he has not availed himself of known material. Some

eight years ago, I drew up a list of the few sites in Britain, which, as it seemed to me, could reasonably be declared to be Romano-British town sites ...The list has appeared in print several times. Mr Bevan takes no heed of it. In doing so he may, of course, be wise: it is hardly for me to say. But I am disturbed at finding that his book suggests to me that he has no very clear conception of what an ordinary Romano-British town was ... (*Class Rev* XXXI (1917): 146).

The matter of republishing outdated monographs was continued in the following year, when Haverfield reviewed the third edition of Codrington's *Roads in Roman Britain* (1918):

...its principal defect is a certain narrowness of aim. It is written very clearly with the eye of a practical surveyor and has the real merit of being based largely on autopsy. But, as so often happens, the surveyor has excluded the geographer. The general bearing of British geography on the lines of Romano-British roads is ignored ...Many questions that curious students might ask, if their interests reached beyond pure topography, get no answer from him. History fares little better than geography. A more serious fault is that Mr Codrington far too often neglects what has been written on the roads of Roman Britain by others before him ...Mr Codrington cares little for what others have done before him, unless, indeed, they lived as long ago as the eighteenth century .... The conclusion of the matter is that if writers on Roman Britain will not read what has been written about it, and do not attain accuracy, and if their readers do not demand such accuracy, the study of the subject will not advance (*English Hist Rev* 34 (1918): 245–7).

Such comments reflect Haverfield's essential optimism about how it was only in the area of archaeological research where there was then going to be any substantial progress. In reviewing, favourably, Rice Holmes' *Caesar's conquest of Gaul*, Haverfield closed by observing that 'I do not in the least believe that "we shall never know much more about Caesar in Gaul than we do now". No archaeologist would admit. Despite Colonel Stoffel's achievements it is practically true to say that archaeological exploration of Caesar's campaigns in Gaul – and for that matter, in Britain also, is hardly begun. We may have to wait for that exploration beyond Mr. Holmes' lifetime and mine...' (*Class Rev* XXV (1911): 258). Above all however, Haverfield's best-known affirmation of the potential of archaeology for the future understanding of Roman Britain was contained in his inaugural address to the newly created Society for the Promotion of Roman Studies (1911a). The presentation was wide ranging and aspects of it have already been discussed and others will be examined later. But with respect to archaeology as a discipline, he was critical of the way some societies had

failed to assist the discipline (with digs at the RAI/BAA and the proliferation of regional archaeological societies). He also suggested that
such societies had often prevented the state from becoming involved
(p. xi) and the reason why so-many societies failed was not so much
with the societies but with the English attitude to learning and expertise and to scientific training (p. xii). After summarizing the progress
in the study of Roman history as a consequence of Mommsen,
Haverfield went on to describe how there were newer forms of evidence to assist in the story, forms of evidence unavailable or unrealized
by Mommsen. In turn, in explaining what he believed archaeological
evidence to be, he revealed something of how his methodological outlook had evolved over the years.

> The fields of non-literary evidence offer a still wider and more fertile
> area of virgin soil. That is, indeed, the chief work to be done in Roman
> history, to wring life and blood out of stone ...The more I study the ordi-
> nary written materials, the harder I find it to learn the truth from them,
> the more often I feel the story which they tell is not the story which is
> worth telling ...It is no doubt hard to construct a 'story' out of archaeo-
> logical evidence, but it is certainly possible to construct history. It is
> possible today to write some sort of history of the Roman frontier in
> Scotland although the facts of that history are known to us mainly
> through archaeological evidence ...Art and epigraphy are old and famil-
> iar subjects for the Roman historian to embrace. We have now to go
> further to forms of archaeology which lack the written element natural
> to inscriptions and the language inherent in pictures (p. xv–xvii).

By this he meant material as diverse as potsherds, fibulae and house
ground plans. Such developments meant '...archaeological evidence at
present helps principally the student of the empire' (p. xviii). These,
and comparable issues, were themes Haverfield was to repeat in subsequent publications. In the report on the stamped samian recovered on
the Corbridge excavations between 1906 and 1914, he wrote of how
the material '...tell us, too, how little we can pretend to know of remains which have not been turned up by the spade' (Haverfield in
Forster 1915: 274). The 'public' recognition of the change to archaeologist came when Haverfield was elected in 1906 for the next year as
the Ford Lecturer in English History at the university. Part of the duties of this appointment was to deliver six public lectures. Those
lectures later formed the basis for one of the two best-known
Haverfield's monographs, *The Roman Occupation of Britain,* published
in 1924 (cf. Chapter 9 for the circumstances behind the delay in its appearance).

The culmination of Haverfield's transformation into an archaeologist in the modern sense can be seen in the debate in which he became embroiled with C.R.B. McGilchrist about Roman roads in Eskdale in north-west England (McGilchrist 1919). In summary McGilchrist disputed elements of Haverfield's projection of the course of the road, based on what he called a cursory visit to the location. This accusation upset Haverfield who countered that McGilchrist's visit was equally cursory and rounded off his response with: 'It does not seem that he used the spade and any exploration of a road must be called cursory which omits the spade ...(the excavator of such a road would be lucky to retrieve finds) few finds may result, and the evidence may be apparently neither proving or disproving, but that possibility does not excuse us from the work of digging when peace lets us resume such archaeological activity' (1919b: 29).

What is most ironic in Haverfield's metamorphosis into an 'archaeologist' championing the cause of excavation and the 'testimony of the spade' is that he was never highly regarded as an excavator by those who knew him. His earliest exposure to the complexities of excavation may have been while he was teaching at Lancing, but if this was so, then it was not recorded. Otherwise there was his association with Chester and later at Silchester. But in both cases, he was not involved in the day-to-day management of the excavations nor, as far as we can see, in the recording and writing up of the results. Instead he usually obtained access to the new inscriptions and the opportunity to provide interim summaries. Elsewhere he frequently used the results of such excavations in his works of synthesis. Haverfield's earliest attested involvement in fieldwork came as late as 1894 and his management of the work of the CEC. His other known excursion into fieldwork was with G.B. Grundy on a Roman road at Blenheim Park in 1897 (Haverfield 1899b). And yet, as early as 1891, commenting on the success of the excavations at Silchester, he was to express the opinion that the '...excavations have another value. They are admirably conducted and will serve as a pattern for similar undertakings elsewhere' (*The Antiquary* XXIV). A year later, the Lancing schoolmaster (or newly ensconced Christ Church fellow), was observing of the Cumberland and Westmorland Society's work at Hardknott Castle:

> One may congratulate the Cumberland and Westmorland antiquaries ...on the good work they have undertaken ...They have set an admirable example to the archaeologists of other counties. Hardknott is only an instance of many smaller Roman sites awaiting exploration, and capable of being thoroughly examined at a comparatively small cost. If every county society would restrict its printing and spend its reserve fund ev-

ery now and then on the scientific examination of such sites, our knowledge of Roman Britain would soon be enormously increased. The pattern has been set in the North: let us hope it will be followed throughout England (*The Athenaeum* 2 October 1892).

Elsewhere, on the back of his growing experience in the directing of excavations, he could more legitimately bemoan the shortage of competent excavators and site assistants as well as the frequently woeful level of on-site recording on many excavations. And it is true he did endeavour to address at least the first of these concerns (e.g. *The Athenaeum* 13 January 1900, 7 September 1901). Of course the irony in all these complaints is that Haverfield's day-to-day engagement did not commence until the CEC programme in 1894. But even then, reservations came to emerge during this project concerning his abilities to direct, record and interpret the results, concerns which seem to have followed him to Corbridge in 1906. While some of his acolytes tried to defend him against such accusations (notably Margerie Taylor, but see also Frere 1988: 1), still the generally agreed view of Haverfield as an excavator was that he was in fact better as an organiser or, better put, a facilitator, than a hands-on site director.

Conclusion

One of the frequently repeated features of Haverfield's career is that it was the involvement with Mommsen and the *CIL*, and the groundwork for the *Ephemeris Epigraphica* which he was to edit that turned Haverfield into an archaeologist of Roman Britain. There is more than an element of truth is these assessments, supported by a number of strands of evidence. As discussed in Chapter 3, the influence of and then contact with Mommsen was decisive in Haverfield's development. Nor is it coincidental that the range of projects and schemes that Haverfield initiated or was involved in show similarities with Mommsen's management of the same in Germany, albeit on a much reduced scale. The Gomme reviews of 1887 signal early on the transition. Pelham's review of the *Ephemeris Epigraphica* must also have had a bearing on the issue. The pattern of publications and the themes therein would seem to support this idea. There is, however, another dimension to the impression that Haverfield changed, if not overnight, but gradually into an 'archaeologist' of a certain type. In the first place his interests when and after he made contact with Mommsen remained strongly epigraphic in tone. And it was to remain so for the rest of the career, even if some have chosen to emphasize the archaeologist of Roman Britain facet. The regular statements he submitted to the *Archaeological Journal* and *The Antiquary* were unashamedly interested in inscriptions first, and only secondarily, excavation. Where he was short of material for the former, then he filled out his statements with progress reports on current excavations. His involvement with the major excavation programmes of the time, was also heavily influenced by the prospect of finding new inscriptions. Chester provided the example in this respect, Silchester the prospect of more. Even his involvement with the CEC was shaped by the plan to support his ideas about the dating of Hadrian's Wall and its components derived as they were, from an analysis of the epigraphic evidence for it.

Haverfield's transition to 'archaeologist' was more as an 'epigrapher-archaeologist' and was more gradual than has been previously thought. Contrary to received opinion, it was not achieved by the late 1880s to early 1890s. Nor was it a consequence of the *CIL* commission. The signs are that it had been going on before then. But what is more striking in this transition is the fullness of his blossoming as an archaeologist in the sense that it is now understood. This was to the extent that it led him to reject the contribution of the classics, to criticize the part played by the universities in producing suitably trained scholars and their reluctance to undertake field research. And yet, another paradox to Haverfield's career is that, despite his criticisms of the nation's universities, he played little or no part in the development of archaeology in his own institution. At best he was prepared to go along with the trend towards its greater integration in the degree of *Literae Humaniores*, letting others make the running. This is more than amply demonstrated in his extolling the virtues of studying ancient history as part of the School of *Literae Humaniores* in 1912 (Haverfield 1912d). In the published version of this lecture one can see how Haverfield believed how comfortably the type of (new) ancient history (where epigraphy rather than archaeology was the major innovation) then being taught at Oxford) could be used to teach students. The lecture demonstrates the fact Haverfield regarded himself in the first place as an Oxford academic in the *Lit. Hum.* tradition with all the strengths and virtues it inculcated rather than as an archaeologist or antiquarian. What the lecture may also indicate is another shift in Haverfield's perception of the work he was undertaking: a move away from the sort of archaeological work with which he had been involved in the 1890s and 1900s. This idea will be explored in a subsequent chapter but, as we saw in Chapter 4, Haverfield was prepared to let Henry Pelham and even more so Percy Gardner fight the cause for making the Ashmolean a centre for the study of the archaeology of classical antiquity. At worst, he was not an enthusiastic supporter of the independence of the subject. Instead he is revealed as an ancient historian with a particular, and perhaps at Oxford unique, interest in the application of inscriptions to the interpretation of classical antiquity. After all, his '...reputation as historian and epigraphist was European' (Carmichael 1919–20: 5). His involvement in other aspects of archaeological research, as it was then understood, were peripheral to these, his other, main preoccupations. Paradoxically despite his attacks on the rather slack contemporary perceptions of what archaeology could achieve along with the amateurism of English antiquarians and their societies, for the moment the thrust of his work continued to be directed through the regional societies and their national counterparts. Surprisingly, given his views in the 1880s, 1890s and 1900s, he remained constant to at least certain societies.

CHAPTER 6

Excavation as 'big business' in Britain

Introduction

Posterity recognizes Haverfield as an excavating archaeologist who through his involvement in a number of projects made a significant – if not defining – part in the development of Romano-British studies. This chapter examines the veracity of such assessments and will explore how his involvement in such work helped shape his published output. The mid-nineteenth century saw the initiation of three major excavations at known Romano-British towns: Wroxeter (1858), Silchester (1864) and St Albans (1869). The publicity and momentum that these excavations generated (coupled with discoveries on the continent) in turn, served to give (Romano-British) archaeology a second wind in the latter half of the century. The results of these (and other continental) excavations stimulated public interest and so, in a concomitant fashion, involvement in more excavation and scholarly publications. An equally important point to bear in mind about the projects that Haverfield became involved with is that they were formulated in the light of work on the continent: Chester, as the exploration of the legionary fortress; Silchester as a site to rival Pompeii (!), according to the proposal put forward by the site excavators; and Hadrian's Wall to match the work on the limes in Germany undertaken there by the Limeskommission.[1]

Exploration by excavation

(a) Chester (1890–92)
The earliest example of Haverfield's involvement in a publicly prominent project (and perhaps his first exposure to field work) was his

---

1. Macdonald 1919–20a: 484: 'Every well equipped scheme of excavation had, of course, his whole hearted support – Silchester, Caerwent, Newstead and Wroxeter' (= Macdonald 1924: 28).

participation in the work at Chester while still a schoolmaster at Lancing (Taylor 1920: 66–71). The discovery of *c.*30 inscriptions from the area of the North Wall at Chester in 1887 during repair work led to excavations in 1888, funded by the Chester and North Wales Archaeological and Historical Society. In the subsequent publication of the results, the excavator, J.P. Earwaker called on the Chester authorities to continue the excavations (Earwaker 1889; 1889–91; cf. Lloyd-Morgan 1996).[2] As the result of the Town Surveyor agreeing to the request, in '... the early part of this year (1890) Mr. F. Haverfield M.A. of Lancing College issued an appeal in connection with Professor Pelham of Oxford and Professor Middleton of Cambridge and other well known authorities on Roman remains, in order to raise funds for further excavation in the north wall' (Earwaker 1889–91: 204).[3] The appeal was supported by John Evans, as well as the bishops Wordsworth and Stubbs, and when it was claimed: 'Of all the historic sites in England, none are so likely to aid our knowledge of Roman history as the Roman military centres' (Scheme for the proposed excavations at Chester, *Archaeol J* 47 (1890): 192). Haverfield's involvement was probably occasioned by his having already advertised his part in *CIL* as well as his damning review of Earwaker's 1889 report summarising the progress to date. In this, he reserved particular criticism for the reading of the inscriptions prepared by de Gray Birch (Haverfield, *The Academy* 22 June 1889; cf. *Archaeol J* 48 (1891): 293).[4] In the capacity of Treasurer, Haverfield forwarded such funds that were raised between 1890 and 1892. In time he could claim that, as a result of his campaigning, both

2. John Pearson Earwaker (1847–1895) went up to Merton where he took his BA in 1872. He was in 1871 elected Secretary of the Oxford Archaeological and Historical Society and in 1873 was describing himself as deputy keeper in the Ashmolean Museum. This would have been an unofficial arrangement – probably for no more than three years – and perhaps one made with the keeper, J.H. Parker (Ovenell 1986: 232–3). Between 1887 and 1880 Earwaker published *East Cheshire, Past and Present or A History of Macclesfield*. He was also an authority on the wills and inventories of the Court of Probate at Chester. His connections with Haverfield overlapped in another context. Earwaker became embroiled in a public controversy concerning the state of the Roman villa at North Leigh, excavated between 1813 and 1816, a site with which Haverfield was later involved (1908–10; cf. Ch. 9).

3. 'I was felicitously able to guarantee a small sum for archaeological work' (Haverfield, *The Antiquary* XXXIII (1890): 9).

4. William de Gray Birch (1842–1922), son of the first keeper of Egyptian antiquities at the British Museum, was educated at Charterhouse and Trinity College, Cambridge. Between 1864 and 1902 he worked in the Manuscripts department of the British Museum. His main interests lay with Anglo-Saxon charters and medieval seals (cf. Astley 1923; obit. *Antiqs J* IV (1924): 323).

Oxford and Cambridge universities were involved, making financial contributions.[5] In 1891, an anonymous commentator of the appeal of Haverfield *et al.* for funds to support the work made a statement which says much about perceptions of the merits of archaeological evidence at this time: 'It must be remembered that the reconstruction of Roman Britain has to be based very largely on inscriptions, one that as a fact, one inscription is worth tons of pseudo Arretine (or Samian) ware' (Anon. 1891: 293). Even Mommsen was recruited. In a reply which says much about their shared outlook, he wrote Haverfield: 'I approve with all my heart the project of taking up on a great scale the excavation at Chester. For the story of the Roman Empire, as far as it has been based on the monuments, there is nothing so instructive as the great headquarters of the imperial army; the cemetery discovered at the beginning of the century at Deayonne has more advanced our knowledge of this period than all the vulgar scribblings which the plebs urbanae have [sic] filled our volumes' (letter, April 1896, Haverfield Archive).

In the light of what resulted, Haverfield's eagerness to become involved in the work at Chester was understandable. The 'reward' for his part, other than his reports on the progress of the work (and reviews of those who also handled the material), was to publish the 40 new inscriptions found.[6] The other architectural features and pieces of significant masonry found during this period were published by a local antiquarian, Edward W. Cox (e.g. Cox 1891–2). Difficult to underestimate is the fact that while still a Lancing schoolmaster, it cemented Haverfield's name in the public domain and not just among the academic fraternity.

5.   In 1891 the work was part-funded by University of Oxford and the Research Committee of the Society of Antiquaries. Later in the same year he could announce that the Craven Committee at Cambridge had advanced £40; cf. *The Antiquary* XXIV (1891). In *The Athenaeum* (31 October 1891), Haverfield reported the award of £60 from Oxford and Cambridge universities.

6.   The publications were distributed among a number of journals: e.g. *The Athenaeum* 13 December 1890, 16 May 1891, 31 October, 16 April and 23 July 1892, 27 January 1894; Haverfield 1889–91. In this respect Haverfield was helped by the appointment of an assistant to prepare the inscriptions, Mr E.F. Benson of King's College, Cambridge. There is something of an anomaly in Haverfield's publication of the Chester inscriptions. He certainly published a very short article on the original discoveries (*The Athenaeum* 13 December 1890, which Macdonald notes was reprinted in the *Archaeol Cambrensis* (1891), but he misses the same in *Proc Soc Antiqs London 1889–91* (pp. 205–7)), and yet Hübner (1890) was also producing much longer descriptions at the same time. One wonders if this situation contributed to Haverfield's dismissive opinions of Hübner, as noted in Ch. 4. Elsewhere Earwaker (1891) also published on the inscriptions.

(b) Silchester (1890–1909)

With his national and international reputation as an epigrapher (and by implication, an archaeologist) established by the *CIL* commission, it is not surprising that Haverfield came to be associated with the major excavation of a Roman town in Britain, that at Silchester (*Calleva Atrebatum*). Systematic excavation here had commenced under the Rev. J.G. Joyce in 1864 and continued after his death in 1884 (Boon 1974: 22–35: Hudson 1981: 31, 58–62). Following the presentation of a proposal to the Society of Antiquaries of London in February 1890 by George Fox (1833–1908) and William St John Hope (1854–1919), assisted by General Pitt-Rivers, a rejuvenated programme commenced in the same year (Fox and St John Hope 1889–91). In their submission, the objective was no less: '...the complete and systematic excavation of the site' (p. 85). 'The result of excavation ...if these excavations are carried on steadily and thoroughly, will be to reveal to the world the whole life and history, as seen in its remains, of a Romano-British city, a city which we already know had a long continued existence' (p. 92). The goal was to produce a site to rival the contemporary discoveries at Pompeii. The results from the Italian town had long exerted an influence on the imagination of British archaeology where, for instance, Joyce's earlier reports had constantly measured and compared his material with that from it. In the Fox–St John Hope proposal however, there was the realisation that the British evidence should be different.[7] The proposal recommended excavation of the site for a variety of reasons, some of which might be characterised today as research priorities, others to elucidate problems or resolve contradictions created by the earlier excavations.[8] Finally there was a call

7. 'The examples at Silchester tell us something of the disposition of such dwellings and also point to the important fact that they differed considerably from the well-known types of the Roman houses as seen in the south of Europe ... The dissimilarity of our northern climate from that of the south of Europe must have induced an equal dissimilarity in the habits of life, and the Greco-Roman or Roman house, as seen in Pompeii would have proved uninhabitable in Britain' (Fox and St John Hope 1889–91: 90).

8. These included the unusual shape and layout of the site for potential explanations for its foundation. The extent of its layout was noted and that earlier excavations at the site had not been as extensive as commonly imagined. As such the ground plans of a number of houses required corroboration, as well ascertaining if the houses possessed bath suites. More specific suggestions included the investigation of the site's public buildings so that they could be compared to those of Pompeii, the excavation of a complete *insula*, discovery of the public bath complex and so the town's water supply and drainage along with its theatre, temples, occupations and trades and cemeteries.

to national pride in supporting such a venture. 'In Italy the government undertakes the exploration of historic cities; in England similar explorations are left to private enterprise, or can only be achieved under the auspices and by the aid of learned societies. Our country has many Roman sites still awaiting the pick and spade, none more promising than Silchester, and it is a reproach to English archaeology that so little has yet been done to make the yield the harvest of knowledge which they would undoubtedly afford' (p. 92; cf. 96).

The society's response to the application of which Haverfield spoke in support was highly favourable. A subscription fund and Excavation Committee were soon established. Excavation began later in the same year and continued for the next twenty years. Annual reports were published in the *Archaeologia* and the *Proceedings* of the excavations' principal supporter (cf. Clarke *et al.* 2001). While he recognised, however, the importance of the site from the outset, describing it at one time as 'the Elderado [sic] of English Antiquities' (*The Antiquary* XXIII (1890): 9), Haverfield does not appear to have been intimately involved in the excavations until as late as 1900 when he appears as a committee member along with Fox, St John Hope, Mill Stephenson and William Gowland – the last two named were subsequently involved with the excavations at Corbridge.[9]

The long-term significance of the Silchester excavations is difficult to understate. It remains one of the best-explored town plans in Europe, if not the best understood (Boon 1974: 31). The results continue to be used today even though they were hindered by the limited excavation techniques of the day and the poor quality of much of the site's stratification. Hudson described the excavations, along with Pitt-Rivers' contemporary work at Cranborne Chase as '...the two most important archaeological laboratories of the nineteenth century where every kind of mistake was made and an encouraging wide range of useful lessons learned' (Hudson 1981: 58). Browning (1989: 354) also made much of the Pitt-Rivers connection and his innovative methods of excavation in her description of how the site was explored. The objective in this re-

---

9. Mill Stephenson (1857–1937; cf. MSG 1937; Hudson 1981: 31–2). William Gowland (1842–1922), later Emeritus Professor of Metallurgy at the Royal School of Mines was a metallurgist with an interest in ancient metal working techniques. He reported on hearths for Bushe-Fox at Hengistbury Head (1911–12). Haverfield consulted him for the *VCH* Northants. volume (p. 178: cf. Hudson 1981: 24; Evans 1943: 108). He is best remembered as an excavator of Stonehenge, a site with which Haverfield had an unusual connection (cf. n. 84 below).

spect was the exposure of as much of the ground plan of the site as possible. But for all the significance of the excavations in the history of Romano-British archaeology, for some, aided with hindsight, the results from Silchester are deemed disappointing, although in truth this was a realization made soon after the completion of the excavations. Haverfield is cited as a caviller in this respect, although it was Collingwood who has been the most influential critic. In the subsequent decades the excavations have been criticised by many (Richmond 1960: 173; Boon 1974: 30ff.). Digging out rooms produced finds in great quantities but not necessarily context. Clarke *et al.* (2001; cf. Fulford and Clarke 2002) note, however, that with the excavators' preoccupation with exploring an entire *insula* (concentrating on *Insula* IX), in the absence of total excavation, the most efficient way was by digging diagonal trenching across the insula. What the excavators apparently did not take into account in their pursuit of ground plan was depth and where a commonly voiced criticism is how the excavators failed '…to record any temporal dimension to the site' (mainly because they did not understand stratification: cf. Browning 1989: 354). Boon claims that Haverfield even denied the existence (or survival) of the 'successive deposits' at the site, citing Haverfield in the *VCH* Hants. (I: 275 = *Proc Soc Antiqs London* XXII: 323; cf. Boon 1974: 30, n. 12).[10] But this is not strictly true. On a number of occasions the excavators did comment on the difficulty of excavating there (Boon 1974: 31). In fact Haverfield was alert to the excavations' limitations too. As one example, he observed that the excavation '…has in one point failed to attain the success which so admirably conducted an undertaking deserves, and which in general it has confessedly attained. No light has yet been thrown on the chronology of the town's history' (*The Athenaeum* 15 December 1894: 836). The sense of reservation, which shows something of Haverfield's maturing into an archaeologist rather than an interpreter of artefacts, is further evident when he wrote:

> The Silchester excavations are of a rather peculiar character. They do not, and in the nature of things they cannot, result in a continuous succession of startling discoveries, each interesting and significant by itself.

10. In the *Proceedings of the Society of Antiquaries of London* Haverfield is reported as having said: 'Hitherto little assistance has been obtained from stratification, internal evidence being relied upon for dating.' In the *VCH*, it is written: 'Its [viz. Silchester's] remains do not even lie in successive strata, like the remains of many long-lived towns.' Haverfield noted that Joyce had seen such deposits in the 1870s, but added that the later excavators had not found the same. He was at a loss to explain the anomaly.

But I fear that many persons expect such discoveries and are disappointed at their absence, and through the disappointment are led to underestimate the real value of the excavations. It may therefore be proper to say that the excavations have a very definite value for historians and archaeologists. This value does not depend so much on individual finds, though they are not by any means unimportant: it depends on the culminative result of the uncovering of a whole town (*The Antiquary* xxxiv (1898): 233).

Reading the subsequent reports of the excavations, one is struck by the way the project seems to have drifted to an end by the years just before the outbreak of the War. Despite his often positive and optimistic summaries in the likes of *The Academy* and the *Classical Review*, not even Haverfield could avoid the feeling that the excavations ran out of steam, as the results seemed not to come up to expectations. What is more, all the reports on the excavations create the same sense that Haverfield was very much a peripheral figure in their execution. This is contrary to some of the obituaries which otherwise imply that he was a major figure in the project. In fact he is virtually anonymous in the credits and there are few instances of him mentioning visits to the site. That said Haverfield profited from his association with Silchester in other ways. What he derived from the excavations was in the first place simply 'association'. This was in the publicity that came from his being on the committee. While others saw to the day-to-day and season-to-season execution of the excavations, Haverfield had access to the otherwise relatively slight number of inscriptions found. What is more, Macdonald's list of Haverfield's publications contains no less than seven major articles which resulted from it. This does not include the numerous commentaries on epigraphic material or general résumés on the progress of the work, access to which was afforded by Fox and Hope (Haverfield 1892b: 182). In these discussions Haverfield displayed a growing knowledge of continental material to elucidate or substantiate his explanations of the Silchester material (e.g. his discussion (1895a) of Roman coinage in the light of a hoard from Silchester and his discussion (1904e) which compared the end of Silchester with the end of Roman life in the province of Noricum Ripense). Not unsurprisingly, the results from Silchester also featured strongly in his major works of synthesis (1905: 193–5; 1924), and in his other publications on the likes of Roman town planning and on the advent of Christianity in Britain. Not for the first time, one is left with the impression that Haverfield benefited from his association with the project with the minimum of commitment on his part.

(c) The Caerwent Excavation Committee (1899–1917)

Haverfield's participation in the excavations at the Roman town of Caerwent in south Wales, even less marginal to that of Silchester, is another example of his gaining access to the progress of on-going projects. For he was not involved in its excavation, nor its management or its finances. Therefore the invitation to become 'involved' has to be a consequence of his national authority. At the same time as the Silchester excavations, in 1899 the Caerwent Excavation Committee commenced the first of a series of excavations. The committee was an adjunct of the Clifton Antiquarian Club, established in 1884 with the intention of arranging excursions in western England and South Wales.[11] According to Boon, although the Caerwent excavations were the inspiration of Alfred Hudd, John Ward and A. Trice Martin, Haverfield managed to have 'planted' Thomas Ashby '...among the amateurs to provide a modicum of control and a direct link back to Oxford if anything of importance was turned up' (1989: 9).[12] The irony of this is that Ashby can have possessed little, if any, excavation experience (Hodges 2000: 22–30) and Haverfield only marginally more. Ashby had previously worked with R.C. Bosanquet at Housesteads on Hadrian's Wall in 1898, where he was responsible for clearing the mithraeum as well as assisting Haverfield in the work of the Cumberland Excavation Committee. How Haverfield managed Ashby's placement is not known. When the excavation committee was formed in 1899, neither he nor Ashby were members. Ashby was added afterwards. Again, supported by the Society of Antiquaries of London and through which Haverfield may have known Ward and the others, unsurprisingly the aims of the committee were to replicate the Silchester exercise (Martin *et al.* 1901; Boon 1989: 9). 'Inspired by the example of Silchester, the committee decided to carry out as far as possible a systematic excavation of the site. It is not often that an opportunity offers (and still less often is it taken) of exploring a greater part of the site of a Roman country town, and if we are able to examine all those parts of it which are not occupied by buildings or which will not manifestly prove unfruitful, we shall be able to supply the only English parallel to the work at Silchester. And, so far, as we have gone, the differences are of sufficient importance to add greatly to the interest of the work' (Ashby 1904: 103). Indeed the reports of the progress of the an-

---

11. Bearing in mind Haverfield's childhood connections with Bath, this might explain his involvement with the society.

12. Hudd (1845–1920) was a local gentleman antiquarian and Ward (1856–1922), the curator at Cardiff Museum. Martin (1855–1927), educated at Worcester College (Oxford) was a schoolmaster at Clifton College.

nual excavations are full of the descriptions, the dimensions and reconstructions of houses. The seasons went from 1900 to 1917 and one of their striking features is how long some of them were.[13] The annual reports, usually published in the *Archaeologia*, were in the early years authored by a combination of Martin, Hudd and Ashby (1899 to 1903 inclusive) with Ashby assuming sole responsibility for the reports 1904 to 1906.[14] From 1907 until 1910 the authors were Ashby, Hudd and Frank King (who had acted as one of the site architects). In the final *Archaeologia* report the sole writer was Hudd.[15] Rarely do any of the reports provide an indication of who was responsible for running the site. In 1907 it was Ashby, Hudd, King and an H.L. Jones and F.G. Newton and in 1909 and 1910 Ashby, Hudd, King, Jones and a (Mr) White.[16] Haverfield's part in the project is supposed to have been as the epigrapher for the annual reports published in the *Archaeologia*. And yet his name is almost entirely absent from these accounts. The one exception is his commentary on what was to become *RIB* 311, the decree of the *civitas* of the Silures (Ashby *et al.* 1904).[17] Otherwise Haverfield does not feature in the excavation and his processing of the inscriptions discovered by the excavations was done in other publications. Ultimately Ashby's involvement withered as he became increasingly committed to the fledgling British School at Rome. He had long severed his association by the time the committee and its excavations folded in 1917.[18]

Other than access to the new inscriptions, it is difficult to see what Haverfield derived from the Caerwent programme other than the same sort of advantages we have seen for Chester and Silchester. It served to

13. E.g. 1907, 29 April until October; 1908, 15 June to 6 November; 1909, 21 June to 6 December.
14. Ward was evidently supposed to be responsible for the exploration of the town's fortifications but progress towards them was slow during which time he became involved in excavations at Gellygaer (1900–01). While what was discovered about Caerwent's walls was included in the main season reports, Ward (1916) was later invited to produce an overview of the Caerwent excavations relative to the fortifications as well as to report in detail his own unpublished work.
15. Interim reports: Ashby 1905; 1906; 1907; Ashby *et al.* 1902a; 1902b; 1904; Ashby *et al.* 1908; 1909; 1910; Hudd 1912–13; Martin *et al.* 1901.
16. Jones later turns up working with the Manchester Excavation Committee. One suspects Mr White is in fact H.G. Evelyn White. Both Jones and Evelyn White are discussed in Ch.8.
17. First published in *The Athenaeum* 26 September 1903: 420.
18. There is only one instance of a potential disagreement between Ashby and his colleagues, in the interpretation of some burials in the 1911–12 report (Hudd 1912–13: 438).

introduce him to a wider circle of fieldwork and fieldworkers, which in turn he was happy to support, advise and publicize. He even contributed to the work of others. Subsequently, familiarity with the Welsh/Celtic connection was to assume a prominent position in his opinions on later Roman Britain.[19] In assessing the work undertaken at Silchester and Caerwent (and the slightly later excavations at Wroxeter), Richmond was critical of the failure on the part of the excavators to appreciate the significance of the stratification at each of the sites. However he had to acknowledge: '...the pioneer work of the nineteenth [century] still remains outstanding for its scope and vigour, and its very negligence has left opportunities, yet to be realized in many places' (1960: 173).

(d) Hadrian's Wall (1894–1903)

One of the reasons that Haverfield was not involved in the day-to-day excavation of Silchester (and Caerwent) lies with his growing commitment to fieldwork along Hadrian's Wall. In fact, work in northern England was to become the focus of his fieldwork for nearly twenty years: '...a district in which he was intimately connected by bonds both personal and professional. For ten years he spent almost his whole leisure time in excavations on the line of Hadrian's Wall in Cumberland, and during all the latter part of his life he was a frequent visitor to Carlisle and a familiar figure in the Museum at Tullie House (Carlisle)' (Collingwood in Haverfield 1922: iii). His affection for the region was such that when he acquired in 1909 in the Headington suburb of Oxford a new house commensurate with the status of a senior academic he named it Winshields after his favourite location on the Wall.[20]

---

19. For example, he was to broadcast the results of the Cardiff Naturalists Society's excavations at the fort of Gellygaer, to which he submitted a short article to its final report; cf. Ward (1903). In that report Ward also recounts (p. 66) the episode of the 'Haverfield posts', where Haverfield, from his experience of excavating in the north of England, advised that the excavators look for a line of postholes which turned out to be the posts to a veranda to a barrack block (cf. Haverfield 1910b: 134–6). The importance of Roman Wales to Haverfield was that it was the epicentre of what he believed to be the Celtic revival of the fourth–fifth centuries and later.

20. Winshields, west of Housesteads fort is the highest point, at 1230ft ASL, on the Wall and therefore enjoys extensive prospects. The closest Wall structure was the MC40, excavated in 1908. There is no record of Haverfield ever conducting fieldwork there. For the background to the development of Headington, cf. Graham 1991. The house was/is in Pullens Lane. Writing to the Newcastle society to thank them for their letter of condolence following the death of her husband, Winifred Haverfield said '..the part of his work

Haverfield's work with respect to northern England went through three phases. His involvement in excavation was an indirect consequence of the invitation in 1888 to participate in the *CIL*. Up to that date he appears not to have published any substantial discussion concerning British inscriptions. Between 1889 and 1893, however, he wrote at least 80 articles on such, of which 25 were devoted to material from the Wall and its hinterland (Macdonald 1924: 43–4). Then there was the work of the Cumberland Excavation Committee (CEC), conducted under the auspices of the Cumberland and Westmorland Archaeological and Antiquarian Society (CWAAS). Finally, there was his involvement, between 1906 and 1913, with the Northumberland County History (NCH) and its flagship excavations at the site of Roman Corbridge.

Yet again, as with other aspects of his career, Haverfield's entry to Mural studies came at an opportune moment. The mid-nineteenth century had seen a number of publications hypothesising on the Wall's function and date along with its components. But it was only relatively recently that local antiquarians such as John Hodgson and John Collingwood Bruce had dared to suggest the Vallum was a military work meant to afford protection to the southern side of the Wall. They also challenged the orthodox view that the Wall was Severan or later, as had been traditionally believed. It was in fact Hadrianic (Birley 1961; Maxfield 1982; Breeze 2003). Although their arguments were vehemently attacked at the time and there was no conclusive evidence or context to prove their claims, their ideas were based on field observations and reading the landscape in a way earlier antiquarians had not appreciated. What is more, they recognised that the various opinions could only be resolved by excavation.

How and why Haverfield came to move to Hadrian's Wall is not entirely clear. Perhaps the earliest indication of Haverfield's interest in mural questions is an unnamed review of G. Neilson's *Per Lineam Valli* (1891) in the *Archaeological Journal* (XLIX: 95–7).[21] It was Neilson's opinion that the Vallum was Hadrianic in date and therefore a pre-Wall construction defence. But the reviewer, if it was or was not Haverfield, noted that: '...Mr Neilson's ingenious arguments will probably convince all his readers who do not know the wall or have only a superficial knowledge of it. Those who do know more, more than a visit of eight days can teach, will probably say with Lord Eldon, curi vult animadversari. Mr Neilson's

---

which gave him most happiness was that done on the Roman wall' (Blair 1919: 117).

21. The author could have been J.P. Gibson or Pelham or Hodgkin. Haverfield offered comments on it in *The Antiquary* XXV (1891).

arguments may be difficult to answer, but there are difficulties he will have to answer when the weather permits of sections and plans being taken; that can only be done in the summer.' Whoever the author was, the significance of the review was that it represented the *communis opinio* of the time.

Haverfield was to write that 1892 was a pivotal year for mural studies (and not least for him). In that year there came together a number of strands of research which were to compliment one another in subsequent years (*The Academy* 28 October 1893). For instance, at about the time of the publication of the Neilson review, he was discussing the date of the Wall. His approach was disarmingly simple. He started by reviewing the epigraphic evidence from it and to a lesser degree the coins found from the same region. Presenting the evidence in a paper to the London society, he concluded the Wall, forts and milecastles had to be Hadrianic and were probably completed or refurbished under Antonius Pius: Severus did not build or repair it (Haverfield 1892a). For the Vallum, he had no evidence. Recognising that Hodgson and Bruce had argued for this date previously, and that all these elements originated with the Stone Wall, Haverfield continued:

> During the last two or three years however there have been signs of a revolt against it (the Hodgson-Bruce view), and in event of a discussion arising, it may be well to state shortly and clearly the evidence which inscriptions furnish ...As is often the case elsewhere, the inscriptions of the Roman wall tell us what historians omit, and are silent about what historians narrate. Their results are, moreover definite and in no way dependent on personal bias. The view which an inquirer takes of a topographical problem is very largely influenced by his own characteristics ...variety of opinion is intelligible when we have to deal with the topographic details of fortifications which stretch some eighty miles (p. 45).

As it transpired, in the absence of state or university mechanisms, the initiative was to be conducted under the auspices of the CWAAS and the CEC. Now, however, the CEC's energies were concentrated on revealing more about the history and development of (the western end of) the Wall and its constituent components. The society had a record of co-ordinating such work in its province. It had previously sponsored systematic work in the region.[22] For instance, in 1886 it established a

22. On the occasion of Haverfield's death, R.H. Blair recalled when Haverfield reminded him how they had met over 30 years previous in the dining room of John Clayton at Chesters (Blair 1919: 117). Clayton died in 1890, so the event must have been in 1889 or slightly earlier. Haverfield's visit to the north must have been occasioned by a trip to examine inscriptions but it may also be significant that the later CEC excavations worked on sites owned by the Claytons.

committee to make the preparations for the (2nd) Pilgrimage to Hadrian's Wall (27 June to 3 July). This involved it marking the course of the Wall and Vallum for the pilgrims with coloured flags. The committee was also empowered to initiate excavations at appropriate locations. It chose to look at sites where the Wall crossed, or bridged, the county's rivers, including work in and around Birdoswald (e.g. at Poltross Burn). The Pilgrimage, described at length in the *TCWAAS*, held a commemorative dinner in Carlisle on 2 July, when it was reported that toasts were made to the call for closer collaboration between the two north English archaeological societies. The representative of the CWAAS, R.S. Ferguson, observed that he believed it to be the first occasion when the two societies had met in joint meeting and perhaps, indicative of previous relations between the two societies, offered he '...would like to arrange that the Newcastle society should make an invasion of the sister society's county' (Anon. 1888: 149). There is no evidence that the offer was taken up in the short-term and the fact there was no mention of the work of the committee after the Pilgrimage suggests that it was very much a one-off arrangement.[23] In 1892 the society patronized explorations at Hardknott which went on until 1894.[24] Indeed Haverfield was to praise this initiative elsewhere. The society, or at least some of its members, had long cherished plans to work at this site. Following a disappointing preliminary season in September 1889 and follow-up work in 1890 and 1891, the society decided to organize '...a proper attack', and offered to find a competent excavator while the site-owner would fund the labour. The society appointed C.W. Dymond as its director. It is presumably through this mechanism, where the society planned excavation and then made a commitment to find a director was how Haverfield ended up working with the CWAAS. With his increasing contribution to northern epigraphy, a consequence of the *CIL*, it is not surprising that when plans were made for the systematic exploration of the Wall and its components Haverfield was an obvious candidate to lead the work. What is surprising is that he had no experience of leading let alone directing any excavation. At Chester, Silchester and Caerwent he was more a passenger than one of the leaders. It has been suggested Haverfield's association with the CWAAS

---

23. There is, however, mention of another committee, established at the last meeting, and meant 'to explore the track of the Roman road across Burgh Marsh' but which had failed to complete the task.

24. There may be some confusion here. R.G. Collingwood (Hardknott Castle. *TCWAAS* 28 (1928): 314–52) reports that the excavations went through 1889, 1890 and 1891 (Anon. 1893; cf. Bidwell *et al.* 1999: 1).

originated with Pelham who had taken an interest in the northern frontier because of developments along the German *limes* (E. Birley to Taylor 11 February 1962, Haverfield Archive). There are, however, problems with this attribution. Pelham was certainly even less an (excavating) archaeologist than Haverfield and had no known record of fieldwork in the region – he was originally from Norfolk. Indeed he only joined the CWAAS in 1895, five years after Haverfield. Elsewhere Haverfield attributed the initiative to the late Chancellor R.S. Ferguson, President of the CWAAS and that this phase of work was inspired by the progress of: '...the scientific labours of the Imperial "limes commission" [which] have made our knowledge of the Roman frontier works in Germany far more minute than our knowledge of the English Wall' (1899a: 337).

There was another important contributing factor to the reasons why the CEC ended up working in the way that it did. The continental, and more precisely the German, connection was vital for what was to become the CEC. For Haverfield (and Pelham), the attraction of the German approach to their work on the *limes* was that it was systematically organised and executed and because it was adequately funded from state coffers (Pelham 1911: 182; cf. Haverfield *The Academy* 28 October 1893). It must be more than coincidence that about the time plans were afoot for the CEC, there occurred the visit of General Otto von Sarwey, the military director of the *Obergermanisch-Raetische Limes* (ORL), to the region in June–July 1893, although again the circumstances behind his trip remain lost. The significance of the visit was that the RLK had only just been created in 1892. The tour, comprising 'a party of Oxford and northern counties archaeologists' (*The Academy* 28 October 1893; cf. Croke 53), was planned as early as March 1893 when v. Sarwey, presumably on Mommsen's suggestion, wrote to Haverfield (Croke 52), and coincided with the CWAAS AGM tour of the Wall. Accompanied by Haverfield, the party visited Hadrian's Wall before moving on to Scotland where William Ramsay joined them for a tour of the Antonine Wall (Croke 53, 9 July 1893; Ramsay to Mommsen, 12 July 1893: 120). Two days later Mommsen was to write and thank Haverfield for accommodating v. Sarwey in a letter that also noted Nettleship's death (Croke 54). Ramsay evidently sent reports of their progress to the newspapers, *The Times*[25] and *The Athenaeum* (15 July 1893: 105–6 and 29 July 1893: 167–8), before returning to Edinburgh from where Haverfield wrote to Mommsen. Following their

25. I have been unable to find any such letters in the indices to *The Times*.

excursion, Haverfield said of v. Sarwey's tour that it '...has done something towards advancing the study of the Vallum in bringing out more clearly the difficulties in the way of considering it a military work. Whether or no my own theory of a political frontier be accepted, I think that the problem has got into a new stage. The possibility of a non-military purpose has been made and the long dominant military view will need fresh evidence before it can assert itself again' (*The Antiquary* XXVIII (1893): 162; cf. *The Academy* 28 October 1893). Von Sarwey's trip was reciprocated when Haverfield accompanied him on a tour of the German frontier in September of the same year (Croke 59). The trip was commemorated by Haverfield writing *A Walk Along the Pfahlgraben*, an open letter addressed to Thomas Hodgkin of the Newcastle Antiquaries (Haverfield 1893b).[26] The letter was directed to Hodgkin because he had published a lengthy description about the frontier ten years earlier (Hodgkin 1883). In his account Haverfield described the organization of research along the German frontier, including the financial arrangements (£2000 for five years) and the competence of the excavators. Interestingly, his attentions were not restricted to the exploration of the system's forts. He acknowledged the existence of *canabae* attached to some forts and noted that similar sites were known in Britain but that it was a pity that they had not previously been explored. Haverfield also described for his correspondent the discovery of an unusual feature, of a small ditch running in advance but parallel to the main frontier line and possibly bridged with crossing points (and further reported in *The Guardian* on 10 October). Haverfield speculated this might have been a non-military boundary marker. He ended his account by noting that v. Sarwey was keen that

---

26. This is a feature of the latter half of the nineteenth and the early twentieth centuries: British visitors, often academics or antiquarians, publishing descriptions of their recent visit to continental museums and sites: e.g. J. Yates 'Limes Rhæticus and the Limes Transrhenæus of the Roman empire – 1852', *Proceedings of the Institute at the Newcastle Meeting* I (1858): 97–134. The example of J. Mowat, who not only walked with H.F. Tozer from Land's End to John O'Groats but also the Pfahlgraben and the Reisenmauer, is discussed in n. 29. In 1904 James Hilton published 'The Pfahlgraben and Saalburg in Germany' (*Archaeol J* LXI (1904): 319–25), which followed up a report in the same journal 20 years before. The most prolific reporter was Bunnell Lewis. As a selection, 'Roman antiquities on the middle Rhine', *Archaeol J* XLVII (1890): 193–214 and 378–405; 'Roman antiquities in the Rhineland', *Archaeol J* LX (1903): 318–73. The tradition of writing synthetic reviews continued into the next century (e.g. Brogan 1933–4; 1935).

similar work should be undertaken in the United Kingdom, and that perhaps Hodgkin, who was then excavating, might undertake it: '...General von Sarwey is most anxious that search should be made along your wall, to see if such a small ditch and stones exist. The search would require great care ...But the search is well worth making, the more as you are actually engaged in making sections' (Haverfield 1893b: 80). Haverfield was to repeat many of these opinions expressed in a letter to *The Academy* (28 October 1893: viz. the Wall to stop incursions and was Hadrianic in date; the Vallum, because it was placed not as near to the Wall in its mid-sections as it could have been, was therefore not defensive in design, and so probably political and so earlier in date than the Wall). Shortly later in one of his regular contributions to *The Antiquary* (XXIX (December 1893), Haverfield went on to outline an agenda for the future study of the Wall.

It is clear the period late 1893 to early 1894 and the contact with v. Sarwey was crucial for the development of Mural studies. It '...is apparent that it was Haverfield who was the one most interested in making sure that advances in knowledge of the ORL was taken into account in research on Hadrian's Wall: witness his letters to Hodgkin reporting in what he had seen and learnt in the course of a visit to the limes in the autumn of 1893' (letter, M.V. Taylor to E. Birley, 11 February 1962, Haverfield Archive).[27] Then there was Jacobi's discovery in September 1893 of the 'stone border' on the German *limes* which in turn seems to have been the inspiration for Haverfield *et al*.'s proposal formulated in mid-1894 (cf. Croke 59 – March 1894, and responding to Mommsen's enquiry in Croke 57). One exchange of opinions was v. Sarwey's belief that the Vallum along the Wall had no military function, a view with which Haverfield at the time disagreed. Whatever the case, in the years after v. Sarwey's visit Haverfield was kept informed, and publicized the results, of work in Germany, not least because he was critical of British scholars inability to read, let alone obtain reports in, German (Croke 59).[28] Such contacts led to an awareness of the achievements of German

---

27. In a letter already cited, Eric Birley wrote Margerie Taylor: '...I tried for a long time to fit into my book [*Research on Hadrian's Wall* – 1961], what will one day have to go into a special paper: namely a survey of the connections between Oxford, the ORL and Hadrian's Wall. The key was 1892–1894' (11 February 1962, Haverfield Archive). It seems that that study was never written. The task was partially but not satisfactorily completed by Browning (1989).

28. In the years after the 1893 excursion, Haverfield was kept informed of work in Germany (e.g. March, July 1894). Von Sarwey is explicitly mentioned as a

work on the *limes* there and in doing so influenced the agenda for the study of the Wall. Finally, it provided an introduction, if not training, to the potential of archaeological research. Haverfield's original interest in the Wall was occasioned by its epigraphy but exposure to the German work led to an appreciation of the limitations of that category of evidence and from this loss of confidence and increasing awareness of what properly conducted archaeological excavation might achieve.

On the back of the contacts and visits made during 1893, in March 1894 Haverfield wrote to Mommsen, outlining his (and Pelham's) plans to excavate on the Wall and the Vallum, perhaps at suitable forts, with the intention of proving once and for all that Bruce on the Vallum was wrong. 'We …are about to issue an appeal for funds to enable …further examination, and in particular to (1) to cut sections thro' and explore the vallum; (2) to dig up one or two suitable fortresses and forts, (I have always thought that Bruce's view of the earthwork is wrong; we wish to go on to certainty' (Croke 59). Later in the same year, Pelham and Haverfield along with J.L.G. Mowat[29] circulated a statement entitled *Exploration of Hadrian's Wall* to the likes of *The Academy* (23 June) appealing for subscriptions to help facilitate the scheme. After summarizing how the exploration of frontier systems elsewhere in the Roman empire had progressed, they proposed systematic excavation of the best pre-

---

source of information in 1893 (in the otherwise undated Croke 61) as was Mommsen (Croke 57 and 60). In July 1894 Mommsen was writing to Haverfield 'Though you won't enter into the Triple Alliance (and you are quite right), I hope regarding the vallum, the two nations will combine their researches and every discovery made on either side of the sea will be an appeal to the other' (Croke 60).

29. John Lancaster Gough Mowat (1846–1894), of St Helen's Jersey, was educated at Exeter College, where he was a scholar from 1865. He was from 1871 a Fellow of Pembroke College, where he was variously lecturer, Senior Bursar and Junior Dean, Librarian and Proctor. He became a student of Lincoln's Inn in 1876. Described as 'an antiquarian, a botanist and a great pedestrian' who had explored Hadrian's Wall, he accompanied T.M. Crowder of Corpus and H.F. Tozer on a walk of the length of the Pfahlgraben in the summer of 1884. A brief account of their tour was published privately by Mowat (cf. *A Walk along the Teufelsmauer and Pfahlgraben* – Oxford 1885; cf. Pelham 1911: 181; Jackson *Proc Brit Acad* 1915–16). Mowat died in sad circumstances. On the evening he returned from Carlisle (7 August 1894) at the end of CEC's first season (for which he was the treasurer), he was found hanging in his rooms in Pembroke. The Coroner's inquest recorded his death as 'suicide in a fit of temporary insanity' (cf. *The Times* 9 August 1894).

served and most elaborate of those systems, Hadrian's Wall. Recent work, along with v. Sarwey's visit, had demonstrated how the interchange of opinions had created more questions than answers. The Pelham *et al.* proposal could therefore set specific objectives: '...that the work had a special aim, somewhat distinct from that of other mural diggings, and was in the nature of pioneer enquiry, it presented problems which were both new and devoid of precedents to guide the workers; in consequences here and there instances mistakes may have been made, which our successors will find and indeed have made the more easy to correct' (Haverfield 1917: 264). Prior to 1894, funds had been voted by the CWAAS. Now Pelham *et al.*;

> ...venture to appeal for subscriptions to be applied, according to need, to these good works. Oxford scholars, much as they have done for scholarship and for research, especially in Greek lands, have too much neglected the treasures at our doors; but many of them know the Roman Wall and may be willing to help in examining it (*The Academy* 23 June: 255).

At the same time as the CWAAS was laying its plans for excavations along the western end of the Wall, the Newcastle society, largely under the initiative of J.P. Gibson was about to embark on their own scheme, concentrating on the eastern-central sector. In July 1894, through unforeseen circumstances, excavations at *Aesica* (Great Chesters) were led by a foreman digger, assisted by regular visits by the Northumberland Excavation Committee (NEC) '...and considerable assistance was given by professor Pelham and Mr. Haverfield and other members of the committee who were in residence for some time at Gilsland and visited Aesica almost daily during the period of their stay' (Gibson 1903b: 21 and 1895: cf. Haverfield's reports in *The Antiquary* from 1894 onwards). The work of the NEC continued in 1895 and 1897, with Haverfield publishing in 1897 its inscriptions (Haverfield 1897c).

From the start, the size of the Cumberland Excavation Committee was small. It consisted of Chancellor Ferguson, Thomas Hesketh Hodgson and the Rev. W.S. Caverley who had a reputation for excavating Roman sites in the region and who pre-surveyed sites for exploration. Haverfield was the CEC's 'mouthpiece and planner' (Birley 1958a: 212) and its 'director and chief expounder' (Birley 1961: 65).[30] We can chart the course of the ten years of work at various locations along the western end of the Wall through a combination of

---

30. Cf. Wilmott 2001: 163–5 for the most recent assessment of Haverfield's work with the CEC.

Haverfield's book reviews, the committee's (i.e. Haverfield's) annual reports in the society's transactions, and from his published lectures and private letters, especially those to Mommsen. The work on the Wall also involved the CEC cataloguing material in Carlisle Museum/Tullie House. The format for the ten reports was set in the first year and remained essentially unchanged thereafter. Opening with a summary of the previous year's results, the season's targets would be summarized and complimented by a short description of the results. After acknowledging the assistance of local landowners and other contacts, there would follow a lengthier description of the various locations and trenches opened. At the end of the report there would be a summary of the season's expenditure with perhaps suggestions for the next year. In these accounts, Haverfield frequently noted who assisted in the work. His staff lists can be supplemented by the much shorter summaries provided by Birley (1961). Haverfield's lists are important for they help to determine how the supervision of the labour was divided between an 'Oxford' group and local archaeologists. The former group included a variety of individuals, principally Haverfield and Pelham, assisted by other 'university' men (Mowat, F.G. Hilton Price – Director of the London Society of Antiquaries (1892–1909), R.P.L. Booker – an Eton schoolmaster, A.H. Smith, Thomas Ashby, and G.B. Grundy). The local antiquarians included C.J. Bates, H.R. Pyatt, Thomas Hodgson and his wife[31], and W.S. Collingwood (father of R.G.), as well as clericals (e.g. the Revs Caverley and A. Wright, vicar of Gilsland) and others (e.g. James Macdonald, father of George). Over the next decade innumerable sites and locations there were explored; innumerable in so much that the exact number of trenches per site is frequently not reported, let alone described. Indeed the inclusion of plans in the annual reports is variable. The method of excavation usually involved opening narrow trenches of varying dimensions across the elements to be examined. Funding was provided by an initial grant from the CWAAS who put up in total £125: £100, paid in two parts in the first two years, with an additional £25 awarded in 1902. Haverfield also raised what he called 'the Oxford subscriptions' supplemented by other awards from named (e.g. the London society) and unnamed sources. From the accounts Haverfield submitted at the end of each of the annual reports, we can see the CWAAS's first £100 was made to last until 1901 when the residue of £4 3s 5d was expended. In the summary of the 1903 accounts, the

---

31. In an obituary of the life of Katherine Sophia Hodgson, daughter of the Hodgsons, Eric Birley noted that she was permitted to 'help' on the excavations (*The Times* 2 April 1974).

Yorkshire Archaeological Society contributed three guineas to the season while £15 of the CWAAS supplementary award remained unspent.

With respect to the progress of the CEC, in the report of the first season of work in 1894, Haverfield repeated the main elements of the Wall (the Vallum, curtain wall and forts) and opinions as to the relationship of Vallum to Wall. Again he gave especial emphasis to Hodgson's and Bruce's opinions about the elements being contemporary and that the Vallum was to provide defence to the southern side of the Wall, as well as to Mommsen's theory. The excavations were to resolve these questions and to establish the relationship of the Vallum to the Wall. Towards this end a number of trenches were opened across the Vallum (at Brunstock, White Moss, Bleatarn, Gilsland). On the basis of the results obtained, the conclusion was there was '...nothing in anyway which suggested any ditch resembling the German frontier ditch' (Haverfield 1895b: 454). Excavations were also conducted close to the fort at *Aesica* as well as at Cragglehill and Harehill, near Lanercost, and Gilsland Station. According to the report published in the *Archaeologia* (Notes on the excavations in 1894, LV (1896): 195–8), in 1894 the south-west corner of the fort at *Aesica* was excavated through July to October (and in 1895).[32] Those involved in the supervision of the various sites included Hodgson, Mowat, A.H. Smith and Haverfield. The Rev. Wright and Hilton Price oversaw the work in the Gilsland vicarage.

In August of the same opening season, Haverfield delivered a lecture, *A New Theory of the Vallum Romanum and Murus by Prof Mommsen of Berlin* (and later published as Haverfield 1894e).[33] This article was a critique of Mommsen, a discussion possible because Haverfield used the occasion to summarize some of the results from the 1894 season and in turn to call for more work to be undertaken. In his translation of the

---

32. In this he was assisted by C.J. Spence, listed as council member of the Newcastle society, a resident of North Shields and a surveyor on site, and Mr Holmes, another resident of Newcastle. In the summary of the excavation accounts in the *Archaeologia Aeliana* (XVII: xxii–xxiii) on 13 November Haverfield donated £3 13s 6d to the excavation fund. The London society gave £10 and an appeal at Oxford £15. The *Aesica* excavations are described as being under the auspices of the Northumberland Excavation Committee of the Society of Antiquaries of Newcastle. Haverfield's report in *The Antiquary* (XXX (1894)) says the season involved Pelham, Mowat, A.H. Smith, Booker and Sheriton Holmes as the surveyor.

33. Mommsen's original, 'Des Begriff des Limes', was published in the *Westdeutsche Zeitschrift für Geschichte und Kunst* (XIII (1894): 134–43) and is republished in his *Gesammelte Schriften* Vol. 5 *Historische Schriften* Vol. 2 (Berlin 1908: 456–64).

original Mommsen paper, Haverfield outlined what Mommsen thought the Roman *limes* to be; a road or path or a strip of land bounded by two sides and not a line; that Roman frontier systems consisted of boundary strips and not lines and that the three best examples of this definition were the German *Pfahlgraben* and the two walls in Britain. In the case of each the physical components of the systems differed slightly, but the basic structures were consistent. The *Pfahlgraben* consisted of a ditch beyond; Hadrian's Wall had a ditch in front of it and the vallum to the rear and the Antonine Wall with its ditch in front and the road to its rear. For each of these systems the elements defined the two boundaries of the two *limites*. With respect to Hadrian's Wall, Mommsen concluded the Vallum was purely civil in character and (following Bruce's earlier suggestion) was contemporary with the Wall. Thus the conclusion was that the area within the two, Wall and Vallum, constituted a demilitarized zone. While agreeing in part with some of Mommsen's conclusions, Haverfield questioned elements of the argument. For instance, believing too that the Vallum was civilian, he argued it may have been a frontier line of a date earlier than the Wall and that it was defended by the forts erected close to it. When this 'civil' frontier with its forts was found to be too weak, the Wall proper was constructed. The next issue was Mommsen's definition of the *limites*. Haverfield emphasised the lack of uniformity between the three systems Mommsen had highlighted. Nor had excavation added much to prove Mommsen's theory, where the evidence was '...unsatisfactory and inconclusive.' He did note however, the recent excavations at Bleatarn (excavated by Calverley) had produced some '...evidence that the Wall and vallum were nearly of the same date, but more investigations is perhaps needed at this spot.' Significant for the future, it was also communicated there might be some problems with the course of the Vallum, not least because it seemed to disappear near certain forts, including Carrawburgh, Housesteads and Great Chesters. In his summing up, Haverfield added:

> A good deal more search seems needed before the mysterious mounds will give up their secret. One gain, however, we have made. We are daily learning what to seek, and the experience of this year may lead to definite results in 1895 or perhaps before the present season closes. It took two years of extensive excavation to find the 'gromatic ditch' in Germany; it may well take us as long to explain our vallum (p. 224).[34]

34. Ironically, in the same month this article was published, Haverfield was writing to Mommsen about his recent work and listing his objections to Mommsen's view on the contemporaneity of the Wall and Vallum in relation

In a more formal context, in a report in the *Classical Review*, Haverfield (1894b: 227) stated the Vallum was earlier than the Wall (citing evidence from Down Hill, excavated by Hodgkin). He also took the opportunity to criticise Hübner's statement that the Wall and Vallum were contemporary. He also expressed the hope that Hodgkin would be able to continue his own excavations.

Following the end of the (1894) season, in August and October, Haverfield returned to Germany and made another tour of the frontier there, accompanied again by v. Sarwey and two unnamed English companions (Haverfield 1894c: Croke 61, 64, 65 and 103). Most of the trip was spent in visiting sites in Bavaria and Württemberg, and in meeting the leading excavators. Another significant introduction was Haverfield's realisation that the study of excavated pottery (in this sense samian) could be used to say more about the date and function of the frontier. As before, the visit produced another report addressed to Hodgkin (Haverfield 1894c) as well as reports in *The Academy* and *The Antiquary*, both on 13 October 1894.[35]

of the Vallum to the forts. 'Three of these are south of the vallum (i.e. outside the Grenzstreifen); elsewhere, wherever the line of the vallum ought to pass close to a fortress, the vallum fades out as if destroyed to make place for the fortress'; Croke 64: cf. 103 (1894 or 1895), 65 (1895), 69 (1896).

35. Of other publications arising from the 1894 tour, a more synthetic piece was a translation of the work of Karl von Schumacher in *The Raetian Limes in Germany* (cf. *Neue Heidelberger Jahrbücher* and reprinted in the *Proc Soc Antiqs Newcastle* VIII 1898). Haverfield perhaps visited v. Sarwey on another tour in June 1903 (Croke 99). Haverfield was to facilitate the visit of at least two other Germans. In 1902 Carl Schuchhardt, accompanied by Emil Krüger (1869–1954), visited southern England (Schuchhardt 1944: 230–42). They stayed with Haverfield at Christ Church (where they dined with Arthur Evans and Percy Gardner). Complimenting Schuchhardts' account of the trip, in September 1902 Haverfield wrote to Thomas Ashby, then involved in co-directing excavations at Caerwent, about the imminent arrival at Chepstow of the two Germans who were planning to visit the site. Haverfield asked Ashby to '...be civil to them' (unpublished letter passed on by Richard Hodges). Haverfield apparently did not know either of them that well. Schuchhardt was a prehistorian, classical scholar and biographer of Schliemann who was later to become embroiled with the Nazis (Marchand 1996). Although complimentary of him elsewhere, Krüger and his opinions on the Roman frontier in northern England were later slated by Haverfield (1904c: 249). Schuchhardt (p. 242–54) also visited northern Britain in 1903, including Scotland on a tour in part assisted by Haverfield. Emil Schulten, the investigator of the Roman camps at *Numantia* in Spain, visited Birrenswark in Scotland as well as Corbridge *c.*1914 (cf. Haverfield 1915a: 61; Macdonald 1929/1930).

The 1895 season was more ambitious than the previous year in the way it was spread among a number of locations between Birdoswald and Bewcastle: at Appletree, Bleatarn, Lanercost and on the Maiden Way (Haverfield 1897a).[36] As a consequence of this work, Haverfield's opinions on the date and rôle of the Vallum underwent a fuller reversal. As has already been noted, the work on and along Hadrian's Wall was occasioned by the progress that was being made in Germany and that the excavators were kept informed about it, as they saw the work in northern Britain as complementing that underway on the continent. But such knowledge and connections could be held against him. The season's most spectacular results came early on. The circumstances of the discovery of what turned out to be the Turf Wall antecedent to Hadrian's Wall is an interesting episode which in many ways typifies Haverfield's approach to excavation work. It is also an interesting example of a sort of resentment the arrival of the 'Oxford school' in northern England created. At the start of the season, on 8 August, Henry Pelham spoke to the CWAAS at Lanercost, on the theme *The Roman Frontier System*. In a wide ranging presentation, Pelham again doubted Mommsen's hypothesis that Hadrian's Wall and the Vallum represented an outer and inner line/*limes* supported by a road within the two. His objection was that the road along Hadrian's Wall (the Stanegate) was on the south side of the Vallum. Instead, he expressed support for Haverfield's idea that the Vallum represented a line of 'demarcation' distinct from a 'military line of defence' (Pelham 1897). That said, Pelham substantiated his lecture with numerous allusions to the frontier in Roman Germany.

The season's most significant discovery was at Appletree where Haverfield reported the discovery of a wall earlier than the stone one, between Birdoswald and the second milecastle west of it (at Wallbar = Milecastle 51 = Wall Bowers: Haverfield 1895b). Although noting that a similar phenomenon had been found on the Antonine Wall, Haverfield commented: '...opinion will not differ as to the importance of the discovery, which has introduced a new factor into the whole mural problem.' He reported the results to Mommsen in the same downbeat manner: 'Our excavations on and near our Roman wall have been continued this summer without much of special importance. At one point W. of Birdoswald ...we have found traces of a [sic] extra wall, built of turfs – a murus caespeticiius ....No such turf wall has ever been

---

36. Those present, according to Haverfield's report, were Pelham, Booker and Cadwallader Bates. Birley 1961 says it comprised Pelham, Calverley and Booker.

noticed by the wall before: we shall search next summer ...to see if it goes all along tho' hitherto unnoticed, or is an exception' (Croke 65; 4 October 1895). The discovery at Appletree may have been the occasion for a September letter from Haverfield to Mommsen, which indicates a greater degree of appreciation with respect to the nature of the evidence. In that letter he noted, as a consequence of his recent visit to Germany and v. Sarwey, he was becoming more sensitive to the growing evidence of differences in the dates of the various lines of the German frontiers and their forts (Croke 103). In fact what had been found was evidence of a turf wall with ditch to the north, running between the stone wall and Vallum, 1½+ miles long until it met at MC 51, the stone wall. A short report of the discovery also appeared in the *Newcastle Daily Journal* in September of the same year, which paraphrased an earlier article in *The Manchester Guardian*. It was the opinion of Cadwallader J. Bates, a noted local antiquarian (cf. Welford and Hodgson 1913; Hodgkin 1903) that neither report afforded him proper credit for the discovery. In truth, in the CWAAS report Haverfield did record in a rather perfunctory manner that Bates had assisted in the season and was '...to whom our principal discovery was mainly due', although his acknowledgement of its significance was decidedly cool. Because of its obscurity, it is appropriate to repeat here the full version of Bates' complaints, not least because it says something about Haverfield's competence as an excavator as well as how he got on with the locals. In writing to the Journal on 14 September, Bates felt the newspaper report belittled the fact he had anticipated the existence of the Turf Wall in his *History of Northumbria* (1895), a wall supplemented by a Severan construction in stone. Indeed he wrote to Haverfield before the season to advise him where to excavate. In turn Haverfield had invited Bates to visit the excavations, which he did on 15 August. Bates' letter to the *Journal* continues:

> ...Great was my surprise and disappointment when Mr. Haverfield told me that though the section was completed, no trace of turves or palisades had been met with. I accompanied him to the spot, and very soon detected three or four black vegetable markings, resembling the remains of soils in the Antonine Wall, exactly where my historical deductions led me to expect to find them.
>
> Mr. Haverfield then very obligingly set out another trench about 300 yards to the east of the one first dug near Appletree. This second section revealed six or seven black lines in strong clay. Still Mr. Haverfield and labourers were inclined to attribute these markings to natural causes. With some vehemence I insisted that it would be a most singular coincidence if a *lusus natura* had inserted these sandwiches of peat and clay

exactly where I was obstinate enough to expect to come on the traces of a turf wall.

Two or three further sections made it impossible any longer to deny the existence of the turf wall. As I knew would be the case, it is now attempted (in your issue of the 4th inst. for example), to minimise the importance of its discovery. I immediately said that the turf wall would be called "a purely local aberration of the Murus in position and texture". It is fortunately easy for anyone possessing the most rudimentary acquaintance with the lines ultimately followed by the stone-wall to see that there are many engineering reasons for concluding that this replaced a previous turf-wall throughout the entire course ... One of the first savants I met after the discovery, when I asked him what he thought of it, replied with ill-disguised contempt of my suggestions (as coming from a simple Northumbrian countryman instead of from a 'Wirklicher Geheimer Oberlimeskommissiondirektor' with all sorts of alphabetical glories after his name) that the presence of the turf wall was very puzzling. 'Puzzling?' I retorted. 'Why, it would have been very puzzling if the turf wall had not been there.'

The subject is one too long and too intricate to be discussed thoroughly except in a separate brochure; so here I must leave it. Mr. Haverfield deserves the highest praise for the perseverance he has shown in conducting these excavations ...but I cannot help thinking it one of the most curious facts in the history of antiquarian discoveries that the actual detection of the turf wall at Appletree should have been the result of a close and searching study of the ancient literature bearing on the Roman wall, and when the same course of study that led to the discovery of this turf wall points to the Emperor Hadrian as having built it ...surely this opinions deserves a little consideration, though it be submitted neither by Prof. Trockenstaabe nor Baron von Moenchenscheune.

The identity of the unnamed 'savant' is intriguing. If it was not Haverfield, then it must have been someone who knew of the seasons' results. The obvious candidate is Pelham. He is the only academic listed on the 1895 staff list and was lecturing there in that year.

The dispute with Bates was one of two instances in 1895 where Haverfield appears to have got into trouble with local archaeologists. Appended to his account of the season is an additional statement written by the excavation's illustrator, Mrs T.H. (Elizabeth) Hodgson (1854–1935), entitled *Notes on the Excavations on the Line of the Roman Wall in Cumberland in 1894 and 1895*. Mr and Mrs Thomas Hodgson had originally been invited to join the CEC because of their local connections and influence, but it was found that he possessed abilities as a surveyor and that his wife was a skilled draughtswoman. The purpose of Mrs Hodgson's report is not made explicit, but it is, in fact, a record of the location, dimensions and general description of Haverfield's trenches, as seen by her and her husband. Indeed if one looks at Haverfield's 1894 and 1895 accounts, one finds that there is virtually no such information therein. His reports provide no substantial records of the location of his trenches, nor their dimensions and often nothing other than a description of what he considered to be significant to his reading of things. The inclusion of site plans with the position of the trenches on them is also variable. Mrs Hodgson provided similar summaries in later years, where the purposes of her descriptions become more apparent (Hodgson 1898; 1899). In her account of the 1896 and 1897 seasons she wrote: 'He [Haverfield] dug many trenches of which I have no measures, as he measured very few except those where the black (a decayed deposit of turves) was found' (Hodgson 1898: 203). She concluded the description with the disclaimer: 'These Notes are a continuation of those which I submitted to the Society (previously). ...They are entirely distinct from the Reports of the Cumberland Excavation Committee ...and are merely an effort to express as exactly as possible the appearance and position of the trenches, so as to enable those who did not see the excavations to understand the method pursued and to see the reasons for the conclusions to be drawn from the work' (p. 210). In her last report, made for the 1898 season, it was repeated that she made her submission: '...without making any suggestions as to the theories to be determined from them' (1899: 365). It is difficult to underestimate the importance of Mrs Hodgson's reports. As her obituarist stated, they '...afford an extremely valuable supplement and check to the generalised conclusions given in Professor Haverfield's reports, and are today a source of information which no students of the problems concerned can afford to neglect.' (Anon. 1936: 238). Ironically, her reports contain very few illustrations – plans – of the whereabouts of the trenches she described.[37]

With the potential significance of the results from 1895 appreciated, Haverfield's attention moved to broader horizons. In the report of the CEC element of 1896, the seasons objectives were (a) evidence for the date of the Vallum; (b) tracing the Roman roads near the Wall; and (c) finding more traces of the Turf Wall discovered in 1895 (Haverfield 1897b).[38] At Birdoswald it was found that the Vallum passed or deviated around the southern edge of the fort. In the same year Haverfield became involved, with Pelham, in excavations at Carrawburgh, '...though

37. Collingwood, and repeated by Simpson (1996: 222), criticized the lack of intellectual rigor behind the CEC decisions where to place its trenches. While Collingwood blamed Haverfield, Simpson blamed the Hodgsons.
38. Haverfield's staff list consists of Pelham and Hodgson. Birley (1961) lists Pelham and Booker.

not part of the CEC', strictly speaking being in the realm of the Society of Antiquaries of Newcastle. The reason for this excursion was because it had been appreciated that the forts at Birdoswald and Carrawburgh both lay in the path of the Vallum and yet did not come into contact with it. With comparable evidence at Carrawburgh, 'a new fact was thus revealed which had been entirely unsuspected before and which makes it probable ..that the Stone Wall, fort, and vallum are of the same age' (p. 413). The conclusion drawn from the results obtained at the two sites was the Vallum was not earlier in date than the two forts. Assuming the two forts were contemporary with those on the rest of the Wall, then the Vallum could not be earlier than the other forts but was later, or what Haverfield called 'coeval'. His preference was for the idea of the forts, Vallum and Wall being contemporary, based on the fact that the epigraphic evidence for the Wall system as a whole that he had examined in 1892 was largely Hadrianic in date and because of the evident relationship of the Vallum and the course of the Wall. Finally, he repeated the Vallum had to be a 'civil' work, as Mommsen had previously suggested. In September, Haverfield could report to Mommsen that the Vallum avoided two of the Wall forts (Haverfield's *Procolitia* and *Ambroglanna*) by going around them. The conclusion had to be the Vallum was not older than the forts but was of the same age (or later). He added: 'This supports your theory (in the Wd. Zeitschrift)' (Croke 69).[39] In contrast to these discoveries, no additional signs of the Turf Wall were recovered, other than in the same Appletree vicinity.

Because of the success of the 1896 excursion, Haverfield continued to wander further afield in subsequent seasons. That that excursion and the work elsewhere in later years were sensitive is emphasised by the pains he went to distinguish between the CEC and other work in the relevant season's reports. For the significance of this move was that Haverfield was 'straying' into the unofficial province of the Newcastle society. In these reports he had to state in bold language what the CEC funds had paid for and how the Northumberland work was covered by his Oxford subscriptions or other sources. In 1897 he was excavating at Chesters (with Bates, Grundy and Hodgson), Housesteads (with Bosanquet) and Rudchester; in 1898 at Housesteads (with Bosanquet); in 1900 at Chesters (Booker and Hodgson); in 1901 at Rudchester;

---

39. Tony Wilmott (pers. comm.) points out that the Vallum goes under Carrawburgh. If Haverfield's original note is correct, then Haverfield was wrong on this.

and in 1903 again at Chesters, all intent on clarifying details or patterns first seen in the Cumberland sector. For instance, at Chesters in 1900 Haverfield wanted to settle a specific question about the Wall. Along the eastern sector it was recognised that virtually all the forts stood on or across its line. An explanation for this phenomenon was that the visible forts were in fact later. Using the results from Birdoswald,[40] he wondered if the sequence was in fact the original erection of forts and wall, followed by the demolition of the fort's northern walls and the filling-in of the ditch. This was then complemented by the forts being extended across the wall and the construction of a new north wall. In the end the Chesters excavation demonstrated that there was a similar story of two periods of activity to that at Birdoswald. The original line of the defences at Chesters was consistently straight and the existing fort, sitting across that line, was therefore of later date. Therefore there was an earlier and later line. However, Haverfield could not determine if the earlier one was of turf or stone, nor if there was any evidence as to whether the earlier fort at Chesters corresponded to the earlier line. At the end of his report he felt it necessary to include a statement justifying his methods of excavation: 'I have heard regrets expressed, and I share those regrets myself, that the trenches at Chesters could not have kept open for the inspection of antiquaries who might wish to see them. But it is a matter which nature and not man decides' (Haverfield 1902d: 19). While nobody could check the veracity of his conclusions here, he claimed it was the poor drainage and subsoil at Chesters that was at fault.

The implications of the Bates and Hodgsons episodes as well as his own (defensive) statements were that there were reservations within the CWAAS about Haverfield's management of the CEC's excavations. His wandering attention may not have helped the situation. There are other strands of evidence which corroborate the impression of some dissatisfaction. The 1899 report contains an otherwise curious statement. The list of supervisors for the season is shorter than previous years, comprising Booker, Hodgson and Haverfield. Haverfield continued:

> One or more of the supervisors named in the Report were present during practically the whole of each working day. We do not claim to have reached any ideal standard in this matter, but we may express our

---

40. The Birdoswald sequence, as Haverfield summarized it, was that there were two distinct lines to the Wall: the stone one and to the south of it, a turf one, each with a ditch in advance of them. The Turf Wall is earlier. There was also the original construction of a fort.

opinion that no ordinary excavation can be said to be adequately supervised where less than this is done (1900: 81).

Although ironically 1899 was the one year he did not work eastwards,
this was the first time in six years Haverfield felt it necessary to refer to
the competence of the supervisors and the degree of supervision they
provided. One suspects his comments were in response to criticisms
then circulating. While it is true that about this time Haverfield was
making similar statements in other journals about supervisory arrangements in general, the reasons for his strictures may be traced
back to his superintendence of the CEC. In 1897 G.B. Grundy joined
the CEC when he put trenches across a stretch of Roman road (High
Street), between Brougham and Ambleside at Loadpot Hill in Cumbria (Haverfield 1899c: 360ff.; Collingwood 1937; cf. Wheeler 1936:
xliii n.8).[41] In the same year, he is also credited with having assisted in
the exploration of Chesters and appears in the staff list for 1898, helping to plan the excavations at the putative fort at Hawkhirst. He was
also supposed to assist Haverfield in the exploration of the Roman
roads south of the Vallum '...but the scheme broke down.' In fact
Grundy worked on other roads with a Mr W.H. Parkin jnr of
Ravencrag. Later in the same year he and Haverfield excavated a
stretch of Roman road in Blenheim Park and indeed Grundy was later
to develop a specialism in Roman and Saxon roads. In his autobiography published 50 years later, Grundy reports a story concerning
Haverfield which suggests there were difficulties that came to a head
in 1898. Although there are some problems with particular details, notably the dates, in Grundy's opinion, Haverfield's methods left much
to be desired:

> ...In the early years of this century I was led by a somewhat devious path
> to a subject of study new to me. It began with an interest in Roman Brit-
> ain, which had been to me, as to many others, a subject of intermittent
> study. It was about 1900 that I began to take it more seriously when, at
> Haverfield's suggestion, I joined him for some weeks each summer in
> excavations on the Roman Wall in north England. Not having had any
> experience of excavation, I accepted Haverfield's methods as examples
> of the right way to set about such work. In the earlier years of that expe-
> rience the work was confined to minor points not calling for excavation
> on a large scale. But I did find Haverfield's superintendence of the men

41. Wheeler's account of the road owes much to information provided by
    Grundy. That Grundy had to write to him with details of the location of the
    trenches and the appearance of the finds says yet more about the CEC's
    quality of record keeping and publishing.

during the excavations was, to say the least of it, spasmodic, and tended to begin late in the morning and end early in the afternoon. I myself, having come to see the results of the work and having nothing better to do when on the spot, was rather assiduous in watching the work as it proceeded. This rather irritated than pleased Haverfield. Also after a year or two's experience I began to have the uncomfortable feeling that we were possibly missing finds of interest and importance by omitting to sift the soil dug up at various sites. But Haverfield pooh-poohed that as a fad. The matter came to a head in the fifth or sixth season of our work in Cumberland and Northumberland when we tackled something on a larger scale, the excavation of the Roman fort at the ancient Procolitia on the high land to the west of the valley of the Tyne at Chollerford Bridge. The whole excavation was hurried, scrambled and very badly done. After that I never worked with him. All I can say – and I say it in the interest of those who shall hereafter explore Roman remains in Britain – that the places we excavated in those years will certainly repay re-excavation (1945: 147).

The implications of the passage are clear. In either 1897 or 1898 Haverfield and Grundy fell out over the competence of the principal excavator, an accusation Haverfield felt he had to defend in the next interim report in 1899.[42] Similar reservations were later repeated by the likes of Leonard Woolley and Robert Forster at Corbridge, and seem to have been shared by at least Mrs Hodgson. But this is to jump ahead. For the 1897 season the plan was to trace the Vallum at Birdoswald and Gilsland and to look at the Turf Wall at Birdoswald as well as two stretches of suspected Roman roads close to the wall, out of Stanwix. At Birdoswald it was found the Vallum returned to its original alignment past the other side of the fort. This was definitive proof that the realignment of the Vallum at this point was due to the existence of the fort. The search for the Turf Wall found that it passed through the fort there, with again the conclusion that the Turf Wall represented a line of defence earlier than its stone counterpart. It was appreciated that this '...discovery is as startling and as important as our last year's discoveries respecting the Vallum introduces a wholly new element into the Mural problem' (Haverfield 1898b: 173). However he could not deter-

---

42. That Grundy has confused or at best conflated a number of events is evident in the fact he is recorded in the CEC reports as being present in 1897, 1898, 1901 and 1902. The fifth or sixth seasons would have been 1898 and 1899. His *Procolitia* is *Brocolitia*, modern day Carrawburgh which Haverfield excavated in 1897. Grundy is credited in the staff list for his work there. It is not strictly correct to describe it as being near Chollerford.

mine how significant.[43] Similar conclusions were reported in the *Classical Review* report for the 1897 season (*Class Rev* XIII (1898): 83). The Vallum and forts of the Wall were contemporary. Therefore the Vallum was not older than the fort and they were all Hadrianic in date. That said, he admitted that he was confused by the discovery of a Turf Wall at Gilsland which was later replaced by a stone Wall (cf. Croke 93). In addition to this work Grundy assisted at Chapelhouse Farm, near Poltross and in a survey of roads out of Stanwix while Haverfield also undertook work at Halton and Rudchester, looking at the Vallum, in the company of Dr Hodgkin and Bates along with Bosanquet.

For the 1898 season the objectives were to complete the exploration of the Turf Wall and Vallum at Birdoswald (and Castleshaw = ?MC 49) as well as two roads nearby and a presumed fort at Hawkhirst, near Brampton (and which turned out not to be Roman: Haverfield 1899, along with Mrs Hodgson's more detailed description). In addition Haverfield worked with the Newcastle society at Housesteads (21 June to 29 October), again not under the auspices of the CEC. The supervisors again included Hodgson, Booker and Bosanquet. Grundy was also present as was Pelham and, for the first time, Thomas Ashby and A.C. Dickie (at Housesteads, with Bosanquet).[44]

---

43. Haverfield records as present, Hodgson, Bates, Booker, Bosanquet, Grundy and Henry R. Pyatt, most of who worked at a variety of locations. Haverfield's report in *The Antiquary* (XXXIII (1897)) says the season also showed that the alleged stretches of Roman roads at Denton, Naworth, and Watchclose were not Roman but the Maiden Way from Birdoswald to Bewcastle was. Part of a road at Burgh-by-Sands, previously said to be Roman was shown not to be so. Seven years later, in an address to the research department of the Royal Geographical Society, in which he made critical comment of the way the Ordnance Survey occasionally indiscriminately accepted the opinion of local antiquaries, Haverfield said that the Maiden Way, running north out of Birdoswald, was traced by the vicar of Bewcastle, Mr Maughan, and was published as such. Haverfield 'endeavoured to trace it, by excavation and by local inquiries. The only result to which I have been able to come to is that the road never ran north of Bewcastle at all, and that both Maughan and the Ordnance surveyors have inserted a fictitious line' (1906b: 170).

44. In his contribution to the revised edition of Traill's *Social England* (1901), Haverfield included photographs of Birdoswald and the Wall in general provided by Ashby. Archibald Campbell Dickie (1868–1941) was an architect employed by the Palestine Exploration Fund in its expedition to Jerusalem (1894–8). He must have gone straight to Housesteads after leaving the Middle East. From 1898 to 1912 he practiced in London and became a Master in Design at the Architectural Association School in 1910. He was Professor of

Prior to or during the 1899 season, Haverfield presented an overview of the previous five years work at the AGM of the CWAAS. While there is nothing especially different to note in terms of the identification and interpretation of features reported in the previous interim reports, the introduction to the lecture is interesting in the way that Haverfield returned to the subject of systematic research along the Wall. Noting that in 1885 Mommsen had observed that the Wall was the best known of Roman military works because it had been so comprehensively (ground) surveyed, Haverfield felt that its pre-eminence had slipped, not least because of the recent work (viz. excavations) of the 'Imperial Limes-commission'. In comparison, Hadrian's Wall was imperfectly understood because it had not been dug.

> ...The spade was rarely used to prove theories which were suggested by the appearance of the ground, and excavations made in some of the forts were incompletely recorded or more often not recorded at all. The result is inevitable. Our best descriptions of the wall contain many statements which are guesses, others which are actually wrong (Haverfield 1899a: 337).

In recent years however, the situation was beginning to improve with the commencement of a number of excavations.

> ...initiated by the Newcastle Society of Antiquaries and by the Cumberland and Westmorland Archaeological and Antiquarian Society, and these, though not comparable with the systematic and extensive operations of the German Limeskommission have produced real advance. Accident has effected a curious but useful division of labour in these excavations. The Newcastle excavations have been mainly busy with forts, Great Chesters and Housesteads: the work of the Cumberland Society has lain along the Wall and vallum and roads outside the forts (p. 338).

In describing the state of knowledge about the wall at the time of the lecture, it was repeated that the 'authorized' view of Bruce and Hodgson was wrong. The Vallum probably had more of a legal purpose than a military (as any military expert knew!). It was Roman in date (because it was straight!) and was built with the wall as a unit. Having resolved the issue of the Vallum, with regard to the Turf Wall, Haverfield admitted they had hit a problem: he could not decide if the

---

Architecture at the University of Manchester and professor emeritus from 1933 (Blyth 1942). As part of the Housesteads 1898 season, Haverfield contributed a report on that year's inscriptions. Bosanquet's report (1904) notes W.H. Knowles produced some of the site plans.

section exposed was representative of a small stretch, a one-off, or in-dicated that the original wall was erected in that fashion before being replaced by a stone one. In his conclusion, Haverfield's presentation validated the work of the CEC.

> I have tried to sum and estimate the contributions made during the last five years to the history of the Vallum and the Turf wall. In doing so, I have fallen among conjectures. But even if these conjectures be as bad as conjectures usually are, the results of the excavations retain definite value. Briefly, they may be said to correct and complete existing maps and descriptions (p. 343).

In other words, the merits of the CEC were that it undertook work which was systematic and recorded and testable. Although he made no reference to it, that they were testable was due in part to Mrs Hodgson's report, noting the 1898 trench locations, dimensions and appearances, which was appended to the CWAAS report for that year.

The 1899 season, conducted in August, continued the pattern of the previous season, where the results were described as 'satisfactory though not sensational' (Haverfield 1900: 80; cf. Haverfield 1899a). The targets were the exploration of Drumburgh, the line of the wall at Burgh Marsh and the Turf Wall at Walby west of Carlisle. Drumburgh turned out to be what was called a small fort or milecastle. The line at Burgh Marsh was not found and there was nothing at Walby.[45] The re-port ended with some general remarks about the usefulness of earlier antiquarian descriptions of the Wall, and in particular MacLauchlan's *A Survey of the Roman Wall* (1852–4). Indeed most of the season had been about checking and confirming what MacLauchlan had claimed as fact.

> The lesson of the past summer is the absolute necessity of excavations to test surface appearances and traditional accounts of the Wall. The lesson has been taught us often before in our six years' work, but the deceptive-ness of surface appearances has seldom shown itself so markedly as this year at Drumburgh ...we have thought it right to use the striking lesson of Drumburgh and its vicinity to point out the true and precise value of a very valuable work. If that work is misused, the advance of Mural investi-gation will not be accelerated; if it is understood, excavation will receive

---

45. Tony Wilmott (pers. comm.) points out that 'Haverfield was investigating a turn in Burgh Lane which might have been the corner of a fort. He found the wall and ditch but no fort. MacLauchlan had this as a milecastle. I identi-fied it as MC62 in the corner of the field in 1999, 100 years later' (cf. Wilmott *Interim Report on the Evaluation of MC62 (Walby East)*. English Heritage).

a substantial impetus, and, in some parts, an excellent guide (Haverfield 1900: 98–9).

The following season (1900) saw the excavation of the Vallum near Cragglehill and Walton and a putative watchtower at Gillalees Beacon. The season seems to have been as low-key as the previous year, assisted as it was by the same colleagues as in 1899 (Booker, Hodgson, along with Bosanquet, and assisted by a R.G. Graham and a W. James; Haverfield 1901a).[46] At the same time Haverfield was excavating at Chesters, independent of the CEC, with Hodgson and Bosanquet. He published the results from Chesters in the *Archaeologia Aeliana*. As noted above, the article is interesting in the way that Haverfield was endeavouring to settle a specific question about the Wall. We have also heard of the criticisms of the season.

By July 1901, writing to Mommsen, Haverfield hoped that the Wall problem was solved. He concluded Hadrian had built it in turf, with forts, some of which were built in stone. Septimius Severus built the wall anew (this time with larger forts in stone). He was to add 'I must also eat many of my own words or at least appear to eat them: however I do not mind' (Croke 93). As events have since developed, Haverfield's adherence to a Severan Wall has also turned out to be incorrect. In this season, work continued on the Vallum at Walton and Castlestead. At the latter site was found that the Vallum avoided the fort there. The supervisors were again Hodgson, Booker, and Haverfield with Grundy reappearing for the first time since 1898 (Haverfield 1902a). Haverfield also continued to work outwith the CEC in this year, this time at Rudchester with the intention of repeating the Chesters experiment of the previous year (looking for the ditch of an earlier fort under the later fort). In the statement of the committee's finances at the end of the report Haverfield could write that the CWAAS had awarded an additional £25 for future work.

In 1902, the ninth year of the CEC, a possible Roman camp at Caermont, Torpenhow was explored while work at Castlesteads fort was nearly completed. Torpenhow was confirmed as Roman in date and the Vallum at Castlesteads was found to avoid the fort. The assistants for this season were Grundy, Booker and Hodgson. W.G. Collingwood helped at Torpenhow along with a Rev. James Wilson of Dalston, the editor of the *Cumberland County History*. But the season's report ended with the statement that the CEC had now run out of

---

46. Birley (1961) records a Frederick Walter Dendy (1849–1940), a stalwart of the Newcastle society, working on the Vallum in this year but gives no other details.

funds and that it threw itself on the generosity of those interested in its work (Haverfield 1903c).

For 1903, in what turned out to be the tenth and final season, Haverfield's report was shorter than usual. He described work searching for the Vallum at Chesters (strictly speaking outside the remit of the CEC), and excavations on the Vallum at Hare Hill, Newton on the Irthington and Burgh-by-Sands. But the season was curtailed by the atrocious weather. Chesters involved Hodgson, Booker and Haverfield, where Hodgson completed a prismatic survey and Haverfield a plane table version. Elsewhere, Newton had been started in the spring of that year, undertaken by Hodgson who was also at Burgh in what was a watching brief as building work went on. In his summary of the accounts, Haverfield noted there was still £15 available for the next year (Haverfield 1904c). On that note the CEC ended.[47]

Re-reading the various reports of the CEC one is left with a sense that the programme was progressively losing direction and starting to drift from the late 1890s. Why? There were the spectacular discoveries at the start of the exercise but with time the results became less noteworthy and increasingly disappointing compared to those of the first three years. For example, for the 1899 season the results were described, as in the previous year as 'satisfactory though not sensational.' The 1903 season was described as a washout. Furthermore, the CEC may have been running out of attractive locations to explore. By and large the CEC work was limited to trenching sections of the Wall and not looking in a systematic fashion any of its forts. As a rule, while it tended to open a large number of trenches each season (e.g. 1894 – 25+ trenches; 1899 – 27+, 1903 – 17), at a considerable number of locations (?25+), it was increasingly restricted to the Wall sector west of Carlisle.

There may have been other factors which explain Haverfield's loss of interest. With regard to the execution of the work, soon after its inception, the CEC lost relatively rapidly most of its supporters in the CWAAS. One of the original members, the treasurer J.L.G. Mowat committed suicide at the end of the 1894 season. Another committeeman, the Rev. Caverley, died in 1898 while the main supporter, the Society's President, Chancellor Ferguson passed away in 1900 (cf. Anon. 1900). Then there is the possibility Haverfield may have become disenchanted with the CWAAS itself. There may too have been the fact the

47. The CEC was replaced by the Durham University Excavations (1927–9) directed by F.G. Simpson, was reconstituted in 1930 down to 1935, under the direction of Simpson and I.A. Richmond. Reports were published in the *TCWAAS* from 1931 onwards (cf. Birley 1961).

committee's finances were drying up. In the end, the CEC put up in total £125 for the work paid in three parts. The rest came from Oxford and other sources. But the overall budget of the CEC was extremely small, especially if one remembers how much the Germans had invested in the same period. To this might be added the criticism Haverfield received from some quarters of the society, as well as from other local antiquarians and archaeologists. One way of charting his engagement with the society is to look at his record of attendance at its AGMs and regular cycle of excursions. In the early years, the excavation seasons usually coincided with these two events. At the start of the CEC, Haverfield is listed as a participant and/or as a speaker at least one of its two or three annual get-togethers and tours, when surely the seasons must have overlapped with the tours. But he failed consistently to show up from 1900.[48] What is more he ceased to publish with its journal until 1911, and only became its president in 1915. That he was increasingly turning his attentions to the east, to the region of the Newcastle society may not have gone down too well either.[49] It seems curious too that a

---

48. Present July but absent September 1893; absent June and September 1894; present (with Pelham) August 1895; absent Hadrian's Wall Pilgrimage June and September 1896; absent July and September 1897; absent July and August 1898; absent June but present (with Booker) August 1899; absent June and September 1900; absent June and August 1901; absent June and August 1902; absent April, June and September 1903. Wilmott (2001: 165) points out that Haverfield never participated on any of the Wall Pilgrimages (e.g. 1886, 1896, 1906). For the 1906 Pilgrimage, the tourists visited Winshields etc. where they were guided by the Hodgsons (cf. Oliver Heslop 1906). In the same year Haverfield's original trench at Appletree was reopened for the delectation of the pilgrims, a tradition that has continued with subsequent visits (up to 1999).

49. In truth Haverfield's attention seems to have been wandering even further. In the Minutes of the Council of the Society of Antiquaries of Scotland (2 December 1899) is noted that Haverfield was: '...proposing with the approval and co-operation of the Society to make trial excavations in certain sites reported to be Roman, with the object merely of determining if possible whether they are Roman are not.' The Council decided to charge the Drs Christison, (Joseph) Anderson and James Macdonald to draft a reply which it approved on 16 December. While the objective of Haverfield's attention and the form of the Council's reply is at present unknown there are one or two potentially relevant points. The Scottish society had for some time been conducting a vigorous programme of excavation on Roman (military) sites, especially in the Clyde Valley, work which Haverfield was more than aware. In addition Christison had presented to the Council in February 1898 a document setting out the case for the continuation of the society's programme of Roman excavations. In his list of preferences, Christison recommended that the society look at Birrenswark. One wonders if Haverfield knew of this and wanted to be at least associated with it.

member of the Excavation Committee, Mrs Hodgson, felt it necessary to submit her supplementary notes to the society's transactions. Were there reservations about the way the work was being conducted and/or the conclusions being drawn? One wonders too about the nature of Haverfield's relationship with (some of) the stalwarts of the society. On 28 May 1901, as part of a Tuesday evening lecture series to the Carlisle Scientific and Literary Society, Thomas Hodgson spoke of the CEC work to date. In his lecture Hodgson said the CEC was a CWAAS project '…in connection with some Oxford antiquarians.' He also noted that he and Haverfield (along with Mrs Hodgson) were the only principals still alive. However his description of the CEC's results omitted to mention Haverfield's part in any other context (*The Times* 28 May 1901). One can only imagine how Haverfield would have reacted to being dismissed as a bit-part Oxford antiquarian.[50] The sum of the evidence lends one to wonder if Haverfield was losing interest in the work of the CEC by the later 1890s to early 1900s. That loss of commitment have been occasioned by a lack of promising data, coupled with problems with the CWAAS.

Sixty years after the CEC, Eric Birley (1961) wrote that Haverfield gave up on mural studies in desperation and frustration, an opinion since repeated by others. In this characterization, Haverfield was simply exasperated by the CEC's inability to resolve the new set of mural questions it had created.[51] While there may be something in saying the end of the CEC was the result of Haverfield simply giving up, it might be going too far to say he '…ended his decade of work on the Wall a frustrated man. Despite the enormous volume of effort which he had led, he was further away from the answer to his questions than when he started' (Wilmott 2001: 165). On a positive note, it is fair to say the CEC, and so Haverfield's, work laid the first secure foundation for understanding of the chronology of the Wall. They did so by identifying hitherto unknown elements of it. In creating a framework, they used dating techniques which had not really been previously applied in the United Kingdom but which owed more to innovations on the

---

50. It is interesting that Mrs Hodgson's obituarist noted it was Haverfield who formed the CEC in 1894, an assessment that is not strictly correct (Anon. 1936: 237).

51. According to Birley: '…his views on the mural problem (showed) signs of hardening into a dogma of despair, assigning a Turf Wall from sea-to-sea to Hadrian …and the Stone Wall to Severus …but J.P. Gibson …remained unsatisfied and it is fair to say that it was his persistence and his vision which kept the idea of research aloof and found in F.G. Simpson the man through which it could be revised and reinvigorated.'

Continent. Another positive feature is that the CEC says much about the field methodology of the day: of the use of excavation in a problem solving capacity. In fact, the issue of the Vallum had been resolved, up to a point, and a model for the interpretation of the Turf Wall advanced. In his publications, certainly up to 1906, there is nothing other than Haverfield being confident he had cracked the problems that originally concerned him in the late 1880s. He had become involved in the 'mural' problem when it concerned the date of the construction of the (Stone) Wall and the function of the Vallum. By perhaps 1901, judging by his letters to Mommsen, and certainly by the end of 1903, the questions seemed to have been answered (it was Hadrianic, to be replaced by a Severan Stone Wall and the Vallum was part of a demilitarized zone). However, the questions had now developed as a consequence of the CEC's work. The committee had concluded the Turf Wall south of the line of the Stone Wall (upon which were the milecastles of Hare House and the turrets of Birdoswald, Hare Hill and Appletree) were Hadrianic and that the stone wall at this point was of later, probably, Severan date. The issue now was the relationship of the Turf Wall it had discovered, relative to the Stone Wall. If the Turf Wall was Hadrianic, did it extend from coast-to-coast or was it a localised phenomenon? Haverfield believed it did stretch so far and therefore in a presentation to the Newcastle society on 29 August 1906, during the first Corbridge season, presented his evidence (Haverfield 1906a; cf. Maxfield 1982: 72–3). Another example of the negative reaction to the German influence on Haverfield's work with the CEC is to be found in this recapitulation of the dating of Hadrian's Wall. Haverfield reported he had once maintained the stone wall had been constructed under Hadrian, but now he presented a paper in which he attributed it to Severus and that it superceded a Hadrianic turf wall. At what must have been a memorable evening, in his summing up and vote of thanks, the President J.P. Gibson blustered that '...academic theory in Great Britain, he rightly or wrongly believed to be somewhat lacking in independence and originality and to have suffered from the dominance of German conclusions reached under conditions different for those of the Roman frontier in Britain' (Neilson 1912: 42; cf. Haverfield 1906a; Bosanquet 1920: 140).

Gibson's criticism of Haverfield's reliance on 'German conclusions' might be indicative of a form of parochialism that explains Haverfield's known antipathy towards local archaeologists. For there are signs of his exasperation with the northern societies from about this time. Almost certainly as a consequence of his experience with the CEC, an indication of how Haverfield believed work on Hadrian's Wall should progress in the light of the German *Limeskommission*'s work and his attempts to institutionalize research is to be found in a letter from Bosanquet to his father-in-law, Thomas Hodgkin, dated 2 September 1904:

> I enclose Haverfield's letter to you and one just received from him in which he has a growl (of a friendly sort) at a phrase of yours. He suggests that the British Academy ...draft a scheme for excavations on the Limes and on the great roads crossing it, all leading up to an official publication. The area involved would cut into the provinces of so many local Societies that they could bear no grudge; and the help of each in its own provinces would be properly sought and acknowledged....The most obvious and necessary help that a local Society can give, is to provide accommodation for the finds; if Newcastle fails to do that, it can't be expected to organise the other departments of an excavation. As to supervision, some day, Newcastle must have a trained expert residing all the year round within her walls; he will be Director of a new Museum, in which the treasures of the Black Gate will be housed and managed as to draw others to them ...But I think it more likely that he will hold a lectureship at the Newcastle University, which will have grown out of the College of Science. It is clear that such a man would organise excavations along the Wall in Northumberland, making use of amateur helpers (Bosanquet 1938: 157–8).

We can see Haverfield's proposal addressing issues evident in the work of the CEC: the split between the two northern societies with the need for centralized direction and the proper funding of future research and the emphasis on studying all aspects of the Wall (the Wall, the Vallum and its roads as well as its fortifications). Interesting is the omission of a specific rôle for the CWAAS in these plans. It is not difficult to see the RLK as the model for this proposal. Haverfield had previously referred to the significance – and uniqueness – of the German programme elsewhere (e.g. Haverfield 1899a: 337–8: cf. Chapter 3). The idea sits comfortably with Haverfield's other, often disparaging, comments on the 'strength' and adverse influence of Britain's regional societies and local antiquarians. While nothing came of the proposal, Bosanquet's prophecy was part confirmed by the appointment of Philip Newbold in 1910 at Armstrong College.

Haverfield's proposal was one solution to a problem others in northern England had appreciated. With the end of the CEC and its own work at Housesteads etc coming to a close coupled with the general failure in the past to undertake careful excavation anywhere along the Wall, Thomas Hodgkin, then a Vice-President of the Newcastle society, in an address to his society in 1902 claimed:

All that is required is that they (the excavations) should be directed by skillful and scientific archaeologists, and that those who cannot themselves either dig or superintend the diggers, but who are interested in the history of the Roman occupation of Britain should contribute according to their ability to the funds of the excavations. Most fairly professor Ganer pointed that the British government, almost alone among the governments of civilized states, refuses to recognize any obligation towards archaeology by the grant of a small pittance out of the vast national store to assist the work of excavation (Gibson 1903a: 10–12, citing P. Gardner's *New Chapters in Greek History* 1892: 176–7).[52]

Returning to whether or not Haverfield had 'cracked' the mural problem by 1904, as it turned out the veracity of his attribution was destroyed by Simpson and Gibson's work at the Poltross Burn milecastle in 1909 and 1910 combined with Philip Newbold's contribution. Unbeknown to itself, what the CEC had found was that the Turf Wall ran no further than the River Irthing. Simpson and Gibson proved there was nothing earlier than the milecastle contemporary with the Stone Wall.[53] Examination of the samian recovered showed it to be of second-century date and what is more that it was possible to distinguish between Hadrianic and Antonine forms.[54] One wonders if it was the occasion of Haverfield's 1906 lecture which led to Gibson joining with Simpson and to their eventually resolving the issue (T. Wilmott pers. comm.). In later years Haverfield seems to have accepted, at least in part, these conclusions, not least because his own work had hinted at aspects of them. That said, even by the time of his death he was still not convinced by all of the reinterpretation. In two

---

52. Hodgkin was also able to report that two 'competent' archaeologists, R.C. Bosanquet and A.C. Dickie, were now available to assist him in seeing through his agenda.

53. In 1912 excavations at MC50 (Limestone Bank turret) and the Turrets 49b and 50a/b also proved them to be Hadrianic.

54. 'The conclusion seems inevitable that the Hare Hill milecastle and the three turrets adjoining were erected simultaneously with the milecastle and turrets along the rest of the line from Birdoswald to Limestone Bank; that certain Flavian–Trajanic fashions in pottery, which are found in the bottom stratum of the Wall structures survived into the early part of Hadrian's reign but had fallen out of use before Corstopitum was laid out as a military depot and Scotland reoccupied in the early years of Pius; and that consequently, the Hare Hill milecastle and turrets, like the rest, were erected at the same time as and formed part of the wall of Hadrian. That they were erected in stone and were contemporaneous and homogeneous with the Stone Wall is shewn elsewhere in this and other reports by Mr Simpson and myself' (Newbold in Simpson 1913: 344).

footnotes complementing Haverfield's fairly negative comments in the (1907) Ford lectures about the sequence of the Wall's construction (viz. a Hadrianic Turf Wall, for 90 years, to rebuilt in stone by Severus, an opinion he based on the ancient literature and inscriptions rather than the archaeology, and the previously generally poor quality of excavation on the Wall), Macdonald adds of Haverfield's opinions:

> It seemed best to let this passage stand as it was originally written. But it is only right to say that, two or three years later, the simple solution here indicated as probable was ruled out by the results of further excavation, the significance of which F.H. was prompt to recognize.

On the quality of excavation, Macdonald noted:

> This criticism is no longer of general application. The series of excavations initiated in 1909 by the late Mr. J.P. Gibson and Mr. F.G. Simpson was carried to completion by the latter with a care and thoroughness which won F.H.'s warmest approval. The result was a most important contribution to the discussion of the problems of the Wall. ...This proved that the stone wall was much older than Severus but it left the turf wall at Appletree as much of a mystery as before. F.H. remained convinced that the latter, whatever its precise significance, must be Hadrianic ... For the rest, he was strongly impressed than ever with the need for systematic and properly directed excavation on a scale hitherto attempted. Since his death substantial progress has been made (Macdonald in Haverfield 1924: 158 n. 1 and 159–60 n. 1).

But this is another matter. In the medium and longer term the CEC results were a disappointment, albeit unwittingly so, not least because the 'chronological model' was soon shown to be wrong, as Simpson and Newbold were to demonstrate within five years. The point is that Haverfield had evidently settled 'The Mural Question', to his satisfaction at least. In assessing the achievements of the CEC, in the short term they could be said to be highly successful (it obtained results and, in doing so rejuvenated work and provided a new model for dating the Wall). Comparing the experience of the Silchester excavations with those of the CEC, Browning has argued Haverfield learnt certain lessons, some of which were derived from developments in Germany. The key was apparently Mommsen's innovation of scientific inquiry in historical research, 'with the preparation of the materials for history and the writing of history' (1989: 355). Now excavation was to complement observation, where specific questions are posed and excavation designed to produce the results which might involve those questions. As it transpired, Haverfield's 'answers' may have been wrong but in

Browning's opinion the methodology he devised was taken to its logical conclusion by Frank Simpson (Browning 1989: 356). The success of the CEC strengthened Haverfield's national and international reputation as an archaeologist. He was already known as an epigrapher, one evidently at the centre of the on-going study of the Roman empire. His work with the CEC, as far as the wider archaeological fraternity (and especially that at Oxford) was concerned, demonstrated his abilities as an excavator. He was now no longer merely the reporter of the work of others, but was the executor of major fieldwork and was producing significant results. It was these achievements which led to the 1906 'invitation' from the Northumberland County History Committee to lead its proposed excavations at Corbridge. Therefore, his work in the north-west contributed significantly to his professional advancement at Oxford. However on the negative side, the impressive early successes became something of a grind – a process in which he and his colleagues came to learn that excavation was a much more mundane, drawn-out exercise than their optimistic earlier statements of what they hoped to achieve. In addition to this there was his progressive distancing from, perhaps even falling out with, the excavation sponsors. Both these suggestions and the sequence of events were to recur in his relations with Corbridge (1906–14), a project from which he became increasingly detached after some spectacular initial discoveries.

This is not to ignore the fact that although the CEC ceased in 1903, the CEC–CWAAS programme helped foster other Haverfield connections in the region. This involved the production of catalogues of certain classes of finds as well as their synthesis (cf. Chapter 7). Assisting Haverfield at various times on aspects of the results generated by the excavations were later Oxford students such as Philip Newbold, Donald Atkinson, and R.G. Collingwood as well as J.P. Bushe-Fox and Thomas May. In the years after the CEC, naturally Haverfield retained opinions as to the date and organization of the wall. For instance, in 1904 he attacked Ritterling's opinions on its date. Ritterling had been as bold to suggest the Turf Wall (discovered by Haverfield) was built in *c*.158. Haverfield disputed the date and went on to make a case of the supremacy of 'English' opinions (1904d: 458).

In reviewing Haverfield's work with the CEC, one is struck by the way it, as we will see below, imitates or – better – is the template for other aspects of his career. There is a belief that some archaeologists are 'lucky', in the sense they have the ability to find the 'right' thing at the 'right time' and to use it to the 'right advantage'. In some ways Haverfield might be described as 'lucky'. We have seen this facet of his character in the way he became involved with the *CIL* and the placing of key articles at the right time. The same phenomenon is evident in his involvement with the CEC. He came to 'The Mural Question' at the right time, when it was recognized that only excavation could settle the question of the relationship of the Vallum to the Stone Wall. He produced the right article (on the inscriptions of the Wall) at the right time. He was there at the right time and was able to call on the right people to support his work (Pelham, Mommsen and more locally the likes of Chancellor Ferguson) and had the advantage of the Hodgsons to compensate for his lack of field experience. What could not have been anticipated were his (under the circumstances, reasonable) ambitions for work elsewhere. But there was still a fundamental flaw in his personality which was to repeat itself at other times in his career: his failure to see a project through to its logical conclusion.

There is one other aspect to Haverfield's involvement with the CEC and his subsequent reputation as the archaeologist of Roman Britain *par excellence*. Up to *c*.1910 he was lauded, certainly in southern England, as the man who had sorted out Hadrian's Wall. His name as an excavator was established. Subsequent developments in the north, in and along the Wall, showed that in fact he had not. In turn, this had implications for his reputation, which was progressively eclipsed in the light of the work of Simpson, Newbold, Birley and later Ian Richmond. While his credentials as the great synthesizer and the principal epigrapher of Roman Britain remained unchallenged it is interesting to see how Haverfield's reputation as the excavator in the north was re-aligned by his successors, mainly in Oxford. In a letter to Haverfield's former assistant Margerie Taylor, Eric Birley wrote:

> ...the more one studies his [Haverfield's] record of the work done under the auspices of the old Cumberland Excavation Committee in the period 1894–1903 the greater one's admiration for his services as a field archaeologist and excavator, even though ...he was not a natural field archaeologist; or rather as I'd be inclined to put it, he was so much a Roman historian and an expounder and director of studies that he could not spare the time for field work and excavation (February 1962).

This is a feature of Haverfield's career which has not previously drawn comment: the redrawing of the Haverfield memory. It is in part evident in the multi-faceted nature of the obituaries that were written of his life, but this is the first instance among other examples of where those who were responsible for the perpetuation of his memory actually articulated that his reputation could, under certain circumstances (normally following the build-up of criticism), retreat from their previous assessments and argue a slightly different perspective.

(e) The Corbridge Excavations (1906–14)[55]

With the end of the CEC in 1903, Haverfield's interest in mural questions shifted to the other half of the Wall and to other problems. In 1906 a sub-committee of the Northumberland History Committee was created to oversee the composition and publication of a history of the parish of Corbridge, something that the local historian and antiquarian John Hodgkin had been advocating since 1890 (Hodgkin 1892; Dendy 1913). Hodgkin proposed that he and Dr Bruce should write the Roman sections. In the spirit of the time, Hodgkin's scheme was eagerly welcomed and a committee formed to prosecute it. Compared to the contemporary *VCH* series, its remit was progressive. 'While preparing a volume of one district [of the county], the editorial committee promotes excavation on important sites in that district, so that the History is an organ of original archaeological research as well as a repository of information already in existence' (Collingwood in Collingwood and Myres 1936: 471). A component of the committee's plans was the proposal to undertake the excavation of the Roman fort at Corbridge then popularly known as *Corstopitum*.[56] In order to elucidate more clearly its history, as the contributor invited to write the section on Roman Corbridge, Haverfield was asked to oversee the excavations although responsibility for the day-to-day management was delegated to others (cf. Birley 1959 for a summary of the progress of the excavations). A year later, the Annual Report of the Newcastle society (*Archaeol Aeliana* IV (1908): xi) recorded the excavations were initiated by Haverfield's Oxford colleague, H.H.E. Craster, and that the organization of the excavation committee was undertaken by William Henry Knowles who had '...succeeded in enlisting members of the other learned societies, of the universities as well as eminent archaeologists.' The results of the first season's work were such that a second season was undertaken in 1907, this time led by Robert H. Forster, assisted by his draughtsman, Knowles. Forster and Knowles, both native Northumbrians who became residents at the site during the excavation seasons, already possessed considerable experience of excavating (Bishop 1994: 10–12). Haverfield would have been intro-

---

55. Much of the work for this section was undertaken by J. Mawdsley Esq. in an unpublished University of Liverpool BA dissertation (Mawdsley 2000). It is used here, with additions, with permission. The site was subsequently thought to be *Coriosopitum* (Rivet and Smith 1979: 322–3), but the evidence of the Vindolanda Tablets proves that the site was in fact *Coria*.

56. The Annual Report of the *Archaeol Aeliana* (III) for 1907 hints too the excavation was linked with the imminent 1906 Pilgrimage to the Roman Wall.

duced to Knowles by at least 1897.[57] With time the excavations continued down to 1914 (Woolley 1907; Forster 1908; Forster and Knowles 1910; 1911; 1912; 1913; 1914; Knowles and Forster 1909; 1915; cf. Birley 1961).[58] During these years Haverfield was involved in an ill-defined rôle but usually bringing with him Oxford students. Contrary to what others of the time may have believed he rarely played a leading part on a day-to-day basis. He did contribute numerous specialist reports and, of course, there was the county history volume.[59] Because the principal sponsors of the excavations were the London Society of Antiquaries and its sister organization in Newcastle, it generally fell that Haverfield would make the statement of that year's progress to the London brethren while the principal site director, Forster, occasionally with Knowles, would deliver a comparable statement to the Newcastle Antiquaries. As Forster was occasionally listed as the British Archaeological Association's (BAA) representative at the excavations and who sponsored them in a small way, he provided short reports for the association and its journal. However, the London and Newcastle lectures remained the main vehicles for the reporting of the excavation's progress. Haverfield's reports, printed in the society's *Proceedings*, tended to be shorter and more general in tone compared to the fuller reports published in the *Archaeologia Aeliana*. The order in which these presentations were made is important, but it is difficult to decide which came first. Forster *et al.* often made presentations at the

57. W.H. Knowles (1857–1943), born in Newcastle-upon-Tyne, was a professional architect there for nearly 40 years. His interests lay with Roman remains and ecclesiastical buildings. He moved to Cheltenham in 1922 and became involved with the archaeology of (Roman) Gloucester (cf. Austin 1943: C. Hunter Blair *Archaeologia Aeliana* 21 (1943): 248–52). Other than at Corbridge, Knowles worked with R.C. Bosanquet at Great Chesters where he prepared in 1897 a plan of the bathhouse which was published by Haverfield in the *VCH* Derbys. (1905) and at Housesteads the following year. He was also at Bushe-Fox's Wroxeter excavations 1911 and 1912. Forster (1865–1921) was a barrister by training and a moderately successful writer (Knowles 1922; Bishop 1994).

58. Also kept in the Ashmolean/Sackler Library in Oxford is Haverfield's own copy of a collection of Corbridge interim reports, *The Romano-British Site of Corstopitum (Corbridge, Northumbria). An Account of the Excavations during 1906–1912: Conducted by the Committee of the Corbridge Excavation Fund*. (Newcastle).

59. This was published as 'An account of the Roman remains in the parish of Corbridge-on-Tyne' in the *Northumberland County History* X (1914): 457–522. Haverfield also contributed to volumes XII and XIII. Collingwood and Richmond were to write for the later volumes.

site of excavations during that season, usually towards its end. More formally, Haverfield tends to have reported to the London society in the May following the season. But it is also evident that he could up-date and lengthen his spoken version, presumably as a consequence of further information received. I assume that the Forster (and Knowles) reports were published later in the year, and so after Haverfield's ut-terances. Irrespective of the obligations that the patronage of the two societies brought, this arrangement of who spoke where was likely to result in differences of opinions, not least because the format of Haverfield's presentations meant that his opinions were often much more generalized and dependent to a degree on rawer data. Under normal circumstances the format of his reports remained consistent. In his presentations Haverfield would acknowledge the assistance of Forster and Knowles, and usually some if not all of the other staff, sometimes referred to as 'resident assistants' or 'Oxford men'. In con-trast Forster's acknowledgements in this respect are often fuller. The majority of his reports usually credit Knowles as co-author of the year's report with the rubric 'with contributions by...' This normally included Haverfield and others such as Craster and Philip Newbold. Following the introductory summary of the season, Forster would then usually make fulsome acknowledgment to Haverfield's contribution before moving on to a more detailed description of the season. This format is visible in the reports from 1907 down to 1913. The first season, 1906, did not follow this pattern because of its exceptional circumstances.

In the first season of excavations, the site director was Leonard Woolley (the circumstances of his appointment are discussed in Chap-ter 8). As the original plan was to conduct just the one season, Haverfield did not have to present a report to the London society. In-stead Woolley provided a summary for the *Archaeologia Aeliana* in which he set out the circumstances of the excavation and acknowledged the assistance of Knowles, Forster, Craster, R.C. Hedley[60] and Mr Simpson, presumably Frank Simpson (Woolley 1907: 162; Bishop 1994: 5–9). Af-ter explaining why, because of the circumstances of the season, the excavations were more diffuse than he would have preferred, Woolley wrote up most of the report including, it seems, the notes about the samian and other pottery. Forster described exploration of the bridge over the River Tyne. Overall, the tone of the report was that the results of 1906 were far better than had been expected.

---

60. At present unlocated, although listed in Birley's (1961) workers on the Wall, Robert Cecil Hedley (1861–1937), a resident of Corbridge.

It was for these reasons that it was decided to resume the excavations on a grander scale in July 1907. Earlier that year, Haverfield, with the Lords Northumberland and Avebury as well as W. Greenwell, was writing to *The Times* outlining their plans and appealing for funds. At this time they envisaged the need for five years' work, promising 'the excavations will be carried out under the personal supervision of a properly qualified archaeologist' (*The Times* 19 March 1907). On 9 September 1907 Haverfield and Woolley were again writing to *The Times* summarizing the seasons results. Haverfield reported to the London society on 14 May 1908 that a 'powerful Committee' had been formed and that there had been '...three months work effected under proper supervision throughout.' The plans for the site were ambitious. The committee hoped to excavate it in its entirety, hopefully within five years at an estimated cost of £2000. The BAA launched the excavation fund with a donation of five guineas.[61] Although there were short progress reports made to the London society (e.g. Chairman's report, 20 April 1908, *Proc Soc Antiqs London* XXII (1907–9: 273; Haverfield's report to the membership, 14 May 1908), Forster provided a fuller account in the *Aeliana*. He is credited with editing this report because Woolley had by then departed for the Middle East. In the initial stages of the season it is reported that Haverfield helped Woolley, as did Forster. Other assistance was rendered by Knowles, Craster, G.F. Hill (of the British Museum), G.L. Cheesman (who was there in July) and two individuals from Armstrong College for the geology and zoology. They were joined by the Silchester veterans St John Hope and Mill Stephenson, and were presumably invited by Haverfield as a fellow member of the Silchester Committee. J.G.N. Clift helped in the winding-up work. Silchester provided another connection with Corbridge. Forster's report for 1907 compared the difficulties of excavating at Corbridge, with its deep over-burden and difficult geological conditions and yet well preserved structures with the easier conditions at Silchester. Such problems made it necessary to cut deeper trenches that in turn cost more in terms of labour. With regard to the season, Forster reported that the results were satisfactory. He also emphasized the fact that the indications were that Corbridge was not an ordinary fortress but rather a town, laid out and

---

61. In a report published in the association's journal (XIII (1907): 69) the members were listed as C.E. Keyser (President), Sir John Evans, the Dean of Durham Cathedral, T.E. Forster, J.P. Gibson, R. Oliver Heslop and R.H. Forster (as Treasurer). There is no mention of Haverfield. The Annual General Report for 1907 in the *Archaeologia Aeliana* records that by that year £2000 had been raised.

built as such but permeated with military elements. In the processing of the finds, Haverfield described the inscriptions while Forster seems to have used Woolley's notes for the samian. Craster was concerned with the coins and Knowles wrote up the 'fountain' structure. In his report to the BAA (read 18 December 1907), Forster noted that the season was much more extensive than the previous year and so the results were equally more important. Now Corbridge was '...an unfortified civil town, though no doubt intimately connected with military life of the eastern wall district' and so supplying the needs of the Roman garrison (Forster 1908: 1). What is striking in this report is that there is no acknowledgment of the work of other members of the 'team' and the only reference to Haverfield is to his reading of an inscription.

Haverfield's report of the July–October 1908 season, read on 17 June 1909 (Haverfield 1909c), opened with the assertion that the excavations '...bid fair to prove the most important work of the kind as yet undertaken in northern England.' In the longer term, the most significant discovery in this year was a '...huge and massive structure [sic] built round a vast courtyard.' While he could not say what its function was, he noted it '...was pretty certainly military, but a choice between obvious alternative explanations could not yet be made.' He then proceeded to describe that year's inscriptions and other finds.

Yet again Forster's report in the *Aeliana*, with contributions by Craster and Haverfield, was a much more substantial affair. Haverfield was thanked in the preface '...for much valuable assistance in the course of many visits during the months of August and September.' Other assistants were Craster, Cheesman, G.H. Stevenson, Norman Whatley, R.L. Atkinson (sic) and M.C. Dodd (sic), Newbold, D.S. Robertson (of Trinity, Cambridge) and Clift. Again, Forster described the results as highly satisfactory with the recovery of masonry of exceptional quality and a hoard of gold coins. An interesting feature of the report was that Forster felt it necessary to repeat his assertion in the 1907 report concerning the form of the site, with the qualifying statement that perhaps there was more of a military component than previously imagined. In the detailed description of the excavations, Haverfield's large building, now called Site XI, was given seventeen pages, another interesting feature bearing in mind that only the western part of the building was explored. Forster did not offer any opinions about its purpose. In the catalogue of reports, Craster described the coins, and Haverfield the fibulae and the pottery including the samian, although James Curle was consulted on the coarse wares in the light of his experience at Newstead.

Forster also provided another report for the British Archaeological Association. In this instance he listed (some of) the season's personnel;

himself with other unnamed members of the BAA, but including Clift and presumably Knowles. He also noted Haverfield, J.P. Gibson and Newbold. The report concluded with the ominous observation that '...as the work is proving more difficult and extensive, and at the same time more important and interesting than was anticipated', he was reduced to appealing to the association's membership for more donations.

Of the 1909 season, read on 26 May 1910, Haverfield described the results as striking and important. That said, their significance lay in the way they contrasted with the elaborate and massive buildings of 1908, when there was found what Haverfield now called for the first time '...the so-called forum, in reality perhaps a storehouse' (and citing a parallel structure from *Carnuntum*).[62] But overall, the buildings explored in this season were much smaller, more poorly constructed and were mostly ill preserved. Perhaps more significantly, there are the first hints of greater problems, which manifested themselves after Haverfield's delivery when Forster added some additional minor details (Haverfield 1910c). As has been noted already, Haverfield was not averse to commenting negatively in public, and criticising the works of others. This was a trait, which developed with age. Some of his reviews were often quite dismissive. The *Proceedings* of the Society of Antiquaries of London frequently preserve his comments of presentations made to its members. Such was his reputation few ever replied – or were afforded the opportunity – to them. However, a slightly different public dispute in which Haverfield became involved concerned the interpretation of some of the structures exposed at Corbridge. It was the arrangement for the reporting of the season's finds that occasioned something of a public spat over the history and function of certain buildings at Corbridge. Elements of their dispute were reconsidered by Eric Birley (1959). The argument centred on the interpretation of what was called Site XI, first exposed in 1908. Superficially, the differences of opinion may have been resolved, although the two continued to broadcast their own views, but more seriously the disagreement may have been, in part at least, at the root of Haverfield's developing detachment from the excavation.

Forster's (and Knowles') parallel report in the *Archaeologia Aeliana* (with other contributors) repeated Haverfield's assessment of the nature of the discoveries. In recognising the assistance rendered by Haverfield, Craster, Cheesman and Bushe-Fox '...as well as other

---

62. In an account of Corbridge 1905–08, addressed to a German readership, Haverfield described the building as 'Hauptgebäude' (*Arch. Anz.* XXIV (1909–10): 241).

friends who gave valuable assistance',[63] Forster alluded to a problem that was to recur in the future.

> It is only by abundance of helpers that the many activities involved in an extensive excavation can be adequately provided, and which it is indispensible that one competent archaeologist should give personal and continuous supervision to the actual digging, it is equally necessary that others should be present to share in the supervision of special buildings and pits and to record and classify.

If these comments were directed at any one person or persons, and this is not certain, then the obvious candidate would have to be Haverfield who was rarely at the site for extended periods. This was an accusation levelled against Haverfield during the work of the CEC. The 'one competent archaeologist' was presumably Forster.

The tensions apparent in 1909 continued to develop in 1910. In November of that year, Forster (with J.G.N. Clift) delivered a paper, *The Forum of Corstopitum*, to the fellows of the London society (Forster and Clift 1909–11). After describing the location, dimensions and appearance of the remains, Forster advanced the argument that the building must date to the Antonine period and was abandoned soon after it was completed, if it ever was. One of the reasons for saying this was the semi-finished condition of the building's lower stonework. All through Forster's account the building was referred to as a 'forum'. In the post-lecture discussion, Haverfield, as a member of the audience, '...regretted that the excavators had not taken their colleague into their confidence with regard to the "forum" but congratulated Mr. Forster on his successful treatment of the building. The question should be worked out on the spot by those familiar with the site, but he himself could not say whether the building had ever been finished' (p. 295). There followed some detailed argument before the discussion was terminated by the President who observed that he had '...been willing to accept Mr. Forster's explanation till he had heard Professor Haverfield's strictures, and now regarded the theory not proven. The paper had lost nothing by discussion, but being full of detail would have been easier to follow if a plan or synopsis had been circulated.'

The matter of the forum-storehouse was not allowed to rest. Haverfield had at least two opportunities to return to Forster's (and Clift's) argument. In February 1911, with Haverfield in the Chair,

---

63. In the Annual Report of the Newcastle society, Haverfield's participation is noted as are his 'other Oxford friends' who attended during parts of August and September.

Frank King on behalf of Ashby, Hudd and himself, described the 1910 excavations at Caerwent to the London society. Again in the discussion following the presentation, Forster observed that the Caerwent buildings seemed reminiscent of the Corbridge forum. More significantly, four months later, in June, Haverfield spoke of the 1910 season at Corbridge. In this presentation he appears to be addressing some of the issues raised in Forster's latest interim report in the *Aeliana* as well as returning to the Forster and Clift's November paper. He prefaced the lecture with grateful acknowledgement to the landowner and the excavation staff, including Forster, as well as commenting on the training component being tried at the site and in particular the Oxford contribution. One is tempted to read these particular comments as a reply to Forster's complaint about the lack of consistent and experienced staff at the excavations. However Haverfield reserved a large part of his presentation to reviewing systematically and rejecting Forster's argument about the form, purpose and date of Building XI, '...called colloquially (if not very happily) the "forum"', and now said to be almost completely excavated.

Having described the physical appearance of the structure Haverfield, threw in asides rejecting previous (e.g. Forster's) explanations of the building's history ('I do not wish to enter into controversy ... but I may say that (as at present advised) I altogether disbelieve a suggestion which has been advanced ...'). While he could not decide if the building was ever completed, the dating of it was refined. With respect to the function of the building, Haverfield then reviewed the evidence for it being a forum/town hall and market place or else the *principia* to a legionary fortress. Reserving more space for discussing the possibility of a forum, and after examining the evidence for comparable parallel structures, he concluded there was no conclusive evidence for either at Corbridge. As a forum, it lacked certain prerequisite elements (viz. – a basilica; a colonnade-cloister around an open court; there were no shops along its eastern side and those chambers exposed in the western range were unsuitable; the building was too massive for a commercial purpose and would have been too costly for a government project; and finally a forum was a facet of a highly developed town life, Corbridge was not a proper town). As a *principia*, the close proximity of two granaries was reminiscent of a fortress layout. That said, there were some problems with ascribing it as a *principia*. Instead, he suggested that the Corbridge building shared more than a passing resemblance to a storehouse recently excavated in the legionary fortress at *Carnuntum*, and associated with a mid-second-century AD store base.[64] Haverfield's lecture then proceeded to outline the other discoveries of 1910. Forster was in the audience and in the post-lecture discussion objected that while Haverfield had rejected the Caerwent forum, still it was similar to the Corbridge building. He also commented on Haverfield's explanation of the condition of the 'unfinished' stonework and the mode of its destruction. Haverfield was allowed to reply, repeating his opinions about the demolition of the building and the accuracy of the Caerwent structure as a forum: 'At Caerwent, and in all fora, there were two features not represented at Corbridge – a large basilica and a corridor and it was therefore useless to compare the two buildings.' The discussion was then deemed to be closed.

It is at this point that one would like to know more about the sequence in which Haverfield's presentations were made relative to Forster's reports. In his account of the 1910 season, Forster (and Knowles, with contributions from Haverfield, Craster and Meek '...and others'),[65] stated that the season's objective had been to find whether the 'forum' was flanked by other buildings. There are no signs that this report was affected by the differences just summarized, which implies that it was submitted for publication before the discussions of late 1910. While specifically thanking the assistance rendered by Newbold, Craster and others (but not Haverfield)[66], Forster returned to a previous theme: 'and it is hoped that the staff of helpers will be further increased during the coming season.' The description of the excavations is largely uncontentious, although Site XI is frequently referred to as the '...popularly known ... "forum"' and its variants. Comparison was again made with the Caerwent example although there was also acknowledgement of the *Carnuntum* building. In the description of the other finds Haverfield reported on the inscriptions, sculpture, brooches and samian pottery with Craster describing the coins.

Haverfield delivered the report of the 1911 season to the London Antiquaries at its meeting on 2 May 1912. Prior to this, in September 1911 Haverfield and Forster had written to *The Times* about the

---

64. Birley 1959: 14–15 noted Haverfield missed another recently exposed structure which might have, in part, supported Forster's interpretation: an extra-mural forum at *Vindonissa* excavated in 1902, and thought to serve the troops and local mercantile community at the same time.

65. The Annual Report of the *Archaeologia Aeliana* notes that Haverfield supervised, as in previous years, in the vacation 'with associates from Oxford.'

66. The Annual Report of the *Archaeologia Aeliana* (VIII (1912): xvii) has work by Forster, Knowles, Craster, Newbold, Meek, Bush-Fox (sic) and Haverfield.

excavations and in particular the Corbridge hoard. In the letter they described the season as very dull and unspectacular (*The Times* 6 September 1911). Forster also spoke to the membership of the Roman society in London on 5 December, at a meeting which Haverfield chaired. Haverfield used the London Antiquaries lecture as the occasion to summarise the previous five seasons excavations and results. With regard to Site XI, it might be noted the plan included with his report is described as being 'adapted' from a copy supplied by Knowles. Constructing a picture of Corbridge as not quite a town nor exactly a fortress, he argued that it was more a store base. Site XI, described as '...the most massive and substantial remains of Roman architecture in this part of the Empire', was labelled as '...perhaps a huge store base' of the mid-second century. The latter part of the report included description of the 1911 season, concentrated at the western end of the site, and in particular a range of oblong buildings with their narrower ends abutting the main east–west road across the site. These buildings he described as a combination of kilns and furnaces (= workshops), some as yards and some as cottages. At Site XI work proved once and for all that the northern half of the building, whilst it had been laid out, was never completed. The eastern range was more problematic. While showing signs of destruction, '...it was also plain that, when it was destroyed, the masonry had not yet been built more than 4 feet high. The theory that angry Britons cast down the walls was thus put out of court; no one would trouble to destroy a wall over which he could jump' (p. 267). In the discussion after the presentation, Forster's only contribution was the observation that he was not sure if the oblong structures Haverfield described were buildings but rather open-air workshops. In addition to these reports, Haverfield also provided short summaries for *The Year's Work in Classical Studies* series for 1910 and 1911, where he reports that the excavations were conducted under the (sole) supervision of Forster (Bruton 1911; 1912).

Forster's (and Knowles') description of the 1911 season, with contributions by Haverfield, Craster and Bushe-Fox[67], acknowledged that in some respects the results were disappointing. The buildings exposed were of poorer quality. The year's major discovery was a hoard of gold coins along with more information from the samian and

---

67. Forster and Knowles were the principal authors with contributions by Haverfield, Craster and Bushe-Fox, along with help from Newbold, Cheesman, Whatley, Collingwood and others. Haverfield in Bruton 1912 notes work on the pottery by Bushe-Fox, Newbold and others.

coarser pottery.[68] Forster's account does not differ significantly from what Haverfield reported, with the possible exception that of the destruction of the eastern side of Site XI, (almost incidentally called 'the forum'), evidently done in the Roman period, 'if that be so, the object was probably hostile – but the whole matter is very obscure' (p. 163).

After Haverfield had written to *The Times* (20 July 1912) about the season, in December 1912, Forster presented a report on that year's season to the Royal Archaeological Institute in London at which Haverfield was not present, although he did contribute a note about one of the inscriptions found that year.[69] Published without the assistance of a site plan, Forster's account summarized work on buildings in the southern part of the site, some of which had been partially exposed in previous seasons. The main discovery was a major building (measuring 65 × 45 feet), comprising what was described as a 'nave' and a slightly later apse and two long aisles dividing the building along its length into three sections. Various floor surfaces were exposed, including one in *opus signinum* dated to Valentinian or later. Superficially resembling the ground plan of the so-called church excavated at Silchester, Forster suggested the building was in fact something to do with government and administration and on the basis of an altar found in it thought it dated no earlier than AD 162. Another inscription evidently recorded the LEG XXX V V. It was this inscription that Haverfield commented upon and concluded that the stone was originally cut as XX with a third X added later. Haverfield speculated on the circumstances of the third X but could offer no solution. Forster must have seen Haverfield's contribution beforehand because he expressed in his presentation reservations about some of Haverfield's suggestions (Forster 1912).

Haverfield managed to present a résumé of the 1912 season, including a narrative of the previous years, to the London society on 8 May 1913 at which neither Knowles or Clift were present.[70] There is no staff

---

68. Knowles offered an account of the season to a visit by the Newcastle society on 6 September 1911. Haverfield and Craster also spoke at the branch of Lloyds' Bank where the hoard was then stored. Haverfield's list of the seasons' staff credits Forster and various 'Oxford Archaeologists' – Cheesman, Whatley, Craster, Atkinson 'and several younger men, along with the present writer, came to aid or to learn.' Knowles's list is fuller, with the same names as well as Bushe-Fox, Newbold, Robin Collingwood 'and others.'

69. The meeting was on December 4. On December 3 Haverfield was speaking at the OGM of the Roman Society about the coastal defences of Britain in the sixth century.

70. On 15 August 1912 Haverfield's will was signed and witnessed by Forster and Newbold which suggests he was on site at least on that day.

list. Opening with a prefatory comment on how difficult it had been to excavate at Corbridge '...since I dug its first trial trenches in 1906', Haverfield provided a résumé of the previous six seasons. Of the 1908 results he referred to the large building 'sometimes called a Forum, but that was probably a military storehouse.' To prove this point he repeated a variation of the argument he had offered in 1911: Corbridge was never a normal place; its buildings cannot be described as being exclusively military or civil in character but a mix of both; whilst there was a military presence there, still there were no signs of the normal castrametation that one might expect; it had no public buildings or well-to-do houses of a town proper. It was also a border town, and so especially liable to attack and destruction. Therefore it had to be a store base for campaigning armies and the garrison on the Wall. It was a semi-garrison town (which he equated with modern Aldershot). That said, Haverfield did note that the year's excavations did not revisit Site XI.

Forster's account of the same year again emphasises a new facet to the work: how the excavations were now leaning towards clearing up problems as well as trying to link areas excavated in previous years.[71] With contributions by Haverfield (on the inscriptions and samian) and Newbold (on the coarse wares) included in the title credits, the staff list names Haverfield, Craster '...and other friends' (p. 231). The one major building exposed was Site XLV which, because of its size and mode of construction, was thought to be an official building, perhaps a court house or other government building, or both, or else an adaptation of a *principia-praetorium* type building, possibly dating to Severus.[72]

For the 1913 season Haverfield presented his London report in May 1914. In this it was stated that the 1912 season had been the most disappointing to date and that 1913 had not been much better. This would explain the relative shortness of his report (being less than 4 pages long). There are no staff credits. In an unusual closing statement, Haverfield hoped that in the ninth season, in July 1914, '...surprises will greet him (Forster) of a more agreeable and important character' (p. 187). Forster, present in the audience, agreed in part with

---

71. For the first time, in the *Archaeologia Aeliana's* Annual Report, the editor makes no mention of work at Corbridge for 1912 (and again in the 1913 report). As will be seen below, the entry for the 1914 season was almost as short.

72. In a summary of the Corbridge excavations up to the end of 1912 and published in the *Archaeologia Cambrensis* (13 (1913): 218–21), there was an additional appeal for funds.

Haverfield's assessment although he added that the excavation was still of a high standard.[73]

Forster offered a fuller account of the season in the *Archaeologia Aeliana*. At face value, something seems to have occurred in Haverfield's (and therefore Oxford's) relationship with the Corbridge excavations in 1913. In this report there are a number of significant differences in the format to that offered in previous years and in the information provided by Haverfield. In the first place Haverfield is not listed in the title credits as a contributor (although he did write sections on the inscriptions and sculptured stone, an arrangement that continued in the next season). Nor is his general or specific contribution acknowledged. That there is no staff list was because, as Forster explained, there were no resident assistants, although he hoped the situation would improve for 1914.[74] Finally, he reported work on Site XI, again described as a 'forum' (and totally omitted from Haverfield's parallel account), although there seems not to have been anything substantially new to report from it. One other innovation is that Forster offered some general remarks about the site – describing it as having seen one trial season and seven years of systematic and sustained work.

Comparison of the two 1913 reports leaves one with the impression that the excavations were in difficulty. A reduction in Haverfield's contribution is evident and might be linked to the drying-up of staff from Oxford. Likewise, Forster's report, this time only 31 pages long, coupled with a combination of disappointing results and the fact that the excavations seem to be increasingly going back to previously exposed sites, leave a sense of the project starting to wind down. The sense of decline is even clearer in the 1914 report. In *Roman Britain in 1914* Haverfield reported that the results were as scanty and as poor as those in 1913 (Haverfield 1915a: 9). Neither did he provide a report for the London Antiquaries, although the society continued to part-fund the excavations, contributing £20 for that year. Forster's report in the *Aeliana*, again omitting a contributions banner, does acknowledge assistance from Bushe-Fox, Atkinson and Craster but not Haverfield who still provided a

73. Haverfield in *Roman Britain in 1913* said the results were for the first time 'scanty' (Haverfield 1914a: 12). In the following year's report, in reviewing Forster's 1913 report, he repeated the results were poor, the buildings insignificant and mostly ill-preserved (Haverfield 1915a).

74. It may be coincidence, but Haverfield had been on the committee promoting excavations at Wroxeter since at least October 1911 (*The Times* 3 October 1911). Excavations at the site, under Bushe-Fox, commenced in 1912, and employed Oxford students. Then there is also the matter of Haverfield's proposed involvement in excavations at *Verulamium* (cf. n.77 below).

report on the stamped samian. The same shortage of skilled and un-skilled labour was also recorded, although Forster was at pains to emphasise this was not due to the outbreak of war, as few of the labourers had joined up, and as it was, the majority of the workers were over-age. Forster concluded the report with a potted history of the site but one without any reference or acknowledgement to Haverfield. After a break of five years, something more substantial than a short summary of the season was offered to the BAA. The editor of the journal's *Archaeological Notes* reprinted an extract from a letter Forster had sent to the secretary of the Newcastle society. In this Forster wrote: 'I doubt whether it will be worth while having a special afternoon as the year's work (1914) is not very spectacular. Apart from the supposed temple, we have only three late rough buildings at the South end of the area. Much of the work has been done in tracing ditches ...I do not suppose I shall be here more than another fortnight, as I shall have to be back in London sooner than usual' (*J Brit Archaeol Assoc* XX (1914): 343).[75] The possibility of another season's work, in 1915, was left open. In the *Aeliana* report Forster hoped that there would be one. As it turned out, the excavations ceased in 1914. The sense of closure is evident in Macdonald's summary of this period some fifteen years after the event. 'Operations came to a close in ...September (1914) and since then the standstill has been complete, nor is there any prospect of a resumption. The somewhat meagre results obtained during the month (and last season) were duly recorded in Roman Britain in 1914, and about the same time a most judicious and readable summary of the whole available evidence was contributed by Haverfield to the Northumberland County History' (Macdonald 1929/1930: 42).

At face value, the reasons for the end of the excavations are not diffi-cult to find. The outbreak of the war could not have helped. More damaging was the fact that the owner of the site, Capt. James H. Cuthbert DSO was reported missing in action in 1915. But looking deeper, there are a number of other factors. The often-amateur enthusi-asm that characterised the early reports gradually disappears in Forster's later reports. So do the references to the Silchester experience. Bishop's characterization of the Corbridge excavations as '*An Edwardian Excavation*' is especially apposite here, where the innocent but still in-formed antiquarianism of the late Victorian–Edwardian age was followed by the excavators' realization that the exercise of digging and the processing of the results was much more than they had imagined in

---

75. The notification in the *Archaeologia Aeliana* is briefer. The Newcastle society was advised to cancel its usual half-day trip because the '...curtailed season's excavations had yielded no 'spectacular' results.'

1906.[76] This was in part caused by the fact that the 'spectacular' results of the early years compared to what was found in the later seasons (according to Haverfield from 1911 onwards) appear to have declined. Hence the progressively downbeat assessments about the seasons that prefaced most of Haverfield and Forster's reports. Richmond (1960: 174) wrote, as with the other excavations of the time, that the monitoring of the on-site recording and so understanding of the stratification was poor on both the CEC and Corbridge excavations. And yet the relatively high standard of the excavation, the quality of the reporting and the desire to resolve specific questions about the site, all in all, a more professional approach, is also evident in the later reports. Woolley's report of 1906 is a mere 25 pages; Forster's for the 1910 season is 67 pages long. Eric Birley (1961: 32–3) believed that by 1907/8 Haverfield had effectively given up any interest in leading the excavations. Possibly because the results at Corbridge in terms of the quality of the masonry were, in his opinion, becoming less and less impressive, Haverfield's interest and commitment to the project waned. As we have seen, the same process seems to have occurred with his involvement with the CEC, where the initial results exceeded expectations but became increasingly less alluring, which in turn explains Haverfield's developing interest in what was happening towards the eastern half of the wall, the 'province' of the Newcastle society. In the case of Corbridge, Haverfield's attentions seemed to have shifted further south and in particular where there were the ongoing London society excavations at Wroxeter under Bushe-Fox.[77] Disputes such as that concerning the interpretation of Site

76. Woolley (a Haverfield protégé of sorts, cf. Ch. 8) was to publish a highly critical assessment of Haverfield's abilities as an excavator. This point was turned into controversy when Wheeler (1961) again demeaned Haverfield's techniques. His views upset Margerie Taylor who in a letter to Eric Birley (2 February 1962, Haverfield Archive) spoke of Wheeler's use of Woolley's comments: 'Of course Wheeler quotes Woolley, who was writing as an old man, his autobiography, and referring to his youth, always a dangerous thing and in any case, as everybody knew, Woolley never hesitated to make a good story. Haverfield was an epigraphist and numismatist, and he was, above all, an historian and not a real field worker, though he went always to see any sites that he wanted to report about.' For further support for Taylor's view on Woolley's ability to tell a good story, cf. Wilson 1989: 127–30. Cheesman, in his 1913 diary, expressed similar reservations about Woolley's reliability. Taylor's assessment, however, should be set against that of one of Haverfield's more 'peripheral' 'students', George Grundy (see above). See also F.G. Simpson's opinion on Haverfield's competence, as reported by Sheppard Frere (1988: 1).

77. There is also a statement in *The Times* (26 April 1910) which has never drawn comment, where there is a notice that the London society was proposing, in

XI may not have helped his mood and sense of engagement. The arguments about what the site represented, may also be indicative of another problem. At the time of the original excavations, for Forster, Corbridge was more a civilian site with a strong military facet. Conversely, Haverfield saw it as a military site with a civilian component. Since this debate, the editors of the Durham University training excavations at Corbridge (1947–73) now consider Building XI, again after more excavation, to be a *macellum* (M. Bishop pers. comm.), contrary to what Birley (1959) had believed in the late 1950s, it was an incomplete legionary headquarters building of Severan date. With hindsight, the distinction may be more to do with semantics, but in some respects it reflected Haverfield's broader European contacts and perspective against Forster's more pragmatic archaeological training. We have seen that at least one contemporary had cause to criticize what he considered to be the overbearing influence of German examples in the conduct and interpretation of the results of the CEC. Irrespective of these sorts of comments from regional antiquarians, in scholarly circles, as a result of this work, and the connections on the Continent to which he reported the results was Haverfield's universally recognized reputation in the centres of European scholarship. 'Abroad he commanded a respect as only a small minority of British scholars have ever enjoyed' (Macdonald 1927: 245). That Forster was clearly a better field archaeologist than Haverfield and his associates – and believed it himself - and was somebody who was prepared to dispute with him, cannot be ignored.[78] It is

conjunction with the landowner, to initiate a programme of excavations at *Verulamium*. Haverfield, the previous day having been elected a VP of the society, was nominated as the society's supervisor of the works. Interestingly, one of the main objectives was to be the search for churches and evidence for late Celtic continuity. Judging by the absence of any other information about this proposal, it seems the plans never got off the ground.

78. Haverfield seems to have had the same problem elsewhere. In his capacity as advisor to James Curle during the Newstead excavations (1905–10), Haverfield occasionally offered opinions on the interpretation of some of the data. Initially at least, Curle seems to have accepted the advice but it is clear that with time and his growing authority, Curle came to question such opinions. For instance, he was to write to Haverfield: 'Thanks for your letter. I am glad to have your criticism. I am quite convinced that the history of Newstead fort …divides itself in to four distinct periods, though I cannot say whether there was much if any lapse of time between them. You are of opinion that an earlier reconstruction of the fort may have taken place [without] during a continuous occupation. You naturally, as the Professor of History, approach it with your knowledge of the Antonine occupation in your mind. I approach it

interesting that in his retrospective study of the excavations at Corbridge, Birley (1959) laid greatest credit for understanding work at the site at the feet of Bushe-Fox and Simpson. Haverfield is little discussed. Indeed his original involvement in the site was more as a figurehead than as the excavation director. Or, as Birley put it, 'under Haverfield's general direction, R.H. Forster and W.H. Knowles were concerning themselves mainly with the planning of structures, and the study of inscriptions, coins and metal objects' (Birley 1954: 310). And it is true that in résumés on the progress in Romano-British archaeology provided for the DAI, and which include summaries of Corbridge, from 1912 to 1914, Haverfield described Forster as 'Leiter des Ausgrabungen' (e.g. *Arch. Anz.* XVIII (1913): 303; XXIX (1914): 399). Forster also seems to have regarded the excavations as a BAA–Newcastle society exercise while it is clear that Haverfield (and others) viewed it as more an Oxford experiment.[79] In his obituary of C.H. Dodd, Caird was to state, erroneously, that he '...assisted Haverfield and Craister [sic] in the excavation of the Roman settlement at Corstopitum' (1974: 499; 'Craister' is repeated in another Dodd obituary in *The Times* – 24 September 1973). Rostovtzeff, who knew Haverfield, in describing the latter's excavations wrote that 'one of the best was his personal excavation at Corbridge on the Tyne' (1924–25: 338).[80]

It has to be said that on current evidence the hypothesis of Haverfield progressively falling-out with the Corbridge excavations is not quite proven. But there are good indications that his part in the project was in decline before the outbreak of the First World War. Con-

---

knowing little history but knowing also that references are sufficiently scanty to leave room, especially in the South of Scotland for an unrecorded period of occupation. Of course I pretend no special knowledge, but in dealing with this case it seems best to state it solely from an archaeological point of view hoping that some day the combine evidence gathered from the forts of this Northern road will lead us to a truer state of knowledge. If you were digging [out] a fort where you had no history to guide you and found an entire reconstruction would you not feel inclined to put it down to having been twice-occupied?' (Letter 14 July 1907: Gordon 2005; Letter 14).

79. In 1906, at least, copyright for the photographs reproduced in the *Archaeologia Aeliana* report was with the BAA. In later years the credits were to Forster.

80. Likewise in a résumé of the contents of the *Archaeologia Aeliana* (VII (1911), an anonymous reviewer wrote of the excavations at Corbridge that they 'have had the advantage of supervision by Professor Haverfield' (*Archaeol Cambrensis* (67 (1912): 330).

firmation of this idea would have been what happened in 1915. Unfortunately, that season did not occur for reasons not connected with Haverfield's attitude. The lack of contact between the Oxford don and his university with the 'professional' archaeologist and his society might be gauged from Knowles' 1923 obituary of Forster. Of Forster's time at Corbridge there is no mention of Haverfield. Many of these difficulties must go back to Haverfield's prickly character. A recurring theme in many of the obituaries of him was not only was he a difficult and trenchant critic and reviewer, but he could never really be described as a team player (cf. Page 1920: 250; Macdonald 1919–20a; 1924 etc.). In turn these factors may have had implications for his willingness to find students at Oxford. Bushe-Fox's excavations at Hengistbury Head (1911–12) and later Wroxeter also drew on individuals associated with Corbridge.[81] In the later years, those who did attend seem to have been employed for their expertise. In one sense, Haverfield's idea of a training project was fulfilled. The centrality of the training component to the Corbridge excavations was emphasized by Birley (1959) in his retrospective of Corstopitum (sic) 1906–58. The initiative of the 1906 season resulted in Bushe-Fox and especially Frank Simpson, in turn Philip Newbold and ultimately, a couple of generations on, J.P. Gillam's work on the pottery from the Wall. In turn, out of the analysis of the ceramics came the four sub-phases of the history of the Wall.[82]

Haverfield's other fieldwork

In addition to the projects described above, Haverfield was involved in a number of other excavations in Britain, some of which have already been alluded to, and all dating to the years before the First World War. Other than his numerous professional and private visits to Europe, he did not undertake any fieldwork overseas although he prepared a report on the inscriptions recovered by J.A.R. Munro, W.C.F. Anderson and J.G. Milne, in 1893 and delivered to the London Antiquaries in 1894.[83]

---

81. E.g. Bushe-Fox's staff list for these sites is as follows: Hengistbury Head – R.A. Smith, F.N. Pryce, A.G.K. Hayter, T. May and G.F. Hill; Wroxeter (1912) – Hayter, Smith, Atkinson, Cheesman and a Mr Asher; Wroxeter (1913) – Smith, a Mr N. La Touche, ?M.S. Smith, Harold Mattingly and Pryce; Wroxeter (1914) – Hayter, Atkinson, Smith and La Touche.

82. 'It seems right that, in taking stock of half a century of work at Corstopitum, I should say so much at least, about its importance in the development of Roman archaeology in this country, and that I should stress the essential connection of the work done there in the past twenty-five years' (Birley 1959: 4).

83. Haverfield commented on inscriptions found by the expedition to the site of Doclea in Montenegro in 1893, the alleged birthplace of Diocletian (Munro *et*

At the time of this expedition the leading authority in Oxford on the archaeology of the region was Arthur Evans. It is not difficult to imagine that Evans would have advised the party that went to Montenegro, and who perhaps recommended Haverfield to the explorers.

Much of Haverfield's other work was small-scale and often came as a consequence of his visits to sites and general regional tours. In many instances he was required to do little more than act as a figurehead or chairman of the excavation committees. To identify such projects, we are normally dependent on Haverfield (or his co-workers) reporting the work, as in the example of his involvement with the crop mark site at Long Wittenham/Northfield Farm (cf. Chapter 10).[84] Elsewhere, in the Roman section of the *VCH* Warks. (1904) Haverfield mentions that he had found, with Mr H. Fowler, Roman tiles and potsherds at Snowford Bridge (in Long Itchington parish) but was at a loss to explain them. The site, east of Leamington Spa, lies off the Fosse Way. The context of Haverfield's interest in the locality is now lost. In 1908, while still working with the Corbridge excavations, it is recorded: 'The

---

al. 1896). Internal evidence shows Haverfield did not go to the Balkans but commented on the squeezes and other copies of inscriptions brought back to Oxford. Elsewhere he published two articles concerning copies of inscriptions from Sardinia and originally sent to the editor of the *Classical Review* (III 1889; IV 1890). There is no evidence that Haverfield ever visited the island. One surmises that he was asked to comment because of his authority as an epigrapher.

84. In addition to his own commitments in Britain, there is the curious episode of Haverfield trying to facilitate German excavations at Stonehenge. Preserved in the Staatsbibliothek in Berlin are three letters from Haverfield to Ludwig Darmstädter. Two of the letters concern Stonehenge. It is clear there is correspondence missing but the outline of the story is as follows: on 16 May 1910, Haverfield wrote to Darmstädter to say he would enquire if he could get the site owner to give his permission for Darmstädter to excavate if he would provide more information about what he wanted to do there. The second letter (22 June 1910) reported that the owner had, to Haverfield's surprise, given his consent on the condition the London society be represented in the field. The society's nominated representative was likely to be William Gowland who had previously excavated there. Two potential problems Haverfield flagged were that Darmstädter's plan to excavate over four or five days was too short (it is interesting to see, in the light of his CEC and Corbridge experiences, Haverfield recommending sieving of the spoil and the need for 3D plotting of the finds) and that Darmstädter's desire to work in July was impracticable (citing a lack of labourers). September was a better option. It may have been the latter consideration, which meant Darmstädter never got to excavate.

(Ribchester Excavation) Committee would also take this opportunity of gratefully acknowledging the ready kindness with which professor Haverfield has helped them, not only by his advice, but by spending several days upon the site in superintending the excavation' (R.S. Conway and J.H. Hopkinson letter to *The Manchester Guardian* 4 May 1908). We have already seen that at the time of the of his work with the CEC in October 1898 he was involved in the exploration of a stretch of Roman road in Blenheim Park (Haverfield 1899b; described as Woodstock by Codrington in *Roman Roads in Britain* (1918: 200; cf. *VCH* Oxon. i). This was executed with the assistance of a CEC associate, G.B. Grundy. Closer to home, Haverfield was also involved in the exploration of the Oxfordshire villa at North Leigh (cf. Chapter 9). None of this work was regarded by his contemporaries as especially significant. Whilst the impression is that he had given up any plans on being involved in excavation in the future (cf. the Old Carlisle address; Haverfield 1920c), there are a couple of indications that Haverfield had plans for others to see through projects commenced before the war. For instance, he intended a survey of the forts of north-west England in the hinterland of Hadrian's Wall. O.G.S. Crawford remembered such plans. 'Much of the information necessary for a complete interpretation is still lacking but some progress has been made since 1914 (e.g. at Ebchester and Ambleside) ...during the period when scarcity of money and labour rendered digging impossible, Haverfield followed up a valuable paper on Old Penrith or Plumpton Wall which he had published in 1913 (e.g. Haverfield 1913e) by similar papers on other forts in the district. The plan was to bring together the known forts regarding each, including as a rule the inscriptions and to state quite tentatively the conclusion to which these seemed to point' (Macdonald 1929/30: 46). The fort surveys that were completed were Maryport, Carlisle, Old Carlisle and their connecting roads.

Conclusion

Corbridge was Haverfield's last substantial involvement in large-scale fieldwork although he was associated with a number of smaller projects in north-west England but again with an even less hands-on capacity. By 1918 at the latest he seems to have given up on excavation work. His illness of 1915–16 must have played a part in this. He continued, however to play the part of patron, committee member, advisor or simply figurehead as well as subscriber to any number of other excavations. In such instances he increasingly appears as the mechanism by which fieldwork was initiated but where the execution was left to others. It was this fact, which explains Margerie Taylor's assessment of Haverfield as facilitator and encourager rather than as a fieldworker. For in truth, repeating the sorts of criticisms that were evident during his lifetime, modern assessments of Haverfield's competence as an excavator are about the one negative feature of his work. The criticisms cover the range of those made of any excavator. Sixty years after his death and writing of the positive influence of his work, still Frere reminisced: 'Like many archaeologists of those times (Haverfield's) digging methods were primitive. I well remember the only time I ever met F.G. Simpson ... I think in 1945. We were all sitting at his feet and asking questions. "How did Haverfield dig?" was one. "He dug like a rabbit" was the stern reply' (Frere 1988: 1). Then there were accusations of uncompleted work and unwritten reports (e.g. North Leigh). R.G. Collingwood claimed that Haverfield excavated the temporary camp at Caermote (sic) in 1900 but '...left no pottery, not even descriptions of what they found' (Collingwood 1921b: 16). This is not strictly true. The site (Camp Hill at Torpenhow, near Caermot) was excavated as part of the CEC's work and was in fact part-published. It was explored in 1902 and the report constitutes one of Haverfield's longer accounts, not least because the site was '...the first Roman camp of earth in the north of England which has been even professionally examined with any sort of care' (Haverfield 1903c: 338).

There may be another reason that explains Haverfield's retreat from fieldwork. While the problems of dealing with co-directors may not have helped and the residual problems of his health post-1915 cannot be ignored, there is the suspicion that in the years immediately before the outbreak of the First World War Haverfield may have begun to evolve (or regress) into a more conventional ancient historian. In this he was one happy to use some aspects of archaeological research (especially epigraphy) but was no longer interested, perhaps disillusioned, with what detailed research archaeological evidence could reveal. Better was to leave the pursuit of such evidence to others, and to use the product of their labours. We have seen there are signs of a comparable shift in his output of published work as well as in some of his public utterances about what ancient history and epigraphy were about.

CHAPTER 7

Improving Roman Britain

We have looked at the evolution of Haverfield's career in terms of his intellectual connections, his evolving research interests and the way he was able to engineer a return to Oxford in 1892. There was also the nature of his participation in a number of field projects. Many of these themes continued to develop in the decades after his return, so much so that the accomplishments culminated in his elevation to the Camden Chair in 1907. However, at the same time as he continued to work on those fronts, he also developed additional aspects to his work. While best remembered today as a scholar of Roman epigraphy and archaeology in Britain, Haverfield retained other research interests. Macdonald said of his range: 'Lexicography, pure scholarship, textual criticism, geography, even botany, art and medieval architecture, have their place alongside of ancient history, epigraphy and archaeology. In the end, of course, the last three overshadowed everything' (Macdonald 1918: 184–5).

One feature of Mommsen's career was the way he was involved in institutionalizing scholarly research as a function of national interests. Haverfield, early in his career, appreciated the advantages of this trend. In 1888 he was to write:

> Among the various methods by which foreign governments contribute to the endowment of research, not the least effective is the foundation and maintenance of Academiae Literarum, which flourish in most European countries, and especially in Germany. Besides publishing regular reports and journals, these 'academies' are often sufficiently well-endowed to subsidise the great literary or scientific work which lie outside the scope of private enterprise, and which in England are usually undertaken by some private society or university press. Thus we owe to the Prussian Akademie der Wissenschaften the great collections of Greek and Latin inscriptions, the ancient commentaries on Aristotle and the 'Monumenta Germaniae' (*The Academy* 21 April 1888).

While it would be going too far to say that Haverfield ever meant to or-
ganise research into Roman history and archaeology in Britain along
the same lines, not least because there was at the time neither a national academy of letters nor a tradition of government sponsorship
(if not royal and aristocratic patronage), still his knowledge of what
was occurring on the Continent cannot have failed to influence how
he saw the need for co-ordinated effort in (archaeological) research
here. Chapters 3 and 4 looked at how Mommsen in terms of his publications influenced Haverfield. Another feature of Haverfield's career
reminiscent of Mommsen is the way that he was either centrally involved with or else instrumental in the initiation of a number of
(non-excavation) projects, whether they be with respect to excavations, the creation of institutions meant to facilitate the study of the
past or collaborative projects to gather, catalogue and disseminate the
progress of recent, dare one say, more scholarly research rather than
antiquarian inquiries.

The Roman Inscriptions of Britain and the Victoria County History

(a) The Roman Inscriptions of Britain

At the same time he was involved in excavation, Haverfield continued
his interest in the Latin epigraphy of the island. The chequered history of the cataloguing of Britain's Roman period inscriptions was
examined in Chapter 2 and where the circumstances to his involvement in Mommsen's *CIL* were summarized in Chapter 4. In time his
participation in this collaborative programme run from Berlin was to
metamorphoze into a wholly British scheme. Following the publication of (Hübner's) *CIL* VII, down to his death in March 1887, W.
Thompson Watkins had been providing periodic reports on new inscriptions found in Britain in the *Archaeological Journal* (e.g. XLV
(1888): 167–86), a series which Haverfield continued whilst preparing
the *Ephemeris Epigraphica* (Haverfield 1890). With the publication of
the ninth volume of the *Ephemeris* in 1913 it was decided not to continue with the series nor to produce a revised version of *CIL* VII, which
left the issue about what to do with a new edition with British scholars.
Deciding to cut out the Berlin co-ordination of the *CIL*, still the objective was to set the same archival standard Mommsen *et al.* planned for
the *CIL* and other aspects of Roman (-German) history. It was
Haverfield who decided on the format (e.g. a publication, unlike *CIL*,
made up of black and white line illustrations) as well as who would assist. He seems to have intended that G.L. Cheesman take on the

responsibility for publishing the definitive corpus of Britain's Roman epigraphy. Indeed Cheesman had been contributing the annual Roman epigraphy updates to *The Year's Work in Classical Studies* from 1909 through to 1913. With Cheesman's death in 1915, however, Haverfield had to rethink the plans, resulting in the intention to do the work himself. While it seems that Haverfield's colleague J.G.C. Anderson was to be part of the project post-Cheesman, the '...scholar who was to execute these line illustrations had been tested and chosen' (Wright 1965: vi). This was to be R.G. Collingwood.[1] Haverfield's death in 1919 meant a temporary suspension of the plans but with the bequest of his estate, its administrators made *The Roman Inscriptions of Britain* (*RIB*) their primary objective. Collingwood was then commissioned to complete not only the copying of texts but also their restoration and interpretation (Macdonald 1929–30: 109). When the Trustees of the Haverfield Bequest choose to reserve a portion of its fund to support the continuation of the work, between 1921 and 1929 (and in 1936) Collingwood continued to make copies of inscriptions, assisted from 1938 by R.P. Wright who, on Collingwood's resignation because of ill health in 1941, became sole editor. Dobson (1998: 229–30) has suggested that Eric Birley's generally negative review of *RIB* (Birley 1966b) was in part due to his disappointment he was overlooked by his friend and mentor Collingwood when the latter choose in the later 1930s to pass on to Wright the task of completing the volume. The volume illustrating and describing inscriptions up to 1954, was finally published in 1965, nearly 50 years after Haverfield had initiated the plan. In the meantime, as the outbreak of the First World War interrupted the publication of other inscriptions the reporting of new discoveries and the re-reading of others from Britain passed to the *Journal of Roman Studies* from 1921, and later, in 1970, to its sister journal *Britannia*.

(b) The Victoria History of the Counties of England
After his return to Oxford in 1892 and other than the summary articles in *The Antiquary* and *The Athenaeum*, and prior to the 1907 Ford Lectures, Haverfield's main medium for articulating his views about Roman Britain were the volumes of the *Victoria History of the Counties of*

---

1. Collingwood claimed in his *Autobiography* (1939: 145) '...Haverfield, almost immediately before his death, had decided to publish a new collection of all the Roman inscriptions ... in Britain', with Collingwood to be the draughtsman but who was soon to become disillusioned with working with inscriptions (cf. Ch.11).

England or *VCH*. The *VCH* was initiated in 1899 by a subsidy from Haverfield's target of old, L. Gomme and A. Doubleday, and was intended to be the definitive regional history of England arranged by its (historic) counties in 160, later 181, volumes (cf. Pugh 1970; Elrington 1990). The original intention was that it was to be a profit-making venture. From the outset the volumes, which started to appear in 1900, were meant to conform to a consistent format. Each county was divided into general and topographic volumes. The former group dealt with natural history, followed by sections by historic periods, political and administrative history, ecclesiastical and religious history, economic history, forests and endowed schools and completed by sections on sports. The topographic volumes are arranged by *hundred* and *wapentake* subdivided into parishes and townships. Each unit is prefaced by a general description followed by sections on manors and estates, economic history, local government, the church and non-conformity, education and charities. This format was a product of the time and the raw material available, for it was a reflection of the way that, throughout the late eighteenth and nineteenth centuries, there had been a steady increase in the number of sub-regional and parish histories published, most written by the minor aristocracy and religious officers (Collingwood in Collingwood and Myres 1936: 469). Hence the emphasis on ecclesiastical matters – documentary and architectural – in at least the earlier volumes.

Despite its good intentions the number of counties completed is small (and remains based on the English counties before the 1974 local government boundary changes). After an initial spurt of what are described as 'general' volumes, as early as 1907 the programme started to falter. This can be seen in economies introduced at this time (i.e. in proposals to drop some sections, the use of more junior editors to speed up the writing and a new reference system). The problems continued into 1908 when the volume prices were increased and the search for a (new) Royal patron failed. The situation, however, improved in 1909 and was stabilized by 1912. But the crisis had had its consequences. In April 1910 the President of the Society of Antiquaries of London spoke of '...the belief then prevalent that the Victoria County History was in a moribund state, though there was a slight hope of its revival. It is with sincere gratification that I am now able to announce that the grave problem of finance has been solved, the work is going on, and there is every prospect of the series being continued as devised by the original authors' (Presidential Address, *Proc Soc Antiqs London* (1910): 182). But there were more changes (e.g. the division of some county volumes into general volumes with 'topographical' sections; Pugh 1970: 9). Indeed for all the changes and others since Haverfield's time, the situation has not necessarily improved in the interim. To date, with 200+ volumes planned, the series is not complete and any hope for the profits has long gone. While there is no *VCH* volume for Northumberland because it was dealt with by its own county history, other counties remain wholly untouched.

Nowadays it is recognized the strength of the archaeology sections of the *VCH* volumes remains with the surveys of antiquarian research in each of the counties. But the format did not provide much scope for advancing models or conceptual frameworks. Collingwood reported some of Haverfield reservations about the arrangements when we wrote:

> ... as Haverfield pointed out in every one of his contributions to this ponderous work, the materials for a topographical survey of Roman Britain are seriously damaged by being forced in to the Procrustean bed of the English county system. This division of facts by counties is harmless so long as the material is merely described, with no attempt at comparison and interpretation: but in an age of scientific archaeological research when comparison and interpretation are indispensable, it is a positive detriment to historical study (Collingwood in Collingwood and Myres 1936: 471).

Powell's (1980) assertion that the original contributors to the *VCH* were not especially distinguished is not entirely fair, for there were, at least in terms of archaeologists in fact a number of noted scholars. Haverfield was engaged as a contributor to the *VCH* at its inception as well as a subject editor until the redefinition of duties following the crisis of 1905–07, after which subject editors are listed as Contributors and Helpers. From the start Haverfield's (and the other contributors) responsibilities were '...to write and or organize the writing of topics in which they were specialists. They had a nation-wide responsibility and did not concentrate on particular regions although they were supposed to keep in touch with local experts.' C.H. Read and R.A. Smith, both of the British Museum, were editors for the Anglo-Saxon period while Haverfield covered Roman remains.[2] 'These men, of course, were not salaried employees. They wrote in their leisure for fees' (Pugh 1970: 4; cf. Powell 1980). At the start Haverfield showed commendable energy in submitting his contributions; four of them within the first three years of the series commencing. The rapidity was no doubt

---

2. Smith is discussed in Ch 8. By the time of his death (in 1940) he had contributed 24 of the 31 Anglo-Saxon articles published in the *VCH* (Leeds 1940).

assisted by being able to call on the advice of certain colleagues (e.g. on place names W.H. Stevenson, P. Gardner and W. Gowland), informed residents and officials of the counties[3] and by acknowledging that he had consulted, often quite closely, earlier detailed descriptions of the counties.[4] He also tended to concentrate and draw on information from recent work with which he was closely associated.[5] By the time of his death, he had contributed the Roman sections for nine volumes: on Hampshire (1900), Norfolk, Worcester (both 1901), Northamptonshire (1902), Warwickshire (1904), Derbyshire (1905), Somerset (1906), Shropshire (1908) and Surrey (1912). But he should have completed more. For instance, when he wrote he was unlikely to deliver sections to the deadlines already set, there was discussion about producing a distinct Roman volume of the six northern counties (a Roman volume had been devised in 1903 but never advertised). The proposal was to cover the counties of Cumberland, Durham, Northumberland, Westmoreland with, in 1905, the addition of Lancashire and Yorkshire (Pugh 1970: 9). The proposal came to nothing. After his death, his contributions to two other volumes were 'completed' by others.[6] The time gap between the Shropshire and

---

3. For those volumes where he made acknowledgments, the lists include: *Norfolk* – J. Evans, C.H. Read, A. Smith, W.H. Stevenson, Jessop, E.M. Belot and others; *Worcs.* – R.A. Smith, R.P.L. Booker, John Amphlett, R.F. Tomes, Rev. J.H. Bloom, Dr Cuthbertson, W.H. Edwards and J. Willis-Bund; *Northants.* – R.A. Smith, T.J. George, Ryland Adkins, J.W. Bodger, W.H. Stevenson; *Warks.* – W.H. Stevenson, G.B. Grundy, Willoughby Gardner, Rev. J.H. Bloom, and S. Stanley.

4. E.g. *Norfolk* – Fox 1889: *Shrops.* – Fox 1897.

5. *Derbys.* – Garstang's work at Brough-on-Noe and Melandra Castle and in a lengthy digression on Roman forts in Britain, on Bosanquet's work at Housesteads and Ward's at Gellygaer; *Hants.* – Fox and St John Hope's excavations at Silchester. Northants. – G.F. Beaumont's (unpublished) survey.

6. Haverfield's posthumous contributions were to the Cornwall volume (vol. 2 (1924), completed by M.V. Taylor and R.C. Collingwood, and Kent (1932, again completed by Taylor assisted by R.E.M. Wheeler). Of the *VCH* Cornwall volume, Macdonald wrote it was '...the last of the contributions which he (Haverfield) made to the VCH. Although it was almost completed at the time of his death, it did not appear until 1924, when it was edited from his papers by Miss Taylor' (Macdonald 1929/1930: 98). There is something of a sleight here. Volume 1 of the *VCH* Cornwall was published in 1906. Volume 2 was favourably reviewed by Maurice Besnier in the *Journal of Roman Studies* (XIV (1924): 275–6). Under the circumstances, one suspects that Haverfield's contribution had lain around for sometime. With regard to

Surrey contribution and the cessation from 1912 of contribution suggests that Haverfield was becoming detached from the *VCH* scheme.
Indeed, for the Shropshire volume (1908), he was assisted by M.V. Taylor, where Haverfield wrote the introduction and the section on
Wroxeter itself, while she was responsible for the rest. More seriously,
his contribution of 1912 to the Surrey volumes was in fact a late contribution. It was supposed to be included in the county's first volume
(published 1902). Just as significant is the fact the entry is credited to
W. Page the editor, no less, of the *VCH* and Edith M. Keate.[7] Haverfield
in fact simply provided a three-page description of Noviomagus and
made some suggestions for the gazetteer of sites.

Another way of gauging Haverfield's increasing detachment from
the *VCH* is to look at who compiled the Roman sections of those counties which were published in his lifetime, when we might reasonably
expect he was available. While it is clear that Haverfield was assiduous
in completing some of his contributions, he seems to have failed in his
capacity of subject editor to delegate commissions to others. We can see
this when we look at the volumes that appeared after his initial burst of
activity. As he retreated from his commitments, not surprisingly we find
gaps in a number of volumes. In their order of year of publication, the
volumes which contained or should have contained 'Roman remains
in...' sections are as follows:

Year	Volume	Contributor(s) and their affiliations
1901	Cumberland	No 'Roman remains' (pre-Roman section W.G. Collingwood)
1902	Hertfordshire	No section
1903	Essex	No 'Roman Remains' (1963 vol. 3 – I.A. Richmond)
1905	Bucks. (ii)	Miss C.S. Smith ('Oxford Hon. School of English Lit.')
	Durham	No 'Roman Remains'
1906	Berks.	P.H. Ditchford, W. Page and Miss C.M. Calthrop ('1st Class, Classical Tripos')
	Devon	No 'Roman Remains'

Kent, Macdonald (in Haverfield 1924: 214 n. 1) reported among 'the unpublished material belonging to the VCH are accounts of Roman
Canterbury and Roman Rochester by F.H.'

7.   William Page (1861–1934), a civil engineer by training, became a professional
     researcher and legal antiquary. He joined the *VCH* in 1902, becoming joint
     editor with Doubleday and sole editor in 1904 (obit. *Antiqs J* XIV (1934): 196).

	Lancs.	No 'Roman Remains'[8]
	Lincs. (ii)	No 'Roman Remains'
	Notts. (ii)	H.B. Walters[9]
1907	Gloucs.	No 'Roman Remains'
	Leics.	The General Editors and Miss Keate
	Yorks.	No 'Roman Remains'
1908	Beds. (ii)	W. Page and Miss Keate
	Dorset	No 'Roman Remains'
	Herefords	H.B. Walters
	Rutland	H.B. Walters and Miss Keate
	Staffs.	W. Page and Miss Keate
1909	London	R.A. Smith, F.W. Reader and H.B. Walters[10]
1911	Suffolk	the late G.E. Fox
1914	Yorks. NR	No 'Roman Remains'

Some of the omissions can be explained. For example, G.E. Fox had previously published on East Anglia, as Haverfield had noted. But his failure to contribute to the Berkshire volume is especially striking, bearing in mind that he had previously worked in the county. The general impression, however, is of Haverfield losing interest in the series sometime between *c.*1904 and 1906, although he continued to be listed as a member of the Advisory Council down to at least 1911. The reasons why this might have been are numerous and perhaps inter-linked. They may be related to his commitments elsewhere. In 1903 Haverfield was appointed the Rhind lecturer for the Society of Antiquaries of Scotland for 1905, lectures which he delivered in late March and early April 1906.[11] It

---

8. In a letter to Charles Roeder of October 1906, Haverfield wrote: 'I believe I am to do Roman Lancs. for the VCH, if time allows.' It appears he had been speaking and so preparing on the subject. For instance, he lectured at Manchester University on *The Roman Occupation of North-West England* (cf. *The Manchester Guardian* 3 December 1912, concentrating on the Manchester area of south Lancs. and Cheshire).

9. Walters, as shown below, was to take on elsewhere a number of other tasks that Haverfield did not complete.

10. Curiously, Haverfield prepared a paper for the Classical Association meeting in January 1912 and subsequently published in the first volume of the *Journal of Roman Studies* on the subject of Roman London. Whilst he had access to some of the material included in the *VCH* volume, notably its plans, his article is replete with carping comments and criticisms of the account in it (cf. 1911c).

11. Indeed it was planned that Haverfield would contribute the section on Roman Essex to the first volume of that county's history in 1903, then to vol.

was planned that he would contribute to the *VCH* Essex volume published in 1903, a contribution that was then held back to the second volume published in 1907, and then for the first of the planned topographical volumes. In the end his contribution never appeared (cf. *VCH* Essex III (1963): xv). Then there was the ending of the CEC's work (1904) and the beginnings of his involvement at Corbridge (1906), the same year was to see the presentation to the British Academy of his first major statement on the condition of Roman Britain. In that year he was appointed the Ford lecturer at Oxford, to present a series of lectures the next year (*The Times* 6 April 1906). And of course the problems of the *VCH* and that it appeared to be failing, may have influenced him to seek out an alternative location for the sort of county overviews that he had been producing since 1888: Sussex (*Archaeol Rev* I (1888)), Berkshire (*The Athenaeum* 26 August 1893), Herefordshire (Haverfield 1896d) and the Upper Thames Valley (Haverfield 1899d). In 1908 he became a member of the RCHM.[12] It is not coincidence that in the aftermath of his appointment, he made occasional overviews and other descriptions to its

---

2 in 1907, if not the 'later' topographical volumes (cf. *VCH* Essex III (1963): xv). Of course none of these ever appeared.

12. There might be one other connection to result from Haverfield's involvement with the *VCH*. In the Bodleian Library, Oxford is preserved a letter (15 September 1914; Bodleian *MS Eng. Lett. E.91 fol.1*) from (the Duke of) Argyll at Inverary Castle. While Argyll is unsure of Haverfield's whereabouts, he invites him and wife for a short stay. 'There is nothing I know of your precise epoch to excite you here unless you detect the hitherto unsuspected.' The writer is the 10th Duke, Niall Diarmid Campbell (1872–1949) of Charterhouse and Christ Church (1896), and where he would have met Haverfield. However Haverfield's connections with the family must go back the Duke's uncle, John Douglas Sutherland Campbell, the 9th Duke of Argyll and Marquis of Lorne (1845–1914). Educated at Edinburgh Academy, Eton, St Andrews and Trinity College, Cambridge, he entered Parliament as the Liberal member for Argyllshire (1868). In 1871 he married Princess Louise, the fourth daughter of Queen Victoria. He was Governor-General of Canada 1878–83. He defected from the Liberals over the Home Rule question. In 1895 he was elected as the Unionist member for South Manchester. He succeeded to the dukedom in 1900. His close association with the Royal court brought advantages but also hindered his political career. A writer, historian and biographer, he was involved at an early stage in the inception of the *VCH*, functioning as the 'literato of the royal family' (Pugh 1970: 2) and the man responsible for obtaining the Queen's interest in the programme. He was succeeded by his nephew.

inventories of the historical monuments for the counties of Hertfordshire (1910), South Buckinghamshire (1912), North Buckinghamshire (1913) and Essex (1916: cf. Collingwood in Collingwood and Myres 1936: 471–2).[13] Described as the chair of the sub-commission (on Roman monuments and earthworks), all of his contributions to this series show signs of passages taken from the earlier *VCH* overviews. More generally the RCHM volumes are more catalogues of (structural) remains and exclude small objects and, as such, are even less so exercises in interpretation. Nor does this summary include his town inventories or descriptions of features such as roads, pottery, inscriptions etc. from individual settlements, regions or counties. In 1914, as a consequence of the Ancient Monument Act of 1913, he was appointed to the English Advisory Board (*The Times* 17 March 1914).

A close reading of the *VCH* various submissions reveals some interesting features and patterns. The structure of his submissions is broadly consistent; opening with general observations on the Roman period in Britain and the county under review, an assessment of the degree or quality of its 'romanization' and then detailed description of site types, usually starting with 'Roman' towns and villas, followed by accounts of other types of sites (temples, industrial, 'native' etc and catalogues of particular types of finds (e.g. for Warwicks., Derbys. and Somerset the lead industry and pigs) or sites (e.g. caves in Derbys.), the roads and finally a gazetteer of relevant sites in the county. This format allowed the author to indulge in a certain amount of recycling and republishing of broadly unchanged (introductory) passages and analogies in the general paragraphs. There are even instances of footnotes being repeated verbatim. This tendency to repeat is especially evident in the later volumes. Each county's description is interesting in itself but there are certain recurring themes. The assessment of the 'romanization' of the counties, or the 'character of the province', is invariably based on the number and quality of Roman towns and villas. There is also an emphasis on the highland/military – lowland/civil divisions of the province. This leads to comments on the variable quality of the evidence for the penetration of romanization. For instance, of Northants., its 'romanization' was assessed as 'tolerably complete' but on a low scale (p. 161).

---

13. The list of those employed to assist in the compilation of the volumes contains names associated with Haverfield, either through Oxford or the *VCH*: *Herts.* Miss E.M. Keate, Miss G. Duncan; the *Bucks* vols. Keate, Miss M.V. Taylor and Duncan; *Essex* Keate and Taylor.

At the time of his death, Haverfield had not completed a substantial analysis of the archaeological history of Roman Britain. At best there was the piece of synthesis on its 'romanization' (Haverfield 1905; 1912a/1915). It was for this reason Bosanquet (1920: 141) suggested that Haverfield's contributions to the *VCH* might be brought together between one cover. While nothing came of this proposal it is testimony to the regard in which the original entries were held. Indeed, according to Macdonald (1924: 34), Haverfield intended to use the various chapters as the basis for a book about Roman Britain. In the intervening decades, the value of Haverfield's original entries remained largely undiminished, forming as they do a start for an understanding of many of the relevant counties. One might question some of the interpretative framework into which the evidence was placed and make allowances for the discovery of evidence since their completion, but their enduring strength lies in the way that Haverfield brought together in generally accurate and reliable syntheses what was known of the Roman material from each of the counties up to his time.

The British School of Archaeology at Rome and the Society for the Promotion of Roman Studies

Haverfield is frequently said to have been instrumental in the creation of two other organizations which are still important in the execution of archaeological fieldwork and the reporting of recent research on aspects of Roman history and archaeology: the British School at Rome and the Society for the Promotion of Roman Studies. It has to be said that his contribution to the former organization was much slighter than his part in the creation of what was to become the principle organization for representing the study of Roman history and archaeology in Britain. The emergence of these two organizations is a reflection of the conditions of the time and a consequence of the international trend towards the institutionalising of the organization of the acquisition of knowledge.

(a) The British School of Archaeology at Rome

The circumstances behind the origins of the British School at Rome have been discussed elsewhere (Wiseman 1981; 1990; Hodges 1989; 1990: 85–7; 1994; 2000; Wallace Hadrill 2001). It is interesting to note that one of the 'reasons' cited for the foundation of the School was to counter American, French and German work in Italy and the Mediterranean (Marchand 1996), as well as to stimulate the teaching of classical archaeology in British universities. A number of foreign schools had already been established in the city throughout the nineteenth century. Their genesis elicited approving comments from the likes of Percy Gardner and William Ramsay. Although relatively late in the day, it was a combination of Henry Pelham and, to a lesser degree, Haverfield, who was the driving force behind the foundation of a school in Rome. In 1898 Pelham and Haverfield visited the city to see the recent excavations in the forum there before touring the Campagna in the company of St Clair Baddeley, Professor Rodolfo Lanciani of the University of Rome and the Ashbys. Thomas Ashby senior, the head of a family company of brewers, had retired prematurely to Rome in 1890. His son, Thomas, went up to Oxford in 1893, where he came into contact with Haverfield. It is therefore not surprising, then, that Haverfield and Pelham used Ashby's hospitality and contacts for their visit. But the tour was double-edged: 'Their hosts evidently left them in no doubt as to their mission' (Hodges 2000: 46). On his return to Britain, Pelham gave notice to the management committee of the Athens school (founded in 1886) that plans for a counterpart in Rome would follow shortly. A Memorandum was published in 1899 followed by the creation of a provisional committee in October.

Haverfield became involved when Pelham, in late 1899, sidestepped the plan to make the new school an adjunct of Athens and proposed that the new institution should be independent. It was at this time that Haverfield was co-opted onto the Organizing Committee. A successful appeal for funds, including contributions from the Ashbys, resulted in sufficient money for the appointment of a director and adverts for students to apply for admission to the school. In truth it has to be said that, other than his participation in the Organizing Committee, his membership of the school's committee and the Ashby connection, with perhaps him also championing the award of scholar- and fellowships associated with it to those he patronised, Haverfield played little or no other part in the subsequent history of the school.[14] After its 'creation', the convoluted and precarious nature of the original school saw G. McNeil Rushforth[15] appointed as its director, with Ashby junior enrolling as the school's first student in 1902. In 1903, with Rushforth's resignation through

---

14. On 4 June 1907 he was co-opted on to the school's Pelham Scholarship Committee (*The Times* 5 June).

15. Gordon Rushforth (1862–1938), St John's, Oxford (1885), lecturer at Oriel (1893), classical tutor (1897), a student of Henry Pelham, was the author of *Latin Historical Inscriptions Illustrating the History of the Early Empire* (1893); cf. Wiseman 1981; Wallace Hadrill 2001: 22.

ill-health brought on by malaria, Ashby became acting-director while continuing to act as the honorary librarian, which brought another benefaction from Ashby senior. Rushforth's official replacement was Henry Stuart Jones who was assisted in his research by A.J.B. Wace from the school at Athens (and librarian 1905–6) and who he subsequently championed for promotion against Ashby when the latter's contract expired.[16] One might speculate on how Stuart Jones was disposed to Haverfield (and indeed Pelham).[17] Ashby's position with respect to his contract remained problematic for the next few years. In 1906 he was made Director in place of Stuart Jones (who '...had to resign on medical advice early in 1905 (so it was recorded)' – Hodges 2000: 48). After a fruitless search for suitable candidates, Ashby, Wace and five others were interviewed for the directorship. Ashby was offered the post for three years and Wace the assistantship, which he turned down, citing ill-health. Ashby was reappointed in 1909, again after trouble with Stu-

16. Alan John Bayard Wace's (1879–1957): cf. Stubbings 1958. Hodges (2000: 46) suggests that Wace failed ultimately to obtain a position in the Rome school because he was too interested in Greek archaeology and because (in Pelham's eyes) he was a product of Cambridge. Bowra, in recounting Arthur Evans' personality wrote: 'He [Evans] was liable to treat intellectual differences as challenges to battle, and when A.J.B. Wace did not accept his views on the Mycenaean civilization and was in fact right where Evans was wrong, Evans saw that he never held a proper position in England and had to spend many years as a professor in Cairo' (1966: 247–8). After a temporary appointment at the Liverpool Institute and a lectureship at St Andrews, Wace became director of the BSA 1914–23. He had been active in Greece from *c*.1902 (Waterhouse 1986). He was friendly with G.L. Cheesman, as the latter's diary shows.

17. The signs are the two may have, periodically at least, not got on. Stuart Jones authored a rather acerbic retrospect about Haverfield. Later on, he was one of the original members of the Haverfield Trustees which decided not to implement all of Haverfield's will. Although he enjoyed a brilliant undergraduate and subsequent career, since his death, Stuart Jones has not enjoyed a good reputation. Sir Henry Stuart Jones (1867–1939), Balliol College scholar 1886 with a First in *Lit. Hum.* (1890) and after various scholarships in 1888 and 1890, and touring Greece (1890–3), succeeded Pelham at Exeter (and at Trinity) as tutor. In 1903 he was appointed Director of the school at Rome. He was elected Camden Professor in succession to Haverfield (cf. Blakiston 1949; Myres 1939; Wallace Hadrill 2001: 27–8; Gill 2004). Haverfield prepared glowing reviews of his *Companion to Roman History* (1912) and *The Roman Empire* (cf. *J Roman Stud* II (1912): 117–18 and 285). Stuart Jones also co-authored, with Haverfield, 'Representative examples of Romano-British sculpture' (*J Roman Stud* II (1912)) and an appendix to Haverfield 1920b.

art Jones, but this time only for two years. Ashby's position was later strengthened by the arrival of Eugénie Strong at the school in 1908. With her social contacts, she secured his position as well as compliment-ing his strengths and making up for what was regarded as his lack of social graces (Wiseman 1990: 7).[18] The subsequent breakdown of their relationship from 1921, however, meant the pair were forced to leave the school in 1925 (Hodges 2000: 50–85; Beard 2000: 24–6). With his diffi-cult character, his age, the fact that he had been out of the country for so long coupled to the death of his academic patrons, Ashby was effectively relegated to the wilderness. But maybe not totally isolated. In 1930 he had been appointed to the only senior research studentship awarded that year by his old college, Christ Church; shades of Haverfield's return to Oxford in 1892. One of the terms of the award was that Ashby had to spend 30 days residence in college. He was on his way to fulfill this in 1931 when he died (Hodges 2000: 1).[19]

(b) The Society for the Promotion of Roman Studies

In the words of one commentator, to 'all intents and purposes the modern organised study in Britain of Roman civilisation began in 1911 with the establishment of the Society for the Promotion of Ro-man Studies' (Croke MS). Up to the moment of its inception, other than the more antiquarian and archaeological societies such as those in London and, to a lesser extent, in Newcastle, as well as the failed societies of the seventeenth and eighteenth centuries, there was no body which looked to the propagation of the study of Rome in Brit-ain. The background to the foundation of what came to be the Roman Society were summarized by Haverfield's assistant, Margerie Taylor (1960). The first moves to create a society 'which should do for Ro-man Studies the work which the Hellenic Society does for the archaeology, art and history of Greece' were made in 1909 (*J Roman Stud* I (1911): 229). The initiative behind its creation evidently came from Haverfield's former 'student' Thomas Ashby and then Director of the BSR. Discussions were conducted between those interested in such an organization and with representatives of the Hellenic Society, the BSR and the Classical Association, after which at a public meeting

---

18. A summary of Strong's career is included in Beard's study of Jane Harrison (Beard 2000: 14–29), with a fuller treatment by Dyson (2004).

19. Ashby died falling from the Southampton to Waterloo express on 15 May 1931. Irrespective of speculation as to the causes of the fall (opening the car-riage door in error, a giddy fall, the product of cerebellum tumour or even suicide), the coroner recorded an open verdict (Hodges 2000: 1).

in June 1910 it was decided to form a society and with it a Provisional Committee. On this occasion Haverfield proposed that classical scholarship in Britain be divided into three parts: the history and art of archaeology of the Greek world should be the remit of the Hellenic Society; that Roman history and art be the responsibility of the Roman Society and that the Classical Association look to the literature, philosophy and grammar of the Greek and Latin languages (*J Roman Stud* I (1911): 228). This proposal, one he was to repeat elsewhere, reflects what he must have thought of the respective accomplishments and abilities of other academic organizations which had an interest in the study of classical civilization, for in fact he was never especially involved with the work of the Classical Association. A member from its outset in 1903, remaining on its list until at least 1917, serving as a VP (from at least 1917), he did speak on a few occasions at its AGM.[20] However he does not seem to have been a 'national' figure. Indeed it is clear that he regarded its remit and work as quite limited for at least his purposes. His only recorded substantial utterance in the association's *Proceedings* is a lecture delivered at its General Meeting in January 1912 (Haverfield 1912c and reprinted as Haverfield 1911c). Critical of the time the association spent on debating the teaching of Greek, the most interesting feature of this talk is the preface, spoken partly in response to the meeting's earlier business concerning why the study of archaeology was so vital to an understanding of the form of the ancient world. In this, Haverfield's theme was the vitality of archaeology over the dryness of text-based analysis, an opinion he had expressed elsewhere.

Further meetings of the fledgling Roman Society were held throughout the summer and into the following year. On the original committee, sometime between June 1910 and May 1911 Haverfield emerges as its chairman, an office he was to occupy down to 1916. In the capacity of the society's first president, he then addressed its first General Meeting on 11 May 1911 in a speech that was not only reproduced in the society's own journal (the *Journal of Roman Studies*) but was reprinted in *The Times* the next day. In this address, Haverfield repeated the proposal for the tripartite division for the scholarly study of classical antiquity in Great Britain (Haverfield 1911a: 228). The society held its first afternoon meeting in December 1911, with R.H. Forster's report on the season at Corbridge.

20. In 1909 he was elected to the board of the association's two journals, the *Classical Review* and the *Classical Quarterly* (*The Times* 7 December 1909).

Haverfield's first presidential speech remains today one of the most frequently cited of all his works, mainly because it is supposed to reveal much about his attitudes to Roman imperialism. Another reason for its 'popularity' lies with the multitude of themes it raises, discussed in general terms, which, in turn, can be adapted to whatever purpose the reader wishes to find. But it should be noted that few of Haverfield's contemporaries or his obituarists regarded the speech as one of his major statements or being otherwise contentious. Because of its importance to some recent writers, its main themes are summarized here. After some introductory comments, Haverfield's observations were as follows:

(a)   a justification for the creation of (yet another) learned society. Recognition of the proliferation of the same in the nation's towns and counties, some of which have filled an important rôle (e.g. bringing together kindred spirits, facilitating publications, and having made unnecessary state intervention), along with their negative effects, including a tendency to be ineffective and to publishing much rubbish

(b)   the problems created by such societies are not entirely of their own making. Reflections on the strength of the English character in the face of concepts of learning (with criticisms of the traditional emphasis on classical learning which has led to a general unspecialized education, one cool to accurate and scientific training)

(c)   that the (nation's) education system has led to the creation of a great number of those with an interest in ancient history and archaeology at the expense of a critical appreciation of how history is put together or an understanding of how to research its problems

(d)   the tendency for even specialists to question the practical value of work at the expense of contemplation of how the data and its interpretation works

(e)   the belief that real progress in the understanding of the past lies with developments in nineteenth century Europe (and in particular in Roman history, thanks to the work of Mommsen)

(f)   the belief Mommsen (i) made sure that there was more to be learnt with respect to the past; it has become more difficult to handle with more facts and it being more technical; (ii) he opened up new (still underdeveloped) avenues of research, making it a more 'progressive' subject which is now never likely to stand still. While some 'truths' had been established, the study of history was now to remove 'falsehoods'; (iii) two particular new avenues were the (fresh) appraisal of ancient texts and non-literary sources

(g)   a defence of the uniqueness of archaeological sources (over traditional literary sources); definition of the sorts of evidence – epigraphy and art and architecture, pottery and house plans.

(h)   the fact that archaeology is most informative about the periods of the Empire, but is also now shedding light on the less well documented period of the Republic

(i)   a digression into why study the past, with the relevance of Roman history to the present day

(j)   the belief that Roman remains in Britain deserve to be studied because they are our past. Recognition of the fact that the London society does some of this, but that a new society could offer a fresh dimension, bringing the universities into the exercise

(k)   some criticisms of the previous lack of university involvement in (the nation's) archaeology

(l)   the acceptance by the public of the British Museum as the guardian of the nation's past. Haverfield is critical of this outlook

(m)   how the universities are beginning to stir and are showing a commitment to excavation. Haverfield hopes that the new society will help continue the trend.

As it has already been hinted, it was the last clause, the part of the universities, which was perhaps Haverfield's favourite theme. He remained the society's president down to 1916 when he stood down (because of his illness or at the end of the original five-year appointment?). He was succeeded by J.S. Reid[21] who occupied the office until 1921 when another Haverfield initimate, George Macdonald became its third president. The list of contributors to the first few volumes of the society's journal reveals a good representation of Haverfield associates: with articles by Mrs S. Arthur Strong (aka Eugénie Strong) and Warde Fowler and reviews by Macdonald, Curle, Matheson and Stuart Jones, with acknowledgements to Percy Gardner and Jane Harrison. From 'students', there were articles by Cheesman, Anderson, Woolley and reviews by Cheesman and Newbold. Haverfield also contributed two articles and four review pieces. It is also interesting to note how the

---

21. James Smith Reid (1846–1926), Percy Gardner's brother-in-law, was a Greek historian, and first Professor of Ancient History at Cambridge, but who in his championing of archaeology has been compared with Haverfield at Oxford. He was also involved in the SPRS and the BSR where he was very friendly with Thomas Ashby (cf. Adcock 1927).

majority of Haverfield's major contributions to the journal were on Romano-British themes.[22] Haverfield was also a stock reviewer for the journal, especially for foreign language publications which he usually praised, and on Roman Britain as well as numerous school texts and primers. In the decades after his death, Haverfield continued to impose an indirect influence on at least the content of the journal. To be sure, after 1919, it was the medium for reporting progress in the archaeology of (Roman) Britain. Not only were there articles and reviews it published but the journal remained for nearly five decades the main mechanism for reporting progress in Romano-British fieldwork.[23] This was accomplished in the 'Roman Britain in 19XX' series which ran from 1921 until 1969 after which the reports were transferred to the society's daughter periodical, *Britannia*.

Membership of other bodies

At the same time he was a full-time Oxford academic, Haverfield was a member of a number of other archaeological organisations and other committees. We have seen his involvement with the Societies of Antiquaries of London (1891) and Newcastle (from 1889) as well as the Royal Archaeological Institute, (and not its rival the BAA) and where he occasionally spoke at its AGMs and summer tours.[24] But, despite his seniority, he does not appear as a council member nor make any substantial contributions to its proceedings. Along with his part in the creation of the Society for the Promotion of Roman Studies, and participation in the establishment of the British School at Rome, Haverfield was a leading member, often officeholder, of a number of regional archaeological and/or antiquarian societies (cf. Chapter 1

---

22. Two articles in *Journal of Roman Studies* II (1912), and two more in volumes IV (1914) and VI (1916).

23. An admittedly rapid survey of the articles about Roman Britain or which have a direct bearing on it (e.g. on Gallic *sigillata*) published in the *Journal* between 1919 and 1939 shows a healthy turnover of contributions, with the caveats that it is in large measure the same old familiar faces who were contributing and that, as often, their contributions were about literary and historical problems. The breakdown of articles by year is: 1919 (3), 1920 (5), 1921 (3), 1922 (3), 1923 (4), 1925 (2), 1926 (1), 1927 (–), 1928 (1), 1929 (2), 1930 (1), 1931 (4), 1932 (8), 1933 (2), 1934 (–), 1935 (4), 1936 (3), 1937 (4) and 1938 (2).

24. Haverfield's election as an FSA was supported by the likes of Mommsen (already a Honorary member), Arthur Evans and Collingwood Bruce (cf. Croke 39 – June 1890).

and n. 28). Other than the excavations discussed in Chapter 6, he was a member of a number of excavation committees, often serving as treasurer while promoting and supporting the (London) Society of Antiquaries' excavations at Wroxeter and his less formal championing of the work at sites like Manchester, Newstead, Gellygaer and Llanwit Major in south Wales, and the work of the Scottish Antiquaries along the Antonine Wall and elsewhere (Craster 1920: 66). Such associations afforded Haverfield a number of advantages that went beyond simply exposure to the results of recent fieldwork in the respective districts. Chapman (1989a: 152) has shown that in the absence of university engagement with the archaeology of this country in the mid-nineteenth century, it was the archaeological societies, national and regional, which controlled fieldwork and methodology of research. Such societies proliferated and declined and at one and the same time encouraged and hindered progress (e.g. Boon 1989 on the societies associated with the excavations at Caerwent). Chapman has also suggested that societies could be politically intellectualized: they '...were battlegrounds for individuals and special groups', whose archaeologists of note '...worked closely, and even conspiratorially together to promote certain ideas and orientations within the archaeological societies of which they were a part. Each nominated the other to offices, made appointments to editorial committees and helped exclude other, sometimes, opposing interests' (1989a: 154).

Haverfield's growing position of authority and his personality ensured that he too exerted a similar influence in those societies that he was member. He was also a member of at least one national organization concerned with the 'nation's heritage', the Royal Commission on the Historic Monuments (of England – RCHME) (Clark 1934). The creation and subsequent development of the RCHM's work is linked with the progress of state intervention in the preservation and management of the nation's heritage. The 'history' of legislation with respect to the nation's heritage has been extensively documented (cf. Boulting 1976; Kennett 1972; Cormack 1978; Breeze 1993). The first attempts to introduce legislation to protect historic sites were led by Sir John Lubbock who was finally successful in seeing through in 1882 the Ancient Monuments Protection Act ('a poor thing'; Kennett 1972: 29; cf. Cormack 1978: 17–18; Hudson 1981: 50–8) and was supplemented by an equally unsatisfactory second act in 1900. The next major development came in 1908 with the creation of the RCHM charged to make inventories of the ancient and historic monuments and constructions, and to recommend those worthy of protection. Under the chairmanship of Lord Burghclere, Haverfield was appointed a commissioner in October of the same year. The commissioners met regularly: at least three times between November and December 1908. The commission's first volume, on the monuments of Hertfordshire was published in 1910. Haverfield started to contribute a series of (Roman) surveys to the commissions' county inventories in the same year. But still the commission remained 'a body of scholars without powers' (Kennett 1972: 30). Despite the moves to a compilation of a list, and so the protection, of the national heritage, the situation was still poor. In 1910 a new Inspector of Ancient Monuments was appointed, C.R. Peers.[25] One of the first things that Peers did was to produce a report of the inspectorate's activities for the year ending March 1911. True to form, Haverfield was not averse to commenting on what he had to say in a review in which he praised the initiative of the report but hoped to see it improve in range and size:

> National care for national monuments has, till the last year or two, been preached and practised more effectively abroad than in England. It is true that acts relating to such monuments were passed in 1882 and 1900 and the late General Pitt Rivers did excellent work, especially between 1882 and 1890, in carrying out the earlier statute. But it was not till the establishment in 1908–9 of Royal Commissions to examine and inventory the historical monuments and constructions of England, Scotland and Wales, till the revival of the Inspectorship of Ancient Monuments in 1910, and till the appointment to that post of a vigorous and thoroughly competent and scientific archaeologist, Mr. C.R. Peers, that real progress began. This progress affects Roman as well as medieval antiquities and deserves therefore the attention of our Society (viz. the SPRS). At present, of course things are still at the beginning. Roman remains do not, and could not be expected to, occupy very much space in the English Commission's recent volume of Hertfordshire ...and the 104 monuments hitherto put under the guardianship of H.M. Office of Works and its Inspector, in accordance with the ...Acts of 1882 and 1900, include only one item which has been ascribed to the Roman period ...But it is plain that more and more landowners will soon place their an-

25. Charles Reed Peers (1868–1953); Charterhouse and King's College, Cambridge (1887) where he read Classics. In 1893 he trained as an architect and worked as such until 1905. He also worked in Egypt in 1897. From 1900 he was editor of the RAI's *Archaeological Journal*. In 1903 he was appointed architectural editor to the *VCH*. After his original appointment in 1910, in 1913 he became Chief Inspector (with inspectors for England, Scotland and Wales) down to his retirement in 1938 (cf. Mann 1953; Ralegh Radford 1953). Peers was certainly known to Haverfield, who advised correspondents to contact him on specific classes of material and objects.

cient monuments under the guardianship of the acts, for the step costs them nothing and may even save them expense, and it ensures the safety of the remains. Then Mr. Peter's modest report will grow into something (say) the *Berichte* of the Provinzialkommission für die Denkmalpflege in der Rheinprovinz and Roman remains will come with the rest within the range of his beneficent activity (1912f: 140).

Ralegh Radford (1953) linked Peers' appointment with the passing of the 1913 Ancient Monuments Act (Consolidation and Amendments) and which established two important principles of state management: (i) the state through the Commission of Works, assumed responsibility for the preservation of ancient sites along with their care. The RCHM was empowered to publish a list of monuments considered by the Advisory Historic Monuments Board to be of national importance; and (ii) the commission was given powers to prevent the destruction of scheduled sites, although any order to that effect had to be confirmed by Parliament. The implication of this clause was that owners had to obtain permission to alter or change monuments in their possession. It also allowed the State first refusal on acquiring such monuments. The 1913 Act really only took effect after the 1920s because of the effects of the war by which time Haverfield was dead.

There was one other national institution to which Haverfield was an elected member. This was the British Academy, the creation of which was a relatively late development compared to its continental counterparts. Indeed, Haverfield had not been unaware of the potential power of such national institutions (cf. *The Academy* 21 April 1888). Although inducted as a member in the second tranche of fellows, in June 1904, he does not really appear as an active participant in the work of the academy (Macdonald 1924: 29). Percy Gardner claimed that the origins of the academy lay with a 'definite scheme for the internationalization of learning' surely accorded with Haverfield's opinions. Gardner also claimed that its creation was his idea when then employed at the British Museum, he wished to see a centralized institution co-ordinating the work then being undertaken by otherwise scattered and weak 'learned Societies of London.' This is presumably the same as his claim he anticipated its foundation with a call for its creation in what was originally an anonymous written review in the *Classical Quarterly* (Gardner 1902b; cf. 1933: 46). Whatever the case, formally constituted on 8 August 1902 by a Charter of Incorporation, the impetus for the creation of the academy eventually came from the Royal Society which, while not wanting to take on the rôle, did offer its assistance and support. Gardner later lauding the academy's achievements still noted:

It marks a distinct advance in English civilization. There is yet left a great deal which it might accomplish by closer organization. It is a source of weakness that the Fellows have usually been elected solely on the merits of their published works, and without sufficient regard to the question how far they could take part in and further the activities of the Society. Many are resident in remote parts of our island, and cannot well come to meetings. This is not to the case in the Academies of Berlin, Munich and Göttingen, all of which stand in close relations with the Universities of those cities, and so have a body of resident members. But at all events every English historical worker knows that there is a learned and influential Society to the membership of which he is eligible, which is sympathetic towards his aspirations, and anxious to help him whenever possible (1933: 48).

In reviewing F.G. Kenyon's history of the first 50 years of the academy, Hugh Last wrote a critical essay. His target was what one might, from knowledge of its continental counterparts, expect from a national academy (Kenyon 1952; Last 1953). Last noted that the academy, because of a lack of public funds, was profoundly under-funded in its first 25 years and therefore unable to offer much by way of practical support for its members. Indeed if one re-reads the contemporary accounts describing the creation of the body, what is striking is the absence of a statement to the effect of defining what the academy was supposed to do (Anon. 1903–04). The financial situation at least was to change from 1924, but still Last painted a depressing picture of a limited, largely irrelevant body which was incapable of taking the lead in initiating or managing the sort of grand projects typical of the German academies. Now, 50 years on, the condition of the academy was somewhat better. Last closed his review with a suggestion for the sort of work it might patronize: 'though those who think that the time is still too soon for a new *Britannia* may be right, there cannot be much doubt that a work about Roman Britain on lines similar to, but rather more ambitious than, those followed by the Römisch-germanisches Kommission in *Germania Romana* ...would meet a widespread need and, if the introductory matter were critically produced, would make a considerable addition to knowledge' (Last 1953: 233). The suggestion was never taken up.

Evidently a regular attendee of its lecture series, Haverfield's contribution to the academy was in two forms: in a lecture delivered in 1906 on *The Romanization of Roman Britain*, which was to be published in a number of revised editions (Haverfield 1912a/1915/1923); and from 1910 presenting to its Fellows annual résumés of progress in Roman Britain and published from 1914 (Haverfield 1914a; 1915a). In the preface to the first (published) progress report, interesting in terms of what it reveals about how he approached Romano-British archaeology, Haverfield protested that he had not wanted to publish his original lectures because of problems with providing what might be incorrect or half-complete summaries, because of the chances of him being accused of 'stealing' other scholars' material and because of the question of obtaining good quality illustrations to complement his reports. He was now prepared, however, to publish his résumés because he thought there were two subjects which merited broadcasting: (i) new epigraphic discoveries; and (ii) new books and other publications about the island (Haverfield 1914a: 56). In turn the reports become longer and more substantial. The series of presentations was only ended by the outbreak of World War One, after which George Macdonald momentarily revived it (1929/1930).

Haverfield and the museums

There was one other element to Haverfield's archaeological work, one which linked fieldwork with his activities in teaching and publication. In addition to his work on epigraphy, excavation and synthesis, all of which enhanced his reputation during his lifetime, Haverfield was also acclaimed as something of a specialist on certain classes of archaeological evidence, notably *terra sigillata* and numismatic evidence. Indeed his research assistant, Margerie Taylor, was to credit him as a coin specialist. His contribution to the study of pottery, in particular *sigillata* and to fibulae, is discussed below. The basis for the acclaim as a numismatist is a number of papers published on Roman coins from Britain and abroad. The interest in this discipline again can be traced back to Mommsen, and a time when numismatics was believed to be one of the two main constituents of archaeology.

Throughout the late 1880s and into the 1890s, Haverfield frequently complained about the quality of Britain's provincial and other museums. This was to become a recurring theme in his published work; a preoccupation with museums and in particular the 'proper presentation' of the material archived in them. The origins of this complaint, as was discussed in Chapters 2 and 4, goes back to his trips to continental Europe and the reports he prepared summarizing what he had seen in various museums there. His concern, however, was not so much to do with the better presentation of their contents for public or lay visitor consumption but rather with the production of definitive catalogues along with commentaries of classes of (Roman period) objects. That museum work was so important, as it formed the basis for creating corpora of reference data, was demonstrated by the volumes of the *CIL*. It would in turn facilitate the more efficient study of the past: the time-consuming exercise of chasing previously published material, would be avoided and definitive descriptions of the objects would permit the advance of knowledge.

Early on in his career, when he was preoccupied with assembling the data for the corrections to *CIL* VII, Haverfield was reporting the frustrating experience of trying to obtain access to public and private collections. For instance, in 1891 in attempting, ambitiously so it seems, to catalogue the Roman material in museums of England, he wrote that the:

> ...following ...paragraphs represent the commencement of an effort to catalogue the Roman remains in our local museums. The work is very necessary for a proper study of Roman Britain, and very little has been done for it in England – Scotland being in this respect, far ahead of us Southerners. The objects preserved in the local museums are of very mixed value...Occasionally I have found that the museums are practically unarranged or devoid of objects worth arranging. Once or twice I have found myself forbidden ...to sketch or make notes without curators' express leave. This seems to me an extraordinary and probably illegal prohibition, for objects are exhibited in public museums ...for the express purpose of making them public (1891a: 168).

The article finished with the promise 'To be continued'. There are no indications that a second part was ever completed. However it was from this basis that interpretation might then proceed. In describing the (early) accomplishments of the Silchester excavations, Haverfield emphasized how artefacts added to the broader picture:

> The importance of the excavations ...seems to me to lie not so much in the individual object or objects, as in the culminative evidence upon the civilization of the town. I am the more desirous to say this because I fancy that the level of the civilization reached by the inhabitants of Calleva is not quite so high as used to be thought (*The Antiquary* XXIV (1891): 212).

Some seem to have appreciated early on the significance of his complaints. In an effusive review of Haverfield's *Roman Inscriptions in Britain II (1890–1891)*, York Powell wrote:

> ...it is something to know that [the] classifying and collecting of the material has fallen into capable hands, and one hopes that the appeal made for help and co-operation from all of who have the good fortune to possess or discover Roman antiquities in Britain will not fall upon deaf ears ...Research is simply methodical scientific investigation and it ought to be carried out in a business-like way, in order that useless time and labour may be spared and the wearisome search through numerous

scattered periodicals entrusted to one or two trustworthy persons once and for all (1893: 228–9).[26]

Five years later, in 1897, James Macdonald completed the catalogue and description of the Roman inscriptions kept in the Hunterian Museum at the University of Glasgow (Keppie 1998a). Haverfield was to write of the *Tituli Hunteriani*: 'I do not know any epigraphic treatise which is better equipped in this respect. The publication of really scholarly and well illustrated local catalogues is among the needs of the time' (*Class Rev* XII (1898): 185). Haverfield omitted to note that Macdonald acknowledged that such merits to the monograph were the results of his advice and comments.

While the call for the systematic reporting and cataloguing of recent finds and museum collections was being recognised by others (e.g. Murray 1904: viii), still progress was not uniform. In 1911, in attempting to republish some inscriptions from Bitterne, Haverfield was to complain of Hartley University College, Southampton that: 'It did not appear to me, when I recently examined them there that the museum authorities attached any great value to them or desired to encourage anyone to study the remains of what is, after all the oldest part of Southampton' (Haverfield 1911f: 139). Later on, when writing about Silchester and the need and problems with compiling corpora, he noted that:

> Even epigraphists, who meet many dates on inscriptions, and whose work leads them to study closely the character and history of single spots, have seldom essayed the task. It needs local knowledge and local activity, for its adequate execution. An exhaustive inquiry into the 'samian' found on any town-site or into the Roman coins picked up there will probably yield dates to show, e.g. when the town began, when it flourished and when it ended. But in England, at least, this generally means a long search through undusted and uncatalogued museums, and through the private

---

26. Frederick York Powell (1850–1904) of Christ Church, Oxford with a First in the School of Law and History (1872), entered the legal profession in 1872, lecturing in law at the same college in 1874 and became in 1894 the Regius Professor of Modern History (cf. Fisher 1912). Haverfield must have been more than a professional colleague. York Powell provided him with an (English) translation of a passage of text in Haverfield's article on a BM MS, *Domitianus I* (cf. The library of Athelstan, the half-king. *The Academy* 12 July 1884). When Haverfield became Librarian at Christ Church, he continued York Powells' work on cataloguing the college's library of music records (cf. Ch. 4. n. 13). In July 1912 the Haverfields attended the wedding of York Powell's daughter to Mr F.H. Markoe (*The Times* 8 July 1912).

collections of persons who rarely know what they actually possess. The inquirer must settle himself in, or repeatedly visit each town in turn, asking often what coins etc, have been found and are to be seen there. At first he will probably be told that there are none. Later on, he will find that some one has remembered that once he, or his great-uncle, had antiquities in a certain drawer, and maybe, inscriptions in an outhouse. Then, if the owner has not at the moment gone suddenly away on a long visit, the inquirer will have to get leave to overhaul and list these antiquities. In short, he must make himself a thorough nuisance to the townspeople, before he attains real results (1920b: 161–2).[27]

One of the consequences of Haverfield's tour of museums was the identification of spurious or misinterpreted objects. Therefore it was natural that he was to produce a number of publications meant to clear up and explain unusual or confusing finds. This included noting

---

27. Haverfield's propensity to recycle his work is evident in this piece. In a lecture on Roman Leicester, admittedly published after his death, but which still enjoyed at least three airings (at the RAI AGM in Lincoln in 1909 (Haverfield 1918a: 1), to the Leicester Archaeological Society and the Roman Society between 1918 and 1919), passages of the piece were re-produced as follows: 'The material for most of the towns, at least in Britain is copious. But it is unsifted and desperately scattered; part lies buried in uncatalogued museums and part in private local collections, which are hard to learn about and almost as hard to get to and get into, but which contain unnoticed but decisive evidence as to the date when a town was founded, when and how long it flourished, what size it reached, and so forth. A really exhaustive inquiry into the "samian" and other datable potsherds found on any town site, or into the Roman coins picked up there, will probably yield dates to prove the facts required. But in England, at least, this inquiry means a long hunt through the archaeological slums of each town in turn. The inquirer must settle himself in one neighbourhood after another, asking perpetually what coins, potsherds, etc., have been found and are preserved there. At first he will be told that there are none; after a while, some one will remember that his great-uncle's great-aunt once had antiquities in a cupboard – even, it may be, inscriptions in an outhouse. In short, he has to worry many folk, and goad them into remembering where things are and where they were found, and make himself a thorough nuisance. Still, the process requires little travelling: once in a town, the enquirer can ferret round it. In war-time we cannot dig up ancient sites, or even cherish hopes that, after peace has come, money for digging will be plentiful, and we might fill the gap be excavating museums, and extracting forgotten stores from their cellars, where, as I know from long experience, much can often be found. Many museums deserve to be labelled as once Lethe and Chaos: they resemble the writing-desk of a busy man, who has been away a while.'

examples of ancient inscriptions brought into Britain, then 'lost' only to be found, republished and then misinterpreted (Haverfield 1891c) as well as anomalous finds of Greek coins (Haverfield and Macdonald 1907; another example of a reinterpretation is Haverfield 1911g where he argued that a piece of sculpture was a forgery).

For all Haverfield's protestations, if his work was to succeed he still had to rely on the assistance of museum curators. While happy to acknowledge the assistance they rendered to the likes of his contributions to *The Antiquary* etc., a number of officials might be described as intimates. For example, he afforded the late Wilfred Cripps (d. 1903) at Cirencester, and indeed his wife, particular praise in this respect (Haverfield 1920b: 161).[28] Elsewhere he worked closely with R.A. Smith and G.F. Hill of the British Museum. And of course he acknowledged those individuals who accompanied him on trips, facilitated his visits and/or provided information with respect to his enquiries.[29]

At about the same time as he was noting his difficulties with accessing museum collections, we begin to find an increasing frequency of Haverfield calling for the systematic preparation of museum catalogues of certain categories of materials. Following on from the *CIL*, he proposed to take the same approach to another class of sub-literary data, that of the potters' stamps on *terra sigillata* and in compiling what should have become a corpus of such marks from Britain. The starting point was to be the marks in individual museums, which in time would be assembled into a national catalogue. This work had been in part anticipated by the earliest attempt in Britain to study this material as a category, when Charles Roach Smith catalogued the samian from London. However his initiative was not followed through (Anderson 1984: 25). In 1890, in a report on new inscriptions found in Britain, Haverfield was writing that he was '...slowly collecting potter's marks, and hope that when I have a sufficient number, I shall be able to publish them in connected lists' (1890: 229–30). The following year he reported in *The Antiquary* (XXIV 1891) that the '...following ...paragraphs

---

28. Haverfield's contact with Cripps goes as far back as the early 1890s; cf. *The Antiquary* XXIV (1891).

29. Among the list of such contacts are those credited in the *VCH* entries, along with J.H. Cunningham at the National Museums, Edinburgh, for assistance in the *VCH* Somerset entry (1906: 232). This Cunningham, John Henry, is not to be confused with H.J. Cunningham at Oxford. J.H. Cunningham (d. 1923) was an Edinburgh businessman and engineer with strong connexions with the Scottish Antiquaries (treasurer, 1891–9 and secretary from 1902. He was also a fieldworker, being, for instance, the planner of Ardoch.

represent the commencement of an effort to catalogue the Roman remains in our local museums. The work is very necessary for a proper study of Roman Britain, and very little has been done for it in Britain' (p. 168). Where there was progress was on the Continent, in Germany and later France. As a result of his second visit to the German frontier in 1894, in an article meant to broadcast the achievements of recent German scholarship, Haverfield was to write:

> ...I may allude to an equally important but no less sensational bit of progress. I mean the increase in chronological data. These data are as yet relative only and shew simply that one work older than some other, but they are none the less useful ...Meanwhile Professor Hettner, the distinguished Curator of the Trier Museum and the archaeological director of the Limeskomission has attacked the pottery found in the various forts and hopes in due course to date its varieties. The attempt is a brilliant one, and if it succeeds its success will be of wide reaching influence; for the present one can only allude to it (1894c: 248).

The results of German work on *sigillata* had implications for the Cumberland Excavation Committee. As an annexe to the report of its 1897 season, Haverfield contributed a description of the samian excavated from Birdoswald. To it he added: 'In Germany various archaeologists, notably Hettner, (Konstantin) Koenen and (Hans) Dragendorff, have attempted to classify chronologically the various sorts of Samian by examination of shape, ornament and general technique. The attempt has aroused little attention or imitation in England, and in the following notes I wish to make what, however scanty and inconclusive, will be at least a beginning of the enquiry in Britain' (1899g: 191).

According to Haverfield, his observations were not followed up. For instance, in the 1903 Gellygaer report John Ward (1903: 74) noted how Haverfield had told him that very little had been done on samian in Britain despite good work on the Continent. Elsewhere, Haverfield commented in glowing terms of Déchelette's *Les vases céramiques ornés de la Gaule Romaine* (1904), although with some reservations about pushing the material too hard with respect to its utility as a dating material. Slightly later, in an appendix to a paper on the Roman military occupation of Wales, Haverfield (1910b: 176–83) added a section discussing the chronology of decorated samian. In this piece he explained to the lay reader the principles by which the material could be used by the archaeologist. Acknowledging the subject was still new, the ground-breaking work having being done by Dragendorff and Koenen assisted by others, the results were scattered among different monographs and periodicals: but 'their work is ...necessarily tentative and some of it necessarily of little value. No one has yet ventured, nor have our studies advanced far enough to justify anyone in venturing, an account of Samian which shall both cover the whole field and cover it in a definitive manner. In Britain, in particular, little has been done. This is partly our own fault; partly also it is due to the deficiencies of our Roman remains' (p. 176). In turn he referred to how difficult it was to master the intricacies of the design on such vessels and potters output. Nor were his opinions restricted to English readers for he offered his opinions to the continentals (e.g. Haverfield 1912g). Here he reiterated that the study of samian had illuminated the otherwise virtually anonymous history of the Roman conquest of Scotland. This was a theme repeated in the inaugural address to the new Roman Society in 1910 (Haverfield 1911a: xvii) and in a lengthy review article of Roman history since the death of Mommsen: the '...study of smashed crockery is perhaps to-day one of the most important and promising studies of a Roman historian' (1912b: 340). As with the CEC, the relevance of *sigillata* studies to the Corbridge excavations was quickly appreciated. Indeed the Corbridge reports were to become the major vehicle for his writings about *sigillata* and the current state of its study.

In 1910, Haverfield spoke at the Society of Antiquaries of London about the 'pottery' shop first uncovered at Corbridge in 1907 and included additional comments about samian ware. In this paper, the crux of his observations was the accuracy of the dates adduced from the pottery related to dating archaeological events/deposits. At the same time he complained about the way that the dates of *sigillata* were both wrong and often incorrectly applied (1910d). The implications of his arguments were that a fresh appraisal of samian (in Britain) was required. A further facet of his concern was developed in the report of the excavation to the same body for 1910 when he repeated his opinion that certain vessel forms enjoyed a longer currency than once presumed. In the report for 1914, Haverfield contributed a *Conspectus of Potter's Stamps on Plain Samian Ware Found at Corbridge 1906–1914* (Knowles and Forster 1915). His observations included how the Corbridge corpus was comparable to assemblages found at other major English excavations, at Silchester, Wroxeter and Newstead. Although refusing to date with any precision the stamps to hand, and decrying German work to do the same as disputable and misleading, he still cited how the study of material such as pottery can '...declare the deceitfulness of appearances: they tell us, too, how little we can pretend to know of remains which have not been turned up by the spade' (p. 274).

In the light of his reservations about the way *sigillata* dates had been applied and in the general state of research on the material in Britain, it is not surprising that the Corbridge assemblages were to be used in another way. Although he took credit for the syntheses of the material, it is also clear that Haverfield used the services of a number of 'students' to help process the raw data. For example, G.L. Cheesman, over 1909–10, produced notes on the potter's stamps from the site. When Cheesman started to specialize in Latin epigraphy, his work on the samian was taken up by two other Haverfield associates, Philip Newbold and Donald Atkinson. In later years Atkinson was to have something of a (archaeological) specialism in the study of (south Gaullish) *sigillata* (Wallace 1994). Atkinson's expertise had been enhanced by his holding the Pelham Studentship at the British School at Rome in 1912, so that he could study the material from Pompeii and which he subsequently published (Atkinson 1914). It was for this reason that one suspects that from an early date in his career, Haverfield intended that somebody, Atkinson as it turned out, should develop this subject (just as Cheesman and later Collingwood were to specialize in epigraphy). Atkinson's rise might have been a consequence of Newbold's retreat from archaeological research. Newbold first worked in the north in 1908 and was Craven Fellow in Rome in 1910 (where he resided with Norman Whatley; cf. Chapter 8). By 1912, if not earlier, he was working with the Corbridge pottery. Cheesman, Atkinson and Newbold's contributions to the study of *sigillata* was noted by Haverfield in the 1914 season report (Knowles and Forster 1915: 267, 275). When Newbold gave up on archaeological studies, Atkinson was the only Oxford-based Corbridge 'specialist' left. Haverfield undertook the synthesis of the samian down to the penultimate Corbridge season (1913) after which Atkinson took over the task in 1914 (and which indirectly might be another sign of Haverfield's developing detachment from the excavation as a whole; cf. Chapter 6). In 1917 Haverfield was to write that Atkinson '...has probably a better knowledge of the dating of Samian ware as found in this country than any other scholar who is available, and I do not doubt that, so far as is reasonably possible, he has exhausted the matter' (Haverfield and Atkinson 1916–17: 238). Towards the end of his life, Haverfield recorded that with '...the aid of Mr. D. Atkinson, of Brasenose College, Oxford more lately Research Fellow in Reading UC, and now Reader in Manchester University, I have been endeavouring in recent years to ensure the compilation of a complete and revised catalogue of the potter's stamps on Samian ware found in this country' (1920b: 193). Later still, in 1919, in describing his attempts to complete a catalogue of the small finds in Tullie House to compliment his original catalogue of its inscriptions and sculptured stones there, Haverfield noted that the samian there had been looked at by Newbold (then at Armstrong College) and Atkinson (at Corbridge), where Newbold completed a list of the potter's stamps and left the manuscript with Haverfield who still hoped to publish. 'I hope when the war is over, to be able to print this, after carrying out some desirable verifications of readings' (1919c: 1). In the meantime Thomas May had also looked at the other Tullie House Roman pottery. His report was then revised by Atkinson. In the end the collection, flagged by Haverfield as far back as 1897, was published by May and the Tullie House collection keeper, Linneaus Hope (May and Hope 1917). At the same time as Haverfield was trying to make plans for his catalogues, others, some connected with him, were working along the same lines. For instance, James Curle (1911) included a lengthy discussion of the *sigillata* from the Newstead excavations. It is clear that Haverfield was instrumental in Curle's growing competence in *sigillata* studies, a fact reflected in his letters to Haverfield (Gordon 2005). Slightly later, in May 1913 J.P. Bushe-Fox, another Corbridge participant, spoke at the Society of Antiquaries of London on 'The use of samian pottery in dating the early Roman occupation of the north of Britain' (Bushe-Fox 1913b), an analysis bringing together the early pottery mainly from Corbridge, Newstead and Cappuck along with that from other fort sites. Bushe-Fox also wrote up the samian from his own excavations at Wroxeter (1912). Curiously, Haverfield consistently failed to acknowledge such work, even when he must have been aware of it. Indeed in the early twentieth century the accumulation of the material and the publication of a British corpus of potters stamps seems to have been the objective of a number of researchers, many of them inspired by, if not associated, with Haverfield. One work on Roman pottery with which Haverfield must have been familiar, even if there is no evidence of him referring to it (nor of the author noting Haverfield's work) was H.B. Walter's *Catalogue of the Roman Pottery in the Dept. of Antiquities in the British Museum* (1908) which was in fact something of a much more substantial affair than the title suggests. This omission is surprising because Haverfield knew Walters and indeed their careers and research interests complemented one another (cf. Chapter 8). And there were others who were also actively researching on the same material. According to one of the obituarists of A.G.K. Hayter, an Egyptologist, but someone who worked extensively in Roman Britain and who appears to have been on the fringe of the Haverfield circle, at the time of his death in 1927 one of his uncompleted projects

> ...which is certainly of more magnitude and perhaps of greater importance than any (of his Egyptian work) is one which has not yet seen the

light. Since 1914 he had been compiling a corpus of the potters stamps of Samian ware. His list is the most complete in existence and was used for reference by scholars in all parts of the country. It is in good order ... It is very much to be hoped that those involved in Roman Britain will see to it that this valuable work does not remain unpublished. For the present it is being kept up to date and added to by Mr. Hayter's son (Peet 1928: 324).

Haverfield certainly knew Hayter but there is no indication that he was aware of this work, and the ultimate fate of the catalogue is not known. Hayter's son, C.F.G. Hayter, continued his father's work on the potter's stamps for Bushe-Fox at Richborough (Bushe-Fox 1928; 1932). Irrespective of Walters' catalogue and the work of others, and despite a number of promises, a complete Haverfield catalogue was not to appear in his lifetime. In the end the task of collating a corpus of British potters stamps was finally completed by Felix Oswald and T. Davies Pryce's *Introduction to the Study of Terra Sigillata* (1920) which drew on progress made in samian studies on the continent rather than Britain (Anderson 1984: 25).

The progress in *sigillata* studies from the late nineteenth century into the years after the First World War mirrors Haverfield's career. He appreciated at an early stage the significance of work in Germany on the subject and in turn used it as a basis for his own work. But some time in the following century there was reaction on his part to the ways that some wished to push the results of its classification to make it do things, notably in terms in dating, which he felt had no secure basis. For this reason we might understand his less-than-glowing acknowledgment of Atkinson's work and that he would not have appreciated how the evidence was used by others in later decades (cf. Chapter 10).

While Haverfield was not to complete the samian catalogue he planned, he did see into print other corpora of inscriptions and sculpture held in English provincial museums.[30] The list of catalogues tends to reflect those areas where he undertook fieldwork, being mainly in north-west England. Many of them originated as articles in the journals of the regional societies which were then expanded into pamphlets or short monographs. For example, in the late 1890s he was invited by the president of the CWAAS to prepare a catalogue of the inscribed and sculptured stones in Carlisle because he was '...the chief authority on Ro-

---

30. Other examples of Haverfield trying to initiate specialist catalogues include his attempt to produce the fullest list of Aucissa type fibulae (Haverfield 1903e), developing on the work of Arthur Evans (1896).

man epigraphy in Great Britain.' It was published as the *Catalogue of the Roman Inscribed and Sculptured Stones in the Museum, Tullie House, Carlisle* (= Haverfield 1899h). At the time of his death he was working on a second edition of the same material in August 1919, with the assistance of Rostovtzeff, now temporarily resident in Oxford and taken up to Carlisle (and also to Cirencester; Haverfield 1917; 1920b) with J.G.C. Anderson, lecturer in Latin epigraphy at Oxford (R. Collingwood 1919; W. Collingwood 1920). It was seen into print by R.G. Collingwood in 1922. Elsewhere he was responsible for the *Catalogue of the Roman Inscribed and Sculptured Stones in the Grovesnor Museum, Chester* (1900: originally published for the Chester and North Wales Archaeological and Historical Society). In this, returning to an old theme, he noted in the introduction, that there was not any inventory of the stones in the museum. Another catalogue which also first saw the light as a journal article was Haverfield and J.P. Bailey's[31] *Catalogue of Roman Inscribed and Sculptured Stones, Coins, Earthenware etc. Discovered in and Near the Roman Fort at Maryport and Preserved at Netherhall* (1915 = Haverfield 1915d).

Along with the country's Roman inscriptions, Haverfield had plans to prepare a similar catalogue on the smaller objects in Tullie House (e.g. its other pottery as well as its brooches) but was unable to do so. He did eventually complete a short article on the fibulae. But the approach to the material was curious. A number of specimens were sent to him in Oxford and he planned to speak about the results of this examination to the society in April 1917, but was unable to honour the arrangement. The results were subsequently published in the *Transactions* (Haverfield 1919c).

Haverfield, Roman urbanism and geography

The best known of Haverfield's 'other interests' were his publications on Greek and Roman town planning. Not surprisingly, with the shift in emphasis from epigraphy to archaeology, his preoccupations with certain aspects of excavation also evolved. Now perhaps best known for his work on and around the Roman wall in England and by association on the Roman military, we have seen to what extent he was also involved in urban sites. On the one hand, there were the major programmes at Chester, Caerwent and Silchester and to a lesser de-

---

31. Bailey (d. 1936) was a noted Maryport antiquarian who had excavated at the site as far back as 1876. It has proved difficult to find out anything about his work, other than generalities and that he watched over the archaeology of the town and its environs for over 50 years (e.g. Bellhouse 1992: 8–9).

gree Corbridge and on the other, the introductory presentations he made of certain Roman towns, often as part of talks for the RAI and/or for the *VCH* volumes. How and why he developed this interest is not certain but it has to lie with his involvement in the excavations at Silchester which had exposed a large part of the town's ground plan. This in turn led to a concern with understanding the principles of town planning. In October 1910 Haverfield spoke on the same subject in the Roman world, to the Town Planning Conference (along with Thomas Ashby; published as Haverfield 1911e; cf. Laurence 1994a: 12–19) while in November he delivered the Creighton Memorial lecture on Greek and Roman town planning.[32] These two works culminated in the publication of his *Ancient Town Planning* (Haverfield 1913c), which, not surprisingly, drew extensively on the results from Silchester and to a lesser degree, Caerwent. An interest in ancient town planning continued in the latter part of his career and was probably stimulated further by the developments he had appreciated in French archaeology (cf. Chapter 5). Just before he died, Haverfield wrote: 'At the present time, there is, perhaps no form of research which would so much advance our knowledge of the Roman Empire as an examination of its individual town-sites. It is only by working out the details of inhabited sites and particularly of towns, one by one, that we can obtain the facts needed to prove various general conclusions as to the development of the Empire and above all, the development of its provincial life.' Research of this type might allow, for example, for the identification of imperial social policies. 'Such things are not told us by ancient writers, not even by Tacitus; for them we must go to archaeology and to history, working in union. ...It is, of course, no easy task.' Slightly later, Haverfield's paper on Roman Leicester, was intended to be a chapter for a book on the towns of Roman Britain, '... a topic which has never yet been treated with adequate fullness, the ten or twelve real towns of Roman Britain' (Haverfield 1918a: 1–2). The book was never completed.

It is interesting in the light of his political and social outlook that Haverfield explained his interest in ancient town planning with reference to the contemporary move towards social engineering with recourse to state legislation. In the preface to *Ancient Town Planning*, and throughout the text, he lamented the lack of originality in much current domestic building work. Here his concern was that most '...of

32. Haverfield (1913c: 3) implies the order of delivery was the other way round: the Creighton and then the conference.

us now admit that if some scores of dwellings have to be run up for working men or city-clerks – or even for University teachers in North Oxford – they can and should be planned with regard to the health and convenience if their probable tenants' (1913c: 4). In turn the monograph, while trying to explain to classical historians some of the principles of town planning was intended to inform modern town planners of some of the achievements of antiquity with respect to '...the well being of the individual' (p. 4). In the light of what follows below, it is worth noting with care Haverfield's conclusions (p. 140–6). In short, he believed modern architects and planners were unlikely to learn much from the Romans directly, for Roman planning (e.g. Roman towns) died away after the collapse of the Roman empire. It is true that Roman town planning 'increased the comfort of the common man; it made the towns stronger and more coherent units to resist the barbarian invaders.' But the benefits soon faded. Roman town planning was only rediscovered – and then adapted – in Europe from the thirteenth century when it evolved into what we can now recognize as the principles of town planning which have a relevance to Haverfield's time. In one sense Haverfield's intentions to offer an introduction to ancient town planning were, like some of his other publications, too successful judging from the general absence of comparable synthesis in the aftermath and by the way the number of subsequent writers who cite him as an authority. In turn however, more recent analyses of his opinions have been proportionally more damming of his conclusions.

The first substantial reappraisal was as late as 1994 when Ray Laurence examined Haverfield's two statements in tandem.[33] In this Laurence situated the contemporary political and social backdrop, which played on Haverfield's opinions. In this analysis, Haverfield's championing of a more socially sympathetic and less economically driven planning movement is still painted in dark shades. The thrust of Laurence's argument is sensible: Haverfield's overemphasis on rectilinear town planning has led to serious misunderstandings of other contemporary 'town' forms. But his largely negative conclusions about Haverfield's contribution to our understanding of ancient town planning are questionable. The criticisms range from highlighting plain factual errors (e.g. Haverfield's misreading of the evolution of Pompeii; his overuse of orthogonal street plans at the expense of less formally

---

33. To reprise what is becoming an old refrain, Laurence described Haverfield's *Ancient Town Planning* as setting '...the agenda for the study of the ancient town' (1994b: 10).

laid out 'Roman' communities – but all a consequence of the limited evidence available to Haverfield) to the more serious: Haverfield being guilty of a form of racial elitism (viz. the distinction between civilized/town dwelling communities using the straight line against barbarian/savage/proto-urban groups existing in their meandering ground plans). In his defence however, it has to be repeated that Haverfield admitted he was entering the discussion about ancient town planning as an outsider and that he was *per force* writing in a generalized manner. The tendency to over-read Haverfield's statements – as in the unfair and unjustified criticism of his use of the word 'civilized and barbarian – is also evident in Haverfield evidently being 'anti-German' because of the apparent recent German predilection for the curve in town planning (Laurence 1994b: 12 n. 19, citing Haverfield 1911a: 12). This in turn is evidence of Haverfield belief in British superiority as an imperial power is patently not so and runs counter to Haverfield's general attitude to Germany and Germans. In short Haverfield has become a convenient target upon who any manner of criticism can be directed, irrespective of the facts that he did not use many of the now prerogative terms in the sense they are now read, that he was writing an introduction to the subject for others, that he was using what is now with the passage of time discredited evidence and that as often as he provided 'questionable' interpretations there are other statements to the contrary that might have been noted.

There is one point Laurence makes which is significant in understanding Haverfield and his legacy. This is the way in his rather naïve – rather than Laurence would have deliberate – characterization of Roman town planning. Haverfield reiterated the division between Roman and pre-Roman urbanism to the point where they became divorced from one another. We have already seen (cf. Chapter 2) how one of the consequences of Haverfield's writings about British antiquarianism and the achievements of its fieldwork was to separate the Roman period from an established conceptual tradition of continuing from the late pre-Roman Iron Age into the Roman period. Unwittingly again, Haverfield's musings on ancient town planning repeated the same conclusion, and so in the process contributed to the sense of stagnation in Late Iron Age studies.

Haverfield's interest in town planning was a facet of a more substantial component to his research; that of 'human geography' in its broadest sense. As Macdonald indicated, another of his innovations in writing about Britain was the emphasis Haverfield placed on the rôle of geography affecting what happened after the Roman invasion. The obituary in *The Times* (2 October 1919) claimed that, as any respectable historian should be, he was a 'good geographer.' Such was the range of his work in the field, another of his obituarists regarded him as a geographer-archaeologist rather than as a historical archaeologist. He had broadcasted the importance of understanding geography and environment in ancient history in a lecture to an audience of Oxford undergraduates and where he added that he had being teaching the subject – or as he called it 'applied geography' 'for a good many years' (1912d: 8–12). And it is true the influence of geography and geology on Haverfield's writings about Roman Britain was crucial.[34] That he appreciated the significance of the subject can in part be attributed to the introduction of geography at Oxford at about the same time that Mommsen and his work was taking effect.[35] In both developments, Henry Pelham had played a major part and he was also an examiner in the Oxford School of Geography, as was later Haverfield.

With respect to geography, Haverfield's interests can be divided into at least four themes. First, there was the way topography-geography as a whole could influence historical events and archaeological patterning. In a lecture of late 1907 at Manchester University on the subject of *The Roman Occupation of North-West England*, Haverfield concentrated on looking at the Roman remains of the Manchester area, southern Lancashire and Cheshire. This led him to emphasize the geographical factors in the development of the region under Roman rule (cf. *The Manchester Guardian* 3 December 1907). Slightly later, his *Study of Ancient History at Oxford* was recommended to those: '...who care to acquaint themselves with the methods of study pursued at Oxford, or maybe interested to read Professor Haverfield's views on the relation of

---

34. Haverfield also produced at least ten papers on (Roman) mining in Britain and four on Roman Ireland, one of which at least was not favourably received by a leading Irish-Celtic specialist, Kuno Meyer (O'Luing 1991: 130).

35. Haverfield attended and spoke at meetings of the Research Dept of the RGS (Haverfield 1906b; *Geog J* 30 (1907): 218; 36 (1910): 677). In an unattributed obituary, it was stated that although he was '...not primarily a geographer, (his) life and work had brought him into close touch with certain sides of geography, and the interests of the subject found in him a warm sympathiser at Oxford', where he supported the School of Geography (Anon. 1919: 395). On 4 December 1915, surely days before his first breakdown, Haverfield was writing to Sir Archibald Geikie (1835–1924), professor of Geology at Edinburgh University and a colleague of Haverfield's in the SPRS, asking for an (geological) explanation why London was where it was and why the Roman settlement was not on the south side of the River Thames.

geography to history and the use of original sources' (cf. Cheesman *Class Rev* XXVII (1913): 103). In time, the significance of geographical factors was to culminate in the 'geographical determinism' advanced by Cyril Fox and O.G.S. Crawford for the development of British prehistory (Ashbee 1972: 66). This approach is now more fashionably known as micro-regional approaches, the template for which is supposed to have been Fox's *Personality of Britain* (1933), based as it was on the results of his earlier pioneering study *The Archaeology of the Cambridge Region* (1923), with its emphasis on the patterns to be adduced by the production of distribution maps of classes of material. In fact, it seems as likely that it was Haverfield who was one of the first to make the distinction between a northern-western highland and militarized Roman province and a more pacified, even romanized, lowland south-eastern district.[36] The consequences of this line of interpretation were most fully developed in the second of his Ford lectures. The origins of his appreciation of the fact may go back as far as the 1880s and in particular to a problematic passage in Tacitus' *Annales*. In describing affairs in Britain in AD47, at *Anns* XII.31 the manuscript reports *detrahere arma suspectis cunctaquae castris antonam* OR *castris Avonam et Sabrinam fluvious cohibere parat*. Over the years a number of emendations were proposed. Henry Bradley, following Hereaus, proposed to emend the passage to read *detrahere arma suspectis cunctaquae cis Trisantonam et Sabrinam fluvious cohibere parat* – 'he prepared to disarm all the suspect tribes on our side of the rivers Trent and Severn' (*The Academy* 28 April and 19 May 1883 and the *Archaeologia* XLVIII (1885)). Haverfield originally disputed Bradley's suggestion, believing the Antontam to be the Trisantona and the modern River Tern rather than the Trent (*J Philol* XVII (1888): 268). He later accepted it (and supporting Mommsen's

---

36. This statement contradicts Estyn Evan's (1975: 1) claim that it was the geographer Sir Halford Mackinder in his *Britain and British Seas* (1902) who was the first to divide Great Britain in to highland and lowland zones (and not Fox). But as Randall (1946: 82, citing Haverfield 1924: 93ff.) noted, Mackinder might have made the distinction but did not emphasize the historical implications. Indeed it still looks as if Haverfield made the identification as far back as 1890s. What Fox demonstrated was the divide between the highland and lowland zones, drawn along the Jurassic Edge (from the Humber to the River Avon), was a conduit for the movement of artefacts from prehistoric times onwards (Crawford 1953: 81). Note too the comments made by Wheeler (p. 43) and Daniel (p. 7–10) about Fox and the Highland/Lowland distinction in I.L.L. Foster and L. Alcock (edd.) *Culture and Environment. Essays in Honor of Sir Cyril Fox* (1963).

emendation in *Rom. Geschichte* V. 152) and that the Trisantona was in fact the River Trent (*Chester Journal* V (1895)). The Bradley reading has since become the accepted version (e.g. Furneaux in *Cornelli Taciti* Vol. II (1891), although occasionally variants have persisted (e.g. Ramsay 1909), preferring the 'Oxford' version of Avonam to replace Antonam; Scarth 1887: 355). With the resolution of the matter of the text, the issue became one of assessing the (strategic) significance of the Trent-Severn and if there were forts associated with it. That this frontier seemed in part to mirror the highland-lowland divide also influenced Haverfield's thinking about the organization of the island. In time it was Graham Webster who fleshed out the idea of a frontier along the Severn-Trent, assisted by an increase in the amount of archaeological evidence to hand to postulate what he came to call the 'Fosse Way frontier' (Webster 1958; 1970; 1980; 1981; cf. Collingwood 1924b). While the veracity of that frontier is now rejected, that it was identified was a consequence of Haverfield's ability to broadcast Bradley's emendation.

A second aspect to Haverfield's work which drew on geography was the use of maps and distribution maps to illustrate and illuminate particular facts and to summarize otherwise voluminous or complex information.[37] This is best seen in his contributions to R.L. Poole's *Historical Atlas of Modern Europe* (1896): xv, with its map of Roman Britain, his updates of the sections in Traill's *Social England* and his works on ancient town planning. In the 1890s Haverfield edited for G.B. Grundy the map of Roman Britain in Murray's series of classical maps. According to Grundy (1935: 99, 104), he also became the editor for the Ordnance Survey map of Roman Britain. In his use of distribution maps, a good demonstration of how these were used to bolster his arguments can be seen in the way Haverfield deployed a series of illustrations to demonstrate the extent of the Roman penetration into Ireland. In responding to claims there had been little Roman influence on the island, he pointed to the fact that the (map) distribution of artefacts indicated an effect in what is now Northern Ireland (*The*

---

37. His interest in maps goes back to Lancing where he made his own (cf. McKenzie in Haverfield 1924: 19). This was followed by him (and Mr J.B. Jordan of the Home Office) producing a relief map of Syracuse. This map was a subject which was to crop up in a number of his reviews and other articles (e.g. *The Academy* 19 February and 19 March 1887). In the *Classical Review* (II (1888): 215–16) Haverfield discussed B. Lupus' *Die Stadt Syrakus in Altertum,* and not only referred to his map but also thanked Heitland for his early comments about it (cf. *Class Rev* I (1887): 73).

Athenaeum 19 October 1912). The same technique (and example) was used in the analysis of the relations between Roman Britain and Ireland (Haverfield 1913d). It permitted him to gauge the extent of 'Roman penetration' of the island based on the distribution of finds of Roman coins and other artifacts. The resulting impression was of a light affect. The conclusion in turn became one of the bases for Haverfield's attribution of a 'Keltic' (sic) religious revival in Britain in the post-Roman era.

Two other manifestations of Haverfield's use of historical geography are his interests in the vestiges of 'ancient' and Roman features in the modern landscape. This was to include his discussions about the survival of Roman period centuriation in Essex (yet another study that was twice published; cf. Haverfield 1918d). Elsewhere he was to research and write, often with Grundy, on the course of Roman roads. The other major facet of Haverfield's publications, and indicative of his research interests, was the critical analysis of the work of earlier antiquarians and so in part to correct the mistakes they had perpetrated with respect to identifying ancient place names and other toponyms. This theme was developed in a lecture to the Royal Geographical Society (RGS) in December 1905, on the weakness of the Ordnance Survey (OS) and its mapping of antiquities (Haverfield 1906b; cf. Hellyer 1989). Judging from the number of references to them, problems with the Survey's ability to place accurately the location of ancient sites was clearly a subject which Haverfield had become aware during the preparation of his contributions to the *VCH* pre-1906. In his presentation to the RGS, Haverfield was at pains to compliment the work of the OS but still harboured reservations about the way it presented antiquities on its maps. 'The general cause of error in the Ordnance maps is the same which is responsible for so many errors in all parts of English life, the absence of trained and expert knowledge'; for the staff of the OS were engineers, not archaeologists. Haverfield went on to highlight four major weaknesses in this respect, although a 'volume would be required to set out the whole available material' (p. 166). The deficiencies were:

(i)   the way 'invisible' archaeological remains were surveyed and published
(ii)   that the OS often used local information without first checking it
(iii)   literary or other forms of printed evidence were used without testing them
(iv)   the way symbols were used to depict facets of the remains mapped

In presenting the case for each of the problems he highlighted, Haverfield cited experiences from his own fieldwork. The lecture became an excuse for him to criticize the work of previous antiquarians (and some societies) that the OS had used as 'authorities'. Some of his comments in this respect have already been noted (cf. Chapter 2). But in the discussion following the presentation, one which discussed the possibility of collaboration in the future between the OS and 'local authorities' (meaning individual antiquarians and local archaeological societies), Haverfield reprised an old tune:

> I must repeat that I am not convinced that the local authorities are by any means the best people to apply to in the matter. Long ago an archaeologist, a tolerably bad one, but still a man of repute in his own day, observed of a local authority that he 'knows nothing outside his parish, and I know nothing inside'. That almost represents the difference between the local and the expert archaeologists in England and in Germany and most other places. The man who is, perhaps, in the best position to judge has not always the local knowledge to know that the thing exists at all. But the lesson to be drawn from the fact, or one of the lessons, is that the opinion of the local men must not be taken as final. It must be submitted to some further decision.

Of the competence of the membership of the Society of Antiquaries of London to help the OS in its work, he added it was '...more useful than mere application to the local societies, which with all due deference to the work they do, contain a considerable proportion of visionaries' (Haverfield 1906b: 175).

Haverfield's other interests

In addition to his teaching, Haverfield was involved in a number of other aspects of the university and its activities that for convenience we might summarize here. *The Times* (unsigned) obituary reports he was '...a shrewd man of affairs and of business' (2 October 1919). The same obituary says a later hobby was university finances and described him as '...a natural economist.'[38] He did undertake some Faculty of *Literae Humaniores* business and unsurprisingly was a member of the Sub-Faculty of Ancient History. Formed in November 1893, this group was originally a dining club, inaugurated by Pelham with Haverfield as its secretary. The club took on more of a business rôle from 1905 when after dinner it started to discuss teaching matters (e.g. lecture lists,

---

38. He did compose, in 1913, a '...list of Periodicals taken by Oxford College Libraries, the Ashmolean, the Taylorian and the Indian Institute' (Macdonald 1924: 54).

degree classes, authors and works for Greats, Greek-less Greats etc.). It was formally constituted in March 1914 (Murray 2000: 344). But the impression of Haverfield as something of an outsider within the university is further implied by his absence from such (social) groups as the 'Tutors Club', '...a dining club, which began about 1820' but which by Warde Fowler's time (a member 1893–1919) '...was a misnomer, for ... it was composed mainly of Professors and Heads of Colleges.' This is presumably the same group Percy Gardner reported of which he was an active member: '...a club of men who dined together once a term and took a line in University business. Among the most prominent members were Pelham, Sidney Ball, Arthur Evans and Lewis Farnell, with several of the Professors of Natural Sciences. It stood for the ideas of Mark Pattison rather than for those of Newman and Jowett. It was certainly not without influence ...But it was loosely organized and its discussions were too discursive to have much practical effect. It was dissolved when the Commission, for which it had striven, was appointed' (Gardner 1933: 71). But the club would have not appealed to Haverfield's personality for it '...was without a serious purpose' (Coon 1934: 72).[39] It was '...apparently in its inception (1820) a protest by the tutorial body against seniority and officialdom, by a class which were beginning to grow more important and self-conscious' (Oman 1941: 199). All in all then Haverfield seems never a major figure within the university, but played a relatively small part. Although Macdonald (1924: 25) spoke of him as a force to be reckoned with on the university's Hebdomadal Council (from 1908), there is currently no evidence to show how much of a figure he was in university politics in a way comparable, for instance, to Pelham. Anderson qualifies this by recounting '...he was shrewd in practical life as in his learned work ... a striking tribute was paid in 1908 to his sanity and independence of judgement when he was returned as a member of the Hebdomadal Council in defiance of all the caucuses' (Anderson 1919: 166). He remained on Council until 1914, when he failed to be re-elected, coming

---

39. It is not clear to what Coon is referring. It reads more as the '"militant" dining club of thirty members' established by Lewis Farnell and the other supporters of research and science at Oxford against the more reactionary Non-Placet Society. The club came together in 1859 (cf. Farnell 1934: 270; Engel 1983: 215). Alternatively, it could be an allusion to the Tutor's Association which came into being in 1853, in reaction to the recommendations made by the 1850 Royal Commission. The association was to play a significant part in the reform of the university in the mid- and later nineteenth century (Engel 1983: 44; cf. Ward 1958).

fourth in a field where only three candidates were elected (*The Times* 24 October 1914).[40] There are also numerous contemporary allusions to difficulties concerning Haverfield at Christ Church and later more so when he moved to Brasenose (Bosanquet 1920: 138). Indeed most of the obituaries refer to the fact that he was what would now be described as 'difficult', which tended to keep others at arm's length. Alternatively it may have been due more to a lack of interest or the traditional college's man's loyalty to his college. Either way, the lack of engagement meant more time and energies for research. This fact may explain that while he must have known most of the leading figures at Oxford in his time, he features so slightly in the memories and retrospectives of many of them (cf. Chapter 1).

Conclusion

It has been the purpose of this and the preceding chapter to demonstrate that there is enough evidence to conclude that Mommsen's involvement in 'big business' archaeology exerted a significant influence on Haverfield, whose involvement in the projects outlined above bears favourable comparison with Mommsen's experience in Germany. Mommsen's success in this respect was due to the strength of his (political) position and his academic reputation which in turn, gave him additional influence, notably through his secretaryship of the Berlin Academy of Sciences. He was also greatly assisted by the State, not least from its financial support. Haverfield in comparison was coming from a position of relative weakness. A junior don at the start of his career (1892) and not possessing the sort of authority and connections that Mommsen enjoyed, most of the German projects described here were well underway, if not finished by the time Haverfield returned to Oxford. Still the parallels between Haverfield and Mommsen are there. His imitation of Mommsen's work can be seen operating on a number of levels. In the first place, the German experience had the effect of establishing a model for the study of Britain's Roman past, initially at the (regional archaeological) society level (with his public statements calling for greater co-operation and a raising of their standards) and then at the national scale. The salient features are the emphasis on collective scholarship (the *RIB*, *VCH* and his other joint publications), the creation of what were intended to be definitive corpora of data and the placement of students and other

---

40. Indeed he failed in 1913 to be elected as one of the two Bodleian curators (*The Times* 14 November).

disciples in positions of authority. There were also the elements of promoting scholarship on the international scene as well as raising standards of description and dissemination, and of the publication of the work achieved. Last but not least, there was the promotion of field-work, first on a national scale (Chester, Silchester) and then to rival continental schemes (Silchester and Hadrian's Wall). Into this category too comes Haverfield's rôle as the 'clearing house' of Roman Britain with his claim to have read virtually all the annual reports of all the regional archaeological societies and his willingness to visit other people's excavations.

But there was a measure of discretion in Haverfield's approach. His was not out-and-out imitation, nor just aping of Mommsen. For the lessons of Mommsen's work could not have worked in Britain if it was total or simple, straight copying of the German example. The different anti-quarian tradition and intellectual structure for the study of Britain's ancient past have be taken into account. This in turn created something even more distinct. In turn, British suspicion of German methods was a sufficient brake on a straight replication of the German model. These limiting factors need to be borne in mind before we consider if Haverfield was of the same sort of temperament as Mommsen, which is unlikely when the English suspicion of government intervention is contrasted to the experience on the continent. But there was also another difference, one due to the weaknesses in Mommsen's approach to studying the past. In other words, what Haverfield believed to be Mommsen's failure in appreciating the strengths of archaeological evidence. Coupled to this was the issue of emulation, a feature to which allusion has already been made.[41]

There was one other major difference between Haverfield's and Mommsen's work. This is the fact that while the motivation might have been similar, in the case of the latter, all that was accomplished was via substantial state funding, if not management, and obviously in the

41. Haverfield, in the light of how the Glasgow society was disseminating the results of its work along the Antonine Wall, suggested the CEC reports should be bound together and sent to certain noteworthy individuals. In February 1900 he wrote to Chancellor Ferguson, president of the CWAAS, asking the CEC reports for the 1894, 1895, 1898 and 1899 seasons be bound into one volume and distributed not least to '...produce some over-the-water notice' (Letter, Carlisle Public Library). Among the recipients were v. Sarwey of the ORL and other (unnamed) Germans. The same practice was continued with the Corbridge excavations – in the Haverfield Library in Oxford is bound Haverfield 1913a summarizing the excavations between 1906 and 1912.

name of the nascent state. Such an arrangement could not have been effected, even if desired, in Britain. With respect to the execution of fieldwork the power of the regional societies was at one and the same time too great and yet too diverse. Often dominated by strong-willed local notables who were not scholars in one sense, they were reluctant to give up their pre-eminence. That the societies were relatively numerous was going to make it doubly difficult, if not impossible to establish a consensus with regard to coordinating a research agenda. Getting the two northern (English) societies to work to a mutual purpose seems to have been an achievement. As it was, the possibility of state interest, especially financial, was lacking, as the failed initiative to create a British equivalent to the RGK showed. The situation in Germany was different, where Mommsen's ability to gain control of the county regional societies along with the creation of a state organization staffed by military officers and other government officials, meant that the participation of the universities there was not so necessary. Indeed the universities could remain indifferent to the progress in Romano-German archaeology.

Another difference was Haverfield's protestations that the universities should be involved directly in the execution of fieldwork. The logical outcome would have been inevitably the introduction of a distinctive archaeology programme at Oxford. But this was not in Haverfield's mind. In Britain, the emphasis on fieldwork at the expense of traditional forms of university scholarship (e.g. teaching and publication) was not coincidental, but was an appreciation of the reality of the situation. That there was no established cadre of academics in post in Oxford (or Cambridge) who were interested in the subject, was a major problem which was an indirect consequence of the structure of those institutions in the first half of the nineteenth century. To establish a basis, one that could benefit from the reforms of the second half of that century, meant at least patronising such a group (at Oxford) and letting them develop the 'agenda' he had advocated from the late 1880s. But there is something of contradiction in Haverfield's demands for improvements in the execution and quality of archaeological research. As we have seen, for all his protestations, he consistently demonstrated a lack of interest in advancing the discipline in an institutional sense. In the first place, in his own backyard he was no great figure in the politics of Oxford University. Haverfield remained, something of an outsider there.

Between 1884 and 1892 Haverfield, as a schoolmaster, gained a reputation as a rigorous and demanding instructor. It would not be surprising that, in the aftermath of Lancing, he would retain opinions about what education should include. But reading between the lines, and looking at other assessments, he does not appear to have been best suited to teaching. Nor would it have necessarily have made him an innovator. Bosanquet suggested that Haverfield's experience of school mastering was influential: 'Seven years of schoolwork, travel and independent research had increased his detachment from the normal Oxford tradition ...uncompromising utterances was contrasted curiously with those of his colleagues ...But if he lacked their urbanity he was free from the intellectual timidity that is apt to sterilize thought in a community of scholars' (1920: 138; cf. Craster 1920: 65). These observations help explain Haverfield's absence from the politics of teaching and had implications for his failure to advocate the cause of archaeology and in turn Romano-British studies there. But his lack of engagement helped maintained the structure and format of *Literae Humaniores*. Another reason for his 'failure' to champion changes to the school, contrary to his reputation among Romano-British scholars, was simply because he remained very much an ancient historian in the Oxford (*Lit. Hum.*) tradition, one who happened to have, as a research by-line, the epigraphy of Roman Britain and, by association, aspects of its other archaeology. This conclusion is corroborated by the way that Haverfield was credited with bringing improved scholarly standards to the writing about Roman Britain and by a concomitant improvement in the organization of that research.

CHAPTER 8

The First World War and Haverfield's 'students'

No city in England is more changed by the War than Oxford (Warren in Fisher 1917)

The success of a university teacher can be measured in people, in those who have been taught or supervised or influenced as colleagues. In particular, leading university teachers will inspire many who go on to posts elsewhere (Aldhouse-Green and Webster 2002: 1).

Having looked at the course of his career up to 1914, we turn to what has been regarded as the third phase of Haverfield's career. Now part of the 'establishment', this period is represented by the consolidation of the work undertaken in the preceding twenty years and his efforts to develop it on the basis of the institutional recognition given to it by his elevation at Oxford. There is also a more negative aspect to this phase of his career, for one of the most frequently repeated facts of Haverfield's career was the way the outbreak of the First World War damaged it, if not indirectly contributed to its end. The harm inflicted was in at least three ways. There was the disruption and cancellation of ongoing work. The declaration of war meant the breakdown in the momentum he had created in the mid-1890s. His personal contacts with the continent, especially with German (and Austrian) scholarship, were, for the moment at least, severed. Finally, there were the losses sustained by a group he is supposed to have been nurturing. In many of the assessments of his career, a recurring theme is Haverfield's creation of an 'Oxford school', although it is perhaps better to define the 'school' not so much by persons but as a mode of instruction which lies with the nature of the Oxford undergraduate degree at that time. While this has become a frequently repeated theme in retrospectives of his career, its requires reconsideration. For there are a number of substantial problems in describing the group as a distinct set of 'students'.

The outbreak of the First World War

With respect to the first and second of the three consequences of the war, it is difficult to understate how much its declaration effected Haverfield. Highly distressed by its outbreak, according to Macdonald:

> In the circumstances the shock of the momentous Fourth of August was violent in the extreme. He was too good a historian not to realize all that was at stake when the nations of the world plunged into an orgy of mutual destruction. He knew that the struggle would be bitter, that civilization itself would be imperilled. He foresaw that, whatever the immediate end, the way of reconciliation would be long and hard. He felt as if the entire fabric of his most cherished plans had been irretrievably ruined. For a week or two, indeed, he was stunned. But the mood soon passed, for on the ultimate question of right and wrong he had never wavered for a moment (1924: 30).[1]

Haverfield's pessimism about the potential consequences of the outbreak of the war was not unique. Percy Gardner was to recount that he had hoped that the series of international conferences held in the years prior to the war would help to maintain peace.[2]

---

1. Cf. Bosanquet 1920: 139–40; Bruton 1920: 74. Indicative of how seriously Haverfield felt it, Macdonald reminisced about the recent declaration of the Second World War; 'It all brings back to 1914 so vividly to mind. I can recollect making more than one endeavour to reassure F.H. You will remember how terribly upset he was...' (Letter to Margerie Taylor, 2 September 1939, Haverfield Archive); 'During the war (George Macdonald) retained his intellectual serenity and balance when others lost heart and hope and during the bleak aftermath ...For Haverfield whose singular energies had given [Romano-British] studies special form and content, was dying, broken in heart and racked in frame' (Richmond 1941: 181). The same sentiments were being repeated 75 years later. 'Haverfield's world indeed disintegrated with the break from his German colleagues and the collapse of international scholarship at the start of the war and with the death in battle of his closest friend and favourite disciple, G.L. Cheesman: he suffered a cerebral haemorrhage in 1915 from which he never fully recovered' (Murray 2000: 356).

2. The congresses Gardner had in mind included: Athens 1905 – International Congress of Archaeology; Berlin 1908 – International Historical Congress; Oxford 1908 – International Congress of the History of Religions; London 1913 – International Historical Congress where the 'undertaking was to English historians a somewhat novel one, and there was a good deal of creaking in the improvised machinery; but the meeting served a good purpose, and our foreign guests learned much of the conditions and working of learned societies in London, Oxford and Cambridge. Our ways seemed to them amateurish; but the amateur is often inspired by an enthusiasm which is apt to

But alas! when the crash of 1914 came, it soon appeared that savants allowed their love of their country to suppress the international love of learning. To me this breach with Germany was especially painful. I had ...maintained close relations with German savants and learned keenly to appreciate their friendliness, their devotion to their calling and their lofty aims. The madness of the war brought these relations for the time to an end. But I never could join in the wave of hostility to learned Germans which swept over England. I know that the German savants had not suddenly changed their nature; they were only swept away by a national impulse (1933: 44).

Following the declaration of hostilities there appeared numerous letters to the press, along with statements and pamphlets by academics, speaking for and against the British government's position. What has come to be called the 'war of the professors' was opened when a number of senior academics from Oxford, Cambridge, Aberdeen (including William Ramsay) and Harvard wrote to *The Times* on 1 August 1914 setting out their opposition to the war. On 20 August two German scholars (the professors Ernst Häckel and Rudolf Eucken of Jena) protested in the *Vossische Zeitung* against England's case for the war. This was reprinted in *The Times* on 25 August. A number of counterblasts followed in the same newspaper in the following weeks. In Oxford the ensuing debate took on high and low intellectual form: from the temporary cessation of electing German Rhodes scholars to Oxford as late as 1916 (Winter 1994: 4), to bringing out the anti-German sentiments of a number of distinguished individuals (e.g. Lewis Farnell, later Chancellor of the university) to the expulsion or the victimising of some academic staff (by undergraduates, Winter 1994: 16; cf. Ferguson 1998b).[3] The best known (British) publication to come out of the posturing was *Why We Are At War* (also known as *The Red Book*) co-authored by a number of members of the Faculty of Modern His-

---

be deadened by elaborate organization' (Gardner 1933: 49, which the writer thought to be the case with the congress' Berlin predecessor). There was also held in Vienna in 1906 the Conference of the International Association of Academies.

3. At Oxford the debate can be charted in the pages of *The Oxford Magazine*. It started with anonymous attacks in the student paper *Varsity* against the Taylorian Professor of German, J.G. Fielder. It elicited letters of support for Fielder (e.g. *Varsity* 16/2/15, 2/3/15, 9/3/15: *The Oxford Magazine* 5/3/1915, 12/3/15 etc.). Elsewhere, T.E. Page denounced Prof. Alfred Marshall in *The Times* (25 August 1914) for advocating respect and friendship to Germans.

tory at Oxford in 1914 (Barker *et al*. 1914; Winter 1994: 15f.; Parker 1990: 104ff.). Another consequence of the early statements about the war was the 'Kultur' debate where the results of German civilization and culture were variously lauded or denounced (e.g. Patterson 1915; cf. Hynes 1990: 67ff.). A facet of this discourse concerned university learning and teaching, between those who championed the merits and methodology of German scholarship and those who rejected them for their rigidity and lack of humanity. In the end, however, the fact that the war was a reality guaranteed that the vociferousness of the anti-war group was at best modified to support for the troops if not the government or else it simply faded into 'silent' opposition.

It is not difficult to imagine what position in either of the debates Haverfield would have taken. His opinions led him to participate in a national debate about whether or not to expel those fellows of learned societies who were from 'enemy' nations. In this he advocated a conciliatory response.[4] His objections ranged to other issues and took the form of letters to newspapers and utterances at public meetings. For example, to the Leeds Classical Association in 1916 he was to question the consequences of the war in terms of what it was doing to Britain's intellectual ties and the cutbacks and closures the war effort involved. More profoundly, he was to articulate what was close to sympathy for German claims for the war (Haverfield 1916a: 1). That said, he was not wholly uncritical of the 'enemy'. Macdonald (1924: 30) noted he championed the cause of Belgian neutrality (but in the climate of the time, who

---

4.   In a letter to *The Times Literary Supplement* (29 June 1916), Haverfield argued against the expulsion of Honorary German members of such societies: 'I fancy it will be a good deal harder than some people think to re-establish intercourse between English and German scholars after the war. Commercial intercourse will no doubt revive quicker. But so long as the German members of English learned societies are not a national danger, what good is gained by expelling them? For all ordinary purposes the war itself has automatically imposed sufficient suspension.' In contrast to the climate in Britain, Haverfield continued as a subscriber to at least the German periodical *Hermes* down to 1917 when it ceased to list them. He continues to appear, with others, as a corresponding member of the DAI until 1916. Manley (2002: 33) has suggested that Haverfield's opinions concerning a three-pronged landing of Roman troops in south Britain in 43 may have been unconsciously conditioned by the prevailing German military plans for the forthcoming war. The strength of the argument is weakened by the fact that there is nothing in Haverfield's writings to confirm – or disprove – him worrying about what might happen if a war with Germany should break out. The references adduced for Haverfield's arguments for the German attack do not stand scrutiny either.

would have not?). In a letter to *The Times* on 9 August 1918, he criticized the Hapsburg monarchy's handling of its Serbian possessions, drawing on his 'intimate' knowledge of the region.[5] Note too his lament to the CWAAS at Old Carlisle in 1919, where the Germans were accused of having harmed learning. To be sure by the end of the war some of his public utterances were almost as bizarre as his prophecies of its outcome. For instance, there is a hint of a degree of xenophobia in his 1918 Presidential Address to the Somerset Society (Haverfield 1919a: xxxvi–xxxvii).[6]

Closer to his main interests, another consequence of the declaration of war was the way that it meant the curtailment if not cessation of field-work and publication, especially in Britain. These were facts he was not averse to raising in public (e.g. Haverfield 1916a: 1–3; 1916b: 29; 1919a; cf. Marchand 1996: 245ff., for the ways work in Germany continued), although he later acknowledged that the interruption in Britain and France at least had not been as severe as he had anticipated (Haverfield 1919a: xxvi).

One other repercussion of the declaration was that life at Oxford was disrupted. The most immediate effect was a massive drop in the number of undergraduates around Oxford which in turn resulted in the colleges experiencing a decline in their income as students' fees dried up. One solution was for professors and readers agreeing to give up parts of their emoluments (Winter 1994: 11). This was followed by the freezing of posts (notably fellowships) and prizes as well as the redirecting of the

---

5. The *Oxford Magazine* reports Haverfield a frequent contributor to the Oxford Fund for the Education of Serbian Refugees. Other comments concerning aspects of the war published in *The Times* were sometimes critical of the Germans and Austrians, sometimes neutral in tone (e.g. 17 August 1917, 14 April, 2 and 27 November 1918 and 26 August 1919).

6. In 1918 Haverfield acknowledged in 1914 he '…ventured to forecast that this war might end through some plague, which would drive Europe into peace. I have no wish to prove a true prophet' and cited Bates Harbin's article on the Black Death in Somerset in 1348 as a model for his prophecy (1919a: xxv). Here Haverfield was probably referring to the influenza pandemic of 1918–19. The war and anti-German sentiments might lie behind Haverfield publishing an otherwise curious piece, discussing the ancestry of the artist Albrecht Dürer (Haverfield 1915c). Haverfield had been reading Thiemes' *Kunstler-lexicon* (1914) in which there was debate about whether Dürer was of German or Hungarian descent. Using his familiarity with the region of Dürer's ancestors (around Gyula, Hungary) and R.F. Kindl's *Die Deutschen in den Karpatienländern* (1907), Haverfield concluded the painter could not have been of German (colonist) blood.

revenue from bequests. Slightly later the vacuum in the atmosphere at Oxford was filled by the increasing number of troops who were garrisoned in the town and even some of the colleges (Stallybrass 1939–40). But for Haverfield the most serious consequence of the outbreak of the war was the great number of students who enlisted from which his circle was not exempt. It meant in turn casualties among them as well as friends and other scholars, British and foreign. For example, he was to lament the loss of the French ceramicist, J.M.J. Déchelette, killed in October 1914, aged 53. In a lecture in Carlisle in 1917 he reported the death of this '...eminent archaeologist' whose work he had previously reviewed favourably (Haverfield 1917: 237; cf. 1914b).[7]

The consequences of the war were still felt in Oxford for some time after. Not only were there the losses in undergraduates and especially in college fellows (Harrison 1994a), but links with central Europe were never properly re-established. 'The First World War severed (the) Anglo-German cultural tie. Despite attempts after the war, both on a personal and an institutional level, to revive the pre-war mood of Anglo-German friendship in Oxford, the old bonds were never fully restored' (Winter 1994: 4). This is best seen in the disappearance of Rhodes scholars from Germany and who were now replaced by candidates from Britain's colonies. More generally, the war had consequences for the development of archaeology at Oxford. For instance, it is acknowledged that the war was a stimulus for the improved standing of scientific work at the university. The retreat of the humanities at Oxford may also explain why archaeology failed to rise to the position in the university's curriculum which its momentum pre-1914 suggests it should have. With respect to Haverfield's work and connections, the seriousness of the war is indisputable. It is with the issue of Haverfield's 'lost' students, however, that we encounter problems.

---

7. Jean-Marie-Joseph Déchelette (1862–1914), author of *Vasés ornés* (1904) and *Manuel d'archéologie préhistoriqe, celtique et gallo-romaine* (4 vols., 1908–14; obits. S. Reinach *Rev Archéol* XXIV (1914): 315–27; C. Jullian *Rev Etud Anc* XVI (1914): 417–21). In a letter to James Curle (December 1914; *Edinburgh University Library Special Collection D: 2268 (+14.6.44, Dr. Curle)*) Haverfield wrote that Reinach had written explaining the circumstances to Déchelette's enlisting and subsequent death. Haverfield's family was not exempt from losses, but there is no evidence to show how he took the deaths of the two great grandsons of John Haverfield (1811–1881) that Macdonald records being killed in 1915 (Macdonald 1924: 15; cf. Ch. 1 n. 23) and the death of a more distant relative, 2nd Lt. Luke Frederick Rennell Coleridge in December 1914.

Haverfield and the Oxford 'group'

According to some of his obituarists, a significant feature of Haverfield's career is the way he built up, some imply almost systematically, a body of 'students'. For instance, Bosanquet (1920: 139; cf. Craster 1920: 66) believed his great 'achievement' was the formation of an Oxford school of Roman historians familiar with inscriptions and the methods and results of excavation. Elsewhere it was lamented he '...leaves no children, unless we may reckon as his spiritual children the group of young scholars who have been formed under his teaching and will surely carry on the work he began so brilliantly' (W.G. Collingwood 1920: 257). The idea of a 'school' seems proved in a statement that was an enlarged version of an article, originally in German for the *Limes Kommission*. Reworked for the International Congress of Pre- and Proto-History in London in 1932, it was asserted:

> Our knowledge of Roman Britain has advanced some way ...and in spite of the vast mass of constantly accumulating material, it is actually the stage of historical revision that is setting in, with the combination of experts on particular points of a recognised provisional picture. This position is substantially due to one man. Both in its place in the history of the island and as a particular aspect of the Roman Empire, Roman Britain was searchingly illuminated by Francis Haverfield, and since his death in 1919 our best work has been concerned and carried out in his tradition, largely by his own friends and pupils (Kendrick and Hawkes 1932: 209).

The creation of a Haverfield, otherwise known as the 'Oxford', group is one of the most repeated features of his career and received wisdom has it that the circle was to carry on the work he had started. From a certain perspective, when we come to look at the structure of the group, a case might be made for saying he did map out a programme, maybe unintentionally at the start, for those who came to work with him. Their training involved them developing particular interests which he came to utilize in his own work. The origins of the arrangement date back to the 1890s and gathered momentum and refinement over the next 25 years. Whether Haverfield had in mind the longer term implications of this arrangement is uncertain, but at least in the short term it resulted in a number of the 'students' developing his work, with some of them continuing to work in 'research' environments (most at Oxford, a few in the expanding group of provincial universities, and one or two in museums and to a lesser degree (public) schools). That it is not possible to say more about the ultimate effects of the scheme is due to the outbreak of the First War.

The preceding paragraphs have repeated the received version concerning the 'Oxford school'. But how accurate it is to label it a 'school' and indeed to call the individuals that have been linked with Haverfield a group? The term came into currency soon after his death. Within a year of it, Stuart Jones, as Haverfield's titular successor, referred to the fact; '...One can render him [Haverfield] no higher tribute than to say that no single scholar can complete that task as he would have completed it; it must, and doubtless will be carried to its conclusion by a band of organized workers. Thanks to his teaching and inspiration we have in Oxford sound and vigorous traditions' (1920: 5). The topos was repeated over the decades by the likes of Bosanquet, Craster, Wheeler and Birley. What made the 'Oxford school' so different from what had existed before it was the emphasis placed on the use of inscriptions to help construct ancient history. According to Frere (1988), the features of the 'school' were the central part of inscriptions and texts to which the archaeological data is applied (this being, in his opinion, Haverfield's main achievement) and its emphasis on scholarship and leadership. The point was brought home by R.G. Collingwood who claimed:

> ...Mommsen had shown how by statistical and other treatment of inscriptions the historian of the Roman Empire could answer questions that no one had dreamed of asking. It was a recently established and exciting fact that by excavation you could reconstruct the history of Roman sites not mentioned in any authority and of events in Roman history not mentioned in any book. Owing to the work of Haverfield ... whose skill and learning as an epigraphist were comparable, we believed, only with those of Mommsen himself, these notions had taken firm root at Oxford and were completely transforming the study of the Roman Empire ...When I began to study Roman Britain the revolution had made little progress but not much (1939: 82 and 124).

Taking up Mommsen's innovation, Haverfield's part in this form of instruction is clear to see. It is evident in his lecture to undergraduates reading for the School of *Literae Humaniores* (Haverfield 1912d). Therefore it is understandable how a connection between Haverfield and those students who read ancient history etc. was made. The 'school' was about a method of instruction, but it is perhaps pushing it too far to claim that those who were instructed in the method necessarily constituted a 'group'. And of course it has to be said that the method emphasized the relationship of epigraphy to ancient history. While at this time epigraphy was regarded as a sub-branch of archaeology, again its connection to the sort of Romano-British archaeology with which Haverfield was associated is marginal.

In addition to the problems in defining an Oxford-Haverfield school, there are a number of other issues which inhibit definition of it as a coherent group. In the first place it was supposed to be forming at a time when the relationship between teacher and (post-graduate) student was far from formalized. Students still tended to work within their college with the appropriate don(s). Therefore, access to instructors outside the confines of college was hampered although this was not an insurmountable obstacle. Haverfield made contact with a number of individuals who were not tied to his college(s) and students could attend lectures outwith the confines of theirs. Another restricting feature is while students might undertake (BLitt) dissertation work with a particular don, which in one sense could constitute a teacher-student relationship, in other cases it may have been little more than a convenient working arrangement.[8] Therefore the structure of the Oxford system made it difficult for an academic to establish the sort of school of

---

8. The minutes of the *Literae Humaniores* Board of Studies record the following supervisory arrangements, usually for BLitt dissertations: Oct. 1901 Haverfield and Pelham to supervise E.S. Bouchier's dissertation on *The Provincial Administration of Diocletian*. The dissertation, on the advice of the examiners, later failed. Ironically Bouchier MA '...author of Life and letters in Roman Africa and Spain under the Roman empire' was to see into print the 3rd edition of W.T. Arnold's *Roman Provincial Administration* (1914); Nov. 1904 Haverfield agreed to supervise R.F. Scholz's (Worcester) on *The Development of Municipal Institutions During the Second and Third Centuries*, although he protested that as a college tutor he was not being paid. The examiners failed it in June 1907; Oct. 1905 Haverfield and Pelham to supervise E.W. Murray's *The Roman Occupation of Illyricum*; May 1907 Haverfield to supervise C.W. Whish, a non-collegiate candidate, for *The Romanization of Gaul Under the Early Empire* for the degree of Bachelors of Letters; in the same month Haverfield was deleted as the supervisor to D. du B. Davidson (Balliol) and his *The Romanization of the Three Gauls*; Oct. 1910 Haverfield and Cheesman appointed to supervise M. Platnauer on the emperor Septimus Severus (Cheesman elsewhere reports meetings between the three in January 1913; of Platnauer's subsequent career see below); June 1917 it was proposed Haverfield or E.W. Watson supervise J.J. Haarhof's [sic] (Worcester) dissertation on schools in later Roman Gaul. Haverfield declined. He did, however, examine and pass it in 1918, with R. Poole. This study was presumably the basis for T. Haarhoff's *School of Gaul: a Study of Pagan and Christian Education in the Last Century of the Western Empire* (1920), reviewed in the *Journal of Roman Studies* (1920) and where the author is described as Lecturer in Latin at the University of Cape Town.

students, let alone a seminar as occurred at continental universities. If it was to happen, then the circumstances ensured that a group at Oxford would be very small. Occasionally, some dons claimed to be a seminal influence on certain students (and students claimed the same) when the relationship was more tenuous.[9] There is one other, perhaps more substantial, problem in talking of a 'Haverfield' group. It is a recurring fact in the obituaries and other statements of his career that the group was severely diminished by the outbreak of the First World War. Underpinning it is R.G. Collingwood's claim that:

> Haverfield, the great master of the subject, died in 1919; most of his pupils had already fallen in the War; I was left the only man resident in Oxford whom he had trained as a Romano-Britain specialist; and even if my philosophy had not demanded it, I should have thought myself, in piety to him, under an obligation to keep alive the Oxford school of Romano-British studies that he had founded, to pass on the training he had given me, and to make use of the specialist library he had left the University. It was this obligation that made me refuse all offers of professorships and other employments elsewhere which I received during the years that followed the War (1939: 120).

In the same fashion is Rhys Roberts' statement: 'One of the tragedies of the war for him was the loss of so many of his gifted Oxford pupils ...Though many others who were influenced by him still happily survive in our midst' (1920: 350). This 'fact', the decimation of the 'Haverfield group', has been repeated over the decades since the war: 'The death of Haverfield in 1919, a few weeks before his sixtieth birthday, it is said to have been hastened by distress caused at the loss of several of his pupils in the Great War, notably Leonard Cheesman' (Wilkes 1989: 245; cf. 2002: 126). The following paragraphs explore the veracity of these sorts of assessments and will try to identify who can be legitimately placed in the 'Haverfield circle'. How the 'students' are identified is based on a variety of sources, many of them with their

9. A good demonstration of this problem is provided by Hill (1937: cf. Boardman 1985) in his description of Percy Gardner's career. Gardner recorded he 'taught' 757 male and 129 women candidates at Oxford. In an obituary published in *The Times* (19 July 1937) it was reported that Myres, Beazley, Casson and Tod were his. Those he did claim as students, but who have also been afforded a link with Haverfield, include Leonard Woolley, J.G. Milne, Guy Dickins, A.M. Woodward, Hugh Last, R.G. Collingwood, Hugh Stuart-Jones and Arnold Lawrence. As we will see elsewhere G.B. Grundy and R.H. Dundas made similar claims.

own problems, where the informal nature of the professor-student relationship alluded to above makes it difficult to identify potential 'students', let alone find a definite link. The obvious sources are the various annual staff lists for the CEC and Corbridge excavations. The reminiscences of certain key individuals are useful, but it is clear that in some instances memories have failed. Some of Haverfield's publications preserve names (for example, those who assisted in the *Ephemeris Epigraphica* and the *VCH*). Elsewhere, university publications such as the Oxford Calendars and College Lists are of use for substantiating the names appearing in such acknowledgements, but they do not normally offer much other information. There is the strong likelihood that Haverfield patronized successful applicants for the likes of Craven Fellowships and the Pelham Studentship at the BSR. Many of the individuals in Wallace Hadrill's list of the Rome students (2001: 208–10) are likely to have had an association with Haverfield but it is difficult to find the definitive proof. Slightly more useful are the obituaries, normally in connection with deaths in the war, published in *The Oxford Magazine*, college journals and other periodicals. Such notices rarely prove a link, but at best indications of the deceased person's interests from which might be extrapolated a connection. As will become apparent, Haverfield contacts comprised a series of layers; an inner circle of 'Oxford' men made up of a combination of contemporaries of his as well as students and outside of this circle, another group, a network of informants, some academics, other 'antiquarians', with whom Haverfield worked. The most difficult problem in trying to assess the precise nature of these relationships are not just into which group or layer a person should be placed, but trying to clarify names. Many have been suggested but often without any further explanation of their relationship with the great man. The situation is not helped by what look like a number of (contemporary) mistakes in the staff lists of excavations (notably Corbridge), which in turn make it difficult to identify such persons or their colleges. It is for these reasons that, to date, a search of the records suggests only two, possibly three, of the so-called Haverfield group were lost during the course of the war with three or four other casualties who might have had a link with him. The fact is the group is not large, which begs the questions who were the other students supposedly killed and how might they be identified? It is the purpose of the next section to disentangle this confusion.

(a) The Oxford connections

Nowadays the best-remembered 'student' is R.G. Collingwood whose career and relationship with Haverfield is examined in Chapter 11. Of the dead, however, George Leonard ('Len') Cheesman (1884–1915) was arguably the greatest professional and personal loss. Like Haverfield, Cheesman was educated at Winchester and went up to New College (1902) where he took a First in *Literae Humaniores* in 1907 before being appointed a 'teacher' at Haverfield's old college, Christ Church. The following year he was elected a fellow of New, becoming a university lecturer in 1910. Cheesman is an intriguing figure, all the more so because, like Haverfield, there survives so little primary material about him.[10] What there is is an extract from a personal diary for 1913 preserved in the Bodleian Library. His diary records friendships with others, many of them were to be killed in the War, and linked with Haverfield at this time.[11] Cheesman's diary is complimented by a memoir by P(atrick) J.

---

10. M.C. Bishop informs me there is in the Corbridge archive a finds notebook in Cheesman's hand. It seems that Cheesman's sister, Margaret, threw out most of his papers after his death. In his will, Cheesman's estate, worth just over £800, went into administration in January 1916 through George Cheesman, solicitor.

11. There are references to meetings, excursions, walks and meals with Norman Whatley, Leonard Woolley, J.G.C. Anderson, Philip Newbold, and Guy Dickins, along with Arnold Toynbee and Joscelyn Bushe-Fox, who though familiar with Haverfield was not a student. Toynbee (1889–1975), a fellow Wykehamist who went up to Balliol (1907–11; cf. McNeill 1977), was to write that Cheesman would have become '...the most eminent Roman historian in the world without dispute since the death of Fraccaro and De Sanctis if he had lived' (Toynbee 1969: 10; cf. 1954: 30 and n. 1; Murray 2000: 360). The value of Toynbee's opinion is slightly diminished by the fact he could not repeat Cheesman's name correctly; Toynbee 1954: 237; 1967: 24 – 'Guy Leonard Cheesman'. There are other individuals in Cheesman's diary who might have enjoyed links with Haverfield, including an Atkinson ('Atters') an undergraduate at New and whom Campbell notes in his memoir was later a fellow of Hertford but was killed. Other names include Arthur George Heath and Cyril Bertram Moss-Blundell. Moss-Blundell, a student elect of the school at Athens (1914–15), does not always appear in a positive light because of his cavalier approach to archaeological research. A scholar at New in 1913, hence the link with Cheesman, he died in September 1915. Again there is no direct connection with Haverfield in terms of fieldwork. On the problems of identifying 'Atters', see below, n. 44. Cheesman was a close friend of Gilbert Murray (e.g. Sherwood 1973: 193). Along with one of Cheesman, Murray kept photographs of other New College fellows, A.G. Heath, Philip Antony Brown and Leslie Whitaker Hunter on his mantelpiece for the rest of his life (cf. Wilson 1987: 244). Heath, fellow of New College, he was killed in the Battle of Loos (cf. *The Times* 16 October 1915). He published posthumously *The Moral and Social Significance of the Conceptions of Personality* (Oxford 1921). The MS was bequeathed to Reginald Lennard (died May 1917; cf. *The Times* 6 May 1917)

Campbell, later headmaster of the preparatory school ('the under school') at Westminster and brother of one of Cheesman's 'friends' at New College, Maurice Campbell who went up to read medicine in the same year as the diary was written.[12] In the same collection there are also twenty Cheesman letters to their mother, covering the period December 1913 to August 1915, just before Cheesman's death, along with ten letters to Patrick Campbell (March 1912 to August 1915). The letters show that Cheesman knew the Campbells before Maurice went up to share the same college stair as the college fellow.

One person in the diary who survived the War was Maurice Platnaeur who, for his BLitt dissertation about the emperor Severus, was supervised by Haverfield and Cheesman, a dissertation '...which was awarded the unusual accolade of praise from a leader writer in *The Times* many years later' (*The Times* 23 December 1974).[13] The dissertation, written between 1911 and 1914, was eventually published after much delay in 1918. In the author's acknowledgements he credited Haverfield 'for many valuable suggestions, in the light of which my essay has been somewhat modified in its present form.' Percy Matheson of New College merited mention too. He reserved, however, his most effusive thanks to Cheesman, to whom he dedicated the book: 'What the

---

and John D.G. Medley, both who appear in the diary, who decided to publish it, after consulting Philip Brown (died November 1915; cf. *The Times* 16 November 1915) and Leslie Hunter (died August 1916; cf. *The Times* 22 and 24 August 1916). In his Cheesman obituary in the *Journal of Roman Studies* (1915e), Haverfield quotes from a letter from Heath about Cheesman's personality. There is another Heath who Cheesman must have known: Roger Meyrick Heath of Oriel, who specialized in Greek epigraphy. With the university diploma in classical archaeology, and once a student at the British School at Athens 1913–14, he died in 1916 (cf. *The Times* 23 September 1916). Toynbee mentions as friends he lost Cheesman, Hunter, A.G. Heath, and Brown as well as A.D. Gillespie, Robert Hamilton Hutchison, Arthur Innes Adam, Wilfrid Max Langdon, Robert Gibson and John Brown (who is discussed below; Toynbee 1954: 29–30; cf. Millar 2004).

12. John Maurice (Hardman) Campbell OBE (1891–1973) was educated at Winchester and New. With a First in Physiology followed by a Senior Demyship at Magdalen, he was a Captain in the RAMC (SR) in Mesopotamia and North Persia (1916–19). He went on to a distinguished career as a heart specialist (obit. *The Times* 9 August 1973).

13. Platnaeur was later an assistant master at Winchester (1910–15 and 1919–22) and variously fellow (1922), Vice-Principal (1936–56) and Principal (1956–60) of Brasenose College.

death in action of Mr G.L. Cheesman of New College means to the study of Roman history in England, only those who enjoyed the privilege of his friendship can say. It is one of the keenest of my regrets that I can never thank him, on the completion of a task, for the constant interest he took in its inception and progress' (Platnauer 1918: vi).

At the other end of the spectrum Cheesman was also on speaking terms with many major scholars and an acquaintance of some of the leading lights of Oxford. The list includes William Ramsay, J.L. Myres, C.F. Lehmann-Haupt, Norman Baynes, Ulrich Wilamowitz-Moellendorff, Eduard Meyer, Mikhail Rostovtzeff and Wilchen (= Ulrich Wilcken). Cheesman also reports his experience as an external examiner at the University of Liverpool. He was also on more than passing terms with a circle that included the poet James Elroy Flecker and his one-time 'friend' (Sir) John Beazley as well as T.E. Lawrence. Above all however, it is his relationship with the Haverfields that is evident in the diary. On at least thirteen occasions he dined with them in the period March to July 1913, often at Winshields. He holidayed with the couple in Devon in April.[14] He reports a number of frank conversations with Haverfield. He was also clearly very friendly with Winifred Haverfield and indeed records a number of picnics with her and other females (including M.V. Taylor and a Miss (M.G.G.) Hugon). Mrs Haverfield was a leading member of the suffragette movement in Oxford and again in a number of entries Cheesman reports discussing with her the subject of women's suffrage and even accompanied her to rallies.[15]

Cheesman's relationship with Winifred Haverfield is reminiscent of what P.J. Campbell wrote of the same man's relationship with his mother:

> The diary shows that Cheesman was fond of his home and very loyal to his parents. But they were conventional, he was not. He visited his home at Hove during the vacations, but he was not sorry to come away. Oxford was the place that he loved. He was a lonely man, with a great need for friendship. Ours was an ordinary happy family, we were fortunate enough to be

14. Just how close the connection was is shown by the fact Cheesman dined with Haverfield in 1913 on March 23, 24 and 28, then at an Oxford dinner held on April 9 for the foreign delegates at the Congress of Historical Institutions, before going on holiday with the Haverfields the next day, and then returning and dining with them in Oxford on April 20, 22 and 29.

15. I have been unable to identify Hugon (d. 1952). Complicating the situation is the other Mrs Haverfield, the Honorable Mrs Evelina Haverfield, to whom Haverfield was distantly related (cf. Ch. 1) and who was even more prominent in the suffragette movement.

able to give him something that he lacked and were repaid with an unusual degree of affection ...His letters (to my mother) ... show a very happy relationship. They are not intimate letters but they show something of himself and of her. They show his understanding of her as well as his gratitude and affection. I think he was frightened of most women, the diary is very interesting about this (Campbell *Bodleian MS Eng. Lett d. 369*).

The impression created by his diary is that Cheesman was a don concerned with and committed to his charges. It has been noted elsewhere that the relationship between the fellows (specifically naming Cheesman and Heath) and undergraduates in New College at this time changed for the better (Ryan 1979). The situation is perhaps best illustrated by Sir William Hayter's memories of New, formed nearly a decade after the First War ended.[16] In his autobiography written some 50 years after the events Hayter recollected how:

... my Oxford failures were not only academic, they were also social. Oxford social life was then very competitive. In the part of it that I knew it tended to revolve round a certain category of don, normally unmarried Fellows living in College and entertaining undergraduates, holding a kind of salon. There was no one like that at New College. At Brasenose there was Maurice Platnauer, who had the best food and wine and the most beautiful rooms. Tom Boase, then a Fellow of Hertford, had interesting guests from other worlds. The most brilliant was Maurice Bowra ... the most important of all these academic salons was that of F.F. Urquhart, the Dean of Balliol, commonly known as

16. Hayter (1906–1995) does not appear to be directly related to the A.G.K. Hayter discussed below. William Goodenough Hayter, Winchester and New where he took a Second, entered the Civil Service and went on to a distinguished career as a diplomat (ending up as HMG ambassador to Moscow in the 1950s). At the time of his appointment to the wardenship of New College (1958) he was Dept Undersecretary of State at the Foreign Office. He was Warden until 1976. His memoirs offer some interesting correctives to received opinions. For instance, he disliked the Winchester emphasis on sporting activities (shades of Haverfield and Cheesman?). He thought his headmaster, the soon-to-retire Rendall, was overrated and claimed he 'molested him' on a couple of occasions. He approved of Rendall's replacement, Spencer Leeson, and his teacher C.E. Robinson. At Oxford he was dismissive of most of his tutors (H.L. Henderson – 'a very incompetent teacher and very disagreeable man', H.W.B. Joseph for philosophy and Alic Smith – 'a great man but not a great tutor'; cf. Lloyd Jones 1972: 396). He did, however, rate his ancient history tutor, C. Cox. Some of Hayter's opinions (e.g. concerning Henderson, but not Joseph and Smith) are validated by Bowra 1966.

'Sligger'[17] ...His other flaw might seem to some people more important though I am not sure that it does to me. David Cecil used to say
when we were electing Fellows of New College in the 1960s, 'What this
College needs is a good old-fashioned homosexual of the best type'.
He meant the kind of bachelor don who would live in College and take
an interest in young men that would be rather more than academic,
and when he said it I used to think he probably had Sligger in mind
(1974: 14–15).

The significance of this passage is two-fold. That there was no 'salon' at
New College when Hayter was an undergraduate was a consequence of
the loss of Fellows in the war, including Cheesman, for the 'Senior
Common Room of New College was still suffering from losses in the
war. Four Fellows had been killed, and since three of these were tutors
in Mods. and Greats, the classics were particularly hit' (Bowra 1966:
101, writing of the years after 1919). Second, Platnauer's 'salon' at
Brasenose must have been at least influenced by his contact with
Cheesman (and others) and New College.[18]

Cheesman was undeniably Haverfield's 'favourite student' and
later a colleague. Bosanquet wrote of '...the sorrow and disappointment engendered by the war itself were deepened by the death of the
man he had expected to carry on his work' (1920: 140). Describing
Cheesman as 'the inheritor of unfulfilled renown', Haverfield expressed his sense of loss in two obituaries, one admittedly a copy of the

17. Thomas Sherrer Ross Boase (1898–1974), Rugby and Magdalen. Director
of the Courtald Institute (*The Times* 15 April 1974). According to Hayter,
Urquhart and Bowra did not get on, but see Bowra 1966: 119–20 for his
opinions on the Balliol man; Sir Maurice Bowra (1898–1971), Cheltenham
and New (1912–22) colleges, fellow of Wadham College 1922; Warden of
Wadham 1938–70, Professor of Poetry 1946–51, University Vice-Chancellor 1951–4. While at New, Bowra frequented the Urquhart and R.H.
Dundas salons (cf. Lloyd-Jones 1972); Francis Fortescue Urquhart
(1868–1934), Beaumont and Stonyhurst colleges and Balliol. A modern
historian, he was fellow and tutor (1896–1934) and Dean (1916–33) at
Balliol. He never married.
18. Platnaeur's obituary in *The Times* noted that 'In his early years at
Brasenose his was a notably "civilizing" influence ...his hospitality was
proverbial. There can have been few university dons who not only royally
entertained so many friends and acquaintances, but also found such deep
and long lasting friendships with each members of each generation. He
was rather shy, of great modesty and his gentleness and courtesy won him
exceptional affection' (*The Times* 23 December 1974). Platnaeur never
married.

other.[19] A number of significant facts emerge from these notices. With parallels with Haverfield's youth, Cheesman travelled extensively through what were described as the provinces of the Roman empire. He had been based for a time in the British School at Athens (1908–09), and which might explain his later involvement in the Oxford Macedonian Exploration Fund (*The Times* 15 March 1911). Between 1908 and 1911, he also worked on (Haverfield's) excavations at Corbridge, producing notes on potter's stamps there for 1909–10) and with Thomas May at Ribchester (1908) as well as at Wroxeter (1912). Cheesman also provided some teaching which complemented Haverfield's. In 1906 he was given leave to introduce a Special Subject in the Honours School of *Literae Humaniores* for 1907 on *The Development of the Roman Frontier Defences in the Western Provinces from 70 to 211*. That said, his publications, whilst perhaps owing something to him, were not really in the sphere one would consider as Haverfield's. Other than a few reviews, he tended to publish on epigraphic subjects. More, by inclination, an historian than archaeologist, he certainly did not write about Roman Britain and, while in his early years was exposed to archaeological fieldwork, it is clear that the subject was not central to his main interests. Indeed, his reputation today is based almost entirely on his *Auxilia of the Imperial Roman Army*. This had commenced life as an undergraduate essay for Haverfield which won the Arnold Historical Essay prize in 1911. In his summary of Roman Britain in 1914 (Haverfield 1915a: 38; cf. 1915b), Haverfield still found space to praise lavishly the book. Macdonald felt the monograph had not received the attention – and so acclaim – it deserved.

---

19. It is difficult to say which of the two notices is the earlier, although the balance favours the *Classical Review* (1915) over the *Journal of Roman Studies* (1915). Less emotional is Haverfield's notice in *The Year's Work in Classical Studies, 1915* (1916: 64). His death was again noted in the *Journal of Roman Studies* VI: (1916): 221); 'This young scholar was a contributor to the journal, and his published work was admirable and full of promise. His death in the war has produced a deep and widespread sense of loss among scholars.' It was left to Haverfield to complete some of Cheesman's unfinished reviews (e.g. W. Fischer's *Das römische Lager inbesondere nach Limes* (*Class Rev* XXX (1916): 59). Even the British School at Athens, where Cheesman had been a student (1908–09), reported: 'His connexion with Athens was not a long one but the School is proud of its association with an admirable student and teacher of Roman history and antiquities, and a growing power in liberal education' (*Annual Brit School Athens* XX (1914–15): 186). There is a dedication too in the second edition of Hopkinson's *Ribchester* (1916) where Cheesman had worked in 1908.

He attributed the failure to the fact that it was published and so 'lost' shortly after the declaration of war (Macdonald 1929/1930: 112).

With the outbreak of war, Cheesman enlisted as part of Kitchener's call for volunteers in late 1914. There are indications that in 1915 some, possibly including Haverfield, tried to get him transferred to a (safer) intelligence posting. Haverfield was severely affected by Cheesman's death to the extent that he became seriously ill on the back of hearing that he was listed as missing in late 1915.[20] He was later confirmed as killed in action on 10 August 1915 at Suvla Bay, Gallipoli while serving in the 10th Hampshire Regiment. When confirmation of his death was received at the end of the year Haverfield's health collapsed.[21] In the aftermath of the news he was to lament: 'We in Oxford have lost many men whose places can never be filled ...But the loss of George Leonard Cheesman is in everyway heavy, to his college, to our educational work, to our Society (the SPRS), to historical study' (Haverfield 1915e: 148). Elsewhere, he was to note a loss of confidence: 'War at all times deters or diverts scholars from learned labours. It calls the younger men to the paramount duty of national defence. It destroys the confidence and quiet of the elder men. It makes research seem valueless and unreal beside its own realities' (Haverfield 1916a: 1). One reason why the loss was taken so badly was that Haverfield was grooming Cheesman to take on

20. A nameless obituarist, perhaps R.C. Bosanquet, described the collapse as '...about Christmas 1916 [sic, an error repeated elsewhere in Bosanquet 1920] his health broke down with a sudden attack or stroke' (Anon. 1920a: 256).

21. Bosanquet (1920: 140) called the cause a paralytic seizure. 'In the latter half of the Long Vacation of 1915 the name of Leonard Cheesman ...appeared among the "missing" at the Dardanelles ...Haverfield said little, but those nearest him knew that he had been cut as with a knife. Cheesman had been his favourite pupil, the most brilliant of the little group of "disciples" that he had gathered round him, the man on who he hoped that his own spirit would in due time rest. And there was more. A strong personal attachment had grown up between the two; the younger of them was almost as much at home in Winshields (Haverfield's Oxford residence) as if he had been a brother. The effect of the blow was to increase the strain on Haverfield to the breaking point. He ended the term in a state of physical exhaustion such as he had never yet experienced. A day or two before Christmas (1915) the climax came in an onset of cerebral haemorrhage' (Macdonald 1919–20a: 487: cf. 1924: 31; Wilkes 1989: 245). Elsewhere the illness was described as a stroke. Haverfield was later to refer to the effects of his breakdown as an '... illness, which has made me incapable of serious work after Christmas 1915 till now' (Haverfield 1916a: np).

the *RIB* he hoped would supercede *CIL* VII (cf. Chapter 7). The sum of the evidence then, is that Haverfield and Cheesman were extremely close. Macdonald notes their exceptional relationship. He also referred to the fact that Haverfield had been brought up in exclusively heterosexual societies. Haverfield married as late as 1907 and again Macdonald notes that he had difficulties adjusting to the change in circumstances. The marriage was childless. At the very least Cheesman's death precipitated a breakdown that meant Haverfield produced relatively less in its aftermath little afterwards little in the period 1916–17. In the six years, 1909–15, nearly 100 articles were published. In the period 1916–21 Macdonald's lists *c*.35 publications.

Cheesman is widely acknowledged as Haverfield's most distinguished 'student' and the one destined for 'great' things. Another 'associate' who was certainly killed is Philip Newbold (1887–1916). One time fellow of Oriel College, Newbold started his excavation career at Corbridge under Forster and Haverfield[22], before being appointed Lecturer in Classics at Armstrong College, Newcastle in 1910. Earlier in the same year he had been a Craven fellow at the BSR. In terms of archaeological research, had he lived (and remained in the subject) it is likely Newbold would have made a more significant contribution than Cheesman, for the latter's interest in archaeology was always marginal to his main interests (ancient history and epigraphy). Under the terms of his Newcastle appointment, Newbold was free to devote his summers to excavation, partly at Corbridge (as in 1912) and partly on the Wall; 'Armstrong College ...lately tried a wise experiment; it appointed a lecturer who should work primarily for it, and from his vantage ground in Newcastle should study the Wall in spare hours' (Haverfield in Atkinson 1916: v; cf. Birley 1949: 13; 1961: 33). Before his death Newbold had undertaken one major piece of excavation there, as well as having collaborated with F.G. Simpson elsewhere and contributed specialist reports to the Corbridge excavations and on the Tullie House collection. But Newbold resigned his lectureship in 1913 and so abandoned the subject which leaves open the question whether he was still part of the 'inner' circle of Haverfield

---

22. M.C. Bishop informs me that one of Newbold's notebooks survives in the Corbridge excavation archives.

'students'.[23] With hindsight, Newbold's major contribution was to over-turn, at least in part, a central piece of Haverfield's research. Some eight years after the Cumberland Excavation Committee had ended its work, F.G. Simpson with a contribution by Newbold published an update on re-cent work, 'The Roman Wall in Cumberland 1909–1912' (Simpson 1913). The circumstances of that work went back to Simpson's excavation of the milecastle at Poltross Burn in 1911, where the results suggested ev-idence that ran contrary to the 'history' of the Wall Haverfield and the work of the CEC had constructed. That 'history' had the Wall originally comprising a turf wall built under Hadrian and a stone wall completed by Septimius Severus. Poltross Burn, built in stone, appeared to date to *c*.120. In the subsequent account Simpson described the excavations of a number of milecastles, turrets and, stretches of wall in and around Birdoswald (49b, 50, 50a, and 50b). Each showed evidence of occupation under Hadrian. Newbold's contribution was to substantiate Simpson's arguments about the structural evidence with an analysis of the pottery from the sites they excavated. He also reappraised the material from the CEC and other Wall sites (including Corbridge and Housesteads) and data from other sites in England and Wales with a Haverfield association (e.g. Gellygaer and Silchester). In what still reads as a brilliant piece of dissection, Newbold demonstrated it was possible to differentiate the

23. Birley (1961: 34). In a letter from Taylor to Birley (6 February 1962, Haverfield Archive), it is said Newbold left Newcastle for South Africa as the city's air acerbated his asthma. There may be some confusion here. Cheesman wrote in his diary that Newbold was heading for a plantation in Uganda. The brief notice of Newbold's death in the *Archaeologia Aeliana* (XIV: 1917) (incorrectly) implies that he was still in post, offering lectures in classics and ancient history. In *Roman Britain in 1913,* Haverfield wrote: 'It is much to be regretted that he (Newbold) has since left England and will help no more in the exploration of Roman Britain' (Haverfield 1914a: 45–6). Whatever, Newbold returned to join up when the First War broke out. In his reply to Tay-lor, (11 February 1962), Birley noted how 'F.G. Simpson always spoke most warmly of him. Incidentally Donald Atkinson once mentioned to me that he was one of the candidates for the lectureship at Armstrong College when Newbold was appointed.' As a 2nd Lieutenant in the Royal West Kent Regi-ment, Newbold was killed in the Battle of the Somme on 13 July 1916. Unfortunately the notice in the *Journal of Roman Studies* (VII: 1917: 303) re-cords him as Newbould. Newbold's publications included the excavation at Limestone Bank which was proofed by Cheesman and F.G. Simpson (Newbold 1913). There were also his contributions to pottery studies for Haverfield. He also authored a report on the pottery from Huntcliff (cf. W. Hornsby and R. Stanton in the *Journal of Roman Studies* II (1912): 214–32).

samian found on these sites between Flavian–Trajanic and Hadrianic and Antonine forms. This meant:

> ...the conclusion seems inevitable that the High House milecastle and the three turrets adjoining were erected simultaneously with the milecastles and turrets along the rest of the line from Birdoswald and Limestone Bank; that certain Flavian–Trajanic fashions in pottery, which are found in the bottom *stratum* of the Wall structures survived into the early part of Hadrian's reign but had fallen out of use before Corstopitum [sic] was laid out as a military depot and Scotland reoccupied in the early years of Pius; and that, consequently the High House milecastle and turrets, like the rest, were erected the same time as, and formed part of, the Wall of Hadrian. That they were erected in stone and were contemporaneous and homogeneous with the Stone Wall is shown elsewhere in this and other reports by Mr. Simpson and myself (p. 344).

What Haverfield made of this argument was recorded by Macdonald (in Haverfield 1924: 159–60 n. 1). While Haverfield was later more receptive to some of the conclusions, one supposes his reservations lay with respect to the ways the *sigillata* was dated and the results then applied. That said, Newbold's use of the evidence of the ceramics was a direct consequence of his working on that material at Corbridge and in the collection stored in the Tullie House Museum in Carlisle.

So far we have two individuals killed in the war who might legitimately be called Haverfield 'students'. Identifying other casualties becomes more difficult because either they do not appear in any of the CEC or Corbridge staff lists or because, while active in Oxford in aspects of ancient history, classics, epigraphy or archaeology, there is nothing to link them specifically with Haverfield. Two examples are Guy Dickins (1882–1916) and Harold John Cunningham (d. 1917). The only indication of a link between them and Haverfield was provided by Hugh Stuart Jones, who in a passage about Haverfield and Cheesman, noted the loss of Dickins (killed in action) and Cunningham '...who did not die by the hand of the enemy' (1920: 5). In either case, however, it is not possible to ascertain precisely what they did for Haverfield. While Cheesman records he and Dickins dined at Haverfield's in February 1913, Dickins is not otherwise credited in any of Haverfield's publications nor appears in any of the excavation staff lists. Dickins MA, resident of Callender, Perthshire and a graduate and fellow of St Johns (elected 1908) was appointed university Lecturer in Classical Archaeology to replace the out-going Rector of Exeter (Lewis Farnell) and to assist Percy Gardner. As an undergraduate, Dickins had specialized in Greek sculpture and was to lecture on Greek art and archaeology. An article (*The Followers of*

Praxitiles) was based on a lecture course he delivered on Greek art at Oxford in the winter of 1913–14 (Dickins 1914–15/1915–16). The résumé of his career, submitted in support of the recommendation to appoint him lecturer notes that he had worked for five years from 1904 on Sparta in the British School at Athens. He had also been in 1905 a Craven fellow based in the BSR and between 1905 to 1909 and 1912 to 1913 was back at the school, latterly working on the catalogue of sculpture in the Conservatori Museum (Wallace Hadrill 2001: 53). Dickins' (Oxford) post was confirmed in December 1914 when it was also recorded that he had accepted an army commission. It is for these reasons that it is difficult, but not impossible, to regard Dickins as a Haverfield student in the strictest sense (cf. Waterhouse 1986). More realistically he was one of Gardner's, who had complimentary things to say about him (Gardner 1926: 11, 15–16; Dickins 1920: vii–ix).[24] Dickins died of wounds inflicted in battle near Pozières while a Captain in the King's Own Rifle Corps in July 1916. If Dickins in reasonably straightforward to locate, Cunningham is more difficult. Born in St Albans, in ?1906 he was Junior Provost of Worcester and was opinionating on the teaching of ancient history in the university in 1907.[25] For the record, he published the odd review (e.g. Frank's *Roman Imperialism* – in the *Journal of Roman Studies* (1914)). Otherwise there is no known Haverfield link.

24. Dickins married Mary Hamilton of the University of St Andrews, who was admitted as a student of the Athens school with a Carnegie Research Fellowship for 1905–07. She and Dickins toured Greece together in 1912–13. Gardner reports how Dickins '...did not, like many young archaeologists, delight in starting brilliant hypotheses: but was ever content in coming nearer to the truth, and setting it forth in orderly and soberly fashion. Such qualities would have made him an invaluable factor in the teaching of archaeology in England ...he set ...a high standard, and had no sympathy with anything which was pretentious or meretricias. The same qualities appeared in two or three courses of lectures on recent excavations, which he gave at the Ashmolean Museum' (Gardner in Dickins 1920: ix).

25. I have been unable to locate with any certainty Cunningham on the Commonwealth War Grave Commissions Roll of Honour. There is a Capt. H.J. Cunningham MC listed in the Bedfordshire Regiment and killed in October 1917. A Henry John Cunningham, of the Machine Gun Corps, was killed in May 1916. Aged 19, he is too young to be our Cunningham. I cannot otherwise explain Stuart Jones' allusion to the circumstances of Cunningham's death, unless he means by illness or what is now described as 'friendly fire'. But surely he should be listed on the Roll? H.J. Cunningham is not to be confused with the Edinburgh Cunningham (and who was a student at the BSR in 1903) discussed in Ch. 7 n. 29.

Two other potential students with obituary notices in the *Oxford Magazine* who, with their particular interests, might be candidates as Haverfield 'students' but with even less certainty are Kingdon Tregosse Frost (*c*.1880–1914, MA and FRGS) and John Rankine Brown (1886–1917). Frost was Lecturer in Ancient History and Archaeology and in Historical Geography at the University of Belfast. His interest in geography implies a link with J.L. Myres rather than Haverfield.[26] Formerly of Brasenose (BLitt 1909) he was killed in August 1914[27] while serving as Lieutenant in the Cheshire Regiment (*Oxford Magazine*, 16 October 1914). A slightly better candidate as a 'student' is John Brown, fellow and lecturer at Pembroke College, and the eldest son of the Moderator of the General Assembly of the Church of Scotland. Brown left Glasgow University in 1905 with a First in classics, and a MA, becoming a Ferguson Scholar and Snell Exhibitioner at Balliol and where he a took First. During his time there he came to know Arnold Toynbee, Cheesman's friend (1958: 237). After Oxford, Brown went to Armstrong College, Newcastle as the Assistant to the Professor of Classics '...and finding the proximity of the Roman Wall a congenial attraction did some useful work there' (*Oxford Magazine* 18 May 1917). I can find, however, no record of what his work in the north might have been. He does not merit mention in Birley's (1961) list of workers on the Wall.[28] But if he did do anything there, then he might be considered in some small way as Newbold's predecessor. He returned to Pembroke in 1911 with a fellowship, teaching ancient history for Greats. After joining up, whilst on active service in Palestine as a Captain in the Highland Light Infantry Brown was sent to Gallipoli in 1915, to be invalided out that autumn. Called up again, he was severely wounded on 21 April 1917 and died two days later.

This accounts for those individuals, certain and possible, who have been described as part of the Haverfield 'group' lost in the war. The

---

26. The *Journal of Egyptian Archaeology* (I (1914): 295) states he previously worked in the Egyptian Ministry of Education and was formerly Lecturer in Classics at Isleworth. He was also an officer of the EEF (1904–05), working under Flinders Petrie. He was admitted as a student to the BSA on his appointment to the Oxford studentship in 1900–01.

27. The *Annual of the British School at Athens* reports it as September 1914.

28. Miss Lindsay Allason-Jones, Director of the Archaeological Museums (University and Antiquaries of Newcastle-upon-Tyne, Newcastle University), informs me that she cannot find any information concerning Brown. In a letter of 26 November 2002, she made the attractive suggestion that Brown may have 'just helped Newbold rather than did anything solo.'

number, contrary to expectations, is not large. Of course it may be a consequence of the factors already outlined and in particular the fluid relationship between teacher and student. Although that many enlisted clearly must have interrupted the momentum Haverfield had been generating, with regard to actual losses, however, contrary to received wisdom, there may be some exaggeration. But while Collingwood and others made much of the fact that Haverfield lost so many students, it is difficult to identify specific individuals (e.g. Jones 1987: 88). In fact, the solution is much simpler because Margerie Taylor (1920: 71) reported his best two students died. But it should be noted that in a passage missed by most of those who have written about Haverfield, Macdonald reported he in fact lost no more than two or three 'students'.

> The active assistance of a number of University men, some of them for-
> mer pupils of his own, gave him much satisfaction. He had often
> lamented that in England there was much scant opportunity for the
> young scholar or historian to obtain a real insight into the mechanisms of
> original research: the absence of a proper discipline of the kind seemed
> to him a grave hindrance to progress. He was sanguine that in the years
> to come the practical experiences gained by these helpers at Corbridge
> would fructify abundantly. Two or three of those for whom he expected
> most were ere long to find a grave on the field of battle. The survivors can
> still justify his hope (Macdonald 1919–20a: 485 = 1924: 28–9).

Given what some have said about Haverfield and the damage inflicted on his 'group', it is inexplicable how this assessment has been over-looked. It is true that parts of it (notably the 'Haverfield' group and the work of the survivors) were picked up by later writers, but it is an inter-esting problem establishing how the idea that Haverfield suffered massive and ultimately destructive losses originated. In reality, what is clear is that there survived a number of other 'students' who went on to enjoy successful careers, a few in archaeology, many of them elsewhere.

Of the other 'students', notable survivors were Thomas Ashby (1874–1931) and John George Clark Anderson (1871–1952). Ashby's career is the subject of a biography by Richard Hodges (Hodges 2000; Wallace Hadrill 2001: 28–34).[29] In some respects he might be described

29. Of his relationship with Haverfield, Richmond (1949) records Ashby as a 'pupil', although Haverfield said that he was '...once a pupil of Professor Pel-ham' (Pelham 1911: iv). Elsewhere, Pelham '...visited Rome in April 1898 with his friend and younger colleague F.J. Haverfield not only to see the ex-cavations in the Forum, but also to view the discoveries made by Haverfield's most able student, Thomas Ashby, in the environs of Rome' (Hodges 1989:

as the original Haverfield 'student'. After Winchester, he must have come into contact with Haverfield almost as soon as he went up to Christ Church in 1892, just when Haverfield was returning to Oxford and the same college. With a First in *Literae Humaniores* in 1897, Ashby won a Craven Travelling fellowship which he took for study in Italy. That said, in his early years Ashby, was involved in excavations in Britain. He appears in the list of assistants who participated on the CEC in 1898 as well as working elsewhere on Hadrian's Wall with R.C. Bosanquet in the same year. Following this exposure, he was involved from 1899 with the excavation of Roman Caerwent. Ashby was to become, in 1901, the first official student at the newly created British School at Rome, its assistant director in 1905 and from 1906 the director until 1925. With his growing involvement in Italy, Ashby's part in Caerwent gradually faded. He was effectively detached from it by 1911. The excavations eventually closed down in 1917 although in truth affairs were moribund from 1913 (Boon 1989; Hodges 2000: 30). Ashby's best-remembered work was to be in Italy, focusing primarily on topographic studies. His DLitt of 1904, supported by Pelham and Haverfield, was awarded on the strength of his work on the Roman Campagna, where his work on recording the landscape established a tradition which continues to exert an influence (Potter and Stoddart 2001). In time Ashby was to be an important influence in Ian Richmond's career.

In contrast to Ashby, Anderson remained throughout at Oxford. After graduating from Aberdeen University as a 'student' of William Ramsay, Anderson moved to Christ Church '...where he came to know Haverfield whose effect on his life was not less strong than Ramsay's' and where he took a First and was Craven fellow (1896) for travel in Greece (Calder 1952; cf. Anon. 1952).[30] In 1903, on a visit to

8). Somewhat surprisingly, in his Ashby obituary A.H. Smith made little of this connection, merely quoting Ashby's friend and contemporary R.R. Campbell that 'Our Greats Tutors were F. Haverfield and J.L. Myres for History and J.A. Stewart and H. Blunt for Philosophy. In after life ...(Ashby) used frequently to say what a fine team they had been' (Smith 1931: 517). Ashby also published work, undertaken by his brother in 1909, on a Roman villa at Harpenden, near Henley (Ashby 1911).

30. Ramsay, in his letters to Mommsen, appears as one of Anderson's patrons, if not his mentor, just as (perhaps more surprisingly) he claimed the same for another Haverfield associate, George Macdonald. In a letter of 7 July 1898 Ramsay wrote: 'After many years of trying and seeking in vain, I have found a successor to explore Asia Minor better than I could do it – J.G.C. Anderson...'

Penzance, Haverfield was describing him as 'his friend' (*Sussex Archaeol Colls* (1903): 159). Anderson appears to have worked with Ramsay at Antioch in Pisidia in 1912 which resulted in him publishing some of the inscriptions found there. Incidentally Cheesman, though not a participant in the field season, was responsible for publishing other inscriptions from the city (Anderson 1913; Cheesman 1913a). With research interests in the Roman eastern Mediterranean and after a series of scholar- and fellowships, at the same time Guy Dickins was made university Lecturer in Classical Archaeology, in 1914 Anderson became university Lecturer in Roman Epigraphy previously having assumed responsibility for some of Haverfield's teaching when the latter was elevated to his chair.[31] Later on, not only did Anderson complete Haverfield's new edition of Furneaux's *Taciti Cornelli de Vita Agricolae* (1922), he ultimately filled the Camden chair (1927–36), after the death of Haverfield's successor, Stuart Jones. In his introduction to the *Agricola*, Anderson paid tribute to Haverfield's efforts to fill out Tacitus' picture of Britain (1922: v).

There are a number of other individuals who in different ways might be called 'students' and who went onto occupy academic posts

---

31. The Report of the Board of *Literae Humaniores* 1913–21 (*FA4/7/2/2*) contains a letter of recommendation (dated 21 February 1914) from Haverfield in support of Anderson's appointment. The letter reveals something of the part of Latin epigraphy in the Oxford curriculum; 'Roman inscriptions now form for the better men as real part of their Roman History as Greek inscriptions of their Greek History. But there has been difficulty in providing regular courses for such students. From about 1897 till 1906 the present Camden Professor gave such courses, and in 1906 the audiences had grown to about 45. In 1907, the Common University Fund established a lectureship in Greek Epigraphy. But no provision has been made for Roman Epigraphy. The Camden Professor has not been able to go on with the courses which he gave as a College Tutor, nor has he found any one else regularly available. As Greek History and Archaeology, &c., are now fairly well endowed with two full-paid professors and two lecturers, &c., it seems time to do something for the Roman students who have only the one professor, and to provide a Lecturer in Roman Inscriptions, primarily (like the Lecturer in Greek Epigraphy), for the purposes of those who are reading Roman History. Mr. Anderson is suggested for the post as being a good lecturer, a well-established Greats tutor, a first-rate epigraphist, and a scholar whose original work in this direction is of the highest order.' Anderson's appointment was confirmed in March 1914, with him to work under Haverfield. However in November of the same year Anderson requested his appointment be suspended until the situation improved in the light of the University's financial circumstances.

outside of Oxford. The career of Donald Atkinson (1886–1963) has been reassessed by Colin Wallace (1994). Born in Birmingham, Atkinson was a classics student at Brasenose (1905–09) during which he worked at Corbridge.[32] Oxford was followed by a period of teaching classics at Stamford Grammar School (1909–12). During his time there, Atkinson, along with H.G. Evelyn White (see below), directed excavations in 1910 and 1911 at the North Leigh villa (Oxon.), a site Haverfield had wanted to use as a teaching model for undergraduates (cf. Chapter 9). In 1912 Atkinson held the Pelham studentship at the school in Rome.[33] Prior to it he conducted excavations in July 1912 at the Romano-British site of Adel (cum Ecup, in Yorkshire (Atkinson 1912–13; The *Report of the Committee on Ancient Earthworks. Congress of Archaeological Societies 1919* incorrectly places this excavation in 1916 or 1917). The report was completed while he was in Italy. In 1913 he was 'Resident Fellow' in Archaeology and Lecturer in Classics at University College, Reading. Whilst there he conducted excavations at

---

32. There is some confusion here about when Atkinson first started at Corbridge. The Corbridge list records him there certainly in 1911 and when he worked on the samian (and maybe 1908). But elsewhere, while at Brasenose Atkinson '...in due course became the pupil of Professor Haverfield ...continuing his interest in archaeology which had been aroused by Haverfield. He, with G.L. Cheesman, Philip Newbold and other pupils, was persuaded by Haverfield to go to Corbridge, where the excavation at Corstopitum [sic] initiated in 1906, was undertaken for the purpose of explaining the site for the VCH then being prepared' (Taylor in an obituary on Atkinson sent to Richard Reece, August 1963; Haverfield Archive). It was at Corbridge, where he was working on the *sigillata*, that Atkinson met Bushe-Fox and was persuaded to go to Wroxeter for 1912–14. For 1912, at least, Cheesman was also present. Atkinson went onto direct his own excavations there – 1924 through to 1927 (cf. Atkinson 1942). According to Bonarkis Webster (1991: 14) for reasons not explained, there were never published any obituaries about Atkinson. This is not strictly true (cf. *The Times* 5 and 14 February 1963 and the draft of an obituary by Taylor sent to Reece, ultimate destination unknown: cf. Haverfield Archive, but perhaps the *Annual Report of the Cirencester Archaeological and Historical Society* 1963: Wallace 1994: 167).

33. Stuart Jones in *A Catalogue of the Ancient Sculptures Preserved in the Municipal Collections of Rome. The Sculptures of the Palazzo dei Conservatori* (Oxford 1928: vi) described how work on the catalogue commenced as far back as 1909 with A.H.S. Yeames, the assistant director at the BSR and then by Eugénie Strong as well as Lewis Farnell, Guy Dickins and Donald Atkinson, who worked on the terracottas.

Lowbury Hill (Berks.; Atkinson 1916) for which Haverfield wrote the introduction to the final report. It was also during his Reading fellowship that Atkinson 'came constantly to Oxford, usually staying with the Haverfield's at Headington Hill and was the greatest comfort and help to the Professor when in the year after 1916 he was recovering from a stroke' (Letter, M.V. Taylor to R. Reece August 1963, Haverfield Archive). Atkinson assisted J.P. Bushe-Fox at Wroxeter (1912–14). In 1914, along with W.B. Anderson, Atkinson completed Thomas May's and Cheesman's work in the *principia* at Ribchester (Atkinson 1928; Wallace 1994: 169). Working at Slack in 1915, he volunteered for war service (as a signaller, and later an officer, with the Royal Garrison Artillery; Wallace 1994: 167). After the war, in 1919, Atkinson moved to Manchester University as Reader in Ancient History and where he was professor from 1929 down to his retirement in 1951. While at Manchester, Atkinson continued to excavate (e.g. at Wroxeter – Atkinson 1942, Ribchester, Caistor-by-Norwich: Wallace 1994: 168). In the subsequent years, Atkinson became curator at the museum at Cirencester until 1963.

In addition to these persons, Haverfield is also associated with a number of individuals who went on to distinguished careers in the archaeology of the Near East. One such person was John Garstang (1876–1956). Garstang, who from 1902 almost single-handedly established the Institute of Archaeology at Liverpool University (Muir 1943: 80: Shore 1985), and was later Professor of the Methods and Practice of Archaeology there, was a Mathematics scholar at Jesus College, Oxford (1895–9). Although he is more closely associated with Egypt, the Levant and Turkey, Garstang's early archaeological career was very much pitched in Roman Britain. Not only were there his excavations, he also produced a number of works of synthesis (e.g. Garstang 1900). In 1895 he undertook his own excavations at Ribchester which he published in 1898. 'This came to the notice of Francis Haverfield ...who encouraged Garstang to take up archaeology.' The difficult post-1899 history of the management of the site has been discussed by Edwards who has suggested that it was '...probably Haverfield who first suggested that he excavate at Ribchester' (Edwards 2000: 25), but this seems unlikely.[34] Garstang went on to devote his vacations as an undergraduate to excavating first at Melandra (1899), then nearby at Brough-on-Noe in Derbyshire (1903) and lastly at Richborough (Gurney 1971: 395), from

---

34. Garstang's interest in the site was supposedly stimulated while still a schoolboy by his regularly cycling past it on his way to an observatory.

which Haverfield drew extensively for his Ford lectures of 1906. The same press reports of Garstang's appointment at Liverpool note that he had been invited to contribute to the *VCH* series. In reality he only completed the sections on early man and Anglo-Saxon remains in Lancashire (*VCH* Lancs. I (1906).[35] He is also listed in later volumes as 'a contributor and assistant' for prehistoric remains although specific entries cannot be found. After Richborough, Garstang devoted himself to Egyptology and Near Eastern archaeology (Gibson 1999).

Another set of interesting Haverfield connections are those with Leonard Woolley (1880–1960), David Hogarth (1862–1927) and a contemporary of Haverfield's at Winchester, and through them, perhaps T.E. Lawrence (1888–1935). Haverfield's contact with Woolley is well documented (Woolley 1953). A graduate in Theology from Magdalen, Woolley was encouraged to go into archaeology by the college Warden, Canon Spooner. It is recorded that Woolley sat in on at least John Myres' lectures (Dunbabin 1955: 351). Woolley met Haverfield through 'a common interest in Robert Buston, the Elizabethan writer who resided for most of his life at Christ Church ... While biding his time at the end of 1906 he had helped Haverfield to catalogue Buston's publications in the Christ Church library' (Winstone 1990: 17–18). In that year, when Haverfield agreed to take on the Corbridge excavations, '...Somebody ...had to be put in charge of the work and because I [Woolley] was an Assistant Keeper in the Ashmolean Museum, my qualifications, were in the eyes of an Oxford Professor, ipso facto, satisfactory. Haverfield arranged with Sir Arthur Evans, the Keeper, that I should go to Corbridge. In point of fact I had never so much as seen an excavation' (Woolley 1953: 14). In another celebrated, if notorious passage in his autobiography, Woolley was scathing about Haverfield's contribution to the management of the excavations (*ibid*. 14–15).[36]

---

35. There was no Roman section in the volume. At the time it was noted the entries concerning early man and the Roman and Anglo-Saxon periods were necessarily short because there was no real interest in them in the region. Haverfield admitted to Charles Roeder that he was to undertake the Roman sections: cf. Ch. 7.

36. Woolley authored a small monograph recounting 'amusing episodes in his career' (1962: 7). The stories are invariably undated and there is nothing directly related to Haverfield in them although there are indirect references to his (Woolley's) time at Corbridge, (p. 7), his working in the Ashmolean (and so pre-Corbridge, p. 14) and a visit to the museum at Chesters, which again must date to his one and a half seasons at Corbridge (p. 13). Best known for his work in the Near East from 1907 onwards, Woolley did not give up en-

Woolley was recruited to Near Eastern archaeology by David Hogarth whose career as an archaeologist is increasingly being reassessed (cf. Hogarth 1896; Sayce 1927; Breasted 1928; Lock 1990). More a protégé of William Ramsay's, Haverfield's contact with him was at a number of levels. After Winchester, Hogarth went up to Magdalen in 1881. Graduating in 1886 with a First in *Literae Humaniores*, he eventually secured a tutorship at the same college. The direction of his career changed significantly later in that year when he became the first Craven fellow (in archaeology), an award that facilitated travels in the eastern Mediterranean, including Greece and Asia Minor (where he toured Lycia in 1887 with Anderson and in 1887–8 with Ramsay and an H.E. Brown). With no known fieldwork in the United Kingdom, Hogarth's archaeological career was to remain exclusively in the eastern Mediterranean and Asia Minor. His first experience of excavation was in 1888 at Old Paphos (Cyprus) with Ernst Gardner and then with the Egypt Exploration Fund in 1893 at Deir el Bahari. Indeed in terms of excavation technique, Hogarth was an acolyte of Flinders Petrie. In 1897 Hogarth was appointed director of the British School of Archaeology at Athens, where he remained until 1900 when R.C. Bosanquet succeeded him. He became keeper of the Ashmolean Museum in November 1908 in succession to (Sir) Arthur Evans, a post he occupied until his death. It would have been at this time that he must have come into close(r) contact with Haverfield. Between going up to Oxford and the keepership, Hogarth had no substantial means of income and was dependent on short-term appointments (e.g. as the leader of excavations) and the authoring of popular books and articles (Lock 1990: 177). In the early part of his career Hogarth co-authored articles with a number of individuals known to Haverfield.[37] With the outbreak of the First World War, after a number of failed attempts to obtain a military post, in 1915 Hogarth was appointed Director of the Arab Bureau in Cairo, part of the Admiralty's Dept of Naval Intelligence. T.E. Lawrence had been seconded to the War Office's Intelligence department in Cairo in 1914, joining the Arab Bureau in November 1916. Hogarth and Lawrence had, however, been working together for some time be-

---

tirely on excavating in Britain. In August 1912, accompanied by Lord Carnarvon, he opened trenches atop Beacon Hill and on a number of barrows in its vicinity: cf. Carnarvon and Woolley 1913.

37. Lock's 1990 bibliography of Hogarth publications includes work with William Ramsay, J.A.R. Munro, E.F. Benson and Arthur Evans.

fore this. Indeed Lawrence regarded Hogarth as his intellectual and professional mentor. The pair first met in January 1909, just after Hogarth had been appointed to the Ashmolean, and when he responded positively to Lawrence's desire to travel in Syria, for which Hogarth offered advice and wrote letters of introduction (Wilson 1989: 53, 988 n. 37: against the incorrect summary in James (1995: 31) which dates the first meeting to when Lawrence was still at school). In fact Lawrence's association with the Ashmolean goes back to 1906 when he, along with friends as a consequence of building work in central Oxford, brought in objects for identification by the assistant keepers, C.F. Bell, and judging from a letter from Lawrence to his brother Bob, dated August, Woolley (Besson 1937: 56; Lawrence 1954: 26). From 1908, Lawrence developed what was to become a second enduring friendship with another assistant keeper, E.T. Leeds (cf. Wilson 1989: 42).[38] The subsequent course of Lawrence's career is well known (Wilson 1989: James 1995). After going up to Jesus College in 1907, in 1909 he made his first visit to the Middle East, surveying Crusader castles in Syria and Palestine. The results of that trip were included in a dissertation (supported by Charles Oman and Leeds) which saw him awarded a First in Modern History in 1910. In the same year Hogarth secured him a senior demyship at Magdalen (where Hogarth and Leeds were already fellows) for the period up to 1914. This award, while ostensibly to support Lawrence's work for a BLitt degree on medieval pottery, allowed him to participate as a non-salaried assistant on the British Museum excavations at Carchemish. Hogarth had (re-)visited the site in March 1908 and applied to the Ottoman authorities for a permit to excavate. The *firman* arrived in September 1910, too late for Hogarth now at the Ashmolean to use. The permit was thus passed to the British Museum, with Hogarth agreeing to keep an eye on the excavations. In 1911, Lawrence was assistant there to R. Campbell Thompson who was the field director under Hogarth's directorship. When Thompson declined a second season, Hogarth arranged for Woolley to be his replacement in 1912 after the latter had finished excavating in Nubia. In the subsequent seasons, down to 1914, the relationship between Woolley and Lawrence was to all intents and purposes cordial and successful. Tensions only became apparent after 1920 (Wilson 1989: 127–30).

---

38. E. Thurlow Leeds (1877–1955), a Cambridge graduate who, after a short spell in the Colonial Service, eventually moved to the Ashmolean in 1908, became its keeper in 1928 until 1945; RLSB-M and DBH 1956; Harden 1956.

The nature of Haverfield's relationship with these three individuals is unclear. The link with Woolley is obvious, but it is surely stretching the facts to claim he was a Haverfield student. There is every likelihood that Haverfield crossed paths with Hogarth in a number of ways. He was to contribute an essay on the contribution of archaeology to understanding the Roman world in Hogarth's *Authority and Archaeology: Sacred and Profane* (1899: 296–311). What, if anything, Lawrence owed Haverfield or what he thought of him is at present unknown. It is certain, however, that Lawrence, through his friend the poet James Flecker, knew John Beazley and therefore Cheesman (as in a letter to Flecker, December 1914; Flecker 1926; 1929: cf. Brown 1991: 67; Hodgson 1925).

Another person occasionally put into the Haverfield 'group' is Norman Whatley (1884–1965). Educated at Radley and Hertford colleges, he was a contemporary and friend of Cheesman.[39] Matriculating in 1903 and with a First in *Literae Humaniores*, he was elected Fellow of Hertford College in 1907 had been out at the BSA as a student in 1907–08 and was a student at the BSR in 1910, interspersed with war service in the university OTC before secondment to the BEF Intelligence Corps. Tutor and Lecturer in Ancient History from 1908 to 1923 and Dean 1912–20, Whatley also worked at Corbridge (variously between 1908 and 1912).[40] In 1923 he left the university to become headmaster of Clifton College (Bristol) until 1939 (and was a member of Bristol University Council 1934–9). Returning to Oxford he became a city councillor for a second time (1944–55, he had previously served 1919–22) and town mayor for 1949–50 (obit. *The Times* 3 April 1965). There is no other evidence for how he worked with Haverfield.

One other individual who cannot but be placed in the inner circle of Haverfield acolytes is Margerie Venables Taylor (1881–1963: obits. *The*

---

39. Dobson (1997) reports the young Eric Birley, when he entered Clifton School, was handed by Whatley, Cheesman's notes for the *Auxilia*. As has been noted, Cheesman and Whatley were close friends but how and why the notes came into Whatley's possession remains unknown. The fate of the notes since Birley's death in 1995 is also unknown.

40. Late on in life, Whatley was persuaded to publish a lecture about reconstructing ancient military campaigns and battles (Whatley 1964). The paper was originally delivered to the Oxford Philological Society in October 1920 but was based on notes assembled in *c*.1913. In the audience which heard the paper were a number of individuals who feature here: J.L. Myres, A.C. Clark, J.A.R. Munro, J.K. Fotheringham, G.B. Grundy, E.M. Walker, W.W. How, J.U. Powell, R.H. Dundas, D.C. Macgregor, N.R. Murphy, G.H. Stevenson, M.N. Tod, H.M. Last, F.P. Long, J. Bell and five other visitors.

Times 27 December 1963; *J Chester Archaeol Soc* 51 (1964): 77–8: Richmond 1964; cf. Anon. 1960). Frere went as far as to group her contribution to Roman studies with that of Haverfield and Collingwood although she was not to produce the sort of works that made Haverfield's name or to undertake major excavation (Frere 1988: 2). Bonarkis Webster (1991: 118) claimed she was introduced to Haverfield when he was at Christ Church but one suspects that their association came through her father Henry Taylor (1845–1927; Anon. 1926), a local solicitor (from 1868) and one-time Town Clerk of Flint (1874–1906). He was also a noted antiquary and formerly President of both the Chester and North Wales Archaeological Society and the Flintshire Historical Society, whom Haverfield acknowledged for facilitating his visits to Chester to see the inscriptions recovered there in the late 1880s. He was awarded an honorary MA by Manchester University for his services to archaeology, principally with regard to Flintshire and was elected a FSA in 1888.

Taylor's second daughter, Margerie, after schooling at Queen's School, Chester, went up to Somerville College in 1900 where she would also have been a contemporary of Winifred Breakwell, the future Mrs Haverfield. In 1903 Taylor graduated with a Second in Modern History. In the years after she worked as a researcher for ten years with the *VCH* and RCHM.[41] Working with the *VCH* brought her into close contact with Haverfield. It has even been suggested that Taylor had hoped to be the first Mrs Haverfield (Bonarkis Webster 1991: 119). She contributed to the *VCH* Worcs. (II: 1906) and was responsible for helping with his Roman section in the volumes dedicated to Shropshire in 1908 and later on Herts. (IV: 1914). After Haverfield's death she completed his contributions to the Cornwall (V: 1924) and Kent (1932) volumes as well as his synthesis on Roman Leicester (Haverfield 1918a). She was also responsible for her own Roman sections in the Hunts. (1926) and Oxon. (1939) volumes as well as developing a special interest, again through Haverfield, for writing up earlier unpublished fieldwork in the vicinity of Oxford (e.g. North Leigh – Taylor 1923; Woodeaton – Taylor 1917). In 1908 she assisted Haverfield, along with Bosanquet, in the preparation of his seminal study of the Roman military occupation of Wales (Haverfield 1910b).

---

41. In a letter to the Manchester archaeologist and antiquary Charles Roeder, in October 1906, Haverfield mentions his (female) secretary, presumably Taylor. Elsewhere in the credits for the 1908 *VCH* Shrops. volume, she is described as 'MA (Dublin), Oxford Honours School of Modern History.'

She also undertook some of the investigative work for the 1916 RCHM Essex volume. In 1913 Taylor is listed as a student at the BSR. Elsewhere it was written she moved to Rome in the same year to work as a secretary to John Marshall.[42] She was forced back to England by the outbreak of the war, where she returned to London to work for Haverfield in 1915 as his secretary and assistant until he died. In addition to her literary work, Taylor made indirectly a considerable contribution to the Haverfield legacy. She became the secretary of the Roman Society from 1923 to 1954 and served as its editor (1923–60). She was the first woman ever to be elected a VP of the Society of Antiquaries of London (1946), was awarded an honorary research fellowship at Somerville in 1947 and made an honorary member of the Newcastle society in the following year. Her CBE in 1948 was for services to scholarship.[43]

From this list of individuals with good or reasonable grounds to tie them to Haverfield, we move to the more contentious. On the margins of the group is the 'problematic' P.W. Dodd. He is a problem in so much that there are so many difficulties in trying to identify if and how he inter-acted with Haverfield. Dodd's path also crossed with a number of other persons who may have had connections with him. Certain facts are clear. Percy Dodd of Wrexham and Jesus College, after taking a Second in *Literae Humaniores*, became Assistant Lecturer in Classics at the University of Leeds in 1911. With respect to Haverfield's excavations he does not appear in the list of Oxford students at Corbridge.[44] However,

---

42. This was presumably John Marshall (d. 1928) a '...dealer in Antiquities who acted for the Metropolitan Museum' (Wallace Hadrill 2001: 73–4). Marshall became a benefactor of the British School at Rome and who in time left part of his library to its collection. At about the same time M(ary) N.L. Taylor of Newnham College Cambridge, was admitted to the School as the Gilchrist Student (1913–14) and who published in the *Papers of the British School at Rome* for 1916, along with her later husband H.C. Bradshaw (the first scholar of the Architectural Faculty in the School), on architectural terracottas from a pair of temples at Falerii Vetres.

43. One other female employed by Haverfield, but otherwise unlocated, was Miss L. Lister of Somerville College who he acknowledged for her assistance in an article about Tacitus (Haverfield 1916e).

44. On the 1908 season at Corbridge is listed a M.C. Dodd as well as R.A. Atkinson. I had previously assumed these were misprints. As already noted, attempts to identify potential Haverfield students are not helped by some confusing or sloppy entries in the contemporary records. In the case of these two individuals, if they are Percy Dodd and Donald Atkinson, not only are their initials incorrect, their college affiliations are wrong. M.C. Dodd and

a P.W. Dodd did assist in the *Ephemeris Epigraphica* (IX Fasc. 4. *Add. quinta ad corpus* vol. VII (1913)). In 1912, he was asked by Atkinson to compile a list 'Previous discoveries at Adel', a site then recently excavated by Atkinson (Atkinson 1912–13). Later, in 1913, Dodd was appointed director of the Yorkshire Archaeological Society excavations at Slack, before enlisting in 1914 as a Captain in the 6th West Yorkshire Regiment. Responsibility for the excavations then passed to his Leeds' colleague, A.M. Woodward, formerly of Magdalen College, until 1915, whom Donald Atkinson assisted.[45] Woodward arrived at Leeds no later

---

R. Atkinson are both listed as Magdalen. They should be Brasenose and Jesus. For the record, there is no Dodd at pre-war Magdalen. Indeed the situation concerning the identity of the Corbridge Dodd is even more complicated. In fact the original reference, M.C., must refer to Charles Harold Dodd, a Classics scholar at University College (1902–07) and who '…assisted Haverfield and Craister [sic = Craster] in the excavation of the Roman settlement at Corstopitum' (Caird 1974: 498; an error repeated in a *Times* obituary notice (24 September 1974). This Dodd, the brother of Percy, was ordained in 1912 and went onto a distinguished career as a church historian. A R.L. Atkinson, who matriculated in 1914, was a member of the university OTC mobilized in that year. He served as a Captain in the 5th Queen's (Royal West Surrey) Regiment, in India (1914–15), Mesopotamia (1915–16) and France and Belgium (1917). He was awarded the MC in July 1917. P.J. Campbell's memoir of Cheesman records an 'Atters' – Atkinson, an undergraduate at New College and who was elected to a fellowship at Hertford. There is no other information other than he was 'killed'. Clearly friendly with Cheesman, does the diary mean Donald Atkinson (which is highly unlikely as he did not die!) or this individual, or is it a confusion of the two?

45. Arthur Maurice Woodward (1883–1973). Given the course of his career it is disappointing to find only one (and short) obituary describing his career (cf. *The Times* 15 November 1973). A scholar who developed multifarious interests in classical antiquity, at about this time Woodward worked in Byzantine history (e.g. along with A. Van Milligen and A.J.B. Wace, he co-authored in 1913, *The Church of St Eirene at Constantinople*; cf. Hill 1945). A fuller report of Ilkley was published by Woodward (*The Roman Fort at Ilkley*, 1927), a reprint of an original report in the *Yorkshire Archaeological Journal*. Dodd was the honorary secretary to the excavation committee. In this he added that the 1919 season was supervised by himself and Dodd. Woodward supervised the 1920 season with a short relief by Dodd. Woodward supervised the 1921 season, but was unable to complete the full report for that year because he left for Athens in October 1922 when he became assistant director of the school there. He had been active in Greece from 1911. He became its director in 1923 until 1929 (Waterhouse 1986). It was Woodward who recommended

than 1913 and his post there must have been the vehicle for his publishing a study of some classical sculpture in the city's museum (Woodward 1914). There is currently no known Woodward-Haverfield connection but they must have known one another. Woodward also enlisted, serving with the Intelligence Corps in Salonika between 1915 and 1918. The decision to suspend work at Slack brought public criticism from Haverfield (1916a: 2) once plans to expand the excavations were stopped when permission from the landowner was refused. In 1919 Dodd (and Woodward) returned to Leeds to find that the Yorkshire Committee had decided to shift its interests, represented by F.G. Simpson, to the fort at Ilkley, a site for which Woodward assumed responsibility with Dodd assisting for only one season. At the same time the pair were left to see the Slack site published (Dodd and Woodward 1920–2; Richmond 1925). In this they were assisted by Bosanquet, Haverfield, Atkinson and F.A. Bruton. Dodd wrote the greater part of the site pottery report, with Atkinson discussing the samian. In 1919 Dodd was elected to a fellowship in philosophy (becoming Senior Tutor in 1926) at his old college, Jesus, where he was heavily involved in teaching for Modern Greats. This necessitated him giving up teaching and research in Roman Britain. His health, wrecked by wartime service,

---

that excavation at Ilkley in 1922 be suspended (Chitty 1987). By 1930/1 Woodward was Lecturer in Ancient History at the University of Sheffield, where he became reader and head of department until his retirement in 1947. I am grateful to Mr L. Aspden, Curator of Special Collections at the University of Sheffield Library for this information. During this period Woodward was responsible for initiating, in 1933, an evaluation excavation at the Roman villa at Rudston (cf. Woodward 1932–4; Woodward and Steer 1936–8, where he is also described as Hon. ARIBA). Woodward served on Council of the Hellenic Society in the later years of the Second World War. What he did after Sheffield is unknown but he seems to have been a man of independent means. He appears to have retired to Tonbridge Wells. He remained an active researcher and publisher down to the mid-1960s. Following Woodward's death in 1973, David Lewis compiled a bibliography of his publications; from the archaeology of Greece, Turkey and Asia Minor, to Attic epigraphy and numismatics to general archaeology, the Renaissance and, of course, Roman Britain (Lewis 1975). The range of his work and the time he was active makes the absence of an assessment of Woodward's career all the more regrettable. Of course, for all this activity there is nothing to show that he was part of the 'inner' circle of Haverfield 'students', although he did provide a short obituary (Woodward 1920).

collapsed in 1931 when he died at the comparatively young age of 42 (cf. *The Times* 25 and 27 May 1931).

An equally enigmatic individual at Leeds who might have owed something to Haverfield was Hugh Gerard Evelyn White (1884–1924), and who at the time of his death was Lecturer in Classical Archaeology in the university.[46] Haverfield was certainly aware of his existence and the range of his work (e.g. Haverfield 1914a: 17). The son of a Cambridgeshire cleric with strong antiquarian interests, Evelyn White went up to Wadham College in *c.*1903 and matriculated in 1907. His subsequent interests in classical archaeology suggest that he was likely to have been one of (P.) Gardner's protégés, even if he does not appear in his list of 'students'. In the same year Evelyn White was given permission to offer a Special Subject for Greats on the *Saxon Shore System in Britain* which implies a connection with Haverfield. Other indications of a link include the fact that, again in the same year, when Evelyn White was involved in the excavation of a Civil War fortification at Earith, Huntingdons. (1907), Haverfield was consulted on the possibility of the earthworks at Cottenham (Cambs.) being a late Roman fort or settlement (Evelyn White 1902; 1904). He suggested it was more likely to be a Norman fort or castle or a Roman fort of the fourth/fifth centuries, citing continental and North African parallels (but with no British examples: cf. Keynes and Evelyn White 1908: 259). In spite of the Oxford permission, in the same year Evelyn White became a schoolmaster at Abbotsholme School, Rochester which suggests he failed to obtain a college appointment. He next appears in 1908 as an excavator at the legionary fortress at Caerleon and then Caersws, excavations conducted under the auspices of the Liverpool Institute's Committee for Excavation and Research in Wales.[47] In 1909 he was working in the British Museum with Aurel Stein[48], before

---

46. The following paragraph owes much to Colin Wallace's work on Evelyn White's career.

47. The report of the 1908 Churchyard excavations at the site, again undertaken by the Liverpool Institute was written by Evelyn White (Liverpool Committee for Excavation and Research in Wales and The Marches 1908/9, 1st Ann. Report). The 1909 season, in the southern fortress angle and evidently minus Evelyn White, was never published although the MS notes are stored in the National Museum of Wales: cf. Nash-Williams 1952: 26. The directors were Bosanquet and Frank King (who, like Evelyn White, had served at Caerwent).

48. Stein was working in 'the Caves' (the Museum's basements), on material from his Second Central Asian Expedition (April 1906 to Nov. 1908; Stein

moving onto fieldwork in Egypt with the Metropolitan Museum of New York, where he continued to work for a number of years.[49] In 1910–11 he was at North Leigh with Donald Atkinson and possibly on the Caerwent excavations (cf. Chapter 6), and in 1913 on the Liverpool excavations at Castell Collen, for which he published that years report as well as the one for work undertaken there in 1911.[50] By 1920 he was at Leeds, which implies he was in some way P.W. Dodd's replacement when the latter returned to Oxford. His last fieldwork was in 1924 when he worked (with Ian Richmond) at the Roman camps at Cawthorn. Richmond was to write of this time at Cawthorn: 'My relations with Mr. White were most happy and his untimely death has made me the executor of a Report which he was looking forward to write' (Richmond 1926–8: 339).[51] Largely forgot-

---

1921; cf. Mirzky 1977: 340–1). In his acknowledgements of the help received, Stein (1921: xiv) noted contributions from ('for a short time') Evelyn White, J.P. Droop, and in particular Leonard Woolley.

49. This period is summarized by Lythgoe in the Preface to Evelyn-White's *The Monasteries of the Wadi 'N' Natru* (Pt.1: 1926) and can be supplemented with the subsequent two volumes of the report (1932 and 1933). Between 1909 and 1911 Evelyn White was at Khargeh Oasis and Thebes, and 1911–13 at Thebes. In 1914 he tried to enlist but was rejected. Returning to Thebes, in the autumn of 1915 he managed to secure an army commission and saw service in the project to construct a railway across the Suez Isthmus to Palestine. 'There his health, always precarious, finally broke down and in 1917 he was invalided out of the army with no hope of further entry.' Returning to work for the Metropolitan Museum, between 1917 and 1919, Evelyn White worked at Cambridge, where he was assisted by the university and many 'friends', whilst through 1919 and 1921 he was back in Egypt.

50. In a report in the *Classical Review* (Evelyn White 1913: 285), he wrote the excavations were for a local committee, which was running out of funds.

51. Evelyn White shot himself in the back of a taxi on 10 September 1924. He was on his way to a Coroner's inquest concerning the suicide of a female who had become infatuated with him (cf. Bonner 1964). Crum, who deposited among his papers in the British Museum a number of pieces of correspondence with Evelyn White, wrote his obituary (cf. Crum 1924). In this there is no mention of the circumstances of Evelyn White's death and only passing reference to a link with Percy Gardner. For the full background of the suicide, cf. *The Times* 10 and 12 September 1924. One point to note is that the night before his death, he had written to the university to tender his resignation. Simpson wrote an introduction to the Cawthorn site (Simpson 1926–8). In this he noted the site had previously been dug in August 1908, the results of which were sent to Haverfield and Bosanquet at Liverpool. Simpson had re-

ten today, Evelyn White was a scholar with an impressive range of interests. His work was not limited to Roman Britain. His earliest publications, many in the *Journal of Hellenic Studies*, covered aspects of Greek sculpture. An Egyptian papyrologist, he also co-authored, with his father, the Cambridgeshire section of the Doomsday Book (1910), translated Hesiod, Ausonius and Statius in the Loeb series and wrote about the Claudian invasion of Britain. Superficially then there is much to suggest more than a passing link with Haverfield but the fact that nobody at the time of his death linked him with Haverfield is suspicious. That said, it is intriguing to find him working through the Liverpool Institute and in particular its main Roman specialist, R.C. Bosanquet (whom Evelyn White acknowledged in his reports for the Institute's excavations).[52] One suspects that this particular connection may owe something to Haverfield's input but this remains unproven.

Complicating the situation further with respect to Leeds and Percy Dodd, Woodward and Evelyn White is Rhys Roberts' (1920: 350) allusion to what he called Haverfield 'students' then employed in the university. It is unclear whom Rhys Roberts meant when he wrote that, in spite of Haverfield's losses in the war, some did survive: 'One of these has the advantage of excellent original work achieved along the Roman Wall; another with an unusually wise knowledge of the different branches of Classical Archaeology has generously offered to undertake a systematic survey of all the remains which the Roman site at Ilkley has hitherto yielded' (1920: 350). Each of Dodd, Evelyn White and Woodward would appear to fit the latter person but the identity of the scholar of Hadrian's Wall is debatable.[53]

---

course to thank 'Miss M.V. Taylor MA of the Haverfield Library and Professor Bosanquet for the opportunity of reading the original notes' (p. 29–30).

52. In the 1913 Castell Collen report, the acknowledgements are to G.F. Hill (Dept of Coins at the BM), Bushe-Fox, Angelo Hayter (then working at Wroxeter and who helped with the pottery) and Bosanquet. There is a brief nod to Haverfield who advised on the identification of some buildings. Bushe-Fox also looked at the coarseware pottery (Evelyn White 1914). Bosanquet is acknowledged in H. Lewis' 1911 work at the same site (Lewis 1912). Haverfield advised on a fragment of an inscription in R. Wellings Thomas' work again at the same site in 1911 (Wellings Thomas 1911).

53. Colin Wallace has suggested to me that Rhys Roberts might mean R.G. Collingwood but I am unconvinced.

On the basis of his date of birth, his years at Oxford and his subsequent career, another potential Haverfield 'student' is Paul Kenneth Baillie Reynolds (1896–1973). Educated at Winchester and Hertford, Oxford, with interrupted war service in the RFA (TF) (1913–19), Baillie Reynolds was, between 1921 and 1923, the Pelham student at the British School at Rome. The outcome of this time was his work on the *castra Peregrinorum* which involved in part his writing-up Thomas Ashby's notes of the same made between 1904 and 1909 (cf. Ashby and Baillie Reynolds 1923; Baillie Reynolds 1923). He was an assistant master at Winchester School (1924) before becoming Lecturer in Ancient History at UC Aberystwth (1924–34). During this appointment he excavated at Caerhun (ancient Kanovium) in the summer vacations of 1926, 1927 and 1929 (Baillie Reynolds 1938). He also supervised for the Wheelers at Verulamium in the 1930s. Baillie Reynolds was later Inspector of Ancient Monuments for England (from 1934) becoming the Chief Inspector (1954–61) and was President of the RAI for 1963 to 1966 (cf. *The Times* 25 August 1973). Other than these facts, there is no known Haverfield connection.

The University of Oxford and its ancient counterparts in Scotland have a tradition of the latter sending students to the former or else of sharing appointments. We have already seen how Rankine Brown was one example. There were two other individuals who made the same journey and who were known to Haverfield. One such was George Hope Stevenson (1880–1952) who worked at Corbridge (1908 and 1910)[54], and later with another Haverfield associate, S.N. Miller, at the Roman fort at Cappuck in 1911 and 1912. Born and educated in Glasgow, Stevenson was Lecturer in Ancient History at Edinburgh University in 1905 before moving to Oxford in 1906 as a fellow of University College (lecturer 1927–35). He went on to a distinguished career there, after wartime service from May 1915 as a lieutenant in the Oxford and Bucks. Light Infantry and in the Intelligence Corps in France (1918). Despite the existence of the connection, Stevenson seems to have made little of his association with Haverfield. There do

---

54. In October 1910 Stevenson was writing from Corbridge to the Society of Antiquaries of Scotland, announcing plans to excavate in the following year at Cappuck (which he did with S.N. Miller). Stevenson said the excavations would be assisted by funds from the Carnegie Fund. The Antiquaries appointed a committee comprising James Curle, George Macdonald and T. Ross, to liaise with Stevenson and even offered to let him use the tools from the Newstead excavations.

not appear to have been written any obituaries of his career, although he was the author of two monographs, *The Roman Empire* (1930) and *Roman Provincial Administration* (1939). Easier to reconcile is the career of Stueart Napier Miller (1880–1952), who was educated at Glasgow University before moving to Trinity College, Oxford. This, coupled with the fact he once worked with Stevenson, and the statement that he was an authority on Roman history and Romano-British antiquities, leads one to suspect Miller had more than a passing acquaintance with Haverfield. In 1909 he was appointed Lecturer in Humanity at Glasgow before becoming the University's first ever Lecturer in Roman History and Antiquities in 1912, and remaining in post until his retirement in 1944. In the autumn of 1911 and spring of 1912 Miller and Stevenson excavated Cappuck. Funded by the Carnegie Trust and supported by the Scottish Antiquaries, they were assisted by the society's Clerk of Works Alexander Mackie, James Curle and George Macdonald for the pottery and coins. In their report of the excavations, there is no mention of Haverfield (cf. Stevenson and Miller 1911–12). Between 1912 and 1914 Miller excavated the Roman fort at Balmuildy. Joining up in 1914, he converted to Catholicism in the same year. After the war he went on to excavate at Old Kilpatrick (1923–4) and later still at York. That he knew Haverfield is implied in the acknowledgment to him in the introduction to the Balmuildy report. That said Macdonald also reported, unfavourably, on Miller's execution of the excavations there.[55] Miller also reviewed some of Haverfield's publications, often quite favourably. And yet, in spite of all this circumstantial evidence there is no definite evidence to link the one with the other.

Yet another individual who comes into the category of possible 'student' is Sir Herbert Henry Edmund Craster (1879–1959). A Northumbrian by birth, but schooled at Clifton, Craster went up to Balliol where he took a First in Modern History and was elected a fellow of All Souls in 1904. His days as an undergraduate therefore overlap with Haverfield's return to Oxford. Joining the Bodleian in 1912, after military service from 1917 in the Intelligence Directorate, he returned to the library, becoming Keeper of Western Manuscripts in 1927 and keeper in 1931 until his retirement in 1945. Craster's original interests

---

55. In another example of Haverfield's negative opinionating, there survives a letter to George Macdonald in which he criticized Miller's management of the excavations at Balmuildy (4 September 1914, Haverfield Archive, Oxford). Miller obits.: Robertson 1952a and b, the latter of which is a reworking of the former.

lay with Northumbrian and northern history, which resulted in his appointment as an editor of the *History of Northumberland* volume (1907–14). Connected with the Northumberland history was the plan to excavate at Corbridge and therefore, not surprisingly, Craster came to participate in its excavation, at least between 1907 and 1912. In 1908–09 he prepared a report on the site's coins, including a hoard (Bruton 1909a: 185). Indeed Richmond (1959: 355) reports that this was when Craster's interest in the Roman archaeology of (northern) Britain started. Post-Corbridge, Craster's interests in Roman antiquities appear to have declined, shifting more to the history and contents of the Bodleian collection. Confusing the matter is the fact that just as some at Oxford appear to have regarded Corbridge as an Oxford exercise, they also thought Craster was on a par with Haverfield there (cf. Caird 1974; Rostovtzeff 1924–5).

So far we have been looking at individuals with certain or potential Haverfield links. The criteria for their inclusion in the discussion is based either on explicit statements to that effect or because their (subsequent) research and activities imply an interest in Roman archaeology. At the same time we have looked at the evidence for a distinct group and examined the nature of its relationship with him. There must be other individuals who could be included in this group but they remain even more illusive.[56] We can, however confidently omit names others have

---

56. Birley (1953) wrote that in his time as an undergraduate at Brasenose (1924–8), a seminal influence was the college fellow Michael Holroyd (1892–1953), who encouraged his interest in Hadrian's Wall. Although there is nothing explicit to link him with Haverfield, the overlap with the end of Haverfield's career is interesting (cf. Ch. 11). Of other potential 'students', one would like to know more about T.D. Atkinson who worked with David Hogarth at Phylakopi on Melos in 1904 and F.B. Welch. Bushe-Fox (1925) notes that Woolley then temporarily directing excavations at Swarling, Kent (1921) was assisted by C.G.H. Dicker and G.H. Lockett, both undergraduates of Oxford and introduced by the Ashmolean Museum. To date I have not been able to trace either person. There was a C.G. Stone (of Balliol) who contributed to *The Year's Work in Classical Studies* on Roman history and inscriptions for 1914. Another individual is a C.L. Stainer of Christ Church who Haverfield reported brought to his attention a fragment of arrentine from near Bicester. From what Haverfield writes, Stainer had antiquarian interests (Haverfield 1907c: 461). Charles Lewis Stainer MA was one of four sons of the (University of Oxford) organist and composer, Sir John Stainer (1840–1901). A fellow of the Royal Numismatic Society (1902–38), C.L. Stainer later published extensively on a range of historical, numismatic and musical subjects, as well as various stories and plays. I am indebted to Colin

suggested. For there are a number of instances where a relationship has been asserted when the evidence points at best to a passing acquaintance. An example of this is the claim that in some way Haverfield was associated with the novelist and civil servant John Buchan (1875–1940). A student at Glasgow University in 1892, where he was taught by Gilbert Murray, Buchan moved to Oxford, to Brasenose, in 1895. Taking a Second in Mods and a First in Greats in 1899, he failed to win a fellowship at All Souls. Following this 'failure', he trained for the Bar and became an administrator under Lord Milner in South Africa. Buchan

---

Wallace for the lead on this. Then there is Henry Beauchamp Walters (1867–1944) who submitted the entries in 1908 and 1909 on progress in Roman Britain to *The Year's Work in Classical Studies*. His interests seem to have lain in things Hellenic: e.g. he read a paper on Greek vases to the Hellenic Society (November 1898), so is more likely to have been one of the Gardner/Myres' group. He went on to a distinguished career as an assistant keeper in the Dept of Greek and Roman Antiquities in the BM where, for instance, he produced the catalogue *The Roman Pottery in the Dept of Antiquities in the British Museum* (1908). Elsewhere Walters partly filled the vacuum Haverfield created for the *VCH* when the latter 'failed' to produce the Roman sections in various volumes. Walters also authored *The English Antiquarians of the Sixteenth, Seventeenth and Eighteenth Centuries* (1934). The Corbridge staff list for 1906 has an excavation assistant called R.C. Hedley, but he is unlikely to have been a student (see Ch. 6 n. 60: Woolley 1907: 162). He is, however, cited as a source of information for Haverfield's compilation of the *Ephemeris Epigraphica*. Other potential 'students' of which more details would be desirable are Henry Robert Pyatt MA (b. 1870), listed in the 1897 CEC season. Birley's (1961) list of mural scholars has him as working at Corstopitum in 1897. In the volume of the *Journal of Roman Studies* which adds the further note about Cheesman's death, the loss of two other Roman Society members is noted: C.F. Balleine (Exeter College, 1912) and A(lexander) D(ouglas) Gillespie (of Linlithgow; died Sept. 1915, aged 26 years and evidently a friend of Arnold Toynbee's and presumably an acquaintance of Cheesman's, cf. Toynbee 1958). In the *Journal of Roman Studies* 1916, are also listed L(eonard) G. Butler (St Johns, MA, a member of the society since 1914) and William Loring (with a private address in Blackheath and who was also a member of the Classical Association). At present there is no further information to link any of them with Haverfield. One other potential Haverfield 'student' might be Edward S.G. Robinson (1887–1976), who entered Christ Church, Oxford in 1906. His mentors appear to have been R.H. Dundas and P. Gardner (cf. obit. *Proc Brit Acad* LXIII (1977): 423–30). Robinson authored a number of obituary etc. notices of a known Haverfield associate, G.F. Hill (see below).

was to report his main influence at Oxford was A.H.J. Greenidge. Irrespective of these facts, in an account *Buchan and the Classics: School and University*, M. and I. Haslett, citing the allusion to Haverfield in Buchan's novel *The Runagates Club* (1928), write that Buchan '...had no recorded dealings with either Haverfield or Mommsen, but almost certainly got to know the former through the college when he became a Fellow' (cf. <johnbuchansociety.co.uk/classics.htm>). The chronology, however, is flawed. Buchan severed his links with Brasenose in *c*.1900. Haverfield moved to the same college in 1907.

Of about the same generation as Buchan was O.G.S. Crawford (1886–1957), who recorded that 'I cannot claim the honour of having been one of his [Haverfield's] disciples except in so far as everyone of my generation must be who is concerned, however, remotely, with Roman Britain which he created' (1955: 73; cf. Myres 1951; Clark 1958; Bowden 2001). After Marlborough (1900–04), Crawford took a Third in Mods at Keble. Withdrawing from Greats he choose to read for the Diploma in Geography, and deciding to study prehistory because he felt that all Oxford had taught him about archaeology was classical sculpture and Greek vases. His mentors at this time were R.R. Marett, H.S. Peake and J.P. Williams-Freeman (Bowden 2001: 30). At his first attempt he only managed to gain a certificate (= third class degree). He stayed on a further year (1909–10) and ended up with the diploma and a distinction. This was sufficient for him to obtain a junior demonstratorship in geography in 1910 which permitted him to explore the relationship of geography to archaeology through distribution maps. In the meantime, in 1909, through Marett, he developed an interest in anthropology. In 1913 he was member of the Routledge Expedition to Easter Island but left ship before it arrived. After working in Egypt in the same year, he excavated in England in 1914. In August that year he enlisted in the London Scottish Regiment but was soon invalided out. Rejected by the Royal Flying Corps, he joined the Royal Berks. Regiment, serving in the Maps section of the 3rd Army before arranging a transfer to the RFC in 1917 and being captured in February the following year. After the war and digging for the summer–winter of 1919, in late 1920 having undertaken voluntary work for it he went to work full-time for the Ordnance Survey as its first Archaeological Officer. According to J.L. Myres, Crawford's interest in maps and archaeology was inspired whilst at Marlborough, while Bowden reports he was already thinking about a map of Roman Britain as far back as 1910 (Bowden 2001: 30–1). Grundy's series of Handy Classical Maps was then coming out, including one of Roman Britain 'mainly edited by Francis Haverfield'. Out of this series, and certainly inspired by the format grew Crawford's Ordnance Survey map of Roman Britain (cf. Myres 1951: 5).[57]

A task that dons were expected to fulfill was to write letters of introduction as well as to respond to inquiries about the suitability of students. With his connections, Haverfield must have had to compose many of these. But it is debatable if such individuals can be realistically described as students. With respect to Haverfield, only one example of this practice seems to survive, where his judgement turned out to be unfair. In April 1899 Haverfield wrote to Mommsen enquiring if there was anyone in Berlin working on the MS of Eusebius' *Chronicle* as he had been contacted by an unnamed Oxford scholar: 'I am not hopeful that he will make much of the job, but if no-one else is doing it, he might try, if he choses.' Mommsen replied in November, saying that the student must be Mr Fotheringham who had already contacted him. After discoursing on the size of the task, Mommsen asked Haverfield for a character reference as it '...is not probable, but not impossible, that our commission would reflect on employing him'. Haverfields' reply was that he did not know Fotheringham but did not think him suitable (cf. Croke 85, 86, 87). In fact John Knight Fotheringham (1874–1936) became an authority on ancient astronomy and chronology. Teaching at King's College, London he became Reader in Ancient History at the University of London (1912–20).[58] He was awarded his DLitt in 1908/9 (supported by H. Turner, C.H. Turner and J.A.R. Munro) on the strength of his *The Bodleian Manuscript of Jerome's Version of the Chronicle of Eusebius* (1905, cf. Myres 1937; 1949). There is no other known Haverfield connexion.

Another equally tenuous Haverfield 'student' is to be found in a recent biography of Thomas Ashby, where Richard Hodges made the interesting suggestion that Vere Gordon Childe (1892–1957) might be

---

57. Crawford (1955: 73) recounted how he once applied, unsuccessfully, to work in a team being assembled by Haverfield to survey some forts in the Lake District. The occasion seems to be *c.*1911 which might tie in with Macdonald's statement that at about the outbreak of the war, Haverfield was beginning a programme of systematic research on the forts of north-west England (Macdonald 1929/1930: 46). There is no other record of that work. In *Roman Britain in 1913,* Crawford was mildly admonished by Haverfield (1914a: 43). For other Crawford memories, cf. Ashbee 1972: 64ff.

58. Fotheringham; Magdalen and Merton, with a First in *Lit. Hum.* (1897), held a senior demyship 1898–1902, was a student of the BSA in 1899 and fellow of Magdalen 1909–16). Before his readership, he taught classics (1904–09) and ancient history (1909–12) at King's.

called one on the basis of a letter from Haverfield of 1918.[59] But this might be pushing the connexion. After graduating with a First in Latin, Greek and Philosophy from Sydney University, Childe was awarded a graduate scholarship to Queen's, Oxford in 1914 where he took the diploma in classical archaeology and a BLitt. His interests, and those of his mentors, were in the archaeology of the eastern Mediterranean. Childe claimed his Oxford instruction was in bronzes, terracottas and painted pottery where he was instructed by the likes of Beazley, Evans and Myres.[60] There is no record of Childe being specifically instructed in Romano-British archaeology (cf. Piggott 1958). Hodges also recorded that, as a child, C.A. Ralegh Radford (1900–98) was introduced by his father to the leading archaeologists of the time, including Haverfield. Ralegh Radford went up to Oxford (Exeter College) to read Modern History in 1918 but claimed to have attended Haverfield's last ever lecture (cf. Hodges 1992).

(b) Other 'students'
In addition to the students of Oxford, Haverfield in the course of his own fieldwork must have come into contact with students of other institutions. It is now difficult, however, to establish precisely who. One person who might come into this category is Francis Norman Pryce (1888–1953). Pryce was a graduate of UC Aberystwyth (cf. Chapter 9 n. 21) when he worked on Evelyn White's excavations at Caersws (1908–09). He may be one of the unnamed young men at Corbridge in 1911 who moved to Bushe-Fox excavations or was one of the Corbridge 'friends' of 1912. He certainly participated on other Bushe-Fox excavations (Hengistbury Head 1911–12; Wroxeter 1913), and led his own excavations at Cae Gaer, Llangurig in 1912 or 1913

---

59. The context of the letter to Haverfield is that after he returned to Australia in August 1917, Childe found it difficult to find a position because of his politics and pacifism. Claiming he was being victimized by the University of Sydney, he wrote to a number of people, including some at Oxford, for their support. One person was Gilbert Murray, a fellow Australian (writing in June 1918). Haverfield was contacted in September and replied in October (Irving 1995; cf. Mulvaney 1994). Childe must have written for Haverfield's assistance for any combination of: (a) he was a 'name' and a leading liberal in the university; (b) he was a personal contact and/or (c) he might have contact with the university authorities at Sydney. The tone of Haverfield's reply clearly indicates he knew Childe well but felt unable or reluctant to assist.

60. On Beazley's instruction of Childe and Joan Evans, Arthur Evans' half-sister, cf. Kurtz 1985: 243; Ashmole 1985.

(Pryce 1914).[61] Pryce went on to a career at the British Museum. Appointed in 1911, he became Deputy Keeper in 1934 and Keeper of Greek and Roman Antiquities in 1936 down to 1939. He also served as editor of the *Journal of Hellenic Studies* between 1924 and 1938.[62]

Strictly speaking not university trained, but one who should be included in the Haverfield 'group' is (Major) Joscelyn Plunket Bushe-Fox (1880–1954). Although Bushe-Fox had no formal instruction as an archaeologist ('...not at all academic, more of a countryman than a classicist' – Fox 2000: 47), Eric Birley said he was '...a man who in his day did more than almost anyone to place Romano-British archaeology on a scientific and humane footing' (Birley 1954: 310). Richmond described him as 'one of the ablest of the young men whom Haverfield gathered about him for the initial exploration of the Roman site at Corbridge' (= 1910–11; *Nature* 6 November 1954: 860), where he specialized in analysing the pottery. But Bushe-Fox's inspiration here lay more with Thomas May than Haverfield, where at Corbridge, 'sitting at the feet of Thomas May, ...he formed his life long interest in Roman pottery' (Anon. 1955). Wheeler, who knew Bushe-Fox intimately, was to eulogize that his 'Corbridge contribution was not so weighty as those

---

61. Pryce excavated, along with A.S. Davies at Mathrafal (Powys) in August 1930 on behalf of the Powysland Club, a rectangular earthwork suspected as being Roman (cf. F.N. Pryce, The tiles of Mathrafal. *Montgomery Collections* 41 (1930): 161–2; S.A. Davies, Excavations at Mathrafal. *Montgomery Collections* 42 (1932): 150–2). I am grateful to Dr Jeremy Huggett for this information.

62. Pryce's brother was Dr Thomas Davies Pryce (d. 1940), a Nottinghamshire GP now best remembered for his work on samian in Britain, first with Eric Birley and then with Felix Oswald (*An Introduction to the Study of Terra Sigillata Treated from its Chronological Standpoint* (1920)). The two worked at Margidunum (between 1910 and 1936), which began when Oswald, F.T. Perry, G.H. Wallis and F.W. Dobson started there at Dobson's initiative. The Pryce brothers excavated the Roman fort at Forden Gaer in Wales in the late 1920s (Pryce and Pryce 1927; 1929). Davies Pryce was also at Richborough (1924), with the Wheelers at Lydney Park (1928–9), at Verulamium (1930+) and Maiden Castle (1934). He also excavated in Wales from the 1920s onwards on Roman and medieval sites, and where he developed a reputation as an expert on the Norman period in the principality. Davies Pryce retired to Woking in 1925 but was an occasional lecturer at the Institute of Archaeology (Davies Pryce is described as close friend and counsellor of Wheeler's, 'a wise elder' – Hawkes 1982: 149: cf. Oswald 1940; Anon. 1940). Oswald (1866–1958), a geologist by training, was Probate Registrar for the same county, and has been described as the last amateur archaeologist in Britain (Comfort 1959).

which came later, but it still remains of value' and that he '...was a pioneer in the fullest sense of the term. Simultaneously with James Curle in Scotland he began the systematic classification of Romano-British pottery on the basis of field evidence, first at Corbridge and later at Wroxeter and Richborough' (Wheeler 1955: 154).[63] Before Corbridge, Bushe-Fox had worked out in Egypt under Flinders Petrie at Gerzeh (1909) and Memphis (1911: cf. Flinders Petrie 1931).[64] Back in Britain,

63. Interestingly, Aileen Fox, once an assistant to Bushe-Fox at Richborough, recollected in her memoirs there 'was a fair amount of rivalry and ill-feeling between Wheeler and Bushe-Fox. I was warned that Rik jumped to conclusion too rapidly and no doubt he thought Bushe-Fox was far too slow. The new Wheeler excavations were better organised and publicized than the long established Richborough undertaking, and provided technical training in recording and interpretation far in advance of elsewhere' (2000: 56). Elsewhere Fox credits Bushe-Fox with a relatively sophisticated understanding of the principles of stratification although she added he was far too cautious in his interpretation of the evidence obtained from Richborough (p. 56).

64. Another person who was at Memphis in 1911 was Angelo G.K. Hayter (1863–1927) who went on to work with Bushe-Fox at a number of (Roman) sites in Britain. A classics scholar at Queen's, Cambridge with a diploma in German and French, Hayter schoolmastered for 25 years. An interest in Egyptology, however, led him to taking courses, from 1901, in the subject at UCL. In 1910 he resigned his position to work with Flinders Petrie. While his main interests were Egyptological, Hayter remained active in Britain. In 1911–12 he was at Hengistbury Head with Bushe-Fox, and in 1912, with T. May, D. Atkinson, Cheesman and Oxford and Cambridge students at Wroxeter. In the same year, with Mr A.H. Cocks and Dr Peake, Hayter was exploring a Romano-British structure at Yewden Manor Farm, Harpenden (cf. Haverfield *RCHM* Bucks. II (1912): 10); in 1913 he was again at Wroxeter, with Knowles, Mill Stephenson, Reg. Smith, D. Atkinson, H. Mattingly and F.N. Pryce and at least nine other university students where, as in 1912, he read the pottery. He did a pottery report for Evelyn White at Castell Collen in 1913. In 1914 he returned to Wroxeter where he worked on the pottery stamps with Donald Atkinson, and in 1920/1, he visited the Oldham antiquarian J.P. Hall's excavations at Caer Llugwy, for which he provided a finds report. He was appointed by its committee to direct excavations at Segontium (1920; cf. Hayter 1921). He was also associated with the excavations at Kenchester, Ariconium, Capler Camp and Caernarvon. At Kenchester, Hayter worked (1912–13 and 1924–5) with the civil engineer and surveyor to Herefordshire County Council, Gavin H. Jack (1874–1952), 'England's greatest bridge saver' and Haverfield obituarist (Jack 1918–20: cf. obit. Mr G.H. Jack MICE, FRIBA, FSA, FGS. Distinguished Career. *Trans Woolhope Natural Field Club* 1952–54: 1–2). Hayter's death notice in the *Antiquaries Journal* lamented he would be especially missed at

he excavated at Hengistbury Head (1911–12), Wroxeter (1912–14, and where Atkinson and other Oxford students participated), Swarling (1921) and Richborough (1922–39). In June 1913, he was in Oxford seeing Cheesman and Whatley. One of the very few Haverfield reviews that Macdonald mentions in the former's list of published work is that of Bushe-Fox's *Excavations at Hengistbury Head, Hampshire* (1915: Haverfield 1916c). The inclusion of the review in the list is curious because it is so uncontentious. It was largely complimentary in tone with some points of issue raised with respect to Bushe-Fox's interpretation of the Iron Age pottery and coins and therefore the significance of the site in late Iron Age Britain-Roman Europe. Bushe-Fox went on to become an Inspector of Ancient Monuments in 1920 and Chief Inspector in 1933 until his retirement in 1945.

Along with those individuals who have been described, on good or less certain evidence, as 'students', there are a number of other persons, some of them eventually colleagues at Oxford, with whom Haverfield not only worked but also taught even if they would not necessarily regard themselves as 'students'.[65] For instance, although better known as a colleague, John Linton Myres' (1869–1954) career, in part, overlapped with Haverfield's and there must have been close contact between the two. The author of numerous books and articles, the chair of a variety of organizations and with a notable wartime career in mili-

---

Richborough (where he and Mill Stephenson had analysed the coins). Before his death, in 1925, Hayter also commented on the Roman coins from an Anglo-Saxon site at Luton. Intriguingly, in the light of Haverfield's long-standing preoccupation with producing a definitive corpus of potters' stamps of Britain, an exercise he tried to co-ordinate on a number of occasions, Hayter had commenced work on a comparable catalogue (cf. Ch.7). I cannot find a clear-cut Hayter-Haverfield link, but all the signs are that Haverfield knew him and his work.

65. Another individual contemporary with Haverfield was Sidney George Owen (1858–1940), originally from near Winchester and educated at Clifton College and Balliol, where he was an exhibitioner (1877–82). With a Second (and a MA – 1886) he became lecturer at Owens College, Manchester and the later Victoria University from 1882. He returned to Oxford and Christ Church (1891–1926). There were, therefore, numerous opportunities for his career to interconnect with that of Haverfield's. He was at one time the editor of *The Year's Work in Classics*, a series of annual statements to which Haverfield once regularly contributed. Between 1926 and 1928, Owen was lecturer in Queen's College. His special interests lay with Ovid and Roman love poetry. He was awarded an honorary DLitt by the University of Dublin.

tary intelligence, it is a pity that Myres declined to write an autobiography (cf. Gray 1954; Dunbabin 1955; Murray 2000: 358). Shortly before his death, however, he did commit some reminiscences to paper (Myres 1979: 5) and there are some other memories.[66] Myres was educated at Winchester, going up to New in 1888, where it is known he sat in on lectures by Oman (for Greek history) and Hogarth (for Greek prehistory, who Myres credited, in 1890–1, with pushing him into research; cf. Fletcher 1928: 328) as well as Macan, E.M. Walker, Haverfield and Pelham (Dunbabin 1955: 349). That said, Percy Gardner claimed him as one of his students (Gardner 1933: 59). It was at this time, while still an undergraduate in 1892, Myres excavated, with Percy Manning, at Alchester on the Akeman Street, work which Haverfield was to praise in print.[67] He also organized a local history museum at Aylesbury. After graduating, with a First in Greats (1892), in a long, varied and distinguished career, Myres was Craven Fellow and Burdett-Coutts Geography Scholar (1892) before excavating on Cyprus. A fellow of Magdalen College (1892–5), he won the Arnold Essay Prize in 1899. He was a student of Christ Church College (1905–07) and was appointed Lecturer in Ancient History in the same college in 1895, where Haverfield was responsible for Roman history. He was also

---

66. E.g. Compton Mackenzie 1931: 249f. – Myres '...a scholar of mundane reputation', an opinion which should be read against Myres' sons' comments (1979: Appdx. 7).

67. *The Antiquary* XXVII (1892): 24. Haverfield knew Manning. He, Myres, Manning, and probably Arthur Evans visited the (crop mark) sites at Northfield Farm at Long Wittenham in the 1890s (Haverfield 1899d: 11). Born in Leeds in 1870 and educated at Clifton and New, Manning had been secretary, *vice* Lovegrove, of the Oxford Architectural and Historical Society, June 1891–March 1892). He was elected a FSA in 1896. His interests lay in the antiquities of Oxfordshire and was a founder member of the Oxford Brass Rubbing Society (1893) which was to become the Oxford Antiquarian Society in 1901. He died of pneumonia in February 1917 (incorrectly dated in Manning and Leeds 1920–1) while 'on service' as a Quartermaster Sergeant with the Oxford. and Bucks. Light Infantry National Reserve. He undertook and completed in 1896 an archaeological survey of Oxfordshire. Failing to see it in to print, he did keep it up to date until 1914, when the outbreak of the war again delayed its dissemination. The task was completed by E.T. Leeds of the Ashmolean (cf. Manning and Leeds 1920–1). In 1927 Christopher Hawkes, in writing up the results of his 1926 excavations at Alchester, mentions that the Myres/Manning records were preserved in plan in the Haverfield Library and with notes and excellent bibliography of the site in the Manning MS, all in the Ashmolean (cf. *Proc Soc Antiqs London* XXI (1916–17): 162).

Lecturer in Classical Archaeology (1903–07). In 1907 he became the Gladstone Professor of Greek as well as Lecturer in Ancient Geography at the University of Liverpool. He returned to Oxford in 1910 as the first Wykeham Professor of Ancient History there.

A closer professional relationship with Haverfield is evident in the case of George Beardoe Grundy (1861–1948), 'B.A. of Brasenose' where he obtained seconds in Classical Moderations and Greats in 1890 and 1891. He assisted Haverfield during his work with the Cumberland Excavation Committee in 1897 when he was described as 'the explorer of Plataea and Pylos'. In the same year he also worked with Haverfield on excavating a part of Akeman Street in Blenheim Park (Oxon.; Haverfield 1899b). We have seen how Haverfield and Grundy may have fallen out in 1898 during the work of the CEC but if this is so then contrary to what Grundy was to claim, it appears that they made up shortly afterwards. The two evidently walked stretches of Roman roads in Worcestershire sometime between 1900 and 1905 (Grundy 1935: 99)[68] and by 1901 (and in 1902) Grundy was working again with the CEC. Between 1897 and 1903 Grundy was the lecturer for the Professor of Ancient History (= Henry Pelham) before becoming fellow and tutor at Corpus Christi until 1931. He was also tutor at Brasenose from 1904 to 1917. With varied research interests, Grundy published on Greek history, Saxon charters and Roman roads (Grundy 1945: 146–60).[69]

---

68. These visits must link with Haverfield's preparations for the *VCH* Worcs. entry, published *c*.1901. If so, Haverfield did not acknowledge Grundy's contributions in the account. He does, however, do so in the *VCH* Warks. I (1906): 235.

69. Between 1876 and 1888, Grundy was variously a schoolmaster and private tutor before going up to Brasenose. In 1892 he held a university geography studentship (which must have come through Pelham's support) for travel in Greece (visiting Plataea). In the following year he was at Trebia and Trasimene in Italy and 1895 at Pylos, reports of which were published in the likes of the *Classical Review*. Following a period of unemployment he was invited to assist Pelham in the teaching of principally Greek history at the University. To be sure, he regarded Pelham as one of his closest friends and strongest patrons (e.g. Grundy 1945: 64, 86–7; 'the best and most effective Professor of Ancient History I have known in Oxford'). He was also complimentary about Nettleship (p. 63), Greenidge (p. 80), Strachan Davidson (p. 64; 160), Munro (p. 158) and Anderson (p. 150, 160). The one omission in this list is Haverfield. Instead, as was noted above, Grundy (1945: 147) was not so generous about him. That said, his opinions and recollections have to be treated with caution. For instance, his claim that Richmond was a student of his is weakened by the fact he could not recollect when he completed his degree

In addition to those who Haverfield 'taught' or worked with at Oxford there is a group of individuals who were approximately
contemporary with his undergraduate days or else were at the university in the years between his graduation and his return in 1892 but who
did not go onto university careers. For instance, there was Robert
Penrice Lee Booker (1864–1922), the one person highlighted by
Macdonald in his summary of Haverfield and the CEC (Macdonald
1918: 185). How he came to be involved with Haverfield is not known.
They cannot have been contemporaries at Oxford, but the notice of
Booker's death in the *Antiquaries Journal* (III. 1923) reports that he was
heavily involved in the Silchester excavations. What is certain is that
they were close friends. Booker was also the son-in-law of Haverfield's
cousin C.C. Mackarness of Scarborough (cf. Chapter 1; *The Times* 2
March 1918) as well as becoming one of the executors of Haverfield's
will. The son of a vicar, educated at Winchester and a scholar of New
College (with a Second in *Lit. Hum.* (1887) and an MA in 1890), Booker
was for a short time (1887) the librarian of the Oxford Architectural and
Historical Society. He became a master at Eton in 1888 where he remained until his retirement in 1920 (he was a house master from 1900).
Booker worked with Haverfield on Hadrian's Wall, as part of the CEC as
well as accompanying him on visits to Bar Hill (in the Septembers of
1903 and 1904: cf. Keppie 2002). In 1923 Booker was described as an
'assistant commissioner' of the RCHM, where is also recorded 'the severe loss suffered by the Commission through the death of Mr R.P.L.
Booker MA, FSA, who freely gave expert assistance to the Commission
on all questions concerning Roman monuments and was primarily responsible for the sections in Volume III (NE Essex) dealing with the

---

(p. 239). His assertion that Donald Atkinson was another one of his is patently
not the case (p. 236, 239). Nor is his recollection of working with Haverfield
strictly correct. Grundy claimed it was in 'the early years of this century'.
Haverfield has it at least three years earlier (1898)! In turn, Bowra (1966: 207)
was not positive about Grundy: '...a tutor in ancient history at Corpus who had
once done good work ...He was now past his prime and had a name for getting second classes for his first class pupils whom he encouraged to read no
books but his own. He was an arrogant, self-satisfied man who paid no attention to what other scholars wrote on his subject and he never revised his views
in the light of new discoveries.' A short death notice about Guy Dickins notes
he argued much with Grundy (*Oxford Magazine* 10 November 1916). Murray's
(2000: 357) assessment of Grundy is more positive.

important Roman remains in Colchester and its vicinity' (RCHM Essex (1923): xix).[70]

(c) Jobs for the boys

From the evidence marshalled so far, it seems clear there was an inner circle of close Haverfield associates, most of them Oxford graduates, some of whom went on to careers in academia. They were complemented by a group of individuals, some 'Oxford trained' who worked elsewhere in Romano-British studies. It is for these reasons that some have called this group of contacts the Haverfield 'school' or 'group' or 'students'. The strength of the attribution is based on the facts: (a) many of them went onto a career in academia, many at Oxford, in *Literae Humaniores* and so to perpetuate the (Haverfield) tradition of teaching; and (b) many of them were previously used by him in the execution of fieldwork, whether in epigraphy (e.g. for the addenda to *CIL* and what was to become the *RIB*) or in the compilation of the likes of the *VCH* and *RCHM* volumes or in excavation. While some continued to work in the subject and others drifted away, that there were so many individuals and because they were seen to complement Haverfield's protestations for the better provision of training and management, they would appear to substantiate the impression that he deliberately set out to create a 'school' of disciples. The origins of the arrangement and the way that Haverfield made contact with those in the first group is uncertain but it commenced after his entry to Christ Church and was initiated by a combination of school and personal contacts, as with Ashby and Cheesman, and by recommendation and reputation (e.g. Woolley and Garstang). Others were presumably drawn to him by his reputation.

The main tool for the attribution of individuals to a Haverfield group lies with the CEC and even more so the Corbridge staff lists. When we look at those who over the years returned to Corbridge it is possible to detect something of a pattern evolving in how some (Oxford) students were employed. We saw in Chapter 5 that from at least the 1890s Haverfield had noted the shortage of trained and competent excavation staff, a deficiency he in part blamed on the failure of the universities. One of the remedies he suggested was for (university) students to be trained to work on site. The idea of training students might go back to the CEC and Thomas

---

70. There is supposed to be an obituary of Booker in *The Times* 13 June 1922, but the reference appears incorrect. A postscript to that notice can be found in *The Times* 27 June.

Ashby who, after working with Haverfield on the Vallum on Hadrian's Wall in 1898 worked with Bosanquet at Housesteads, where he was '...entrusted with the further excavation of the Mithraeum' (Birley 1961: 181). Ashby subsequently went on to Caerwent (1899+). That said, in the subsequent years of the CEC, there do not appear to have been any other students comparable to Ashby. Instead the idea of a 'training excavation' seems to have crystallized in Haverfield's mind after the 1907 Corbridge season. In 1908 he was to write that, along with Forster, Knowles, Craster and a Professor Monk, the excavations were marked by a '...new and interesting feature ... the co-operation of young Oxford men, five tutors and as many undergraduates who have in turn lived on the spot for two or three weeks each and taken a share in the work. Thus may Corbridge become a school of practical archaeology, where scholars may handle realities and learn the exercise that competent supervision without excavation is criminal' (*The Times* 19 September 1908). For the 1910 season Haverfield reported that three or four (Oxford) fellows and five or six younger men were present (Haverfield 1911h: 178). However, in the same year, Haverfield's co-director, Forster, complained of a shortage of supervisors and expert staff on site. In 1911, along with familiar names, Haverfield added that '...several younger men' joined them. Was this comment Haverfield's response to Forster's 1910 complaints? If so, the situation did not improve. In 1913 the '...excavators had not the advantage which they have enjoyed in previous years of the help of resident assistants during at least some part of the season' (Forster and Knowles 1914: 281).[71]

---

71. Of the Oxford (Cambridge and other) students who worked at Corbridge, the following list is compiled from the interim reports published in the *Archaeologia Aeliana* (vols. III–VII) and Haverfield's reports to the Society of Antiquaries: Atkinson (1908, '11, '14), Cheesman (1908, '09, '10, '11), Collingwood (1911, '12), Craster (1906, '07, '08, '09, '10, '11, '12, '14), C. Dodd (?1908), Newbold (1908, '11, 12), Stevenson (1908, '10 – on the basis of a letter discussed in n. 54 above), Whatley (1908, '11, '12) and Woolley (1906, '07). Others who were present but for whom it is difficult to establish precisely when include Hayter, Bushe-Fox and so T. May. In the preface to Woolley's *As I Seem to Remember* (1962), N. Teulon Porter reported that he too had worked at Corbridge: 'We first met as fellow navvies, but under different foreman ... It was his very first dig (=1906) and being Victorians, we were still living and working in an era of pick and shovel technique and would today have been dubbed "Potato Diggers" ..he became known at Corbridge as "The Gent" while I, having fallen into a dirty ditch on my arrival, was "Mucky Lad" and "Mucky" for short.' Teulon Porter (*c*.1884–*c*.1958) was probably originally a Cambridge student. He was a friend of Cyril Fox, who with Teulon Porter and others formed, in Teulon Porter's front room in Shaftesbury, Dorset, what was

In later years, along with their involvement in the management of the excavations, following a process of 'trial and error', in the refined format, other Haverfield 'students' were encouraged to go to Corbridge where, in either their first or second years they would be given responsibility for a particular aspect of the season's report. Bosanquet (1920: 139) described the arrangement as one where Corbridge furnished the 'pupils' with material which they worked up, under Haverfield's eye, over the winter. For example, Craster was on the first Corbridge season and by 1908 was contributing to the coin reports and later helping Simpson (1913). And, as was summarized in Chapter 7, various other 'students' were used to process the site's assemblage of *sigillata* in anticipation of Haverfield's plans to work up a definitive catalogue of the British material. For in addition to his strictures about the training of university students as field workers and the excavation supervisors, we have seen how Haverfield frequently berated the poor quality of cataloguing of the various categories of archaeological data.

From Corbridge some of its staff moved, perhaps encouraged so, to other sites. Cheesman subsequently worked at Ribchester in 1908, while Atkinson was there in 1913/4 (along with W.B. Anderson, Professor of Imperial Latin at the Victoria University, Manchester) and 1920–1 (cf. Hopkinson 1911). Corbridge students and others were employed at Bushe-Fox's excavations at Wroxeter (1912 – Atkinson, Cheesman; in 1913 – R. Smith, Atkinson, H. Mattingly, and F.N. Pryce, whilst 'the Universities are using the site as a training ground for archaeologists. Four students from Cambridge, three from Oxford, one from London and one from Birmingham' (Bushe-Fox 1914: 2) – a development for which Haverfield, as a member of the excavation

---

to become the Vernacular Architecture Group in 1952. He appears as a member of the Cambridge Antiquarian Society from 1914 (ceasing in 1935–6). He and his wife oversaw War Office diggings in the coprolite beds around Grantchester (Cambs.) on behalf of their Society between 1917–18 (*Proc Cambridge Antiq Soc* XXII (1917–18: 124–6) before Cyril Fox took over the responsibility. Mrs Teulon Porter subsequently opened trenches for Fox when he was excavating in The Fen in early 1921 (*Proc Cambridge Antiq Soc* XVIII (1921–2): 26; cf. Scott-Fox 2002: 34f.; Grimes 1967). Teulon Porter moved to Shaftesbury where he founded the local history society and its museum. 'He had unlimited enthusiasm and the gift of imparting it to others, an immense amount of uncoordinated knowledge and no power of organisation' (de Zouche Hall 1974: 4).

committee must have been instrumental; 1914 Atkinson, Smith: Bushe-Fox 1913a; 1914; 1916).[72] After gaining experience at Corbridge in at least 1908 and 1910, Stevenson (along with another potential Haverfield student, but one without any certain association with Corbridge, Stueart Miller) went on to run their own excavations at Cappuck. This arrangement for the training of students culminated with Collingwood, after an introductory season at Corbridge in 1911, assuming responsibility for Haverfield's excavations at Ambleside in June 1913 (Haverfield and Collingwood 1914). At the September 1913 dedication of Queen Adelaide's Hill, Ambleside, to the National Trust, Haverfield spoke at Borran Hill on the location of the Ambleside fort, while Collingwood summarized the results of his excavations (*The Times* 12 September 1913). Haverfield later delegated Collingwood to explore a number of other fort sites.

Other 'associates' and informants

The discussion so far has concentrated on Haverfield's Oxford links. But the form and strength of his group of co-workers was not restricted to 'Oxford men' or students from other universities. It is clear that he knew most, if not all, the leading non-Oxford and other non-University practioners of the day in a variety of capacities. This could be as the reporter of ongoing work from the 1890s, as a member of their excavation committees or ultimately as the leading figure in the field of Romano-British archaeology. For great as his reputation was as the synthesizer of the evidence for the Roman period, Haverfield could not have been able to do this without the considerable help that he received from a network of correspondents and friends around the

---

72. Wheeler reports that '...of five university students who worked together in the Wroxeter excavations of 1913, only one survived the war. It so happened that the survivor was myself' (1956: 60–1). One of those who might have died is the otherwise unknown N. La Touche (present in 1913 and 1914). There was a Geoffrey George Digge La Touche at Trinity, Cambridge in 1910) and the Roman Society pre-War members lists a C.D. La Touche at a Dublin address. The La Touches were an established Dublin family with links with the Church. Wheeler was at Wroxeter as the Franks student and was 'sent' by C.H. Read. At Read's instigation, the studentship was created in memory of Sir A. W(ollaston) Franks, a former president of the London Antiquaries and Keeper of Antiquities in the British Museum and was attached to University College, London. Wheeler was to be supported for research on Romano-British pottery. Franks had previously assisted in the compilation of Haverfield contribution to the *Ephemeris Epigraphica* (see above Ch. 4).

country (Bosanquet 1920: 140–1). On current evidence, it is difficult to disentangle how Haverfield made their individual acquaintances, but we have seen that the foundations of the network were laid in the 1880s when he:

> ...spent his holidays in visiting British and continental museums, thus he established ties with local societies at Chester, Carlisle, Newcastle, Glasgow and elsewhere ...For some of them he drew up detailed catalogues of their inscriptions ...By papers read at their meetings or contributed to their proceedings, by correspondence with curators, collectors and excavators he kindled a new interest in Roman Britain remains which had been gathering strength since then... His reputation was well established when in 1891 he was recalled to Oxford (Bosanquet 1920: 135; cf. Craster 1920: 65).

Throughout his career Haverfield was a keen visitor to the excavations of others, visits which often caused panic amongst the hosts (e.g. Macdonald and Park 1906; Wheeler 1961). Then there were his periodic visits to the museums in the provinces as well as his association with organizations such as the Royal Commission on Historical Monuments in 1908 and his seat on the Board of Ancient Monuments in 1914.[73] And we have seen how Haverfield was a regular attender, participant and speaker at meetings of the London Society of Antiquaries, where he was elected a Fellow in 1891. Such appointments not only afforded an unparalleled knowledge of recent developments, but also gave him innumerable opportunities to publish interim reports on recent work and new data (e.g. 1914a; 1915a; the numerous letters to newspapers and his public lectures: cf. Macdonald 1924: 40–57). Representative of the extent of his circle of contacts, the list of acknowledgements in his 1914 statement on *Roman Britain in 1913* notes Bruton, Miller, Simpson, the professors Newstead and Elliott at Chester, Arthur

---

73. 'A multitude of articles in many periodicals, each of them succinct and directly to the point, made his name a household word to students at home and abroad. Local correspondents flooded him with letters ...Lest he should miss anything of note, he joined innumerable societies and read their publications. Nor was all this enough. Between terms his chosen recreations were the carrying out of personal examinations of Roman sites, and the scrutinizing of Roman remains in museums and private collections'; '...as one of his friends has said, he was for many years "the clearing house for Roman Britain." Every discovery was reported to him directly or indirectly and everything of moment was scrupulously recorded' (Macdonald 1919–20a: 481 and 484; cf. 1924: 23 and 24; Carmichael 1919–20).

Acton, Hugh Evelyn White, John Ward and F.N. Pryce (Haverfield 1914a). There were those Oxford students who went on to direct their own excavations (e.g. Ashby at Caerwent, Atkinson at Ribchester and elsewhere) and who more importantly brought other connections. Others were Oxford contemporaries who went into other vocations but retained an interest in archaeology (e.g. Booker). In a similar fashion, such was the nature of the work he 'championed', notably at Corbridge, Haverfield invariably came into contact with graduates and students of other universities. Of the Corbridge season of 1910, along with the Oxford representatives, Haverfield (1911i: 478) said he knew of at least one schoolmaster who had served there who was now doing good work in his own area. Other fieldworkers, being of a comparable age to Haverfield must have made contact through other means: as contemporaries at university or in subsequent years, as his reputation grew. And there were those individuals not holding university posts, but who were established as researchers at the regional level, including the likes of F.A. Bruton, Bushe Fox and Simpson. Then there was a group of other less well-known Roman workers, including Willoughby Gardner in north Wales, Heywood Sumner and the Cunningtons in the south-west.[74]

Haverfield's network of informants was extensive and in being so provided him with comprehensive coverage of on-going work throughout the country. He relied upon them from the early 1890s for his quarterly statements in *The Antiquary* and *The Athenaeum*. When we look a little more closely at what he said in such reports, what is note-

---

74. An example of such a local antiquary was R.H. Walters who reported on his antiquarian fieldwork at a Roman site near Stoke-near-Ham (Somerset; Walters 1907). Richard Hensleigh Walters (d. 1924) was a noted Somerset antiquarian best known for his family's collection of artifacts retrieved from the quarrying of the Iron Age hillfort and Roman site at Ham Hill. In the 1907 *Proceedings* of the Somerset Society, Walters reported his work in and around the vicinity of Stoke-under-Ham, but without making any mention of Haverfield. On 23 July 1918, at the meeting where Haverfield was elected President of the Somerset Society, and in part to commemorate the occasion, Walters gifted his collection of Ham Hill artifacts to the Society. Walters was lavishly thanked for his generosity, which included a gracious acknowledgement from the chair by Haverfield, although one suspects he did not really know him. Walters was elected an FSA in 1918 (obit. St George Gray 1925). In the *VCH* Somerset (1906: 295) Haverfield mentions, in the context of Ham Hill, the work of the late W.W. Walters of Stoke-under-Ham, the father of R.H. Walters.

worthy is that he rarely credited individuals with the information. When and where he did acknowledge them, they were usually personal associates or else connected with Oxford. Nor was he above assuming responsibility for reporting recent results if he thought that individuals were not up to the task.[75] That said, a major feature in the assessments of Haverfield's career is the sense of loyalty shown to him from workers in the provinces. This fact is reflected in the number of obituaries that were published in regional journals. It is interesting to speculate on why this should have been so, as his personality would have made it difficult for him to get on with such persons automatically. The devotion may have been due in part to the fact that as the 'great man', he was prepared to visit them and to take an interest in what they were doing. This sense of *auctoritas* helped him to dominate the situation. Even James Curle in his review of Atkinson's *Lowbury Hill*, to which Haverfield had contributed, could not conclude without adding:

> Professor Haverfield in his introduction to the volume has well emphasised the undesirability of excavation undertaken by workers without adequate training. The progress of our knowledge of the Roman Empire during the last years has been rapid, and a higher standard of results is to be looked for. That such is the case is in no small measure due to the stimulus and encouragement which Professor Haverfield

---

75. 'Sometimes after a personal visit, he would publish an account of a notable find, more especially if it were an inscription. But he was always ready to leave the task to others, *if he was reasonably satisfied of their competence*' (Macdonald 1919–20a: 481 and 484; cf. 1924: 23 and 24; Carmichael 1919–20). In Easter 1905, Haverfield was writing to Lord Abercromby, mentioning that James Curle had taken him to Newstead, where the excavations had just begun (13 February 1905; *Edinburgh University Library Special Collection, Lord Abercromby 136*). 'It promises to prove an interesting site – a fort considerably larger than the average, and just possibly some traces of two periods. But the job is not very easy, and I ventured to suggest to both Dr. Christison and Mr. Curle that it was rather too hard for Mackie by himself – one might put it stronger but that is perhaps enough.' Alexander Mackie (d. 1926) was the Scottish Society's Clerk of Works. He had previously supervised its work at Birrenswark, Camelon, Lyne and Inchtuhil (1901). He also excavated, with James Marr, at Castle Law fort (Abernethy) as well as the native forts of the Poltalloch estate. That Curle acknowledged Mackie's experience and 'valuable service in working out the problems of the site. He stuck to his post undeterred by weather, and by shrewd observation contributed in no small measure to the success of the understanding' (Curle 1911: xvii) shows that he ignored the advice.

himself has given in the conduct of so much of the archaeological work of recent years (*J Roman Stud* VI (1916) 269).

Perhaps more important in his relationship with the societies is the fact that Haverfield championed a message which was attractive to a new generation of workers who were beginning to dominate the regional societies. But in his contact with the societies, Haverfield still had firm opinions as to what should be their part in the progress of Romano-British archaeology.

The origins and nature of the individual relationships are difficult to establish, so what follows is likely to be only a few of those contacts.[76] Some of them have already been noted (e.g. Mill Stephenson and George Fox). Many of them are more than likely to have been friends of Haverfield, nevertheless in some instances there are signs of a tetchy relationship with others. The nature of the relationships can be gauged by his otherwise neutral acknowledgements for information they might have provided him. In other situations he seems to have been prone to falling out with them, as shown by critical reviews or other negative criticisms in the same sort of reports. We have seen how he variously fell out with or harboured reservations against the likes of Simpson, Grundy, and Miller etc. Another contact was John Ward, who in particular, relied on Haverfield to broadcast and support the excavations at the Roman fort of Gellygaer in south Wales. However in his *Roman Britain in 1913*, Haverfield acknowledged receipt of information about the site from a J.W. Rodge (Haverfield 1914a: 18). Had Haverfield also fallen out with Ward?[77] But there again, there are

76. A good example of an individual with whom Haverfield must have been in contact but for which the records are deficient is Harold John Edward Peake (1867–1946). Peake was an anthropologist and archaeologist of independent means who also held a number of national and local offices (a VP of the Royal Anthropological Institute, and its president 1926–8, a member of council of the Society of Antiquaries (1928–30), president of the Newbury and District Field Club (and Honorary Curator of Newbury Museum), as well as chairman of governors of Newbury Grammar School etc.) which permitted him to indulge in his interests in archaeology, antiquarianism and anthropology. He did his own excavations, largely on prehistoric sites. A prolific writer (e.g. *The Corridors of Time* series (1927–56) with H.J. Fleure), he was especially expert on Berkshire (*The Archaeology of Berkshire* (1931). He is not to be confused with A.E. Peake who Taylor (*VCH* Oxon. I: 330) says advised about the villa at Asthall on Akeman Street (cf. *J Roman Stud* XII (1922): 254–5; Kendrick and Hawkes 1932). This Peake was another antiquarian with interest mainly in prehistory, where he best known for his work at Grimes Cave.

77. Ward (1856–1922) was appointed in 1893 Curator of Cardiff Museum (when he was elected a FSA) and later, from 1912, the first Curator of the National

also indications that such breakdowns could be temporary and relations later be restored.

The range of Haverfield's contacts extended from the great and the good to the more ordinary. An example of somebody at the top end of the social scale was John Abercromby, the 7th Lord Abercromby (1841–1924). Following a brief army career, from 1860 Abercromby developed antiquarian interests, especially in language. He became a fellow of the Scottish society 1879, a VP in 1897, its secretary between 1901 and 1905 and its president 1913–18. Not only did Abercromby personally fund much excavation in Scotland, he published numerous articles in the society's proceedings, including on the chronology of Beaker vessels and on cinerary urns. To be sure his major work of scholarship was *Bronze Age Pottery of Great Britain and Ireland* (1912), the first attempt to arrange chronologically such pottery by types. While Haverfield was writing to Abercromby about aspects of prehistoric pottery and to offer his regrets when the latter resigned as president, Abercromby also discoursed in 1902 on the society's excavations at Inchtuthil in 1901, noting a disagreement about the site's location which might have included Haverfield's opinions (cf. Abercromby 1901–02).

Museum of Wales. He was awarded an Honorary MA in 1917 by the University of Wales in recognition of his services to archaeology. Gellygaer was 'the site of the first full-scale excavations of a Roman fort in Wales' (Randall 1946: 98), lasting 1899 to 1913. The author of a highly regarded text book on Roman Britain (cf. Ch. 9), he also produced an overview of Romano-British buildings (Ward 1911a and 1911b). Ward has been described as '...the formidable and cantankerous curator' (Scott-Fox 2002: 61) and '...a gruff, self-educated but competent archaeologist with a thorough knowledge of Roman Britain as is evidenced by his two volumes in Methuen's Antiquities Books' (Randall 1946: 98). In the light of their personalities, it would be interesting to know how Ward and Haverfield got on. Significantly, I have found no substantial obituary of Ward. Of the excavations at Gellygaer, 'Ward recorded the mistakes that the excavators had committed and learnt to avoid. The main cause of error was that the excavation was superintended by members of the committee working on a rota with inevitable differences of knowledge, method and competence. The result was a loss of record of important detail and lack of unity of command, for a committee can no more conduct an excavation than it can fight a battle. In all subsequent excavations, this basic error was avoided and the change of method was facilitated by the foundation of the National Museum of Wales, for it could provide the skilled commanders' (Randall 1946: 82).

A more ephemeral Haverfield connection is the elusive John George Neilson Clift, described from 1907 to 1914 as joint honorary secretary of the British Archaeological Association and who last appears in its list of members as Major (RE) in 1922. However, he seems to have been elected to its membership as late as 1914. Up to that year Clift was a regular contributor on antiquarian subjects to the association's journal.[78] Intriguingly, before he disappeared from the BAA's list of members, he gave as his forwarding address a variety of London and Home Counties addresses. There is an interesting reference to Clift in a letter from Winifred Haverfield to Taylor in which she wrote: 'He (Haverfield) has never forgotten Mr. Clift – in fact it is unlikely that that young man will appear again, I should think. I suppose that you heard of that episode?' (6 September 1911; Haverfield Archive). Whatever Mrs Haverfield may have prophesied, Clift appears in a report of the 1912 season and where Haverfield speaks of his plans and description of a building there (Haverfield 1913f: 153). Clift's connection with the excavation must lie with one of the two principal field directors there, William Knowles, who was a VP of the BAA (1911–22). Later on, Clift participated in Bushe-Fox's excavations at Richborough (1922–3; Bushe-Fox 1926: 1). Clift's position with the BAA also afforded him the office of Commissioner with the RCHM(E). He was appointed in 1913, Haverfield in 1908. In the same 1920 *Annual Report of the Earthworks Committee* of the Congress of Archaeological Societies which recorded Haverfield's death, it is reported that 'a further loss (is) owing to the resignation of Mr J.G.N. Clift, a member since 1909, on account of ill health due to active service, which will oblige him to reside abroad for some years ...the loss, it is hoped only for a time, of Mr Clift's services will be much felt owing to the active interest he has taken in the Committee's work' (p. 6). Clift was well enough to rejoin the committee in 1922 and continued to serve down 1930 when he, along with others, was stood down when the committee was replaced by a research committee. What happened to him after 1931 is not known.

Another contact was Thomas May (1842–1931), a prodigious excavator and researcher, who was widely acknowledged to be Bushe-Fox's

---

78. Despite his association with the BAA, Clift was also from 1912 a member of its 'rival' organization, the RAI, as was his fellow Corbridge worker, R.H. Forster (a member since 1909).

mentor.[79] He is best remembered for his excavations in and around Warrington at Wilderspool (1895–1905; cf. May 1904) and Ribchester (1906–08) and at an advanced aged and under difficult circumstances at Templeborough in 1916 and latterly Strafford-on-Avon (May 1922; Simpson 1976). He was a pottery assistant to Bushe-Fox and a co-worker at his excavations at Richborough, Wroxeter, Hengistbury Head, Ospringe, and Swarling. He wrote catalogues of the 1890–1909 pottery excavated from Silchester in Reading Museum (May 1916) as well as for the Colchester, Carlisle (May and Hope 1917) and York collections. Although he did not publish the Templeborough coarse ware pottery, the task was completed by Grace Simpson (1976: 84) who wrote that as a ceramicist May was the equal of James Curle, Frank Simpson and Philip Newbold, even if Anderson (1984: 27–8) is slightly more cautious in her assessment of his qualities. How May interacted with Haverfield is unclear. The two clearly knew one another and on occasion worked together. Haverfield appears to have visited the Wilderspool excavation before the end of November 1899 (cf. *The Antiquary* 1899, Report xxx). And yet in at least his interim reports for the same excavations in the first decade of the new century, May makes no reference to Haverfield. It is also possible May served at Corbridge. He, with Donald Atkinson, worked on the Tullie House Carlisle pottery, as Haverfield acknowledged (Haverfield 1917: 237). Wheeler (1955) linked Bushe-Fox's interest in Romano-British pottery with Corbridge and implies that he was inspired there by May. If so, the year is uncertain. Bushe-Fox was there 1908, 1910 (when he provided his first ceramics report), 1911 and 1914. In its second season of excavation (1908), May worked at Ribchester with J.J. Phelps and Cheesman. As already noted, Haverfield is also credited with superintending at Ribchester in the same year (*The Manchester Guardian* 4 May 1908). May and Cheesman wrote up the site with the latter treating on the site's garrison and the inscriptions. In his history of the excavations at Ribchester, B.J.N. Edwards has shown how Haverfield pulled rank and changed the plans of the site's *principia* May produced in 1911 to fit his own expectations. 'This change can be traced back to a piece of intellectual chicanery, for in Haverfield's *Roman Britain in 1914*, the principia is

---

79. Born in Cambridge but educated in Edinburgh, May was a fellow of the Education Institute of Scotland. He was also an Inspector of Inland Revenue to Warrington until his retirement in 1903. He became an FSA in 1916 and received an honorary degree from Manchester University in 1919 (obit. *Antiqs J* 12 (1932): 352).

...pruned' (Edwards 2000: 32). While it transpired that Haverfield's alteration of the plan was to be vindicated, May's original account was dismissed as 'incorrect' although he had merely hypothesized about the plan rather than having presented it as fact. The damage in relations between the two, if there was any, was later sorted out. On 15 September 1915 Haverfield performed the opening ceremony of the Ribchester Museum an occasion which coincided with a visit to the site by the archaeological section of the BAAS then meeting at Manchester.

In terms of scholarship Haverfield's successor is widely recognized as R.G. Collingwood, but this misses the contribution of (Sir) George Macdonald. Indeed, what Macdonald did was to make the results of his and other labours in Scotland readily available to Haverfield who then used them in his own better-known works (Richmond 1941: 180). Later on he became Haverfield's literary executor and was responsible for continuing the British Academy reports on recent progress in Romano-British studies he had started (Macdonald 1929/30).[80] Although he never produced the kind of overviews that made Haverfield's reputation nationally, Macdonald published a number of important books and articles on aspects of Roman Britain. He therefore merits closer examination.

George Macdonald, born at Elgin in 1862, was the son of a schoolmaster and noted local antiquarian and archaeologist William Macdonald with whom Haverfield worked on the publication of the Latin inscriptions in the Hunterian Museum at Glasgow University (Keppie 1998a). Educated at Ayr Academy, Macdonald junior went on to Edinburgh University in 1878. Graduating in Classics in 1882 with a first class honours (MA) degree and after winning awards for study in Germany, Italy and Greece, he proceeded to Balliol in 1884 where he took a first (1887). After Oxford he was appointed a master at

---

80. For instance, 'Collingwood on whom (Haverfield's) mantle fell ...dominated Romano-British studies in the 20s and 30s and because he could write English like an angel his views had an astonishing influence' (Frere 1988: 1). Although '...Macdonald made no claim to expert knowledge in epigraphy, something of Haverfield's mantle fell upon his shoulders' (Curle 1939–40: 128); '...on (Haverfield's) passing, the mantle fell upon Macdonald, who with truly Roman pietas, recognised that one of his first duties was to see that the massive expressions of Haverfield's exceptional powers of restrained synthesis ...was not lost' (Richmond 1941: 181). '...I must mention the names of three great scholars who placed the study of Roman Britain on a scientific basis, F. Haverfield, Sir G. Macdonald and R.G. Collingwood' (Charlesworth 1949: 83).

Kelvinside Academy, Glasgow where, in 1892, he was made assistant in Greek at Glasgow University when Gilbert Murray, then Professor of Greek, requested leave of absence due to illness.[81] Through a combination of teaching courses in Greek history and the work he had undertaken on behalf of the university's Hunterian Museum in 1903, following a reorganization of the museum, Macdonald was appointed Curator of 'Coins, Pictures, Prints, Books, Manuscripts and other objects of artistic or archaeological value' for the next five years. At the same time he was also made the University's first Lecturer in Classical Archaeology, when he proposed to offer a course for Candlemass term 1902–03 on *The Early History and Art of Sicily and Magna Graecia*.[82] In what must have been embarrassing circumstances for his patrons at the university, in 1904 he resigned both positions, transferring as Second assistant secretary in the Scottish Education Department, and becoming in 1922 its secretary, a post he occupied until his retirement in 1928. In his later years, with the honorary curatorship at the Hunterian he had held since 1905, he continued his antiquarian researches. It was Macdonald who replaced Haverfield as the second president of the Roman Society in 1920 (Richmond 1941).

Macdonald's interests lay in two fields. He was originally a numismatist with a special interest in Greek and Hellenistic coinage. Such work was presumably stimulated by his close proximity to the Hunterian collection, which he was heavily involved in cataloguing and publishing.[83]

---

81. In June 1899 Ramsay was writing to Mommsen enclosing a copy of a testimonial he had prepared on Macdonald's behalf. referring in large measure to Macdonald's *Catalogue of Greek Coins in the Hunterian Collection* (published between 1899 and 1905), in which he included, with permission, some observations made by Mommsen. The purpose of the reference is unclear but seems to have been for a lectureship in the university, for in October Ramsay reported that Macdonald had been unsuccessful. Ramsay's note adds that he did not know Macdonald (but respected his father's work) and emphasized the son's work as a Greek historian.

82. This post was, in part, to be paid for by a group of private donors. The lectureship was originally to be in Greek Archaeology but was changed to Classical (cf. *Glasgow University Minutes of Senate and Glasgow University Court Minute Book*). It was not filled after Macdonald's departure. For a reminiscence on Macdonald and in particular the way he came to dominate Scottish archaeology in the 1920s and 1930s, cf. Graham 1981.

83. E.g. 1899–1905; 1911 and numerous contributions to the likes of the *Numismatic Chronicle* as well the *Proceedings of the Society of Antiquaries of Scotland* and the *Journal of Roman Studies*. A list of Macdonald's publications was published in the *Journal of Roman Studies* XXII (1932): 3–8 and updated after his

Out of this grew an interest in Roman coins, and especially those from Scotland and northern England and to a concern with the location of their find spots and so the Roman presence in Scotland. This naturally enough meant a preoccupation with military sites and in particular with the function of the best known Roman military installation in Scotland, the Antonine Wall. Out of a number of articles reporting fieldwork, excavation and works of synthesis brought together as his Dalrymple Lectures in 1910 came *The Roman Wall in Scotland* (published in 1911 and revised 1934). How Haverfield made the younger Macdonald's acquaintance is a source of confusion.[84] Other than Haverfield taking a close interest in Macdonald's other fieldwork (e.g. at Bar Hill in 1903, cf. Keppie 2002: 31), the pair eventually worked together in what was described as Haverfield's 'flying column' in July 1913 on the fort as Ythan Wells, Aberdeenshire (cf. *The Times* 10 December 1913) and in 1914–15 at Raedykes.[85]

---

death by J.G.C. Anderson (cf. *J Roman Stud* XXX (1940): 129–32.

84. According to Alexander Curle, it was his father's (Macdonald's) excavations at Birrens from 1895 which indirectly brought the younger Macdonald '...into contact with Francis Haverfield who was to become to later years, a close friend as a fellow worker in the study of Roman Britain' (1941: 441). Elsewhere James Curle attributed, wrongly, their meeting to 1912 when Macdonald was 'invited by the Treasury to report ...on an important find of gold coins discovered in the course of excavations at Corbridge' (1939–40: 126: cf. Macdonald 1912). This is in spite of Taylor setting out in a letter to Curle that she believed the two were meeting in Oxford as far back as 1900 and corresponding as early as the mid-1890s. Contact must surely have been established through Macdonald's father in at least the 1890s when Haverfield assisted in the preparation of the first full account of the Roman inscriptions in the Hunterian Museum (Keppie 1998a: 42). A letter from Haverfield to Macdonald, dated 12 July 1893, discusses v. Sarwey's recent tour. Haverfield also thanked Macdonald for receipt of two 'papers' (one on Burghead Church, the other on Ptolemy's *Geography; Edinburgh University Library Special Collection*). At present, with its reasonably impersonal tone, this is the earliest contact between the two.

85. Macdonald's other fieldwork included the 1902–05 excavations at Bar Hill (Macdonald and Park 1906; Keppie 2002); in 1914 leading work at Raedykes (although Macdonald 1929/1930: 36 says he was also there in 1916), 1923–8 with A.O. Curle at Mumrills; 1932 at Westerwood and 1920, '31 and '35 at Croy Hill. Haverfield and Macdonald's first joint publication was a short piece on Greek coins in Exeter (*NC* VII. 1907). Of Macdonald's (and Park's) 1906 report of the Bar Hill excavations, Haverfield noting his own involvement, still lauded 'I am convinced of both the special value of

Another professional academic who was a significant Haverfield associate was Robert Carr Bosanquet (1871–1935; cf. Hughes 1935), a graduate of Trinity College, Cambridge who held a studentship at the British School in Athens (1892) and a Craven travelling studentship in 1895–7. How and when Bosanquet came into contact with Haverfield again is not known. The posthumous publication of some of Bosanquet's letters by his widow is uninformative (Bosanquet 1938). The only allusions to Haverfield in this collection are when Bosanquet attended a lecture at the Society of Antiquaries (London) in May 1899 at which Haverfield reported progress at Silchester. Their association has to go back to Haverfield's work around Hadrian's Wall, where Bosanquet was born and later farmed. After conducting excavations at Housesteads in 1898 on behalf of the Newcastle society (which provided an outlet for Haverfield during certain years of the CEC), Bosanquet became assistant director (1899) then director (1900) of the school at Athens, in succession to David Hogarth. He was Professor of Classical Archaeology at the University of Liverpool from 1906 to 1920 and from 1907 chair of the Institute's Excavation and Research in Wales and the Marches Committee.[86] In 1908 Bosanquet was appointed a commissioner for the Royal Commission for the Ancient and Historical Monuments of Wales and Monmouthshire (RCAHM(W)). He retired prematurely in 1914 in order to farm his family's estate. Bosanquet was widely commended by Haverfield and others for his university's work in Wales and the Marches. This involved excavations at Caersws (1908 and 1909), Caerleon (1908) Gaer Noddfa (autumn 1909, ?Carno, both for the RCAHM(W) Monmouthshire), Parc-y-meirch, near Abergele (1912) and Castell Collen (1913). One of his duties as a commissioner was to tour the principality as part of the process of recording and describing its remains. Normally the entries for the commission's inventories were written by its Secretary but in a number of cases Bosanquet contributed descriptions of certain Roman sites (eg. Castell Collen, The Gaer (Clyro), The Gaer (Newchurch, all RCAHM(W)

the Barrhill [sic] excavations and of the great merits of Mr. Macdonald's account' (*Class Rev* (1907): 119). Also in Scotland, Haverfield must have been aware of the noted Glasgow solicitor and antiquarian, David Murray (1842–1928). The two certainly corresponded and they shared some mutual interests, not least with Murray a strong advocate for the better preservation, protection and cataloguing of the nations antiquities (Murray 1896; 1904).
86. Bosanquet married, in 1902, Thomas Hodgkin's eldest daughter (Ellen). Haverfield's relationship with Hodgkin is noted below.

Radnorshire (1913), Dolaucothi (RCAHM(W) Carmathenshire (1917), Caergai, Cefn-Caer (= Pennal) and Tomen y Mur (all RCAHM(W) Merioneth (1921)). It appears that Haverfield accompanied Bosanquet on some of these tours.[87] Many of these entries refer to Haverfield's overview of the Roman military presence in Wales (Haverfield 1910b), which had involved him making a number of visits to the region. In 1909 the pair obtained permission to clear some watercourses and a reservoir at the site of Dolaucothi (Bosanquet; cf. RCAHM(W) Carmathens. (1917): 28 and written up by Haverfield (Haverfield 1909b: 14 which 'is virtually identical with Bosanquet's account'; Lewis and Jones 1969: 247 n. 1).

As Macdonald was Haverfield's principal correspondent for developments in Scotland and Bosanquet was his contact and companion for work in at least parts of Wales, so F.A. Bruton filled the same capacity in the Manchester and western Pennines region. Francis Archibald Bruton MA (1861–1930) is another Romano-British antiquary who is likely to have been at Oxford at about the time Haverfield was a student. They remained friendly correspondents down to Haverfield's demise. Indeed he knew Haverfield sufficiently well to be writing to him shortly before the latter's death and was to provide an obituary about him (Bruton 1919). Bruton was a renowned field naturalist as well as an archaeologist with strong links with Manchester University while at one time an assistant master at Manchester Grammar School. He was also intimately involved with the work of the Manchester and District branch of the Classical Association, which in addition to undertaking its own work in the city, had previously worked at Melandra (1905) and later on at Toothill (1913+; Conway 1906). Elsewhere its members were also involved in the excavations at Castleshaw and Ribchester (1914; Atkinson 1928). Bruton edited the branch's reports of its excavations on the Roman fort at Manchester (Bruton 1909a). Before this he had been the honorary secretary of the committee for the excavation of Melandra Castle and Toothill (Conway 1906; Bruton 1909b). He also undertook work at Castleshaw (in 1907 and which he wrote up for S. Andrews in 1908) and may have worked with Garstang at Ribchester in the same year. He also submitted the entries on Roman Britain to *The*

---

87. Bosanquet recorded his tours in the Annual Reports of the Liverpool Institute: Sept. 1909 inspecting sites in Radnors.; 1910–11 visits to Radnors. and Denbighs.; 1911–12 visiting Flints. and Radnors.; 1912–13 Denbighs. and Radnors.; 1913–14 Denbighs. and Merioneths.; 1914–15 Pembrokes. and Carmathenshire.

Year's Work in Classical Studies series from 1910 through to 1914 and then for 1916, 1918–19 and 1921–2. He worked with Bushe-Fox at Wroxeter and later edited Hall's *Caer Llugwy* (1923). Last but not least, he wrote a *History of Lancashire* (1921).

The committee for the 1906–07 Manchester excavations was an impressive list of individuals, some of who appear at various times elsewhere in Haverfield's career.[88] He was certainly closely consulted on the progress at Manchester, being a frequent visitor to the excavations. In press cuttings reporting the progress and in appeals for subscriptions for more excavations, Bruton frequently used Haverfield's opinions as proof of the necessity and quality of the work undertaken (e.g. *The Manchester Guardian* 3 and 11 January, 25 June 1907). The work of the Manchester committee has been reassessed by Grace Simpson (1976). She reports that its work was partially flawed in so much as the excavators did not seem to have had the confidence to 'push' the evidence they had recovered. Whilst they consulted every noted archaeologist of the time for their opinion, the final report was unambitious in its interpretations. But such was the quality of the records in the 1907 report made by the committee, Simpson was able to re-date the Manchester fort. Of the Manchester staff, one individual might be highlighted. John Henry Hopkinson (d. 1951), once of Magdalen College, was a Craven fellow at Oxford in 1899–1900 and 1900–01. He was previously Lecturer in Greek at the University of Birmingham (1901–04) and was retained as Special Lecturer in Greek and Classical Archaeology when he moved to the University of Manchester as Lecturer in Classical Archaeology. After his ordination, he became Vicar of Colne and was also formerly principal of Hume Hall, Manchester and a schools inspector. As secretary of its excavation committee, he excavated at Ribchester, for which he wrote a report on the fort there (Hopkinson 1911). Haverfield was not entirely complimentary of the first report (*J Roman Stud* I (1911): 244) which brought a

---

88. James Tait (Professor of Ancient History, University of Manchester), Harold Williamson (sixth form master, Manchester Grammar School), H.L. Jones (headmaster at Willaston School, Cheshire – in a report to *The Times* (6 April 1907) Bruton wrote that Jones 'was for a number of years Mr T. Ashby's right-hand man in well-known and remarkably successful excavations at Caerwent', Miss Dora E. Limebeer, J. McInnes (senior lecturer in the university) and G.C. Brooke (of the Dept of Coins and Medallions, British Museum). Other contributors to the Manchester (and other reports) included Sir William Boyd Dawkins DSC, FRS, FSA (1838–1927); 1873–1908 Professor of Geology and Paleontology at the university (cf. Anon. 1928).

comment from the Manchester Committee and a riposte from Haverfield (*J Roman Stud* II (1912): 120). Hopkinson was also responsible for the second edition of the Ribchester pamphlet (1916) which in turn was updated in a third edition by Donald Atkinson in 1928.

There is one other Manchester antiquary and archaeologist with whom Haverfield was at one time in regular contact. Charles Roeder (?1848–1911) was a native of Gera in Thuringen, but a Manx scholar of some repute and the author of *Roman Manchester* (1900) in which is noted 'I have also to thank Professor Francis Haverfield for much help and information.' The pair had originally made contact as far back as 1889 when W.T. Arnold was writing to Roeder on Haverfield's behalf. On at least one occasion Haverfield cited Roeder as an authoritative informant (Haverfield 1899d: 12). Over the next few years Haverfield wrote either to thank him for letting him see material from the Manchester area or for answering specific questions about it. A number of Haverfield's letters are pasted into the copy of Roeder's *Manchester* held in Manchester Public Library and which often contain *marginalia* and comments disputing points of opinion in the text. Significant features which emerge from their correspondence are Haverfield opinionating on the dates of samian ware and of aspects on the Brigantes. Other than a letter of thanks from Haverfield for a presentation copy of Roeder's book, the last two (surviving) letters between the two date to 1906 and, judging from their tone, imply a cooling of relations. Indeed the evidence suggests Roeder was as difficult a character as Haverfield, coming over as self-confident and arrogant and with time, defensive of the magnitude of his contribution to the study of Roman Manchester. For example, in a letter to *The Manchester Guardian* (16 December 1906) commenting on an article on the Roman town previously published in the newspaper, Roeder added: 'I alone am responsible and have been concerned in the practical investigation and conclusions of Roman Manchester in the past. Mr Phelp's particular share has been ...excavation of part of a bath complex.'

It would be interesting to know more of what Haverfield thought of the Manchester group: the branch of the Classical Association, along with Roeder and Bruton. In a lecture delivered at Manchester University in December 1907 on *The Roman Occupation of North-West England*, Haverfield said of the exploration of the Roman site that what had been achieved was largely due to Roeder and Bruton but '...there was perhaps not very much more to find and yet not very much could be said to be known of it'. Instead he urged the Manchester antiquaries make up for the destruction of the Roman fort and settlement at Manchester by focusing on the site around it (*The Manchester Guardian* 3 December

1907). But surely this was precisely what the local branch of the Classical Association had been doing in the early years of the new century?

Haverfield had access to a group of friends, associates and informants for the Hadrian's Wall region. We have seen, however, that in his part of the CEC and Corbridge excavations, he appears to have had, on occasion, difficulties with some local archaeologists and antiquarians there, perhaps as he was regarded as an outsider. Therefore the closeness of his circle of informants is harder to assess. Some of them he appears to have got on with. Notable among these was the patron of the CEC excavations, Chancellor R.S. Ferguson of Carlisle (1838–1900), an antiquarian with a broad range of interests (obit. *Archaeol J* 57 (1900): 170–3). As noted in Chapter 6, Haverfield evidently met John Clayton just before the latter's death (Blair 1919: 117). Clayton (1792–1890), a man of independent wealth, after a career in local government service retired to his estate at Chesters to continue his interest in local antiquities and to purchase sites on the Wall which became available (obit. *Archaeol Aeliana* X (1913): 182–5). Frank Simpson (1882–1955) played something of the same rôle with respect to passing on information in northern England. For some Simpson and, to a lesser degree, his mentor John Pattison Gibson (1838–1912), remain the unsung heroes of work on the Wall (Birley 1955; 1961: 65; Richmond 1956; *Nature* 6 November 1954: 860; Wilmott 2001). Gibson was a Hexham chemist by profession, with interests in photography which took him into recording the region's antiquities, and in particular its medieval churches as well as Hadrian's Wall (Anon. 1913). In time, following the deaths of Clayton and Collingwood Bruce, Gibson came to be recognized by the likes of Chancellor Ferguson as *the* local authority on the Wall. Indeed it has been claimed that he was the leading figure in the next twenty years in revitalizing mural studies, and was an individual central to the prevailing atmosphere of feud and controversy which thrived at the time. Gibson interacted with Haverfield in at least two ways. After his first attempt at excavation at Mucklebank Wall Turret in 1892, between 1894 and 1896, Gibson excavated at Great Chesters (Aesica) and where he was joined by Haverfield who was officially working for the CEC. In time Gibson was involved in a public spat with Haverfield over the date of the stone wall. In the past Gibson had maintained the Wall was Severan in date with the Vallum as Hadrianic. In time he changed his position, and recognized that the Wall was Hadrianic and the vallum, Severan. There is a synchronicity in this change of mind, for Haverfield had originally thought the Wall to be Hadrianic in date. At a lecture in 1906, however, he argued that the Wall was Severan and that what the CEC had found near Birdoswald represented the last vestiges of an earlier Hadrianic fortification (Haverfield

1906a; cf. Chapter 6). Of the debate it was said '...it admirably illustrated the peculiar service to archaeological science to be derived from minute local knowledge and special structural study when applied in criticism of more general academic history' (Neilson 1912: 42). How the disagreement between the two affected their future relations is unrecorded, although it was said that Gibson '...could show touches of archaeological feud' (Neilson 1912: 44). One wonders at the subsequent nature of Haverfield's relationship with Gibson (and Simpson). For example, when Gibson returned to excavation in 1907 (the first time since Great Chesters), at Haltwhistle with Simpson (who apparently paid for it), followed by Poltross in 1911 and High House near Birdoswald in 1911, Haverfield is conspicuous by his absence from the reports of these excavations although Craster and Bosanquet are credited (cf. Gibson and Simpson 1911; Jones 1987: 88–9 and Birley 1959 for an assessment of Gibson and Simpson).[89]

It has been recently re-argued that it was the method of systematic enquiry, which Simpson and Gibson employed, which Haverfield adopted

---

89. Haverfield's relationship with Simpson seems, superficially, to have been good, but as he was not part of the 'Oxford group' of contacts he was treated with suspicion. In January 1908 Craster was writing to Haverfield about arrangements for the publication of an interim report of the Corbridge excavations. In that letter Craster notes William Clayton (owner of the Chesters estate) '...has appointed F.G. Simpson to be warden of the Wall; a mysterious transaction suggesting tufa and paludan mertum [sic]. I understand however that he is to be a sort of archaeological land-agent with instructions to keep in repair the camps and so-much of the wall as are on the Clayton property. He is rather an ass, but the intention is a good one.' Something of the tension that the work in and around Hadrian's Wall at the turn of the century occasioned might be gauged from an (unpublished) letter from Winifred Haverfield to Taylor (6 September 1911): 'My Lord is a little disturbed because there is a vague sort of idea that Mr. Simpson has got "something up his sleeve". It is rumoured that all his Hadrianic excitement may be due to the fact that he got some evidence at Winshields milecastle which he has suppressed. It is all much more vague than it seems when one puts it in words, but my Lord is prepared to regard him and all his works with loathing if anything of the sort transpires' (p. 74 of the 1911 Report of Haverfield's own copy of the Corbridge Excavation Reports 1908–1914 and Northumbria and Scottish papers, Haverfield Archive). Mrs Haverfield must be referring to Simpson's excavations in the vicinity of MC50, where he clarified the Hadrianic date of the stone wall between MCs 49 and 51. The significance of the Poltross Burn excavations was discussed in Ch. 6.

and developed, even if the chronology is wrong (Browning 1989; Haverfield commenced work before the Gibson and Simpson alliance). The essence of Simpson's methodology was the selective use of excavation at locations chosen to maximize the amount of information that might be obtained, in terms of the quality and wider utility, to solve specific problems. The technique was applied at Haltwhistle Burn (1907–08), Poltross Burn (1909–10) and from 1911 along the Stone Wall (Richmond 1960: 174), before being used by others elsewhere (e.g. S.N. Miller at Balmuildy, 1912–13) and ultimately by Ian Richmond. Simpson's contribution to the teaching of archaeology at the University of Durham through the work of the University's Excavation Committee has already been discussed. The date of his first meeting with Haverfield, whilst now lost to the former's biographer, was no later than 1906 (Simpson 1976: 2). Of Simpson's work along the Wall between 1909 and 1912, Haverfield was to write: 'It is a matter for real regret that Mr. Simpson's work on the Wall has come to an end' (Haverfield 1914a: 39–40).

Simpson and Gibson were just two northern antiquarians with whom Haverfield interacted. Others have already been noted in the discussion of the work of the CEC. Thomas Hesketh Hodgson (1841–1917) was the sort of 'modern' antiquarian of which Haverfield approved (Haverfield 1917: 264). He was formerly a civil servant who retired to Cumberland to become involved in local affairs. In terms of archaeology, he worked with Haverfield and the CEC, where he and his wife served as illustrators and surveyors and he as an excavation supervisor. Superficially Haverfield and the Hodgsons appear to have got on well. However, how well is questionable. We have seen something of the tensions which existed between Mrs Hodgson and Haverfield with respect to the way he conducted the excavations of the CEC. And there were Mr Hodgson's comments in a 1900 lecture about Haverfield's part in the work of the CEC. Other Haverfield northern connections-cum-informants included Charles Henry Hunter Blair (1863–1962), one time secretary and president of the Newcastle society. Over the years, certainly in the 1890s, Blair was a major source of information for new inscriptions found in the north and frequently provided illustrations of the same for Haverfield's summaries. It is also clear there was a degree of familiarity between the two (Blair 1919: obit. Richmond 1963). Another close friend and confidant was James Curle (1862–1944), while at the same time Haverfield was also very friendly with Curle's brother, Alexander. James Curle was educated at Fettes College and Edinburgh University, becoming a solicitor by profession. A member of the RCHM, Curle is now best remembered as the excavator of the Roman fort at Newstead (1905–10), published as *A Roman Frontier Post and its People. The Fort at*

Newstead in the Parish of Melrose (1911).[90] How, why and when Haverfield made his acquaintance is now lost. It must lie with Haverfield's visits to Scotland in connection with the Society of Antiquaries of Scotland's turn-of-the-century excavations on and around the Antonine Wall. In the spring of 1905, soon after the excavations there had commenced, Haverfield, accompanied by Curle, visited Newstead and knew him sufficiently well to offer advice on the competence of his principal excavation supervisor. He continued to offer advice and support – and to commend its achievements – over the next few years (Gordon 2005). In December 1914 Haverfield was writing to Curle about a number of matters, including business related to the *Journal of Roman Studies*. What is interesting in this letter is that Haverfield writes of Macdonald having recently stayed with him at Oxford. In addition, he reports he had visited Wroxeter in September but was so '…tired I funked the long journey on, and came home again.' Haverfield was clearly not well, and his condition must have been that which Macdonald and Taylor discussed 25 years later and how the outbreak of the First World War depressed him. The visit to Wroxeter must also be the occasion of Wheeler's anecdote of the prospect of a Haverfield visit terrorizing Bushe-Fox. Curle possessed other skills. For instance, he compiled, at a distance, the pottery report for the 1906–07 excavations at Manchester, material at which Haverfield also looked (Bruton 1909a). He helped Macdonald in the compilation of the Haverfield bibliography (Macdonald 1918; 1924).

Finally, there is one other name from northern England who deserves mention. Whilst never explicitly stated as a close associate, Haverfield profited from knowing Thomas Hodgkin (1831–1913), a Northumbrian banker, antiquarian, stalwart of the Society of Antiquaries of Newcastle and an amateur historian of some note who was awarded a DCL by Oxford University in June 1886. Given what has already been said about Haverfield's career and his (European) contacts, Hodgkin might well be described as an important figure in his development. For instance, as early as *c.*1883, Hodgkin was lecturing on the results of German work on the Pfahlgraben, where the lectures 'principal value lay in its suggesting to northern antiquaries interested in the British frontier walls, that comparative method of dealing with discov-

---

90. The acknowledgements in the introduction to the report includes Capt. H.G. Lyons, R. Smith (British Museum), A.G. Wright (Coldstream Museum), A.O. Curle, H. Jacobi (of Saalburg Museum), E. Krüger (of Trier Museum) and Prof. Schumacher (of Mainz). The biggest thanks were offered to George Macdonald and Haverfield.

eries on either frontier' (Dendy 1913: 80; cf. Hodgkin 1883; Tout 1913–14). Haverfield was to compose (public) letters to Hodgkin about his own visits to the *limes* which were updates to Hodgkin's original essay (Haverfield 1893b; 1894c). Similarly in 1890 it was Hodgkin who made the initial suggestions for a new county history of Northumberland – a project with which Haverfield became intimately involved and was to spawn the excavations at Corbridge. However the contact was not entirely slavish. In 1887, Haverfield was taking Hodgkin to task on aspects of Roman Dacia (cf. Haverfield 1887).

In Haverfield's description of them, his northern contacts were, in many respects, in the tradition of late nineteenth century antiquarians. In the case of the individuals just discussed, Haverfield retained a generally positive, favourable opinion of their abilities. This is in contrast to his otherwise generally gloomy, albeit generalized, assessments of other workers from the region. We have already seen a few instances of those persons for whom he had mixed opinions. They include Watkins, Scarth, Harbin and Cadwallader Bates, most of who were of the generation of the first and second phases of Haverfield's career. Haverfield was more positive in his opinions of the works of Scarth and Harbin but less so of Bates, who, as we have seen, clashed with Haverfield during the 1895 season of the CEC. Twenty years after the CEC, at the AGM of the Somerset society, Haverfield praised Harbin and his work. In the published, tidied up, version of his lecture, Haverfield wrote that Harbin was:

> ...one of those local archaeologists who, though little accounted of by most modern historians in our Universities, do really deserve the title of 'scholar'. He was a relative of other not unknown men of his name – among them the late Cadwallader Bates of Northumberland, a brilliant if at times speculative historian (1919a: xxv).[91]

There is one other corps of expert wisdom upon which Haverfield was able to draw. As it became increasingly a centre of expert knowledge, Haverfield had recourse to the services of some of the staff of the British Museum. Reginald Allender Smith (1873–1940) was another regular 'specialist' contributor to projects with which he was involved. Educated

---

91. The Rev. E.H. Bates Harbin (1862–1919), educated at Edinburgh and Jesus College, Cambridge, with a BA in 1884 and a MA 1890, was ordained in 1889 and eventually came to minister in his home county. His particular interests, unsurprisingly, related to ecclesiastical issues and the medieval period (cf. Maxwell Lyte 1918). Haverfield also contributed an obituary to *The Times* on 24 September 1919.

at Christ's Hospital and University College, Oxford, in 1898 he was appointed Deputy and then (from 1928) Keeper of the Dept of British and Medieval Antiquities. His successor was (Sir) Thomas Kendrick (1895–1979), a late contemporary of Haverfield's. Kendrick went up to Oriel College (matriculating 1913), who after enlisting as a Lieutenant in the 2nd Warwickshire Regiment, transferred as a Captain to the Lancashire Fusiliers before being wounded in 1916. In 1918 he returned to Oxford to take the diploma in anthropology (and was still there in 1920) before joining the British Museum in 1922, becoming its Keeper of Medallions etc. in succession to Smith in 1938. Kendrick is now best remembered for his monographs on medieval antiquarianism in Britain (Kendrick 1950; 1971). Smith was a fellow candidate for the 1913 archaeological studentship, which effectively launched Wheeler's career (Wheeler 1956: 26). Some obituaries note that, for a time after the First War, Smith was the leading expert on later prehistoric, Roman and Saxon archaeology in the country, although he was rapidly superceded and became increasingly the representative of the old school of archaeological research. E.T. Leeds in his memoir of Smith described his (archaeological) interests as those of a generalist but with a preference for the Paleolithic and, perversely, the Dark Ages and the Anglo-Saxons. He contributed numerous sections on all these subjects to the *VCH*. Haverfield cited him as an informant for his sections in the *VCH* volumes. Leeds believed Smith's work was '...essentially thorough, and though at times dry and presented in a rather didactic manner, much of it reached a high standard' (Leeds 1940: 293).[92] Smith also worked with Bushe-Fox at Hengistbury Head (1911–12) and Wroxeter (1912–14).

Another member of the staff of the British Museum with whom Haverfield was familiar was the numismatist (Sir) George Francis Hill (1867–1948). As far back as 1890 he had praised Hill's article on Leicester in *The Antiquary*. Not only did the pair work together, but Hill was one of the two individuals (the other being James Curle) who assisted George Macdonald (and Margerie Taylor) compile a bibliography of Haverfield's publications (Macdonald 1918). Hill was educated at University School, UCL and University College, Oxford where he was an exhibitioner (and honorary fellow from 1931). In his final year at Oxford, Hill worked closely with Percy Gardner on aspects of Greek art, architecture and numismatics. With a double first (1891), Hill planned to stay on at Oxford but his failure to obtain a fellowship meant that in 1893 he joined the staff of the Dept of Coins and Medals in the British Museum, becoming assistant keeper in 1911 and keeper from 1912 to 1931. Hill entered '...the museum at a moment of great activity in Greek numismatics, when largely through the work of the keeper, Barclay V. Head, scholars had begun to realize how great a contribution this science could make to the study of the ancient world' (Robinson 1950; 1959). Hill became Director and Principal Librarian of the Museum (1931–6), succeeding Frederic Kenyon. Elected an FBA in 1917, editor of the *Journal of Hellenic Studies* between 1898 and 1912 and a Commissioner for the RCHME, Hill retained a wide range of interests and was a close friend of Charles Peers. His principal area of research was Greek and Hellenistic history through its coins. He is also described as one of the prime movers in establishing the Roman Society (cf. Allan 1949).

Conclusion

This chapter was prefaced with a statement taken from Aldhouse-Green and Webster's introduction to a set of essays offered as a *Festschrift*, dedicated to W.H. Manning to mark his retirement from the department at Cardiff. In some respects the sentiments expressed in that passage can apply as much to Haverfield. But in one particular sense they do not. We have spent time trying to disentangle the facts, as to whether or not it is legitimate to say that Haverfield consciously set out to create a group or school of students to continue his work in Romano-British studies. By extension we have also considered whether or not it is legitimate to say that his decline after 1915 was caused by the severe losses that 'group' suffered as a consequence of the war. In either respect, the conclusion has to be that he did not deliberately set out to create a 'group', indeed the conditions at Oxford were not conducive to one and, as it is, Haverfield was not temperamentally nor professionally inclined to do so. This opinion is complemented by the conclusions drawn in Chapter 6. Instead, it is better to say that he influenced certain students with a mode of instruction and a way of approaching (epigraphic) data which had a utility across the spectrum of classical antiquity. While he might have taken a professional pride in seeing how his teaching influenced such individuals, to describe them as a 'school' or a Haverfield 'group' is pushing the evidence. In fact the identification of the group was the invention of the generation that followed Haverfield – interestingly not by those of Haverfield's inner circle. Instead it was left to 'outsiders' to claim him as the teacher or mentor.

CHAPTER 9

Haverfield's reputation and influence

To write a good monograph on a Roman province requires qualities rarely found in conjunction: minute observation, in order to interpret correctly the details of local archaeology, and breadth of view to envisage the general conditions under which the Roman empire has developed. The excellence of Professor's Haverfield's study devoted to Roman Britain lies in the rare union of these two qualities (Cumont 1912: 113).

Professor Haverfield in Oxford, der einzige Gelehrte in England, der sich lebhaft um die einheimischen Altertümer kümmerte (Schuchhardt 1944: 231).

Introduction

Haverfield's death was sudden. He suffered a seizure late in the evening of 30 September and died within 30 minutes, expiring early the next day.[1] Although he had suffered a breakdown in late 1915 that was widely attributed to the stress brought on by the reported loss of Cheesman at Gallipoli, the seriousness of his condition was recognized at the time and a fact he was to acknowledge, still, some believed he had recovered by 1917. Macdonald recounted he was superficially in good health ('…physically and mentally …he was more like his old self than he had been for years') after returning from a tour of Cirencester and Hadrian's Wall. With hindsight and the benefit of the obituaries, however, it is clear his recovery was never totally effected. Blair (1919: 117) reported how, a few weeks before his death, Haverfield had been

---

1. There is some confusion as to the cause of death. It was variously described as 'a paralytic stroke' (R.G. Collingwood 1919: 118) and as angina pectoris (W.G. Collingwood 1920: 257). His funeral took place on 4 October. The mourners included Charles Oman, Sir Herbert Warren, Sir Paul Vinagroff, Gilbert Murray, the professors Margoluith, Stewart, Gardner, Geldorf, Grenfell, Thomson, Wright, Sherington and Messrs A.C. Clark, C.H. Firth and R.L. Poole.

at the Blackgate, Newcastle, looking at inscriptions which was presumably tied with the occasion when, in mid-August 1919, at Old Carlisle in Cumberland he had to return home feeling unwell (W.G. Collingwood 1920: 257). Bosanquet summed up the reality when he wrote that following Cheesman's death, Haverfield '...worked on but in 1916 [sic] a paralytic seizure was followed by a long illness from which he never wholly recovered' (Bosanquet 1920: 140).

Confirmation of the fact that post-1915 there was a decline in Haverfield's powers is reflected in his output of publications. Furthermore there was, after Corbridge, his retreat from fieldwork, being reduced to patronizing that of his societies and supporting the work of associates such as R.G. Collingwood in north-west England. The post-war years were also marked by him making a series of very public, but broadly negative, assessments of the progress of excavation in the UK and with it the provision of training and instruction in the discipline. As we will see, Haverfield repeated many of these reservations and complaints on a number of occasions and in different contexts (e.g. Haverfield 1920a). But still the situation failed to improve. No matter how much he pontificated on the situation or agreed to let his name be appended to appeal lists there was no substantial change in the situation. Following his death, the question is what happened to Romano-British studies?

In examining Haverfield's achievements, it is clear that for different writers they were different things. Macdonald eulogized the range of his interests: 'lexicography, pure scholarship, textual criticism, geography, even botany, art and medieval architecture, have their place alongside of ancient history, epigraphy and archaeology' (1918: 184–5). We have already seen how, for instance, he was regarded as the epigrapher *par excellence*. For Page it was '...as an epigrapher and student of Romano-British archaeology that he will be remembered' (1920: 250). For others, it was the breadth of his involvement in the subject that was significant. R.G. Collingwood described him as 'one of the greatest English antiquaries' (1919: 118). Elsewhere his part as the synthesizer of the archaeology of Roman Britain was noted. More specifically, for Bosanquet (1920: 141) it was the 'masterly' contributions to the *Victoria County History*, his accounts of Roman Wales and the chapter in the *Cambridge Medieval History*. In a characteristically provocative manner, Wheeler (1961) believed that Haverfield's place in scholarship lay with the chapters of the *VCH*, his contribution to *CIL* and *The Romanization of Roman Britain*. Elsewhere he was a field archaeologist, although there are those who have come to question this (cf. Chapter 6). Other obituarists highlighted other facets of his work. An unnamed writer in the *Geographical Review* wrote: 'Not only a learned archaeologist and historian, Haverfield was a keen and accurate thinker, an unusually gifted writer, and, of even more importance to us, a geographer at heart' (*Geog Rev* 15 (1925): 510), a fact repeated in another anonymously authored obituary in the *Geographical Journal* (1919: 395). Haverfield's former secretary and assistant Margerie Taylor believed that perhaps '...his greatest contribution to the study of archaeology and history was the encouragement he gave to it when he himself became Camden Professor of Ancient History, by interesting the younger members of the University, by training a school of Romano-British archaeologists and by promoting excavations in every part of Britain' (1920: 66). The establishment of a 'school' of Romano-British archaeologists was noted by Bosanquet (1920: 139) which others have tended to call the 'Oxford school' (e.g. Collingwood, Stuart Jones, Wheeler and Birley). Taylor later modified her opinion in a letter to Eric Birley, where she re-emphasized Haverfield's part as the instigator of collaborative research.

> Haverfield was never really a fieldworker or pretended to be; he was what you call an expounder, and his aim was always to bring together the Roman historian and archaeologist ...He it was who urged all his pupils to come up to the Wall. I think he thought that the various problems [of the date of Hadrian's Wall] could only be solved by excavation and that the running of an excavation was not his job, but the expounding of the results and getting people together and even raising money for them. That is, I think, why he was interested in Corbridge (6 February 1962, Haverfield Archive).

Of all the opinions expressed about Haverfield's work, this is the most balanced, not least because it benefits for being written 50 years after his death. As we have seen, he did employ a number of Oxford associates and the concern with developing a group as archaeologists ran parallel with his preoccupation in raising general standards of (archaeological in its general sense) work with respect to the study of the history of Roman Britain. In a number of public statements, Haverfield, in lamenting the previously generally poor quality of antiquarian accounts, used this as the vehicle to call for better standards in the investigation and interpretation (cf. 1911a; 1924: 59–88; Appendix 3). Such demands were typified by his contribution to *CIL* and the re-reading of a number of inscriptions which had been incorrectly published by Hübner. The experience also shaped the format of what was to become the *RIB*. Elsewhere Ramsay, in a review of Macdonald's *The Roman Wall in Scotland* (1911) wrote:

Dr. Macdonald's book is an excellent piece of work. Without impairing his credit, we may also reckon it as one of the many brilliant examples of the influence that professor Haverfield is exercising on the organisation and the right method of studying the history of Roman Britain. The author is by natural bent and by inheritance an enthusiastic and scientific archaeologist; but without the example and practical influence of the Oxford Professor it may be doubted whether he would have enjoyed the same advantages in the performance of his task. The school of British archaeology, of which Professor Haverfield is the centre, or at least the constant and trustworthy adviser, is doing a great deal of excellent work (1911: 177).

Work promised and projects uncompleted

At the time of his death it was widely lamented that Haverfield had not produced *the* major overview of Roman Britain that a man of his repute should have. His Oxford contemporary Charles Oman believed '...great learning that perished with the owner of it was really exasperating and useless... he could point to his life long friend and fellow Wykehamist Haverfield, as signal proof of his principle' (Robertson 1946: 302).[2] R.G. Collingwood (1919: 118) offered a more explicit regret: 'It is to be deplored that, owing to various causes – his early immersion in teaching and later the war, ...he has left no great work behind him. Two or three such works were planned and some actually begun; but they can never now see the light. His reputation with posterity will rest on a few monographs and numerous short papers.' Collingwood could not have anticipated that this deficiency would be partially resolved by the posthumous publication of Haverfield's *The Roman Occupation of Britain* in 1924.

With the unexpected circumstances of his death, it is no surprise that Haverfield left a number of projects in progress or planned or unfulfilled. The list is impressive. The problem is trying to disentangle what were realistic from those that had been on-going for some time, and others with little or no prospect of completion, or which were no more than flights of fancy. For Haverfield was a great one for flagging work which he never managed to complete. As far back as 1893, York Powell (1893: 229) reported the subject of Roman Britain needed a complete history and that he was happy to report that Haverfield was already working on one. Later on, Cheesman (1913b: 105) hoped that Haverfield would produce something more substantial than the second

---

2. Oman repeated the same accusation, perhaps with less justification, with regard to the work of the Doomsday Book historian, J.H. Round (Stephenson 1980: 1–2).

edition of *The Romanization of Roman Britain* (1912): 'May we hope that the increased material at his disposal will induce Professor Haverfield to embody his conclusions in a more comprehensive work at no distant date?' Rhys Roberts (1920: 349) noted that Haverfield had not lived to complete the authoritative work on Roman Britain, while S.N. Miller added '…students of Roman Britain long looked to Francis Haverfield to give them after nearly a 100 years a successor to Horsley's *Britannia Romana*. That hope was disappointed by his death' (1925: 262–3). Craster (1920), however, suggested he had given up on the idea of a 'big book', a view corroborated by Bruton (1919), who says he had not been working on it, and Bosanquet (1920: 141) stating that Haverfield was never confident it would appear. Perhaps written too far ahead of his death to explain his failure to write that definitive work (but another example of a passage which he was to recycle elsewhere), Haverfield did once observe:

> Roman Britain has no history of its own … With the Roman conquest our island began to be one of the countries known to us historically, and some at least of the persons who lived in it, and the events which occurred in it have been definitely recorded in literature. Nevertheless Roman Britain has …for no country or person or thing has its history unless it possesses or has possessed a definite individuality which has existed continuously for some perceptible period of time. It is not enough that the man or thing should have existed during a period known to us from history: there must have been in some way or other, an independent existence and independent unit. But under the rule of the Roman Empire was merely one province, and in general an unimportant province, of a vast and complex state which stretched over three continents from the shores of Ocean to the sands of the eastern side (*VCH* Norfolk i (1901): 279).

Presumably calling on personal information, Macdonald claimed, however, he did plan to consolidate all his contributions to the *VCH*, once they were completed, '…into a definitive *Britannia Romana*. When war and illness interrupted the current of his life, the hope was regretfully dismissed. But even had the break not occurred, the dream might have lacked fulfillment' (Macdonald 1924: 34). On a more positive note, Read (1919–20) reported that Haverfield was planning, and had in fact, begun a new edition of the seventh volume of the *CIL*. Bosanquet (1920: 141), once fearing that the drive for Haverfield completing the *RIB* was going to be lost was glad to report that Anderson had informed him that the OUP was considering such a work. Bosanquet also wanted Haverfield's students to complete either this and/or see into print the 'failed' *VCH* volume on the six northern English counties, a suggestion repeated by Craster, who noted that in

preparing his assessment he had consulted Taylor for information regarding unpublished and planned work. Other projects in the
pipeline included what became Anderson's edition of Furneaux's
Tacitus for which he had begun a new appendix (completed by Anderson), on minerals in Roman Britain (Haverfield 1924: 254). There was
also a new edition of the catalogue of inscriptions in Tullie House on
the way, while there was still the problem of a definitive work on
Romano-British samian, although a start was promised with the publication of Newbold's catalogue from stamps of Hadrian's Wall
(Haverfield 1919c: 1).

With respect to the military history of Roman Britain, James Curle
lamented that '...no one in his day had done more to encourage the
study of Roman Britain and to gather together the details of the latest
discoveries, and yet the great work on the Northumbrian Wall which he
might have written never saw the light' (1939–40: 127–8). Craster
(1920: 68) reports the same intention. Whilst the impression is that he
had given up any plans on being involved in excavation in the future,
there are a indications that Haverfield had plans for others to see
through projects commenced before the war. For instance, there was the
survey of the forts of north-west England in the hinterland of Hadrian's
Wall (cf. Chapter 6). O.G.S. Crawford remembered such plans. 'Much
of the information necessary for a complete interpretation is still lacking but some progress has been made since 1914 (e.g. at Ebchester and
Ambleside) ...during the period when scarcity of money and labour rendered digging impossible, Haverfield followed up a valuable paper on
Old Penrith or Plumpton Wall which he had published in 1913
[Haverfield 1913e] by similar papers on other forts in the district. The
plan was to bring together the known forts regarding each, including as
a rule the inscriptions and to state quite tentatively the conclusion to
which these seemed to point' (Macdonald 1929/1930: 46). The fort surveys completed were Maryport, Carlisle, Old Carlisle and their
connecting roads. After Haverfield's death, Collingwood continued the
survey. This sounds reminiscent of Haverfield's proposal to submit a
Roman volume to the *VCH*. Finally, in a letter replying to Atkinson in
April 1918, Haverfield wrote he had delayed responding because he
had been away at Hindhead (Surrey) 'recruiting', which begs the question, for what?

Last but not least, as was discussed in Chapter 7, a relatively late developing theme in Haverfield's work was (Roman) town planning and
the writing of town histories. Indeed, in 1918 he claimed to be planning
a book on the towns of Roman Britain (Haverfield 1918a: 1–2). This
proposal was given fuller description by Macdonald who wrote that the

'special interest in the civil as distinct from the military side of Romano-British life, which Haverfield developed in his later years, showed itself in his *Romanization of Roman Britain* (4th ed. 1923) ...Had he lived longer, it would have found still firmer exposition, for at the time of his death he was collecting material for a book on the towns of Roman Britain. Two of the preliminary studies for this had been published from his papers by Miss M.V. Taylor' (viz. Leicester and Cirencester: 1929/1930: 81). In July 1904 at the Bristol meeting of the Royal Archaeological Institute, Haverfield read a paper on Roman Somerset 'as an interesting subject which had not been properly worked out' (*Archaeol J* LXI (1904): 209). At least part of this must have been seen through in his 1906 contribution to the *VCH* Somerset.

What these anecdotes confirm is that while Haverfield might have had much to do at the time of his death, no major statement of his choosing had appeared. But it is striking how such opinions reflect what people thought he might or should have done rather than Haverfield's plans. That with one exception (and one not noted by any of his obituarists), none of these plans came to anything suggests that either they were never near completion or that he, indeed had no plans to develop them. If the latter is the case, then it is another piece of evidence that indicates that Haverfield's commitment to Romano-British studies as a separate discipline was waning. If any pattern can be extracted from the plans attributed to him, and in turn indicative of what was required, it is perhaps recognition of the need for fuller and more considered interpretations of certain subjects, whether it be the history of the Roman Wall, the military presence in north-west England, the urbanization of the province or continuing the compilation of national catalogues of classes of material or even an overview of the Roman period. That none of these plans were ever completed means that we have to use what he had managed to publish and, in particular, his two major monographs as well as what can be extracted from his various papers, many of which served as markers for future work. But such works have to be handled with caution as they may not have been intended as definitive statements. But before we look at the implications and influences of the core arguments that underpinned Haverfield's major works it is necessary to look at the state of the discipline of Romano-British archaeology up to about the time of his death.

Roman Britain in 1919

In assessing the condition of Romano-British archaeology at Oxford and ultimately Britain at the time when Haverfield was at the height of his powers (e.g. 1907–14), we are presented with a number of conundrums. At the time of his death Romano-British studies stood at a crossroads. In a certain light the situation looked healthy. Received wisdom has it that Haverfield had come to be regarded as the personification of the subject. His reputation was established within his university where he was pre-eminent as well as further afield, in the national and regional societies as well as overseas. With his death, the creation of the Haverfield Bequest seemed to be the harbinger of even better things, with a relatively large fund dedicated to supporting the advance of the subject by the careful placing of its resources on a number of fronts.

Beneath the surface, however, the situation was not so comfortable. Following his funeral, the contents of Haverfield's will were revealed. Its terms divided into two parts: the personal bequests to family and friends and those clauses concerned with 'research' and establishing what came to be known as the Haverfield Trust. With respect to research the will stipulated that:

a: his archaeological, historical and topographical books be bequeathed to the university and the Ashmolean Museum

b: the monetary worth of his real and personal estate not otherwise disposed of was to be realized for the creation of a trust fund to be deployed for '…the promotion of the study of Roman Britain (including the comparative study of Romano-British and other Ancient remains in and outside of the British Isles) either by defraying the expense of excavations (including the adequate remuneration of competent directors) or by endowing a Readership or Lectureship on the subject or by a combination of the two methods or in any other way which the University or the persons entrusted by the University with the management of the fund judge from time to time likely to promote the objects of my bequest.'

c: the Society of Antiquaries of London be consulted for advice with respect to the bequest. In addition the Society was to be represented by two delegates in the management of the Trust and that it was essential that graduate members of Oxford as well as members of the (then four) University ladies colleges be equally eligible ('but not necessarily to the exclusion of others') for the Readership/Lectureship or other post.

In making these conditions, it would appear Haverfield was intent on trying to maintain the momentum his (pre-war) work had created and, in doing so, to reconcile some of those tensions he believed had hindered the progress of Romano-British archaeology and perhaps archaeology in general. In his conception of the future of

(Romano-)British archaeology as outlined in the 1911 address to the SPRS, the rôle of the (regional archaeological) societies was a subservient one, one meant to support the (growing) university involvement in excavation and to assist in the production of data for interpretations. For the antiquarians of the mid- and late nineteenth century (just as their earlier forefathers) who had dominated the societies had demonstrated, in Haverfield's opinion, their unsuitability for such work. Instead they were now to work to the universities' (meaning above all, to an Oxford) agenda. It was contacts such as this along with others which in turn this led him to formulate a number of recommendations for the societies post-1918. Such is the sub-text to his address to the Somerset society in 1918. While praising the achievements of the society up to that date, his main proposal was a call for the greater accessibility of society and museum collections, preferably with the publication of detailed catalogues of their holdings as well as for improved library holdings. While the 'amateurs' might continue to excavate, improved standards were still needed. For this reason excavation had to be the preserve of the qualified researcher, who should come from the universities. What is surprising, however, is having seen how Haverfield's work owed much to the German model for institutionalizing research, that he did not propose to entrust the task of compiling the corpus of Roman inscriptions to, for instance, the British Academy in imitation of the German academies' control of national projects. That he did not make the suggestion may reflect his opinion of the value of the British counterpart. In fact, on the basis of the will, managing the 'agenda' was to be managed by handed by his University and the London society.

This is the impression at face value but the situation is slightly more complicated. In assessing the significance of the will, it has to be remembered that it was drawn up in August 1912, that is at the time of his greatest optimism for the subject but before his hypothesized distancing from it.[3] Instead of seeing the will as his legacy for the subject, it

3. Once realized, the estate amounted to £12,330 6s 3d. Probate was granted in December 1919 to R.P.L. Booker and the Rev. Claude Martin Blagden, Clerk. Blagden (1874–1952), Corpus Christi, Oxford (1894–6), held a number of college teaching and university church appointments. He was Canon of Coventry (1918–20), Archdeacon of Warwick (1920–3) and later Coventry (1923–7) before becoming the Bishop of Peterborough in 1927. Other than his religious offices at the University, there is nothing to link him directly with Haverfield. Each of the executors was to receive £25 for their trouble. Other 'personal' bequests were to his widow who was to receive £500 plus all his possessions (other than their house), his mother-in-law an annuity of

should be treated as a product of the circumstances in which it was composed. The situation had changed eight years later, even if the will had not been amended. Some of his wishes seem to have been resolved very quickly. In February 1920, Stuart Jones proposed that the university's General Board of the Faculty make a grant of £400 for equipment and the upkeep of the ancient history library, the nucleus of which was to be formed from Haverfield's collection. An additional £200 p.a. was required to maintain the collection. Later in the year, in summarizing the contents of the will to the AGM of the Congress of Archaeological Societies, J.N.L. Myres reported that the library was to be left to the Ashmolean with the rest of his estate to be held in trust by a representative committee. The trust was to have two objectives. It was to oversee the completion of the compilation of a corpus of inscriptions and secondly, to encourage and facilitate archaeological survey of Roman remains reduced to map form. In the discussion after Myres' statement, Collingwood explained that he was already at work on the corpus, but with 2000+ inscriptions to examine, he hoped delegates and the members of their societies would be able to provide photographs and squeezes for him.[4] In summing up the discussion, the Congress President (C.H. Read) concluded he '...was glad to think that the great name of Professor Haverfield would be perpetuated by the trust formed by his will to carry on his work' (*The Programme of the Haverfield Trust. The Year's Work in Archaeology 1921 Published by the Congress of Archaeological Societies* 1922: xi–xii).

£120 per annum in the event of his wife predeceasing her (which occurred in 1920) and M.V. Taylor £150. Winifred Haverfield's life after his demise was far from happy. Having moved from Oxford to her parents' home in Leamington Spa, her body was found in the River Leam on 21 July 1920. Evidently suffering from 'failing health since the death of her husband and an operation had been followed by acute melancholia', the verdict on her death was reported as 'Suicide whilst temporarily insane.' Aged 41 years, she is buried alongside Haverfield in a cemetery off Dunstan Road, Headington (cf. *The Times* 30 July 1920). Blagden conducted her funeral service at St Hugh's College Chapel, Oxford where she was a tutor. The mourners included her father, brother and uncle as well as representatives of St Hugh's and Somerville colleges, Arthur Mackarness, Booker (from Haverfield's side), the Warden of Wadham, C.B. Heberden, Professor and Lady Gilbert Murray, Professor and Mrs Stewart, Myres, Miss Moberly formerly of St Hugh's, C. Bell and a Dr K. Ley (*The Times* 2 August). When her will was completed (probate March 1921 to Mackarness), she left nearly £3250.

4.   At the same meeting Cyril Fox, perhaps making a claim for support from the Trust, reported he was surveying in south Cambridgeshire.

Whatever Haverfield might have had in mind when the will was drawn up or how his thinking evolved in the years after it, what resulted was slightly different (and was amended further in 1966: Todd 2003). After settling his other requests and payment of outstanding bills, the Trust received £11000. The next step was the creation of a committee of Administrators rather than Trustees (as the fund is still a bequest and not a trust), made up of the Warden of Wadham (Joseph Wells), Stuart Jones, Whatley, Macdonald, Anderson and Collingwood.[5] The committee reported to the Board of *Literae Humaniores* in February 1921, when it was noted that the interest accruing from the Bequest would be in the order of £400 p.a. The committee resolved to create a standing committee which was to disperse no more than £200 p.a. to assist excavations, and £75 p.a. towards the completion of the *RIB* with an additional £120 to be put aside as a contingency fund for the same. The committee also felt it should look to supplement its funds from other sources. As Haverfield had wished, the committee was to seek close links with the London society.

The clause in Haverfield's will concerning the appointment of a Lecturer in Romano-British studies is interesting. Its inclusion was at a time when other universities were making innovations with respect to appointing staff with at least an interest in Roman Britain. So there may have been an element of keeping up with developments elsewhere. But we have also seen that after the First World War (and possibly a few years beforehand) Haverfield was becoming disenchanted with the subject, as reflected in his publications and the 'failed' projects. Therefore the survival of the clause might be seen as an anomaly in an unchanged will from an earlier, more optimistic time. Assisting the committee in its decision was the fact that Collingwood was apparently prepared to take on Haverfield's teaching and so to solve its problem, at least in the short-term. If so what the committee could not have anticipated was Collingwood's growing disenchantment with the subject and his drift away from it. However this is assuming too that Haverfield's desire was to establish Romano-British studies as a permanent feature in the Oxford curriculum. Alternatively, the wish to appoint an occasional lecturer is indicative of the peripheral nature of his work in Roman Britain relative to the main thrust of his teaching (if not research) at the

---

5. Todd (2003: 37) lists as early administrators Henry Stuart Jones as its first chairman, to be followed by Anderson, Collingwood, Hogarth and G.H. Stevenson '...both holders of Oxford posts but having little evident connection with Roman Britain', along with Macdonald and Wheeler. In fact Hogarth and Stevenson were Haverfield intimates.

university. Whatever the factors, the committee's most significant decision was that '...it would not be desirable to endow a permanent Readership or Lectureship in the subject of Roman Britain, but that it would be possible and desirable from time to time to provide for the delivery of lectures or courses of lectures in Oxford, with special reference to the work carried on by the means of the fund.'[6] Although the reasons why the committee decided not to see through the suggestion for a permanent lectureship in Romano-British studies are not recorded, we might gauge how the discipline and Haverfield's proposal were regarded at Oxford from a number of contemporary publications. For instance, Cheesman noted that the study of archaeology and that of Roman Britain in particular was '...nothing but an intricate mass of technical detail, in which none but specialists can find their way, and from which no conclusions of general interest are likely to emerge. From this narrowness of vision even archaeologists are not always exempt, and the dating of pottery and the study of architectural detail become ends in themselves, not means for reconstructing the development of culture or filling up gaps in a defective historical tradition' (Cheesman 1913b: 102–3). While Cheesman went on to exonerate Haverfield from this tendency, similar sentiments are evident in the opinions of other Oxford contemporaries. If more proof is required, one detects a hint of the writing on the wall in Anderson's Haverfield obituary:

> His special work – not always appreciated and sometimes deprecated as a specialism even by University teachers – gave to all his teaching and writing that firm grip and that note of reality which are denied to more and more book-learning (1919: 166).

If we run with the accepted version that one of Haverfield's accomplishments was that he made Roman Britain a respectable subject for university students, then there is equally a case for regarding his contribution in the professional sense as something of a (long-term) disappointment, if it be judged on the criterion of his establishing the subject as a university based discipline. That is, of course, if it was his

---

6. Such an ambivalent attitude to formal instruction and ultimately degree qualifications in archaeology persisted for at least the next 30 years. Grahame Clark reports that in Christopher Hawkes' inaugural lecture as the first occupant of the new Oxford professorship in European archaeology in 1946, Hawkes believed it impossible to imagine the University setting up a Hons. School of Archaeology (Clark 1989: 12 citing Hawkes, *Archaeology and the History of Europe: An Inaugural Lecture* (1948)).

intention. It may not be coincidental too that in a report in *The Times* (13 October 1919) summarizing the new academic session at Oxford, it was said by the anonymous contributor '...the teaching of ancient history has suffered an irreparable loss with the death of Professor Haverfield.' For some, Roman Britain was still a part of ancient history.

The fact is that the teaching of Roman Britain at Oxford does not appear to have featured prominently in Haverfield's portfolio. Indeed looking at the courses he taught brings home the facts: (i) he was, for the purposes of teaching an epigrapher and (ii) how much teaching he did in Roman history (cf. Appendix 4). It is therefore not surprising how virtually all of those of his 'students' who went on to university careers are better characterized as ancient historians. The list includes the obvious and more speculative persons (e.g. Cheesman, Anderson, Stevenson, Atkinson and Miller). For those individuals who are now remembered as archaeologists other than Ashby, (e.g. Woolley, Garstang), their connections with him are more difficult to assess. All of them got jobs outside of Oxford but did not become Romano-British specialists. Likewise, for all the effort at setting up excavations designed in part to train (Oxford) students, again we cannot really say Haverfield pushed the issue. He had not developed a programme in this respect, but seems to have been content to take the opportunities as they arose. After Corbridge, he no longer had the need to do so. Elsewhere there are signs, from at least 1915, and very likely beforehand, of a growing sense of his disenchantment with the subject as a lack of interest on his part to see the discipline of archaeology better integrated as a University subject. The point is demonstrated in a lecture he delivered to an audience of Oxford undergraduates in which he extolled the merits of the way ancient history was taught as part of *Literae Humaniores* (Haverfield 1912d).[7] In his presentation of the subject, archaeology, and especially epigraphy, was merely a facet of ancient history and should be treated as such. In the sentiments he expressed, the archaeological Haverfield of the 1890s and 1900s have metamorphosed into those of an ancient historian. It is for these reasons that one might suggest that for Haverfield, by about 1914, Roman Britain was something he did for himself, almost as antiquarian exercise, to which were applied more rig-

---

7. For example, 'I do not know whether I shall seem an unbending conservative or a hopeless optimist or a liberal who is trying to make the best of a bad business. But the fact which I have just stated suggest to me that, in respect of the training which they give in historical method, Greek and Roman history, as studied in Oxford, fit into each other and supplement each other in a most happy manner' (1912d: 24).

orous scholastic standards: he remained at heart an Oxford ancient historian wedded to the tradition of *Literae Humaniores*.

These facts explain Oxford's decision not to take on Haverfield's (academic) legacy. During his lifetime the strength of the discipline there was almost entirely focused upon him, albeit precariously given his growing distance from it. If he were to go, a vacuum would be created there. And this is what precisely happened. In the years after his death what is striking is how his work appears to have been overthrown at least at Oxford. With virtually no roots there and no real support within the institution, there was no substantial case for continuing his work. Therefore it is not surprising that the subject there faded in the decades after his death, unassisted as it was by R.G. Collingwood and others' half-hearted commitment to it in terms of provision for its formal instruction there. In reality, the best prospects for the subject's development lay away from Oxford (and Cambridge), in the newer provincial, metropolitan universities, in institutions not so wedded to the classics and the traditions of the ancient universities. This meant the likes of Liverpool, Birmingham, Leeds and Manchester, in communities with a prosperous middle class prepared to patronize as a matter of civic pride, the formal co-ordination of instruction in archaeology via an institution of higher education. These sentiments went in tandem with the way the same groups frequently funded excavation in cities which were experiencing rapid urban growth. In turn, in these new seats of learning there were the authorities keen to create departments of archaeology and make innovative appointments. This was something that the traditional universities could not accommodate, a fact recognized by Percy Gardner (1926). But even with the new university departments, (undergraduate) students were not really a priority because an established career path for graduates in the subject was yet to develop. For this and other reasons, the new departments remained in some respects aloof from the teaching and creation of a new generation of instructors. The change in this respect came only in the generation after such departments were established. It is for this reason then, that it was not the institutions which took up Haverfield legacy. In fact, the vacuum created by his death was filled by the main English national archaeological society (that based in London), the British Museum and, to a lesser extent, its regional counterparts, including the National Museums of Scotland and of Wales as well as the Ashmolean at Oxford. Of these organizations, the British Museum, in some respects became in the short term the engine house of research in this country, certainly until the newer universities had established themselves and a state archaeological service had been created. This took some time to achieve, during which time the momentum in Romano-British studies, evident up to 1914 was left in a state of limbo if not stagnation until 1919, after which it proceeded to lose focus in the two decades thereafter.

'Other Universities are bestirring themselves' (Haverfield 1911a: xx)

We have seen how Haverfield had for a number of years been critical of the way that Britain's older universities had failed to contribute to advancing knowledge of the country's Roman past through its archaeological remains (cf. Chapter 7 and Appendix 3). Through the 1890s and into the 1900s his criticisms became more explicit and his observations increasingly trenchant. The focus of his complaints was more to do with the fact the institutions (and so their staff) had not become involved in fieldwork, which he presumably imagined would generate the data to permit fresh interpretations and theories. At the same time, the progress would marginalize what he saw as the damage that the provincial antiquarians could cause. There was a problem, however, in how to make the point. Other than the press, there was no other national medium in which he could broadcast his opinions on how future progress could be effected. He could only do so in the papers delivered to and published in the journals of the regional archaeological and antiquarian societies. But in using such outlets, there had to be a degree of moderated opinions and reserve in such utterances. His comments, however, could be more explicit in those publications which were traditionally not the preserve of the antiquary (the *Geographical Journal* etc.) or else when he set up his own mouthpiece (the *Journal of Roman Studies*). Either way, we can detect an evolution in his thinking about the relationship of universities to archaeological societies to research.

It is difficult to pinpoint when (Romano-British) archaeology was first offered as a separate or distinct topic of instruction in a British university. Levine's (1986: 135–63) discussion of the use of history as an academic discipline in the (oldest) universities does not include archaeology, although elsewhere the use of Romano-British archaeology was attributed to the likes of Collingwood Bruce (p. 97). Over the centuries there had been created a number of university posts where the incumbent was expected to be familiar with British antiquities, if not to offer instruction in them. The oldest of these positions was the chair established by William Camden at Oxford in 1622 with the purpose of reading lectures '...on Florus or other ancient historians, twice a week, Mondays and Saturdays' (Piggott 1976: 41, citing Gough's *Life of Camden*, preface to the 1789 edition of the *Britannia*; Stuart Jones 1943–4).

In Haverfield's opinion, the chair, or the subsequent occupants were typified by their inactivity and a failure to work to the spirit of Camden's intentions. The situation only really changed in the later nineteenth century. Perhaps more surprising was John Anderson (1726–1796; Professor of Natural Philosophy at the University of Glasgow 1757–96) and his desire, following his falling-out with his employers, to create a professorship of Roman antiquities at the new university he wished to see established in the city after his death. That institution became Anderson College, later to become Strathclyde University. His collection of curiosities and other objects was eventually transferred to the Hunterian Museum at Glasgow University in 1887 (Murray 1904: 161). Another ultimately stillborn proposal made in Scotland was the offer to create a professorship in archaeology at Edinburgh.[8] Other notable professorships created at about this time include the 1851 Disney chair at Cambridge, endowed by John Disney ('...an amateur of Classical Archaeology' – Clark 1989: 28) and dedicated to delivering 'in the course of each academic year six lectures at least on the subject of Classical, Medieval and other Antiquities, the Fine Arts and all matters and things connected therewith' (Daniel 1981: 83). The significant feature of the professorship, described by Percy Gardner (its holder 1880–7), as a lectureship, was that the post did not require residency in Cambridge, so permitting the holder to occupy posts elsewhere (Gardner 1933: 52). The earliest incumbents possessed diverse 'archaeological' interests (John Marsden and classical statuary; Churchill Babington and multifarious; Gardner, G.F. Browne and Anglo-Saxon studies; and William Ridgway in anthropology – Clark 1989: 26–9).[9] With respect to archaeology, Oxford created its first professorship in classical archaeology in 1884. Because the appointment involved residency at Lincoln College, the post came to be known as the Lcincoln hair. The first incumbent was William Ramsay appointed in 1885 but who left a year later citing a lack of support

8. In 1862 Alexander H. Rhind bequeathed his estate to the Scottish Society of Antiquaries, originally planning to create a professorship of archaeology at the University of Edinburgh. The money, however, was eventually transferred to the Antiquaries to endow an annual lectureship to provide courses in archaeology and ethnology. His bequest led to the appointment of the first Rhind lecturer in 1876 (cf. Stevenson 1981: 157).
9. In 1880 Charles Waldstein was appointed Lecturer in Greek Art. Reid lectured on Roman antiquities, with Gardner elected to the Disney chair to teach Greek archaeology. These appointments and developments led to an expansion of teaching resources in the university.

from the university authorities.[10] He was replaced by Gardner who occupied the chair between 1887 and 1925. In 1892 the Edwards Chair in Egyptology at UC London was established specifically for Flinders Petrie. The examples summarized here show that while there were the beginnings of establishing teaching posts in archaeology in some of Britain's universities, these were one-off appointments where the incumbents were expected to offer irregular programmes of lectures on matters antiquarian and archaeological, which might include British material. Still in the spirit of the early nineteenth century however, there was no cadre of coherent teaching or plans for the development academically and pedegalogically of the discipline archaeology. Instead in the universities the subject, if it was even noted, remained a minor facet of classical studies.

The first instance of Haverfield's opinionating on the subject of archaeology and the universities dates back to his initial foray into fieldwork. In 1891, describing some of the inscriptions recently uncovered at Chester, he noted that for once the universities were beginning to take an interest in Roman Britain (*The Athenaeum* 31 October 1891: 590–1). His first substantial published statement about the state of archaeology in the academic environment, however, was as part of a paper on the administration of Roman mines delivered to the Chester Archaeological Society. In his introduction he stated:

> Archaeologists may be divided into two classes. These are firstly, the local archaeologists, who devote themselves mainly or entirely, to the study of their own particular neighbourhoods, and there are, secondly, the general archaeologists, if I may so call them, who deal with details collected from all quarters with no geographical limit. The first class is very common in England; you may find it in any town which has an intelligent and educated population. The second is almost confined to our universities. The two are mutually necessary, the one to supply local details; the other to compare, estimate and explain. Local workers, if left to themselves, are likely to misunderstand, to over or undervalue the importance of discoveries; general archaeologists, unless they have local details, have but a poor collections of facts on which to base their inductions (1892d: 80).

Five years later, in the pages of *The Antiquary*, commenting on plans to compile an index of the publications of (British) archaeological societies,

---

10. The University apparently forgot the provision to pay him (cf. Boardman 1985: 44f.; Murray 2000: 337). Periodically funded by Merton and later Magdalen colleges, the funding of the chair was not properly established until 1925.

he reported: 'I regret... that the scheme is not carried further and made to include other articles on English antiquities ...One of the most serious defects of archaeological work, so far as my own subject is concerned is the separation of local or district work from work done, for instance, in the Universities. This separation is not confined to England, nor is it all a new feature, and the blame for it rests quite as largely on the Universities as on district workers. It is, however, a serious evil and should be combated on all suitable occasions' (*The Antiquary* XXIII (1897): 105). He raised a related issue in *The Athenaeum* of 13 January 1900, although in this instance, the criticism was relatively mild, with Haverfield pointing out that there was a potential problem looming in excavation projects: a shortage of competent supervisors. His immediate solution to the shortfall was a call for more and better-run excavations. This would then create more and better supervisors who could record the results and so avoid the problems in the day-to-day running of excavations. By the next statement, again in *The Athenaeum* (January 5 1901), he was asking: 'Why do not a few of our capable university archaeologists turn their attentions to the antiquities of their own country?'

Contrary to what some might suggest about a rise in interest in Romano-British studies in Britain, Haverfield seems to have been less positive. In a lecture delivered about Roman Yorkshire to the Annual Meeting of the RAI at York in July 1903, he made some trenchant comments explaining why Romano-British studies had stagnated in Britain, and why the situation might be changing:

> ...the subject of Roman Britain was not very popular, on account of its being difficult and distant. It was difficult because it involved the study of the whole Roman Empire, because during the last fifty years the study of that empire had expanded with amazing rapidity, and it was hard to keep up with the development. It was also a distant subject. Do what they would, Roman remains never came home like medieval. We felt indistinctly that between us and the Romans there was a great gulf fixed, that we could not make a national hero of Caratacus, and unless the question was one of local topography, the consideration of Romano-British life seems a far off alien study. The state of things, he thought, would not last long, because the growth of Imperial sentiment in England would soon awaken an interest in other Empires. He went on to say that we should consider Roman Yorkshire rather as illustrative of the Empire than as a topographical area of roads etc. (Haverfield 1903f: 382).[11]

11. This account was missed by Macdonald in his bibliography of Haverfield publications. I owe sight of it to Ebbatson (1994: 57–8). However the use of the quote is selective. I repeat it here in full because it reiterates a number of other issues dear to Haverfield.

In 1907, in the Ford lectures, he was again calling for the universities to become involved in the proper training of field excavators (Haverfield 1924: 160). The failure of archaeology to develop in Britain's universities was attributed to the institutions being over-concerned with antiquity viewed through the perspective of the classics (Haverfield 1924: 86–8). To solve the problems he highlighted, in the same year in the report on the season's progress at Corbridge he asserted it had become an excavation, in part, to train Oxford students (*The Times* 19 September 1908). Haverfield returned to the part of the universities and the practice of archaeological excavation in a lecture delivered at Manchester University in December 1907. As part of a presentation on *The Roman Occupation of North-West England*, it was reported:

> Dr. Haverfield commended the work of the newer universities in the attention to archaeology. Liverpool hoped to examine the Roman remains of Wales; Sheffield and Leeds had formed a Yorkshire committee for a similar purpose. Manchester has its own appropriate portion in the plan of Manchester and the neighbours, as Prof. Conway had already fully recognised (cf. *The Manchester Guardian* 3 December).

The rôle of Britain's universities in the development of archaeological research was not allowed to rest. A more explicit assessment was made to the Cambridge Antiquarian Society in February 1910 (cf. Appendix. 3). He returned to the same issue in his inaugural address to the newly created Society for the Promotion of Roman Studies, in a speech meant to set the course for the evolution of the study of Roman 'history' in Britain. The first part of the speech was a call, with acknowledgement to some university staffed excavations, for the integration of Romano-British studies into the university curriculum. 'It is the more necessary that the Universities should help because ...the whole of Roman archaeology and history has become of late years far more difficult and technical than it was when most of us began our studies, and the general knowledge of the Roman Empire is therefore more indispensable than ever to the student of Roman Britain' (1911a: xx; cf. *The Times*, 12 May 1911).[12] He also noted that an unnamed university was offering courses in Roman Britain in place of Latin prose. Comparable sentiments were expressed in a talk to the Leeds branch of the Classical Association in

12. While it has been claimed that Haverfield '...made Roman Britain a study suitable for universities, although this was first realised by Gerald Simpson in 1924' (Simpson 1976: 3), courses were being introduced in Oxford as early as 1909–10, and at other universities (e.g. Liverpool).

1916, a version which had already been delivered to the AGM of the Roman Society in the previous year. In the published version of the lecture he referred to the fact that 'Our British Universities ...have been, throughout indifferent to national antiquities, like the German Universities till quite recently' (Haverfield 1916a: 3).

Similar sentiments were articulated in his introduction to Atkinson's report on excavations at Lowbury Hill (Atkinson 1916). For instance, British archaeologists, while generally better than their German counterparts, still required better training. Returning to the issue of Britain's universities and archaeological research, he opened with criticisms of the way that the ancient universities (Oxford and Cambridge along with Glasgow and Edinburgh) had done little or nothing in the study of Britain's national antiquities – a phenomenon shared with Germany. He blamed the deficiencies on the literary and linguistic traditions of these institutions as well as their inability to teach subjects like topography in the way that many of the (self-instructed, non-institution based) antiquarians had appreciated. Instead, innovation in the study of the past had been occasioned by the rise of the new universities. 'Partly, perhaps from a pardonable wish to advertise themselves and to justify their own existence, they have taken up what older institutions have neglected: and actually they have done much good in a brief span of time' (Haverfield in Atkinson 1916: ii). Because of the progress that was underway in some of these institutions, Haverfield was able to highlight progress of Romano-British studies at Manchester, Liverpool, Leeds and Durham ('with its Newcastle annexe': p. v).[13] But still there was work to be done. The new universities should continue to train archaeologists, ones familiar with the work of others, notably on the continent. Secondly they should encourage regional work and the continuation of current projects. In this respect the new universities, with their links with the regional societies, should consider co-ordinating training excavations in order to raise standards. Thus Durham and Armstrong College at Newcastle should be looking to Hadrian's Wall, Glasgow and Edinburgh to its Antonine counterpart and even University College Reading to Silchester. This was an advantage which he felt Oxford did not possess: proximity to a suitable Roman site in its own backyard. And still the problems he had originally highlighted lurked.

---

13. In her recollection of the work of the Yorkshire Roman Antiquities Committee, Chitty (1987) writes that when Haverfield spoke at the Committee's inaugural meeting at York in March 1906, he '...stressed the necessity of co-ordinating archaeological work with the bookwork going on in the Universities of Leeds and Sheffield.' I owe this reference to Colin Wallace.

The obvious solution to the problems Haverfield highlighted would have been for him to contribute more explicitly to, if not establish, what would now be called a research centre at Oxford, one which offered 'training' in both traditional academic disciplines as well as in the methods and practice of excavation. But as we have seen this failed to happened even if in a certain light it appears that he attempted to do so; viz. through the courses he taught at Oxford, by the number of scholars for whom he obtained posts there or in the provincial universities and by taking control of field 'training'. The first of these developments was examined in Chapter 8. An extension to excavation was to use fieldwork to supplement teaching. For example, he was involved in a scheme to display and excavate North Leigh villa (Oxon.) in 1908–10. Some excavation, unpublished, was completed but was then interrupted by the outbreak of the war (Haverfield 1924: 220). North Leigh seems to have been conceived as part of a scheme to establish an Oxford training excavation, closer to home than Hadrian's Wall: '...I once tried ...in Oxford the experiment of dove-tailing a set of lectures to a small class into a series of visits to selected sites, Silchester, North Leigh etc. The class seemed interested in the experiment but did not think much of the sites. Nor have I ventured to repeat the experiment' (Haverfield in Atkinson 1916: vi).[14] Elsewhere, Margerie Taylor, in bringing together the scattered remains which had been recovered over the years from the site of Woodeaton (Oxon.) noted that there had not been the exploration the site merited: 'The academic atmosphere at Oxford, sympathetic enough to the pen, has never been kindly to the use of the spade, and other obstacles which need not here be particularised, were, still recently, insuperable' (1917: 99).

14. Haverfield (1899d) had already published some epigraphy (discovered in 1892) from near the site. The North Leigh villa was first excavated in 1813 by the Rev. W. Brown, Rector of Handborough. Taylor (1939: 318) reports excavation resumed in 1910. She also records that the excavation in ?1911 was the result of an appeal by Haverfield who had obtained a permit from the site owner, the Duke of Marlborough. The entry in Haverfield's *Roman Occupation* (1924: 221, Fig. 51) says the excavations were between 1908 and 1910. The same entry reports they were halted by the War but that the Haverfield Bequest Committee retained the permit and had arranged for public access to the site (the excavation subscriptions also having paid for roofing over the site's principal mosaic). The excavations were directed by Donald Atkinson and Hugh Evelyn White. No report of the work was published. Taylor claimed that Evelyn White's MSS was with the Haverfield papers in the Ashmolean. Atkinson said it was missing.

If Oxford and its staff and students were lukewarm to what Haverfield might have planned, still his chivvying may have had an effect elsewhere. There was, for instance, his acknowledging the increase in university supported excavations.[15] With regard to offering (non-)professorial instruction in the archaeology of the Roman province, however, the situation is less clear. This is in part a consequence of the way that the subject tended to be the innovation of instructors who were initially appointed to posts as ancient historians or classicists but who, at the same time, had interests in other facets of the study of antiquity. With respect to the newer institutions Haverfield praised in 1910, the contribution of the Liverpool Excavation Committee and, in particular, its sub-committee for research in Wales to the development of British archaeology both in the UK and overseas, remains to be written (Freeman in prep.). A start can be found in Shore (1985; cf. Kelly 1981: 149–51, 224–5 and 353–5). Whilst the committee was more concerned with fostering work in the eastern Mediterranean, Haverfield saw that it had an important rôle in Britain. The committee was part of the Liverpool Institute of Archaeology which was affiliated to the city's university. The origins of the institute go back to 1902 when John Garstang was made Honorary Reader in Egyptology in a university without a department in the discipline.[16] Garstang used the appointment to canvass support from the city's mercantile community. By 1904, having raised £10,000+, the institute was created with the appointment of four staff. Haverfield was a member of the institute's Consultative Committee in 1909–10. The relationship of the institute and the university at this time is fascinating. Notionally affiliated to the university, the institute's staff offered both public lectures and other courses for fee-paying members of the university. Its main thrust, however, was research funded mainly by Liverpool benefactors. It was therefore essentially a group of researchers, where the staff undertook their own (private) work. Another striking feature is the flexibility of the institute's appointments. Because it offered teaching to support the university rather than serve its own degree program, the resignation or other movement of staff did not automatically mean that a replacement

---

15. By *c.*1918, the universities would have been Oxford, Cambridge, London, Durham, Manchester, Birmingham, Liverpool, Leeds, Sheffield, Bristol, Wales, St Andrews, Glasgow, Aberdeen and Edinburgh (cf. Fisher 1917; Jones 1988).

16. His appointment was facilitated by letters of support from the likes of the professors Maspero, Sayce, Pelham and Rhys as well Arthur Evans, Haverfield, Madan and Quinbell of the Egyptian Archaeological Survey (cf. *The Liverpool Mercury* 24 November 1902).

in the same area would be made, but that the institute would appoint in whichever field it desired. That it shared appointments in such diverse departments as the School of Local History, Palaeography and Diplomatics, Welsh and of course History, Classics and Ancient History simply added to its vibrancy. In the early years of the Institute's existence it '...was the boast of the University Council in its annual report of 1905-06 that the University was now equipped for the study of archaeology "on a scale without parallel in other British Universities"' (Shore 1985: 2: cf. Muir 1943: 80) and where Percy Gardner (1926: 23) could assert its library collection ranked mention with those at Oxford, London and Cambridge. At one time or another up to the First World War, the institute's interests ranged from Egyptology to the archaeology of the Sudan, to Greece, the Levant and Asia Minor, to central America. It retained lecturers in Assyriology, ancient geography, classical archaeology, numismatics, medieval archaeology and even a fellow in the archaeology of music. In 1906–07 it even offered lectures on the archaeology of embroidery. Such was its reputation, the Institute was able to recruit from the European centres of learning. In 1911 it appointed C.F. Lehmann-Haupt from the University of Berlin as Gladstone Professor of Greek and Lecturer in Oriental History and Archaeology when John Myres resigned the chair (and so his lectureship in Ancient Geography) to become (Wykeham) Chair of Ancient History at Oxford in 1910. Lehmann-Haupt left his position and returned to Germany at the outbreak of the war.[17]

It goes with out saying that the institute possessed strong links with the university's classics and ancient history departments as well as with anthropology. But it was never a centre of Romano-British archaeology. Of its original staff, R.C. Bosanquet, appointed Professor of Classical Archaeology in 1905 and yet another Haverfield confidant, provided a course of lectures on the theme *Tacitus' Agricola and the Roman Conquest of Britain* in 1909–10, one of the earliest instances of a university department offering a course on the archaeology of Roman Britain. By

---

17. Liverpool employed at about the same time Kuno Meyer, Professor of German and Honorary Professor of Celtic, who was the brother of the distinguished ancient historian, Eduard Meyer, and one of the Vice-Presidents of the fledgling institute. Kuno Meyer severed his Liverpool connections acrimoniously in 1914 (Kelly 1981: 174–5; O'Luing 1991). Elsewhere, Haverfield was complimentary of his work and especially his 'Learning in Ireland in the fifth century' (Haverfield 1914a: 35). Cheesman and Myres dined with Lehmann-Haupt in Oxford in January 1913, the connection would have been through Liverpool, (Myres once Professor of Greek and Cheesman an external examiner).

1919–20 the course had become 'Roman Britain'. With respect to Roman Britain the Institute's work in Wales appears to date from *c*.1907.[18] In the summer of 1909, Bosanquet was conducting excavations at Caersws (in conjunction with the Powysland Club: Bosanquet 1911). In the institute's report for 1908–09, he reported that as a consequence of his appointment to the Royal Commission on Ancient Monuments in Wales and Monmouthshire he toured Roman sites in the area, while still conducting his own excavations at Caersws and helping at Caerleon. This work lasted until late 1909 when it seems he gave up directing excavations if not continuing to support them; for instance with the excavations at Parc-y-meirich near Abergele in 1912. Bosanquet was responsible for other, potentially radical, proposals for the future of archaeological research in Wales (Bosanquet 1912). At the August 1911 National Eisteddfod he called for a properly equipped National Museum of Wales, a decent catalogue of sites in the principality (e.g. British camps) and above all a streamlining of excavation work. 'We must get rid of the personal equation. The digging should, so far as possible, be superintended by the same person or persons. It follows that they should devote their whole time to the work.' As to the qualifications of that person it was stressed he should possess certain technical knowledge. 'The excavator must be competent to preserve the evidence.' What was required was an archaeologist-surveyor. In a tone reminiscent of Haverfield, Bosanquet went on to argue against the regional societies taking on the task. They could not compare or correlate the results of different hands. Experience had shown that local societies were unable to provide skilled supervisors on a regular basis. 'Excavation without supervision is almost a crime.' Of the universities he believed they could play a part in the vacations, but the problem was their academic sessions. Instead, he recommended that excavation should continue for at least nine months a year. In the end although the Honorable Society of Cymmrodorion endorsed his opinions, nothing seems to have come of the proposal. Bosanquet's suggestions ran in tandem with suggestions that Haverfield had made a couple of years

---

18. In November of that year *The Times* (23 November) reported, under the banner 'Welsh Research', the outcome of a meeting in Liverpool and a proposal to create a national committee to study through excavation the Roman and prehistoric remains in Wales in order to compose a 'complete history of the Celtic people.' The work was to be coordinated by the Liverpool committee with Bosanquet as its main fieldworker assisted by a general management committee consisting of Garstang, Myres and Newberry for Liverpool and Haverfield as an external member.

earlier, calling for the institutionalizing of research. In a paper again delivered to the Cymrodorion in 1909, Haverfield had proposed:

> It would ...be worth while if Welsh archaeologists would combine to compile a complete set of uniform drawings or photographs of all the pieces of decorated Samian and all the *fibulae* found in Wales, outside of Caerleon and Caerwent. Such a set would include everything that could be heard of as stored away in private collections or in private houses, as well as all specimens which exist in museums. When completed it could be kept at some accessible centre, perhaps in a Welsh National Library or Museum, or it could be multiplied by a mechanical process and copies distributed to numerous centres. It would, I am sure, aid the student very greatly. Not only would it encourage a belief in the intrinsic value of trifles; it would immensely facilitate the comparison and interpretation of fresh finds. A similar list, without drawings or illustrations, should be made of all the coins found in Wales. Then the historian could begin his task of describing Roman Wales with a light heart (1910b: 59–60).

When Bosanquet retired prematurely in 1920, Liverpool's already marginal involvement with Roman Britain came to a (temporary) end. At the time the Liverpool Institute was becoming active, Armstrong College, then an adjunct of Durham University but later to become Newcastle University, was also innovating. As one of England's oldest universities, in 1841 Durham was conferring honorary degrees to local archaeologists and antiquarians. However writing in the mid-1930s, Eric Birley observed, '...it is only in the past quarter of a century that the University has done more than recognize archaeological distinction' (1937: 65). In fact the first Roman archaeologist to be appointed in the region was made at the relatively newly created Armstrong College in Newcastle. In 1910 the college appointed its first Lecturer in Roman Archaeology, a Haverfield 'student', Philip Newbold. But '..that appointment was a personal one, and when the lecturer's health broke down (in 1913), there was no one to succeed him' (Birley 1937: 65). In 1924 Durham University created its Excavation Committee with F.G. Simpson as director. The purpose of the committee was firstly to promote research into the Roman occupation of the region and second, to provide practical experience of archaeological methods for students at the university as well as at Armstrong. The arrangement was supported by the creation of a new lectureship divided between the two institutions and Birley's appointment in 1930. Such was the burden of work, in 1935 Birley managed to effect a change in his appointment when he became the resident Lecturer in Roman Archaeology at

Durham while his duties at Armstrong passed to Ian Richmond. From 1937 the emphasis on the teaching at Durham was on Roman Britain. But for all these developments, still there was little support within the university for the creation of a degree in archaeology, as it was felt there was no prospect of a career in the subject. In the meantime Birley (1937: 65) was to admit that the majority of those who passed through his classes up to at least the Second World War were students in History and to a lesser extent Classics (cf. Anon. 1937: 252).

The innovations at Liverpool and Durham (and Newcastle) were replicated in other institutions, albeit on a less ambitious scale. A number of the newer metropolitan universities appointed staff who among teaching duties in the likes of classics and ancient history, offered some sort of instruction in archaeology, usually in its classical form. Of the universities that existed at the time that Haverfield could refer, Leeds University appointed Percy Dodd to a lectureship in classics in 1911 (cf. Stephens 1975). A.M. Woodward arrived in the same university pre-1914. He was followed there by H.G. Evelyn White in 1920. With regard to Manchester University, the career of J.H. Hopkinson, brother of the University's Vice-Chancellor and formerly of Birmingham University, was summarized in Chapter 8. He was Lecturer in Classical Archaeology there between 1901 and 1904. The work undertaken in the Manchester area was in the name of the Excavation Committee of the regional branch of the Classical Association, with which Haverfield enjoyed close ties, as well as by staff in classics. The situation is slightly clearer at Birmingham. The new university was the outcome of the expansion of Mason's College which originally had its own chair of classics held by E.A. Sonnenschein (1851–1929), a post he continued to occupy in the new university.[19] He was also a leading figure in the foundation of the Classical Association. In 1912 the university was moving towards creating a number of new honours schools including one in classics. At that time the most pressing need was for a professor of Greek while the requirements of Greek archaeology were also urged. The 1914–18 war delayed the matter and a full chair was not established until 1924 (Vincent and Hinton 1947: 101–5). A chair in Latin came in 1919, just after Sonnenschein's retirement. The *Proceedings of the Classical Association* for 1917 report a Mr C.D. Chambers, described as lecturer at the

---

19. For Sonnenschein cf. Brodie 1924: 7; Mackay 1978. Haverfield knew Sonnenschein, for the former corresponded with the latter about Roman antiquities in Warwickshire (cf. *VCH* Warks. I (1906): 240).

university, speaking to the Bristol branch in December 1916 about *The Frontier Defences of Roman Britain*. Chambers published at least one article on a Romano-British theme, on the island's dovecotes (Chambers 1920).[20]

In addition to these universities there were a number of institutions which do not appear to have offered any teaching in the subject of (Romano-British) archaeology but whose staff were involved in excavation of Roman period sites. For instance, in 1912 or 1913, F.N. Pryce of UC Aberystwyth and another person who was at least on the margins of the Haverfield 'group', excavated Cae Gaer, Llangurig, Montgomeryshire with a group of students. This was a site Haverfield had discussed previously.[21] It is not clear if this excavation was a university exercise. It certainly did not possess at that time, and

20. Charles Chambers MA (*c*.1867–1924), Harrow and Hertford College, Oxford, with a 1st in *Literae Humaniores* and the Ellerton Prize for an essay on Old Testament and Egyptian monuments, was originally appointed in 1904 (cf. *The Times* 12 February 1924). He was to become Reader in and later Chair of Greek at Birmingham (1921–4), having previously been a schoolmaster at Bromsgrove School. Again, I owe some of this information to Colin Wallace.

21. There is some confusion in the reports of this work. The Report of the Committee of ancient earthworks and fortified enclosures at the Congress of Archaeological Societies (26 June 1914) has the work in July 1912, '...by Welsh and other archaeologists under the direction of Mr F.N. Pryce of the British Museum' (p. 11). A report by Pryce (1914: 205) says work was undertaken in August 1913. The participants listed are mainly UC Aberystwyth people with others from elsewhere in Wales. Haverfield in *Roman Britain in 1913* (Haverfield 1914a) implies that Pryce was at Cae Caer in the summer of 1913. It would be useful to know more about how Pryce became involved in archaeology. It might have been due to Herbert John Fleure (1878–1969). Fleure, originally a student in zoology at UC Aberystwyth (1897–1901), became a research fellow in the department before holding a research studentship at the University of Zurich and then returning to lecture in zoology, geology and botany. He was elected Professor of Zoology in 1910, becoming its head in 1917 and in 1918 the first Professor of Geography and Anthropology which allowed him to create the first combined department of Geography and Anthropology. In 1930 he became the first Professor of Geography at the University of Manchester before he retired in 1944. I.C. Peate (d.1982, aged 91 years) who with a research degree from UCA in geography, anthropology and archaeology (1924), certainly was a student and was later to hold the position of Keeper of Welsh Folk Life at the National Museum of Wales. He was, from 1927, the curator of the Welsh Folklife Museum (*Antiqs J* 63 (1983); 546). Fleure, with particular interests in studying how man evolved as a result of his physical and social environment, was a close co-worker with H.E.J. Peake (cf. Bowen 1969; Garnett 1981; Scott-Fox 2002: 88, 216).

still does not, a department of archaeology. At the University of Glasgow, S.N. Miller excavated a number of Roman forts in Scotland, most notably the Antonine Wall forts of Balmuildy (1912–14) and Old Kilpatrick (1923–4) before being invited by the Yorkshire Archaeological Committee to lead its 1925–7 excavations at York. In the 1930s A.M. Woodward, formerly of Leeds but by then lecturer in ancient history at the University of Sheffield, was excavating the Roman villa at Rudston in Yorkshire (Woodward 1932–4; Woodward and Steer 1936–8).

It is these developments up to *c*.1912, which possibly explain the clause in Haverfield's will concerning the potential appointment of a lecturer at Oxford. But for all these advances, however, virtually none of the institutions offered degree qualifications in archaeology. At best, there were diplomas (as at Oxford, in classical archaeology pre-First World War (cf. Chapter 4) – and where a diploma in archaeology was a product of the period after the Second World War, and Liverpool from about the same time) and certificates etc. One of the reasons for the reluctance was the common belief there was no prospect of a career in archaeology (e.g. Birley 1937), not least because there was only just emerging post-1919 a state-funded archaeological service and so a career structure. In 1975, J.N.L. Myres in the capacity of President of the London Society of Antiquaries recounted that:

> When I was an undergraduate more than fifty years ago, persons who could be properly described as professional archaeologists were very rare birds indeed. A few posts in two or three departments of the British Museum, one or two more in the National Museums of Scotland and Wales and in university museums, then almost confined to Oxford and Cambridge, two or perhaps three professorships, none of them with any departmental staff, and a minimal number of very badly paid posts in the Royal Commissions and the Ancient Monuments Inspectorate of HM Office of Works. Finally, of course, there was ...O.G.S. Crawford, who had just forced himself as a more or less self-appointed Archaeology Officer upon a reluctant, and somewhat resentful Ordnance Survey. That was about the lot, and, even if one includes more or less learned Secretaries of three or four learned Societies and the Directors of the British Schools in Athens and Rome, the total number of scholars who could be properly described as professional archaeologists at that time was probably no more than twenty-five or thirty at the outside. When I inquired, on taking my degree, about the prospects of archaeology as a career, I was firmly warned off by mentors, for all practical purposes, I was told, there was

no careers in archaeology, and, if one had to earn a living, as I had, one must find some other way of doing it (1975: 5).[22]

It was for these reasons that the award of degrees in the subject in the United Kingdom was to remain an innovation for the decades after the Second World War and especially in the 1960s and 1970s. Before this, in all these instances archaeology was usually taught as an adjunct to departments of classics, ancient history or even extra-mural studies and continuing education because this was where academic staff were located. Elsewhere it was included as a part of a general degree. It does not require emphasizing that the introduction of archaeology degrees does not mean that Romano-British studies were necessarily a part of the instruction.[23] Continuing the pattern, the Scottish universities were as equally slow as their English counterparts: Edinburgh created the Abercromby Professorship (with Gordon Childe) in 1926, while at Glasgow a separate archaeology department, with its first professor (Leslie Alcock), was born out of Geology as late as 1972.

If the pre-war situation Haverfield was once pleased to highlight seemed rosy with respect to the universities' provision for instruction in Romano-British archaeology, after the First World War, however, the situation, rather than continuing to make the progress, was in retreat. While Oxford failed to grasp the initiative in 1920, at Cambridge the subject went off in another direction. Since the early 1880s the university had enjoyed something of a tradition in classical archaeology, a reputation cemented in 1883 with the construction of a new Museum of Classical Archaeology which brought together the Fitzwilliam Museum with the holdings of the university's own Antiquarian Committee and those of the Cambridge Antiquarian Society. This collection was administered by the Antiquarian Committee which indirectly also influenced decisions about teaching. But now the emphasis was on as much British anthropological (i.e. as a form of prehistory) as classical material (Clarke 1925). In 1920 the Board of

---

22. In the same vein, in 1940, Kendrick in a tribute to his successor at the British Museum wrote of R.A. Smith: 'British archaeology did not possess in those days (e.g. 1898–1920) the wide following of students that have been attracted to the subject in recent years, and while it would be untrue to say that Smith was ever "a solitary pioneer" he did make his contribution' (*The Times* 23 January 1940).

23. By 1953 Leeds had in post W.V. Wade (*c.*1911–1955), described as Lecturer in Romano-British archaeology (cf. Moore 1939), and a numismatist and excavator of Roman sites in Yorkshire (cf. obit. *CW* 55 (1956): 368–9). I owe this information to Colin Wallace.

Archaeological and Anthropological Studies was created, as an amalgam of the 1883 Antiquarian Committee with the 1904 Board of Anthropological Studies coupled to a subtle redefining of the remit of the Disney chair. The outcome of this was to ensure that Cambridge's reputation for the study of British and international prehistory through anthropology was now established while classical archaeology, without a Romano-British element, was left essentially as an adjunct of Classics (Clark 1989: 23–7).

Outwith Oxbridge the situation was similarly grim. In truth, the newer universities were not yet sufficiently established to change the situation. Where there was potential was with the newer institutions, such as Liverpool and Manchester. But such institutions continued to make appointments looking to classical archaeology, and of individuals who at best might have possessed an introductory grounding in Romano-British work, but who had moved on to wider (e.g. Mediterranean or Near Eastern) horizons. Instead there were still not yet any dedicated Romanists comparable to Philip Newbold at Armstrong College, with the possible exception of Donald Atkinson (now Reader in Ancient History at Manchester) at any of these institutions. The changed economic climate did not help the finances at those institutions that relied on endowments and gifts to finance their activities. This was especially so at Liverpool. The innovativeness of its Archaeological Institute could only continue as long as the subscriptions and gifts flowed. Although it is commonly, if somewhat erroneously, believed to have went into 'decline' after the War – the seeds for its 'decline' were there pre-War – that the institute failed to develop its resource base meant the university increasingly had to intercede to 'protect' it (Freeman in prep.). The institute's financial situation continued to worsen in the years after the War and with the recession and the decline of the city's mercantile community, it was finally fully absorbed into the university in 1948 as the School of Oriental History and Archaeology. In turn there was a shift in the emphasis towards teaching over research and over the years the Institute staffs' teaching was more and more integrated into the University's degree programmes. Meanwhile, at Birmingham the circumstances did not permit the innovations that were planned at the outbreak of the war.

The failure of (and failings in) of Romano-British studies in an academic sense after the First World War is exemplified in two different ways. In 1935 B.H. Garnons Williams submitted an account to *Greece and Rome*, the mouthpiece of the Classical Association, of an innovation he had recently attempted with the sixth form at his 'northern public school' (p. 129), namely a course on Roman Britain (Garnons Williams

1934–5).[24] That it was so innovative, the author wanted to share the results with his readers. The reasons why Roman Britain, 'a study which is generally regarded merely as an interesting by-way' (p. 130), was selected as a course lay with the facts that Sixth Form (boys) were not likely to be incapable of being interested in Roman Britain. Roman Britain was also a byway of ancient history, so the subject could be used as a complement to Roman history. It was also regarded as an 'atypical Roman province' and therefore relatively unimportant and paradoxically more interesting and stimulating. Elsewhere it was argued that educationally the subject taught the student not to take anything for granted but they should question everything (p. 137). This last point owed something to Garnons Williams admitting he had enjoyed, while an undergraduate, hearing R.G. Collingwood's lectures. And of course the location of the school made it possible to visit some impressive Roman remains. The reading list for the curriculum is instructive: A.R. Burn's *The Romans in Britain*, T. Kendrick and C. Hawkes' *Archaeology in England and Wales, 1914–1931*, Furneaux's *Tacitus*, Haverfield (and Macdonald), Collingwood's *Archaeology of Roman Britain* and *Roman Britain* and Ward's *The Roman era*) as well as the Ordnance Survey's maps. The core components of the course included the Roman Wall, towns, villas, religion and the end of Roman Britain. It is impossible to say to what extent Garnons Williams initiative was unique, although it seems A.R. Burn may have attempted something similar for the Sixth Form at Uppingham in 1930–31 and which resulted in his *The Romans in Britain: an Anthology of Inscriptions* (1932).

In spite of these innovations at school-level, Romano-British studies in the schools and universities seems not to have made much progress judging from the quality of discussion among some members of the SPRS in January 1937 (Anon. 1937). Present at a meeting chaired by R.G. Collingwood, were A.R. Burn, Richmond, R.H. Barrow, Eric Birley, Philip Corder, R.W. Moore, C.E. Stevens and Ronald Syme. The breakdown of the individuals affiliations is instructive; at least eight Oxford MAs and one at Glasgow (but originally Oxford).[25]

24. Basil Hugh Garnons Williams (1906–1992), Winchester and Hertford College Oxford, with Firsts in *Literae Humaniores* 1929; Head of Classics at Sedbergh School 1930, followed by appointments at Marlborough (1935), Plymouth College, as headmaster (1945) and headmaster of Berkhamstead School 1953–72; cf. *Who Was Who* IX (1996): 199; *The Times* 11 and 13 April 1992. I owe these references to Colin Wallace.

25. Barrow (former senior scholar at Exeter College), Corder (then based at York), Moore (from Shrewsbury School), Stevens, Syme, Birley, Richmond and Collingwood were all Oxford MAs. The 'outsider', Burn, in fact went up

Reading the account of the meeting (*Report on the Discussion on 'Roman Britain' as a Subject of Teaching*) it is difficult to discern what was the purpose of the exercise, although it seems to have been part of a series of meetings discussing issues in education.[26] The comments reported are disjointed and are largely anecdotal to which Collingwood struggled to provide a coherent overview. The opinions, however, are informative of what some saw as the merits of studying Roman Britain. For instance, Barrow commented on certain strengths inherent in the subject (e.g. its emphasis on local and English history as a part of world history, that it facilitated the teaching of Latin and the way it served as a gentle introduction to Roman provincial administration, literature and epigraphy for the study of Roman imperial history). On the negative side he was concerned that it ran the risk of creating false perspectives, of over-emphasizing the local dimension, that the subject could not be treated on its own but had to be seen as a part of the Roman empire for which there were limited chances of teaching at most schools. Above all, it could err in to superficiality. In comparison, Birley reported on who was required to read the subject at Durham (e.g. modern historians and very few classicists). He also bemoaned the absence of decent textbooks for teaching, especially for Britain's Latin inscriptions (but ignoring Burn 1932?). This was a point taken up by Burn who made some suggestions to improve the situation, not least the compilation of a book containing all the literary sources for Roman Britain. As a schoolmaster, Corder could speak with a greater degree of familiarity with the problems of teaching the subject and noted that schoolboys, with their natural enthusiasm, readily participated in training-cum-research excavations. Returning to the academics, Moore argued the wider scale teaching of the subject was hindered by the structure of the current School Higher Certificate. But the subject had its merits not least because, echoing a line of Haverfield's, 'Rome's chief work was done in the provinces.'

The most striking observations were to come first from Richmond, then Stevens and finally Syme. Richmond, after recounting his story of finding an uncut copy of Haverfield's *The Romanization* in his school library and how it opened up a new world because it showed that original work demanded creative work, still opined: 'On the other hand, as there was no place for archaeology in school examinations, it

---

to Christ Church before ending up at Glasgow (1946–69).

26. In the *Journal of Roman Studies* XXIX (1939): 231–5 was published *Report on the Discussion of 'the Problem of Teaching Republican History in Schools'*.

was likely to attract only the less intelligent and because it offered small opportunities for a career, it could not be encouraged.' He also advised that the best training excavations for schoolboys were in gravel pits because there would be few finds but good stratification. Stevens offered an even harsher appraisal about whether '…archaeology had educational value, of which he was not sure.' Last but not least, and perhaps most surprising of all given his absence from the subject as a whole, Syme recommended that the discipline archaeology deserved study because it not only concerned the history of the island but also served as an introduction to primary source evidence (literary and archaeological) and because it was not so prone to facile generalizations. In other words Syme was repeating the established opinion on the relevance of archaeology to ancient history (at Oxford), one previously articulated by Haverfield.

In his concluding comments, with sentiments that underpinned his general attitude to what he thought was the longer-term relevance in studying Roman Britain, Collingwood observed:

> …the discussion had revealed the fact that Roman Britain had found its place in the teaching of schools and universities. Some speakers deplored the fact: but could we now alter it? To him the value of historical study depended less on the importance of the facts studied than on the student's manner of approaching them. The student must feel that they are facts closely concerning himself; and the methods used must be the best possible, with every freedom for the critical and constructive faculties. The value of this movement towards archaeology in education was clear from the previous speaker's [Syme] description of the response it aroused in their pupils and from the way in which they had adapted methods of research to the purposes of teaching. Because it was a short period and a small subject it made use of very delicate instruments, and this trained pupils in accurate thinking. The recent increase in accuracy of historical thought in this country was exemplified in the popularity of this subject, and thus the study of Roman Britain was symptomatic of the desire for a further increase in accuracy, which was bound to improve the standard of historical studies as a whole (p. 253).

Just as the pre-war innovations in the university sector heralded a false dawn, there were other indications that (Romano-British) archaeology was not in the best of conditions at the outbreak of the First World War. When one looks at the amount of excavation work which was undertaken, the period 1900 to 1910 was important for Roman archaeology in Britain as a whole. Not only was there Haverfield's involvement with the CEC and then Corbridge but there were a number of other equally large as well as smaller long-term on-going projects (e.g. Silchester 1910;

Corbridge and Wroxeter 1914; Caerwent 1917). To be sure it is clear that Haverfield was an important part in trying to get other excavations started – he was on the Wroxeter Committee (1911) which was appealing for funds (*The Times*, 3 October 1911), while still broadcasting the results of on-going excavations. Indeed, the amount of excavation which went on in this period is impressive. The same rosy impression of the strength of the subject is evident in assessments of the publications of the period. With respect to the publication and interpretation of these labours, a recurring theme in Haverfield's work before the First World War, was a call for an improvement in the quality of the dissemination of the results derived by excavation, the cataloguing of classes of finds, the reading of inscriptions and in the general interpretation of the data. It is indisputable these improvements were beginning to occur in the early twentieth century. After the War, superficially the situation looked as good as it had been five years earlier. Macdonald (1929/1930) provided an overview of progress between 1914 and 1928. After 1918, the large-scale excavations resumed: Richborough (1922–4 and 1926–7), Caerwent (1923–6), Wroxeter (1924–8), Lydney Park (1928–9) and St Albans (1930+), the majority supported by the London Society of Antiquaries and in part by the Haverfield Bequest (cf. Todd 2003: 38). In his summary of Romano-British archaeology between 1910 and 1960, Richmond (1960: 173) could point to much activity in the 1920s, and to the kind of large, flagship excavations typical of the last decade of the nineteenth and the first decade of the twentieth centuries had just about ended. There was also Miller's work on behalf of the Yorkshire Archaeological Committee at York (1925–8). Such was the scope of this work, in his retrospective on Romano-British studies after the First World War, Frere claimed there came to exist two separate (university based) groups doing research, mainly through excavation: '...between the Simpson-Richmond school in the North, patiently unraveling the problems of the frontier, in carefully planned small-scale work, and in the South, the great green-field programmes at Silchester, Caerwent, Wroxeter and Caistor-by-Norwich, culminating with Wheeler at Verulamnium between 1930 and 1934' (1988: 2–3). On the province's Roman frontiers, Richmond was to write: 'In the annals of archaeology on Hadrian's Wall the decade 1929–1939 will always stand out as the time when the principal periods in the history of the monument were firmly fixed and the complicated relationship between its component parts was securely defined' (1950: 43). This was when the chronological history of the Wall was refined, when Birley and Richmond followed up Simpson's excavations at Birdoswald to formulate a new interpretive framework for the evolution of Hadrian's Wall (Breeze 2003). It is for these reasons that, reflecting the same optimism, Jones

(1987: 88–9) suggested that while difficult, it was not impossible to construct for the decade before the Second World War the sort of prosopographical structure for Romano-British studies he proposes for the post-Second World War era. The pre-First World War years were difficult because, as Jones appreciated, it was difficult to identify who might have been in the one 'school' of the time: that of Haverfield. He argued, however, it becomes easier for the years 1919–45 when there were then three figures who dominated the subject: Simpson, Wheeler and Collingwood, aided and supported by such 'junior' figures as V.E. Nash Williams, Eric Birley and Ian Richmond. This conceptualizing seems somewhat forced. Jones, while missing that Wheeler claimed to have 'students' at Cardiff, accepts that he never really established a 'distinctive' school, indeed was unable to, not least because of his subsequent peripatetic existence. Simpson was temperamentally and professionally unable to effect an influence other than by helping a small and intimate band of personal contacts. And, as will be argued below, by this time Collingwood's commitment to Romano-British studies was on the wane.

In fact the closer one looks at it, the stronger the impression is that Romano-British studies were not in the healthiest of conditions. This is so post-1918 and as likely to be pre-1914. While this impression benefits from hindsight, the problems of the post-War years were already there before the outbreak of the War. It is noteworthy that in the pre-War years, from *c*.1901 onwards, Haverfield in his various annual statements on progress in Roman Britain, increasingly noted how the amount of excavation being undertaken was slipping from a high in the late 1890s, a decline caused in part by the refusal of landowners or their agents to grant access. The situation was acerbated by the outbreak of the war. Another part of the problem was finance. Excavation was becoming more expensive and the changed economic climate post-1914 made for additional difficulties. But this was symptomatic of another issue. What was inhibiting research at this time was the combination of the dependence of excavation committees as well as public beneficence to fund increasingly expensive excavations. The division of responsibility between a director and his committee was bound to create tensions. Ward's experience at Gellygaer and Caerwent had demonstrated the need in committee-run excavations for 'clear direction entrusted to one person' (Boon 1975: 52).[27] Garstang ran into similar problems at Ribchester

---

27. The 'learning' process is evident in Ward's correspondence with Mill Stephenson in the preparation of what was to become an unpublished chapter in Ward's *The Antiquary's Book* (1911). Asking about Stephenson's experiences at Silchester, according to Boon, Ward had not had an entirely enjoyable time

(Edwards 2000). The situation was made all the worse by the increases induced by inflation and the increasingly complex – and hence costly – process of excavation. National and local government refused to support the burden consistently and properly. In the relatively prosperous decades before the war, it was possible, if not always easy, to raise subscription funds. The number of major and long-term excavations undertaken in this period is proof of the fact. But even then there was recognition of problems to come. The insidious dependence on public generosity was noted as far back as the 1890s. In 1906 an anonymous reviewer (perhaps H.B. Walters) of the Melandra report lamented:

> In Germany, where the public support of natural, historical and linguistic science is intelligent, organised and methodical, there is no especial need for drawing upon private beneficence. In America the public-spirited millionaire is found to take upon himself some part at any rate of the debt which riches owe to research. But in this country the shortcomings of the national administration are but too rarely compensated by the enlightened liberality of the opulent. Let the magnates of commerce at Manchester ...be stirred at least by the Committee's appeal to their local patriotism, and determine that the new investigations at Toot Hill and Castleshaw which the Committee propose, shall not languish for lack of funds (*Class Rev* XX (1906): 290).

Elsewhere, this time to the British Academy in February 1911, Haverfield reported on recent research in Roman Britain and prefaced his talk with an assessment of its state. In his opinion, 1910 was something of a watershed. But access to sites and the increasing expense of excavating was becoming a problem. Later in the same month, Haverfield was in the chair at a meeting of the Society of Antiquaries of London, when he learnt that Caerwent was probably going to close down because of problems with the landowner. And again in the same month it was reported he had said: '...the past year constituted in some ways an epoch in Romano-British studies' (*The Times* 23 February 1911; cf. 24 February 1910), for the year had seen the end of work at Silchester, Caerwent and Newstead. The termination of these excavations was a combination of them reaching the end of their natural lives but more worryingly, it was becoming more difficult to obtain financial support from public sources. The situation was made all the more difficult by the events of 1914–18

---

at Gellygaer and Caerwent. Part of his problem was finances, another the way that the excavation was governed by the interference of a committee and lay-partners. Note too Hayter's (1921: 22) observations that he could employ fourteen labourers on pre-war excavations for the four in 1920.

and their aftermath. Of the larger projects, only Corbridge was still going. Plans for *Verulamium* had been still-born although the hopes for Wroxeter were advancing.

The implications of this résumé are that, rather than being in a healthy condition, in the period between at least *c.*1914 and 1929 Romano-British studies were at best marking time in reworking the same approaches to field work and returning to old themes with respect to their interpretation. What was left of the momentum generated up to 1914 had come to a halt. Once peace returned, it was difficult to revitalize it. The loss of staff, rising costs, and the changed social climate now made it difficult to return to the optimistic archaeology of the late Victorian–Edwardian era. Nor was Haverfield, in the capacity of 'facilitator' *par excellence*, in a position to contribute. The collapse in his health in 1915 was matched by what appears to be a change in his attitude to excavation. His experience of the Corbridge excavations might have played a part in this respect. With hindsight, Haverfield made what reads now as an acknowledgement to how such times had gone forever. At what was to be his last public engagement, speaking to the autumn meeting of the CWAAS in August 1919 he observed:

> I can imagine few sites in West Cumberland which would better deserve excavation than this site of Old Carlisle ...I will confess that some years ago I had hoped that the site ... might have been purchased and excavated by a wealthy Cumbrian, but that hope did not materialize, and the recent war, which has in so many ways wrought untold harm to archaeological study, has put the excavation of such sites beyond the means of an ordinary subscription list. Before the war, it is possible that a fort of this character might have been cleared out for £500. Today, when, as I am told, is the case on a site in Yorkshire, the labourers have to be paid wages which exceed those of a fairly well paid University lecturer, I imagine that they who would clear Old Carlisle had better see their way to a full £1000 before they begin. ...Therefore, I will not urge on any one present the undertaking of any such scheme. But I am clear that if good future should ever make it possible, abundant reward would follow (suggesting work on the left flank of the wall, at Maryport or Netherhall). ... But in the new world and the new Europe that are before us, much that used to be possible must be surrendered as beyond attainment, and we can only do what we can individually, not altogether by spending money, but by solid work, to minimise the evil, which one of the learned nations of the world has in our time brought upon learning (1920c: 149–50).

A new world of 'professional' archaeology of a sort had arrived, perhaps the natural culmination of his efforts of the previous thirty years. The outbreak of the First World War effectively terminated a bygone age of leisurely research and excavation and 'antiquarian' publication. One can detect what reads almost as an air of desperation in C.H. Read's observations in his presidential address to the London Antiquaries in April 1913. Read's opinions are so important it is worth quoting some of the relevant points at length.

> I have more than once in this room pointed out that our old Society should keep a watchful eye on the progress of specialization in the archaeological world. Past centuries have shown that this process is both continuous and inevitable, and, in most aspects, of great practical use. The question we have to ask ourselves is, how the process will affect us; what will be the result, if archaeological study continues to be subdivided into a still greater number of bodies with interests limited to specific fields? It is clear that we cannot complain, any more than the father of a vigorous and intelligent family can resent their taking the initiative at their own time. The defect of specialization is well known and recognized, though perhaps recognition alone hardly meets the evil. Archaeology is a wide field, and, both in space and method, is daily widening. No single life would suffice to master it under modern conditions, and the specialist must needs content himself with a knowledge of the science, rather than to attempt completeness of knowledge of its manifestations. Among workers in this field, and equally among those who train them, the tendency is set strongly towards specialization, and the graduate in archaeology, as I may call him, is summoned, almost peremptorily, to devote his energies to some definite and limited study, epigraphy, early Greek culture, Roman trade, the prehistoric ages, or what not. His teachers and associates think they are consulting his best interests in urging upon him the desirability of tilling his own little plot of this archaeological field, without trespassing more than is necessary on the ground of his predecessors or contemporaries. ...If there be any truth in it, and I think the experience of the past ten years makes it clear that there is, our problem is, what particular function is the body-politic will be performed by the Society of Antiquaries of London in twenty or thirty years' time? As I have said before ...I am inclined to think that in the past half-century the Society has been too retiring, that it has not sufficiently asserted itself for the public good in the dignified way that is its right, that it has not been at the pains to claim its place in the front ranks of scientific work, where it should always have the right to stand. While I confess to a sympathetic feeling towards so modest and retiring a pose, I am compelled to doubt its wisdom, and even its propriety. However modest we may be individually, however averse to submit to the glare of the footlights in our proper persons, we dare not forget that in our corporate capacity, we are, as our Charter amply shows, nothing less than trusties, the purpose of our trust being the furtherance of archaeological science, while the beneficiaries are the British public an the world at large. In so far as we allow opportunity, or those who can help us to make opportunity, to drift by our doors we are false to our

trust, and a persistent policy of the kind will surely lead to stranding in a backwater. …Another result of our present condition is that many memoirs of high quality, of a kind eminently suited to our publications, are read in other places and ultimately produced in a very inadequate manner. This is nobody's gain, and yet our loss. (*Proc Soc Antiqs London* 1912–13: 141–2).

Read then went on to criticize the rather cosy, unchallenging nature of the Society's weekly meetings, where the fellows had come accustomed to 'an evening's entertainment.'

There is another way in which we can see the moribund condition of Romano-British studies at about the time of Haverfield's death. As already noted, Randall suggested that, with hindsight, a pivotal moment in the improvement of publication came after Conybeare's *Roman Britain* (1903: Randall 1946: 80). In the succeeding decades there appeared a small number of monographs which consciously attempted to synthesize for the general public, but to a better standard than previously, the results of the work of the preceding twenty odd years. For instance, in 1912, on the advice of (the late) G.E. Fox and assisted by Mill Stephenson, A.H. Lyell completed his bibliography of Romano-British monuments in the United Kingdom arranged by county, a work that anticipated Bonser's Romano-British bibliography by nearly 50 years (Bonser 1964). At about the same time, the excavator of Caerwent and Gellygaer, John Ward reported he had proposed to '…write a volume on Roman Britain, but I soon found the subject was too large and complex to be treated comprehensively, and at the same time to place the reader *en rapport* with the results of the systematic excavations of the last twenty-five years. These have vastly increased our knowledge of Roman Britain, especially its "major monuments" – the towns, forts, public buildings, and houses – and to these I confined myself in *Romano-British buildings and earthworks'* (1911a: v; cf. 1911b). As its title suggests, this was a monograph that concentrated on the architecture of Romano-British archaeology. Towards this end, Ward had two explicit objectives: to describe the remains and to interpret the evidence. At the same time, however, he returned to his original proposal and completed *The Roman Era in Britain,* a monograph representing a major innovation in the way that Roman Britain was presented. Ward was able to draw on the preceding 50 years work, including that supported by the Society of Antiquaries of London, to publish 'a volume …which for its day carried a volume of detailed information quite unsurpassed in any other province of the Empire' (Richmond 1960: 173). It was the first synthesis of the island's Roman history and archaeology for nearly 25 years. After an introductory chapter which made general observations about the island, its archaeology, its geology, and its

natural resources, Ward then summarized the qualities of earlier literature on Britain in the Roman period and concluded with a résumé of the
country's museum collections. The core of the text is a series of chapters
which describe the evidence, by categories ranging from bridges and
military remains, through to religion, pottery, metal implements and ap-
pliances and coins. The monograph was, in fact, the sort of 'finds of
Roman Britain' that was later superceded by Collingwood's (and later
Richmond's) *Archaeology of Roman Britain* of 1930. That Ward could complete such a book was a reflection not just of the accumulation of the
evidence of the preceding years but equally was due to the results of the
more systematic analysis of the range of finds that excavation was producing (cf. the very favourable review in the 1912 *Archaeologia
Cambrensis*). It also indicated a conceptual shift, where the Roman period
in British history, in terms of its archaeological evidence, could be seen as
something distinct from other periods. In both aspects, as we have seen,
Haverfield had played a part.

Ward was an acquaintance of Haverfield's but the latter is not credited in the Preface of the *Roman Era* (and his *Romanization of Roman
Britain* is missing from the bibliography, although his opinions are occasionally noted throughout the text, a fact noted by an unnamed
reviewer in *The Times* (31 August 1911)). Haverfield's absence implies
another trend that began to emerge in Romano-British research at
about this time. The success of the progress to which Haverfield contributed was such, it was inevitable he and his ilk would be increasingly
marginalized. His difficult personality with his ability to alienate others
may have contributed here. Similarly his problems post-1915 must
have added to his detachment. But above all, if he was to retain a pivotal
position, he had to continue to control the dissemination of information, especially if he gave up his part in directing excavation. It is
interesting to note how his direct influence in a number of excavations
of the time that one would have expected him to have been interested
in, was slight or even non-existent. Representative of this new type of
work was Taulford Elly's work at Hayling Island, published in 1908 as a
monograph incidentally submitted in part for the requirements for a
DLitt. at the University of London. The site was recognized, significantly for what follows below, as a non-villa establishment and
excavated as such, annually between August 1897 and 1907. Haverfield
certainly knew of Elly's work; he wrote summaries of the early years of
excavations in the likes of *The Antiquary* while Elly provided Haverfield
information about it for the *VCH* Hants. (although in the end
Haverfield did not complete it). In his final report, however, Elly did acknowledge the assistance of A.S. Murray, H.A. Grueber, S.G. Starling,

Mill Stephenson and C.H. Read (at least two of who were associated with the British Museum). What is striking is that the sort of works summarized here represent a form of publishing to which the academic fraternity, with one or two exceptions, was not contributing. This is certainly true up to 1914 and still partially so post-1918. The strength of the relationship between non-university researchers and fieldwork is emphasized by the appearance of the Methuen County Archaeologies series edited by T. Kendrick. In a review, by ?Crawford, of the first volume in the series, H.J.E. Peake's *The Archaeology of Berkshire* (1931), it was noted that the series was the next stage after the VCH volumes. They were the '...children of that weary Titan, the Victoria County History. They attempt to condense with a single octavo volume the gist of these five heavy Victorian tomes. But, we hasten to add they achieve both more and less than their progenitors' for they were more up-to-date, cheaper and usable but otherwise less detailed. 'They are conceived on a scale befitting the generation that is to use them ...the County Archaeologies do not cover the same ground as the Victoria County History; they are primarily archaeological, whereas the Victoria County History is primarily historical.' The County series was also meant to engage a wider public readership, while bringing to the reader the results of 25 years of progress. 'During this period of accumulation, synthesis has been impossible. The present series is a successful attempt to consolidate our achievements' (Anon. 1931).

It was for these reasons that in an overview of Romano-British studies, it was asserted: 'In 1910 when the Society for the Promotion of Roman Studies was founded the study of Roman Britain was already firmly set upon its path. Earlier brilliant treatments by Francis Haverfield, in Traill's Social England, in the Victoria County History and his own Romanization of Roman Britain had set a general picture which was attractive and cogent synthesis of the evidence provided by literature and archaeology' (Richmond 1960: 173). But things were not to move on significantly. In his summary of Romano-British studies between 1914 and 1920 Macdonald (1924) listed what he considered to be the major publications. And yet the list is surprisingly slight which is turns leads one to ask, unlike the overviews which profited from the rosy tint of hindsight, if in fact Macdonald was inadvertently offering a more realistic reflection on the condition of the subject.[28] Slightly later, in 1930, Kendrick and Hawkes could speak of Haverfield's *Roman Occupa-*

---

28. It included Oswald and Pryce 1920, Haverfield 1924, R.G. Collingwood 1923, Anderson's new edition of Furneaux (1922) along with May's descriptions of the pottery from Silchester (1916) and Carlisle (May and Hope 1917).

tion, Collingwood's *Roman Britain* (1932 edition) and *The Archaeology of Roman Britain* (1930). Macdonald's 1914–28 survey, Anderson's edition of Furneaux's *Tacitus* and Oswald and Pryce's *Corpus*.[29] It might also be noted that these were exactly the same texts that Garnons Williams was recommending to his *school* class at Sedbergh.[30]

Whatever Haverfield's reputation, the sum total of the preceding paragraphs is that study of Roman Britain had failed to establish an institutional basis at least in the universities. What is more, after the War, the climate and the economic situation was not conducive to such developments. Elsewhere, the newly created British Academy was still too weak to take the lead and the State was only just beginning to get to grips with preserving and managing the nations' monuments let alone fostering research. Outside of the institutional framework there was, however, a rise in the amount of low-scale work undertaken by archaeological societies and in particular more skilled researchers across a range of non-urban and non-military sites. At the same time there were the more systematic programmes of cataloguing and description, with their emphasis on non-destructive examination, that the various Royal Commissions on Ancient and Historic Monuments were undertaking.

Although before the War the State was slow in taking the initiative, a reticence for which there were consequences especially concerning the legal protection of the nation's archaeological resources, the post-War years saw the rise of the Inspectorate (and the likes of J.P. Bushe-Fox and Paul Baillie Reynolds), itself a consequence of the greater efficacy of State intervention in the preservation and management of the nation's heritage. At the same time some of the country's museums contributed significantly to fieldwork. In fact from the mid-nineteenth century, the British Museum was in many respects the (nation's) centre for research, with its specialist experts and the knowledge of its keepers. By the 1920s the Museum's British and Medieval Antiquities depart-

---

29. There are some surprising omissions in this list. For instance E. Foord's *The Last Age of Roman Britain* (1925), which the author started in 1910. His self-imposed remit is interesting. The book was meant 'to treat the history of Britain as a part of the Roman Empire and Europe as a whole. I found the many modern works on Roman Britain of very slight value in comparison with their literary bulk, and in the end I jettisoned the greater part of the mass' (p. 5). Interestingly, Foord, more a popular writer than a scholar, felt confident enough to criticize a couple of Haverfield's published opinions.

30. And to round off the point: 'Since the war research into the history of the Roman Province of Britain has been so widespread that it was high time that the results were collated and published in the form of a continuous narrative' (Baillie Reynolds 1937: 451).

ment constituted its largest antiquities department (Miller 1973: 338). Its staff were regular contributors to excavation reports. The primacy of its position was reinforced by the 'authoritative' guides to the collections that it produced (e.g. Smith 1922; Walters 1899; 1903). Such was the range of its staff's activities it could be said: 'The Museum anticipated British universities in its appreciation of the educational value of archaeology' (Clark 1989: 5).[31] By the end of the nineteenth century, the part of the regional and provincial museums had also increasingly come to the fore. This was a trend already apparent in the 1890s – note many of Haverfield's associates in this respect – but again it is from this period that we see the rise of a number of pivotal individuals whose careers commenced in museums as well as the Royal Commission as later still the Inspectorate.[32] We have already seen that the excavation of Roman sites in Scotland had been the preserve of the Society of Antiquaries of Scotland since the 1890s.

It is a significant fact that, while the provision for Romano-British studies was at best stagnating, if not declining, in the universities, the one exception to this general decline occurred in Wales, not in a university but in a museum. Here the creation of the National Museum initiated a series of relatively well-run and well-published excavations (Randall 1946). The new museum was created by Royal Charter in 1907 and, being based in Cardiff, initially drew its staff from the city's municipal museum. Separate departments, including archaeology under the direction of John Ward, were established in 1914. Following Ward's retirement coupled to the appointment of a replacement Keeper of Archaeology at the National Museum of Wales at Cardiff, a lectureship in archaeology was created and based in the University College of South Wales and Monmouthshire (e.g. in Cardiff). R.E.M. Wheeler, as Ward's successor, was appointed to both posts in 1920, where he saw part of his task 'to secure for archaeology a recognized place in the curriculum of the Welsh university, where I was the first holder of the first lectureship in the subject' (Wheeler 1956: 63). In his version of events, Wheeler claimed he decided as part of his task as keeper and later as di-

---

31. This impression is confirmed in Aileen Fox's memoirs where she wrote that the leading figures in archaeology in her early years (the 1920s and 1930s) included F.N. Pryce, Reg. Smith, T. Kendrick and C. Hawkes, all based at the British Museum (Fox 2000: 53).

32. For example, Wheeler first with the Commission in Essex and at Colchester and especially the National Museum of Wales and then the Museum of London, as well as Cyril Fox at Cardiff, Hawkes at the British Museum, and Philip Laver and Rex Hull at Colchester.

rector of the Museum, that the archaeology department should be an aggressively fieldworking and excavating entity. He therefore initiated a series of campaigns under his direction at such Roman sites as *Segontium* (1921–3) and Gaer Brecon (1924–5) while lieutenants, such as V.E. Nash Williams, worked away at Caerwent and Caerleon (and Cyril Fox at Offa's Dyke and later on a range of prehistoric sites). On Wheeler's departure for London, the lectureship was filled by his successor to the keepership, Fox, and then later by Nash Williams (who Wheeler claimed was one of his 'students' in his time there).[33]

What these developments in the museums and the inspectorate represented was that the part previously played by the (gentleman) antiquarian had now been subsumed by the rise of national organizations and, to a lesser degree, the regional societies but, with regard to the latter, not necessarily with any substantial improvement in the quality of fieldwork. And that there were so many of them meant their efforts remained fractured and multi-directional. The national societies (the London society, the BAA and the RAI), after momentarily rising to the fore, had largely missed the chance. In England, only the London society offered any direction, with its patronage and publishing of a series of research excavations undertaken by Bushe-Fox and later Donald Atkinson in the years just up to and after the war, followed by Hawkes at *Camulodunum*, and the Wheelers at St Albans. That this occurred was flagged by its president C.H. Read in his 1913 address, which has already been noted. In that largely negative speech, Read was happy to note that two years after he had first proposed it, he was:

> …happy to be able to announce that the Franks Scholarship is now under way …In suggesting it to you, I was chiefly influenced by the need for a bond between the Society and some centre where teaching in archaeology was a permanent feature of the curriculum. That a bond of the kind would be welcomed by such an institution as the University of London …could scarcely be doubted. The advantage to the Society ..can hardly be expected to be so immediate, though there would be few to question the Society's ultimate gain. Meanwhile the arguments I advanced originally are, I think, still as valid as they were. Educational

33. In fact Nash-Williams took a First in Latin in 1919 (MA, 1923 and D.Litt. 1939). He was the assistant keeper in archaeology at NMW from 1924 and its keeper in 1926. He excavated at Caerleon between 1926 and1931 (cf. HJR 1956). When Nash-Williams joined up in 1939, Aileen Fox took over his lecture courses until 1945 when Nash-Williams returned to resume his duties (Fox 2000: 97; 99). A Dept of Archaeology at the university, one separate from the museum, became a reality in 1958 with a chair of archaeology created for Richard Atkinson along with the appointment of Leslie Alcock.

science in this country is hardly on so sound a practical a plan that we can afford to neglect an opening when it is found. The lines on which the Franks student will work are clearly defined: when followed they will certainly produce good results, and increased knowledge in the sample field of the archaeology of Britain, while the work performed in each year by the student will inevitably create in him, if it does not already exist, a feeling for archaeological research, an interest in the history of past times and their products that cannot but react to the benefit of such a body as ours. These reasons alone justify the action of the Society, but I venture to go even further ...The institution of this scholarship gives, even now, in its first year of existence, signs of a useful development. The broad lines for study or research laid down by the Joint Committee of London University and the Society limited the field to the archaeology of the British Isle and its continental relations, limits sufficiently wide to provide a training in the culture of northern Europe, even when interpreted in their narrowest sense.

Read could report two recent offers to develop the scholarship: one where its scope might include research in Spain while Arthur Evans offered £25 '...to enable the present holder of the studentship to go abroad to study the pottery of Romano-British times, the subject he had offered'. The student was R.E.M. Wheeler.[34] While the Joint Committee was, for the moment, unable to accept the first offer, Evans' offer was (*Proc Soc Antiqs London* 1912–13: 143–4).

Towards the end of the 1920s, the society also sponsored the appointment of a succession of 'archaeological officers' for London, with duties akin to what would now be called watching briefs in the developing city. Eric Birley was the first appointee, in August 1928 and, after he resigned because of his appointment to a teaching position at Durham in March 1929, was replaced by the Franks student G.C. Dunning, and he, in turn, by Frank Cottrill. The innovation, however, was not necessarily occasioned for academic reasons:

> The necessity for a more thorough supervision of excavations in the City of London has for a long time had the particular attention of the Council (of the Society), which is now able to report that by means of a fund initiated by our Fellow Mr Holland-Martin and subscribed to by many important bodies in the City, it has been possible to put this supervision on a satisfactory footing (*Antiqs J* IX (1929): 293).

The fact is that it was non-university bodies which were at the forefront. Haverfield had effectively dominated the dissemination of

---

34. The circumstances behind Wheeler accepting the studentship and Evans' offer are reported slightly differently by Hawkes (1982: 50).

knowledge through the 1890s and for the next twenty years. And yet despite his best endeavours the initiative had not really been taken up by the 'students' or the universities. In the years immediately before the outbreak of the First World War and in the post-war period, it was non-academics who were producing the discussions of that work.[35] But this non-academic fraternity was different to the gentlemen antiquarians of the mid-nineteenth century. Whilst still 'amateurs' by profession, writers such as John Ward, James Curle, Peake and Elly were far more competent than their predecessors. This development went in tandem with the emergence of far more skilled archaeological excavators.[36] Again largely 'amateur' and non-academic in content, individuals such as Bushe-Fox, Robert Forster and Frank Simpson (until his association with Durham, commencing from 1924), and the rising group of university-trained (public) school masters and many others were the ones doing the excavation. The impression is that it was the national societies and the museums that were in different ways setting the pace with respect to archaeological research in the 1920s. In more than one sense Haverfield had been instrumental in this progress but which still begs the question why had the subject of Romano-British archaeology failed to establish itself in the universities? Why had this part Haverfield's work apparently failed?

The answer parts lies in the fact that the question is wrongly phrased, predicated as it is on the assumption that Romano-British studies was or is a discipline which merited separate treatment. It is the same assumption which underpinned the SPRS survey discussed in Chapter 1. Another element which contributes to the issue is the primacy that is given to Haverfield in establishing the subject, with the corollary that as

---

35. The list of acknowledgements in Ward's *Roman Buildings and Earthworks* (1911b) is instructive. Those credited read as a Who's Who of Roman-British archaeology: Joseph Anderson, R.C. Bosanquet, J.P. Gibson, the late G.E. Fox, F.A. Bruton, J. Curle, James Barbour, A.E. Hudd, T. Ashby, Frank King, F.G. Simpson, St George Gray, George Macdonald, Dr Cox, W.H. Knowles, Col. C.E. Ruck, Thomas May, Charles Bathurst, W. Clarke, L.P. Salmon, Mill Stephenson, St John Hope. It goes without saying how few of them held university appointments.

36. 'Archaeology in Britain in the early part of (the century was firmly established by the excellent work of amateur archaeologists like Henry and Philip Laver. They were similar in background and outlook to Dr. Arthur Bullied in Somerset and the Curwens in Sussex: a generation of amateurs who spent most of their spare time devoted to the detection of and excavation of archaeological sites' (Foster 1986: 9; cf. Anon. 1942–5).

an academic, the subject had to be based in an academic institution of higher learning.

The building of Haverfield's reputation

Despite the negative impression of the realities of Romano-British archaeology post-1919, Haverfield's reputation went from strength to strength. 'Anything that Professor Haverfield writes about Roman Britain, of course, will be welcomed by all antiquarians. He writes with the authority of an expert who has specialized in the subject and he would be a daring critic who would attempt to discover errors in his work.' So wrote a nameless reviewer in Haverfield's lifetime (Anon. 1915). Miller said of Haverfield, six years after his death, he:

> ...was able to impress upon students the need of technical training, of familiarity with the researches of continental scholars, and of co-operative effort, especially co-operation between local archaeological societies and the universities (1925: 264).

Continuing in the same vein, in 1920, again recalling Haverfield on Roman Wales, W. Rhys Roberts (1922: 140) claimed 'Among modern classical scholars who have interested themselves in the archaeology of Wales the late professor Haverfield holds a foremost place with his palmary papers ...What a fine plan of campaign was there sketched out for the Welsh-Latin archaeologist, and with how keen a sense of proportion and of telling phrase.' Thirty-five years after his death, the historian of the centenary of the Leicestershire Archaeological Society could write how 1919 '...saw one other outstanding event. Professor F. Haverfield's lecture on Roman Leicester, delivered here less than six months before his death' (*The Leicestershire Archaeological Society 1855-1955* (1955): 21). Much later, Chitty was to reminisce:

> The 'Roman Antiquities Committee for Yorkshire' was inaugurated at York, in the Yorkshire Museum, in March 1906 ...Part of the programme was a lecture by the great Professor Haverfield, and much that he said is still our concern. He stressed the necessity of coordinating archaeological work ... of uniting the professional and the amateur in the field, of keeping bibliographical and field work going together. He added – as we should all agree – that Yorkshire is a county of exceptional interest in Roman history, two-faceted military and civil (1987: 3).

Elsewhere, Wheeler, in a rather purple passage, expressed the view that:

Haverfield was admittedly never notably susceptible to the niceties of field techniques …(yet) it is an astonishing fact that the broad outlines of our picture of Roman Britain remains very much as he left them. The truth is that Haverfield was concerned primarily with the landscape; he was little interested, or interested very secondary, in botany. The wide expanse of woodland, rather than the species and incidence of trees, were his theme. He was an artist: he thought and wrote as an artist. Any fool can be a sort of botanist. Almost any student with a *beta* mind can dig and record the minutiae of an individual site and sort out its potsherds. But there have been very few artists. Haverfield was one …The accumulative cleverness of a subsequent century of busy little men and women will not improve the intuitive and essential rightness of [this] artist (1961: 158).[37]

Another example of Haverfield's 'bequest' can be found in Bruton's introduction to J.P. Hall's *Caer Llugwig* (1923) which is full of the dialogue between Mommsen and Haverfield concerning the nature of the Roman occupation of Wales. Taking up this theme, in an overlooked paper exploring the romanization of Wales and building on Haverfield's 1910 survey of the Roman frontier in the Principality, Wheeler acknowledged the discoveries '…made since he (Haverfield) wrote have amplified rather than amended his tentative conclusions, and there is no limit that the preliminary deductions, supported by excavations in North, middle and South Wales are likely to undergo serious modification' (1922: 40). That said, Wheeler wanted then to look at a question not appreciated by Haverfield, a problem 'without precise analogy in the history of the Roman Empire.' One has to look hard for what Wheeler was getting at, but it would appear to be the romanization (of a sort) of the 'Welsh'. Curiously, given his acknowledgement of Haverfield and his work, Wheeler says that the process is best summarized in W.B. Henderson's *Companion to Roman Studies* 2 (at p. 372).

Other than some reservations about his competence as an excavator, in the years after his death Haverfield's reputation generally remained largely intact. His opinions still counted for something if, on occasion, the effect was in the long term negative. For example, in discussing the date of the erection of the walls around the towns of the province, Philip Laver argued that Haverfield's assertion that most of the walls in Britain were probably put up in the third or fourth century '…seems to be

---

37. The impact of Wheeler's assertion is somewhat diluted by the fact that three years earlier, in an assessment of the life and work of O.G.S. Crawford, he wrote there were three '…real progenitors of modern archaeology' – Pitt-Rivers, Arthur Evans and J.L. Myres. Crawford was in the first brood of their students (cf. *Antiquity* 32 (1958): 1–4).

utterly erroneous' (Laver 1920: 24, citing *The Romanization of Roman Britain* p. 76). Cyril Fox in his seminal *Archaeology of the Cambridge Region* (1923) challenged Haverfield's opinion about the degree of Roman intervention in the landscape in the region (Scott-Fox 2002: 42).[38] Elsewhere Haverfield has been blamed for creating false impressions and even hindering research. Randall (1946: 81) corrected the incorrect use of the name *Isca Silurum* as the Roman name for Caerleon: 'The title is of course a misnomer. The Roman name was Isca, and the tribal suffix was appropriate only to a cantonal capital: it was never applied to a legionary headquarters, nor to a fort. Yet Haverfield used the erroneous version, and it is a great consolation to amateur antiquarians to learn that great scholars can make big mistakes.' Such comments, however, might be read as more points of detail than important issues. Elsewhere, Cunliffe (1971: 22) claimed that Haverfield's 'cursory summary' of antiquarian work at Bath was 'scathing and grossly unfair' and 'deflected later archaeologists from serious reconsider(ation).' Then there was A.L.F. Rivet's criticism about the creation of a military/civil division of the province:

> Haverfield corrected [the] impression (viz. rich Romans on the one hand and seething masses of savage blue-painted Britons on the other) pointing out that Britain and Roman were not mutually exclusive terms and that in fact most of the Roman civilization had a British content. But this has resulted, through no fault of Haverfield's, in the new myth, admittedly less harmful than the old, of a province so thoroughly British that no foreign landowner would dare to show his face in it (1964: 29).

Haverfield's major statements

Along with his fieldwork and other acts of organization, Haverfield's lasting reputation rests on the durability of certain of his publications which in turn have been credited with continuing to influence the way that the subject is taught and researched. But the absence of a major statement on the subject make for problems in assessing what he thought was the real state of the discipline at the time of his death. It forces us to plunder his many articles for information. If we wish to obtain an insight into what Haverfield thought were the major features of the Roman period, we have to use isolated statements in his many articles and contrast them with his two major works, *The Romanization of*

---

38. Scott-Fox has to be treated with caution. He can be rather one-eyed and reports a number of errors. His two references to Haverfield are misleading and at least one of them is patently wrong. His mother's (Fox 2000) memoirs are less problematic.

Roman Britain and *The Roman Occupation,* both of which are discussed below in more detail. Along with these two monographs, there are a number of other publications which might be considered as approaching overviews or syntheses. The principal of these were the contributions to the *VCH* which allowed Haverfield to discuss the nature of the Roman period at a regional level, and could then be adapted to an impression on a national scale. The same sort of opportunity was also afforded by a number of other commissions, including the reports in the newspapers of lectures he had delivered to the likes of the British Academy, the Classical Association and the Roman Society. It is interesting to note that usually in these utterances Haverfield rarely gave credit to others. When he did so, it was limited to a few personal acquaintances.

In the long term Haverfield was to exploit these formats to great effect. At the start of his career, however, and before his reputation as the great synthesizer had been established, his utterances were limited to a slighter format. It has already been noted that the nineteenth century witnessed an explosion in the amount of archaeological excavation undertaken in Britain. With this expansion was a commensurate increase in work on Romano-British sites. Up to the 1890s, however, there was no co-ordinated or consistent format available on a national scale, where even the most preliminary results of that work might be reported. The likes of the Society of Antiquaries in London had tried to initiate a programme of summarizing the Roman remains of a number of English counties, but the project seems to have soon run out of steam. Of particular sites, excavators were forced to have recourse to local newspapers or occasionally the national press (e.g. *The Times* and *The Manchester Guardian*) or else to the journals of the local and regional societies. As we have seen, one of Haverfield's accomplishments was that he was to become, between 1890 and 1915, the conduit for reporting of the fieldwork of others on a national basis and thus anticipated the dedicated Roman Britain section in the *Journal of Roman Studies* (from 1921) and later its sister journal, *Britannia* (from 1971).[39] Prior to

39. On Haverfield using the results of others, see his entries in the *Arch. Anz.* (1901 to 1905 and 1909 to 1914) where he describes the progress of a large number of sites in the UK but with relatively few credits, acknowledgements for information received or even recognition of who actually undertook the work. The names provided are the usual suspects (Curle, Macdonald, Bushe-Fox, the Liverpool Committee and to a lesser degree Atkinson, Simpson, Newbold and Miller). There is the odd surprise in the lists, including the Cunningtons and their work at Casterley and Heywood Sumner at Rockbourne. Haverfield's reporting of work at Northfield Farm, Long

1907 Haverfield's statements tended to be published as annual updates in the likes of the *Archaeological Journal, The Antiquary* and *The Athenaeum*. After his elevation to the Camden chair, he continued to submit occasional reports, with the only other major pieces of archaeological synthesis he was to produce being the Roman Britain series (in 1912, 1913, 1914 and 1915) summarizing the previous year's work for the British Academy, with the later ones published in its *Proceedings*. The series was cut short by the outbreak of war. The academy statements shared the same common format with his other overviews, reporting the results of recent excavations, the discovery of inscriptions and the more 'acceptable' recent publications. The start of the series was not auspicious, being an abrupt summary of a lecture delivered to the academicians in February 1912. The main element of the lecture was criticism of 'the excess of tinkering at sites', of work begun but not completed, published and/or incompletely executed. 'More has been attempted than the supply of good men and subscriptions warrant' (Haverfield 1911–12: 409). The reports Haverfield provided for subsequent years were much more substantial and positive in tone. These reviews were also circulated separately and so were subject to comment. Of the 1913 statement an anonymous reviewer observed:

Wittenham typifies how he could monopolize the scene. In 1893 the tenant farmer, H.J. Hewett, noticed differential growth in his fields and then recorded, excavated and proved them to be the indications of a Romano-British site. What he had found was a crop mark site. While Haverfield, in the company of others, visited the site over the next few years (and indeed published something about it with Arthur Evans, cf. *The Athenaeum* 26 August 1893: 297), he reprised the results at length in an article about comparable sites elsewhere in the Upper Thames valley (Haverfield 1899d; *The Athenaeum* XIII (1900): 56 – where he was advising watching barley fields as they tended to produce better marks than wheat or root crops). What Haverfield did not emphasize was that Hewett had already published the results elsewhere, creating the impression that Haverfield was the man responsible for appreciating the significance of the discovery. Elsewhere he published a report of A. Acton's excavation at Holt (Cheshire). Haverfield had already mentioned it in his British Academy report for 1915. But since it still had not been fully published, Haverfield decided to republish his own summary (cf. Haverfield 1916d; *VCH* Berks. 1: 219). The site was also written up for the RCAHM(W) Denbighs. volume (1914). In the end Acton, who died in 1925, passed the excavation archive to the National Museum of Wales. But such was the poor condition of the records W.F. Grimes had a considerable task extracting any meaning out of them (Macdonald 1929/1930: 110).

Papers like this one are the justification for the existence of academies. It is most necessary that all who have a real interest in a subject have their knowledge kept up to date, yet few have either the ability or the opportunity to cover the whole field. In England since the days of Camden at least, Roman archaeology has been a favourite study, as a rule those who have pursued it have had a zeal much in excess of their knowledge. Not the least of the merits of Professor Haverfield's little book is that it discriminates the work that is well done and scholarly from that which has not these qualities and so helps to raise the standard of Romano-British antiquarianism generally (*Oxford Magazine* 22 January 1915: 148).

The position of authority Haverfield came to acquire meant that he became responsible – in the early years at least – for the Roman Britain reports in the Classical Association's *The Year's Work in Classical Studies*. He contributed to the 1906 and 1907 reports as well as on Latin Epigraphy and later, on Roman History with Epigraphy during the war years (1915, 1916 and 1917). With respect to these annuals, it is interesting to note how some of those who had been associated with him previously came to provide reports. For instance, Cheesman took over the Latin Epigraphy section from 1909 to 1912 and added the 1911 Roman History entry. When he enlisted in 1914 he was replaced by C.G. Stone, assisted by Cheesman.[40] Elsewhere, Haverfield was occasionally asked to lecture about Roman Britain.[41] Why he should have ceased making the sort of contributions which he had done for the previous fifteen years is unclear. The answer may lie in the fact that, with a growing reputation, his increasing involvement in work at Corbridge, which was followed by his elevation to the Camden chair and then the effects of the war, the impetus was lost. The fact that some of his public lectures were reported in the

40. Anderson contributed the 1912 Roman History bulletin. For Roman Britain post-1907 responsibility for the 1908 and '09 reports passed to Walters. From 1910 however, Bruton contributed the reports until 1914 and then for 1916, 1918–19, 1921–2, 1923–4, 1925–6 and 1927–8. With Bruton's death in 1930, the next report was made by Collingwood and in 1939 by Myres, after which the series ceased. Before this however, the importance of the reports had been diminished by the progress statements in the *Journal of Roman Studies*, starting from 1921.

41. There were also a number of other (English) publications which appear to be one-off statements: Roman Britain *Edinburgh Review* CLXXXIX (1899) and Roman Scotland *Edinburgh Review* CCXIII (1911), which was meant to be a review of five recent publications on Roman Scotland. It ended up as Haverfield attempting to write a history of the Roman conquest and occupation of Scotland. The ideas contained in this paper were developed in a later review of Roman Scotland (Haverfield 1918b).

national newspapers may have been sufficient for his purposes. Another factor is that it is possible to detect a slight shift in his research output after 1904, with a greater emphasis on Roman history as well as with articles which looked at broader non-British issues in Roman archaeology. It may not be coincidental that the first edition of the work, one of which he is now best remembered, *The Romanization of Roman Britain*, appeared in 1906. It is as if the years up to this publication were the formative period.

The natural consequence to Haverfield's growing eminence in Romano-British studies was that he was increasingly invited to produce overviews in more general publications. The first of these came in 1902 and the entries for H.D. Traill's *Social England* (1893). This phase of work culminated with his entries on Romano-British themes in the 10th (1902) and 11th (1910) editions of the *Encyclopaedia Britannica* and statements in 1911 on Roman Britain for the *Cambridge Mediaeval History* (Haverfield 1911d). Commissions such as the Cambridge entry were the outcome of a process of limited synthesis, which went back as far as 1902. The ability to prepare such summaries was as much a product of private research as Haverfield becoming a conduit for and the advisor to on-going projects. Finally, there was one other medium which Haverfield continued to use to broadcast his views on Roman archaeology as well as what was being achieved by others. This was in his letters and articles to the national press and in particular *The Times* and *The Manchester Guardian* as well as reports in the provincial press.

The 'major' works

It is a principal contention of this study that Haverfield's pivotal position in Romano-British scholarship was due in part to the way he meant different things to different people. To demonstrate this point we might look at how readers, or more accurately reviewers, reacted to his major publications. For all his various publications and diverse interests, Haverfield's reputation rests largely on two works, his *The Romanization of Roman Britain* which in many respects was the culmination of all the years of annual statements and reporting, and to a lesser degree a collection of lectures adapted to a publication format, *The Roman Occupation of Britain* with a third monograph, *Ancient Town Planning*, relegated to the realms of the specialist. The second, however, has to be used with a degree of caution which is not usually employed. The last was certainly not intended to be definitive. Indeed its publication was something of an afterthought, where it did not go into print until after his death.

It is unfortunate that, in spite the range of his work summarized in the preceding chapters, Haverfield's is now best remembered for the first two monographs. For their existence has tended to distract appreciation of the principal point of his work. In the subsequent decades, and especially more recently, his various contributions to the development of Romano-British archaeology have been progressively played down, if not forgotten. Instead scholarly attention has shifted to assessing the relevance of his opinions as articulated in the two monographs and in particular the implications of the Roman occupation. In this respect, the debate has polarized between those who broadly accept his interpretative framework, and those who dismiss him as a product of Britain's colonial experience. Part of the problem in this debate is that despite the primacy given to Haverfield's opinions about the 'romanization' of the province it was not necessarily a central component of his time and work. Instead his main concerns were for the best accumulation and presentation of the evidence that formed the bedrock for his and any others interpretations. Such an approach, following in the Rankeian tradition of letting the evidence speak for itself – and so requiring the systematic and 'correct' accumulation of the data to be deployed – is yet another of the legacies Haverfield left for his successors. His superficial neutrality in writing about the past with regard to Roman Britain was noted by Jones (1987). But there is another dimension to it. Jones drew attention to the fact that both Haverfield and Collingwood '...felt the need to preface their works with almost an apology for writing on Roman Britain' (1987: 86) and that it was indicative of a lack of confidence in archaeological evidence in the face of the more authoritative and 'reliable' literary evidence. If Jones is correct, then is it also reflective of the fact that Romano-British studies were still not quite a respectable field for the classicist, ancient historian and even the philosopher. It might in turn explain why Haverfield was not so bothered with producing the great work of interpretation or chronological narrative of Roman Britain.

(a) The Romanization of Roman Britain
The Romanization went through a number of editions which permit us to see evolutions in Haverfield's thinking. It first saw the light as a lecture delivered (and repeated) at the British Academy in November 1906 and subsequently published in its *Proceedings*. The significance of the original version was noted by an unnamed reviewer in the *Journal of the British Archaeological Association* (XII (1906): 63–4). 'Into the thirty-three pages of this pamphlet, Dr Haverfield has condensed much material which, in view of the limitations of our knowledge of the periods under consideration, is of surpassing value.' Noting how Haverfield suggested that the evidence showed that Latin was now

widely understood (as reflected on coins and inscriptions), the best evidence of what occurred in Roman Britain lay with 'the material class', meaning buildings, pottery, glass, metal and wood and even the bodies of the dead. Continuing the laudatory tone, the reviewer added:

> Dr Haverfield dwells on the value of material evidence and touches on the fascinating subject of Celtic influence in the design of pottery and metal objects ...Conditions of space forbid the insertion of a one-tenth part of all we would wish to say on various points suggested by this valuable pamphlet, but we must remark how conclusively evidences show that, in the more civilised portion of Britain, at least, the average conditions of life were favourable to enterprise.

He rounded off his comments with 'We have but one fault to find with respect to his work: that Dr Haverfield has not given us more' (p. 64). The salient feature of this review is how little it informs the reader about what the central theme to the pamphlet might have been, although the writer did like the idea of the Celtic revival in late Roman Britain.

The second edition of *The Romanization*, expanded and printed in 1912 in larger numbers because the first edition had sold out, was reviewed more widely. It was discussed by A.M. Woodward in the *Archaeological Journal*, where it was noted that Haverfield had largely overthrown the ideas 'of the older archaeologists, who saw in every excavated site a military environment.' Now the emphasis was on the way that the Roman empire affected life in the provinces.

> It is here that archaeological evidence, when accurately read offers a tardy justice. The function of history lies with the ruled as well as with the rulers,[42] and if the historian's treatment of Roman Britain has lacked a due sense of proportion between frontier organisation and internal development. Professor Haverfield's interpretation of the positive evidence of archaeology convincingly restores the balance. In The Romanisation of Britain we find a process that is consciously constructive. Incorporation in the empire involved more than denationalisation; it meant absorption in the material civilisation of Rome, resulting in a Roman fabric to which the native elements in their more essential features almost entirely conformed. It meant that, while this, absorption was not wholly uniform, and that here and there conditions of locality or of especial fitness show indigenous survivals, yet in the main in the lowlands of southern and eastern Britain the difference between Roman and provincial practically vanished. The process was a conscious one;

---

42. Woodward is referring here to Haverfield's comments on this (Haverfield 1911a).

the method was the alluring admixture of suggestive example with a certain measure of local devolution.

The reviewer's only reservations were how far the Latin language was adopted by the populace, and how deep the process penetrated the rural context. In contrast the evidence suggests that 'Wales, and the north and the extreme south-west were left essentially Celtic.' It was these survivals which formed the basis for a Celtic revival in the later empire. However, the 'Romanisation of Britain is shown to have been more than a merely transitory interlude, rigidly marked off by the arrival and departure of the legions. In spite of a Celtic revival and an English invasion its influence could still be faintly traced even in the sixth century' (Woodward 1912: 373–4).

Cheesman reviewed the same edition in a complimentary but ultimately anodyne review (Cheesman 1913b). In this description, noting that it still remained little more than an interim statement, Cheesman emphasized Britain's links with the Continent and the way Haverfield had managed to incorporate the results from such sites as Silchester and Corbridge along with those from the North Leigh villa. Cheesman concluded that:

> ...this book should be in the hands of both archaeologists who wish for a clear definition of the goal towards which their efforts can be directed, and of historians who wish to know something of the evidence of which are based those results which the barrenness of the literary tradition of this period of English history compels them to utilize.

In making this recommendation Cheesman drew attention to the fact Haverfield had to marshal:

> ...an intricate mass of technical detail in which none but the specialists can find their way and from which no conclusions of general interest are likely to emerge. From this remoteness of vision even archaeologists are not always exempt, and the dating of pottery and the study of architectural detail ends in themselves, not means for reconstructing the development of culture or filling up gaps in a defective historical tradition. The value of this book lies in the clearness and precision with which Professor Haverfield sets forth the historical conclusions which are both the results of years of minute archaeological research and its justification.

A European perspective on the 1912 edition can be found in Franz Cumont's 1912 review. Since Haverfield had previously lauded Cumont and his work, not surprisingly, the reviewer's comments were highly complimentary. While acknowledging it was a 'popular book in the best sense of the word', Cumont commended it to specialist readers too.

As the author points out, the great work of Rome is to have won over to her civilization the whole western world. It is particularly interesting to show how this civilization succeeded in taking root in the very extremities of the empire, in an island which seemed to stand at the verge of the habitable world.

Finally, he observed that the principle features Haverfield adduced were relevant to Roman Gaul. His one criticism of the text was that Haverfield had underplayed the part of the Roman army in the process of romanization.

The Romanization went into a third edition in 1915. In its fullest developed form, it contains many of the themes Haverfield had articulated in the previous twenty years. This edition was again reviewed for the BAA's membership, again by an anonymous reader. This time the résumé was much more substantial and, unlike the 1906 review in the same journal, the reader found more to Haverfield's account than just a mere exposition of the evidence of what happened in Roman Britain. Now Haverfield:

> ...sees the Roman Empire as the whole of the civilised world, and how the safety of Rome constituted the safety of all Roman civilisation. Outside roared the wild chaos of barbarism. Rome kept it back from end to end of Europe, and across a thousand miles of Western Asia. Had Rome failed to civilise, had the civilised life found no period in which to grow firm and tenacious, civilisation would have perished utterly. The culture of the old world would not have lived on, to form the ground-work of the best culture of to-day ... Professor Haverfield proves how real this Rome was, how it produced unity of sentiment and culture among the conquered nations, an assimilation of rulers and ruled and a civilisation which they passed on to later ages. Rome had a great tolerance, and never tried to enforce uniformity ...In all their ways (viz the move to urbanism, adoption of language, in government, the arts, religion and material civilisation) the subject nations followed the lead of Rome, and framed their lives in accordance with Roman modes, manners and customs, though the process was gradual and the results by no means uniform. That is the general view of the spread and development of the Empire, but Britain seems to have been somewhat exceptional and Professor Haverfield ...shows how far the country was Romanized, and how large stretches remained that were not brought under Roman influence (*J Brit Archaeol Assoc* (XXI (1915): 65–6).

With one or two quibbles the latter part of this summary is a fair reflection of the totality of the work (the reviewer drew attention to the sections on language, housing, Roman art, religion and the idea of a Celtic revival), but the first part is surprising and seems more to be a product of the reader's own opinions. It is an easy accusation to suggest that the reviewer may have been influenced by contemporary events in his summation, especially when, in returning to reality, he notes that the 'Roman' influence in Britain was in fact so variable.

(b) The Roman Occupation of Britain

Unlike *The Romanization*, *The Roman Occupation* did not benefit by going through a series of revised editions but was rendered into shape by George Macdonald. The monograph commenced life as a series of public lectures Haverfield delivered in the spring of 1907 when he was the (1906) Ford lecturer at Oxford, but came to include much material prepared for his 1906 Rhind lectures in Edinburgh (Bosanquet 1920: 141). The background to the circumstances of Haverfield delivering those lectures is instructive. In 1902 the Scottish Antiquaries were undertaking yet another review of its programme of excavations on Roman sites. In May 1903, with the question of it appointing a Rhind lecturer for 1905 raised, the society's council asked its Secretary, Dr Christison, to enquire if (George) Macdonald, the lecturer in 1903–4, and in the light of the recent research in Scotland, was likely to publish his lectures on the same theme. Christison reported in June that Macdonald had said he did indeed intend to publish, after the completion of the excavations at Rough Castle. The council therefore decided to let the matter rest. And yet for reasons that are not explained, by November of the same year, the council had chosen to appoint Haverfield as the lecturer for 1904–5 to speak about Roman Britain.[43] One of the major reasons for the council's desire to appoint him was the absence of a (recent) synthesis of archaeological progress in Britain. In the meantime Haverfield had been appointed in April 1906 as the Ford Lecturer in English History which, as part of its remit, required a series of public lectures on aspects of the history of Britain. Following the delivery of the Oxford lectures, Haverfield planned to publish them in a much-expanded form, but progress on putting what were public orations into printed form was delayed. Some work was managed over 1913 and 1914 with the insertion of new paragraphs and the addition

43. There is something amiss here in the chronology. The Rhind lectures were delivered between 28 March and 10 April 1906. Appointed the lecturer as early as November 1903, the delivery dates were agreed between Haverfield and Christison in the spring of 1905 when the two met in Edinburgh (Letter, Haverfield to Lord Abercromby *Edinburgh University Library Special Collection 136*; cf. Minute Book of the Society of Antiquaries 1901–13; 3 November 1903; 20 March 1906). The enquiry to Macdonald is ambiguous. He does not appear to have been involved in the excavations at Rough Castle, 1902–3.

of footnotes, but he then seems to have given up. In the aftermath of his death, Macdonald (and to a lesser extent M.V. Taylor) completed the process of working up the lectures to an acceptable state, satisfying Haverfield's original plan to provide 'the general reader with a trustworthy introduction to the problems of Roman Britain' (p. 8). Macdonald's main contribution to the exercise was completing the insertion of the footnotes, many of which referred to Haverfield's publications relevant to particular subjects post-1907. He also offered correctives to some of Haverfield's (spoken) opinions. Re-reading the lectures the impression of the publication of *The Roman Occupation* was in part a salvage job, one endeavouring to get out a 'major' work to perpetuate Haverfield's reputation for posterity. Unfortunately if this was the intent, the consequences were double-edged. Because *The Occupation* remains one of Haverfield's two major statements, even if the intention was a general introduction on the topic, subsequent generations, naturally enough, have had to use it, but perhaps in a fashion with which Haverfield would not have been entirely happy.

The reception to the monograph was again generally enthusiastic (Wheeler 1923). But this might have been as much to do with the circumstances of its publication. Another Haverfield associate, Mikhail Rostovtzeff reviewed it in the *American Historical Review* (Rostovtzeff 1924–5). In truth, the review provides little, being in the main a repetition of Macdonald's preface. What is of interest is the way Rostovtzeff believed Haverfield:

> ...combined in his person the best features of both the German and English scholarship. Thoroughness of information, strong critical attitude towards the sources, painstaking accuracy in the preliminary work of copying and commenting upon the inscriptions and in classifying the archaeological material were the features Haverfield took from the Germans (p. 337).

These strengths were coupled with such 'English traits' as lucidity, clear-cut ideas, a sense of humour and the ability to grasp the importance of the evidence. These assessments hint at the fact that Rostovtzeff thought Haverfield was in the first place an epigrapher who moved to the history of Roman Britain, with his site visits, the cataloguing of the material and his initiating excavations. In contrast to these opinions, a short, anonymous review in the *Geographical Review* (15 (1925): 510–11), naturally enough drew attention to the way Haverfield argued how the geography of Britain conditioned its 'romanization'. The reviewer also noted how Haverfield emphasized the 'traditional' error of not seeing Britain '...as part of a greater political and economic unit of which it formed a small and relatively unimportant part.'

A more substantial assessment was provided by Stueart Miller. Again the comments draw extensively from Macdonald's introduction but, in contrast to Rostovtzeff, Miller offered his own view on the themes addressed and made his own constructive criticism about the text. Acknowledging that this may not have been the work Haverfield had planned, still '...it is (it not need hardly be said) by far the best book upon the subject. To say that the chapters dealing directly with the history of Roman Britain contain little that is new is really to pay a tribute to the influence of Haverfield's own teaching and of the work he published.' In thanking Macdonald for his efforts for seeing the lectures into print, Miller added:

> In this volume, as elsewhere, Haverfield's writing – easy, vigourous, idiomatic, economical of ornament and emphasis – always conveys the man's strong sense of actuality. It was this sense that made him concentrate his Roman studies upon his own Province, and turned him from disputation upon meagre and dubious texts to the continuous and tangible evidence of archaeology ... It is clear that he always had in his mind the question of whether anything of Roman Britain survived into our later history. In general, he saw no connexion between Roman Britain and later Britain, and there was, perhaps, something of disappointment in the asperity with which he occasionally turned upon less critical writers who had little difficulty in finding the Roman survivals they looked for (1925: 262).[44]

With regard to specific themes, Miller suggested the text was relatively weak on the question of Romano-British Christianity, noting that Haverfield had in fact written elsewhere useful contributions to the subject (cf. Haverfield 1896a; 1918c) which indicated 'the changed direction it gave to that Celtic resurgence upon which Haverfield in recent years put so much stress' (p. 263).

In addition to his two main monographs, among his contemporaries, there was one other Haverfield publication that was regarded as one of his most important statements – a contribution to the *Cambridge*

---

44. Crawford (1928) used Haverfield's opinions as the basis for an indirect attack on Hilaire Belloc's *A History of England, Volume 1 to 1066* (1921) in which Belloc argued for a far greater degree of continuity from late Roman to early medieval Britain than the likes of Haverfield had imagined. In praising advances in knowledge on the issue in the past twenty years (and all of it down to excavation), Crawford concluded that Haverfield was correct in arguing for a (cultural) hiatus between fifth century and later Britain.

Medieval History (Haverfield 1911d). Overlooked today, the importance of the essay is its lateness in his career as well as its succinctness. The account opens with the bold statement that '...the character and history of Roman Britain, as many other Roman provinces, were predominantly determined by the facts of its geography' (p. 367). It then develops into a narrative history written against the literary sources of the early history of the island. Significant points which come out of the account is the relatively insignificant contribution made by the army's distribution in the process of 'romanization': 'From the standpoint alike of the ancient Roman statesman and of the modern Roman historian the military post and their garrisons formed the dominant element in Britain. But they have left little permanent mark on the civilisation and character of the island' (p. 370). Instead, the military's part was to create the peaceful conditions whereby Roman civilisation could spread. The degree of assimilation was unsurprisingly greatest in the south-eastern parts of the island, a process which predated the invasion. The process was later facilitated by the government's policy of founding 'municipalities', where Haverfield could draw extensively on the results from recent excavations at Silchester and Caerwent. But above all, the process was accelerated by the 'automatic movement' of Italian traders and commerce. In the towns, the civilization there '...appears to have been of the Roman type' (p. 375), with its emphasis on (Latin) inscriptions and art at the expense of Celtic equivalents. However, the degree of penetration in the towns could not have been that deep because of the way the towns declined and disappeared in the following centuries. In contrast, the clearest manifestation of 'romanization' was to be found in the countryside of second and third century lowland England, with the full flowering of what was called the 'rural system', of land division, villas and farmhouses. The 'end of Roman Britain' was, in Haverfield's view, a consequence of the political problems elsewhere in the fourth and fifth century empire. The collapse of central authority in Italy meant governors and other officials as well as troops were not sent to protect the island; 'No one went: some persons failed to come' (p. 378). This leads to discussion of the degree of British culpability in the end of (Latin) civilisation. Once attributed to a British rejection, Haverfield argued that the '...old idea that the Britons and Roman were still two distinct and hostile racial elements, has, of course, been long been abandoned by all competent inquirers' (p. 378). That Roman civilization disappeared was not because of its rejection by the natives. It was too slightly established to survive the chaos of the period. It declined as the towns and countryside wilted under the pressure of economic dislocation in a process not aided by attacks by invaders. It was to be 'replaced' by a Celtic revival which had survived in the less romanized marginal regions to the north and west of the romanized districts. The idea of the significance of Celtic on Britain and as the basis for the 'Keltic' revival of the fourth and fifth centuries was developed in the *English Historical Review* (1913d).[45] The idea of a revival originating from Wales (and ultimately from Ireland) at this time had previously been advanced by Haverfield in a debate with Mommsen in which Haverfield had also pointed to a much more substantial Roman presence in the principality than had previously been accepted (cf. Hall 1923: 9).

Much of Haverfield's explanation for the course and outcome of the romanization of the island still looks familiar today. There is the emphasis on the geographical division of the island and the way that it conditioned the cultural development of the island. There was recognition of the pre-AD 43 acculturation of the island along with the fact that the process speeded up after 43. Haverfield repeated these opinions in an article looking at Britain's late Roman coastal defences. Over time they remained largely consistent so it is worth repeating them here at length:

> It is a commonplace that Britain is an island. The further truth, that it is an island which is very closely tied to the continent lying east of it, is a good deal less familiar. Geography units are apt, even for historical purposes, to emphasise instead those two features of the island which Mr. Mackinder (cf. *'Our own islands': An elementary study of geography*) ...has called its insularity and its universality, its separation that is, from Europe, and its central position in the world. I feel, however, that both students of ancient history, and also modern men at this particular moment are more concerned with the peculiar relations of Britain to Europe. It is not the insularity of the island but its dependence on the continent which really matters. This dependence dates from the days long before the appearance of man; it is due, indeed, to the conjunction of western Europe in remote geological periods. That part of Britain which faces the continent is the low-lying part ...It is therefore fairly flat and it offers no strategic obstacles to invaders. Its only features, its forests and its fens, are hardly large enough even to divert the march of armies and have been over-rated by writers ...The really difficult regions

---

45. E.g. 'The Kelts are the spiritual heirs of the Roman empire more truly than even than the Italians or the Romaic Greeks. Nearly every Keltic tribe in central and western Europe fell under Roman rule, accepted Roman culture, used Roman speech and save where it perished before Slavonic assault preserved Roman civilisation to later Europe. One land alone remained Keltic and not Roman – Ireland' (1913d: 1).

of Britain, the tangled uplands of Wales and west Yorkshire and the north, lie far away from the path of European aggressors. They might assist the rulers of Britain in checking an Irish invasion; they do not protect it from European influences. Britain is a land which was made to be invaded from the continent ...The earlier history of the island shows the results of these geographical features (1912e: 201).

There is not much in this characterization that sits uneasy with modern opinions. There is one significant feature in Haverfield's appreciation of the mechanics of 'romanization' which does not accord with modern explanations: the relative unimportance he placed on the direct part played by the army in that process. Urbanization and changes in the countryside, at least in south-eastern England, are recognized as the markers by which any assessment of romanization are to be judged. Finally, his views on the end of the Roman island are significant. Not only did he break from the prevailing view that it was a reflection of British independence but he also looked for the gradualist explanation which is evident in recent works.

Such conclusions were widely accepted at the time and his work was rightly acclaimed. Indeed as the development of Roman Britain as a legitimate field of study was recognized, so Haverfield's observations about romanization '...effectively set the agenda for Romano-British studies for more than sixty years' (Jones 1987: 87). Indeed Frere believed; 'what was awaited was a synthesis, and this was the great achievement of Haverfield in his Victoria County History articles and in his two great books... His influence ...extended over the whole country' (1988: 1).

Knowing what has been said about Haverfield's difficult but ultimately open personality, he must have appreciated that with time many of his conclusions would have to be modified, if not abandoned. For example, there was his belief that '...Romanisation in general extinguished the distinction between Roman and Provincials alike in politics, in material culture and in language' (1912a: 18). Such conclusions were a consequence of his overstating or over-emphasizing certain types or pieces of evidence, itself a consequence of the limitations of contemporary knowledge. There was also his preoccupation with the conclusions drawn from the excavations at Silchester (e.g. 1924; cf. Jones 1987: 87), technically limited as they were, as well as his propensity to seek parallels from Europe to validate the British material. Likewise there was his over-enthusiastic reliance on the apparent distinction between a civil (civilized), south-east, lowland province and a military (barbarian), highland district in the north and west. The accumulation of more evidence and information aided by advances in data recovery and new research techniques has also changed the picture since Haverfield's time. His treatment of villas and their economies now reads as naïve, as was his treatment of other types of rural settlement. He failed to treat in any detailed manner the nature of Romano-British religion which he would have found does not rest so comfortably with his notions of a classicizing trend throughout the islands. His conclusions on language and the universality of Latin have since been undermined where the common observation is that an absence of evidence cannot be taken as decisive.

Haverfield as a popularizer?[46]

From knowing the sort of statements that he published, we come now to assess why Haverfield wrote in the fashion that he did. To what extent might Haverfield be described as a popularizer? Indeed did he regard this as part of his mission: the better and wider dissemination of knowledge about Roman Britain? Richard Hingley has highlighted how, at the end of the nineteenth and the start of the twentieth centuries, there was an explosion in popular accounts about Roman Britain, and in particular with regard to novels and school texts. It was often linked with popularist, jingoistic language extolling the benefits of the Roman empire. The phenomenon was for reasons peculiar to itself. But from where were these authors deriving their information? An obvious source, given his position and his public utterances and one preferred by Hingley, would be Haverfield. So to what degree was he a popularizer? The simple answer is he was not, which leads to the question who was using his work and how?

In the first instance, Haverfield even at the height of his powers cannot be described as having produced literature aimed at a popular readership. To be sure, there is not much in his character to suggest that he was sympathetic to the general reader. It is true that in the early phases of his career down to *c*.1907, he was contributing overviews and updates to some of the more public journals, but still ones aimed at an educated and informed readership (e.g. *The Academy* and *The Athenaeum*). Otherwise the nearest he got to the genre were his dictionary and encyclopaedia entries and the guides he prepared of museum collections. It is difficult to imagine his contributions to regional archaeological societies etc. attracting a wider audience. Indeed many of his major statements, notably the *VCH* series, were published in reasonably inaccessible places. The chronology of his output similarly

---

46. In an account of the life of A.H. Sayce, Gunn (1949: 787) described his subject s 'a great vulgurisateur.'

militates against the idea he was the great popularizer. *The Romanization* monograph first went into a relatively inaccessible pamphlet of 1905–6 although it did admittedly soon go out of print. Expanded versions of the same only became available from 1912 onwards. *The Roman Occupation* volume was only published after his death, over fifteen years after the first version was offered for public consumption. Therefore these works cannot have had that much of a popular influence.

Another factor which might have inhibited Haverfield producing popular accounts of the archaeology of the island must lie with academics and their developing (élitist) attitudes. Stray (1998), echoing Engel (1983), has suggested that one of the consequences of the debate, interventions and reforms of the (ancient) universities in the nineteenth century was that by the end of that century, classical scholarship had been marginalized in English culture. Dons were no longer amateur scholars but players in a research environment where 'advances' in knowledge and the integration of inter-disciplinary approaches were more important than the moral training of students. While some might have regretted that this involved the writing of 'little books' at the expense of more substantial publications (e.g. Rhys Robert's comments reported in Chapter 2), such an impression is visible in Haverfield's output (cf. Chapter 5, Tables 1 and 2). There was, for instance, the shift from the more populist statements in the likes of *The Antiquary* and *The Athenaeum* in the 1890s to those in the *Classical Review*, the *Proceedings of the British Academy* and ultimately for the SPRS and its *Journal of Roman Studies*. This preference for more specialist vehicles is also reflected in Haverfield's increasing desire to use the universities and their infrastructure to drive research at the expense of the archaeological-antiquarian societies, that he had used in the 1890s and early 1900s. The evidence points then to the fact that there is little to show that Haverfield would have been in sympathy with the popularizing of archaeological research. We have already seen he was generally contemptuous of the work of other non-university workers or those he did not know personally. He also relied on the prejudices of others to inform his opinions. Nor did he have high opinions of the work of earlier and later antiquarians, some of whom he believed masqueraded as archaeologists. Indeed this might have been Haverfield's major contribution to the popular perception of Roman archaeology: the way he made earlier antiquarian accounts more accessible while at the same time being at pains to debunk their incorrect identifications and interpretations. As Hingley observed, he left the detection and the identification of the mission of Roman civilization in Britain to other, more popularizing, authors.

So what was the undertone of Haverfield's work? In short, as the preceding sections have argued, it was to improve the quality of work on the archaeology of Britain in the Roman period. This was necessary because of what he believed to be a particularly British phenomenon; the poor, unanalytical publication of archaeological material. The entire situation was to be changed by a combination of mutually supportive elements; (a) by a more rigorous (re-)cataloguing of museum collections and the reporting of recent work, publicized in keynote publications, of which the *VCH* was but one part; (b) by the fostering of close relations with foreign colleagues and institutions as well as creating a familiarity with their work and methods; (c) by the promotion of a number of 'big' excavation projects (e.g. Silchester and along Hadrian's Wall) which were to improve standards of excavation and publication; and (d) by the patronizing of certain individuals, or 'students', to undertake the work and to continue it in the future. It is a not insignificant fact that Haverfield closed his inaugural address to the Roman Society with the hope that '..if our Society can do anything to bring about a good understanding between workers in the Universities and workers up and down the country, we shall not have laboured in vain' (1911a: xx). Haverfield was later to speak of the relatively slow progress of Romano-British archaeology as a recognized discipline. He attributed its progress in the nineteenth century originally to developments on the continent and then, in Britain, firstly to developments in religion, the Victorian trend to forming societies and the impetus given by the (temporary) '...antiquarian zeal of the early Victorian age touch(ing) all classes' (Haverfield 1924: 82). He certainly did not believe that the universities had helped the cause, but that their emphasis on Latin had produced a false sense of superiority among historians. 'Our dominant education has been classical and linguistic, even history has been taught hitherto as a matter of words. There has been little care of things, and in consequence archaeology is in our Universities a somewhat novel study today, still regarded with a faint suspicion and occasional jealously' (1924: 87; cf. Appendix 3). The sum of these observations, contrary to expectations, is that little else other than these priorities concerned Haverfield between 1890 and his death.

We are left, however, to explain why Haverfield had recourse to the sort of explanation of cultural change that he used. One of the most important implications of the scope of Haverfield's work, whether it be with respect to its epigraphy, to the excavation of Roman period sites (towns, its frontier installations or its road network) as well as his works of syntheses, was that in creating a distinct Roman period in British history, he indirectly established the tradition of debating the consequences of that period on later (post-Roman) society, a question to which he, in turn, contributed. The mechanism for assessing that sense of continuity was the idea of romanization. At the opposite end of the time spectrum, Haverfield did not make any substantial contribution to the archaeology of late pre-Roman Iron Age Britain. This failure has been attributed to his imperialist attitudes. But it is as likely to have been a consequence of his (over-)emphasis on the Roman period. The advantage of his form of romanization was that as well as providing a framework for exploring late Roman – early Dark Age Britain, at the same time it also permitted him to re-establish the linkage between the indigenous Iron Age population and what came after it. The veracity of this conclusion will be examined in the next chapter where we will explore where Haverfield might have derived his models and to what extent, if any, his ideas were influenced by the prevailing political, intellectual and social climate.

Mythologizing Haverfield

The preceding chapters have examined Haverfield's work and his contribution to Romano-British studies. At the same time, as much emphasis has been placed on the opinions of his contemporaries as those of Haverfield. The reason why the former group is important is because it was this body, comprising academics and archaeologists, who perpetuated the memory of his work. Closer examination of the opinions of the group, however, suggests a number of misconceptions have developed concerning Haverfield's legacy: misconceptions in the sense that the memory of his work may not correspond with the reality of his accomplishments. For want of a better way of expressing it we might call these representations the 'Haverfield myth' to which there are a number of components. The most obvious is the magnitude of the losses he is supposed to have suffered in the First World War. Examination of the evidence suggests the numbers involved are questionable. Then there is the issue of his involvement in excavation. By the time of the outbreak of the First World War he had been involved in two major programmes of excavation (the CEC and Corbridge) but, with both, he had become increasingly detached. In both instances too, it was appreciated by his co-workers that he was not especially skilled as an excavator. We have already seen that contrary to what some of his obituaries might suggest, Haverfield's involvement in excavation was much more peripheral. This was a fact recognized by some of his contemporaries. For instance, M.V. Taylor was happy to offer a defensive corrective on Haverfield's ability as an excavator to Eric Birley (cf. Chapter 6). In fact Haverfield's only experience of hands-on-management was during the CEC campaigns but there are indications that as far back as the mid-1890s others were questioning his competence. His retreat from day-to-day management may have been in recognition of his abilities but there are also indications that he was sensitive, excessively so, to criticism. The other striking feature of all the excavation projects with which he was involved is they all started with spectacular discoveries: this applies to Silchester, Chester, the CEC and Corbridge. But after the early successes of each of these projects, they seem to have dissipated into annual grinds, where one senses that in the absence of matching finds in the subsequent seasons, Haverfield's interest waned. The decline in his interest may also be a consequence of the projects not really possessing coherent ends or objectives. In such instances the original excavation designs seem to have been limited to variations of 'the complete excavation' of the respective sites. In this sense, we can see his waning interest during the CEC and his wandering attention during the Corbridge excavations. In the case of the latter, his withdrawal from the project was as much to do with his relations with his co-director as with the excavation losing direction. One suspects that if the circumstances had permitted (e.g. the outbreak of the First World War and his subsequent breakdown, which effectively ended his career as an excavator) he might have substituted Corbridge with involvement at the fledgling Wroxeter excavations, directed by a closer associate, Bushe-Fox. But as the circumstances fell he did not and this speculation has to remain just that. Elsewhere his engagement with excavation was merely as a subsidiary and/or as a figurehead. Finally, there were his works of interpretation, or lack of them. In blunt language, he left no really satisfactory syntheses on any of the many aspects of Romano-British history with which he was concerned. Two of the enduring works (his *Occupation* and the *RIB*) appeared after his death owing much to the labours of others, notably Macdonald, Taylor and Atkinson. What had not appeared were the works of synthesis and the numerous (national) catalogues he is supposed to have commenced, including those of the inscriptions and samian and fibulae of Roman Britain. At best the groundwork for a number of major statements had been completed (e.g. the *VCH* and RCHM entries). Expressed in blunt language, Haverfield's career might be described as him regularly manoeuvering or getting himself into position, initiating the work that was desirable or necessary and saying the 'right' things, all for the opportunities to be lost, either through the force of circumstances, or else his inability to see the initiatives through to their logical conclusion or because he became alienated from them.

The more one looks at Haverfield's career the stronger the sense that the period *c.*1910–15 was the turning point. It is true that the significance of the latter year was appreciated by his contemporaries but more in terms of his health. But there is more to it. For from about this time there seems evident a change in his outlook on Romano-British archaeology. We have already noted that the head of steam that had been built up in the years before the outbreak of the war was interrupted. Then there was the falling off in his publications and a diminution in his range of activities. There is another dimension to the sense of failure. His reputation was and is still based on his work on the archaeology of Roman Britain, but in terms of his Oxford career, his duties were more that of a (Roman) historian with a particular interest in epigraphy for Roman history and with a subsidiary interest in teaching Roman Britain. We see this in the range of courses he offered and the dissertations he supervised. If in some respects the outcome of a lifetime's work was disappointing, if due in part to the fall of the circumstances at the time, then how are we to explain the memory and reverence in which Haverfield came to be held after his death? While the importance of his work and influence was recognized by numerous lesser individuals, there would appear to be three persons who were responsible in large measure for developing the 'myth'.

We have seen how George Macdonald, a close friend, became Haverfield's literary executor. He was responsible for the publication of arguably Haverfield's most accessible publication, *The Occupation*. His processing of the Ford lectures into an intelligible form, he admitted, was undertaken as an act of *pietas*. The significance of *The Occupation* to the Haverfield memory goes beyond the text. As important is Macdonald's biographical sketch in the introduction. Written in an idiosyncratically florid style, the sketch was originally prepared for the British Academy obituary and was then repeated almost verbatim in 1924 (and later). In its preparation, Macdonald acknowledged assistance from Taylor and Collingwood. Indicative of its influence, Miller (1925: 264), in lauding Macdonald's editing of *The Occupation,* complimented him for having done so much to perpetuate Haverfield's memory. In turn the extent of the 'debt' can be gauged in the way reviews of *The Occupation* invariably repeated 'facts' derived from Macdonald's introduction and biographical note. Indeed elements of the notice are still being repeated in the most recent assessments of Haverfield's contribution to Romano-British studies. As we have seen, closer examination of some of these facts reveals a slightly perspective on Haverfield's actions. The Macdonald notice has come to form a corner stone of the perpetuation of the Haverfield story, and has contributed to mythologizing his reputation. In turn, as Macdonald was asked to provide the kinds of overviews of Roman Britain that Haverfield had once provided, he had numerous opportunities to carry the Haverfield torch. Macdonald also succeeded J.S. Reid as (the third) President of the Roman Society (1921–6, as well as serving on its Editorial Committee) and so occupied a position of some influence.

Macdonald acknowledged how much his work post-Haverfield owed to the help and assistance of Haverfield's research assistant, Margerie Taylor. That said, her part in the perpetuation of the 'myth' is much harder to assess. She is, by any criteria, a difficult person to write about. There are many anecdotes about her, some of which are repeatable. Wheeler's assessment of her character is reminiscent of contemporary opinions about Haverfield; 'She has cloaked a tireless generosity under a veil of intolerance which has deceived only those who do not know her' (1961: 157). Haverfield's death in 1919 left her in a difficult position. She had no visible signs of employment other than what Haverfield had provided. Unable to establish a career in academia, it is in the years immediately after his death that she comes to fore. It was presumably this 'weakness' which explains how she managed to establish herself in the Ashmolean Library. In the same review of *The Roman Occupation*, Miller noted '...the Society of Roman Studies with its Journal, the Haverfield Bequest Committee and the Haverfield Library at Oxford give promise that the study of Roman Britain will continue along the lines (Haverfield) would have approved' (1925: 264). In leaving his personal library to the Ashmolean, it has been said, erroneously, Haverfield asked that it should be cared for by Taylor: '...thus giving her a place, though at first a rather uncertain one, in the field of Romano-British archaeology' (Bonarkis Webster 1991: 120).[47]

It cannot be a coincidence that Taylor came to occupy pivotal positions in all these organizations. Although it has not been possible to establish how, and whether legitimately, she soon appears as the 'guardian' of the two collections – the library and the archive. One would like to know more about how she came to be involved in these 'organizations', especially the Ashmolean (where she would sit in the open library with an eye to those who entered the Haverfield Room), where there are indications that she saw part of her 'job' to edit the collections and in particular what was left of Haverfield's correspondence. If in the five years or so after Haverfield's death, Taylor managed to manufacture a niche for herself at Oxford via the Haverfield Archive, still in the long-term the archive

---

47. This statement is dubious because there is no clause or other provision in his will for Taylor to curate the library.

failed. It does not seem that she was delegated to manage the archive, at least under the terms of the will. So, if she was authorized, then the offer must have been at least permitted by the Bequest Committee, where the trustees evidently hoped the library would become a central store of information relating to Roman Britain and that reports of finds and related information be sent to it.[48] In the aftermath of Haverfield's death excavators and other field workers were asked to deposit at least copies of their reports, if not their archives, in the collection so that it might become a central store of information about Roman Britain. Taylor would have been the obvious person to coordinate receipt of the material and provide access to it. But the combination of Taylor's personality and in particular the way access to the collection was effectively restricted to those (Oxford) persons she approved, meant that as the amount of excavation that took place in the years after Haverfield's death stagnated, so the archive failed to develop. The situation was made all the worse by the failure of Oxford staff to excavate. In the end the archive became increasingly irrelevant and superfluous. The archive's homepage on the World Wide Web reports it contains the occasional element which post-dates Haverfield's death and so indirectly reflects the piecemeal nature of the later additions to the collection. The effect of the archive, however, was minimized by the way the *Journal of Roman Studies* from 1921 (and through its regular reports on recent progress in the archaeology and epigraphy of Roman Britain) came to be the mouthpiece for disseminating knowledge about the Roman province. The reports were prepared, coincidentally, by Taylor and Collingwood. The original report said that the series was initiated by the Haverfield committee, with information that was to be sent to Taylor, which would then be filed (and made available for consultation) and to be published in a manner established by Haverfield in the British Academy series of reports (cf. *J Roman Stud* XI (1921): 200). It is indisputable that Taylor shepherded the Roman Society through difficult times, notably the 1920s and early 1930s, whilst continuing to make a considerable contribution to Romano-British studies: 'Her own special task, carrying on Haverfield's tradition, has been to compose the annual accounts of excavation in Roman Britain which

---

48. On 20 June 1921 *The Times* published a letter from Stuart Jones on behalf of the committee asking fieldworkers send to the Haverfield Library at the Ashmolean information concerning recent discoveries and the results of fieldwork in Romano-British studies. The information would be published in the *Journal of Roman Studies* and correspondents would be duly credited. There is no mention of Taylor as the person to whom the information should be forwarded.

forms so valuable a feature of the Journal' (Anon. 1960: xi). In 1923 she became it's membership secretary, a post she occupied until 1954 ('...the distinguished list of Presidents whom she has controlled' – Wheeler 1961: 157). She was also the journal's editor from the same year down to 1960 and its President 1955–8. 'It was her devotion to Haverfield's memory and principles, her stern scholarship and intellectual prestige – exercised through her annual report (in the *Journal of Roman Studies*), through the administration of the Haverfield Bequest for the furtherance of Romano-British studies, and through the editorship of the *Journal of Roman Studies* for so many years – that was largely responsible for keeping the subject on course through the 40s, 50s and 60s' (Frere 1988: 2).[49] With regard to the Haverfield Bequest Committee, Taylor became the secretary to its administrators. 'Although not formally an Administrator, her work on behalf of the Bequest was of enormous importance and was by no means confined to the paperwork which meetings called into being. She travelled widely on behalf of the Bequest, at minimal cost, and her always trenchant views on the progress or otherwise, of projects supported by the Bequest were an invaluable source of informed comment ...no-one did more to ensure the effective operation of the Bequest than Margery [sic] Taylor' (Todd 2003: 38).[50] Taylor also used her position in Oxford (and London) to exert a less obvious, but still as influential, effect on Romano-British studies. As the unofficial curator-cum-guardian of the Haverfield archive, she also effectively controlled who had access to the material therein. Numerous publications of the 1920s and 1930s on the archaeology and sites of Roman Britain acknowledge her assistance in

---

49. Taylor's determination, understandable in the circumstances, to establish herself might be gauged in a tribute offered on the occasion of her 80th birthday. An unnamed writer observed: 'The upsurge of feminine achievement that has been an outstanding feature of the last one hundred years is now much taken for granted. Our Editor's generation was in the forefront of the movement, and her own zeal for a scholar's life was of a steady purpose not to be denied. It is permissible to pay this tribute. Not a few women who ardently advocated emancipation lost in the process the pleasanter characteristics of their sex, exchanging daintiness for vehemence and femininity for self-assertion. Margerie Taylor has left none of the charm of her generation behind; adding wisdom to charm, she has carried both with her to grace and dignify her ideals while ever revealing her keen and indomitable personality' (Anon. 1960: xi). Taylor was also interviewed for a lengthy piece that appeared in *The Times* 31 July 1961.

50. It is a pity that Grace Simpson's claim that '...thanks to the watch kept from 1920–1939 by Miss M.V. Taylor and Collingwood, from their base in the "Haverfield library" in Oxford, standards of excavation distinctly improved' (1996: 224) is not explained further.

providing material from it.[51] In turn her position enabled her to exert a degree of patronage, which would appear to be out of proportion to her position at Oxford. In short if she liked a person she was prepared to help further their careers. For instance, she seems to have taken a liking to the young Christopher Hawkes. Writing of Wheeler's 1924–5 excavations at Brecon Gaer and the students employed there, Jacquetta Hawkes noted: 'It is proof of the high reputation of the Wheelers had already established that a formidable lady, Miss M.V. Taylor, who presided over the Haverfield Library at Oxford, decided to dispatch ...two star scholars (C. Hawkes and N. Myres) to learn from them the rudiments of excavation and the archaeology of Roman Britain' (Hawkes 1982: 90). Taylor later persuaded Hawkes to take on the excavations at Alchester in 1926–7 on behalf of the Oxford Classical Association, in which she was a leading figure (Hawkes 1927). Conversely, those who dared to comment critically on Haverfield and his work (and in turn others in the group), could become targets. The most graphic example of this was (the non-Oxford) Wheeler and his criticisms, published in the pages of *Antiquity*, of the Jubilee volume of the *Journal of Roman Studies* and especially Richmond's second part of the Hod Hill report (cf. Chapter 10). The public respondents to Wheeler's criticisms included a number of leading figures at Oxford and Cambridge. Taylor was not listed as a signatory to the complaints, but it is certain she was there in the background. While similarly critical opinions have continued to appear, and whilst there is some anecdotal evidence to the contrary, it may not be coincidental that critical appraisals about Romano-British scholarship up to the mid-1960s and published from the 1970s have not attracted the same degree of opprobrium. The reason for this must lie with the passing of a generation.

The third individual who helped foster the Haverfield 'myth' was his best-known (surviving) 'student', R.G. Collingwood, whose career and influence will be examined in the next chapter. It will suffice to say here that Collingwood was extremely friendly with Taylor and Macdonald. Collingwood's contribution to the story was that his earliest major works of synthesis were focused on Haverfield and his opinions, even if they were in part written as critical responses which could not be answered. In his autobiography Collingwood constructed a picture where he felt obliged to persist with his work in Roman Britain out of another sense of *pietas* to Haverfield. In the first instance there was seeing

51. For example, in the Preface to his *Archaeology of the Cambridge Region* (1923), Cyril Fox wrote: 'I have also to thank Miss MV Taylor, of the Haverfield Library Oxford, for access to MS. Records bearing on the Roman occupation of my district' (p. vi).

through the *RIB*. As the process of collecting the primary source evidence continued, however, so Collingwood became increasingly disenchanted with the way that Haverfield had used such material, and ultimately the conclusions he had drawn. As such, Collingwood saw his work as offering the necessary corrective to the Haverfield version. Whatever, Collingwood's work served to keep Haverfield and his work in the public domain for at least another generation. In time, Collingwood was also extremely friendly with Eric Birley and Ian Richmond, the next two major figures in Romano-British studies after Collingwood's death. Both publicly venerated Haverfield. Both were on friendly terms with Collingwood and Taylor. Richmond, also a product of Oxford and later resident there, was another individual preferred by Taylor. The sum consequences of this group of individuals and the positions they occupied was the propagation of the idea, spurious for all that, of an 'Oxford school' and Haverfield simply the master of Romano-British studies when in fact he was more than that.

CHAPTER 10

Haverfield into the next millennium

You know that the nineteenth century is coming to an end, though when it will end is a matter of dispute. I suppose that now and through next year, in articles and on platforms, hundreds of attempts will be made to characterize or to appreciate the nineteenth century, and certainly to take stock of its failures and successes and of the progress made in one department or another (Pelham 1899: 6).

Haverfield and the phenomenon of 'romanization'

Other than the correction of points of detail, the framework of Haverfield's work remained largely unchallenged in the decades after his death and, until relatively recently, unchanged. That they have endured can be seen in a number of ways. To varying degrees subsequent scholarship continues to graft or integrate new archaeological evidence to that framework. Likewise, the structure of many of the standard textbooks, and therefore much of the teaching, of Roman Britain continue to share a common underlying format based on inscriptions (in the so-called 'Oxford' tradition) that make up in part for the deficiencies of the historical sources. In the same manner there is the legacy of interpretative themes that Haverfield identified and in particular identification of the phenomenon of the romanization of the island. It is this aspect that has then occasioned critical reappraisal of Haverfield's influence, although we might note it does not seem to have been so much an issue for his generation. At that time it was accepted as a fact of life: empires and imperialism brought assimilation and civilization, and in this case, the positive benefits of 'romanization'. It is only now that the 'positive' consequences of Roman government have come in to question.

For some commentators of Romano-British scholarship there is one overriding influencing factor in Haverfield's conception of 'romanization'. In recent times, there has developed a concern with the assessing to what extent Haverfield's perception of the British empire influenced his outlook on the Roman (cultural) empire and in turn its 'romanization'. This is the one aspect of his work which has generated the debate: to what degree were Haverfield's opinions influenced by his attitudes to the British empire of the late Victorian and Edwardian eras? In the late nineteenth and early twentieth centuries, when the existence of empire and its colonial 'civilizing' were extolled and justified so (ancient) empires and the virtues of their methods of acculturation were regarded as perfectly natural and praised for their accomplishments. This might be described as the 'apologist' explanation. More recently, as attitudes to imperialism and colonialism have become more critical, acculturation is seen as a tool of oppression and accordingly condemned. This line of logic underpins, for example, post-colonial resistance approaches to the study of imperial systems. The dominant view seems to be that Haverfield was prone, explicitly or implicitly, to such moralizing, which conditioned how he saw romanization being transmitted. In other words, Haverfield's attitude to the British empire affected how he explained the workings and ultimately the mission of the Roman empire (Hingley 1994; 1996a; 1997; Freeman 1996a; Edwards 1996). The way that this can be detected is to see Haverfield in the spirit of the age and to see who and what was being written about the British empire. It should then be a relatively straightforward exercise to see such attitudes in a number of his keynote statements. The four most significant of these are his two monographs, his first presidential address to the Roman Society (Haverfield 1911a) and a contribution to a debate on ancient imperialism in which Haverfield spoke on the Roman example (Haverfield 1910a). In these statements, one, or so it is believed, can see Haverfield apologizing for colonial empire and that he sought to legitimize its achievements in its Roman predecessor.

From at least the late nineteenth century, for scholars of classical antiquity the fact there existed a 'British empire' made comparison with its ancient counterparts, notably the Roman, attractive, if not inevitable. The comparisons were being made almost as soon as a British empire was appreciated for what it had become and the implications then applied to other historical imperial systems (Brunt 1964–5). The tradition continues down today. Out of any number of examples one might cite, this line of interpretation is evident, for example, in the synopsis of a paper presented by Stephen Dyson at the 92nd Annual Meeting of the American Institute of Archaeology (Dyson 1991). A fuller working-up of the paper does not seem to have been published and judging by the lack of references to it, it has not been noticed by many. And yet the thrust of the paper seems very similar to what has been argued subsequently by others. It is therefore worth summarizing the core of Dyson's argument. Entitled *Ancient Im-*

perialism and Modern Nationalism in the Study of Romanization in Nineteenth Century Britain, France and Germany, and claiming an influence from Foucault, Dyson argued:

> ...our understanding of how we approach a field of knowledge can only come from a consideration of the intellectual and ideological forces that have shaped the study of the field. The Romanization of western Europe is an especially rich area for such studies since scholars in centres like Germany, France and Britain had to combine a profound respect of Classical civilisation, an enthusiasm for imperialism that led to a strong identity with Rome and a growing sense of nationalism that forced the identification of resistance to Rome.

Using three case examples of such tensions, Dyson highlighted the 'archaeological policy of Napoleon III', and in Germany' ...the complex intellectual and ideological forces that led, on the one hand, to pioneering archaeological work at Roman sites on the Rhine and Danubian frontiers, yet also the promotion of the cult of Arminius as hero in the anti-Roman struggle'. In contrast, Britain 'had much less a formal archaeological policy. Similar conflicts, however, were present in the popular imagination', citing the glorification of Boudicca and the depiction of Roman Britain in Kipling.

Dyson does not seem to have developed these arguments, although the spirit of them seem has been repeated by others. Therefore some of the same criticism might apply and will be discussed below. I have summarized elsewhere some of the limitations of this sort of analogy, not least of which is that the propensity to draw analogies usually ignores the uniqueness of the Roman version (e.g. Freeman 1996a). For instance, the summary is too generalized with regard to nineteenth century attitudes to imperialism. Likewise there may be too much over-statement on the 'archaeological policy' of the respective governments.

In the revival in the discussion of the condition of Romano-British studies, one of the most significant discussants has been Richard Hingley who, in an impressive series of publications, has contributed much to invigorating the issue of relating Romano-British archaeology to our understanding of the present (1984; 1991; 1993; 1994; 1996a; 1996b; 1997; 1999; 2000; 2001a; 2001b). The core of his argument, one following a tradition evident in other disciplines, is that Haverfield's and his generation's explanation of the purpose and progress of 'romanization' was heavily conditioned by their exposure to the consequences of nineteenth century British (and European) colonialism. This they used to validate their own eulogistic attitudes to the benefits of imperial government. Such attitudes, perhaps not fully appreciated at the time, were in turn the consequence of such factors as the prevailing educational system with its emphasis on the classical languages combined with the strong sense of public (= imperial) service on the part of a social elite. There was also uncritical acceptance of the long march of British history and an insular form of manifest (British) destiny. The rule of the British, like its Roman counterpart, was almost inevitable and in that case, its mission had to be explained. While this summary perhaps over-simplifies Hingley's argument, I have argued elsewhere that the various components that he marshals to formulate his argument do not stand up to close scrutiny: in short the parts do not match the whole. Not least his characterization of Haverfield and his work is flawed, although this is in part a consequence of accepting the 'received' version of Haverfield and his work.

This is not the occasion for a detailed critique of Hingley's opinions but is something for elsewhere. An in-depth review is necessary not least because his ideas have evolved in response to the issues they created and the responses elicited. There are, however, a number of points, which might be drawn out here. Our starting point is a symposium on the theme of *Roman Imperialism: Post-Colonial Perspectives* organized by Webster and Cooper. One of a number of interesting contributions to the proceedings was Hingley's *The Legacy of Rome: the Rise, Decline and Fall of the Theory of Romanisation* (Hingley 1996a). In this Hingley explored a number of themes. The issues were, first, '...how some British academics, administrators and politicians actively used the Roman Empire to help identify and define their own aspirations and in so doing drew a parallel between Britain and Rome ...Second I will show how some contemporary scholars retain a positive conception of the Roman experience ...' (p. 35).

In the examination of his themes, Hingley repeated a number of points, which had been flagged in earlier publications. For instance, there was the tendency for Victorian (and earlier) writers to use the past to inform the(ir) present. Then there was the way that modern writers used the Roman experience to validate their attitudes to the British empire. 'I have argued elsewhere that some Edwardians came to draw upon Rome as a means of identifying Britain's imperial purpose; however, some qualifications are required here. First, only certain aspects of the Roman imperial model were felt to be relevant, and most British authors who envisaged a parallel between the British and Roman imperial systems were highly critical of the despotic nature of the rule of the Roman emperors. The British Empire was felt to be highly superior in political terms' (p. 36). Elaborating on these points, Hingley cited a number of administrators, politicians and educationalists who wrote in this fashion. Haverfield is said to be one example. After discussing some of the reasons why writers made such analogies (including the influence of the prevailing system of education and the effect of the developing rivalry between Britain and Germany which, in part, resulted in a drive towards greater administrative efficiency of the empire, a process which might have benefited from taking on board the lessons of the Roman example), Hingley looked at Haverfield's contribution to these developments. The core to the argument is the material contained in the 1911 Roman Society address and, in particular the themes relating to incorporation and of assimilation and denationalisation. 'In his 1911 paper, and also in the 1915 republication of The Romanization of Roman Britain, Haverfield clearly identified these two aspects in arguing that the efforts of the Romans took two forms – the defending of the frontier and the development of the civilization of the provinces during the resulting peace' (p. 38). These concerns were supposed to be manifested in Haverfield's involvement with the CEC and his work at other sites in and around Hadrian's Wall and in the message of assimilation presented in *The Romanization* where the process was envisaged as directional and progressive.

The second part of Hingley's paper looked at the efficacy of the concept of romanization as a mode for explaining the past. In this sense, there had been a shift, away from the 'moral' dimension of the process to the ways that native society adapted 'Roman' culture in response to their changing circumstances. After citing a number of examples of this line of reasoning, Hingley offered the counter-argument: the problem is that '...the study of Roman Britain in the past has been partly determined by its context within the society in which he (Haverfield) developed.' Still this problem offered a potential solution; by the use of revisionist attitudes to imperial rule, typified by 'post-colonial analysis'. Rather than such approaches providing a framework for definitive explanation, Hingley argued what they permit is understanding of past perspectives and to imagine new attitudes. In this sense post-colonial analysis offers insights to three interrelated themes: to de-centre study, which seems to mean listening to the opinions and reactions of the governed, exploited and oppressed to imperial rule (in other words those not at the centre of power), to identify the range of responses to colonial contact and to demonstrate instances of overt and covert opposition to the domination of external powers.

Some of the ideas contained in the *Legacy* paper were developed in a contribution to a collection of essays on the theme of *Dialogues of Power and Experience in the Roman Empire* (Hingley 1997). Here Hingley 'looked specifically at how the indigenous population of Britain might have reacted to the Roman conquest and occupation of these islands'. The influence of post-colonial perspectives is clear. Repeating the format employed in his previous discussions, the first part of the paper attacked the traditional pro-Roman perspective on romanization. Drawing on progress in other disciplines to realign Roman studies, Hingley assessed Haverfield's attitudes to pre-Roman native society in Britain and Europe, where he saw them '...as an archaic projection of modern European society – uncivilized but intelligent' (p. 86). Instead of this outlook, Hingley preferred to let the archaeological evidence speak for itself, unencumbered by the sort of prejudices that Haverfield typified, to examine a much more socially sophisticated, multi-identity society than Haverfield could have ever imagined.

The points raised in this paper were developed elsewhere in an article Hingley included in another set of essays on recent innovations in historical archaeology. Here he summarized the thrust of his contribution as:

> ...an account of the context of the theory of 'Romanization' as it developed in Britain in the twentieth century. I also develop a critique of the dominant explanation for changes in Romano-British society and material culture through time and review the potential for developing an alternative perspective based on a more complex interpretation of human behaviour (Hingley 1999: 137).

Now it was argued that the tradition of romanization studies was directional and one of a progressive process of social change: 'the assumption that natives wished to become Roman, or more Roman, is argued to be the motivation behind the gradual transformation of material culture in the provinces from native to Romano-British throughout the three and half centuries of Roman rule' (p. 137). But Hingley replied that (modern) interpretation failed to understand the social context which conditioned such views of knowledge, believing that before any interpretation can be valid, what was required is 'a critical review of the literature produced by those who created the modern discipline of classical studies, and in particular Romano-British archaeology' (p. 138).

As these comments imply, for Hingley the problem with Romano-British archaeology went back to the influences of the late nineteenth and early twentieth centuries and the prevailing attitudes to empire, which, in turn, drew comparisons from what the Roman examples were thought to be and where the academic study and interpretative framework for Roman Britain was derived from Britain's own imperial history. This led to him trying to identify the British imperial mission. In this he cited Haverfield as a leading influencing authority (ultimately down to today), where even the great man considered the 'poor' wanted to be, and were ultimately, 'romanized'. It was argued Haverfield regarded this as positive force. And again the validity for this argument was found in his 1911 address to the fledgling Roman Society. In contrast, or so Hingley maintained, 'It is significant to anyone who wishes to take a different look at the evidence that this progressive and pro-Roman way of understanding our Roman past, has, to an extent, created the information that we have available' (p. 141). To prove the fact, there is repetition of the point made in earlier papers concerning the over-emphasis previously placed on the excavation of certain categories of sites (e.g. military and 'prestige' at the expense of the (non-villa) countryside and the 'poor').

The culmination of Hingley's work was the bringing together many of the themes articulated in his previous articles, along with some new ones in a substantial monograph, the ambitiously titled *Roman Officers and English Gentlemen. The Imperial Origins of Roman Archaeology* (2000). For our purposes here, its main points are how images of the Roman past contributed to the late Victorian/Edwardian own sense of empire at a general level (often invoking the denigratory nature of the British under Roman rule). This in turn nurtured the belief that the experience of the Roman conquest contributed to the formation of the English character, embracing those who stood out apart from the Roman empire in the cause of liberty and so, the rôle of Haverfield in making Romano-British history/archaeology a respectable subject for study.

The reviews of *Roman Officers* were generally positive. Reece (2001) thought: '...Hingley has demonstrated well the interlinking of Imperial discourse and the writing of Roman Britain well into the second half of the twentieth century ...The person who perhaps comes out of the description and analysis best is Collingwood'. Where the reviewer had reservations, they concerned the introduction of 'theory' into the debate.

It is only in the last three pages of the conclusions that I really take issue with Hingley. He demonstrates well how Imperial discourse acted as a theoretical template in the study of Roman Britain and rightly says that this led the subject astray. He thinks this is because Imperialism is the wrong theory and a good dose of better theory will do us all good. The only thing it is likely to do is provide material for another author in 50 years time to demonstrate how new theory led us equally astray. If theory is needed let it be centred round the hedging of fields and the milking of cows and things that really matter (p. 226).

In the opinion of a second reviewer:

Hingley discusses the conceptual framework in which Haverfield operated, his substantial contributions, and the enduring strength of his views on the Romanization of Britain. R.G. Collingwood's often variant views receive considerable attention, while those neo-Haverfieldians like S.S. Frere are passed over more quickly. Hingley closes with a demonstration that the operative cultural models that guide archaeological research do matter. Statistical tables of the types of sites excavated in Roman/Britain since the early 1920s show the domination of military sites and villas. Such an agenda reinforced models of rural Romanization and prevented the emergence of alternative hypotheses that focused on continuities from pre-Roman cultures and cultural resistance to Romanization. Overall the book provides a nice demonstration of the importance of placing archaeological research in its wider historical and cultural context (Dyson 2001a: 712).

The final sentence is undoubtedly so, but Reece and Dyson missed some crucial points which have a bearing on Hingley's presentation of the past. First, his study managed to examine Roman archaeology in Britain without reference to how it was developing at least in Haverfield's time. In fact, in Hingley's account, up until Haverfield Romano-British studies appear to be the product of writers of fiction or of antiquarianism. Then we are presented with a picture of Haverfield's ideas being largely set by *c*.1900 and remaining in essence unchanging. Likewise those ideas were formulated against a particular agenda. Both these characterizations are debatable. We have seen how contemporary developments continuously influenced Haverfield's ideas and we have also examined how he was a product of his time. In the third instance, Hingley confuses Haverfield's output with how his opinions were used and reinterpreted by others. What *Roman Officers* is about is the way that non-archaeologists used Haverfield's interpretations. What Hingley's account is more about is the way non-archaeological writers used the notion of Rome. The authorities examined are largely politicians, educationalists, some historians and others little better than jingoistic pulp writers. It goes without saying that he may or may not have agreed with how they were deployed. The brotherhood of archaeology is conspicuous by its absence in the account. The only 'archaeologist' noted is R.G. Collingwood. Last but not least, the strength of Hingley's exposition lies, as Dyson notes, with some of the data he assembled from some of his earlier publications, some of which is questionable.[1]

A third review raised a number of important reservations (Wilkes 2002). For instance, it drew attention to the way Hingley failed to note how strong had been the English engagement with Hellenism in the

---

1. A frequently-made accusation levelled at Haverfield is that he was preoccupied with the 'Roman' attributes of the province with a relative disregard of the 'native' and that he was only ever interested in the forts, towns and villas (e.g. Hingley 1984; 1989; 1991; 1994 etc.; Scott 1990). According to Hingley, it was Haverfield (and admittedly to a lesser extent Collingwood), who was responsible for such a skewed emphasis in research in Roman Britain, as reflected in the quantity of excavation undertaken on villas, walled towns and forts and the relative absence of detailed study on non-villa settlements and unwalled small towns. In Hingley 1989 this data is tabulated in two bar graphs, his Figure 2 ('*Proportion of villa in relation to non-villa excavations*') which shows the number of villa sites excavated relative to non-villa sites. It would appear to demonstrate (a) the past biases in favour of the former; and (b) how the balance has been redressed, with in recent decades a greater number of non-villa sites being explored. But the initial assessment of Haverfield is not entirely fair. As we have seen, he was not necessarily a fieldworker or excavator, whatever he might have said, but more a mechanism to support the work of others. This rôle, in turn, placed him in a position to synthesise and interpret the broader picture. Nor was he unaware of the existence of non-prestige sites. Indeed on numerous occasions he was calling for their exploration in order to correct potential imbalances in contemporary perceptions of the Roman occupation. For instance, in *Some Remains in the Upper Thames Valley* (1899d), Haverfield reported on 'peasant' sites, 'more probably pastoral than agricultural, not highly civilized.' Elsewhere, as late as 1912, he was stating, 'a proper understanding of Rome was dependant on a knowledge of non-Roman peoples' (*J Roman Stud* II (1912): 289). In actuality, the categories of rural and small urban sites discussed by Hingley are exactly the same as those deployed by Haverfield. Where he and Hingley differ is in the way (a) Hingley is able to add more subtle shades to the various site types and (b) to relate them to newer forms of data derived from more recent anthropological studies and, in particular, a new appreciation of what constitutes the family unit. Still the conclusions drawn are largely either fleshing out and/or negating Haverfield's basic conclusions. Put another way, in this argument Hingley is merely tweaking the evidence to create a picture which still owes much to Haverfield. Furthermore, two comments might be made with regard to the graphs in Hingley's 1989, Figure 2. In the first instance, to show how Haverfield (and his successors) introduced a research bias in Roman studies, the figure consider the decades 1920–90, with data derived from the

nineteenth century, and that what occurred in Roman studies slightly later, was in part a reaction to this. Wilkes also pointed out that contrary to Hingley's description of the period under review, Haverfield was perhaps less central than he argues. 'He [Haverfield] seems to emerge as a rather passive figure engaged in making his notions of Roman Britain more palatable to the educated classes in the high summer of Empire'. Hingley also failed to note the way Haverfield challenged parallels with the Roman and British empire and the passivity of English scholarship:

---

annual reports originally published in the *Journal of Roman Studies* and later in its sister publication, *Britannia*. Other potential sources reporting comparable work are omitted. This is not so serious for the period after 1920. One assumes that if the journals of the regional societies had been utilised, still the magnitude of the biases adduced would remain largely consistent. What Figure 2 does fail to consider is what was happening before 1920 and therefore in Haverfield's lifetime. It is highly likely that a table for the period, of say, 1800–1920 would show the same sort of biases that Hingley identified for the first half of the twentieth century, for a popular activity for nineteenth century antiquarians was villa excavations. So in one respect to blame Haverfield for the picture of the twentieth century is unfair. Secondly, Hingley's interpretation of the data overestimates what he calls a research bias, as if the excavations he tabulates were driven exclusively by a research imperative. Equally valid, if not more so, are factors such as who was conducting the excavations. It was invariably the local antiquarian and archaeological societies, and inherently amateur, as part of their annual summer activities who undertook such work, and who were naturally enough preoccupied with obtaining tangible results for their efforts. This fact is also reflected in the way the annual excursions of the archaeological and antiquarian societies of the Victorian and Edwardian eras focused on the likes of churches and castles and upstanding Roman sites as well as the better known examples from prehistory because there was otherwise so little else for them to see (Hudson 1981: 47). In this sense villa excavations offered a better prospect than any other sort of rural site and would be better suited to the competence of the excavators. Being able to identify and then recognize a site for what it is is essential, whether it be manifested as stone masonry, mosaics or tesserae etc., and will in turn focus attention and (future) research. In a comparable fashion Hingley fails to take into account the popularity of school(boy) training excavations (Corder 1932–3; Garnons Williams 1934–5). Therefore Hingley's identification of a bias, while accurate, can be attributed to other factors as much as the pernicious influence of Haverfield (and Collingwood).

'a more balanced picture perhaps demands close attention to the rôle of Haverfield as purveyor to the British, of the fruits of Mommsen's revolution in the study of ancient Rome' (p. 127).

Following the publication of *Roman Officers*, Hingley published two other statements on the themes of Victorian and Edwardian English perceptions of Rome, on romanization, and post-colonial resistance. In *Images of Rome. Perceptions of Ancient Rome in Europe and the United States in the Modern Age*, Hingley contributed two pieces: an introduction and a longer article (Hingley 2001a; 2001b). In the second of the essays, *An Imperial Legacy: the Contribution of Classical Rome to the Character of the English*, the main issue was the ways '...images provided by classical Rome were used to help define ideas about English origin and imperial purposes *c.*1880 and 1930, a period when new intellectual currents developed to define and provide support for British control over large parts of the world' (p. 145). A debate concerning English origins (but not explained why) evidently developed in the late nineteenth and early twentieth centuries. Up to that time, the prevailing explanation for the origins of the English drew on Teutonic racial origins, themselves a consequence of the Anglo-Saxon invasions. The reaction to the established view was to see Englishness as the product of a mixed genetic inheritance combining ancient Britons, classical Romans, Anglo-Saxons and Danes, with the emphasis on the Roman aspect. It is with this background in mind, Hingley looked at the way the ideas of 'Roman' and native were incorporated into ideas of Englishness (aided by archaeology). Because it was Haverfield, at one of the nation's leading universities, who was instrumental in making Roman archaeology intellectually credible, so his contribution to the debate takes central position in Hingley's text. As a product of his time, the '...relevance of Roman archaeology to the imperial spirit seems partly a result of the value of Haverfield's focus upon the importance of 'Romanization' in defining the English character' (p. 146). Romanization was thus a concept developed to explain the passage (or to correct the previous idea of light romanization) of civilization to the ancient Britons. The theory thus conveniently fitted the contemporary search for continuity in images of English national life. For many writers of the period, the passage of civilization from Rome also included the transfer of the imperial spirit of Rome, English civilization, religion and even imperial ability, all to be lauded as the Roman legacy. Not surprisingly, the sense of continuity that such opinions represented permeated academic and popular works. And this was all due in part to Haverfield and his work, where he added substance to the crude notions of the Roman legacy:

> The type of analogies which were drawn between Britain and Rome dur-
> ing the nineteenth and early twentieth century deeply influenced the
> character of Haverfield's studies and have in turn influenced his succes-
> sors (p. 147).

With respect to analogies, Hingley identified five topics to illustrate
the way images of the classical Roman contributed to representations
of the English. For convenience, I combine the first and second – as
the ancient Celt as Indian and Englishmen as classical Romans – using
British India as the motif. In these juxtapositions, the Romans were
popularly seen as officers and imperial administrators living with the
trappings of Roman government (in their towns, forts, villas etc., just
as did the British in India) with the Celts, otherwise the Indians, living
as an inferior, subjugated population. Incidentally the analogy also
demonstrated how the Britons had learnt the lessons of the Roman occupiers, irrespective of whatever damages had been inflicted by the
Germans. In contrast to the experience of the Britons, the Celts said to
derive their ancestry from the islands pre-Roman population, were
largely unaffected by the Roman occupation which permitted the late
Roman Celtic revival, with ancient Britons believed to be 'ancestral'
parents of the Irish, Welsh and Scots (citing Haverfield 1912a: 19).
The departure of the Romans left the Celts as unencumbered as they
were first found. But following the departure of the Romans they were
either massacred by Teutonic invaders ('the freedom loving Teutonic
ancestors of the English' p. 150) or were driven to the western extremities of the island.

The third of Hingley's topics is native resistance (to Rome), as exemplified by Boudicca, and the way that it brought out, even in defeat, the
independent 'spirit' of the English. And of course, there was the aspect
of the British turning the lesson round and becoming the coloniser.
The fourth topic is the inheritance of the imperial torch of 'civilization',
an idea drawn from a variety of sources (e.g. the Roman history of the
island; the legacy of the classical education; and the then current Dar-
winian concept of progress). All emphasized the element of destiny as
well as the way that the British had improved the inheritance. Then
there was the way that Roman attitudes of *humanitas*, 'an ideological justification for the Roman elite that supported conquest and domination'
(p. 153), were hijacked by Victorian/Edwardian Britons. Here Hingley
highlights inconsistency in such arguments.

The fifth and final of Hingley's topics is 'Englishness' itself, a debate
the product of a crisis in English politics in the 1880s. Uncertainty in
English society at this time resulted in positive assertions of what English cultural attainment was supposed to be. The response reached its

peak in the inter-war years (and focused on ideas of stability and unity and permanence). The response tended to emphasize the English as a mixed island race, one which drew its inheritance from a greater range of peoples from Britain's past. This explanation effected something of reconciliation of earlier explanations of the origins of the English. On the one hand it acknowledged the legacy and bequest of Roman civilization as it was passed down, while on the second, recognized that (at least some of) the ancient Britons survived the Anglo-Saxon assault and in doing so bringing those (Roman) attributes to subsequent generations (citing Rhys (1884/1908) and Scarth (1883)).

In this interpretation, the ideas of the Roman legacy were expounded and given intellectual credibility by Haverfield; 'romanization' was the mechanism by which Roman civilization was communicated to ancient Britons. Now, in place of an influx of Roman colonists, the Britons themselves became romanized. One problem however was to explain whether the results of that assimilation were passed on, if the Anglo-Saxons had massacred the romanized Britons. The solution offered by some writers was some of the population must have survived the onslaught (as in the persistence of Christianity).

In Hingley's version of the developments, the various interpretations and ideas summarized here were then picked up by certain historians concerned with grander (imperial) issues (e.g. Charles Lucas' *The British Empire* (1915) and *The Story of Empire* in H. Gunn 1924)) who grafted onto the genetic legacy of the Roman occupation a Roman spiritual counterpart. Taken together, the successive racial and spiritual virtues served to explain 'Englishness' and its (positive) characteristics. Conveniently, such explanations also served to modify the overbearing influence of the Teutonic effect (especially as it was a politically sensitive time). Equally important is the fact, as Hingley puts its, that for Haverfield the romanization of the English was at the expense of the romanization of the Welsh and Scots. 'Roman Britain therefore had significance in the definition of modern English imperialism and civilization' (p. 158). The influence of the idea of racial strength derived from racial mixing is then supposed to be visible in the years after the First World War, when, for instance, R.G. Collingwood in *Roman Britain* (1923: 100) argued that Britons must have survived the Anglo-Saxon assault, as evidenced by the way the work of the great artists owed much to Romano-British models and in arguing so created' …a linear conception of British history' (p. 158).

While the Teutonic 'myth' of English origins did not die immediately, the idea of Romano-English inheritance became popular from the 1890s, peaking in the 1920s. The advantage of the theory lay in the way it combined a variety of themes and interpretations supported where appropriate by archaeological work.

> I have suggested that ..it became politically useful for the imperial elite to us both the idea of the inheritance of bravery from the ancient Britons and the notion of the civilizing of the native Britons by imperial Rome. To carry these inheritances into the modern world required at least a partial survival of the Romano-British population during the Anglo-Saxon conquest, hence the decline of the Teutonic myth. The idea of racial mixing has also become the acceptable archaeological interpretation for the history of Britain during the 20th c. (p. 160).

In the process of intellectualizing the problem, and explaining the racial melding Haverfield is credited with making a major contribution, even if, as Hingley acknowledges, many of his ideas were taken on-board and re-interpreted by others. But still:

> Haverfield's work had a major part in the development of [the] nationalistic emphasis in the Roman archaeology of Britain. His theory of Romanisation served to support a tradition that was developing during his lifetime. He provided academic credibility for the idea that a direct racial link carried Roman civilization through to the modern English. Others may have used Haverfield's work in a way that he did not intend … it is likely however, that Haverfield's work was inspired by an unconscious desire to establish lines of continuity in national history through England's inheritance of European civilization. This may have formed a logical way in which to develop an idea of Romanisation in the Edwardian period but I would argue that these concerns with the inheritance of Western conversation have created a particular national emphasis in the approaches to Roman Britain and Western identity We have inherited this national emphasis and we may now wish to reconsider our approaches to the Roman past to meet the context of the present day (p. 162).

There are many points here with which one might take issue. In the first place, as plausible as Hingley's reconstruction of the general tone of the discussion of the origins of Englishness in the nineteenth century is and the connection made between Haverfield and the European inheritance is especially interesting, he overstates Haverfield's direct contribution to it. It is undoubtedly the case, as Hingley notes, that Haverfield's writing struck a resonance with the opinions of other writers of the time, but as we shall see, there is very little in Haverfield's output which shows an interest in the sort of issues that are highlighted. More specifically Hingley's summary of Haverfield's presentation of the (late Roman) Celts of Britain is not strictly accurate but somewhat garbled. Nor does the summary of the chronology fit the facts. Instead of it being a phenomenon of the post-Roman, or at best, the very end of the Roman period, Haverfield actually argued that much of western Britain remained relatively untouched by Roman (cultural) influences to the extent that there was a revival in Celtic motifs in the Roman period, one where the influences could co-exist, if not expelling the light degree of romanization elsewhere in the province.

One of the reasons why nineteenth-century Britons were able to look back on the Roman past with such a positive outlook was thought to be because of the emphasis on the 'classics' in the education system of the time as a major prop to this attitude. The analysis operates at two levels. On the one hand there is that which compares and contrasts the ideology, structure and dynamics of the two empires. This is often thought to be a phenomenon of late nineteenth to early twentieth century scholarship and a product of the height of imperial confidence (Cannadine 2001). A second form of treatment is how and why those who made such comparisons did so; what were their motives? This is more of an issue in late twentieth-century scholarship. Such Victorian/Edwardian writers are invariably characterized as apologists of empire and or at worst, as out-and-out imperialists. But again in this generalized condemnation something is lost in the detail. For instance, with regard to the leading ancient historians of the time, few of them seem to have operated in the first mode. If this were so, then it would nullify the significance of the second trend (Freeman 1996a). Because of the connection, however, between the classics and the contemporary system of education the assumption made by many is that the origins of such comparisons lies with university teachers who in turn shaped their students and who were increasingly being trained to run the empire. But it is too easy an exercise to select authors and titles from the late nineteenth and early twentieth century to prove that historians of the time were making what they believed to be valid comparisons between the Roman and British empires and which Haverfield it is assumed would have been in sympathy. For instance, Evelyn Baring's (Lord Cromer) *Imperialism: Ancient and Modern* (1910), Lord James Bryce's (and a friend of Haverfield's) two volume *Studies in History and Jurisprudence* which included *The Roman and the British Empire* (1901) and Sir Charles Lucas' *Greater Rome and Greater Britain* (1912) have been used as examples. Indeed, Lucas has become a widely cited exemplar for those examining the Victorian link between Rome and the British empire. The apogee of the Oxford influence is to be found in the way, according to at least one historian of the 'Kindergarten' and the 'Table', some Oxford classicists were influential tutors of some who were to become members of the movement. Their teaching:

…helps explain the group's deep respect for the growth of western civili-sation. (Lionel) Curtis, especially tended to identify British culture with that of Greece. The Oxford system also emphasized Britain and Euro-pean history and (Philip) Kerr's tutor was H.A.L. Fisher, the famous historian of Europe whose instruction was reflected in his early articles in The Round Table. Imperial and colonial history was not yet an inte-gral part of the Oxford syllabus (Kendle 1975: 18).

If this were the case, then with the world of classical antiquity as the back-drop it would be reasonable to expect it was (Oxford) classicists and ancient historians who promulgated the outlook and sorts of compari-sons which are to be found in Bryce, Cromer *et al*. The evidence is, however, surprisingly slight. It is clear that a number of Haverfield's col-leagues and contemporaries did make such cross-imperial comparisons, but those most frequently cited today were not ancient historians but rather medieval and modern historians who used Haverfield's writing. A good example of a leading historian who did so to his own effect is Charles Oman, a well known arch-Tory. A contemporary of Haverfield, Oman claimed he was extensively influenced by him. In the fifth edition of his *England before the Norman Conquest* (1921, although the core re-mained that prepared for the 1910, second edition), Oman noted debts to H.C. Davis (Professor of Modern History at the University of Man-chester), T. Rice Holmes and Haverfield[2] and, later on, Leonard Wooley (sic). Haverfield helped in the drafting of Chapters V (the Roman con-quest), VI (the conquest of northern Britain) and VII (the period of Domitian to Commodus). Oman's use of archaeological evidence, evi-

---

2. This does not miss the fact that Oman was a friend of Haverfield, and it was a friendship reciprocated ('my friend, Professor Oman': *The Times* 14 April 1919). Not surprisingly Oman's acknowledgement was expansive: 'I am no less deeply indebted to the help of the present holder of the Camden Chair of Ancient History, Professor Haverfield, I was indeed fortunate to obtain the assistance of such an unrivalled specialist in all that concerns Roman Britain. He placed at my disposal a number of pamphlets and papers which would otherwise have been practically inaccessible to me – for many of them were scattered broadcast among the proceedings of learned societies, Eng-lish and foreign, where they are hard to find without a guide. He put me under a still greater obligation by looking through my chapters, and furnish-ing me with much comment, and a considerable number of corrections. The extent to which I have been aided by his published treatises may be best gauged by a glance at the footnotes to Chapters V, VI and VIII' (p. ix–x). Simpson (1996: 219) suggested that Oman's first visit to Hadrian's Wall, in 1891, was made at Haverfield's suggestion.

dent in the earlier chapters but not so much in the later Roman period when he relied more on documentary sources, includes information from the excavations at Gellygaer, Caerwent, Templeborough, Brough-on-Noe, Melandra, Slack and Castleshaw. The result was a narrative history. For our purposes, Haverfield's 'influence' is apparent in Chapter VI and the early years of the occupation '...in which all Southern Britain was being rapidly and steadily Romanized' (p. 105), after the model set by Agricola and to be seen in language, the growth of towns and roadside settlements. Oman goes on:

> Nothing can be more definite and well marked than the evidence that the higher civilisation of the conquerors destroyed within two or three generations the lower national culture of the conquered. Celtic art had a peculiar character of its own, which it is impossible to mistake, and countless British finds bear witness to the fact that it was alive and flourishing when Claudius crossed the Channel [with a footnote 'For all these see Haverfield's Romanization of Roman Britain, *Proceedings of the British Academy* for 1907']. But it could not stand against the world-culture of the Romans. The Briton preferred the classical type when it was presented to him, even in inferior and second-hand examples, to his own ancestral work, just as the native artisan of India to-day is prone to cast away the time-honoured patterns of the East and to copy the most commonplace European models. On the whole it is true to say that from the second century onwards there was hardly any Celto-Roman art in Britain, but only Provincial-Roman art, an art that cannot easily be distinguished from that which prevailed in other remote and rough parts of the Empire (p. 106).

The impact of Rome could be traced in the likes of religion and especially in pottery: 'even the ordinary better-class crockery of daily life was imported from Gaul, or copied at second-hand from the Aretine [sic] ware of Italy itself.' Elsewhere some Celtic traditions survived in some pottery, notably Castor Ware of the East Midlands and New Forest Ware, 'survivals of an isolated sort in an ocean of commonplace work, directly borrowed from the conquering race. Nor is it even the case that the town, with their partially immigrant population, shared in the monotonous culture of the Empire, but that Celtic life survived in the villages ...Rural Britain soon grew to be provincial and not barbarous in its outer aspect, though it was but a poor province' (pp. 106–7).

Oman is but one example of a writer who although not a classicist by training went through *Literae Humaniores*. While other writers of medieval and later British history, can be cited it makes the point that in the general picture of late nineteenth century it appears to be that a preoccupation with melding the accomplishments of the Roman empire with the British empire was more a concern for the modern historians and their political contemporaries than their classical counterparts. Indeed, contrary to received wisdom, not all were convinced by Lucas' opinions, least of all Haverfield. What has been largely ignored is that he reviewed Lucas's arguments. His conclusions are instructive to the point they require no further comment:

> The excursions of modern statesmen into ancient history have always an interest and often an importance for historical students, even though the statesmen be not (as for example, Mr. Bryce) scholars versed in the technicalities and the minuter results of historical research. The admirable little volume on *Ancient and Modern Imperialism*, which was issued by Lord Cromer ..is a first-rate instance of such an excursion based, be it added, on a very useful knowledge of much ancient history ...The volume before us is perhaps less likely to attract the student. The most interesting and valuable, as well as the fullest and most detailed parts of it, so far as one can judge, are those which deal with Greater Britain. Greater Rome, that is the Roman provinces, receives both a briefer and in some points, perhaps a disappointing treatment. The reader who does not know the subject is likely to be led astray at the very outset. ...The great feature of the Roman empire, at least in western and central Europe and in Africa, was its Romanisation of the native peoples. That is a feature which does not, and which practically cannot, recur in the British empire, and it supplies perhaps the most fundamental contrast between the two states. Those who fail to realise it can never fully understand what in the end the Roman empire achieved. The Roman in their first days of empire hardly understood it ...Another contrast which Sir Charles mentions in language scarcely likely to enforce it on his readers is the following. The world in which the British empire exists is one which contains much older European civilization and the civilization seems strong and unlikely to perish; the Roman had to fence his frontiers in order to keep any tolerable civilization alive in the world at all. Sir Charles tells us that 'taken as a whole, British trade and colonization, have known no limits. The policy has not been that of the Roman Wall'. But Roman walls were not barriers against the expansion of Rome, nor as many finds in Germany show, did they mark the limits of Roman trade ...On the other hand, the whole drift of recent colonial policy in respect to Chinese and other immigrants into Australia, New Zealand, South Africa, British Columbia, has been precisely the policy of the Roman Wall, expressed in legal rather than military forms. It has set a barrier against the incoming of peoples who have been judged likely to weaken or damage the European type of civilization (*J Roman Stud* II (1912): 279–80).

I have spent so much time looking at Hingley's opinions for a number of reasons. His work now represents the most substantial current appraisal of Haverfield and his influence on Romano-British studies and shows signs of becoming the new orthodoxy. Some of his conclusions about the intellectual climate in which Haverfield existed are indisputable. Similarly, one would concur with many of his perspectives on what was being written at the time and for what reasons. His, and others', characterization of Victorian/Edwardian attitudes to the Roman past and the contemporary Britain is superficially attractive and certainly fashionable. But in its generalizations of the situation many of Hingley's points lose, if not ignore, much important fine detail. Everybody of that time is labelled as sharing the same common opinion about the British imperial mission and acceptance of the social values of the moment.

But in fact there was a substantial body of opposition. Haverfield's often negative attitudes to the relevance of the classics were by no means unique. Other academics condemned the emphasis that had been placed on them for the training of teachers (cf. Chapter 3). Percy Gardner, shortly after Haverfield's death argued:

> No doubt 50 years ago the Classics occupied too great a part in education; and the consequence has been a reaction, which has gone too far in the other direction. But a counter reaction is setting in ...The English universities and schools which have most strongly experienced both the undue stress laid on the Classics and the prejudiced reaction against them are beginning to feel the force of a fresh tide. But the new teaching of the Classics must be wide and more comprehensive than the old, directly its attention not to the mere words of ancient writers, but to all aspects of the life of antiquity (1926: viii).

Among the critics of the Greater Rome-Greater Britain analogy, Gardner too was by no means unique in this respect. This is an important point missed by Hingley: the way that many classicists of the time defended the teaching of the ancient languages, not because of the way they were supposed to reinforce the prevailing social order, but because it was felt, rightly or wrongly, that they inculcated intellectual discipline and the search for real 'meaning'. The example of the classics in turn demonstrates another problem: Hingley's failure to explore, in any depth, Haverfield himself. Conclusions are derived from Haverfield's works that were prepared for other purposes. On the contrary, there is sufficient evidence in Haverfield's writings to demonstrate his opinions were far more sophisticated and modulated than Hingley would give credit. In fact they were not written for the way some have subsequently elected to interpret them.

In assessing Hingley's work we can see that the thrust of his research has been preoccupied with the link between the British imperial experience and the Roman example and how one has shaped interpretation of the other. His assessments of Haverfield's work, naturally enough, have drawn on examples of his published work and, in particular certain public utterances. The three works that continually reappear are Haverfield's address to the Roman Society (Haverfield 1911a), the 1915 version of *The Romanization of Roman Britain* and, to a lesser extent (the posthumous) *The Roman Occupation of Britain* (1924). With respect to the latter two we have seen that if we take into account their origins and subsequent development neither of them can necessarily be regarded as definitive statements indicative of Haverfield's thinking although they have come to treated as such. We have already examined the themes central to them and have also seen how different contemporary reviewers drew differing interpretations from them. The same sense of ambiguity continues to affect modern readers, including Hingley. We have also considered the third of these works, the Roman Society address (cf. Chapter 7), to see how representative of Haverfield work the points made in it are. Re-examination of it shows how others have used the speech in the years after it was delivered. We can see from his résumé of the speech how it, in large measure, underpins many of the critiques of Haverfield's work. And yet in reality this constituted a very small part of the main point of the speech. We might note too the real purpose of the speech – the future realignment of archaeological research in Britain. Indeed, as at least one modern reader has noted, the speech was essentially the justification for the creation of yet another 'learned' society (Majeed 1999) which, we could add, Haverfield had to justify because there were potentially rival bodies whose work might be said to overlap with what was proposed for the new organization. Taken at face value, the point of the speech was an attack on previously poor English appreciation of what the classical past was and how the situation might be improved. It is with this purpose that the other themes raised, some below the surface, should be viewed. Despite his appreciation of some of this, in a line of argument comparable to that followed by Hingley, Majeed still used the address as an instance of how some late Victorian/Edwardian scholars believed Roman history can inform 'our own Empire', especially with regard to issues such as the assimilation of imperial subjects and their denationalization. In this sense, Haverfield's work is described as being typical of a literary genre of his time, where 'allusions to Rome had become a "heuristic refinement" in British Imperial thought' (Majeed 1999: 89 citing Betts 1971: 158). To illustrate the point, Majeed proceeds to dissect the works of two other historians – Lucas and Bryce – who like Haverfield, used present/past comparisons and contrasts to the Roman Empire to discuss race, identity and assimilation in the British Empire. Crucially, like Haverfield, 'both authors refer in particular to British India in their comparative arguments' (Majeed 1999: 89). I have already discussed the utility of this line of argument elsewhere. The problem with reading the speech in this manner is that it is selective in what is used. In turn it has to work what evidence there is to hand. For instance, India crops up in only one sentence in the speech. As it is, the same passage (why study of the past is relevant to the modern day) seems not so much to do with a compare and contrast exercise, but is more an allusion to the dangerous, ongoing situation in Europe. While it is true that Haverfield was on (friendly) terms with Bryce, he was also critical of the sort of comparisons that he made (Freeman 1996a). Furthermore a close reading across the range of Haverfield's published opinions would show his use of allusions to British India are extremely rare. Few can be cited, and as many examples used to show that he disliked making analogies between it and the Roman empire.[3]

Haverfield's romanization

Hingley's characterization of Haverfield and his work can be tested in other ways. For instance, it is worth looking from where Haverfield

---

3. As just one example, Haverfield recounted how he had given a course of lectures which considered 'various likenesses and unlikenesses of the Roman provinces to British India', during which at '...the end of, one of the audience came up and asked if he might put me a question. "You seem (he said) to know something about India. Can you advise me which would be the best province for me to choose if I get into the Indian Civil Service."' Disappointed by the way the audience may have misunderstood the point in the comparisons he had made, Haverfield concluded the story by observing 'Young students of ancient history do not always recognise ...They know – in general – little of the of the institutions of their own land or age – far less probably, than their predecessors 80 years ago – though they know much more of the personalities... Though they often possess a good knowledge of ancient history, a comparison between Greece and Rome and the things of their own day has little meaning for them' (Haverfield 1910a: 106).

might have derived his ideas about 'romanization'. I have argued elsewhere that he may have taken it from Mommsen (Freeman 1997), but the picture may be slightly more complex than I originally thought. Haverfield seems to have first used the word in an explicit sense in his first report on recent discoveries in Roman Britain in *The Antiquary* and written towards the end of 1890. In the context of buildings then just found he wrote:

> Roman remains are speaking generally, comparatively rare in England, and it is only by the combination of individually insignificant details that we can adequately measure the Romanization of Roman Britain (*The Antiquary* XXIII (1890): 8).

In the same journal there was also the existence of 'Romanised natives' (p. 229). But from where did Haverfield learn to appreciate such sensitivities? It seems likely he could not have 'lifted' the concept from a British tradition, for there is nothing evident in earlier publications upon which he could draw. While Wilkes (2002) notes that the word 'romanization' was associated with adherence to the Roman Catholic Church, the earliest attested (archaeological) reference to it, according to the second edition of the OED, is the assimilation of Roman customs or models, citing Whitley's *Study in Language* (1876: 'Italy after its first romanization...') and A.J. Evans' *Antiquarian Researches in Illyricum* III and IV (*Archaeologia* XLIX (1885): 27 – 'we are struck by the evidence they (inscriptions) supply of its thoroughgoing romanization'). In both these examples the term is linked to language and in particular the adoption of Latin. Mommsen had also used the word and defined the parameters for the western empire's acculturation in the same way when he contemplated the provinces of Roman Europe, which Haverfield read as an undergraduate (cf. Chapter 3 and 4). It is for this reason then that it is likely that Haverfield drew yet again on Mommsen and developed one of the 'minor' themes in the projected volume IV of the *Römische Geschichte* (1885). With his interests in epigraphy, it is not surprising that Haverfield had recourse to the rôle of language as a mechanism for the transmission of culture and so its change in his earliest publications. His view was that Britain became romanized, where Latin was adopted universally as the *lingua franca* of the province at the almost total expense of Celtic. There is another strand of evidence which may have clarified to Haverfield how the process was manifested materially. There are good indications that he was alert to a process of cultural transmission and modification by the late 1880s. In discussing the towns and museums he had recently visited in Galicia and Transylvania (in 1887), of the town of Czernowitz in Bukowia (sic), an area which had been occupied by the Austro-German colonists since the late eighteenth century, he was struck by how similar were its communities.

> One interest, indeed, the town has which can hardly be matched in Europe. The Bukowina[4] was annexed to Austria in 1775, and the capital and chief towns were garrisoned by German colonists, who have held their ground more or less completely till this day. Accordingly, here at the meeting place of Ruthenian and Rouman, 300 miles from any Teutonic land, the astonished traveler stumbles upon a town where the streets are named with German names, and the local politicians, in the local newspapers assault one another in the German tongue. But, though, the townspeople are still in great part, German-speaking, they have not lived in the midst of Ruthenes and Roumans for nothing, and the place struck me as German in a limited sense (fn.: Czernowitz and Suezawa returning three German liberals in recent Austrian elections). Things are very different in the German settlements in Trasilvania, which I visited afterwards. There the 'Saxons' have maintained their nationality through – perhaps, because of the troubles which have beset them. Here the German element seems likely to merge in the surrounding populations, and the future struggle in Bukowina politics will be that between Ruthene and Rouman. In any case, the place has an interest for the student of nationalities – perhaps even for the anthropologist" (1891b: 3).[5]

In this respect we can see Haverfield deploying some of the same criteria that Mommsen had devised to assess acculturation (language and political institutions), but at the same time it compliments some of the criticisms he made elsewhere about Mommsen's (archaeological) work. Whereas Mommsen emphasized language as a determining feature, Haverfield's strongest evidence for 'romanization' was to be found in what he called 'material civilisation'. Whilst acknowledging there could be some distinctly non-Roman traits in this (i.e. in the

---

4. Bukowina, modern Bukovina, is now a district of the Ukraine. Czernowitz (or Cernauti), the major town of the region, is modern day Chernovtsy. Suezawa is Suceava in Romania.

5. The ethnic origins and their vestiges of the German colonists in central Europe was a subject to which Haverfield returned in his discussion of the ancestry of Albrecht Dürer (Haverfield 1915c).

form of private domestic dwellings) and the perpetuation of some other Celtic traditions (e.g. some pottery, brooches, some art etc.), still Haverfield argued '...the material civilisation of the province, the external fabric of life was Roman in Britain as elsewhere in the West' (1912a: 30). This he saw manifested in public buildings, in the fittings of private housing, in art and craft (p. 39) as well as in the structure of local government and the organization of the land. What is more he saw this transition pervading most elements and aspects of life in Britain. He reiterated the point elsewhere.

> First, and mainly: the Empire did its work in our island as it did generally on the western continent. It Romanised the province, introducing Roman speech and thought and culture. Secondly, the Romanisation was perhaps not uniform throughout all sections of the population. Within the lowlands the result was on the whole achieved. In the towns and among the upper class in the country Romanization was substantially complete ...But both the lack of definite evidence and the probabilities of the case require us to admit that the peasantry may have been less thoroughly Romanised. It was covered with a superimposed layer of Roman civilisation (p. 59).

With regard to Roman Britain and its 'romanization', the elements he found to be indicative can be quickly enumerated. For instance, in his contribution to the 1908 *VCH* Shropshire, significantly as part of a digression, he noted:

> Mr. J.R. Green's[6] idea of rural Britons who remained apart from the Romans, spoke British, owed some allegiance to their native chiefs and retained their native system of law, like the Zulus and

---

6. John Richard Green (1837–1883) was a cleric, writer and honorary fellow of Jesus College, Oxford who despised the tendency for writing 'drum and trumpet histories' of Britain. He was the author of *A Short History of the English People* (1874 with numerous editions). In the 1898 illustrated edition it was written he 'was the first English historian who had either conceived or written of the English from the side of the principles which his book asserted' (e.g. the People). He also wrote *A History of the English People*. Green's opinions in *The Making of England* (1881) were roundly assaulted in Haverfield's discussion of the circumstances behind the end of Silchester (cf. 1904e; 1912e). And yet in the Ford lectures, in the lecture on the end of Roman Britain, he was more complimentary about Green and his style. Indeed in June 1909, Haverfield attended a commemoration and dedication service in his honour at Jesus College, Oxford.

Maoris of our Empire, is, I think, mistaken. Celtic may have been spoken and the Celtic law recognised (like other systems of native law elsewhere in the Empire), and the great native families may have kept high social and local position, though definite evidence of all this is wanting. But the gap between Roman and Briton is (I believe) a gap which was soon completely bridged in most parts of the province, and the Celtic elements which survived here survived in harmony with the Roman civilization and not in contrast to it (p. 208).

Having seen that Haverfield derived his ideas of romanization from Mommsen as well as a European rather than a British context, we now move to how his views were used by his contemporaries. In a series of articles exploring the consequences of Haverfield's work on late Victorian – early Edwardian perceptions of the British empire, as well as the invention of a concept of 'Englishness', Hingley drew attention to a number of potentially important trends which might owe more than just passing reference to the influence of Haverfield and his writings. For instance, he has pointed to what seems to be an upsurge in the later nineteenth century in publications about Roman Britain, although it has to be said that the range and quality of the output he cites is limited to children's stories, school history books and low brow novels rather than higher quality publications (Hingley 1997: 2000). Hingley had recourse to such works because of the scarcity of quality discussions concerning Roman Britain available up to this time. From the material he cites, Hingley suggests it is possible to detect broad shifts in the message that such literature tried to put over, although again, on the basis of what he uses, the oscillations may not be so clear-cut as the understandably generalised picture suggests. The earliest version, promulgated in works such as B. Windle's *Life in Early Britain* (1897), was that there was a distinction between Roman settlers and the indigenous population. The Roman input or influence was thus minimal. The *Leitmotiv* for this explanation was the British experience in India. Hingley adduced the beginnings of a shift in the explanation which is supposed to be evident from the 1880s onwards, but typified by H.E. Marshall's *Our Island's Story* (1905). In this version, the Roman occupation came to be the beginning of English/British history (which ignores early histories, such as David Hume's *History of England* (1754–62)). The cause of this changed view was due to a number of contemporary developments. There was the growing public acceptance of British

imperialism and its accomplishments which were seen as sufficient justification, if not its *raison d'être*. Coupled to this
acceptance was what Hingley calls the particularly Victorian cy-
clical vision of history. After the Roman empire and its
undoubted success, the wheel had come full circle 1500 years
later, with the emergence of its British counterpart. In addition
to these factors Hingley attributed the shift to a rising
Germanophobia. Accepted explanations of the origins of the
English linked them with the arrival of the Anglo-Saxons (while
the Celts were the ancient Britons who survived the 'Saxon onslaught'). To play down the Teutonic link (with all the negative
characteristics attributed to the Germans) there evolved a mode
of explanation which argued that the English strength of
character was derived not solely from the 'German' invaders but
from the admixing of a variety of cultural influences over time.
This logic could accommodate the positive (civilizing) consequences of the Roman occupation along with the Celtic
renaissance (as well as the post-Anglian, Scandinavian and
French influences in British history).

The mechanisms which brought Roman civilisation to the island, as cited by Hingley, are to be found in the likes of the
Scarth's *Roman Britain* (1883) where Roman colonists intermar-
ried with natives. Elsewhere it was attributed to high-rising
Britons working in the imperial system and so taking on the trappings of Roman culture. In this respect, Haverfield apparently
provided the intellectual model for the way that Roman civilisation spread to the ancient Britons, citing Haverfield's 1905
lecture *The Romanization of Roman Britain*. In Hingley's opinion
the:

> ... theory of Romanisation served to support a tradition that was devel-
> oping during his academic lifetime. He (Haverfield) provided
> academic credibility for the image of a direct racial link for the inheri-
> tance of Roman civilisation by the English. I am not suggesting that
> Haverfield was motivated by a conscious wish to create such a teleologi-
> cal image of English origins but that his work was used in this way by
> others.

The strength of the point, however, is diluted by the fact that *The
Romanization*, Haverfield's first major statement, was a lecture delivered to a restricted audience in 1905 and only published in
1912, some years after most of the defining literature, such as
Scarth, Hingley cites. This is tantamount too to putting the cart

(the interpretation) before the horse (viz. Haverfield then coming up with the intellectual or academic justification for the interpretation). There is the possibility that some of Haverfield's earlier works and opinion, notably his reviews of and later contributions to Traill's *Social England* (1894 down to 1902) might have been used by other authors. But there is no proof that he had written anything of this sort before the *VCH* entries. It is true there was something of a boom in published works at this time. It includes Hodgkin and Oman and more specialized literature such as Sagot, Ward and Lyell (cf. Chapter 2). Alternatively one could suggest Haverfield was influenced by the sort of writers that Hingley discusses and that later authors picked up the same ideas via him. A particularly interesting idea is the potential influence of Scarth who has already been noted (cf. Chapter 1). From where Scarth drew inspiration for his ideas is another interesting question, not least because he was known to be critical of Mommsen's conclusions if not his methods (Scarth 1887). Another influence could have been H.C. Coote's *Romans of Britain* (1878) with its theme of the survival of Roman law and practice in post-fifth-century Britain. Otherwise there appears to be little in contemporary British publications of the time that he could use and Mommsen's *Roman Provinces* (1885) had not yet been published. And then there is the problem that, as we have seen previously, Haverfield had little or no time for Coote's and Scarth's scholarship. To conclude, there is no reason to link Haverfield's opinions with contemporary Romano-British scholarship, not least because the alleged sequence of developments do not fit, let alone share similar views. At best he may have been used by others, but he had no control over how.

Haverfield's politics

Another way of assessing Haverfield's opinions on the Roman-British empire analogy is to take account of his own political outlook. We can look at this subject in a number of ways. In the absence of a clearly expressed set of values we might look at his reputation and the opinions of others on this subject. Then there are his utterances on contemporary events and finally in the way he related politics to learning and scholarship. I have already alluded to the fact that Haverfield at Oxford was known for his Liberal politics. 'In academic as in national politics he invariably leaned to the liberal side. Sometimes indeed, he left even his fellow-liberals behind' (Macdonald 1924: 26). But there again it was a liberalism of an idiosyncratic sort to the point it is hard to disentangle any consistency in his opinions. This need not necessarily rest uncomfortably with the signs of his association with the 'High Church', certainly in his early years. For instance, he supported Lord Hugh Cecil's candidacy as a prospective MP for the vacant Oxford University constituency in 1909 (cf. *The Times* 7 June 1909).[7] Elsewhere there are indications of Haverfield's relatively liberal attitudes in contemporary social issues. He was a strong advocate for admitting women to higher education.[8] In a related way, Cheesman, in his diary for 1913, records Mrs Haverfield's part in the suffragette movement in Oxford. And it appears that Haverfield was sympathetic to the cause, if Cheesman was not necessarily so.[9]

In his personal politics, Haverfield's liberalism is equally evident. It is no surprise that he was not a complacent acceptor of government foreign policy. In the admittedly few extant observations about contemporary political events, Haverfield often expressed views counter to the prevailing climate. We have already seen his opinions about the justifications for what became the First World War and how badly he took its outbreak (cf.

---

7. Hugh Richard Heathcote Cecil, Baron Quickswood (1869–1956) was elected unopposed the following year as a Conservative noted for his unwavering Anglican principles.
8. For example, Haverfield was also a supporter of the University Extension Movement. He spoke, with others (including Eugénie Strong), at the Oxford Summer School of the University's Extension Delegacy in August 1913, where the general theme was *The Place of France in World History* (*The Times* 25 July 1913).
9. She was the secretary of the Oxford branch of the National Union of Women's Suffrage Societies through which she was a correspondent with Bertrand Russell. In 1913 she opposed the proposed Election Fund to support women candidates in parliamentary elections. Momentarily accepting the policy, she resigned in 1914 (cf. Crawford 1999: 483). Three years earlier, Haverfield was signing a memorandum to *The Times* (24 June 1910) in support of women's suffrage. Nor is it surprising that he was a signatory to a petition from some leading Oxford academics, again published in *The Times* (17 February 1917), requesting the government give women the vote in recognition of their contribution to the war effort. He was also a supporter of other public causes. For instance, in 1907 he was contributing to the Russian Famine Relief Fund (*The Times* 9 March).

Chapter 8).[10] Just as significant are his opinions on the Boer War. At the end of the 1890s, Britain's involvement in the war in South Africa served to polarize at Oxford who supported or opposed the government's decision to declare war in October 1899. The identity of the pro-government party is well-documented, but in the anti-war group Haverfield was in good company. Following a series of disastrous military setbacks, British successes reversed the decline with the prospect of victory. When the war entered a new phase of guerrilla engagements, attrition and concentration camps meant to corral the Boers and their families, the pro-Boer Liberals attacked the Tory government's policy that was regarded as more 'patriotic' ('...mounting concern at home among humanitarians, left-wing Liberals and Socialist who refused to believe that the ends justified the means'; James 1995: 267–8). The government called a snap election, the so-called 'Khaki election' in October 1900, resulting in a Tory landslide, which was regarded as an endorsement of their advocacy of imperial expansion. The war dragged on until May 1902. Haverfield was evidently opposed, like other (Liberal) Oxford academics (e.g. William Warde Fowler, Gilbert Murray and elsewhere William Ramsay), to the government's position (cf. Thomson 1957; Henderson 1971). He referred to this in a letter to Chancellor Ferguson of 2 February 1900: 'Of course the war kills all other interest, but not quite. I find many a man glad to turn to anything else for a while' (Unpublished letter, Carlisle Library). Later in the same year, in a letter to Mommsen, he noted: 'For us in England I think this will not be a happy Christmas though our imperialists may try to consider it so' (Croke 90). Mommsen's reply three days later mentions how '...old friends of old England mourn with you and with the small party that feels the moral falling off and the political dangers of your great nation.' (23 December 1900: Croke 91). Evidently not in the best of moods, in a late night letter on July 1901, Haverfield wrote: 'The war causes me much sorrow: it is still near midnight – mia nyx and it is my own country.' Finally, in another letter to Mommsen, on 30 December 1902, he wrote: 'It is not a good New Year for all of us. We have got out of our South African War, but the fogs, for which our island has long

10. Haverfield's upset at the outbreak of the war was shared by Warde Fowler whose '...distress over the (First World) War was so profound that for some time he could do no serious work. Though he had strongly disapproved England's official attitude in the Boer War, and had even blamed himself because, as a teacher of the British youth, he had indicated sympathy with imperial ideals, he did not doubt the entire rightness of the Allied cause in the war with Germany' (Coon 1934: 118).

been celebrated, have got into our politics and our politicians and strange things get done in fogs' (Croke 97).

In fact, the list of anti-imperial Oxford Liberals contains some impressive names. Obviously exceptions can be named or imagined, but one of the reasons why the classicists would be less well-disposed to this sort of analogy making goes back to what was regarded as the intellectually purer expectations of the degree of *Literae Humaniores* and its emphasis on learning for learning's sake. This ran counter to the type of institution and form of instruction that Benjamin Jowett was thought to prefer. It cannot be coincidence that the most vociferous anti-imperialists happened to be the strongest proponents of the School. For instance, W.J. Arnold, an Oxford graduate, and his editor at *The Manchester Guardian*, C.P. Scott, influenced by developments in South Africa, could be described as anti-imperialist in outlook. Likewise, Gilbert Murray co-authored with F.W. Hirst and J.L. Hammond *Liberalism and the Empire* (1900), a critique of empire where the authors feared that contemporary events were the result of and were, in turn, being used to permit state-sponsored aggression being '...too often employed as means towards good or tolerable ends, but actually worshipped and glorified as ends in themselves' (p. vi). Murray's contribution concentrated on the way imperial systems exploited 'inferior races' while Hammond discussed Britain's foreign and colonial policy in relation to the tenets of liberalism. Hirst's essay was, in the main, an attack on Cecil Rhodes and an explanation of 'the finance of imperialism, and to show how militarism and excessive expenditure upon armaments both feed and are fed by calculated promises and "inevitable wars" which serve at the same time another purpose – that of preventing reforms at home' (p. xvii). 'Murray ...believed that the British were the only people in the world who attempted to be really just towards inferior races; but he was haunted by the lessons of Greek history and the memory of how Athens had forsaken democracy, had become corrupted by Imperialism, and had gone to its friendless doom' (Symonds 1986: 92). Perhaps in reaction to the use of classics to bolster imperial aspirations, Murray was one of those who did not support the continued compulsory requirement of Greek and Latin for undergraduates (cf. Chapter 3). This debate was in addition to the thrust and counter-argument of academic publication (Turner 1981).

Haverfield and the idea of history

Haverfield's non-partisan attitude to the British empire can be seen in another sphere: in his opinions about the purpose of history. R.G. Collingwood was to accuse Haverfield of being the least philosophical of historians, and by implication castigate him for not possessing a sufficiently rigorous conception of how the historian constructed his idea of the past. In terms of his political outlook, there is little to suggest that Haverfield was likely to be prone to drawing the same sort of comparisons and analogies between the Roman and British empire that other contemporary historians and more populist writers did. This impression is substantiated when we look at how Haverfield wrote about the past. On a number of occasions Haverfield complained about the damage that making such comparisons could do (Freeman 1996a). In fact he retained a more sophisticated appreciation of the purpose of history. His most frequently quoted (and indeed his only) substantial statement on comparative imperialism was made in his Presidential address to the Roman Society. For instance, Haverfield asked, what was the purpose of historical (and archaeological) research?

> Need I ask, what is the use of it all? ...This only will I say, that Roman history seems to me at the present day the most instructive of all histories. ...It provides us few direct parallels or precise precedents; the wise man does not look for that in history. But if offers stimulating contrasts and comparisons and those glimpses of the might-have-been which suggest so much to the intelligent reader. Its republican constitution offers the one true analogy to the seeming waywardness of our own English constitution. Its imperial system, alike in its differences and similarities, lights up own Empire, for example in India, at every turn. The methods by which Rome incorporated and denationalised and assimilated more than half its wide dominions, and the success of Rome, unintended perhaps but complete, in spreading its Graeco-Roman culture over more than a third of Europe and a part of Africa, concern in many ways our own age and Empire. Another, and even vaster achievement of Rome may seem to-day less important. We know that by desperate efforts it stayed for centuries the inrush of innumerable barbarian tribes and that the pause insured to European civilisation not only a survival but a triumph over the invading peoples. We know also, or fancy we know, that our own civilisation is firmly planted in three continents and there is little to fear from yellow or other peril. Yet if the European nations fall to destroying each other, such dangers may recur; we have still to look unto the pit whence we were digged. The man who studies the Roman frontier system, studies not only a great work but one which has given us all modern western Europe ...Even the forces which lay the Roman Empire low concern the modern world very nearly (1911a: xviii).

Taking this passage at face-value Hingley believed it to be '...the logic behind the academic study of Roman Britain as it developed in the first half of the twentieth century' (Hingley 1991: 91). But this is perhaps reading too much into an innocent declaration. We should keep

it in proportion when applying the wider implications of this statement. In the first instance, this was a public address to a general
meeting and to a society which, in its advertisement for members, had
called for men of learning as well as for patriotism. What Haverfield
was arguing for was the way history illuminated the present, not to justify it. He made similar comments, which it is true, could be as misread
as the Roman Society lecture. In an address of 1912 to an audience of
Oxford undergraduates in the School of *Literae Humaniores*, the study
of Greek and Roman history was useful:

> ...in respect of the historical problem of political life and of human na-
> ture which they bring before us. In one way or the other of them we find
> most of our modern difficulties somehow raised.

This is not to deny that he made reference to the lessons of Roman history relative to the issues facing the British empire.

> ...the administration of a great Empire concerns many men to-day and
> in a very vital manner. Our age has not altogether solved the problems
> which Empires seem to raise by their very size – the gigantic assaults of
> plague and famine, the stubborn resistance of ancient civilizations to
> new and foreign ideals, the weakness of far-flung frontiers; it can hardly
> find men enough who are fit to carry on the routine of government in
> distant lands. The old world was no better off: too often, they survived
> only through cruelty and massacre and outrage. Rome alone did not
> wholly fail. It kept its frontiers unbroken for centuries. It spread its civili-
> zation harmoniously over western and central Europe and northern
> Africa. It passed on the classical culture to new races and to the modern
> world. It embraced in its orderly rule the largest extent of land which has
> ever enjoyed one peaceable and civilized and lasting government. It was
> the greatest experiment in Free Trade and Home Rule that the world
> has yet beheld (1912d: 25 and 28).

Nor does it ignore the fact that this lecture, like the Roman Society address is full of references to, for instance an oriental threat (the 'yellow
peril') to the West. Then there is the summary of the Haverfield lecture
to the RAI in 1904 where he acknowledged that there had been a recent
revival in Romano-British studies, '...because the growth of Imperial
sentiment in England would soon awaken an interest in other Empires'
(1903f: 383). Elsewhere, in a lecture *The Frontiers of the Roman Empire and
Roman Britain* delivered to the Lancashire and Cheshire Antiquarian Society in January 1907, it was reported Haverfield said that the reason for
the Roman invasion of Britain lay with the need to protect Gaul: 'Britain
acted on Gaul very much as the Irish-Americans seem to act on Ireland,

and aided to foster a spirit of independence which might in a crisis be dangerous, and which on one occasion actually was so' (*The Manchester Guardian* 11 January 1907). But he made as many references to the lessons of more recent European history too. For example, in his assessment, questionable as it is now, of the survival of Roman templates in modern British towns, Haverfield observed: 'We in England tend perhaps to overrate the likelihood of such survivals. Our classical education has, until very lately, taught most of us more of ancient than of mediaeval history' (1913c: 140). Nor does it ignore that Haverfield was alert to the validity of cross-empire comparisons but those he made were intended to elucidate points rather than to confirm facts.[11] At the same time he was just as prepared to draw parallels from other periods and situations. This is in contrast to many recent assertions about (Oxford) Roman historians of this time (Hingley 1994; 1996a; cf. Freeman 1996a). While it is true that Haverfield might have extolled ancient Roman culture, in the absence of any statements to the effect, linking him with the mission of the British empire is at best tenuous. Macdonald's bibliographical list of Haverfield's work notes only two potentially pertinent articles (1910a; 1916a). This failure is all the more surprising given what was happening in contemporary Oxford.

But, in general he seems to have been dismissive of such attempts. In fact the evidence suggests that Haverfield was consistently uneasy with mixing politics with learning. In his biography of Thomas Ashby, Richard Hodges reproduced a letter from Haverfield to Gordon Childe of November 1918 in which the former observed:

> Generally, I have a great dislike to mixing up politics and learning. At the same time, I am bound to remember that learned men do sometimes say things which upset politicians; and that, in university matters, action is occasionally taken on one ground and defended and justified on another ...I feel it will remain true that unpopular views are unpopular, and no indignation will get round this awkward fact. I am afraid that we in Europe will have a good deal of friction over the leavings of the war ...For a historian, it is a stirring time: every morning one wakes to find a monarch or a monarchy gone: Europe's but a battered caravanserai (2000: 26 citing Mulvaney 1994: 67–8).

---

11. As one example, in 1900, when describing the recent discovery of inscribed lead pipes at Chester, Haverfield wrote that the individual named on them, Agricola, 'pursued a forward policy, which was apparently revered on his recall. One might compare him to Sir Bartle Frere, perhaps, or to some of our Indian Viceroys' (*The Antiquary* XXXVI (1900): 6).

It is this sort of attitude which explains at one and the same time Haverfield's close association with Mommsen the Liberal as well as his frequent condemnation of the latter's' tendency to allow his politics to cloud his judgment. In this he seems to have believed 'culture no longer held primacy over politics; his ideal of man was the *homo politicus*, and the aim of writing history was "political pedagogy". Pedagogy always requires models, and such a model Mommsen discovered in Republican Rome' (Demandt 1990: 287). For Mommsen the purpose of historiography was '"political education in the service of national-liberal propaganda"' (Demandt in Mommsen 1996: 5). In turn his writings were heavily influenced, if not conditioned, by the events of his time. The fact was Rome had created a unified, world state, just as the various German states now needed. In effect Rome could act as a model for German unification. And yet Mommsen was alert to what brought about the fall of the empire – in part unbridled imperialism and which he was at pains to condemn in all its forms. On another occasion Haverfield was to recollect:

> Mommsen, in one of those addresses on politics ancient and modern, which foreign custom occasionally requires of University Professors, traced the strength of the Principate to a feature which he found also in the position of the Hohenzollern rulers of Germany. The Princeps, he alleged was not a mere despot; he combined some sort of despotism, or constitutionalism, in any case some supreme military authority, with the idea of office, of presented duties or responsibilities – responsibilities, not to a parliament but to his own and his peoples conscience. How far this is a true view of the position of the King of Prussia and the Empire of Germany, I cannot now ask. Everything depends ...on how the institution be actually worked. The 'servants of the state', such as Mommsen tells us the Hohenzollern rulers are, may so easily become its masters if they wish. One can see that in the Roman Empire some rulers were actually what we should call 'servants of the state', spending their whole activity in its cause ...Others, also able rulers, were emphatically, for good or evil, 'autocrats' (1916a: 12–13).

This is one of the ways where Haverfield differed from Mommsen and his agenda. Unlike Mommsen it is difficult to discern any political agenda in Haverfield's scholarship. Time and again the extant material reiterates a commitment to European scholarship and the development of Romano-British studies through archaeological investigation, while a preoccupation with imperialism or missionary civilizing or the extolling the benefits of colonial administration is consistently absent. This view is in accord with Haverfield's (and other Oxford classicists') opinions about the function of history; debunking easy assumptions and popular analogy.

The same liberalism seems to have influenced his opinions on education. His allusions to teaching and research to advance knowledge for the sake of knowledge would have been at variance with the sort of training school for professional administrators in the practical university that Jowett championed in the latter third of the nineteenth century. As his defence of the teaching of ancient history as part of the School of *Literae Humaniores* at Oxford demonstrates, he was not pre-disposed to the utilitarian function of learning. Nor does he appear to have been receptive to the arrival of the (American) Rhodes scholars in late 1902 (cf. Chapter 3). These were sentiments he shared with others. His Oxford colleague, William Warde Fowler in a collection of essays '...nearly all written during the early stress of the battle of Verdun, and helped to carry me through the strain of that very critical time' (1916: 1) drew parallels between the contemporary European experience and the past. Elsewhere he was stimulated to respond to the analogies drawn by others, principally Germans, about German and British culture and history and the Roman experience.[12]

The sum of the evidence then is that Haverfield would not have been disposed to the sort of crass or gung-ho eulogizing of the benefits of Roman rule of which some would believe he was guilty. It is indisputable that he saw more benefits to be derived from it than the damage it inflicted, but relative to his contemporaries his opinions were much more moderate than those of others. Where such opinions are articulated they have to be seen in the context of the utterance. Instances of such pane-

---

12. Warde Fowler's biographer also noted that: 'Protest has been made against the tendency to drag ancient history with modern analogies. It has often been done to little purpose. Fowler used analogy cautiously. And his parallels are more than superficial. The little volume entitled Essays in Brief For War Time, in which comparisons are found, contains two essays. "The New Tyrannus" and "Civis Germanus Sum". In the former he contrasts great tyrants of Greece ...with the striking personality and brilliant restlessness of William the Second' (and in the latter, a rejection of the German-Roman, British-Carthage analogy made by the Kaiser; Coon 1934: 260–1). Warde Fowler's *Roman Essays and Interpretation* '...involves literary, legal and especially natural history comparisons. I like to show that the apparently marvellous may be sometimes wholly or in part authenticated by modern parallels ...It is not beside the mark to mention these comparisons of a broad political nature and points of detail, for they suggest the author's modern historical interests ...and show that only ancient history ...was one, but that all history was an unbroken evolution' (Coon 1934: 261).

gyrical work was usually as public lectures and popular literature and were they taken up and manipulated by others. Equally so, it is unfair to damn him where his opinions are not palatable to modern tastes or where his use of now such politically loaded terms as 'barbarian', 'savage' and civilization are regarded as elitist and even racist. What is more significant in his work is his appreciation of the historical continuum of Western Europe rather than the benefits and justification of empire.

Conclusion

In the end we then, we are left to explain why Haverfield had recourse to the sort of explanation of cultural change that he used. Hingley's work places Haverfield's ideas of 'romanization' into the wider context of British colonial and imperial attitudes but without demonstrating Haverfield as part of the same. If it was not meant to be congratulatory or self-sustaining with respect to the British empire, why did he use it? The argument preferred here is it was more the case of Haverfield taking up and expanding on something Mommsen had discerned. One of the most important implications of the scope of Haverfield's work, which went back to Mommsen, whether it be with respect to its epigraphy, to excavation (whether it be of towns, frontier installations or whatever) and his works of synthesis was that, in isolating a distinct Roman period in British history, he indirectly divorced it from what is now called the late pre-Roman Iron Age. It cannot really be said that Haverfield was interested in the pre-Roman, Iron Age population/period in this island, although he did not ignore it. But what he could not escape, not that he wanted to, was the more established tradition of debating the consequences of that period on later (post-Roman) society, a question to which he in turn contributed. The mechanism for assessing that sense of continuity was the idea of 'romanization'. This explains, in part, why he did not make any substantial contribution to the archaeology of late Iron Age Britain. Anathema today, the failure has been attributed to his imperialist attitudes, where he was supposedly not interested in the 'barbarians'. But the reality is perhaps more prosaic. It is more likely to have been a consequence of his (over-)emphasis on the Roman period. However, the advantage of his form of romanization was that as well as providing a framework for exploring late Roman – early Dark Age Britain, at the same time it also permitted him to re-establish the linkage between the indigenous Iron Age population and what came after it. This line of explanation has Haverfield's concept of romanization developed more as an inadvertent consequence of his other Roman work. While some have endeavoured to isolate an intellectual and conceptual undertone to his work, an alternative case can be made for the agenda as an indirect consequence of the creation of the Haverfield 'myth'. In reality, his life's work came to be geared to improving the presentation of the discipline. But compared to his university work, his interest seems tantamount to a hobby, coincidentally a comment made of Collingwood's approach to Romano-British studies. What others chose to see as his legacy was their own choice, of which the most influential has been Collingwood. But as we will see in the next chapter Collingwood's method was to take a facet of Haverfield's work and to manipulate it to his own intellectual predilection. It was the results of this marginalization which later generations of scholars have picked up on and which has perpetuated the myth.

CHAPTER 11

Haverfield, R.G. Collingwood and beyond

I will not be drawn into discussion of what I write. Some readers may wish to convince me that it is all nonsense. I know how they would do it; I could invent their criticisms for myself. Some may wish to show me that on this or that detail I am wrong. Perhaps I am; if they are in a position to prove it, let them write not about me but about the subject, showing that they can write about it better than I can; and I will read them gladly. And if there are any who think my work good, let them show their approval of it by attention to their own (Collingwood 1939: 118–19).

Introduction

Haverfield's death marked a watershed in Romano-British studies, even if it was not necessarily appreciated by his contemporaries. We have seen how damaging the First World War was for him (Macdonald 1919–20a: 486; cf. 1924: 30; Bosanquet 1920: 139; Richmond 1941: 181). While it is clear, contrary to popular opinion, he did not lose that many 'students' – the most notable survivor was R.G. Collingwood and whose preservation was due to his serving in Naval Intelligence – there were the various interruptions to his work. Field-work and research temporarily ceased with the distinct possibility that the advances made up to the outbreak of the War would be at least halted. Then there was the severing of his contacts with continental scholarship. And there was the change in the social climate that followed the war where the universities had to accommodate a new age of teaching and associated activities. What was worst of all, his death demonstrated how marginalized his work was still regarded at Oxford. In the short term the question was who would continue the work that he had commenced? As it transpired, according to the principal individuals of the time, the situation was saved almost entirely by the self-sacrifice of one person. While Macdonald took on the part of the leading Romano-British scholar of his day, in the opinion of most, Collingwood was the next 'great' in the field: 'He took up the mantle of Haverfield and became the leading authority on this field, the guide and counsellor of all younger scholars in it' (McCallum 1943: 160).[1]

Haverfield and Robin Collingwood

Today Collingwood is remembered as a philosopher, interest in whose work has undergone something of a renaissance (cf. Parker 2000; Johnson 1998; Helgeby and Simpson 1995). In this respect his two interests, philosophy and archaeology, are often regarded as running in parallel through the course of his career. But in fact a distinction needs to be introduced. Collingwood's academic career may be divided into three distinct phases, with the first and third being more pronounced (Johnston 1967). The earliest spanned 1912–25 and concerned mainly archaeology, with some excursions into philosophy (with in 1916, his first book, *Religion and Philosophy*). Prominent in the second phase, 1925–33, was his work on the philosophy of history relative to archaeology, although the latter became progressively less significant. The third and final phase began *c*.1933 and was almost entirely devoted to the philosophy of history. As van der Dussen observed, although Collingwood understated his own historical and archaeological work, it did have a profound effect on his philosophical outlook: 'Collingwood himself considered philosophy as his primary occupation and his work in archaeology and history as that of an amateur ...In his own thinking there was always a close relationship between philosophy and archaeological and historical practices' (1981: 1).

---

1. Collingwood '...occupies a leading place with Haverfield in the fine Oxford tradition of Romano-British scholarship. That tradition is now being carried forward by living Oxford men, without a break, into the realm of post-Roman history and early Saxon settlement' (G.M. Trevelyan *The Times* 13 January 1943); 'Collingwood was also a distinguished philosopher and probably the most substantial intellectual among all Romano-British scholars.' Of his contribution to the Oxford History of England, Jones observed that it '...was much more ambitious than Haverfield, making the first authoritative synthesis of the history of Roman Britain. Its influence has been enormous, expressing the views derived from the rapid expansion of field research in the 1920s and 1930s forming the framework of argument through the 1950s and 1960s and still being regularly quoted in the 1980s. His book was ...much more than an attempt at a simple narrative. Collingwood made full use of archaeological data, but retained a predominantly narrative form. This book was a thorough and commanding analysis of all the major issues, drawing conclusions that were controversial' (1987: 87–8).

Analysis of Collingwood's *oeuvre* has been the preserve largely of philosophers and historians of that discipline. Examination of his work in archaeology has been in terms of how it interplayed with his wider philosophical outlooks. The same approach has recently underscored how some archaeologists have tried to apply his methodology to broader archaeological interpretation theory (e.g. Hodder 1986). What there has been is a relative failure to contemplate the longer-term implications of what he saw happening in Romano-British history. Indeed we should also be alert to the fact that, because received wisdom repeats Collingwood as something of an intellectual 'giant', his reputation goes before him. As Parker expressed it: 'many of those who took Collingwood as a starting point, not only for the philosophy of history but for other philosophical issues as well were not really attempting a full understanding of Collingwood but were pursuing their own particular interests' (2000: 163). To be sure, in Parker's opinion, it is philosophers rather than historians (and archaeologists) who possess the best working knowledge of Collingwood and his methods (e.g. Hodder 1986: 90–102; 1995).

Robin George Collingwood was born at Cartnell Fell on 22 February 1889. Following what reads as an idyllic childhood but an unhappy schooling at Rugby, he went up to University College (Oxford) in 1908 (Johnston 1967: 6ff). It would have been at this time that he came into closer contact with Haverfield, although it was through his father, William Collingwood, a noted antiquarian of northern England as well as secretary and close confidant of John Ruskin, that he first made his acquaintance. He is listed as a participant on the CEC excavations in 1903. At Oxford he sat in on Haverfield's lectures and was encouraged to participate at Corbridge in 1911. The two later worked together in the field. Collingwood helped at Ambleside when work began there in 1912 and down to 1915 (and later in 1920). He also co-authored two papers reporting their work.[2] In addition to this, prior to the First World War Collingwood was also '...employed by Professor Haverfield to survey a number of Roman forts for an account of the Roman Britain History of the Northern Counties for the VCH' (Taylor, Haverfield Archive). Before the announcement of his final university results in

---

2. Haverfield and Collingwood 1914; Collingwood and Haverfield 1914. In the second paper, Collingwood completed those sections which Haverfield due to the illness was unable to finish. Collingwood wrote the subsequent seasons reports (1915; 1916; 1920; 1921a).

1912, Collingwood accepted a fellowship in philosophy at Pembroke College. In Collingwood's version of events, following Haverfield's death and the fact he was now the only 'trained' Romano-British archaeologist left in Oxford, he felt obliged to take on Haverfield's teaching, so that in the early 1920s Ian Richmond reported how Collingwood was teaching Hadrian's Wall for Greats as well as courses in philosophy.[3] In 1934 Collingwood was elected a fellow of the British Academy, and in the following year became the Waynflete Professor of Metaphysical Philosophy at Oxford, a chair he held until his resignation in 1941. Collingwood's academic appointments far from inhibited his work as a historian and archaeologist, an interest originally stimulated by his father. Having joined the Cumberland and Westmorland Society in 1909, the younger Collingwood became the editor of its *Transactions* in 1920 (Jt. Editor 1924–33), its president for the period 1932–8, and an honorary member from 1938. With respect to excavation, after a spell with Haverfield at Corbridge, Collingwood's first independent work was at Papcastle in 1912, a position he obtained on Haverfield's recommendation to the Cumberland and Westmorland Society (Collingwood 1913). This was followed in 1926 by Bainbridge and finally in 1937 and 1939 excavations at King Arthur's Round Table, near Penrith (Collingwood 1938; 1940; cf. Bradley 1994; Helgeby and Simpson 1995).

Collingwood's rise to pre-eminence in Romano-British studies was indisputably a consequence of Haverfield's death. According to Taylor, the war '...stopped all excavation, and when [it] ended and Collingwood returned to Oxford in 1919 he at once threw himself into archaeology, all the more so because Haverfield died and all the responsibility for certain aspects of research in Roman Britain passed to him' (unsigned, undated obituary note, Haverfield Archive). One of those 'responsibilities' was the *Roman Inscriptions of Britain* which at the moment of his death, Haverfield was planning to supercede the unsatisfactory *CIL* VII

---

3. Van der Dussen (1981: 433–4) records that for 1921, '22 and '23 Collingwood offered lectures on *The Roman Wall; History and Archaeology*. From 1925 down to 1931 and in 1933–5 and 1937–8 this was replaced by *Roman Britain*. Collingwood's title at Pembroke seems to have evolved. In 1915 down to at least 1919 he was described as Lecturer in Classics and Philosophy. By 1928 this had become Lecturer in Philosophy and Ancient History. Between 1927 and 1935 his title was Lecturer in Philosophy and Roman History.

(Craster 1920: 64; Macdonald 1929/30: 109; Keppie 1998b).[4]
Collingwood was happy to repeat the idea that he was the only person
who could fill the vacuum. In spite of what he considered to be an overly
burdensome teaching load, in explaining why he chose to remain at
Oxford, Collingwood cited he:

> ...was already committed. Haverfield, the great master of the subject died
> in 1919: most of his pupils had already fallen in the War: I was left the only
> man resident in Oxford whom he had trained as a Romano-British spe-
> cialist: and even if my philosophy had not demanded it, I should have
> thought myself, in piety to him, under an obligation to keep alive the Ox-
> ford school of Romano-British studies that he had founded to pass on the
> training he had given me, and to make use of the specialist library he had
> left to the University. It was this obligation that made me refuse all offers
> of professorships and other employments elsewhere which I received dur-
> ing the years that followed the War (1939: 120).

This version of events has Collingwood in large measure the natural
'successor' to Haverfield and that he was happy to fill the rôle. It is a
version frequently repeated in Romano-British historiography. In
time, he might have returned to his philosophical interests to the
point that the two ran in tandem. But the impression needs correcting.
What has not been widely appreciated is, despite the evidence being
there, Collingwood had relegated Romano-British studies by the
1930s. He was to claim that his contribution to *Roman Britain and the
English Settlements* in 1936 was his swan song in a subject he now
thought worked out. In 1937 occurred his '...venture into prehistory at
the site known as King Arthur's Round Table' (Helgeby and Simpson
1995: 2ff.). His 'resignation' from *RIB* came at about the same time. In
fact, his sense of dissatisfaction and disaffection as in his *Autobiography*
and as his criticisms of Haverfield demonstrate, went back well into
the 1920s. It is for these reasons it is not insignificant that Collingwood
increasingly regarded himself as a historian first rather than an archaeologist, a subtle transition indirectly appreciated by Johnston
(1967) and Parker (2000: 164), following the publication of *Speculum*

---

4. Collingwood also saw into print a new edition of Haverfield's *Catalogue of the Roman Inscribed and Sculptured Stones in the Tullie House Museum in Carlisle* for which
   he had completed the notes but whose death 'prevented him either writing it or
   (as with his habitual generosity he had undertaken to do so) advancing the
   money to pay for its production' (Collingwood in Haverfield 1922: iii).

Mentis in 1924.[5]

Assessing the nature of Collingwood's relationship with Haverfield and particularly the influence of the latter is difficult. A difference in style between the two was recognized by Rich (1987: 3–4) who noted that Collingwood's '...intellectual approach promoted inquiry, whereas Haverfield himself was so authoritative that he almost silenced it' (pp. 87–8). Birley, among others, wrote of Haverfield's tendency to overpower the opposing view merely through his authority. A slightly different picture, however, might be obtained from two other notices, both by Collingwood, one an obituary, the other a review. It is worth looking at these two assessments before we examine how his own work related to that of Haverfield's. In the first place, it has to be emphasized that Collingwood was generous in his recognition of Haverfield's work. He invariably spoke of his 'mentor' in positive, if occasionally critical, terms. The obituary yet again acknowledged Haverfield's '...European reputation as the leading authority on Roman Britain while engaged in the work of a schoolmaster at Lancing' (1919: 117). More negatively, he described him as an 'antiquary' and spoke of him as a 'dangerous critic and a difficult colleague' (pp.117–18). He lamented the failure to leave 'no one great work behind him' and concluded his 'reputation with posterity will rest on a few monographs and numerous short papers' (p. 118). This is in sharp contrast to Macdonald's view that Haverfield thought his most important work was the 1913 addenda to *CIL* VII (1924: 33).

Some of Collingwood's observations were developed in a review of the delayed 1907 Ford lectures (Haverfield 1924). Some of his earlier opinions were corrected. For instance, he acknowledged that for: '...the general reader, the present volume will long be the one book necessary; for the specialist it serves up in a unique manner the present state of knowledge and serves as the indispensable base for all further research' (Collingwood 1924a: 435). But still there were a number of weaknesses (e.g. a roughness of style, colloquial sentences and disproportionately abundant references to Oxford). Such weaknesses were a reflection of the circumstances of its publication. While acknowledging that it '...rarely happens that the work of a single man changes the aspect of any study so completely as the work of Haverfield changed the study of

---

5. Potentially relevant here is the aside in Wheeler's review of *Roman Britain and the English Settlements*, where it was reported during a recent illness Collingwood had given away all his archaeological books. Wheeler (1939: 87) hoped this did not mean he had given up completely on the subject.

Roman Britain' (p. 435), Collingwood referred to the extent of Haverfield's debt to the labours of others, a fact glossed over by Macdonald. More substantially, Collingwood made reference to some contemporary reservations about Haverfield's methodology. For instance, there was an (over-) emphasis on archaeological evidence at the expense of a general treatment of the history of the island. We have already seen this tendency and the reasons for it in Haverfield's address to the Roman Society (Haverfield 1911a), as well as a propensity to exaggerate or overstate a point. Another failing noted by Collingwood, which again went back to the influence of Mommsen, was Haverfield's relative reluctance to footnote or explain statements of fact. In another passage from his *Autobiography* which reiterated the connection between Mommsen and Haverfield, whilst setting out his rationale to excavation, Collingwood recorded that when he was an Oxford undergraduate:

> ...archaeology began to invade ancient history at the other end of its timescale. Mommsen had shown how by statistical and other treatment of inscriptions the historian of the Roman Empire could answer questions that no one had dreamed of asking. It was a recently established and exciting fact that by excavation you could reconstruct the history of Roman sites not mentioned in any authority and of events in Roman history not mentioned in any book. Owing to the work of Haverfield, whose interest embraced every branch and twig of Roman archaeology and whose skill and learning as an epigraphist were comparable, we believed, only with those of Mommsen himself, these notions had taken firm root at Oxford and were completely transforming the study of the Roman Empire ....When I began to study Roman Britain the revolution had made little progress but not much (pp. 82 and 124).[6]

That said, it has been pointed out that:

> ...it has to be doubted, though, if Collingwood is altogether correct in crediting Haverfield with the scientific revolution in archaeology. It is more probable that he projected his own idea and ideals on to his

6. There is an interesting issue here. In his editing of Haverfield's *Roman Occupation*, Macdonald noting Haverfield's assertion 'where Roman and native elements combine (notably in religion), the Roman appears to be predominant', the editor added 'This is a point which FH was wont to insist. Some may be disposed to think that he pressed it too strongly. It might be argued that in Britain Roman forms are no more inconsistent with Celtic content than are Greek forms with Oriental content in the eastern provinces' (in Haverfield 1924: 247 n. 1).

teacher, whom he valued so highly, the more so because he admits that
Haverfield himself was not conscious of the novelty of the approach.
There is more reason to believe that it was [F.G.] Simpson …who worked
out the principles of 'scientific' archaeology apparently at the beginning
of his career with J.P. Gibson (1838–1912) (van der Dussen 1981: 205).

Elsewhere Johnston has pointed to a passage in Collingwood's
Speculum Mentis, published in 1924 which alludes to an earlier time. In
the extract, referring to his appointment to the Pembroke fellowship
in 1912, Collingwood wrote: '"…Philosophers," wrote a great historian
to a young friend appointed to a philosophical fellowship, "are my
natural enemies."' Johnston suggests that the historian was Haverfield
(Johnston 1967: 94 on p. 308 in the *Speculum*).[7] Collingwood was critical of Haverfield's lack of 'historical' methodology. We have already
seen that Haverfield was credited, with others, in introducing a revolution in Roman history at Oxford. Yet still Collingwood claimed:

> Haverfield himself, least philosophical of historians, cared nothing
> about the principles or the potentialities of the revolution he was lead-
> ing. He never even seemed aware that a revolution was going on. He
> once complained to me that examiners in 'Greats' seemed bent on ig-
> noring his lectures in the papers he set; and that in a general way his
> colleagues did not share his own attitude to history; but I did not think it
> occurred to him that there might be a reason for this neglect, or that dif-
> ferences between different historians' attitudes towards history might be
> worth reflecting upon (1939: 83).[8]

A difference in Collingwood's approach to the material of Roman archaeology becomes even more apparent after Haverfield's death. Of
the *RIB* 'bequest', which Collingwood (with his father) worked on
through the 1920s and is a work which many believe to be his most enduring contribution to Romano-British studies, as an epigrapher,
Collingwood later wrote: '…on the questions which I particularly

---

7. Parker (2000: 176; cf. Boucher 1989) notes Collingwood also tended to ridicule nineteenth century positivist philosophers, who were impressive only in
   their passion for facts. Might this be read as an indirect criticism of
   Haverfield and his 'mania' for catalogues and indices?
8. In the light of Oxford's later decision not to follow his work, I suspect
   Collingwood misunderstood Haverfield's complaint. Rather than ignoring
   his courses because they were 'traditional' in method, Haverfield's problem
   was that his type of history, as represented in Roman Britain, was not recognized by the examiners as pedagogically significant.

wanted to ask, it happened that inscriptions threw hardly any light, I felt therefore, that by my work in Romano-British inscriptions I was rather building a monument to the past, to the great spirits of Mommsen and Haverfield than forging a weapon for the future' (1939: 120). Elsewhere Collingwood, in assessing the relative importance of Latin epigraphy in Britain concluded that:

> ...inscriptions constitute a source of high importance. In Britain, however, their distribution is curious and gives rise to some difficulties. Throughout the lowland zone they are relatively rare; in the highland zone they are extremely common. The result is that for every aspect of the life of the frontier armies ...they give us voluminous evidence; for the more civilised parts of the country they give us very little indeed, and this is one of the reasons why archaeology is so overwhelmingly important as a source of information in the general life of the people (Collingwood in Collingwood and Myres 1936: 464).

This was clearly a major break from Haverfield. The difference went even further. In his review of *The Roman Occupation*, Collingwood believed that Haverfield's principal interest was:

> ...the Romanisation of Britain. It was and still is, a timely contention; it was this that earlier students had failed to see and it is that the general reader has least recognized. But in making his point, Haverfield was led to exaggerate both the degree and the extent of this Romanization: to understate the degree to which Romano-British culture, even where it was most Roman, remained British, and to overstate the extent to which it affected the poorer classes of the population. At one end of the scale, the village-dwellers in all parts of the country were affected indeed, but not very deeply affected, by Roman civilization; and the habits of life which they reveal always continued to show profoundly unRoman elements. Haverfield was not in fact blind to this; on the contrary, he often called attention to it; but often, for the sake of making a legitimate and important point, he understated it, and left an impression of seeing nothing in Romano-British culture except the Roman element (1924a: 436).

The accusation that Haverfield might have pushed the evidence too hard is interesting, bearing in mind that one of the most common criticisms made of Collingwood's archaeological (and indeed his philosophical) work was a tendency to do the same with a resultant distortion in interpretation. For instance, Baillie Reynolds (1937), in his review of the first edition of Collingwood and Myres' *Roman Britain and the English Settlements* (1936), was especially critical of Collingwood's over-reading of the ancient sources (notably his use of the lost books of Tacitus and his 'imaginative' views on the Claudian conquest).

In contrast to Haverfield, Collingwood's 'interests' lay with:

>...the state of the people rather than with military or political history. He was careful to present a picture of the appearance of the countryside, the distribution and occupation of the inhabitants, and the factors which led ultimately to change ...A further set of factors which Collingwood emphasized were those which concerned the decline of Roman civilization in Britain... The picture of Roman Britain which Collingwood presented was not so crowded with detail as to leave a blurred impression, nor so vague as to lack precision. Information acquired locally was organised; and a harmonious whole constructed from innumerable fragments. The trade of the country, its agriculture, its administration, the pattern of its society, were surveyed, and the ordered city within the Roman wall, the villa with its mosaics and bath portrayed. The result was the visualization and reconstruction of a civilization by a process of historical archaeology (Schneider 1952–3: 179 and 180).

We have seen how Collingwood became increasingly disinterested in the application of epigraphy to his work. As an excavator Collingwood was as good, and as poor, as Haverfield. Obituaries of the former, notably that penned by Richmond, tended to be critical of his excavation work.[9] One of the problems was his use of excavation as a specific question solving exercise where, in his hands, it often became self-satisfying, proving what was wanted. In turn this tendency, especially in his later work (but explained in part by his poor health and complicated personal life), led to Collingwood pushing his interpretations too hard, a problem exemplified by his King Arthur's Round Table excavations which have been described as an unfortunate example of his drift into speculation and even fantasy. For this reason, it is for his works of synthesis and interpretation that Collingwood was and remains best remembered. Three major

---

9. In a not particularly distinguished notice (it makes no mention of any of Collingwood's major books), Richmond wrote: 'Though R.G. Collingwood's primary interest was in philosophy, he was attracted to the study of archaeological methods as a philosophic problem, and became one of Professor Haverfield's most distinguished disciples, specialising in topographic and epigraphic studies ...His remarkable powers on incisive and lucid description and his philosophers outlook made him an inimitable writer of text-books reviewing the whole field of Romano-British studies from the subjective and objective standpoint' (1943b: 254).

publications can be highlighted.[10]

In 1923 there appeared *Roman Britain*, Collingwood's first major archaeological monograph, (with a second edition in 1932), which '...served to lay down once and for all my general attitude towards the problems and even more important my general conception (partly due to Haverfield) but partly different from his of what the problems were' (1939: 121). J.N.L. Myres reviewed the second edition in the *Journal of Roman Studies* (1932). Significant for our purposes, he could point to the way that Collingwood's thinking about his subject had evolved between the two editions. While this usually meant subtle rewriting of passages, some of the changes had major implications. For instance, Myres drew attention to the way the 1923 edition emphasized the uniqueness of Romano-British civilization in its fusion of classical and Celtic elements, while the 1932 version argued for a failure of fusion.

> The emphasis has been shifted from the notion of a well-blended fusion of distinct elements which only failed to secure permanence because of the excessive pressure of external forces to the nation of 'a scale of Romanisation', from the villa owners and townsmen who in outlook as well as in law were Romans, down to the remoter country peasantry among whom 'unromanizied' remained all but complete. The disappearance of the upper classes allowed the Saxons to impregnate (culturally) the masses (p. 253).

Elsewhere, the second edition was reviewed by Hawkes in the 1933 *Antiquaries Journal* where it was observed that the author was at his best in the appreciation of Roman art, an opinion many would now challenge. From the perspective of the philosopher, van der Dussen (1981: 241–7) has also shown how *Roman Britain* changed in the light of an evolution in Collingwood's outlook. The volume was the outcome of lectures he delivered in 1921, and '...represent almost the first attempt anywhere to describe the state of Romano-British studies in simple language, aimed as much at amateurs as professional' (Johnston 1967: 39). In van der Dussen's opinion, the questions adduced and the an-

---

10. I recognize how this assertion omits an enormous number of publications, ranging from the posthumous *RIB* (seen to completion by R.P. Wright in 1965), through to Collingwood's pivotal part as the 'public' voice in the debate on the date and function of Hadrian's Wall and his contribution to overviews of Britain in the Roman years. For a fuller list, van der Dussen 1981: 455–8; Richmond 1943a: 481–5; *Trans Cumberland Westmorland Antiq Archaeol Soc* XIII (1943): 211–14.

swers advanced to explain a number of events in Roman Britain, in the 1932 edition are much more tightly argued. This was in addition to the increase in information to hand and changes in interpretation which came with his rephrasing of the questions which had preoccupied him in the first edition. Collingwood's concern was to place Roman Britain in the context of British history in a way which had not been attempted before. As part of this there was his concern with trying to assess the nature and cause of 'The End of Roman Britain'. In the first edition this was explained by reference to external factors or events (the attacks of the Saxons, Picts and Scots as well as the corrosive consequences of the British usurpers). In the second, however, his views had changed. Now it was attributed to the superficial veneer, even penetration, of romanization. 'The business of this book is to show how this happened, to show in what ways the Britons became Romans and in what ways they remained Britons ...We must discover exactly what kind and degree of Romanization came about in Britain: and if we can do that, the ultimate fate of Roman Britain will become intelligible, and the Roman occupation, instead of seeming a mere irrational episode in English history, will reveal a logic of its own' (1949: 12–13). In another break with Haverfield, Collingwood believed that it was not possible to quantify 'romanization' because it differed in kind and degree in its components:

> ...we cannot be content simply to assert that Britain was Romanized. The civilization which we have found existing in the towns, the villas, and the villages is by no means a pure, or even approximately pure, Roman civilization bodily taken over by the conquered race ...In a sense it might be said that the civilization of Roman Britain is neither Roman nor British but Romano-British, a fusion of the two things into a single thing different from either. But this is not a quite satisfactory way of putting it; for it suggests that there was a definite blend of Roman and British elements, producing a civilization that was consistent and homogeneous throughout the fabric of society. The fact is rather that a scale of Romanization can be recognized. At one end of the scale come the upper classes of society and the towns; at the other end, the lower classes and the country. The British aristocracy were quick to adopt Roman fashions, but the Roman fashions which they adopted were rather those of Roman Gaul than those of Rome itself, so that their borrowings are already Romano-Celtic rather than Roman. But this Romano-Celtic civilization gradually becomes less Roman and more Celtic as we move from the largest towns and largest villas to the small towns, the small villa of humbler landowners, and lastly to the villages. Here we encounter a stratum of the population in whose life the Roman element hardly appears at all; if we must call their civilization Romano-Celtic, it is only about five per cent Roman to ninety-five Celtic (1949: 91 and 92).

It was this superficiality which explained why the Roman element largely disappeared from political post-Roman Britain, where it was the wealthier, more Romanized components of the population who bore the brunt of attacks which '...thus de-Romanized the ...countryside by the simple process of sacking the villas. Consequently, from the late fourth century onwards Britain became less Roman and more purely Celtic, not because the Roman elements was composed of foreigners who left Britain at the so-called "departure of the Romans", but because it was composed of a minority of wealthy Britons of the upper classes, whose wealth and power, indeed to a great extent their very existence, came to an end in the troubles that marked the close of the Roman occupation' (1949: 93).

Roman Britain was followed in 1930 by *The Archaeology of Roman Britain*: 'Collingwood's most successful book and its influence in archaeological circles can only be compared with that of [Collingwood's] *The Idea of History* among philosophers and historians, although it has been far less controversial' (van der Dussen 1981: 121). In contrast to the themes in *Roman Britain*, *The Archaeology* was written as a response to the growing over-specialization in Romano-British literature. 'The time seems ripe for some one to make a first attempt to digest the mass of technical detail into manageable form ...It is strictly, as the title of the series implies a handbook of archaeology, not an history' (Collingwood 1930: i). The trend towards specialist texts was started by Haverfield with his catalogues of elements of museum collections and then the cataloguing by others, of other categories of material (e.g. samian). However there is something of a contradiction in Collingwood's approach, as it was still an attempt to synthesize the results of the past 50 years of fieldwork, in fact since Haverfield started work. Not surprisingly, the *Archaeology* was widely reviewed. Ralegh Radford in the *Journal of the British Archaeological Association* (1930) noted the pressing need for coordinating the increased output of archaeological literature, of which Roman Britain was the most urgent problem. Acknowledging how Collingwood was the first to attempt to digest this evidence, he saw the main conclusion of the work as: '...Mr. Collingwood holds that subsequent discoveries have endorsed Haverfield's view that in this field (native sites) the trace of Rome are definitive and unmistakable even though they vanish, when they the bottom of the scale is reached' (p. 428). One of Haverfield's contemporaries, R.C. Bosanquet, reviewed the same monograph in the *Journal of Roman Studies* (1933). In this he called it a compendium of the highest value, one which replaced the earlier works by John Ward. Placing Collingwood's contribution in context, Bosanquet observed:

> In his Ford lectures, delivered 25 years ago, Haverfield, spoke with something like despair of the neglect of archaeology, particularly that of Roman Britain, by the older universities. Nothing could better demonstrate the change that was already coming about and the progress made since, mainly through his teaching and example, than that the first adequate handbook of the subject should be produced by an Oxford tutor, one of his own pupils (p. 101).

The last of Collingwood's major statements came in 1936 and in *Roman Britain and the English Settlements*, the first volume in the Oxford History of England series co-authored, although separately written, with J.N.L. Myres. It has been described as the first ever continuous narrative history of the four centuries of Roman rule in Britain (Baillie Reynolds 1937: 451). Still widely appreciated, reviews of it at the time of its publication were mixed. G.M. Trevelyan said of Collingwood's contribution; 'In the present state of knowledge, I suppose that that volume is the best that can be put into the hands of the general reader' (*The Times* 13 January 1943). In a largely complimentary review Baillie Reynolds added:

> Since the war research into the history of Britain has been widespread that it was high time that the results were collected and published in the form of a continuous narrative. No one is better qualified to perform this task than Professor R.G. Collingwood, who now gives us for the first time in this book, the history of the four centuries of Roman rule in this country ...Book III is a review of the conditions of the province under Roman rule. This is an extremely valuable section of the work and though it cannot supercede Haverfield's Romanization it may be said to be a simplification and correction of it in view of the evidence accumulated since 1915, especially that from Wroxeter and Verulamium (p. 451 and 452–3).

Ian Richmond provided a less contentious summary, but still referred to the author as a 'philosopher by profession' (*J Brit Archaeol Assoc* (1937). True to form, Wheeler penned a more hard-hitting critique of the second edition for the 1939 *Journal of Roman Studies*. This was, by Wheeler's own admission, a delayed review but he decided to submit it as '...an opportunity to tell something of the debt which, on every sort of ground, the post-Haverfield generation has owed to RG' (sic) and where '...no archaeological (or semi-archaeological) work in our time is likely to be so widely read or to deserve so wide a popularity.' But this was merely the preamble. For Wheeler was highly critical of Collingwood's 'personal and subjective attitude towards History that must either be accepted or rejected by the reader at the outset; it admits no compromise. He interpolates motives, builds characters, constructs episodes with a liberality or even licence that is great fun' (p. 87). Owing a debt to Haverfield and Fox on the importance of the island's geography, still fact and speculation were intermixed, with little discrimination or citation of primary sources. Paradoxically, where Collingwood had access to decent documentary sources, Wheeler thought him weak, but better when there were no such authorities (p. 88). With respect to the contents, recalling his own work on Iron Age hill forts, Wheeler argued that Collingwood (and Haverfield) were too dismissive of Celtic urbanization:

> Roman Britain was, in fact, a two-dimensional thing, an elaborate variegated transparency through which one continually sees the outlines of Celtic Britain blurred and distorted, but still essential and solid. I am afraid that Roman Britain was on the whole bogus, and would not depreciate the unambitious but honest 'Celtic' material on which it precariously stood (p. 89–90).

If it was any consolation, while Wheeler was complimentary of Collingwood's 'reasoned' imagination, he was even more critical of Myres' contribution.

So far we have looked at the points of influence and difference between Haverfield and Collingwood. One other element worth emphasising in the light of what has been discussed above is a comment made by A.R. Burn, a Collingwood contemporary:

> Collingwood, following Haverfield, was fond of emphasising the thorough Romanization of the Roman Empire which made Roman Gaul or Roman Britain very different from British colonial India or Africa. He was particularly hard on Kipling, for pictures in Puck of Pook's Hill on Roman Britain conceived on British India lines, with a sharp line between Roman and 'natives'. In this he was clearly right. With all their faults, the Romans never drew any such line (1932: 66).

What should be evident at this juncture is that the basis for Collingwood's arguments and conclusions owe as much to the groundwork laid by Haverfield as Collingwood's intellectualizing of the issues. In this sense, there are innumerable passages which reflect a debt to Haverfield. What is apparent is that the framework within which Collingwood's arguments were essentially structured with regard to issues Haverfield had established. This is manifested in the chapter headings in *The Archaeology of Roman Britain*, where categories of information that Haverfield had utilised (types of forts, villas, pottery (fine and coarse) and brooches etc.) were reused and the volume of data merely increased. Indeed, Haverfield had been writing small monographs, often based on museum collections, since the late 1890s. Collingwood's volume was the natural culmination of this process. Today the logic underpinning such an approach is questionable: '...the austere flesh of [an] invaluable exercise in taxonomy' (Salway 1981: 766), continued by Richmond and still applies even today (e.g. de la Bédoyère 1989). Where there was a difference in approach between the two it was that Collingwood used Romano-British studies as a collection of data which he could apply to his philosophical dialogues.

Collingwood's innovation, relative to Haverfield, was to make the process of assimilation constantly dynamic and not just a one stage hybridization of Roman and Celtic elements.

> Historians have sometimes spoken of the provincial life of the Roman Empire as though its civilization were a stagnant, monotonous flood that swamped every vestige of racial individuality in the various provinces, and presented a face everywhere, the same, everywhere fixed in the expression of a dull cosmopolitan mediocrity ...in Britain at any rate this was not so. Towns, villas, villages, pottery, metal work - in all these spheres we have found not a cosmopolitan Roman culture, but one compounded of Roman and Celtic elements (1949: 111).

The same process could be seen in Romano-British art, and especially sculpture. To a lesser extent it was visible in language, where among the less romanized natives 'British' was spoken. When Romano-Britons wanted to write they had to do so in Latin (!). Religion too was affected, in the gods worshipped and at cult centres (e.g. temples of the Romano-Celtic form) – 'this type seems to be a genuinely Romano-Celtic thing, in the sense that it grew up in the Celtic provinces under Roman rule and under the influence of Roman architectural ideas' (1949: 137).

We can also look at Haverfield's influence on the structure of Collingwood's thinking when we consider the form of empire with which they were preoccupied. In this respect Haverfield set a framework which Collingwood then realigned. Like Haverfield, Collingwood possessed a largely culturally uniform conception of the Roman empire. Collingwood claimed Haverfield was over-fond of the Roman empire-British India, although as we have seen, there is little (published) evidence to that effect. Whilst he was implicitly critical of Haverfield's, and others', occasional propensity to compare the Roman empire with its British counterpart, Collingwood was even more reluctant to draw such parallels. Instead, he saw the Roman version as unique in the way it:

> ...could claim kinship, physical and spiritual, with everyone from the Tyne to the Euphrates and from the Sahara to the Rhine. It is this that makes the Roman Empire a quite different thing from all modern empires ...The Roman Empire was a society of peoples in which intercourse was nowhere checked by barriers such as separate races or even nations in the world of to-day. That can be proved by the three tests of travel, residence and marriage. In these three ways the Roman Empire was far more cosmopolitan than modern Europe.

The three criteria, paraphrased by van der Dussen as '...examples of certain habitual practices' were later modified to race, language and civilization, all of which were deployed to demonstrate the cosmopolitan character of the Roman empire (1981: 243). And yet, in spite of this more flexible perception of the structure of the empire, Collingwood failed to examine, or even to recognize, the relationship of this to the material culture which he used to assess the scale of romanization. Instead his vocabulary, and so his understanding of Roman material culture is limited solely to the broad categories Roman, Celtic and Romano-Celtic.

Still Collingwood believed that one of the consequences of his work on '...historical methodology led me to an entirely new treatment of archaeological material' (1939: 137). This involved him posing what he considered to be penetrating questions of accepted facts or evidence. This in turn allowed him to formulate '...questions to which not only do literary sources give no direct answer, but which cannot be answered even by the most ingenuous interpretation of them' (p. 134). He illustrated this principle by examination of the size of the population of the island in the Roman period (pp. 135–6; cf. 1949: 261–76) and the working of Hadrian's Wall (Couse 1990).

Another example of this line of reasoning is Collingwood's (pp. 137–44) assessment of the extent of the romanization in Britain of indigenous art. To be sure, he believed the best example of his work was Chapter XV on Art in *The English Settlements:* '...a chapter which I would gladly leave as the sole memorial of my Romano-British studies, and the best example I can give to posterity of how to solve a much debated problem in history, not by discovery of fresh evidence, but by reconsidering questions of principle' (pp. 144–5). This opinion was based on the argument he formulated in a chapter assessing the quality of Romano-British art, one in which he posed a question; 'Why was that art so bad?' and then endeavoured to answer it by reconsidering the validity of the question first set. As his starting point, Collingwood took issue with Haverfield's contention that Celtic civilisation in Britain had been '...replaced by one of the "cosmopolitan" pattern to be found, with local differences but not very important ones, in any province of the Roman Empire' (p. 137). And yet, according to Haverfield, there occurred a Celtic revival at the end of the Roman period. Collingwood's objection to this, as it was expressed elsewhere, was how could the Celtic revival have occurred if its model had been eradicated earlier, and why anyway should there have occurred the reversal to the 'old ways'? Cutting through current explanations of the problem, Collingwood believed that the answer lay with; 'Where you find ...new ways of thinking and acting never displayed with more than a low degree of success, you may take it as certain that the discarded ways are remembered with regret, and the tradition of their glories is being tenaciously kept alive' (p. 143).[11] In this context, for the failing of the new ways, read 'Classical art', the discarded ways 'Celtic' and the glories being kept alive, the putative Celtic revival. 'The general position ...implies that the less successful the Britons were in Romanizing art ...the more likely they were to cherish the memory of their own fashions and ensure that the fashions were never wholly lost to sight by the rising generation' (p. 144).

Today many of Collingwood's assessments are untenable and have been criticized from a number of perspectives. Indeed, in spite of his pride in it, *The English Settlements* has been the most widely criticized of his major works. One weakness is that Collingwood was too rigid in his conception of the categorizing of cultural identities. For art, this meant the way that Britons produced 'Celtic art' and that there was a classical pattern which they attempted apparently *en masse*, to emulate. His opinions are wholly subjective in their outlook. For example, Phillips (1977) noted that he assumed that all Romano-British sculpture was produced by native Britons and that such craftsmen were simply trying to imitate classical models. It goes almost without saying that Collingwood's original question (why was Romano-British art so bad?) was not necessarily the right one. The irony in all this is that Collingwood recognised a more crucial problem in this debate, but one which he did not try to explore: 'what exactly does Romanization mean? What was it that really happened to people when they became what is called Romanized?' (1939: 140).

---

11. These were: (i) Celtic traditions must have survived throughout the years of the occupation but have not survived archaeologically; (ii) not all the Celts became subjected to the Roman occupation and which in turn left seed beds of Celticism for the future; and that (iii) 'Celtic art was a product of the "Celtic" temperament, and that the Celtic temperament blossomed into artistic expression only under conditions of a certain kind' (1939: 139).

As noted above, Collingwood's contribution to Romano-British studies had a second facet: that his philosophy (especially of history) drew on his archaeological experience and, in turn, may have shaped his views on Roman Britain. Put bluntly, Collingwood's historical outlook was '...you have to understand the thought of someone by understanding the object of their thought, as opposed to having an abstract presumption about the way their minds work' (Parker 2000: 166). In other words, in order to know the past, the historian has to re-enact that past in his or her own mind. In the *Autobiography*, he reported that archaeology, and in particular excavation, had taught him that the historian was in the business of posing questions and seeking out answers rather than relying on what he called 'authorities'. Archaeologists did the same in showing that history had to be reconstructed without 'authorities' and dealt with things not mentioned in them (Parker 2000: 205; cf. Johnston 1967: 10). This was a criticism, as we have seen, frequently made of his later major work, typical of which was *Roman Britain and the English Settlements*.

It is natural that (Romano-British) archaeologists and philosophers have seen aspects of Collingwood's fieldwork influencing and shaping his philosophical work (cf. Browning 1995). For instance, in assessing his work at Hardknott fort in Cumbria it has been said the:

> ...site was essential to understanding the history of the Lakeland forts, a question that occupied Collingwood in his most active period of fieldwork, from just before the First World War until the early 1930s. Throughout these years he used the archaeology of Roman Britain as a laboratory to develop his idea on the nature of history. His position was that in philosophical terms, history consists of actions arising from thoughts and that all history is essentially the history of thought (Bidwell *et al.* 1999: 1).

After his death, and indeed as early as the mid-1920s, Collingwood's reputation as a philosopher went into decline, at least among philosophers, which in turn affected his reputation as an archaeologist (cf. Hodder 1995; Helgeby and Simpson 1995). Johnston (1967) has summarized the thrust of the criticisms levelled at his philosophical work: his outlook was underwritten by the increasingly unfashionable concept of the 'freedom of will' that came in the years after the First World War. This coincided with the general rise of specialization in higher education, both at undergraduate and postgraduate levels. The emergence of academic specialists, including those in philosophy, meant that they worked in disciplines in relative isolation. Philosophy became a matter of logical analysis and a technical subject detached from the sort of wider 'social' applications that Collingwood had been trained to believe. In this respect, the problem was that the two strands to his career, philosophy and archaeology, appeared to be so closely intertwined. That he believed this to be so lay with his experience as an Oxford undergraduate reading for *Lit. Hum.* Recurring criticisms were his tendency to over interpret the evidence to hand and to drive it too hard in support of the conclusions he wanted to draw. In the first instance his approach to history was conditioned by his initial training in archaeological excavation which involved careful planning and execution. Excavation meant the recording of artefacts, the significance of which the archaeologist had then to assess. Thus questions were asked of the data and answers formulated. At Oxford this approach was modified, encouraged as it was by the prevailing *Literae Humaniores* programme of instruction which Collingwood (1939: 12–14; 1949), like so many before him, came to extol as the finest form of analytical training that a student could receive. In this arrangement, philosophy constituted a major component to this degree. This approach came to be the methodology which he adapted to his work in the philosophy of history and intellect. He believed that every idea (or question and answer) is formulated in response to a specific problem. Never mind if the question was the wrong one. In the archaeological dimension this meant that each object found on a site must have fulfilled a function or purpose in the life of the users and/or inhabitants of the site. This approach to evidence led Collingwood to reject the sort of scissors-and-paste approach or philological and textual criticism that other historians deployed in interpretation.

The criticism of his philosophical work in turn led to assaults on his work in archaeology. Specialists in the field, if not prepared to accommodate intellectual pontificating were less disposed to accept the conclusions derived from a subject (history) perceived to have less and less relevance to archaeology. Collingwood's position was not helped by the fact that in searching for 'answers' to his 'questions', he often distorted the evidence to fit his solutions. Richmond noted "...that the fertility of imagination which led Collingwood to pose questions ...sometimes induced him to misinterpret the results of excavation. Too often Collingwood had formulated in advance what he expected to find through excavation and that was all that he found. Others who explored the same evidence later would discover things which Collingwood had overlooked and which sometimes undermined his conclusions" (Johnston 1967: 40; Helgeby and Simpson 1995). These and other reservations concerning Collingwood's work were brought together by Hodder (1995). The problems of Collingwood as an interpreter of archaeological evidence included the way he handled the raw data (viz. his use of imagination, his field methods, his tendency to generalize and his refusal to consider different opinions and interpretations but often to ridicule them). Therefore for Hodder there was not so much a rejection of Collingwood's 'shaky' philosophical position but of his loose practices ('insufficiently self-critical'; Hodder 1995: 374–80). But slack practices also meant he was forced to publish numerous retractions and explanations for earlier mistakes. One other element Hodder missed in assessing Collingwood's work is the fact his thinking and so writing was liable to review and substantial reworking which, in turn, made it difficult for lesser lights to assimilate whatever was to be said about aspects of the subject.

Despite the fact Collingwood's reputation as a philosopher declined, he continued to exert a significant influence in pre-Second World War British archaeology. Not only did he excavate, but he published on the subject. With his growing interest in philosophy it was inevitable that his commitment to Roman Britain was going to wane but for the period up to the early 1930s he continued to give the subject academic credibility, not least because he was the only one writing about the broader picture of the island at this time. Collingwood's reputation as a philosopher, however, has clouded his position in Romano-British studies. His great reputation in the former has given his opinions a degree of primacy in the latter.[12] His contribution to the subject, other than correcting (or contradicting) some of Haverfield's opinions is supposed to be his emphasis on the 'little' people and 'issues' of the province. Irrespective of his philosophical pontifications which had minimal relevance to the understanding of Roman Britain and archaeology (and regardless of what the modern generation of post-processualists might believe), and despite his position of 'influence' at Oxford, there are grounds for arguing he hindered the progress of the discipline post-Haverfield. In actuality his long-term contribution has been over-stated. We can see this in a number of ways. With respect to his output, Johnston (1967:

---

12. For instance, he 'never lost interest in, or relinquished his rôle in the historical and archaeological work, even after his retirement to the chair of metaphysics at Oxford in 1935. Indeed the appointment increased his determination to keep both professional interests, philosophy and history, as he pursued his grand strategy of a rapprochement between methods in archaeology in the nineteenth century as part of a methodological revolution which incorporated ancient history, had done nothing to liberate students from the tyranny and limitations of the textual authorities and elevate them to a new science' (Parker 2000: 205).

39) noted how Collingwood, between 1913 and 1939, authored an impressive 125 papers, five books and 21 reviews on archaeological subjects (by way of comparison, Haverfield is supposed to have published three monographs and 500+ papers in *c.*30 years). But most of Collingwood's articles were usually no more than ten to twelve pages long. Then there is his archaeological fieldwork. Close examination of his output reveals the bulk of his active fieldwork was undertaken in the 1920s. Work undertaken in the 1930s was much more limited and included King Arthur's Round Table (1937) which, as we have seen, was not widely regarded. Furthermore, those excavations that he did undertake were invariably published in the same (regional) journals with very few exceptions (e.g. in *Antiquity* and more synthetic pieces in the *Journal of Roman Studies*). Indeed, as much of his fieldwork was in field survey as excavation, as many of his publications comprised 'overviews' and syntheses on a range of topics of all periods. In short his work does not show the degree of coherency and direction as that of Haverfield. At face value in an earlier time Collingwood would not have been out of place as a regional antiquarian.

The biggest gap in Collingwood's career was his failure to establish a group of 'students' any thing like the Haverfield group. It is near impossible to identify any individual who owed their career to his teaching or patronage, although some have claimed a link of sorts. At best what we can see instead is the way that he influenced certain (Oxford) students of his time.[13] At the same time, Collingwood's published statements on the province were of less and less relevance. Indeed he regarded his *Roman Britain and the English Settlements* (along with his contribution to Tenney Frank's *Economic Survey of Ancient Rome*, both in 1934) as his farewell statements to the study of the past (1939: 121). Richmond (1943a: 480) claimed that illness in 1932 was the beginning of Collingwood disassociating himself from archaeology. In fact his disengagement with the subject predated this and to have begun in the late 1920s. But such was his and Haverfield's authority, few if any were able to write about the province for the next 25 years. Collingwood had become part of the problem.

---

13. Birley and Richmond attributed their introduction to Hadrian's Wall to him (Birley 1961: 68). Birley (1958a: 212; cf. 1961: 200) says that Collingwood encouraged younger men to work in Cumbria (e.g. citing F.G. Simpson) with funds from the Haverfield Trust. Meanwhile, A.L.F. Rivet's interest in archaeology was aroused by his lectures (cf. Todd 1994).

The preceding paragraphs have looked at Collingwood's intellectual bequest to the discipline of Romano-British archaeology. Nearly 60 years after his death, to judge from the number of laudatory references to him, Collingwood continues to exert a powerful influence on Romano-British studies. Part of this is due to the understandable wish to claim him as a leading figure because of the kudos of his being an eminent philosopher linked to archaeology. The first to claim such were his obituarists. Richmond continued to repeat this theme in later publications. In his 1957 Oxford inaugural lecture, Richmond, in paying '...homage to two Oxford professors whose work has been a potent source of inspiration and emulation', spoke of Collingwood as an '..inspiring formulator, whose cool thought, crisp diction and beautiful prose fascinated all who came under his spell. He was an artist ...with the grace of vision given to such men, so that his teaching was especially creative and stimulating. But the balance between artistic creation and historical formulation is delicate, an equipoise almost beyond the wit of man. The effect of this dichotomy in Collingwood's intellectual approach was to provoke inquiry where Haverfield might almost have silenced it' (Richmond 1957: 3–4). The logic underscoring this opinion is inverted. Collingwood used archaeology to inform his philosophy, but still he regarded it as a component. In the cult of veneration, Haverfield was indisputably a 'great' name with an equally great reputation. But the social and academic climate of the time combined with the peculiar legacy he left (to Collingwood and Taylor) did not, could not, permit 'criticism' and revision of neither Haverfield nor Collingwood. The fact that the next generation of scholars (Birley, Richmond, and to a lesser degree, Wheeler) and those on the margins (Taylor and Simpson) said that Haverfield and Collingwood were 'greats' has served to preserve their reputations and therefore their standing. In fact, a more critical reading of Collingwood's life, his work and his opinions reveals a slightly more jaundiced approach on his part to Romano-British studies. But in the climate of the times after his death, it would have done the same discipline no service to articulate these opinions. Instead, continuing to link Collingwood with the subject gave the fledgling discipline a sense of intellectual respectability and rigour. This sort of characterization served to give the subject a sense of relevance and a general value. It is this fact, that of contributing to a scholastic tradition, which is as much Collingwood's legacy as Haverfield's.

Romano-British studies post-Collingwood: R.E.M. Wheeler and Eric Birley

As has been indicated, Collingwood's retreat from Romano-British studies had implications for the subject, not least at Oxford. The fact that, other than his own books, no other (major) monographs were published in the 1920s and 1930s highlights the degree to which the subject was grinding to an (academic) halt. For there were there no 'major' or dedicated practitioners or other scholars there at this that time. Instead, the future of the discipline lay away from it as shown by the fact that the leading 'scholars' of the period 1920–39 were not at that university. Although now more usually lauded for his contribution to the development of excavation techniques, R.E.M. Wheeler's early career was based squarely in Romano-British studies. Indeed, in the immediate post-Haverfield period the range of his work bears comparison with that of Donald Atkinson. The course of Mortimer Wheeler's (1890–1974) early years is well documented (Wheeler 1956; Hawkes 1982; McIntosh 2004). An important fact is that he was not part of the Haverfield (Oxford) group, although he did do one season at Wroxeter (1913) and could count on Bosanquet as a referee. Wheeler was a graduate of University College, London (1907–13), where he regarded Ernst Gardner as his mentor. This was followed in 1913 with his obtaining an archaeological studentship and working for the RCHM in Essex, indirectly for Haverfield's *VCH* volume of the same county. Wheeler's first own excavation was at Colchester in 1917, whilst still serving in the army. Returning to the RCHM in 1919, he moved to the post of Keeper of Archaeology at the National Museum of Wales and with which went a lectureship in archaeology at the University of Wales. In 1924 he became museum director before he left for the keepership of London Museum in 1926. The years in Wales included the systematic excavation and publication of three Roman sites; Segontium (1921–2), Brecon Gaer (1924–5) and Caerleon (1926–7). The move to London was matched by work at Lydney Park (1928–9), Verulamium (1930–3), Maiden Castle (1934–7) and Brittany (1937). He also authored four period catalogues of the City's museum collection (in the Roman, Saxon, Viking and later periods) and in 1928 the RCHM inventory of the Roman city. In 1934, largely under his initiative there was inaugurated the Institute of Archaeology. His move to India in 1944 effectively ended his career as an excavator in the United Kingdom. The rest, so to speak, is history.

In his later years, especially in the pages of *Antiquity* (under the editorship of his friend and television colleague, Glyn Daniel) Wheeler seems to have reveled in criticizing the (Romano-British) archaeological establishment (Snodgrass 2002). He was to criticize the tradition out of which Collingwood and Richmond, emerged and so indirectly Haverfield, even though elsewhere he could be complimentary about him (cf. Chapter 9).[14] In this respect Wheeler saw part of the task to improve on what he regarded as their flawed methods of excavation. Citing Woolley's criticism of the Corbridge excavations, Wheeler added his opinions on St John Hope's work at Silchester and Bushe-Fox at Wroxeter (Wheeler 1956: 60–1; and of his work at Richborough – Fox 2000: 56). He also contributed an essay to the journal in 1934 on the subject of the topography of Saxon London and its relationship to its Roman predecessor. This was attacked by J.N.L. Myres and elicited a riposte from Wheeler. Controversy between the two continued when Myres slated Wheeler's Verulamium report in the pages of *Antiquity* (1938) to which Wheeler felt he had to reply (Wheeler 1938; cf. Cunliffe 2002). More generally Wheeler made a number of critical, even disparaging, commants about the post-First World War and pre-Second World War achievements of Romano-British archaeology (cf. Appendix 5 below). Elsewhere, on two occasions, Wheeler continued his sniping at Romano-British scholarship. In 1961 he provided a corrosive review of the jubilee volume of the *Journal of Roman Studies*. Snodgrass, in speculating whether Wheeler asked Daniel for the commission in order '...to let him have a real crack at the Roman Society' saw it as 'an obituary for the subject' (of Romano-British archaeology). Although the review was more to do with the limitations about 'traditional' approaches to the subject, it implied criticism of Haverfield, Taylor, Collingwood and Richmond. More damaging, however, was the controversy caused by his review of the posthumous second volume of Richmond's Hod Hill report (Wheeler 1968). If Wheeler's reputation with the 'establishment' was already sour (with reservations about the validity of his earlier archaeological work, and above all his propensity for self-advertising and his celebrity status – where for instance, Bushe-Fox was less 'of a showman than Mortimer Wheeler' – Fox 2000: 48), then this review sealed it. Such were his criticisms of Richmond the person, according to Snodgrass, that Daniel was

---

14. Wheeler was also on more than passing terms with the likes of Macdonald. A letter of June 1936 with Wheeler's felicitations to Macdonald and his wife includes mention of a book (presumably his and Tessa Wheeler's *Verulamium: a Belgic and Two Roman Cities* (1936)) he was gifting to Macdonald. To the letter is added 'She had a great affection for you' (*Edinburgh University Library Special Collection: Letters of Sir George Macdonald I Letters (24) to Sir George Macdonald. Misc.*).

'hounded' into printing a collective rejoinder from five of Richmond's friends and colleagues (A. Fox, J. Toynbee, S.S. Frere, and J.K. St Joseph and separately from G. Boon; cf. Snodgrass 2002: 1103). Wheeler was permitted a reply and in typical fashion, by dismissing their competence to criticize him (they were variously described as an art historian, an air photographer and two defaulting excavators), claimed to answer their objections. Only Fox, as a prehistorian (with a European perspective as well as Wheeler being a friend of her and her husband) was exempt. Forty years on, however, as Snodgrass (1999: 104; 2002: 1104) acknowledges, what Wheeler was arguing in both the original review and his reply was that Romano-British studies had to assimilate to what was going on in archaeology as a whole or else become shunned. It is difficult to disagree with Snodgrass' assessment that Wheeler's observations were prophetic. The subject had become sidelined and only regained a sense of vitality when it did assimilate. One cannot help but suspect that part of the root cause of the argument was that Wheeler was not part of the Haverfield-Oxford set. His (professional) career developed outside the universities (until he established the Institute of Archaeology).[15] This left him free to operate as something of a maverick on the edge of the discipline. Within the discipline, Wheeler's reputation with respect to Romano-British archaeology has not suffered well. It has either been forgotten or otherwise criticized. We have also seen that while he claimed V.E. Nash Williams (and Richmond) as 'students' of his during his time at Cardiff, this is pushing the facts. Part of the problem was his character combined with the fact he was regarded as something of an outsider, one without a 'real' academic post. His methods and tendency to self-advertising did not go down well either. That he dared to make critical comments about Richmond did not endear him to the leading figures of the time. The sense of antagonism is still evident in Frere's (1988) retrospective of Roman Britain since Haverfield and Richmond.[16]

If Wheeler is now a marginalized figure in Romano-British studies, a contemporary of his with a much more secure reputation is Eric Banff

---

15. 'Mortimer Wheeler was a museum man by profession' (Clark 1989: 13). To be sure, Clark's brief summary of Wheeler's career fails to mention anything of his Roman work.

16. E.g. 'Wheeler I never encountered in those early days – I have always been profoundly thankful that I was digging at Little Woodbury when he was digging at Maiden Castle. (p. 2); Wheeler's *Verulamium* '...a coherent, if inaccurate, picture of the social and economic rise and fall of towns in Roman Britain' (p. 3); 'Charlatan though he was in some aspects of his character...' (p. 4).

Birley (1906–1995: cf. Bowman 2004). If one accepts Jones' (1987) debatable identification of 'schools' with 'masters' and 'pupils', sometime by the mid-1930s (a date which coincidentally compliments the argument here for the final decline of the subject at Oxford), the initiative in Romano-British studies shifted to Durham and to Birley. That he has only recently died makes it difficult to assess the lasting significance of his contribution to Romano-British archaeology (James 2002). As it is, his work is beyond the immediate scope of this study.

Birley went up to Brasenose College, Oxford in 1924 where he came under the influence of Collingwood. His interest in Roman archaeology was evidently due to his headmaster at Clifton College, Norman Whatley, a known Haverfield 'student' and from whom Birley received Cheesman's notes for his *Auxilia* which had been given to Whatley before Cheesman was killed in 1915 (Dobson 1997: 215–17). Although he claimed his first introduction to Hadrian's Wall was through Collingwood, elsewhere Birley recorded he owed his initial interest there to Michael Holroyd, his tutor, and the fellow and lecturer in ancient history at Brasenose. It was Holroyd '...who persuaded [me] to make Hadrian's Wall and the University of Durham [my] main fields of work – and who took practical steps to enlist the active interest of that university ...there can have been few teachers of Ancient History at Oxford, since Haverfield's day, who exerted so great and lasting an influence over their pupils, or were so greatly loved' (1953: 255; cf. Chapter 8 n. 56).[17] After graduating with a double First in 1928, Birley spent three years excavat-

---

17. Again, I owe this identification to Colin Wallace. Holroyd (1892–1953), the son of a former Director of the National Gallery, was educated at Westminster and Christ Church College. He took a Second in Class. Mods. in 1914 but did not go onto Greats because he enlisted in the same year. He served in the 3rd Hampshire Regiment (BEF) before being wounded in 1915. Capt. Holroyd was then transferred to the fledgling MI5. After the war, in 1919, (incorrectly listed as 1915 in *The Times* obituary), he was elected to a fellowship at Brasenose, where Haverfield in his capacity as the Camden Chair was attached and where Holroyd became lecturer. Holroyd excavated, with Birley, at Birdoswald. I have not established Holroyd's patrons but he was an FRGS with a well-known interest in geography and ancient history. He was also acknowledged as not being especially productive in terms of research (some entries in the original edition of the *Oxford Classical Dictionary* and a contribution on Greek and Roman art in F. Marvin's *Art and civilization* (1928)), but was appreciated for his sense of taste, exceptional social connections and his interest in his students (obits. *The Times* 14, 16 and 19 October 1953; *Antiqs J* 35 (1954): 154).

ing, mainly in the capacity of watching briefs in London for the Society of Antiquaries (and where he met Wheeler and J.A. Stanfield and developed an interest in samian studies). Prior to this he had worked at Bainbridge with Collingwood and in 1927 at Birdoswald (again with Collingwood and Frank Simpson, whom he came to revere). In 1929, along with Ian Richmond, Birley worked under Simpson at Birdoswald. The following year Simpson resigned his position as Director of the Durham University Excavation Committee and was succeeded by Birley. In 1931 he was appointed lecturer at Armstrong College, Newcastle, before moving to Durham in 1935 as Lecturer in Roman Archaeology (where he became Professor of Romano-British History and Archaeology in 1956), with Richmond as his successor at Armstrong. The pre-war years were spent excavating in the north, along Hadrian's Wall, at Chesterholm and Birrens and, in particular, in establishing in 1934 what was to become the Durham University training excavation at Corbridge, with Richmond in joint charge, and continued with interruptions down to 1973. After writing about the pottery from Birdoswald under Simpson in 1933, Birley, at Bushe-Fox's invitation, wrote the official guide to Corbridge and which led him to a reconsideration of the site 1906–58 (Birley 1959). He had previously been asked to sort out the 1906–14 finds for display in the site museum. One of the outcomes of this phase of work was an acerbic argument between Birley and George Macdonald, played out in a number of journals, concerning the dating of the northern frontiers (cf. Chapter 12 n. 2 for references).

The more one looks at Birley's career, the more striking become the similarities with Haverfield.[18] It can be said however, and, following James, that up to the outbreak of the Second World War, of the three, Collingwood, Birley and Richmond, it was Birley who worked most closely in the spirit of Haverfield. Birley's interests in the Roman army, stimulated while at school, led to Roman epigraphy and ultimately Roman prosopography. His early professional years saw him heavily committed to excavation and research projects (including the creation of a long-term training excavation at Corbridge for university students). As a sideline, Birley developed interests in samian studies. Post-1945, his involvement in excavation lessened. In contrast, his work

---

18. Birley wrote to Margerie Taylor: 'I only wish that I had been old enough to have met him in the flesh but I have studied his writings so much, and in my time have learnt so much about him from RGC as well as from you, that I feel as though I had in fact met him' (Letter, 11 February 1962, Haverfield Archive).

came to concentrate on the structure of the Roman army (itself a consequence of his wartime service in military intelligence where his task was to analyse the organization and strength of the German army from his knowledge of its Roman counterpart), on works of synthesis and an interest in (northern) antiquarianism (James 2002: 18ff.). It is interesting that Birley never wrote a 'big book' about Roman Britain. There were numerous articles on aspects of the subjects and something more substantial planned or else unfinished (e.g. a text on the Roman garrison in Britain and the province's *fasti*, both of which were completed by others (Holder 1982; Birley 1981). Unlike Haverfield however, he was to establish a 'school' – again in terms of committed students with a particular approach to the study of the past – reminiscent of, but ultimately more successful and influential than, that associated with Haverfield (Jones 1987). This has also been represented as a 'northern' Roman military Durham school against a 'southern' civilian Oxford school. But still with the former, there was a clear link back to Haverfield, with its emphasis on texts and above all epigraphic sources. The one point of difference, according to James, was Birley's rejection of archaeology as the arbiter of literary sources. Bearing in mind the problems one encounters in assessing Haverfield and his 'group', it is interesting how at least one associate of Birley has written about his group. 'These pupils, a title claimed by many who had no formal instruction from him, formed a distinctive "Birley school". They were trained in a particular way, to seek out the basic evidence and they found kinship with one another in a shared teaching and a shared affection for their teacher ...They have been accused of arrogance, but would argue this only means that they were taught to look at the evidence for a hypothesis, not at the reputation of the scholar advancing it' (Dobson 1997: 228).

Ian Richmond

In spite of what Wheeler and Birley were doing, with Collingwood's death in 1943, in the received version of the 'history of Romano-British scholarship', the '...succession passed from Collingwood to Richmond' as the 'leading Romano-British scholar' of the day. '...Posterity will remember him and treasure his writings as those of a great archaeologist and historian in line of succession to Haverfield and Collingwood' (Birley 1966a: 302). Note how the assessment emphasizes the Oxford link. Richmond continues to exert a profound influence on the nature and progress of the subject. This has been in respect to the work he undertook and the body of students he fostered. His reputation is as much to do with his enthusiasm for the subject, in to which he threw himself, not least in fieldwork (Frere 1988: 1; Cowan

1966). Most his contemporaries continue to write positively of him. For example, 'Richmond was indeed a very remarkable figure, both physically and intellectually, combining the great learning of Haverfield with the great field experience of a Wheeler; his sense of fun and his love of his fellow men made him a wonderful companion on field trips' (Frere 1988: 2). Then there is the fact that he was pivotal to the creation of a large body of students who went on to occupy academic posts. Surprisingly, it was not so much in the corpus of literature he produced, even if, according to one of his contemporaries, '[f]ew writers have equalled Richmond's felicituous blend of Classical learning and archaeological expertise and none successfully imitated his style – though several have tried' (Salway 1981: 766).

Born in 1902, one of the twin sons of a respected local doctor, Richmond was educated at Ruthin School, Rochdale. In 1919 he went up to Corpus Christi, just too late to meet Haverfield although yet again it is striking how much he features in his work. Richmond (1957: 3) was to write: 'I read and read again everything he wrote and for me he being dead yet lived.' G.B. Grundy, however, was to claim him as one of his (1945: 236, 239), as did Percy Gardner (1933; cf. Boardman 1985: 48). Richmond eventually took a Third in Classical Moderations in 1922 and a slightly better Second in Greats two years later, but still managed to publish his first article while still an undergraduate (Richmond 1922). Part of his failure in this respect was attributed indirectly to Haverfield, for when;

> ...convalescing from a serious illness during his last year at school a book of Haverfield's inspired in him an interest in Romano-British studies, so that, though to his great regret he never met Haverfield ...he spent more time than his tutors wished in reading archaeology' (*The Times* 6 October 1965).[19]

During his undergraduate years Richmond attended Collingwood's lectures and could remember hearing Macdonald speak at the university in 1920 (Richmond 1941: 181). In time he was to pen at least three obituaries about Collingwood and his contribution to Romano-British

---

19. There are preserved a number of variations of this story. For instance, 'Richmond referred to his own experience as a schoolboy when he found an uncut copy of Haverfield's Romanization of Roman Britain in the school library and being bored with ordinary school work, found here the entrance to a new world. The study of the subject was a stimulus to original thought because it demanded creative work' (*J Roman Stud* XXVII (1937): 253).

studies (Richmond 1943a; 1943b; 1943c). Despite his connection with Collingwood, Richmond (and his students and disciples) did not rate the former's published work as highly as others have done:

> Richmond with great tact wrote of him 'He was an artist also, by hereditary instinct and developed power, with the grace and vision given to such men, so that his teaching was especially creative and stimulating. But the balance between artistic creation and historical formulation is delicate, an equipoise almost beyond the art of men'. This view led Richmond to omit Collingwood's great book in the Oxford History of England series from his bibliographies (Frere 1988: 1–2).

It was during his time as an undergraduate that Richmond gained his earliest experience of excavation, when he worked under Wheeler (at Segontium 1921–2, '...then a young undergraduate ...but already alive with the intellectual agility and imagination which were to distinguish his mature scholarship'; Wheeler 1956: 68; cf. Wheeler 1965) and at Cawthorn Camp 1921 with Frank Simpson, another Haverfield associate, and Hugh Evelyn White. It was at this time too that Richmond wrote the first of a number of regional and site histories. The termination of the Yorkshire Archaeological Society's excavations at Slack led to plans to consolidate the results into a history of Roman Huddersfield and its environs. One of the original directors of those excavations, A.M. Woodward, was to write it but had to withdraw upon being appointed director of the British School at Athens. In his place Richmond agreed to take on the task (having already excavated at Roman Meltham (1923) and a section of the Roman road at Blackstone Edge). In the resulting volume Richmond was assisted by Collingwood and by Donald Atkinson who studied the pottery. In 1925 he published *Huddersfield in Roman Times*. After graduating in 1924, Richmond won a Gilchrist studentship to the British School at Rome. This studentship was originally meant to support research on Roman housing, but Richmond changed it to the monumental walls and gateways of Rome. Prompted by Collingwood and Taylor he was also a Craven Fellow and a Goldsmith's senior student. 'Up to the time when he went to Rome his main inspirations had been the writings of Haverfield, the teaching of R.G. Collingwood at Oxford, and the introduction to the art and methods of excavation which he had received from Mortimer Wheeler at Segontium' (Birley 1966a: 293). At Rome, between 1924 and 1926, while '...F.G. Simpson influenced his archaeological career ...it was under Thomas Ashby ... that he found what seemed to him then and for several years later to be his primary vocation, namely the study of Roman buildings in all their aspects' (Birley

1966a: 294). In time, with Ashby's death in 1930, Richmond saw into print his *Roman Aqueducts* (1930; cf. Hodges 1990: 87). In 1926 he became Lecturer in Classical Archaeology and Ancient History at Queen's, Belfast. With Ashby's removal from the Rome school, Richmond became its director for the period 1930–2 until forced to resign, citing ill-health (there were unfounded rumours of his involvement in a scandal fabricated by the Mussolini regime; cf. Wallace Hadrill 2001: 80–6). Although Wheeler claimed Richmond on his return to the United Kingdom was for a time likely to be Bushe-Fox's replacement as the Chief Inspector of Ancient Monuments (Wheeler 1965: ix), after effectively two years of unemployment and following a conversation with Birley at Birdoswald in 1935, Richmond was recommended for the post of Lecturer in Romano-British History and Archaeology at Armstrong College (later King's College and later still the University of Newcastle). This appointment made Richmond the third occupant of the post Bosanquet had prophesied as far back at 1904 and the successor to Philip Newbold's appointment in 1910 and later Birley. Richmond was to remain at Newcastle until 1955 (with a Readership in 1943 and a personal chair in 1950) when he was made the (first) Professor of the Archaeology of the Roman Empire at Oxford, a creation which perhaps marked the culmination of Haverfield's work with respect to Oxford: a dedicated senior academic post in Roman archaeology.[20] In a similar way, Wheeler could not fail to pass judgement. Richmond's place '...lies in the direct line of descent from R.G. Collingwood and, behind him, Francis Haverfield, who made Roman Britain a specifically Oxford tradition, and it is entirely appropriate that Richmond should have returned there ...Whether or not of the overall stature of Haverfield, Richmond has left us work of which an unusual proportion will live, and the general indebtedness of

---

20. Richmond received honorary degrees from Edinburgh, Leeds, Belfast, Manchester and Cambridge universities, was a VP of the London Antiquaries (1945–9 and 1957–9), later its director (1959–64) and president (1964). He was elected an FBA in 1947, made a CBE in 1958 and knighted in 1964. Richmond's reputation was, at the time of death, almost as great as that as Haverfield's; 'Richmond was one of the greatest Roman scholars that this country has produced. His scholarship was internationally recognised and his visits were welcomed in every country from Scotland to Transjordan ...All students of the Roman period appreciated his scholarship ...No excavation was too insignificant for him to visit and study with the greatest care' (Gracie 1965: 230–1).

Romano-British studies to his wise encouragement and ready advice is beyond calculation' (1965: x).

Richmond's academic work divides into two spheres of activity: excavation with its publication and in synthesis. With regard to the former his reputation lies mainly with the Roman army and the excavation of its fortified sites. In this respect he is commonly associated with an idiosyncratic form of excavation; slit trenching and key-hole sondaging of sites to confirm hypotheses and check building alignments. Richmond learnt of the advantages of the method from his contact with F.G. Simpson, who had devised the technique in his pre-War excavations along Hadrian's Wall and in its environs (Helgeby and Simpson 1995: 3; Simpson 1996: 222; Frere 1988: 2; cf. Wheeler (1965: x – his 'preference for carefully selective small scale-operations rather than for the big battalions')). The technique, with all its drawbacks, worked best on sites which were expected to exhibit standardized or consistent ground plans. It was thus best employed on Roman military sites.[21] Richmond's preference for excavating forts and camps is a bias reflected in his excavation reports, the best known being his *Hod Hill. Excavations Carried Out Between 1951 and 1958. Volume II* (1968), published shortly after his death. We have seen how this report, and in particular Wheeler's review of it, was to become a point of controversy. Developing criticisms he had made previously, Wheeler not only took the opportunity to pass comment on Richmond's poor record in publishing his results but also his methods of excavation (Wheeler 1965; 1968; Hawkes 1982: 353–6). The reaction to these comments reiterated the high esteem Richmond was held by his colleagues and students and the way that Wheeler was,

---

21. Towards the end of his time at Newcastle, and during almost all his Oxford years, Richmond, along with J.K. St Joseph of Cambridge University, excavated the legionary fortress at Inchuthil in Scotland. Richmond first saw the site in 1937, just as he and J. McIntryre were finishing their excavations at Fendoch, but he did not commence work at it until 1952, believing it would take ten years to excavate. Employing no more than six or seven men per annum and excavating only a fraction of the total site, Richmond and St Joseph were able to elucidate the history of the site just before the premature death of the former. The site was eventually seen into print by St Joseph assisted by Lynn Pitts (Pitts and St Joseph 1985), with the omission of Richmond's name from the title credits drawing some comment.

as far as Oxford was concerned, an outsider.[22]

Other than his excavations, although he published what were recognized as sound introductory texts and other more specialized monographs, Richmond did not produce the sort of major synthesis that an academic in his position could have been expected to author. The circulation and reception of his opinions about Roman Britain were helped by the medium in which he published. His best known statements include his *Roman Britain* (Britain in Pictures, 1947). Even more successful was another *Roman Britain* (1955), this time published in the Penguin paperback format and variously reprinted over the next 25 years (with a second edition in 1963 and a third in 1995). Of the pair, one reviewer stated '...both give readable and stimulating surveys ...Both books give a highly subjective view of the subject, and both deserve to be read and re-read, in company with Haverfield's *Romanization of Roman Britain* and M.P. Charlesworth's *The Lost Province*' (Birley 1966a: 298–9). Later on there was the edited collection of essays *Roman and Native in North Britain* (1958) which along with Salway's *The Frontier People of Roman Britain* (1965; 1967) has been described as the '...only full length stud[ies] of the Romanized civilian population of the frontier region' (Salway 1981: 769). Other than the invitation to produce a new edition of Collingwood's *The Archaeology of Roman Britain* (1969) – which after Richmond's death was completed by his 'student', D.R. Wilson – Richmond produced no other major statements.[23] Looking at his output, it is debatable how far Richmond's influence with respect to interpreting Roman Britain has survived. It is true that his contribution to Collingwood's *Archaeology of Roman Britain* remains a stalwart on Roman Britain bibliographies but it is questionable whether his one major work of synthesis, *Roman Britain*, even in a revised third edition, is relevant today (Reece 1997).

---

22. E.g. 'Anyone who has worked with Ian Richmond will remember with gladness his enthusiasm, his lively and disciplined imagination, his humanity and his friendship' (Wilson in Collingwood and Richmond 1969: xxv; Wheeler 1965: x–xi).

23. Wheeler (1965: ix–x) wrote that Richmond's interest focused mainly on Roman Britain (although by the time of his death, he was beginning to shift his interests to Roman Spain), where his '...work lay primarily, though not exclusively, in the field.' Wheeler drew attention to his work on the Roman military, the baths at Bath, the Silchester church, Chedworth Roman villa and Hod Hill but failed to note his contributions to Roman religion, especially that of the army.

It is therefore disappointing that Richmond, other than a few isolated statements, did not produce a detailed overview of the nature of romanization. He hinted at what might have been significant in his inaugural lecture of 1957 and where he identified themes for future research (e.g. the recording of surviving architectural details, work on small towns, villas, military *vici* and the Roman penetration of Scotland, progress which was then assessed by Frere nearly 25 years later (Richmond 1957: 18–20; Frere 1988: 5). He was invited to update Collingwood's *Roman Britain and the English Settlements* in the Oxford History of Britain series. But his premature death halted the plan. It was completed by Peter Salway (1981). Therefore '...some indication of what Sir Ian's ...full scale survey of Romano-British history might have been is preserved in his Penguin Press *Roman Britain*' (1955 – Salway 1981: 765).

In his (major) works of synthesis on Roman Britain, Richmond, like Haverfield and Collingwood before him, referred extensively to the phenomenon of romanization. What is apparent is a conviction that romanization as civilization was in various ways a tool of Roman imperial government: '...The instrument of civilisation used by Rome in achievements such results was the town and the many sided attainments of amenity and social grace which successful civic organisation involves' (1955/63: 66, 79, 85). The rise of towns therefore showed how some elements of the tribal aristocracy now followed Roman attitudes, of using the facilities of town life for at least part of the year. Proof of the validity this statement was found in the urban experience in Gaul. The criteria by which he identified it remained largely unchanged to those deployed by his predecessors although he did introduce some interesting ways of explaining why it occurred. Thus we see the appearance of (Roman) urban forms (p. 67ff.; 186), villas with their accoutrements pp. 109–25),[24] evolutions in religion (p. 180f.) and especially with the arrival of the Imperial cult and the syncretistic marriage of Roman and native cults. All of these developments were attributed to the Roman conquest and in at least the case of 'building fashions' were adapted

---

24. Of villas, it was asserted: 'Nor are they to be connected with Roman immigrants rather than native Britons. Roman settlers there were retired soldiers, administrators or even investors, but these were a minority compared with native British land-owners, the principal farmers and notables of the tribes. The villas mostly represent the adoption of Roman standards in greater degree by natives of substance' (1955/63: 109). Components of the 'acceptance' of such values included the use of mosaics (p. 121).

within a generation of the conquest (p. 110). Never stated explicitly, the objective of the conquest seems to have to bring civilization to the island. In explaining who and what drove the process of romanization, Richmond attributed the dynamics almost totally to the imperial authorities, to both individual emperors and to their agents in the field (governors, army commanders and administrators: cf. Richmond 1955/1963: 71–2). Their main vehicle for this was urbanization: 'The instrument used by Rome in achieving such results was the town and the many sided attainments of amenity and social grace which successful civic organisation involves' (1955/63: 66).

Richmond characterized the process of change as benign in nature. That it could happen was because of the Roman government's usual way of handling its provincial subjects which was very much flexible and hands-off in the way it dealt with local populations: '... nothing is more characteristic of Roman imperial development than a readiness to work within existing arrangements provided these could be assimilated to Roman form' (1955/63: 79; cf. p. 85). In this treatment then, the natives were allowed or encouraged to make the transition to a romanized state seemingly by their own process of discovery and assimilation. In this process Richmond saw the transition as a deliberate, conscious set of choices of actions made on the part of the provincial populations: '...The foregoing review of the various British towns and cantons plainly shows that as in Gaul, they (the natives) were left to feel their own way towards a Romanization which proceeded wherever possible within the native framework' (1955/63: 85). Elsewhere it was argued that:

> The choice ...becomes something purposeful. ...It becomes a reflection, however pale, of classical culture ...There is no doubt, then, that the richer villa-owners appreciated classical themes, and it is certain that many of their choices were directly linked with classical habits of mind or behaviour (p. 122).

The variable degree of romanization apparent in the regions was attributed to the fact that the:

> ...inhabitants of such places were as Romanised as their means permitted them to be. Some other explanation of the state of affairs is therefore required, and the way thereto is cleared if it can be accepted that the Romanized villa and the native form started from the same cultural level; for it then becomes necessary to suppose that the difference must lie in the social relationship of their occupants (p. 124–5).

In his explanation of that relationship and the consequences of romanization, Richmond introduced a number of subtle innovations which have influenced subsequent interpretations. So for instance, he made the appearance of the Roman patron-client relationship a positive factor in the transition.

> If the difference between the Romanized villas and the farms of primitive native style can be recognised as corresponding to the social distinction obtaining within the tribe between landowners and tenants, then its continuation may be explained by the freedom from interference which tribal custom enjoyed under Roman rule so long as the terms laid down by the treaty of settlement were observed (p. 125).

Richmond's enduring reputation has been assisted in a way that neither Haverfield (contrary to received wisdom) nor Collingwood were able to accomplish: by the evolution of the academic-postgraduate relationship that was in a fledging state when Haverfield was active. Unlike Collingwood, Richmond was able to bring on a number of students who went on to occupy academic posts and so to undertake fieldwork. Jones (1987: 30) identified this as an 'Oxford school' which was in contrast to a developing Birley 'Durham' or 'northern' group. The difference between the two groups is that the Birley group tended to be concentrated on study of the structure of the Roman imperial army with some reference to mural issues and Roman castrametation. The 'Oxford school', other than some who researched on the archaeology of the Roman Empire, was more oriented to the archaeology of the southern part of Britain and therefore a greater range of themes, military and non-military. Richmond's influence continued into the 1970s and 1980s and even into the 1990s through a succession of postgraduate students who went on to occupy academic (and other professional) posts, mostly in the United Kingdom. The majority of his students were to obtain appointments in north and central England which may be significant. Most of them were also appointed before the full effects of the 'New Archaeology' and the excavation revolution occasioned by the development boom of the early 1970s. For this reason it can be said that many of his students, along with those of the 'Durham school' represent the last generation of a 'conservative' or 'traditional' approach to Romano-British studies that goes back to Haverfield.

Romano-British studies after the Second World War

The preceding paragraphs have explored the strength of the line of continuity from Haverfield to Collingwood and on to Richmond. It is this line that allows us to assess their influence in the works of most later (academic) authorities on Roman Britain. What is evident from the outlines of the career and work of the three is what they failed to develop, even

address. The common feature is that they all published in varying degrees works of synthesis on the social and economic life of Roman Britain
and, in doing so, broke from a politico-military approach. In their discussions a principle issue was to assess the degree or depth of penetration of
Roman culture in the island. Haverfield had been at pains to demonstrate just how romanized Britain had become. This was evident by the
categories of data he adduced as showing it; categories such as inscriptions, *sigillata*, coins and fibulae. As we have already seen the
identification and manipulation of these categories as 'Roman' was based
on the existence of comparable evidence from the continent. It was this
general theme and these criteria, but not their veracity, which
Collingwood took up as he attempted to argue for the less universal penetration of romanization in Britain. But for all this, his interpretations,
like those of Richmond, worked with the idea that degrees of
romanization could be adduced by the presence of the categories of evidence which Haverfield had defined.

With the benefit of hindsight it might be said that it is a fact that the
(major) publications on Roman Britain in the period 1945 to the late
1980s were largely unoriginal, lacking the innovative approaches to the
framework that Haverfield and Collingwood had created. Between
Collingwood and the late 1960s there were published few, if any, enduring overviews about Roman Britain which deployed new thinking in the
reasons for and the outcome of the Roman occupation of Britain. This
was, after all, the time that Collingwood's *Archaeology of Roman Britain*
was to be updated. But this is not to deny that there did appear some
monographs which may not have the authority of text-books but still
were influential. In this group I would include most, if not all, of Richmond's work. One work of the post-Second World War period which
was highly rated at the time of its publication was Charlesworth's *The
Lost Province or the Worth of Britain* (1949) which started as the Gregynog
lectures at Aberystwyth in 1948. Written, in part, in response to the consequences of the last war and to emphasize Britain's European links.
Charlesworth set himself two questions: why did Rome choose to annex
the island and what were the consequences of the decision on both the
Britons and the Romans. The answer devised for the first question was
it was for the Roman military and the economic advantages the island
promised. The consequences for the Britons were even greater.
Charlesworth enumerated the benefits as language, communications
(which means roads and site placements), culture (= agriculture, including changes to the island's flora, reading and the alphabet), the
arts (meaning cookery, construction, sculpture etc.) and religion and in
particular with the introduction of Christianity. We might also add to

this list 'the tradition of the Roman occupation'. It does not need repeating these were criteria familiar to Haverfield and Collingwood. But having listed the features, it is curious that Charlesworth did not use the word romanization. Instead:

> If we ask ourselves what we owe to the Roman occupation one fact stands out clearly. For the first time in its history our country emerges as a whole, one unified territory, organized and governed from a centre, intended to function as a unit, 'the Britains' ... This unity was at once manifested in and strengthened by language, communications, culture, art and religion and at the present day we are still being influenced by them, in so far as they are the bone and marrow of modern culture (1949: 64).

It is difficult to assess just how influential were Charlesworth's conclusions. *The Lost Province* continues to enjoy a reputation that seems curious today. For passages of it read as if they were the template for the dialogue among the revolutionaries in Monty Python's *Life of Brian*. Populist in tone, it was highly regarded in scholarly circles of the time. Of about the same vintage, and as significant, if now not more so, was the appearance of A.L.F. Rivet's *Town and Country in Roman Britain* (1958). It is a work which has been consistently rated alongside Richmond's output (e.g. Salway 1981: 766). In part reaction to Haverfield's emphasis on certain types of data, Rivet broke new ground in the way he addressed Romano-British studies from an economic rather than a chronological perspective, although with the same emphasis on urban and rural conditions. As part of this approach, Rivet also criticized the overuse of Haverfield's emphasis on the British content of Romano-British culture as well as the preoccupation on the highland, military zone and a civil, lowland one. But other than Rivet, there is little that was published in the years down to the mid-1960s which has borne well the passage of time. Useful more as a curiosity is Bonser's *A Romano-British Bibliography* (1964) which '...marks the end of the era of Romano-British studies characterized by Collingwood' (Salway 1981: 758).

A more enduring contribution to the history of Roman Britain, not least because it went into a number of subsequent editions, was Richmond's titular successor at Oxford Sheppard Frere's *Britannia: A History of Roman Britain* (1967/1978/1987). It was to become the acknowledged textbook for experts and undergraduates alike for the next twenty plus years (Jones 1981: 88: Salway 1981: 765). In the preface to the first edition, Frere envisaged it, written as part of an ongoing series on the provinces of the Roman empire, as an update to Collingwood's *Roman Britain and the English Settlements*. His approach to the evidence was traditional (Frere saw his debts in this respect to Haverfield, Collingwood and Sagot), following Haverfield in particular, with the marriage of the available literary and epigraphic evidence supplemented with the results of archaeological research. In other words, typical of the 'Oxford approach' to Roman Britain. What it was not to be was an 'archaeology of Roman Britain', but a historical interpretation rather than a general description. As might be expected with all 'great' books, *Britannia* has meant different things to different scholars. Jones (1981: 88) noted in this respect it drew heavily from Frere's own excavations at Verulamium (just as Haverfield utilized the Silchester excavations and Collingwood Wheeler's work at Verulamium). Salway (1981: 765) says that Frere is especially good with its footnotes and bibliography. Perhaps most important of all is the fact that it was the first major monograph on the subject to be published in the past ten or more years which had the advantage of bringing together the results of recent work. In other words it was the right text at the right time.

Britannia dominated university teaching for over two decades. With hindsight it is an infuriating text to use, not least because of the inadequate footnoting and the absence of archaeological details (features thought to be innovative at the time). Its primacy lasted until the 1980s when coincidentally there appeared in the same year (1981) two new monographs on the subject: Malcolm Todd's *Roman Britain* and Peter Salway's more weighty volume of the same name which was in many respects the revised version of Collingwood and Myres. Indeed the latter consciously limits itself. It was originally going to be prepared by Richmond, but his death halted the plan. Salway was asked to take on the task but, with the need for extensive rewriting, it was decided in 1967 to commission a new volume. But still the influence of Collingwood is there to be seen in the new volume, in its emphasis on archaeology rather than in documentary sources and in its structure and format, including a critical bibliography.

Salway's detailed study of Roman Britain recognized a distinction between political and cultural romanization;

> …'Romanisation' in the commonly assumed sense of a conscious spreading of Roman amenities at Roman expense to provincials is a misunderstanding; pressure and the offering of advantages to men of local influence was the method of attempting to ensure loyalty and it was as these leading provincial families came to emulate and identify themselves with Roman political and social culture that the Romanization of the provinces which we can recognise archaeologically followed (1981: 113).

That said, the same categories of material that we have seen Haverfield and Collingwood utilizing are used here. There is also consideration of the mechanisms by which romanization could be affected (pp. 505–7). In contrast, the latest edition of Frere's *Britannia* is more traditional in its approach, with conclusions reminiscent of Collingwood, in its belief that Romano-British civilisation was; 'outwardly ...Roman, inwardly it remained Celtic, yet it would be wrong to suppose an inner conflict between the two aspects. The result was a synthesis, included by Rome and welcomed by the British people as they came to realize the advantages of peace and wealth conferred by membership of the empire' (p. 295). In turn, the same previously employed criteria appear (urbanization, villas, mosaics, games, language and law, coinage, art and architecture). The one concession to the present is recognition of the variables in this synthesis caused by social stratification and the varying conditions of life and opportunity. The agents of change were the army, merchants and the policies of governors and emperors. The underlying trend in these sorts of characterizations is that Roman material culture is used as some sort of absolute indicator whose presence or absence is the basis for assessments. The meaning or potential regional meanings attached to such cultural objects is largely left unexplored.

Over and above the advances in information available however, there was a more serious methodological drawback in Haverfield's work, one which was in turn not adequately addressed by his successors. Some of these problems might be dismissed as semantics, but their significance with regard to romanization is crucial in how we interpret the objectives of the process. At no time did Haverfield attempt to explain what he saw as 'Roman' or 'Roman material civilisation'. Instead, his approach was to seek out the same features and types of objects in Europe and in Britain. The similarities adduced represented 'romanization' with the implication that Britain was or had become increasingly similar to its European counterparts. What Haverfield was in fact doing was drawing upon the archaeological and epigraphic similarities of the Roman province in the same way that Mommsen had tried to homogenize the Roman empire. But in either case there was little consideration of the presumptions which shaped these judgments. Having identified similarities, Haverfield's next step, and the one used by his successors, was to explain why they occurred. In short, all changes adduced were thought to have had a meaning, one which transcended the mere functional explanation of the objects. It was this assumption which his successors, from Collingwood onwards, have repeated almost verbatim.

We can see now how many of these assumptions were made. In the first place there was the prevailing social climate. Ideologically, Haverfield's opinions were composed at a time when the 'mission of empire', not only in the political and military senses, but also in the cultural and economic dimension, were being confidently extolled, although it is debatable if Haverfield was ever prone to such crass moralizing. Nor was Haverfield exempt from such sentiments. In a paper of 1916 (see also Haverfield 1910a), surprising in its comment on contemporary events, Haverfield looked to the complementary achievements of the Roman and British empires. But when it came to the Roman period and in the case of Britain, he never really satisfactorily explained why such acculturation occurred, nor what caused it. This means that one is left to speculate by what mechanisms it occurred. There are admittedly hints at something. The model was established by Mommsen. For instance, the passage from Tacitus' *Agricola* (21) was used to imply a state-managed, and by implication controlled, exposure to Roman culture. Such problems as those highlighted here have only been partially treated by Haverfield's Romano-British successors.

It should be apparent that the questions posed and the methodologies used in addressing romanization are now considerably more sophisticated than in Haverfield's day. This has been due to advances in the methods of data collection, in the understanding of such objects and in the willingness of archaeology to assimilate the advances in kindred disciplines. But certain fundamental facts remain unchallenged. All approaches accept as fact that the data accumulated has an embedded meaning and thus a rôle which can be discerned by the researcher, if it is looked at correctly. In conjunction with this view is the one that the recipients of it – and probably the donors too – were conscious players in its transmission, where each party was aware of the significance of their acts and their adoptions. Secondly, while it is now accepted that 'real' romanization affected only part of native society – its élite – and that for the vast majority of the population it had little consequence, it is maintained that those affected had subliminal reasons for using Roman culture. As Frere put it:

> ...Haverfield long ago made the point that when the provincial adopted the use of Roman things he could be declared civilised enough to realise their value and further, could be seen to have abandoned any inherited hostility towards them... (1987: 296).

This was a view reiterated later by Richmond and his statement that the use of mosaics reflects a '...choice (being something purposeful) ...it becomes a reflection, however pale, of classical culture ...There is no doubt, then, that the richer villa-owners appreciated classical themes, and it is certain that many of the choices were directly linked with classical habits of mind or behaviour' (1955/63: 22).

Because it was the likes of Richmond and Frere and to a less degree Salway and Todd who dominated teaching at that time, they became the focus of attack for a new generation of Romano-British archaeologists in the late 1980s. In the lead of new approaches was Millett's *The Romanization of Britain*, a title redolent of an inheritance back to Haverfield. Millett was in the vanguard of a fresh way of assessing romanization, which in turn inspired yet more, more 'theoretically' driven research. In turn the 'conservatives' have not been so convinced that anything new was being revealed. Unsurprisingly, the anti-theoretical reaction to Romano-British studies is more evident in the work of 'established' scholars of an older generation. The most recent summary of progress in Roman Britain (Todd 1989) differs in no significant way from the themes and categories of data outlined in its predecessor volume (Kendrick and Hawkes 1932). Complementing this failure has been a conservative reaction to the application of a more critical methodology in Romano-British studies. In its most modest form, it has been quite reasonably been said that: '...We are far from being against new approaches (as long as they are couched in a language that does not instantly mystify)' (Potter and Johns 1992: 9). More depressing, in a résumé of recent 'major' work, Frere was largely dismissive of alternative ways of looking at the evidence. The core of his criticisms was aimed at the rise of archaeological units, problems with what he believed to be poorly supervised research and the access to easy publication, but above all:

> ... we need to teach the new generations of archaeologists the virtue of clear selective reporting, and to show them that Roman Britain was an outpost of the classical world, where wild anthropological or sociological theories and their accompanying jargon, introduced from the shadowy and de-personalized world of prehistory has little place ...We want fewer Central Places, Gift Mechanisms and such like Models and more study of the almost illimitable resources of the archaeology of the Roman empire (Frere 1988: 6).

In this version of the Rankeian outlook to the philosophy of history, and following the precepts of the Oxford school, 'Let the data speak', irrespective of the mechanisms which might have conditioned its definition and its interpretation. Unfortunately the same attitude is to be found in Salway's *Roman Britain* (1981).

Along with these reservations, a number of problems persist with all characterizations of romanization as currently articulated. Frequently the conclusions drawn from the identification are as weak as the categories of data which supposedly identify it. In this respect I accept the premise that archaeological evidence retains a detectable, often coherent meaning but a common example, although not so frequent today, is where the quantity and quality of material relative to adjacent districts leads to the drawing of conclusions that certain peoples or sites enjoyed preferential treatment from the Roman authorities. In other words, that those authorities – even the emperor – could and did enjoy control of who had access to its (material) culture. Such conclusions are frequently validated by reference to literary sources which cite imperial attempts to restrict or limit the activities of (Roman) traders (e.g. Fulford 1989: 90–4). Of course the very existence of such strictures only serves to emphasize that trade did go on and that the emperors were largely powerless to stop it. But again, we must not lose sight of reality. Would the state be that interested, all the time, in what crossed from one side of the Rhine or Danube to the other?

In the absence of statements to the contrary, the impression generated by such statements is that we are dealing with a homogeneous, uniform Roman culture reacting with an indigenous one. Such comments apply even to the newer generation of analyses. To be sure, what most 'new', theoretical Roman approaches were doing was asking what they believed to be new questions of the same established types of data, data which they believed by dint of its very existence to have a detectable meaning or significance. They and their predecessors believe that romanization as acculturation had to happen and that it occurred consciously to the actors. And yet there is no consideration of why this should have to have been so. Whilst it is recognized that the outcome of this interaction need not be the implantation of the same in virgin areas, still there is a failure to consider exactly what was being implemented. For example, it is common to find it concluded that the greater the quantity and quality of 'Roman objects' recovered from a site or region, so the greater the degree of penetration. This in turn leads to questions about why it occurred and the medium for its execution. Those most cited mechanisms are the army (both deliberately and inadvertently), merchants and imperial administrators (Frere 1987: 296), as well as the indigenes actively desiring it. The primary rôle given to the army in this capacity explains in turn a preoccupation with discussions of romanization and acculturation in what are termed frontier regions and at the almost total exclusion of regions to the rear of them. A point made by Slofstra drew attention to the fact that:

> ...Many studies of acculturation ...barely discuss the dynamics of culture but confine themselves mainly to the psychological aspects and the final results of cultural contact. They often focus on a highly descriptive trait-list approach of elements transferred from one cultural context to another (1983: 72).

This observation, whilst not explicitly stated, clearly applies to most discussions of the sort of romanization discussed by Haverfield *et al.* The point was developed further by van Es in that:

> ...Romanisation is not the importation of a neat finished culture and it is certainly not a one time event in the Roman period ...it is a continuous process that began with the physical presence of the first Roman and in fact earlier than that (1983: 5).

In turn:

> ...The degree of acculturation depends at the level upon which it takes place, which may be state or civil law, administration and organisation: it may concern matters of spatial organisation, the economy or religion. On all these levels a distinction must be made between form and content, especially in the early stages of the process of acculturation" (pp. 161–2).

If, then, the native and Gallo-Roman content were constantly evolving, by implication, so 'Roman' culture must have been equally prone to evolution. It too can never have been static. Thus, with this reasoning, it becomes impossible to arrive at a satisfactory position as to what is Roman culture. Assessments of romanization on a temporal plane become equally difficult; it is not impossible, but yet ultimately irrelevant. That said, we return to an observation that has been repeated almost *ad nauseum* in the preceding chapters. All theories of romanization, imposed or passive, as well as the counter arguments to them still circle around the debate of how to interpret the material. There has been no contemplation of the evidence upon which the interpretation, and subsequent detail, is based, even in the more 'theoretically' driven contributions to the series of Theoretical Roman Archaeology Conferences. As in the past it is based on passive acceptance of categories of data, which are perceived to be Roman. We have seen how Haverfield and his generation might have made that connection, but it should be clear now that the confidence with which they made the link requires reconsideration. Until this is attempted, all theories of romanization remain self-fulfilling, if not pointless and ultimately worthless.

CHAPTER 12

Romano-British studies in the new century

The preceding chapters have explored the course of Haverfield's career relative to the development of Romano-British studies as well as his immediate legacy. We now come to assess the importance or, better put, his relevance today. The first point which has to be made is that this study was never meant to belittle his achievements or to denigrate his accomplishments. Nearly 100 years on, one is struck by the range of his interests and his degree of expertise in them. But there is one other aspect of his career which is relevant: the way his reputation has evolved in the light of that work, both at the time he lived and in the decades after his death. That is the acceptance of the oft-repeated achievements of his career. Here I have concentrated on what I call the Haverfield 'myth'. And this is where this study has tended to be critical: of the way others have used his name and work, either to further their careers or in trying to advance a particular line of interpretation to the point where they have distorted his work.

As explained in Chapter 1, one of the reasons for this study is assessing how valid is the cliché 'Haverfield set the agenda for ...' The concern was to trace how Romano-British studies were founded and have evolved in the way they have. In turn this study has become an examination of the condition of Romano-British studies at the end of the millennium. This may have been an issue that has concerned some previously, some in the more distant past (Wheeler) and others more recently (Cunliffe, Snodgrass, Hingley etc.), but that said there had been not much progress. In exploring the relevance of the discipline today, we have covered a number of themes, not least the intellectual evolution of Romano-British studies, and the part of the intellectual community, and especially in the universities, in its development. This has permitted examination of how Haverfield interacted with and contributed to a number of debates. For instance there was his relationship with respect to contemporary debates concerning the relevance of ancient history and in particular Roman imperialism to Britain's colonial empire. The emphasis has been on the implications of the events and publications of the time and in their context, rather than on formulating assessments based on the benefit of hindsight and on statements accorded magisterial status that some have elected to repeat verbatim without appreciating their context. Despite the scope and depth of his accomplishments, today Haverfield is best remembered for defining of the phenomenon of the 'romanization' in Britain. The preceding chapters have spent some time examining a number of themes pertinent to this legacy. We have already looked at the genesis and implications of those of his (major) works relevant to the phenomenon and found that the circumstances behind each of them was peculiar to themselves and which might serve to diminish their utility as definitive statements. As we have seen, consideration of Haverfield's attitudes to the publication of his views, as well as his attitudes to contemporary events, do not appear to have overly influenced his professional work. The sum of this reappraisal is that there is little or nothing to show that any of these criteria overtly influenced how he wrote of the process of cultural assimilation. Part of the problem is that scholarship subsequent to Haverfield persists in characterizing 'romanization' as an absolute issue: an inevitable consequence of the Roman empire, with Haverfield as the messenger, rather than seeing it more as a product of the time when the theory was originally formulated. In reality the situation is rather more straightforward and one-dimensional in its treatment of the issue. For some the issue of the Roman cultural mission has been resolved. This was effectively the point Wheeler was making as far back as 1961 and beyond and his opinion that Roman studies in Britain were not evolving – where progress was being made it was merely in the accumulation of more of the same sorts of data familiar to Haverfield and his generation to flesh out the same skeleton constructed by him. Alternatively, there are those who would reject entirely Haverfield's conclusions. The drawback to either position is that neither of them offers more than the minimum of concern with considering why Haverfield followed the course he did. At best they seem content to draw rather crude analogies between late Victorian scholarship, society and the possession of an empire forming a keystone to either his writings or his outlook. Such accusations are too simplistic and do him little service. They demean his scholarship, which was more that of a world historian than these sorts of characterization would imply. Instead he was much more catholic in his use of the past to inform the present than those who would emphasize how his work on Roman Britain was designed to be an exemplar on later nineteenth pro-colonial attitudes. Instead of this I have tried to show how the work that made Haverfield's career was formulated in the light of a European perspective and in the pursuit of a more rigorous standard of scholarship and knowledge. Close reading of his work suggests, however, that one cannot detect in Haverfield any real link between contemporary politics and his writings. While he could not have existed in a (intellectual and social) vacuum, in this case one cannot argue for a concealed agenda in Haverfield's work. Perhaps he may have thought about and even believed in them, but he never bothered or chose to articulate them in his writings to the extent that we can confidently assert that he was so influenced. Instead of this the impression is of a man preoccupied with his subject and who, having set himself objectives, rigorously pursued them to the expense of other interests. On the other hand, the current propensity to criticize Haverfield merely serves to prolong the life of that mode of interpretation that enjoyed a relevance to the time he wrote, but which is now redundant.

These conclusions are validated by an appraisal of the evolution of Haverfield's career. In Chapter 1 it was noted that at face value the course of his career could be divided in to three distinct phases (pre-1892, 1892–1914 and 1914–19). Examination of the evidence suggests that this periodization is broadly accurate but the significance of the various stages also explains how Haverfield's relationship with (Roman) archaeology evolved. The first phase – from the time to his going up to Oxford through his time as a schoolmaster – is indistinct, but for a progression from philological, to epigraphic to antiquarian-archaeological interests. This phase morphs, with the return to Oxford in 1892, into something approaching Haverfield as a full-blown archaeologist in the late Victorian sense. It included his involvement in fieldwork (and in particular that with the CEC and at Corbridge). Then there was his work with inventories of sites and cataloguing types of material (the plans for a corpus of *sigillata* etc. along with his various museum catalogues etc), which in turn facilitated his works of synthesis (e.g. for the *VCH* and RCHM, along with other overviews). There was also a preoccupation with organizing archaeological research (with his patronage of organizations and suggestions for reform as well as the issue of (university) students and their work). The third and final phase is again not so clearly delineated, but with the transition occasionally slightly earlier, from *c.*1907, than previously assumed. This phase of his career is marked by the beginnings of a reduction in his archaeological work, at the expense of an increase in other interests historical. Then there was the retreat from the *CIL* and the rise of *RIB*, which was intended to be another tool for the historian. His reluctance to countenance archaeology as a separate subject at Oxford and his championing of the cause of the School of *Literae Humaniores* in the university confirmed his evolution into an academic in the established Oxford sense. This transition, as much a consequence of his elevation to the academic elite was in part due to something of a disillusionment of what archaeology could achieve. Of course, as with all summaries, the divisions between the various phases appears to be more abrupt than they were in reality. It explains how Haverfield appears to be a mishmash of paradoxes and contradictions which range throughout all facets of his life and work. So his politics and personal attitudes were a mix of opinions and values which on occasion seem not too consistent. On the one hand there was his alleged 'liberalism' and his support for contemporary political issues (women's suffrage, university reform, criticism of (Conservative) government foreign policies) and yet the potential influence of his church background and his conservative attitudes to other aspects of educational reform (the introduction of higher degrees, the status of archaeology in the university) and, his friendly association with known Tories. But we should perhaps not be so surprised at these contradictions. Who can claim any comparable consistency in their attitudes and opinions? In spite of these subtleties, however, those who have used Haverfield's work in the aftermath of his death have tended to treat his career and so his work as being coherent and consistent from their outset. In this he was from the start a Romano-British scholar. In the version preferred here he was an Oxford ancient historian whose happened 'to do' Roman Britain.

We have seen the various ways Haverfield and his work meant different things to different people. He was variously an epigrapher, a historian, an archaeologist, a numismatist and even a geographer. Just as significant is the way his memory was used in the subsequent generation to perpetuate one version of his contribution to scholarship – the Romano-British scholar par excellence, but an impression largely at the expense of his other work (as well as his limitations). This in turn is a consequence of the canonical status of Macdonald's life of Haverfield, where the subject emerges simply as (a fully evolved) scholar of Roman Britain. Macdonald has no depth or appreciation of the subtlety to Haverfield's other work. But it is this version which has, over time, been accepted and repeated. In this Haverfield has been placed on a pinnacle of sorts as a consequence of the subsequent development of the discipline. In his lifetime, certainly up to *c*.1914, he was regarded by his associates as a, if not the, leading Romano-British archaeologist in the country and what is more, as an excavator. But it is clear that some of those who worked with him harboured reservations about his capabilities and competence in this respect. We see this most clearly in his relations with the CEC and with the subsequent Corbridge excavations.

It seems too that such criticisms became more widely appreciated after 1914 with the consequence that his closer associates were forced to re-draw his reputation as an excavator. Shortly after his death he was no longer being presented as the excavator *primus inter pares*, but had become the great facilitator and organiser. Such an assessment is true to a degree. But why was he able to initiate and organize (the start of) programmes of research, but rarely able to complete them? This is a re-curring feature of his career: a capacity not to see projects or programmes to their natural or at least neater ends. There are other facets of his career which, under close(r) scrutiny also seem to run coun-ter to the tradition. We see this in his gradual distancing from the annual updates in the journals of the 1880s and 1890s, from the *VCH* and the way *RIB* was passed on to others, with the latter only to become a reality nearly 50 years after his death. 'Failures' such as these were un-deniably due in part to the force of circumstances, notably with the outbreak of the First World War. But perhaps more important was a flaw in his personality, where he lost interest with those who were not with him, as was recognized by many at the time of his death. There is also the element of his ambition, a facet of his character which has been vir-tually ignored in all assessments of his career. It cannot be denied that Haverfield had an eye for the main chance. Again, those obituarists who endeavoured to rebalance his reputation and competence as part of the assessment of his 'achievements' consistently ignore or miss these points. In the repetition of the key 'facts' of his career, the salient fea-tures may not be as they seem. For instance, there are the circumstances to the invitation and his subsequent part in the *CIL*, all at the expense of Hübner, which have been conveniently forgotten or else ignored. The evidence suggests that Haverfield manipulated his part in the pro-ject to a degree previously unappreciated. Then there was his ability to place the right publication in the right place, especially those of the 1890s. He was involved in a number of major excavations at the right time. Finally there is the idea of the loss of the majority of his students. Examination of the records suggests that to call it a coherent group is the product of a rosy hindsight. As it is, the group of students was small and the losses proportionally difficult to identify. Of those he is sup-posed to have nurtured to carry on his work, only one can really be said to have continued it (Donald Atkinson), while the others who stayed in academia, virtually all disappeared back into Oxford and the world of *Literae Humaniores* from which they had emerged.

These facets of Haverfield's career which could have been identified relatively easily. That few have done so begs the question why not? When were these 'distortions' first propagated, and by whom and why have they been repeated for so long? A rather obvious explanation may lie in the structure of Romano-British studies, where it has been said:

> Roman Britain has always been a small academic field, where most of the main figures have been personally well-known to each other. This means that it is not always easy to disentangle who influenced whom, and who was friendly with whom (Jones 1987: 85).

Such insularity has meant that, with the hierarchical nature which has long been associated with the discipline, it has often been difficult for some to write as openly as they would like about the state of the subject and the influences of its (leading) figures. It is equally the case, for many of the 'establishment' to accept constructive criticism of the previous generation. It has been a recurring theme throughout this study that there is a tradition in British scholarship for presenting the invention and development of Romano-British studies in terms of a series of major or 'great' figures, each of whom in turn, has in some sense passed on a baton or legacy to his successor. It does not require emphasis that the formulation of and ultimately the perpetuation of this line of descent, is the product of the generation after the last of the 'greats' and that it therefore becomes self-perpetuating if not self-aggrandizing. This sense of continuity is apparently supported by the way that the development of the subject was marked by each of the 'greats' producing for their time 'the great book'. In this portrayal of the evolution of the subject, the lineage commences with Haverfield, 'the father', who brought a new rigour to the discipline, to Collingwood, the man who in some respects gave intellectual respectability and on then to Richmond who, with his appointment to the Chair of the Archaeology of the Roman Provinces at Oxford in 1956, represents the acceptance of the subject of Roman archaeology as a legitimate discipline as far as the universities were concerned.

Although superficially attractive, there are a number of weaknesses in such a characterization. In the first place, Haverfield is made the focus of the subject, while belittling what had been done in the 50 or so years preceding him; in both the tradition of British antiquarianism and the contribution of specific individuals. Secondly, we have seen that, as great and as innovative as Haverfield's work was, whatever progress he had made was largely stopped dead in its tracks, certainly with his death in 1919, possibly as early as just before the First World War. For with his demise, other than the raising of standards in terms of the recording of data he had always advocated, there was no real continuity in his work. The academic losses as well as the economic climate of the time coupled with his university's retreat from the subject meant that the sort of work he had practiced was not continued with the same sense of authority he had once exerted. The burden of academic research in terms of fieldwork was not developed but remained the concern of the two major antiquarian societies as well as numerous regional ones. Otherwise, the management of the academic study of Roman Britain was left in the hands of one person based in the Ashmolean Museum at Oxford, but without a secure institutional position. The pivotal position the Haverfield Library and Archive was meant to play in the management of the subject lasted no more than ten years after his death. With respect to teaching at Oxford, nobody else was in place. Instead, the teaching of Roman Britain was done more out of a sense of duty by Collingwood rather than because of the intrinsic sense of the value of the subject. Elsewhere, the provincial universities largely ignored the teaching initiative too. In many respects, then, following Wheeler it is fair to describe Haverfield's work as ending up in something of an intellectual, institutional siding.

Of course what is missing from these assessments of Haverfield and his legacy is what he thought of himself. The perception preferred here is one substantially different to that which sees him simply as the 'father of Romano-British studies'. Instead he should be regarded as an Oxford academic before a Romano-British scholar. It is undeniable that in one sense he was such a scholar but at the same time he saw such scholarship as a facet of a new type of ancient history, one that joined – albeit it uncritically – the textual (written and especially epigraphic) with the archaeological (= antiquarian = topographic/place names etc) with excavation and catalogues. But in the latter part of his career he was not a sufficiently committed archaeologist in the sense he regarded Romano-British archaeology as a subject in itself. It was still to be part of ancient history. In other words he may not have been as much of an archaeologist, as he probably realised by the end of his career. If this summary is valid it would help explain how Haverfield's writing about Roman Britain tended to situate it as part of Roman Europe. For Haverfield, the archaeology of the Roman empire had to be that of its provinces. It was this which made it a legitimate discipline for university students. Nor was he so preoccupied as some would have with the self-justifying or lesson-learning comparisons of empire. He may certainly have had opinions about the world around him but these had little bearing on the admittedly blinkered mission that he set himself. Working as something of a 'pioneer', this outlook and methodology was bound to have consequences on his followers. Circumstances dictated that the most important of these disciples was Collingwood, who had his own agenda to settle, one consciously derived from Haverfield. The essential point about Haverfield and Collingwood is the link between the two requires no underlining discourse. Collingwood's work on Roman Britain might in some respects be characterized as an intellectual exercise – a case study for much of this general theorizing on history. His work has a propensity to over-generalize and, despite his claims to do so, failed to consider the 'little man' at the expense of the same 'grand themes' he accused Haverfield of pursuing. In time the conceptual framework and therefore the questions that concerned Collingwood became those which Richmond and others assumed generally to accept, and only occasionally to refute and redefine them as they saw fit. It is for these reasons that Collingwood's contribution to Romano-British studies is better described as leading the subject up an (intellectual) siding, if not a cul-de-sac. The fact that Haverfield dominated Romano-British studies at Oxford combined with the consequences of the war meant that his death created a vacuum there. If Collingwood valiantly stepped into the breach, in the longer term his parallel career in philosophy meant he had little or no chance to form a group of students. Judging from the dearth of significant Collingwood philosophy students, he may not have been disposed to bringing on researchers anyway. Collingwood's 'failure' to train a new generation of Romano-British scholars explains in large measure why Haverfield's influence has persisted. Haverfield might have had 'students' Collingwood did not. With Haverfield's work regarded as more practical to Collingwood's rather intellectualised view of Roman Britain, there was another reason to extol Haverfield.

As we have seen, Haverfield did not complete, and perhaps never intended to, his *opus maior* on Roman Britain. Other than the foray into ancient town planning, his two best-remembered publications are *The Romanization of Roman Britain* and *The Roman Occupation of Britain*; the former (in its last edition) completed four years after his death, the other five years after the same event. The circumstances of his death, however, ensured the two monographs assumed a greater importance than they were perhaps meant. Influential as the two continue to be, the signs are that they may not have been entirely indicative of Haverfield's opinions on the subject at the time of his demise. We can speculate on the reasons why he did not. The circumstances and events of his career cannot have helped. Temperamentally he may not have been suited to such a work or more provocatively his interest in Romano-British studies led him to conclude there was no need for such a work. The subject material did not necessarily merit the effort. Whatever the explanation, the point is that the strength of Haverfield's reputation today is dependent on what happened in the aftermath of his unexpected death.

With the publication of *The Roman Occupation* that was, in part, achieved. For a better understanding of what Haverfield thought the study of Roman Britain was about, one has to look at the extensive list of his other articles, chapters and contributions to understand his thinking. In this respect the priority was the compilation of properly marshalled corpora of data before interpretation could commence. Equally as significant, it was those who were responsible for seeing it into print who are vital in the formulation of the myth. George Macdonald did not have an academic position to fill or justify. Margerie Taylor was forced to create her own niche in the vacuum created by Haverfield's demise. Certainly in her case, keeping alive the Haverfield reputation benefited her, possibility at the expense of aspects of Haverfield's work. For instance, judging from its contents pages, the *Journal of Roman Studies* became increasingly focused on (ancient) historical and classical literature, contrary to Haverfield's original plan for the Society which published the journal. Roman Britain was slowly but increasingly marginalized in the range of articles published in its pages, a phenomenon which was itself perhaps a reflection of the parlous state of Romano-British studies in the country. Instead, the subject came to be represented by the 'annual reports' on Roman Britain until these were superceded by the creation of *Britannia*, a journal of Romano-British studies. The inception of that vehicle meant an even greater emphasis on historical, literary and philological matters in the pages of the Roman journal at the expense of Roman archaeology in general.[1]

It is the culminative effect of these facts which permits us to speak about a dislocation on a far greater magnitude between Haverfield and his successor, Collingwood, than is usually acknowledged. The situation was made all the worse by the fact that Collingwood's work in the subject, originally undertaken as an act of *pietas*, was secondary to his other interests. Not surprisingly, his engagement with the subject progressively diminished, first in terms of actual research, then in the teaching he offered, then merely to the production of textbooks, enduring as some of them have become.

Indirectly then, rather than deliberately, Haverfield's work put the subject along a course of development from which it was, and probably is still now, unable to break loose. It explains in part the relative stagnation of the discipline in the years up to and after the Second World War.

---

1. That this has occurred is brought home by the rise of another recently created Roman periodical, the *Journal of Roman Archaeology*, which fills a vacuum created by the shift of emphasis within the Roman Society.

It may not be coincidence that the longest lasting of the 'text books' about Roman Britain, from the period up to the Second World War are John Ward's *The Roman Era in Britain* (1911a) and Collingwood's *Archaeology of Roman Britain* (1930), both of which might be said to be manuals describing types of archaeological finds. The other major literary product of Haverfield's time was the appearance of specific types of textbooks describing specific forms of archaeological monument (e.g. Roman roads). Again it may not be coincidental, but following the SPRS meeting in 1938 R.H. Moore, the Shrewsbury schoolmaster, published *The Romans in Britain: a Selection of Latin Texts Edited with a Commentary*, reviewed, with some reservations, by Baillie Reynolds (1939). Moore acknowledged debts to Stevens and R.H. Dundas at Oxford, C. Clement Whittick at King's College, Newcastle upon Tyne and Garnon Williams. Moore, in his preface, also recommended as secondary texts Collingwood's contribution to *The Oxford History of England*, Anderson's *Furneaux* and Rice Holmes's *Caesar's Gallic War*. It is true that what Collingwood, in his pomp as a student of the subject (e.g. in the first part of the 1920s), was offering it as a corrective to the Haverfield approach. But I have tried to argue that in terms of the bulk of his fieldwork (in north-west England) Collingwood is in some respects reminiscent of the polyglot antiquarian that was his father. The range of his (non-excavation) fieldwork projects, with the focus on what we might label non-Roman indigenous sites, were of a type not explored by Haverfield. But it is a pity that Collingwood did not take this work further. Despite the nature of his fieldwork, he continued to write books on Roman Britain on the small and grand scale (his *Roman Britain* through to the sections in the *Roman Britain and the English Settlements*) and was involved in the same tradition of cataloguing and organizing (his contribution to *RIB* until he gave up on it, and the inventory approach in *The Archaeology of Roman Britain*). As we have seen, his work on Roman Britain was for him at least peripheral to his main interests. The fact is that his work would seem to indicate that, like so many of his (Oxford academic) contemporaries, whether they be historians or ancient historians or epigraphers or classical archaeologists, he regarded it as something that respectable scholars did as a sideline to other more substantial interests. Typical of this time Wheeler, in writing about Richmond's time at Oxford as undergraduate and his interest in Roman Britain considered that, '…he (Richmond) probably spent a disproportionate share of his time upon what was then an esoteric sideline' (Wheeler 1965: ix). Based on his fieldwork, had Collingwood realized that Romano-British archaeology was not an intellectually meaningful discipline or period? If he had made such a realization then it is not especially explicit in his written work but is manifested more by his retreat from the subject from the late 1920s, a withdrawal that was otherwise explained by his curtailment of activities through illness. In some respects, however, Collingwood's work still represented something of a cul-de-sac in that what he was doing was not taking Romano-British studies substantially further. Instead, what he did was to perpetuate and repeat the Haverfield tradition – cataloguing, with the *RIB* and other museums descriptions and, of course, with *The Archaeology of Roman Britain*. Collingwood assessed the great man's interpretative framework by referring to the categories of evidence and so the issues he had delineated. The exceptions to this tradition were the likes of Donald Atkinson, Eric Birley and Ian Richmond employed in the universities, and non-university researchers Joscelyn Bushe-Fox and certainly Mortimer Wheeler, and their range of non-Roman or marginal Roman sites explored through the late 1920s and 1930s.

As already noted, the creation of the Haverfield 'myth', and by implication of its continuation by subsequent scholars of Roman Britain, was in large part the work of Taylor, Macdonald, Richmond and to a lesser extent Birley and even, indirectly, Wheeler. Macdonald and Taylor represented an older world and the establishment, but an increasingly out-moded approach to the study of Roman Britain, one which originated from a particular way of approaching the subject. Both remained outwith the university system and so to newer ways of instruction. Neither of them was entirely necessarily sympathetic, by training or character, to some of the methodological and interpretative advances that the discipline underwent in the first half of the twentieth century.[2] While the importance of this line of descent is more likely important to these individuals, there were others at the time who appreciated in one way or another that there were problems with the subject. Those who dared to question the received version of Haverfield's work and reputation could expect retribution. One who did was Wheeler who was to remain – perhaps by his own willing participation – an 'outsider' to the

---

2. A good example of this marginalization was the friendly debate Macdonald entered into with Birley and T. Davies Pryce concerning how far one could use *sigillata* to deduce historical events, viz. to date the development of the Roman military occupation of northern Britain (cf. Macdonald 1935; 1937; 1939; Davies Pryce and Birley 1935; 1938). In the collection of Sir George Macdonald's papers in the Special Collection of Edinburgh University Library are two or three letters between him and Birley and drafts of Macdonald's articles related to this controversy.

establishment (one based principally at Oxford or with its emissaries in other institutions) and who was censured for having the temerity to criticize the great man, his work and in particular his intellectual heirs. Nor were his comments about the subject as a whole likely to win him friends and influence. Other forms of exclusion for those who stood outside the 'tradition' included access to the Haverfield Archive. To progress in the subject one had to be acceptable to that establishment. Of course none of this situation was necessarily Haverfield's intent, although it is clear many of his opinions ran parallel to the attitude of the 'establishment' after his death. But what it did mean, as an Oxford-based discipline, in the main Romano-British archaeology remained impervious to the developments that prehistoric archaeology underwent through from the 1930s onwards. The discipline in itself remained aloof but intellectually moribund as it merely perpetuated the same sort of things that Haverfield had initiated. One might argue the subject only came out of this self-imposed hibernation in the late 1960s with the rediscovery of landscape and therefore of those who inhabited it. But the shackles were broken not so much because of an assault on Haverfield and the Roman Britain tradition, as by developments in British archaeology and the management of the archaeological stock: by the rise of rescue archaeology, its concomitant developments, and the greater use of regional survey of a type the RCHM and Haverfield had not attempted. In turn the challenge to the framework of interpretation came later, in the 1980s, and again for reasons found not in Romano-British studies itself but changes to research in history and the social sciences.

What this study has emphasised is two aspects to Haverfield's contribution to Romano-British studies. On the one hand, there was his move towards the institutionalizing of knowledge. This was to be effected by the call for a rise in standards in the presentation of work but which he wanted done through the universities, especially Oxford and in turn Durham and Birley, but with the condition that it remained part of the study of ancient history or as part of other centralised institutions which either way would reduce the influence of the local or the amateur. The precedent for this approach was a combination of the spirit of the time grafted on to the German experience with respect to *Altenwissenschaft*. It involved the systematized critical analysis of inscriptions on a national and regional scale and, less successfully (although this was not his fault), pottery (as samian), coins and fibulae as well as the aborted efforts to describe the Roman collections in the country's provincial museums. Haverfield's annual reports on the state of Roman Britain form another aspect of this cataloguing of knowledge. The *VCH* and RCHM contributions, as proto-SMR descriptions, are as pertinent here. In all this work, the plan was to marshal the raw data so that the study of Roman Britain could proceed in a more secure, scholarly fashion. In turn it led to works of synthesis and interpretation, his second contribution, in which the emphasis came to be his work on the romanization of the island's population. Of the two facets, it was the former accomplishment which was lauded by his contemporaries while it is the latter, that of his output, which has been regarded as his bequest by the modern generation and more pertinently has become that element which has been most often challenged.

But there is something more to Haverfield's work than these two (positive) legacies which has failed to draw comment. As we know Haverfield has often been called the 'father of Roman Britain' in the sense that he started it all. But this attribution has a double edge. For what Haverfield managed to achieve, if unintentionally and certainly unwittingly, was to divorce Romano-British archaeology as a discipline from mainstream British archaeology. His works of cataloguing, of drawing what are considered to be stereotypically Roman categories of data, had the effect of emphasizing, if not creating, an (artificial) divide between pre-Roman and Roman Britain. In doing so while he might have made Britain as a Roman province a subject worthy of independent study, still something was lost in the exchange. In the long term this separation was extremely damaging. For his work had the effect of placing Roman Britain firmly in the realms of classical archaeology with the way it deployed the same sort of categories of evidence as the basis for interpretation and the way he tried to link the island with Roman Europe. And of course, in this way, the developments in Romano-British archaeology mirrored processes and developments which had long been underway on the Continent. In the same way the definition of Roman Britain on the basis of certain categories of artefacts was also damaging for the way archaeological research was undertaken in Britain.

We have seen the way that (British) antiquarianism from the sixteenth century could, in many ways, be said to be indiscriminate in what it chose to record and the way it offered to explain the monuments described. In time Haverfield was to be highly critical of what he regarded as the negative influence of the untrained and fanciful opinions of such writers. While he acknowledged the competence of a small group of writers, in general his opinion of writers, notably those of the nineteenth century, invariably characterized by him as amateur and dismissed as 'antiquarians', was far from complimentary. As much a product of the spirit of the age, and with the systematizing of knowledge and training, such was the strength of his opinions, he effectively marginalized the accomplishments of antiquarianism and the part to be played by the lay worker. Antiquarians were tolerated, humoured or regarded as proto-archaeologists rather than students proper. This attitude with respect to Romano-British antiquarianism is one of Haverfield's less well-documented legacies. In reality, their unique initiative, with its emphasis on landscape and the strength of being multi-period and non-discriminating, that had been gathering momentum in the nineteenth century were lost in Haverfield's dismissal. Appreciation of this fact remained largely so for the next 40 or 50 years and has only been redressed in the recent interest in antiquarianism. That the full implications of Haverfield's contribution in this respect were not appreciated at this time was due in large part to his obituarists and close associates, notably Taylor, Macdonald and to a lesser degree Birley, along with the passive acquiescence of the majority. What his dismissal failed to appreciate was the way that this traditional antiquarianism had, and continued to, developed an increasingly sophisticated understanding of landscape and the layering of human action on the ground. Indiscriminate and unselective as it was, still such writers were not driven by the identification, and so filtering-out, of the Roman in that landscape. Nor were the antiquarians, broadly speaking, especially preoccupied with the parcelling-up of the monuments they described by period, but were concerned more with form and function. Likewise in their written accounts, there is often an almost seamless continuity from what are now regarded as prehistoric to the Roman to the post-Roman/Dark Ages period. Haverfield's 'achievement' was that his work, albeit unwittingly, was to insert an artificial divide between the periods, certainly between the former pair but with more subtler shades between the latter coupling. Haverfield was never especially interested in the what is now known as the pre-Roman Iron Age in this country, although he was, contrary to popular criticisms, aware of the native population in the full Roman period. That said he was sufficiently alert to the fact that whatever happened in the Roman period was in large measure dependent on what preceded it. In turn, his attempts to reconcile at least the former divide, was the exploration of romanization and the consequences of the Roman presence/period on the island's indigenous population.

The implications of Haverfield's introduction of a period divide had consequences for archaeological research, although it is questionable how much this was all his fault. In his dismissal of much British antiquarianism, what he chose to overlook was the way certain antiquaries appreciated how a simple reading of landscape and topography could elucidate so much. This was, as noted already, a continuation of a medieval tradition. We have also seen that it was the methodology used by the likes of the pioneers of the study of Hadrian's Wall in the mid-nineteenth century, where they began to construct reasoned inter- pretations on the features and evolution of the frontier system without the benefit of excavation. But they also appreciated that excavation would be the arbiter of their opinions. What Haverfield did, in his own small way, was to use excavation but still choose to ignore such opinions, or in the case of the CEC to use excavation to challenge and ultimately denigrate them without giving credit for the fact that their opinions were the reason why the excavations were initiated in the first place. In the spirit of the age, with an admittedly enlightened, certainly econom- ically efficient, understanding of using excavation to solve specific questions or general problems, the broader potential of archaeological research was compromised. Excavation now became the way that (Ro- man) archaeology was executed in this country. But this is not to push the point. Others were as guilty in this respect. But Haverfield's defini- tion of an archaeological cultural period in Britain on the basis of a political event (when parts of Britain came under Roman political con- trol) meant excavation now became the process of exploring Roman towns, Roman villas, Roman temples etc. in the search for Roman in- scriptions, Roman coins and Roman pottery etc. This shift in the pursuit of the past was partially validated by the corresponding con- temporary emphasis on work on Roman forts and Roman frontiers. It was this development which effectively wrote the pre-Roman Iron Age indigenous population out of the picture of Roman Britain, even though Haverfield was more than aware of its existence. This explains why Haverfield then had to come up with an explanation to reconcile the two periods; this was the theory of 'romanization', one which re-es- tablished a linkage between the two periods. The distinction was not so pronounced at the other end of the spectrum and what happened with 'the end of Roman Britain'. This was because it was a period which had long interested Haverfield and was one where there was better evi- dence, primary and secondary, for him to work with.

So where does this leave Haverfield and Romano-British archaeol- ogy? How are we to account for the failure of the subject to develop after him? If we accept that he saw as a necessary task the better compilation of the various categories of (archaeological) data, which he regarded to be the product of the Roman period of the island's history, before any form of broad sweep interpretation could commence, then the problem has only really come to the fore in the decades after his death. We return to the expression which recurs throughout this study, Wheeler's assess- ment of Haverfield and the tombstone metaphor: where the subject effectively stopped still with his death. In looking at Haverfield, his two-fold contribution to Roman studies endured after his death. The data driven approach, which in turn complemented the chronological framework derived from the (limited) literary sources and the better corpus of the epigraphic evidence, retained a utility down to today, or put another way, cannot be ignored. This was a point Snodgrass (1985) made in his discussion of why 'New Archaeologists' might profit from a closer familiarity with the achievements of traditional classical archaeology. Haverfield's second legacy, the formulation of the interpretative issue, also persisted. But in this instance, the debate proceeded along the lines of supplementing and supporting his basic framework for the romanization of Britain or, in the mould of Collingwood, challenging, gainsaying and treating the distaff side to the Haverfield version.

The explanation offered here for Haverfield's legacy has not reconciled the current preoccupation with attacking Haverfield's work on the grounds that it served little more than to reinforce (British) ideas of the merits and mission of colonial rule. Superficially this link is attractive, but using Haverfield as the focus of the attack is a red herring. As with much of his work, the intent is clear on his part but the outcome or, better put, the way others, archaeologists, historians and politicians, chose to interpret his conclusions could not have been anticipated and were beyond his control. The current propensity to criticize Haverfield merely serves to prolong the life of that mode of interpretation that enjoyed a relevance to the time he wrote, but which is now redundant. In this there is a certain irony, with the shades of the ways Romano-British scholars have done the same in the decades since 1919. Indeed the signs are that, where Haverfield was aware of the ways what he had said were being used, he was not averse to reacting to them. It is for this reason then that, while some of his conclusions might have suited the purposes of more overtly politicized writers, Haverfield remained merely the researcher.

To all intents and appearances, Haverfield was simply an Oxford trained and based ancient historian who happened to do work on Roman Britain. Whatever his heirs may have thought, the evidence suggests Haverfield's own work implies appreciation of the fact that Romano-British studies was a relatively minor subject. It was certainly not as significant as some of his successors would have us believe. But there again, being in post, such writers had a vested interest in arguing the case. One certainty is there are many of Haverfield's statements to the effect that Romano-British archaeology was in reality best treated as a facet of European archaeology, and so history, and that it could not stand alone in other ways. Whether or not his reasons for arguing this are still valid today (the thrust of the argument here suggests not; defining a discreet Roman period in Europe is as perverse as arguing the same for Britain), this is what his reworking of romanization tried to do – to link Britain to Europe, however one wants the reasons why he felt romanization occurred. This was perhaps the greatest and yet the most unappreciated facet of his legacy to the twentieth century.

The Haverfield 'myth' has not only distorted aspects of his career and therefore misinformed the subsequent generations of Romano-British scholarship, but it has also masked the latent weakness of the subject at the time of his death. It is a fact that by 1919 Roman Britain was still not an accepted aspect of 'real' archaeology in Britain's universities. It was not quite classical archaeology and it certainly did not merit comparison with the conditions of a fledgling British prehistoric archaeology nor its medieval counterpart. In reality it continued to remain one step up from the sort of antiquarianism of the nineteenth century, against which Haverfield had railed. It was not established at Oxford for the reasons already noted. In the short term Roman archaeology's progress in the universities was rendered static with the decision of the Haverfield Bequest Committee. But the committee's decision was a reflection of reality. In the longer term – perhaps with Haverfield's connivance – it had failed to put down roots within the teaching for *Literae Humaniores*. That failure persisted under Collingwood and in fact deteriorated as his commitment to the subject waned. Other than his writings, the period 1924–50 was marked by the absence of the publication of any (lasting) monographs on the subject. Nor had the discipline managed to establish itself in the newer provincial universities. There were signs of a degree of acceptance up to the outbreak of the First World War but the momentum was lost in the aftermath. As it is, for all the foresight that such institutions showed, the indications are that the subject was still taught in the Oxford fashion, where it was regarded as an interesting side line but one that remained an adjunct to the skills required for ancient historians or the classical archaeologist (e.g. competence with inscriptions, coins). The same sort of sentiments permeated how many of the leading members of the Roman Society, some with what are regarded as strong archaeological credentials, viewed the introduction of Romano-British studies in teaching in the (public) schools in the 1930s. That there was confusion in what the teaching and ultimately the practice of Romano-British archaeology was about is evident among those teachers who introduced the subject at such schools, where the justification for their 'innovation' of introducing sixth formers to such treasures was linked to the progress in ancient history and in the (easier introduction to) intellectual training the subject offered. Thus instruction in Romano-British archaeology could be described in the way of the title of this study. There is more than a grain of truth in Frere's statement (cf. Chapter 1) that Romano-British studies were an excellent training ground for fledging archaeologists who went on to other things.

The failure of the universities to take up the task is reflected in the way research in the post-Haverfield years evolved, or rather failed. Because there were so few university staff specializing in the subject, the universities remained little involved in the major excavations of period. Other than Atkinson at Manchester, Miller at Glasgow and towards the end of the pre-Second World War period, Eric Birley and the Durham training excavation, who was there? The big excavations of the period, supported by the likes of the Society of Antiquaries of London, were conducted by non-university persons such as the Wheelers and Bushe-Fox. Elsewhere, at Oxford R.G. Collingwood was progressively doing less and less in this respect. It is also true that Frank Simpson enjoyed an extraordinary appointment at Durham while Richmond was still flitting about before settling at Armstrong College in 1935. But it does not need emphasizing that these excavations were almost entirely not linked specifically to the teaching of (undergraduate) students, although they could participate, but rather to the advancement of the careers of the excavators, some with at this time a tenuous link with Romano-British archaeology and for the organisations that patronised them. We can continue with a list of those who were regarded as leading Roman Britain fieldworkers and specialists of this time who were not linked to the universities (e.g. Wheeler, F. Oswald, T. Davies Pryce). The subject remained then as much the preserve of the enthusiastic amateur and the layman working through the regional archaeological societies and other lesser organisations (e.g. the schools) as it had been the clerical antiquarian of the mid-nineteenth century.

In this rather pessimistic picture of the state of Romano-British archaeology post-Haverfield, there were two bodies that might have advanced the cause and taken the subject to a higher state of integration: the country's museum, the British Museum, and the Inspectorate. In terms of the museums as a whole, the situation had undoubtedly improved in the time between Haverfield becoming involved in Romano-British archaeology and his death. We can see this in the way that the provincial museums were producing more and better dedicated catalogues of their holdings – a process partially initiated by him. We can also see the improvements in the way that museum curators and keepers were becoming increasingly recognised as authorities in their own rights (e.g. E.T. Leeds, L. Hope, C.F. Hawkes and R. Hull etc.). The general improvement in the competence of curators in turn reflected the improved quality of graduates who went into the museum service. But as in the past such individuals were largely the recipients and conduits of data spewed forth in excavation reports etc., and cataloguers of their museum's holdings, rather than being the initiators of the collection of data. In short, they remained little more than the specialists they were. The same sort of process occurred at the British Museum. We have seen how by the late nineteenth century, the museum possessed in many of its departments scholars of ability and imagination who were driving forward the study of their respective disciplines. In turn with the likes of the guides and handbooks to their holdings, there were authors who were able to provide overviews. However the initiative was lost because of a number of developments after the First World War. The fact that the museum did not patronize excavation in the UK meant that its keepers remained largely passive. Furthermore many of those who were employed in museums and who started out with an interest in Roman Britain drifted away – one might say, grew out – of the discipline.

The post-First World War decades witnessed the creation, strengthening and ultimately the rise of the Inspectorate responsible for the preservation of the nation's archaeological (and other) heritage. There was some hope, not least with the likes of its senior officers Joscelyn Bushe-Fox and Paul Baillie Reynolds, especially when calls on their time was sufficient to permit them to indulge their interests in 'research' excavation that the Inspectorate might take the initiative in advancing Romano-British studies. Into this group also comes O.G.S. Crawford at the Ordnance Survey. But again the initiative was lost. Officers of the Inspectorate were increasingly diverted to involvement in management and conservation issues. To this was added the rise of archaeologists, both within the Inspectorate and in other institutions, with interests in other periods of British history and not just Roman.

With hindsight comes 20/20 vision, where the condition of the present becomes explicable and the evolution of the current situation obvious. This work started off as an exploration of the influence that Francis Haverfield is thought to have exerted over the development of Romano-British studies. In Chapter 1, the possibility of a decline in the provision for instruction in Romano-British studies at least in the country's universities was noted. The reason for this crisis was laid at the door of the product of the times, where the discipline was the victim of developments elsewhere which have had a knock on effect. An alternative explanation was to attribute the situation to an inherent weakness in the discipline, a weakness some would blame on the structure of the subject and therefore, at least in part, the fault of the 'father of the subject', Haverfield. The subsequent chapters have explored the origins and development of the subject in the time that Haverfield flourished and in the years where his legacy was most immediately felt (from the 1880s down to the end of the 1930s). The conclusion is that there were fundamental structural weaknesses in the subject but that it is unfair to level them at Haverfield. Contrary to received wisdom, it is true that he did not take the subject forward from the substantial progress he made in organizing and marshalling the raw data for the study of the subject. Nor was his initiative followed by his university or by its provincial contemporaries. But it is also evident that the 'ground' plan for the subject which some are happy to believe he had in mind never really existed. For the fact is that Haverfield remained an ancient historian but one with an advanced and relatively sophisticated appreciated of the potential of archaeology. But he was not prepared, or else was unable, to take the subject that bit further. The crucial weakness in the subject that became evident at the moment of his demise was made all the more apparent in the subsequent two decades. Superficially, after this death there was much progress in the subject in terms of excavation but still the period is marked by the leading practioners of the day, whether they be in the universities or the museums or the Inspectorate, failing or refusing to move forward. The subject thus was relatively moribund in its progress in spite of the credit and adulation afforded R.G. Collingwood.

In many respects the current concerns about the failings of the subject, with the associated sense of incredulity that Romano-British archaeology might not be as important as some would like to believe, is indicative of the sense of false importance afforded the subject. Instead of asking why the subject is in 'decline', perhaps the question should be why the subject in the first place? What are the merits of the subject Romano-British studies as a distinct period of study? That it has become such a subject is due to Haverfield. It was his principle achievement in many respects to divorce the Roman period in Britain clearly from that which preceded it. His own research interests ensured that the issue of (cultural) continuity into the fifth century and beyond remained at the fore. In establishing the subject 'Roman Britain', it was Haverfield who emphasized a break from the Iron Age antecedents and influences in the period of the Roman occupation which have in the long-term created more problems than solutions. To emphasise the importance of the Roman era, we see his preoccupation with the romanization question, which has in turn misdirected the efforts of subsequent generations. What is all the more sadder about Haverfield's separating Roman Britain from Iron Age Britain is that the emphasis placed on the evidence of the former period was at the expense of other developments in British archaeology. Late nineteenth century antiquarianism, building on the traditions of the preceding three centuries, had been increasingly moving towards a more sophisticated understanding of the importance of landscape and monuments in the understanding of ancient societies. Haverfield's work, with its preoccupation with the creating corpora and excavation of sites (of whatever time) pushed to the fore the evidence of a 'Roman' period. It was to be another 75 years, not until the late 1960s, that the significance of landscape was once again realised by Romano-British archaeologists.

A sub-text to this study was that in accepting that there was something of a general decline in the status of Romano-British studies in the universities and therefore in the public dimension, it has tried to explain the current malaise in the discipline identified by (university-based) practioners in the discipline. In explaining the condition there are two broad schools of opinion. On the one hand, there is that which attributes the decline in Romano-British studies to recent developments in archaeology as a whole, where there has been the growth of archaeology as prehistory, of its medieval counterpart and, of course, the expansion of the contribution of (British) archaeology elsewhere in the world. Contributing to the situation has been the influence of what some regard to be more challenging intellectual theorising about the subject and what it can tell us about the human condition. This line of argument maintains that Romano-British studies, as a branch of classical archaeology, has failed to develop its own 'theoretical' (whatever that term means), or until relatively recently, basis. Instead, it is has been wedded to the importance of the creation of databases as the bedrock for interpretation, as well as to the primacy of literary evidence over the relatively muted voice of archaeological evidence. The 'decline' of Romano-British studies has also been linked to the fact that in terms of where the majority of instruction in the subject is offered – in the universities and the country's colleges of higher education – the discipline has allegedly lost out in the rewards offered for innovations in teaching and in the awarding of research grants. A recurring feature in this explanation for the decline of Roman Britain as a subject for instruction has it as more the victim of circumstances, one which has lost out, almost passively, to the advance of its archaeological sisters.

A second school on the current condition of the same subject offers a slightly more sophisticated version of the same explanation. In this respect, the problem goes back to Haverfield and in turn the influence, good or bad, that he continues to exert over the subject. In this respect it is the models (viz. the interpretative model romanization combined with primacy of literary sources) and, to a lesser degree, the categories of evidence with which he was involved coupled to the islands epigraphic evidence and then such classes of data as sigillata, coins, villas and forts) which has been the problem. This line of argument, whilst acknowledging Haverfield's contribution to the subject, tends to reduce his intellectual modelling of Britain as a Roman province to the unhealthy product of our Imperial past and one too heavily influenced by that experience. Instead, as would be argued by post-processualist archaeologists and some of the newer generation of Romano-British scholars, the subject only really commenced with the work of Collingwood. But even then they would maintain that still Haverfield exerts an unhealthy influence on how we view, and continue to write about, Britain simply as a Roman province. We have seen, however, that this version of Haverfield is more of a caricature of later twentieth century prejudices than Haverfield's own opinions.

There is one other problem which is relevant here; that is the intellectual framework in which romanization studies remain stuck. Some of the problems were highlighted in Chapter 1. The fact is that Romano-British studies have failed to recognize that romanization theory was as much a product of its time, as are the criticisms which have been raised in how the theory justifies and explains itself (Freeman 1997). The discourse remains set in the idea of either, 'there was positive, passive, romanization', or 'it was imposed on the unwilling', or 'it was subverted' which leads to arguments about those who might in turn 'protest' or resist in their own way. The argument remains fixed on the idea that the identification of the phenomenon of Roman acculturation with all its baggage *did* exist. It is acceptance of this, which means that the debate about the degree and depth of penetration can persist. There are undoubtedly valid points in both these explanations. And, as a result, as we have seen, it is for this reason that Haverfield continues to exert a profound influence on how the subject is treated even today. Most obviously, his legacy is to be seen in the format of the standard textbooks on the subject, in which in large measure the chronological framework upon which the accumulated archaeological data has been pegged. Roman archaeology is general still fails to get to grips with what makes Roman material culture Roman. This is why the on-going cycle of Theoretical Roman Archaeology Conferences has been largely disappointing (Laurence 1999; and the essays in the proceedings of the TRAC 2005 conference). If not just a vehicle for presenting papers on something 'Roman', rather than questioning the evidence to hand, most contributors seem intent on looking at some of the more obscure facets of romanization or wish to advance grand theories based on little subjects. In reality, for all the recent discussion about the forms of 'romanization' that might be discerned, contemporary Roman archaeology has still not managed to explain what it understands to be 'Roman material culture', the foundations upon which all discourses of romanization are built (Freeman 1993).[3] But not only is there the chronological and interpretative framework which most continue to accept and others 'reject', but which really means rejigging the status quo. This is another facet of the serious point about Haverfield and his career. This is the creation of the 'Haverfield myth' and in turn the creation of a hierarchy of order by those who originally propagated it. Indeed the (Macdonald's) version of Haverfield's life is as much a product of the time and its social values.

In a typically perceptive and yet curiously largely ignored review of Malcolm Todd's new and revised third edition of Richmond's *Roman Britain* (1995) compared to Millett's *Roman Britain* (1995), Richard Reece (1997) just about hit the problem nail on the head. The 'problem' is the tradition out of which Richmond's efforts were constructed. In short Reece saw Richmond's *Roman Britain* being driven by established 'facts', one usually drawn from the literary sources about the island. In this approach, apparently derived from Haverfield, the historical sources are marshalled into an account 'of what actually happened' onto which are grafted selections of archaeological material to illustrate the story. After this, where there is little or no literary evidence, come 'the text-free compilations of the countryside, economics, religion and art' (p. 476). This approach tends to produce, in Reece's opinion, an easy, non-challenging non-questioning narrative, one that is easy to digest. The first signs that it could be challenged came with the publication of A.L.F. Rivet's *Town and Country in Roman Britain* (1964). Its significance, according to Reece, was it broke the mould of 'The One Great Book'. It did not present a cosy, problem-free explanation of Roman Britain. It paved the way for an approach radically different from

---

3. It would be an interesting exercise to compile the number of times where (recent) conference proceedings and other publications are prefaced by assertions that the author is 'bored' with the romanization discourse, or else prefers not to use what has come to be known as the 'r' word but then proceeds to do just that. I fail to understand how, if the problem of romanization is an issue, why there has not been attempted a systematic analysis of what makes certain classes of (material) evidence – or behaviour – peculiarly or exclusively 'Roman' in content and value. Alternative terms such as 'discrepant experiences' and creolization are equally as pointless in this respect, as they argue for the creation of a hybridized outcome created from the meeting of what are still perceived as essentially monolithic, homogeneous cultural blocks; Roman and the other.

that used by Richmond (and according, to Reece, Haverfield – although this opinion might be questioned) and more recently, in the same tradition the likes of Frere, Todd and Salway. Now, in contrast to Richmond and 'the Oxford school', a new generation of Romano-British archaeologists starting with Millett have attempted to break from this generation by writing about the sort of themes that the historical sources ignore. Where there might be some documentary evidence that has a relevance to the subject under review, Reece points out that the archaeologically driven approach runs the risk of misunderstanding or over-emphasising the significance of the material, a problem not restricted to the archaeologists. The problem then, is to what extent one feels that the interpretation of and writing about Roman Britain has to include the integration of the historical evidence, and, by implication the chronological framework and how far the archaeology can stand independent of it. To my reading this was precisely the problem Haverfield was trying to grapple with. His approach, with its emphasis on the accumulation of data, whether it is as inscriptions, pottery, coins, brooches and ultimately excavation was the first steps to breaking away from the traditional primacy of the historical sources. That this was his attitude can also be seen in his criticisms of the teaching of ancient history at Oxford and in his protestations to the Roman Society.

Reece's solution to the impasse he identifies is to reconcile the two approaches in what he calls a 'historical text book', with critical apparatus assessing the context and reliability of much data that has been reused and rehashed over the decades so that the significance and relevance of this sort of material can be relegated to its proper place. To his eyes, this would immediately, mercifully, shorten the vast majority of 'text' books and even force others into extinction.[4] One might add that this sort of approach was in part attempted by Braund's *Ruling Roman Britain* (1996), where the author dissected the available literary sources for Britain in the late first century BC and first century AD to gain insight into Roman understanding and attitudes towards the island, even if Braund is weak on the archaeological evidence. This sort of close reading then opens the way for Reece's second, and in his opinion, far more potentially profitable approach. Citing how Collingwood (but overlooking Ward 1911a) had written *The Archaeology of Roman Britain* without reference to any historical framework, Reece took this as evidence of the fact 'we already have the ability to see Roman Britain as a

---

4.   Reece's argument also fails to note at least Burn 1932, Barrow 1934, Moore 1939 and Mann n.d.

material picture within an ornate historical frame. The frame limits the picture but does not dictate its composition' (p. 477). In this respect, Reece argues that the future of Romano-British studies lies with improving our understanding of the various archaeological histories of the regions of the island. If this were true, then I would argue that coincidentally this was precisely what Haverfield was attempting to do up to the First World War, with his contributions to the likes of the *VCH*, his other regional surveys (e.g. Scotland, Wales etc.) as well as his town surveys. This was before he ever contemplated the compilation of an archaeological history of the entire island in the Roman period.

In the end, if Romano-British archaeology is to (re-establish) itself as a distinct, vital and challenging discipline, then Reece is not optimistic for the future. 'The idea of a single basic text has lingered on because many people want to be told "What happened in Roman Britain"' (p. 476). The problem is '...the general reader, and even the archaeological consumer, craves warmth, status and decoration' (p. 477). Traditionally the sense of comfort was derived from the classics and ancient history, with their emphasis on a higher civilising/cultural plane. In contrast, Millett and his ilk have, in Reece's reading, rejected such props and used less humanistic traditions, ones which in part are taken from the social sciences. In this respect, there are two lines of interpretation: one which used the past to either explain the present or to make the past seem relevant to today (e.g. with the current interests in the colonial experience and in turn such fads as post-colonial analysis) or else to argue in a circular fashion. In this instance, drawing perhaps on a technique used, or certainly a theme favoured, by Collingwood, Reece highlighted the example of Romano-British art. The 'Traditionalist's' approach to it is to define it and to draw from this, with the modern eye, the aesthetics of the ancient Briton (p. 471). Reece's point is that the initial definition is arbitrary and invariably negative about what Romano-British art achieved. Neither of these approaches reveals anything of merit or value about Roman Britain. Instead, his preference is to let the product (of the period) speak for itself: let the producers and consumers of the time and the success of their products be the judge of what Romano-British civilization was about. One can only concur. Indeed this is how Haverfield and his legacy should be treated today; not by looking for romanization but trying to make sense of the evidence.

APPENDIX 1

The Berlin Letters

Introduction

Stored in the Berlin Staatsbibliothek are collections of letters involving Haverfield and a variety of German scholars. There are also comparable collections between other German and British academics, including Ingram Bywater, Henry Pelham and William Ramsay.

The Mommsen-Haverfield Correspondence

The largest extant corpus of Haverfield's letters anywhere is that to and from Theodor Mommsen. It is kept in five files, in which most of the letters have their own index number, but with the occasional oversight. The files, with their contents, are as follows:

Mommsen 46	Bl. 1–22	(14 Briefe, 6 Postkarten). Philologie	(i) 1883–9
Mommsen 46	Bl. 23–54	(11 Briefe, 3 Zettel, 11 Postkarten).	(ii) 1890–4
Mommsen 46	Bl. 55–86	(18 Briefe, 3 Postkarten, 2 Zettel)	(iii) 1895–1903
Mommsen 46	Bl. 87–95	(6 Briefe, 1 Weihnachtkarte)	(iv) undated
Mommsen 11	Bl.1	(1 Korrespt.?)	'auß einem' Sir ...von fremder Hand) to FJH 11.1.89.

While I examined the collection during a short visit in August 1999, the letters are also being studied by Brian Croke as part of his study on Mommsen and Britain. He has kindly provided transcriptions of most of the letters (all but thirteen). A number of texts still need to be transcribed (almost invariably copies of letters from Mommsen to Haverfield, and because of the former's abysmal handwriting). There are 32 letters from Mommsen to Haverfield and 75 the other way round. There are two letters from Haverfield to Mommsen's son, Wolfgang and one from Mommsen to a Miss Anna Parker. The correspondence starts 1/5/83 (FJH to TM, a copy of which is also preserved in the Ashmolean

Collection at Oxford) and ends 26/8/03 (FJH to TM – just before the latter died). The gap between the receipt of letters and replies is often very short, although there are occasions when the time span in longer. In certain instances this is a result of circumstances (either party being away or through illness). Unsurprisingly there are instances were letters have not been preserved. There are also a few undated letters. Most of the letters tend to contain reports on epigraphic matters (normally FJH asking for advice, enquiries about British inscriptions, details about the *CIL* and *Ephemeris Epigraphica* etc.) and Mommsen's request for information about manuscripts in Oxford and collations. Occasionally there are snippets of information about ongoing archaeological work as well as, more rarely, some personal statements. Naturally enough, some of the letters have a bearing on what is argued in this text. Because Croke's work is ongoing, I have decided to keep reference to the letters, and especially their contents, to a minimum, and to where they have a bearing on this text. Where a letter is discussed, the translation is usually Croke's. As the Berlin index system is cumbersome, Croke has also allocated his own numbers to each of the letters, which I have used in the main text. I include here a concordance of the Staatsbibliothek and Croke's system. The letters cited in the text are as follows:

Croke 1	(Mommsen 46 Bl 1–22: 1–2)	Haverfield to Mommsen, 1 May 1883
Croke 8	(Mommsen 46 Bl 1–22: 8)	Haverfield to Mommsen, 21 February 1884
Croke 10	(Mommsen 46 Bl 1–22: 10)	Haverfield to Mommsen, 13 April 1884
Croke 11	(Mommsen 46 Bl 1–22: 11)	Haverfield to Mommsen, 13 June 1884
Croke 12	(Mommsen 46 Bl 1–22: 12)	Haverfield to Mommsen, 20 June 1884
Croke 22	(Mommsen 46 Bl 1–22: 18)	Haverfield to Mommsen, 31 July 1887
Croke 24	(Mommsen 46 Bl 1–22: 20)	Haverfield to Mommsen, 18 October 1888
Croke 34	(Mommsen 46 Bl 23–54: 31–2)	Haverfield to Mommsen, 28 March 1890
Croke 36	(Mommsen 46 Bl 23–54: 33–4)	Haverfield to Mommsen, 3 April 1890
Croke 39	(Mommsen 46 Bl 23–54: 36)	Haverfield to Mommsen, 6 June 1890
Croke 47	(Mommsen 46 Bl 23–54: 41)	Haverfield to Mommsen, 19 October 1891
Croke 48	(Mommsen 46 Bl 23–54: 44)	Haverfield to Mommsen, 5 February 1892

Croke 52	(Mommsen 46 Bl 23–54: 46)	Haverfield to Mommsen, 28 March 1893
Croke 53	(Mommsen 46 Bl 23–54: 47)	Haverfield to Mommsen, 9 July 1893
Croke 54		Mommsen to Haverfield, 14 July 1893
Croke 55		Mommsen to Haverfield, 14 January 1894
Croke 56	(Mommsen 46 Bl 23–54: 49)	Haverfield to Mommsen, 18 January 1894
Croke 57		Mommsen to Haverfield, 25 February 1894
Croke 59	(Mommsen 46 Bl 23–54: 52–3)	Haverfield to Mommsen, 21 March 1894
Croke 60		Mommsen to Haverfield, 8 July 1894.
Croke 61	(Mommsen 46 Bl 87–95: 93)	Haverfield to Mommsen. [July – if it's a reply to Letter 60]
Croke 63		Mommsen to Haverfield, 20 July 1894
Croke 64	(Mommsen 46 Bl 23–54: 54)	Haverfield to Mommsen, 27 August 1894
Croke 65	(Mommsen 46 Bl 23–54: 46)	Haverfield to Mommsen 4 October 1895.
Croke 67	(Mommsen 46 Bl 55–86: 60–1)	Haverfield to Mommsen, 16 November 1895
Croke 69	(Mommsen 46 Bl 55–86: 63)	Haverfield to Mommsen, 10 September 1896
Croke 85	(Mommsen 46 Bl 55–86: 75)	Haverfield to Mommsen, 8 November 1899
Croke 86		Mommsen to Haverfield, 13 November 1899
Croke 87	(Mommsen 46 Bl 55–86: 76)	Haverfield to Mommsen, 17 November 1899 [should this be 2/12/92, as in Wilcken's biography of Mommsen?]
Croke 88		Mommsen to Haverfield, 2 December 1899
Croke 90	(Mommsen 46 Bl 55–86: 77)	Haverfield to Mommsen, 23 December 1900
Croke 91		Mommsen to Haverfield, 26 December 1900
Croke 93	(Mommsen 46 Bl 55–86: 78–9)	Haverfield to Mommsen, 11 July 1901
Croke 97	(Mommsen 46 Bl 55–86: 82–3)	Haverfield to Mommsen, 30 December 1902
Croke 99	(Mommsen 46 Bl 55-86: 84)	Haverfield to Mommsen, 25 March 1903.

Croke 103   (Mommsen 46 Bl 87-95: 92)   Haverfield to Mommsen,
                                        Friday 20 September 1895. [Must

                                        surely be 1894?).

The Mommsen-Pelham Correspondence
There are nine letters, all in English, from Pelham to Mommsen ar-
chived in Berlin. The earliest is dated 26 November 1887, the latest 26
August 1894 with three undated.

The Mommsen-Ramsay Correspondence
There are approximately 149 letters between Ramsay and Mommsen
archived in Berlin. Like the Haverfield and Pelham collections there,
they have been checked by Croke who has been unable to locate the
parallel Ramsay collection in the UK, and which makes the Berlin collection all the more important. The earliest letter appears to be
January 1883, the latest August 1901, with seventeen undated. Superficially there is nothing of interest in the letters concerning Haverfield
but. again, there are odd snippets about archaeology at Oxford.

APPENDIX 2

Haverfield and *The Antiquary*

(a) *The Antiquary*

In the mid-1880s, prior to Haverfield's return to Oxford, and presumably in response to a (growing) market for 'popular' archaeological-antiquarian publications that went beyond the proliferation of the more high-brow regional journals, *The Antiquary* was launched. The following passage is the preface to the first issue written by its editor, Edward Walford. It is repeated here in its entirety for a number of reasons. It defines in one relatively short piece what archaeology and antiquarianism was thought to be at a time when standards in fieldwork and the reporting of it are supposed to have improved from their rather parlous state at the start of the century. This introduction thus highlights the sort of problems that Haverfield had to face in trying to improve standards. Agreeing to contribute, from 1890 onwards, quarterly statements on recent discoveries and publications to its readership, this was Haverfield's first step towards establishing himself as the authority on the island's Roman archaeology.

> 'Out of monuments, names, wordes, proverbs, traditions, private recordes and evidences, fragments of stories, passages of books, and the like, we doe save and recover somewhat from the deluge of time' – Lord Bacon

> 'Time doth consecrate;
> And what is grey with age becomes religion' – Schiller

As a Preface to the First Volume of *The Antiquary*, I think that I cannot do better than reprint my original Prospectus.

It is with a firm belief in the above sentiments that *The Antiquary* has been projected. In spite of the fact that this age lives so much in the present, worships progress so keenly, and looks forward to further progress so hopefully, there is in the breast of our 'nation of shopkeepers' a deep-seated reverence for antiquity, a *religio loci*, which shows itself in the popular devotion to ancient art, whether in architecture, in painting, in design, or in furniture, and in the eager reception accorded to fresh discoveries of relics or works of antiquarian interest, and which finds its expression in the hearty and general welcome accorded year after year to our leading Archaeological Societies when they make their annual excursions and hold their 'Congresses' in pleasant places.

It is hoped that a magazine devoted to the work of cherishing and fostering the antiquarian spirit in the various paths of inquiry and research, will meet with the support which it aspires to merit. *The Gentleman's Magazine* has for some time ceased to fill the position which *Sylvanus Urban* once held as the organ of all students of antiquity; and we desire reverently but hopefully to take up the work which he too hastily abandoned.

We shall not, however, allow ourselves to be so restricted in our choice of subjects as was our predecessor half a century ago. We have many other questions to discuss which were unknown to our grandfathers, or at all events unappreciated by them. The more intelligent study of History, the wide spread of Art education, the increased interest felt in the study of local traditions and dialects, as shown in the establishment of societies for promoting it; these and other causes have enlarged not only our sphere of knowledge but also our sympathies.

Our pages will furnish original papers on such subjects as fall within the scope of our Magazine, as indicated generally in the following list; and our columns will also be freely open to correspondence to Old Abbeys, Alchemy and Witchcraft, Ancient Ballads and Drama, Ancient Castles and Seats, Local Antiquities, Archaeology, Architecture, Arms and Armour, Ancient and Modern Art, Articles of Vertu, Autographs, Bells, Books and Bookbinding, Bibliography, Eccentric and Forgotten Biography, British and Anglo-Saxon Literature, The Calendar, Cathedrals, Ceramic Art, Church Furniture, Church Restoration, Curiosa, Dress and Vestments, Early Voyages and Discoveries, Early Printing and Block Books, Epitaphs and Inscriptions, Engravings, Excavations and Explorations at Home and Abroad; Exhibitions of Paintings, Sculptures, &c.; Family Pedigrees, Genealogy, Heraldry, Illuminated MSS., Inns and Hostelries, Letters and Extracts from Family Archives, Local Traditions and Folk Lore, Manorial Customs and Tenures, Meetings of Learned Societies, Monumental Brasses, Numismatics, Obituary Notices of Antiquaries, Old English Poets, Travellers &c., Parish Registers, Picture and Art Sales, Provincial Dialects, Archaeological and Historical Books, Seals, and English and Foreign Topography.

On all these subjects we shall endeavour as well to elicit the opinions of others as to teach and supply information ourselves; and we trust that our pages will form a medium of intercommunion between persons of common tastes and pursuits wherever the English language is spoken.

With this object in view we invite correspondence from those who have a right to speak on their special subjects because they have studied them deeply and lovingly; and we do not doubt that the result will be acceptable to a large and increasing number of readers. It is hoped that in this respect our efforts will be largely seconded by the secretaries and correspondents of local societies.

We shall provide a column for inquiries on all subjects of antiquarian interest, without in any way trenching on the domain of our pleasant and instructive contemporary, *Notes and Queries*, for whom we feel a love and veneration second only to that which we reserve for the laced coat and ruffles of *Sylvanus Urban*. In another column our Subscribers can make known their wants of scarce volumes, engravings, prints, &c. We shall also give prominence to all information relating to art sales, whether past or approaching, while books of an antiquarian and retrospective character will be duly noticed, or reviewed at length

It is for my readers to decide how far the above professions and promises have been realized: my duty is to thank most sincerely those writers whose pens have enabled me in some measure, I hope, to keep faith with the public.

(b) Haverfield, *The Antiquary* and progress in Romano-British archaeology

Haverfield's increasingly distanced relationship with *The Antiquary* can be charted through his incidental comments on how Roman archaeology was progressing through the 1890s. The relevant entries are as follows:

Antiquary volume	Roman Britain report	Comment
Vol. XXIII	i (7/12/90)	Haverfield is writing after a request from the Editor. Submission to be every three months and appeals for more information.
Vol. XXIV	ii (5/3/91)	Winter has effectively stopped work.
	iii (14/6/91)	Complains that there are not enough people sending information. Material also being found and displayed without being reported.
	iv (13/10/91)	Silchester and Chester still the most important excavation, the rest being of the second class. The recent literature was just as poor.
Vol. XXV	v (6/12/91)	Nothing of substance accumulated.

	vi (12/3/92)	'even less than usual seems to have been accumulated.' Partly his own fault (a change of residence), but doesn't think he has missed that much of importance.
Vol. XXVI	vii (14/6/92)	Not much to report.
	viii (14/9/92)	Complaints about archaeological congresses and societies spending too much time on tours and excursions at the expense of excavation.
Vol. XXVII	viii (sic – 8/12/92)	Lots of material.
	x, xi, xii (15/8/93)	Haverfield been ill which means that his reports have fallen behind – so will be combining the three missing reports.
Vol. XXIX	xiii (20/12/93)	Only one major find.
	xiv (no date, but April 1894)	Several interesting discoveries
Vol. XXX	xv (14/10/94)	Submission delayed by Haverfield having to complete two major articles.
Vol. XXXI (1895)	xvi (15/1/95)	Last few months have not yielded much
	xvii (10/6/95)	More promise than performance. Numerous and interesting discoveries but not specifically remarkable. Some important excavations about to start.
	xviii (no date)	Discoveries encouraging and 'almost' exciting
Vol. XXXII (1896)	xix (5/1/96)	'For once a lean quarter.' Report delayed by one month in hope of ...'
Vol. XXXIII (1897)	xx (13/12/96)	The year delay caused by factors beyond his control so is a summary of the past eleven months.
	xxi (4/3/97)	Few finds in past three months, but still of some interest
	xxii (10/7/97)	No comments
	xxiii (12/11/97)	Some finds of real importance

Vol. XXXIV (1898)	xxiv (12/2/98)	As winter, few things to report
	xxv (6/7/98)	In past five months, few finds to report
Vol. XXV (1899)	xxvi (18/12/98)	Report has been delayed by other causes, but much to report
	xxvii (20/1/99)	Apologies for the delay
	xviii (18/7/99)	Discoveries not few or unimportant
	xxix (10/11/99)	Lots of results of variable quality, but as a body, valuable
Vol. XXXVI (1900)	xxx (30/11/99)	No comment
	xxxi (6/3/00)	Considerable number of discoveries in southern Britain. Unequal in importance, but excel the usual winter yield.
	xxxii (15/10/00)	Recent results demonstrate the value of the spade and excavation
Vol. XXXVII (1901)	xxxiii (6/12/00)	No comment
	xxxiv (10/10/01)	Non-archaeological circumstances have reduced his ability to compose the Notes. Is more a struggle. Hopes to be able to get things back on track.

APPENDIX 3

British universities and British antiquities

The following is an extract from a lecture preserved in the Haverfield Archive and delivered by Haverfield to the Cambridge Antiquarian Society on 8 February 1910. It is repeated here with permission of the Haverfield Trustees. Whilst there is correspondence in the archive that suggests the Society wanted to publish it, it seems to have remained unpublished. There are, however, passages in it that are reminiscent of public statements Haverfield made elsewhere (cf. *Cambridge Antiquarian Society Proceedings* 14 (1904–10): 140). Part of the lecture is reproduced here not only because of the issues it raises but because it reveals what has been outlined above about what Haverfield saw as one, if not his main, task as an Oxford academic.

> ...the Universities [i.e. Oxford and Cambridge] neither helped nor heeded. In the long history of a splendid and massive erudition, maintained through ten generations, the Universities had no share. Once or twice a University Professor has broken loose and joined the antiquaries, but it has been a Professor of Botany like Babington or of entomology like Wedgwood. In the list of intermittently distinguished men who have held the Camden chair at Oxford from 1624 till 1909, not one of them has touched the national antiquities which Camden loved.

> In part, this severance of academic studies and antiquities is due to geography ...In part again, it maybe due to those fetters which Henry VIII and Laud and Whitgift laid on the independence of the two Universities and which have not been yet wholly and altogether removed. But the evil is not restricted to two special Universities. It is equally apparent in the Universities in Scotland, France, Germany. Its main cause must, I think, be sought in the educated character common to all Universities. The medieval Universities trained students for the three professions in which educated men could win a livelihood and organised for the purpose their three 'Superior Faculties' – superior not in intellectual merit but in pecuniary profit. Modern Universities provide approaches for more professions – schoolmasters, public officials, engineers, chemists –

and attempt a liberal rather than a merely professional education. But the educational work thus required has throughout been a work that stands by itself. The teachers engaged in it have been, alike by habit of life and habit of thought, remote from the world of public men: their methods have been linguistic and till some fifty years ago, their two languages were Latin and Greek; their organisation has been bureaucratic and they have been slow to change. In the interests of education, as they conceived it, they have therefore excluded large fields of intellectual activity and knowledge. Just as they admitted natural sciences only in the primitive and cumbersome garb of conjectural emendations, so they have ignored history and archaeology not directly concerned with classical texts and have classed the study of man' s town or nation or national literature among the interest and amusements, not among the real occupation of a student or a scholar.

Much evil has followed. The Universities, shut up to linguistic studies, have dwelt on the nature of form and manner so long that academic has become a byword for those who fail to grasp the substantial reality of the facts before him, and a contested election or statute is fought not on the principle of many voters persuading themselves to vote against their real convictions. That, no doubt, is harmless. It is serious that liberal culture has been divorced from civic duty and a right understanding of one' s own country. It is serious that the study of history and archaeology, where they have been omitted, have been cut off from their plainest and most accessible illustrations and fields of study. It is serious, that research, moving for long years on linguistic lines of Euclideantemnity, has failed to raise its head at all. It need not be argued in Cambridge, but it wants saying in some other University that education, without research is an ignistatuus. I do not mean that in order to become educated a pupil must do research work. I mean that unless a body of teachers includes some men of learning and originality, some who can and will in the cause of truth extend the bounds of knowledge, its teaching will be poor stuff. That leaven there must be or the bread will be a stone. The researcher and the learned man are not popular in England. The ordinary man and still more, the ordinary woman, thinks them oddities and the educationalist, who ought to sympathize, has often a panic fear, that they will make a mess of his educational system. Yet they are indispensable, and if examination-ridden Universities are to gain an infusion of them, it must be through an admission of the studies of national history and antiquities and literature.

No less harm has come to the study of national antiquities. As I have said, ten generations of men from the days of Elizabeth to the days of Victoria have worked with a splendid result. If there has been little co-operation or combination single men have been as giants. But, except in some of the best books, there have been serious faults, and that stratum of antiquarian activity which has been visible in our so-called archaeological Societies, has often shown these faults on a colossal scale. The workers are, many of them, University graduates. But they have left the University unused to severe or accurate logical thinking and ignorant of the historical framework which conditions the study of national antiquities. Where they have done good work, it has often done ill. England is wealthy and they have been able to afford a decent print and page for their fancies. England has kept to the classical traditions and dim recollections of Latin in Littlego has lent a classical colouring to their compositions. The British people, which combines a real love for an expert's opinion with a complete incapacity to distinguish an expert and a charlatan, has taken them to be authorities. But anyone who has to use their work must at once recognise that much of it is ignorant and slovenly and inaccurate and much of it lacks that sense of the meaning of antiquarianism studies which alone can make them fruitful. Antiquarian has become as much a byword as academic. One praise alone these men deserve. They have saved from forgetfulness much that would otherwise have wholly perished. If they have not saved wisely, if they have often preserved the unimportant and let the valuable slip, they have in a fashion done their best. After all, when fools rush in where angels fear to tread, its not always the fools who are to blame.

I have been criticizing the three centuries which began with Camden – let us say roughly the years 1586–1886. Since their close there has come a great change. In the last twenty-five years our medieval antiquities have received increasing attention in the Universities ...Thus taught from outside the Universities have realized both that ...economic history has national importance and that it can be recovered not from the pages of literary historians but from archaeological work, amidst the fields and earthworks of the countryside ...Unfortunately this growing interest in national antiquities has not yet spread to the earlier, prehistoric and Roman and Saxon remains. Here some of the younger Universities have made efforts. The Liverpool Committee for Excavation and Research in Wales and the Marches has done in two years good work in Wales and it owes its origins and most of its success to the efforts of Professor Bosanquet and some of his colleagues and pupils in Liverpool University. But much more is needed and at once. Recent research has so enlarged and developed the study of Roman antiquities that it is passing beyond the limits of the local antiquary and demands of knowledge and method and experience of the trained scholar. A hundred, nay even seventy years ago it was otherwise; then the amateur could handle his Roman remains with some hope of success. Mommsen has changed all that; the study is now both technical and elaborate. The local antiquary, I think, is beginning to realize this and to understand that the old notion that any Englishman can go anywhere and do anything without any sort of training has broken down as completely in this subject as in many larger aspects of life. The outer world has not yet realized it, nor I am afraid, have all scholars. I heard the other day an archaeologist trained in the British School at Rome deplore the work of a good man's time on so easy and exhausted a subject as Roman Britain. It was a piece of ignorance which perhaps may give our teachers of Greek archaeology cause to think.

The place which such a subject claims in a University is plain enough. It concerns a part of our British antiquities which is remoter from our present life than most medieval matters but which yet ...has some practical importance still. It concerns also a section of a chapter in Roman history just as the study of Greek 'protos' belongs to the preface of Greek history. We need not exaggerate its value. If anyone cares to quote the truism ' a verse of Homer is worth all the crockery of the Aegean' – or (for that matter) of North Britain, we shall only say that their truism is a truism. Greek pottery and Greek sculpture and Roman history have a supreme value and whatever the triumphs in stone for human intellect ...many generations must pass before the world will be rich enough to turn its back on them. But all that goes towards them is, in its degree, valuable. The man who digs Romano-British potsherds deserves the same praise that we give Bentley for excavating the digamma. Distinct from art there is a science of archaeology which aids to the perfecting of our knowledge, now of art and now of history and that archaeology has its place amongst the proper studies of the University both as a subject of research and, in due measure, as a subject of education. More particularly has it a place when it concerns itself with the antiquities of our own land and our own past and when the objects of its study are close around us, collected in our museums or scattered through our fields and downs.

APPENDIX 4

The teaching of ancient history and archaeology at Oxford 1915

In 1915 J.L. Myres, summarized in a lecture, *The Provision for Historical Studies at Oxford*, what was offered in his university between 1913 and 1915 with regard to archaeology and classical antiquity. The following table summarizes the situation. Omitted are most of those entries which list courses in anthropology, post-Roman, medieval and modern British, European and international history. I have retained, however, those courses, which relate to classical antiquity in all its forms, not least because the list of teachers is informative, containing as it does names intimately associated with Haverfield. The figures in the right hand columns indicate the number of lectures per week in the relevant term.

| | | Course begins in | | |
		Oct.	Jan.	Apr.
Primitive Culture				
The Bronze Age & early Iron Age	Leeds	*	*	*
Greek History				
Recent Hittite research	Hogarth	*	1	*
Introduction to ancient history	Myres	*	*	2
Methods & authorities	Myres	*	*	*
Introductory lectures	various	*	*	1
Introduction to the study of Greek history	Whatley	*	*	2
Influence of the geography of Greece on its political history	Toynbee	*	*	1
Greece & Persia, 550BC–322BC	Myres	2	*	*

The Greeks in the west	Dundas	1	*	*
Secondary powers in Greece	How	*	1	*
Greek commerce	Myres	2	*	*
Political institutions of the Greek city states	Myres	*	2	*
Aristotle's *Constitution of Athens*	Walker	2	*	*
Problems of early Greek history	Myres	*	*	2
Questions in early Greek history	Dundas	*	*	1
The 6th century BC	Tod	*	*	2
Foreign policy of Sparta in the 6th & 5th cent. BC	Dickins	*	1	*
Herodotus	Underhill	2	*	2
Herodotus	Toynbee	*	*	1
Herodotus	Cunningham	*	*	2
Introduction to 479–404BC	Stevenson	*	*	2
479–432BC	Tod	2	*	*
Peloponnesian War	Walker	*	2	*
Thucydides	Underhill	*	2	*
Thucydides	Henderson	*	2	*
Thucydides VIII & Xenophon *Hell*. I, II	Grundy	*	2	*
Development of Euripides thought	Prof. of Greek	*	1	*
Diodorus xvi	Walker	2	*	*
The city state after Alexander	Myres	*	1	*

Roman History

Rome, Italy & the sources	Henderson	*	*	1
Problems in Roman history	Benecke	1	*	*
Army, frontiers & provinces	Hardy	2	*	*
Roman religion & folklore	Bailey	*	*	*
Constitution of the Republic & early empire	Haverfield	*	*	2
Constitution under the republic	Grundy	*	*	2
Constitution under the empire	Grundy	2	*	*

Constitutional history with Appian	Strachan-Davidson	*	*	3
Roman municipal sources	Henderson	*	1	*
Polybius	Benecke	*	*	1
Economic and social causes of the fall of the republic	How	*	*	2
Italian land problem	Toynbee	*	*	2
Questions from the Gracchi to Caesar	Hardy	*	1	*
146BC–AD69	Brown	*	*	1
78BC–43BC	Wells	3	*	*
Cicero *Letters*	Matheson	2	*	*
Caesar's Dictatorship & the early empire	Hardy	*	*	2
Caesar The Civil War 44–31BC	Anderson	*	*	1
Roman empire: frontier geography & Monumentum Ancyranum	Haverfield	2	*	*
The provinces: Europe & Asia	Haverfield	*	2	*
The provinces: Asia & Egypt	Anderson	*	2	*
Sources for the period 43BC-AD117	Cheesman	*	*	1
Senatorial & equestrian careers	Hardy	*	1	*
Tacitus *Annals*	Cunningham	*	2	*
The Flavian emperors	Cunningham	1	*	*
The years 80-120 with Suetonius	Haverfield	*	1	*
Pliny *Letters*	Stevenson	1	*	*
Roman Britain (two lectures)	Haverfield			

Aids to the history of the Graeco-Roman world

Greek sculpture – early	Gardner	*	3	*
Greek sculpture – 450–320BC	Gardner	3	*	*
Greek sculpture – selected works	Dickins	*	*	1
Greek sculpture – passages of ancient writers	Dickins	*	*	1
Greek coins	Gardner	*	1	*
Origin of Greek coins	Gardner	1	*	*
Greek vases	Gardner	*	1	*
Classification of the Minoan periods	Evans	*	1	*
Homeric religion & ritual	Farnell	*	1	*
Homeric archaeology	Farnell	1	*	*
Homeric archaeology	Myres	*	1	*

Homeric archaeology	Allen	*	3	*
Excavations at Delphi	Gardner	*	*	1
Early religious monuments in the Mediterranean area	Farnell	*	*	2

Epigraphy, Papyrology & Palaeography

Origins of the Greek alphabet	Tod	*	*	1
Greek epigraphy	Tod	1	*	*
Greek historical inscriptions	Tod	*	2	*
Roman epigraphy	Anderson	*	1	*
Roman municipal inscriptions	Brown	*	1	*
Papyrology	Hunt	1	1	*
Latin palaeography	Loew	2	*	*

English History

Roman Britain	Haverfield	1	*	*
English history before 1066	Lennard	3	1	*

Geography

Influence of the geography of Greece on its political history	Toynbee	*	*	1
Geography of Roman Britain	Haverfield	1	*	*

APPENDIX 5

Mortimer Wheeler and the progress of Romano-British archaeology

Towards the end of completing this monograph I managed to consult one of R.E.M. Wheeler's least frequently cited works. *Alms for Oblivion* (Wheeler 1966) is a collection of essays and lectures put together at a time when Wheeler was becoming an increasingly forgotten figure as a (Romano-British) archaeologist. There are two essays in particular which contain opinions that have a significant bearing of what has been argued in this monograph, notably in Chapters 1 and 11. Their significance lies not least in the fact that they articulate views which Wheeler must have formulated in the years immediately after the Second World War – if not before – and certainly long before his more infamous 'personal' attacks on the state of Romano-British archaeology.

In 1948, as his inaugural lecture (*The Archaeology of the Roman Provinces and Beyond* – Wheeler 1966: 73–98; cf. Hawkes 1982: 260; 262–3) to mark his installation as the first (part-time) professor of the Provinces of the Roman empire in the University of London, Wheeler attempted '…to define a practical approach' to the remit of his post (p. 73). Here it was asserted that Roman archaeology in general approached its subject from the wrong perspective: 'Our concern here and now, however, is less with the central Empire itself than with its victims – victims who in a measure were also its masters. And at the outset, I would get this important matter of orientation clear. It was long our normal habit to survey the Roman Empire through the eyes of Rome or Byzantium, to regard the provinces primarily as imperial problem children with troublesome idiosyncrasies, rather than as integral personalities…' (p. 75).

As part of the problem, he believed Ian Richmond and Eric Birley were working to an agenda created by Haverfield '...both working primarily (though by no means exclusively) upon the seemingly infinite potentialities of northern Britain. This small provincial fragment has already been explored with more loving care than any other part of the Empire and should now by rights be secure from major threats' (pp. 81–2). The idea that work on Hadrian's Wall and its environs was now little more than an exercise in dotting the i's and crossing the t's was to be repeated elsewhere, but still Wheeler argued that Romano-British studies had still not started to address the '...unsolved problems of the Romano-British countryside' (p. 82). But even then there was a sting in the tail. While work might still be necessary, Wheeler puzzled why Romano-British archaeology as a discipline was as important as some would have him believe.

> Even in the present difficult times, more work and better work, is being done of Roman Britain than any other of the Roman provinces. We are certainly cultivating our garden, and there is sometimes a risk lest that tiny allotment should usurp too large a place in our affections. Let us get this matter right: what is the value of Roman Britain in our humanistic or even, more narrowly, in our Roman studies? We are compelled, I am afraid, to confess that that value is not very high ... For the abundance of our ancient insular cultures, the variety of the surviving evidences ...and above all, the geographical compactness which ensures constant and effective criticism, combine to make the archaeology of Britain the best training-ground in the world for the young archaeologist. If Britain is not and never can be a major battlefield in the study of ancient civilization, it is at least the ideal training ground for our field armies. The battles will no doubt be fought elsewhere – on the European continent ...But do not let us turn our recruit, as we have too often done in the past, onto the battlefield until he has passed through our Aldershot discipline. In too many parts of the world ... have I beheld the ignorance and malpractices of the untrained archaeologist. Were it within my power, I would insist upon the qualification *PRB* – 'Passed Roman Britain' – from every British field-archaeologist before licensing him to practice abroad, whatever the nature or period of the chosen objective there. And, conversely, I would insist upon PRBs extending their studies overseas to the maximum many possible, certainly to a far greater extent than at present (pp. 93–4).

The idea of Roman Britain as a training ground in which to qualify archaeological practitioners is reminiscent of Frere's later assessment of its virtues as a training ground (cf. Chapter 1, n.1).

Some seven years later, on the occasion of the Marett Memorial Lecture (*Archaeology and the Transmission of Ideas* – Wheeler 1966: 47–72), Wheeler reprised some of the sentiments he had expressed previously:

> Our trouble is that we are, as it seems to me, becoming excessively insular in these matters …The work which in fact we do is on the whole pretty good within its limits: but its limits are pitifully too narrow. The great Haverfield did us for a time a sterling service in giving our classics a local application; Romano-British archaeology has reached an uncommonly high level of technical excellence but it has diverted into a relatively insignificant channel talent which might have been more amply deployed. Not long ago a young Cambridge graduate came to see me for advice as one about to undertake the study of Roman Britain. My advice was that given once by Mr. Punch in other circumstances. *Don't.* Instead I bade him to take a jeep, go to North Africa, stake out a strip of Libya fifty miles wide and in depth …and make a complete surface record of what he saw there… (p. 50).

The identity of the Cambridge student remains elusive but at least one might conclude that Wheeler was being consistent in his opinions. It is not known how well received – if at all – they were.

BIBLIOGRAPHY

Abercromby, Lord 1901–02 Account of the excavation of the Roman station at Inchtuthil, Perthshire undertaken by the Society of Antiquaries of Scotland in 1901. *Proc Soc Antiqs Scotland* XXXVI: 182–242.

Adamson, J.W. 1930 *English Education 1789–1902*. (Cambridge).

Adcock, F.E. 1927 James Smith Reid (1846–1926). *Proc Brit Acad* 1927: 335–45.

Aldhouse-Green, M. and Webster, P. 2002 Introduction: Archaeology is about people. In M. Aldhouse-Green and P. Webster (eds) *Aspects of the Celtic and Roman World*. (Cardiff): 1–5.

Allan, J. 1949 Sir George Francis Hill (1867–1948). *Antiqs J* 29: 246–7.

Allen, C.K. (ed.) 1955 *The First Fifty Years of the Rhodes Trust*. (Oxford).

Anderson, A. 1984 *Interpreting Pottery*. (London).

Anderson, J.G.C. 1911 Review of H.F. Pelham's Essays. *Class Rev* XVII: 258–9.

——— 1913 Festivals of Mên Askaênoi in the Roman colonia at Antioch in Pisidia. *J Roman Stud* 3: 267–300.

——— 1919 Obituary. Professor Haverfield. *Class Rev* XXXIII: 165–6.

Anon. 1888 Excursions & Proceedings: A pilgrimage along the Roman Wall & Examination on the line of the Roman Wall. Report of the Committee appointed April 20 1886, laid before the Society at Kendal, Sept. 8th 1886. *Trans Cumberland Westmorland Antiq Archaeol Soc* IV: 124–51 and 162–77.

——— 1891 The excavations in the North City wall at Chester. *Archaeol J* XLVIII: 293.

——— 1893 The Roman fort at Hardknott known as Hardknott Castle. *Trans Cumberland Westmorland Antiq Archaeol Soc* XII: 375–438.

——— 1900 In memoriam (Richard S. Ferguson). *Trans Cumberland Westmorland Antiq Archaeol Soc* XVI: vii–xx.

——— 1903–04 A brief account of the foundation of the Academy and the Presidential address. *Proc Brit Acad 1903–04*: vii–ix and 1–16.

——— 1906 Review of Haverfield 1905. *J Brit Archaeol Assoc* XII: 63–4.

——— 1913 John Pattison Gibson (1838–1912). *Archaeol Aeliana* X: 300–3.

——— 1915 Review of Haverfield 1915. *J Brit Archaeol Assoc* XXI: 65–6.

——— 1919 Obituary. Professor Francis J. Haverfield. *Geog J* 54: 395.

——— 1919–20 Francis John Haverfield. *Proc Soc Antiqs London* XXXII: 164–5.

——— 1920a In memoriam. *Trans Cumberland Westmorland Antiq Archaeol Soc* XX: 255–7.

——— 1920b Professor Francis John Haverfield. *The Annual Register 1919: Obituary*. (New York): 208.

——— 1926 Henry Taylor. *J Chester Archaeol Soc* XXVII: 192–5.

——— 1928 Obituary. Sir William Boyd Dawkins. *Archaeol Cambrensis* LXXXIV: 157.

——— 1931 Review of H.J.E. Peake's The Archaeology of Berkshire. (In T. Kendrick (ed.) *The County Archaeologies*. London). *Antiquity* V: 388.

——— 1936 In memoriam (Mrs T.H. Hodgson). *Trans Cumberland Westmorland Antiq Archaeol Soc* XXXVI: 237–8.

——— 1937 Report on the discussion on 'Roman Britain' as a subject of teaching held on January 12 1937. *J Roman Stud* 27: 251–3.

——— 1940 Dr Thomas Davies Pryce. *Antiqs J* 20: 426.

——— 1942–5 Obituary. Philip Laver. *Trans Essex Archaeol Soc* XXIII: 196–204.

——— 1952 Obituary. Professor J.G.C. Anderson. *J Roman Stud* 42: 110–12.

——— 1955 Joscelyn Plunkett Bushe-Fox. *Antiqs J* 35: 283.

——— 1960 To Miss M.V. Taylor CBE, MA, FSA. A Tribute. *J Roman Stud* 50: xi.

Arnold, W.T. 1914 *The Roman System of Provincial Administration to the Accession of Constantine the Great* (3rd edition by E.S. Bouchier, 1974 reprint).

Ashbee, P. 1972 Field archaeology: its origins and development. In P.J. Fowler (ed.) *Archaeology and the Landscape. Essays for L.V. Grinsell*. (London): 38–74.

Ashby, T. 1904 Excavations at Caerwent in Monmouthshire. *Man* IV: 101–7.

——— 1905 Excavations at Caerwent, Monmouthshire, on the site of the Romano-British city of Venta Silurum in the year 1904. *Archaeologia* 59: 284–310.

——— 1906 Excavations at Caerwent, Monmouthshire, on the site of the Romano-British city of Venta Silurum in the year 1905. *Archaeologia* 60: 111–30.

——— 1907 Excavations at Caerwent, Monmouthshire, on the site of the Romano-British city of Venta Silurum in the year 1906. *Archaeologia* 60: 451–64.

——— 1911 A Roman villa near Henley. *Archaeol J* 68: 43–8.

Ashby, T. and Baillie Reynolds, P.K. 1923 The Castra Peregrinorum. *J Roman Stud* 13: 152–67.

Ashby, T., Hudd, A.H. and King, F. 1908 Excavations at Caerwent, Monmouthshire, on the site of the Romano-British city of Venta Silurum in the year 1907. *Archaeologia* 61: 565–82.

——— 1909 Excavations at Caerwent, Monmouthshire, on the site of the Romano-British city of Venta Silurum in the year 1908. *Archaeologia* 62: 405–48.

——— 1910 Excavations at Caerwent, Monmouthshire, on the site of the Romano-British city of Venta Silurum in the years 1909 and 1910. *Archaeologia* 62: 1–20.

Ashby, T., Hudd, A. and Martin, A.T. 1902a Excavations at Caerwent, Monmouthshire, on the site of the Romano-British city of Venta Silurum in the year 1901. *Archaeologia* 58: 120–52.

——— 1902b Excavations at Caerwent, Monmouthshire, on the site of the Romano-British city of Venta Silurum in the year 1902. *Archaeologia* 58: 391–406.

——— 1904 Excavations at Caerwent, Monmouthshire, on the site of the Romano-British city of Venta Silurum in the year 1903. *Archaeologia* 59: 87–124.

Ashmole, B. 1985 Sir John Beazley (1885–1970). In D. Kurtz (ed.) *Beazley and Oxford. Lectures Delivered at Wolfson College, Oxford on 28 June 1985*. (Oxford): 57–71 (reprint from *Proc Brit Acad* 56: 433–61).

Astley, H.D.J. 1923 Obituary Notice. Dr W. de Gray Birch FSA. *J Brit Assoc* XXIX: 185–8.

Aston, M. and Rowley, T. 1974 *Landscape Archaeology. An Introduction to Fieldwork Techniques on Post-Roman Landscapes*. (Newton Abbott).

Atkinson, D. 1912–13 An excavation at Adel. *Yorkshire Archaeol J* 22: 287–93.

——— 1914 A hoard of samian ware from Pompeii. *J Roman Stud* 4: 27–64.

——— 1916 *The Romano-British Site on Lowbury Hill in Berkshire*. University College Reading Studies in History & Archaeology.

——— 1928 *The Roman Fort at Ribchester*. (Manchester).

——— 1942 *Report on Excavations at Wroxeter (the Roman City of Viroconium) in the County of Salop 1923–1927*. (Oxford).

Austin, R. 1943 Obituary. W.H. Knowles. *Trans Bristol Gloucester Archaeol Soc* 63: 271–4.

Bailey, C. 1927 (Sir Thomas) Herbert Warren (1853–1930). In Weaver 1927: 891–3. Revised by M.C. Curthoys in Matthew and Harrison 2004 57: 481–2.

Baillie Reynolds, R.K. 1923 The troops quartered in the Castra Peregrinorum. *J Roman Stud* 13: 168–89.

——— 1937 Review of R.G. Collingwood and J.N.L. Myres *Roman Britain and the English Settlements* (1936). *Antiqs J* 17: 451–3.

——— 1939 Review of R.H. Moor *The Romans in Britain* (London). *J Roman Stud* 29: 271.

——— 1938 *Excavation on the Site of the Roman Forts of Kanovium at Caerhun (Caernarvonshire)*. (Cardiff).

Baldon, E. 1998 The problem-orientated scientific biography as a research method. *Norwegian Archaeol Rev* 31: 79–96.

Balme, M. 2001 *Two Antiquaries. A Selection from the Correspondence of John Aubrey and Anthony Wood*. (Durham).

Bamford, T.W. 1960 *Thomas Arnold*. (London).

——— 1975 Thomas Arnold and the Victorian idea of a public school. In B. Simon and I. Bradley (eds) *The Victorian Public Schools. Studies in the Development of an Educational Institution*. (London): 58–71.

Barker, E., Davis, H.W.C., Fletcher, C.R.L., Hassall, A., Wickham-Legg, L.G. and Morgan, F. 1914 *Why We Are At War. Great Britain's Case*. (Oxford).

Barker, K. and Darvill, T. 1997 Introduction: Landscapes old and new. In K. Barker and T. Darvill (eds) *Making English Landscapes; Changing Perspectives*. (Oxford): 1–18.

Barnard, H.C. 1947 *A Short History of English Education from 1760–1944*. (London).

Barrow, R.H. 1934 *A Selection of Latin Inscriptions*. (Oxford).

Bate, H.N. 1937 Cuthbert Hamilton Turner. In J.R.H. Weaver (ed.) *Dictionary of National Biography 1922–1930*. (Oxford): 861–4. Revised by R. Brown in Matthew and Harrison 2004 55: 603–5.

Beard, M. 2000 *The Invention of Jane Harrison*. (Harvard).

Bédoyère, G. de la 1989 *The Finds of Roman Britain*. (London).

Bell, A.S. (ed.) 1981 *The Scottish Antiquarian Tradition. Essays to Mark the Bicentary of the Society of Antiquaries of Scotland and its Museum, 1780–1980*. (Edinburgh).

Bellhouse, R. c.1992 *Joseph Robinson of Maryport. Archaeologist Extraordinary*. (Otley).

Besson, C.F.C. 1937 In A.W. Lawrence (ed.) *T.E. Lawrence by his Friends*. (London).

Betts, R.F. 1971 The allusion to Rome in British imperialist thought of the late nineteenth and early twentieth centuries. *Victorian Stud* XV: 149–60.

Bevan, J.O. 1890–2 Certain useful subjects of scientific investigation. *Trans Woolhope Natural Field Club*: 211–20.

Bevan, J.O., Davies, J. and Haverfield, F. 1896 *An Archaeological Survey of Herefordshire*. (Westminster).

Bidwell, P., Snape, M. and Croom, A. 1999 *Hardknott Roman Fort, Cumbria*. Cumberland & Westmorland Architectural & Archaeological Society Research Series No. 9.

Bill, E.G.W. 1973 *University Reform in Nineteenth Century Oxford: A Study of Henry Halford Vaughan, 1811–1885*. (Oxford).

Birley, E. 1937 Archaeology. In G.E. Whiting (ed.) *The University of Durham 1937*. (Durham): 65–7.

—— 1949 *The Centenary Pilgrimage of Hadrian's Wall, 4th–9th July 1949*. (Newcastle).

—— 1953 Michael Holroyd MA, FSA. *Trans Cumberland Westmorland Antiq Archaeol Soc* LIII: 255.

—— 1954 In memoriam. Joscelyn Plunket Bushe-Fox. *Trans Cumberland Westmorland Antiq Archaeol Soc* LIV: 310–11.

—— 1955 In memoriam (Frank Simpson). *Trans Cumberland Westmorland Antiq Archaeol Soc* LV: 359–65.

—— 1958a The archaeology of Cumbria and Westmorland. *Antiqs J* 115: 209–14.

—— 1958b John Horsley and John Hodgson. *Archaeol Aeliana* XXXVI: 1–46.

—— 1959 Excavations at Corstopitum 1906–1958. *Archaeol Aeliana* XXXVII: 1–31.

—— 1961 *Research on Hadrian's Wall*. (Kendal).

—— 1966a Sir Ian Archibald Richmond 1902–1965. *Proc Brit Acad* 52: 293–302.

—— 1966b Review of R.P. Wright (ed.) *The Roman Inscriptions of Britain* (Oxford 1965). *J Roman Stud* 56: 226–31.

—— 1981 Richmond. Sir Ian Archibald. In E.T. Williams and C.S. Nichols (eds) *Dictionary of National Biography 1961–1970*. (Oxford): 882–3. Revised by M. Todd in Matthew and Harrison 2004 46: 876–8.

—— 1991 Überlegungen zur Entwicklung der Limesforschung. In H. Vetters and M. Kandler (eds) *Akten des 14. Internationalen Limeskongresses 1986 in Carnuntum*. (Wien): 9–17.

Bishop, M.C. 1994 *Corstopitum. An Edwardian Excavation. Photographs from the 1906–1914 Excavations of the Roman Site at Corbridge, Northumberland*. (London).

Blair, R.H. 1919 (Monthly meeting 29 October 1919). *Proc Soc Antiqs Newcastle* IX: 117–18 and 125.

—— 1920 Report of Council for 1919. *Archaeol Aeliana* XVII ³: xiii.

Blake, L., Jones, A. and Madden, L. (eds) 1990 *Investigating Victorian Journalism*. (London).

Blakiston, H.E.D. 1949 Jones Sir Henry Stuart-. In Wickham-Legg 1949: 496–8. Revised by D. Gill in Matthew and Harrison 2004 30: 521–4.

Blyth, E.M. 1942 Professor A.C. Dickie, ARIBA. *Brit Museum Quart Explor Quart* 1942: 5–7.

Boardman J. 1985 One hundred years of classical archaeology in Oxford. In D. Kurtz (ed.) *Beazley and Oxford. Lectures Delivered at Wolfson College, Oxford on 28 June 1985.* (Oxford): 43–55.

Bonarkis Webster, D. 1991 *Hawkeye. The Early Life of Christopher Hawkes.* (London).

Bongard-Levin, G.M. 1999 M.I. Rostovtzeff in England: a personal experience of west and east. In G.R. Tsetskhladze (ed.) *Ancient Greeks: West and East.* (Leiden): 1–45.

Bonham, V. 2001 *A History of Clewer. Canon Carter Centenary Lecture.*

Bonner, G. 1964 The Crum Papers. *Brit Museum Quart* 28: 59–67.

Bonser, W. 1964 *A Romano-British Bibliography (55BC–AD449).* (Oxford).

Boon, G.C. 1974 *Silchester. The Roman Town of Calleva.* (London).

––––––– 1975 Edwardian management and excavation costs in Britain. *Antiquity* 49: 51–4.

––––––– 1989 Archaeology through the Severn Tunnel: the Caerwent Exploration Fund, 1899–1917. *Trans Bristol Gloucester Archaeol Soc* 107: 5–26.

Bosanquet, E. 1938 *Robert Carr Bosanquet. Letters and Light Verse.* (Gloucester).

Bosanquet, R.C. 1904 Excavation on the line of the Roman wall in Northumberland. The Roman camp at Housesteads. *Archaeol Aeliana* XXV: 193–300.

––––––– 1911 The Roman fort at Caersws, Montgomeryshire. *Trans Hon Soc Cymmodorion 1909–1910*: 1–3.

––––––– 1912 The organisation of Welsh historical and archaeological research. *Trans Hon Soc Cymmodorion 1910–1911*: 125–9.

––––––– 1920 Francis John Haverfield. *Archaeol Aeliana* XVII: 137–43.

Boucher, D. 1989 *The Social and Political Thought of R.G. Collingwood.* (Cambridge).

Boulting, N. 1976 The laws delays: conservationist legislation in the British Isles. In J. Fawcett (ed.) *The Future of the Past: Attitudes to Conservation 1174–1974.* (London): 9–33.

Bowden, M. 2001 Mapping the past: O.G.S. Crawford and the development of landscape studies. *Landscapes* 2: 29–45.

Bowen, E.G. 1969 Obituary. Professor H.J. Fleure, DSc, LLD, MA, FRS. *Archaeol Cambrensis* CXVIII: 148–9.

Bowersock, G. 1974 The social and economic history of the Roman empire by Michael Ivanovitch Rostovtzeff. *Daedalus* 103: 15–23.

––––––– 1986 Rostovtzeff in Madison. *The American Scholar* 55/3: 391–400.

––––––– 1993 The south Russia of Rostovtzeff: between Leningrad and New Haven. In H. Heinen (ed.) *M. Rostowzew Skythien und der Bosporus, Band II. Wiederentdeckte Kapitel und Verwandtes.* (Stuttgart): 187–97.

Bowman, A.K. 2004 Birley, Eric Barff. In Matthew and Harrison 2004 5: 843–4.

Bowra, C.M. 1966 *Memories 1898–1939.* (London).

Bradley, H. 1885 Ptolemy's Geography of the British Isles. *Archaeologia* 48: 379–96.

Bradley, R. 1990 Review of Todd 1989. *Britannia* 21: 393–6.

—— 1994 The philosopher and the field archaeologist: Collingwood, Bersu and the excavation of King Arthur's Round Table. *Proc Prehist Soc* 60: 27–34.

Brand, V. (ed.) 1998 *The Study of the Past in the Victorian Age.* (Oxford).

Brandt, R. and Slofstra, J. (eds) 1983 *Roman and Natives in the Low Countries: Spheres of Interaction.* BAR Int. Ser.184. (Oxford).

Bratchell, M.E. 1969 *Edward Augustus Freeman and the Victorian Interpretation of the Norman Conquest.* (Ilfracombe).

The Brazen Nose 1919 (Haverfield). *The Brazen Nose* III. November: 5–7.

Breasted, J.H. 1928 David Hogarth. *Geog Rev* 18: 159–61.

Breeze, D.J. 1993 Ancient monuments legislation. In J. Hunter and I. Ralston (eds) *Archaeological Resource Management in the United Kingdom. An Introduction.* (Stroud): 44–55.

—— 2003 John Collingwood Bruce and the study of Hadrian's Wall. *Britannia* 34: 1–18.

Brock, M.G. and Curthoys M. (eds) 1997 *The History of the University of Oxford. Vol. VI. Nineteenth-Century Oxford, Part 1.* (Oxford)

—— 2000 *The History of the University of Oxford. Vol. VII. Nineteenth Century Oxford. Pt. 2.* (Oxford).

Brodie, W. 1924 *Kelvinside Academy 1878–1923.* (Glasgow).

Brogan, O. 1933–4 An introduction to the Roman land frontier in Germany. *Greece & Rome* 3: 23–36.

—— 1935 The Roman limes in Germany. *Archaeol J* 92: 1–41.

Brown, M. (ed.) 1991 *The Letters of T.E. Lawrence.* (Oxford).

Browning M. 1989 Archaeology historicized: Romano-British frontier studies and German historiography at the turn of the century. In V.A. Maxfield and M.J. Dobson (eds) *Roman Frontier Studies 1989. Proceedings of the XVth International Congress of Roman Frontier Studies.* (Exeter): 354–7.

—— 1995 A Baconian revolution. Collingwood and Romano-British studies. In D. Boucher, J. Connelly and T. Madood (eds) *Philosophy, History and Civilization. Interdisciplinary Perspectives on R.G. Collingwood.* (Cardiff): 330–63.

Bruce-Mitford R. 1971 Envoi. In G. de G. Sieveking (ed.) *Prehistoric and Roman Studies Commemorating the Opening of the Dept of Prehistoric and Romano-British Antiquities.* (London): 8–15.

Brunt, P.A. 1964–5 Reflections on British and Roman imperialism. *Comparative Studies in Society and History* VII: 267–88.

Bruton, F.A. 1908 and 1911 *Excavations of the Roman Fort at Castleshaw.* (1st and 2nd Reports, Manchester).

—— 1909a *The Roman Fort at Manchester.* (Manchester).

—— 1909b *Excavations at Toothill and Melandra. Second Annual Report.* Classical Association of England & Wales. (Manchester).

—— 1911 *The Year's Work in Classical Studies.*

—— 1912 *The Year's Work in Classical Studies.*

—— 1919 Appreciation. *The Manchester Guardian*, October 4.

631

———— 1920 Roman Britain. In W.H.S. Jones (ed.) *The Year's Work in Classical Studies 1918–1919*. (London): 71–4.

Burn, A.R. 1932 *The Romans in Britain. An Anthology of Inscriptions*. (2nd edition, 1969; London).

Burrow, J.W. 1981 *A Liberal Descent: Victorian Historians and the English Past*. (Cambridge).

Burrows, M. 1890 Oxford as a factor in the progress of archaeology. *Archaeol J* 47: 351–8.

Bury, J.B. 1906 Review of Haverfield 1923. *English Hist Rev* 21: 759–60.

Bushe-Fox J.P. 1913a *Excavations on the Site of the Roman Town at Wroxeter in 1912*. Report of the Research Committee of the Society of Antiquaries of London. No.I. (Oxford).

———— 1913b The use of samian pottery in dating the early Roman occupation of the north of Britain. *Archaeologia* 64: 295–314.

———— 1914 *Second Report on the Site of the Roman Town at Wroxeter in 1913*. Report of the Research Committee of the Society of Antiquaries of London. No.II. (Oxford).

———— 1916 *Third Report on the Site of the Roman Town at Wroxeter in 1915*. Report of the Research Committee of the Society of Antiquaries of London. No.iv. (Oxford).

———— 1925 *Excavation of the Late Celtic Urn Field at Swarling, Kent*. Report of the Research Committee of the Society of Antiquaries of London. No.V. (Oxford).

———— 1926 *Report of the Excavations of the Roman Fort at Richborough*. Report of the Research Committee of the Society of Antiquaries of London No. VI. (Oxford).

———— 1928 *Report of the Excavations of the Roman Fort at Richborough*. Report of the Research Committee of the Society of Antiquaries of London No. VII. (Oxford).

———— 1932 *Report of the Excavations of the Roman Fort at Richborough*. Report of the Research Committee of the Society of Antiquaries of London No. X. (Oxford).

Bywater, I. 1894a Nettleship Henry. In S. Lee (ed.) *Dictionary of National Biography XL (Myllar–Nicholls)*. (London): 236–8. Revised by R. Stearn in Matthew and Harrison 2004 9: 453–4.

———— 1894b Conington, John. In L. Stephen (ed.) *Dictionary of National Biography XII (Condor–Craigie)*. (London): 13–17. Rewritten by R. Smail in Matthew and Harrison 2004 12: 954–6.

Caird, G.B. 1974 Charles Harold Dodd, 1884–1973. *Proc Brit Acad* 60: 497–510.

Calder, W. 1952 Obituary. J.G.C. Anderson 1870–1952. *The Oxford Magazine* 22 May.

Cannadine, D. 2001 *Orientalism. How the British Saw Their Empire*. (London).

Cannan, C. and Allen, P.S. 1918 Obituary (Ingram Bywater). *J Philol* XXXIV: 1–11.

Carmichael, Lord 1919–20 Anniversary Meeting. *Proc Soc Antiqs Scotland*⁵ LIV: 5: 1–11.

Carnarvon, Lord and Woolley, C.L. 1913 Excavations on Beacon Hill, Hampshire, in August 1912. *Man* XIII: 8–10.

Chambers, C.D. 1920 Romano-British dovecots. *J Roman Stud* 10: 189–93

Chapman, W. 1989a Towards an institutional history of archaeology: British archaeologists and allied interests in the 1860s. In Christenson 1989: 127–35.

—— 1989b The organisational context in the history of archaeology. Pitt-Rivers and other archaeologists in the 1860s. *Antiqs J* 69: 23–42.

Charlesworth, M.P. 1949 *The Lost Province or the Worth of Britain*. (Cardiff).

Cheesman, G.L. 1913a The family of the Caristanii at Antioch in Pisidia. *J Roman Stud* 3: 253–66.

—— 1913b Review of Haverfield 1912a. *J Roman Stud* 3: 102–5.

—— 1914 *The Auxilia of the Roman Imperial Army*. (Oxford).

Chitty, M. 1987 A personal record of Roman Yorkshire 1906–1943. *Bull Yorkshire Archaeol Soc Roman Antiq Sect* 4: 3–13.

Christenson, A.L. (ed.) 1989 *Tracing Archaeology's Past. The Historiography of Archaeology*. (Carbondale)

Christie, R.C. 1895 Pattison Mark. In S. Lee (ed.) *Dictionary of National Biography XLIV. (Paston–Percy)*. (Oxford): 58–63. Rewritten by H.S. Jones in Matthew and Harrison 2004 43: 115–20.

Clark, A.C. 1913–14 Robinson Ellis 1834–1913. *Proc Brit Acad 1913–1914*: 517–24.

Clark, G. 1934 Archaeology and the State. *Antiquity* 8: 414–28.

—— 1958 O.G.S. Crawford, 1886–1957. *Proc Brit Acad 1958*: 281–96.

—— 1989 *Prehistory at Cambridge and Beyond*. (Cambridge).

Clarke, A., Fulford, M., Rains, M. and Shaffrey, R. 2001 The Victorian Excavations of 1893. Silchester Roman Town – The Insula IX Town Life Project. <http://www.silchester.reading.ac.uk/victorians> accessed 1 Nov. 2006.

Clarke, D.V. 1981 Scottish archaeology in the second half of the nineteenth century. In Bell 1981: 114–41.

Clarke, L.G.C. 1925 The University Museum of Archaeology and of Ethnology at Cambridge. *Antiqs J* 5: 415–22.

Codrington, T. 1903 *Roman Roads in Britain* (revised edition 1918, London).

Collingwood, R.G. 1913 Report of the excavations at Papcastle, 1912. *Trans Cumberland Westmorland Antiq Archaeol Soc* XIII: 131–41.

—— 1915 The exploration of the Roman fort at Ambleside: Report of the second year's work (1914). *Trans Cumberland Westmorland Antiq Archaeol Soc* XV: 1–62.

—— 1916 The exploration of the Roman fort at Ambleside: Report of the third year's work (1914). *Trans Cumberland Westmorland Antiq Archaeol Soc* XVI: 57–90.

—— 1919 (Haverfield). *Proc Soc Antiqs Newcastle* IX: 117–18.

—— 1920 The provisioning of Roman forts. *Trans Cumberland Westmorland Antiq Archaeol Soc* XX: 127–42.

——— 1921a Explorations in the Roman fort at Ambleside (Fourth year 1920) and at other sites on the tenth iter. *Trans Cumberland Westmorland Antiq Archaeol Soc* XXI: 1–42.

——— 1921b Hardknott Castle and the Tenth Antonine Itinerary. *Archaeologia* 71: 1–16.

——— 1921c Hadrian's Wall: a history of the problem. *J Roman Stud* 11: 37–66.

——— 1923/1932/1949 *Roman Britain*. (with a revised and 2nd edition: Oxford).

——— 1924a Review of Haverfield 1924. *Antiqs J* 4: 435–7.

——— 1924b The Fosse. *J Roman Stud* 14: 252–7.

——— 1930 *The Archaeology of Roman Britain*. (London).

——— 1937 Two Roman mountain roads. *Trans Cumberland Westmorland Antiq Archaeol Soc* XXXVII: 1–12.

——— 1938 King Arthur's Round Table. Interim report of the excavations of 1937. *Trans Cumberland Westmorland Antiq Archaeol Soc* XXXVIII: 1–31.

——— 1939 *An Autobiography*. (Oxford).

——— 1940 King Arthur's Round Table. Final report including the excavations of 1939. *Trans Cumberland Westmorland Antiq Archaeol Soc* XL: 169–206.

Collingwood, R.G. with Haverfield, F. 1914 Report on the exploration of the Roman fort at Ambleside. *Trans Cumberland Westmorland Antiq Archaeol Soc* XIV: 433–65.

Collingwood, R.G. and Myres, J.N.L. 1936 *Roman Britain and the English Settlements*. (Oxford).

Collingwood, R.G. and Richmond, I.A. 1969 *The Archaeology of Roman Britain*. (revised edition, London).

Collingwood, W.G. 1920 In memoriam (F.J. Haverfield). *Trans Cumberland Westmorland Antiq Archaeol Soc* XX (NS): 255–7.

Collingwood Bruce, J. 1957 *Handbook to the Roman Wall*. (XIth Edition: ed. I.A. Richmond: Newcastle).

Comfort, H. 1959 Felix Oswald (1866–1958). *Am J Archaeol* 63: 194.

Conway, R.S. 1906 *Melandra Castle: Being the Report of the Manchester and District Branch of the Classical Association for 1905* (edited by R.S. Conway, with an introduction of E.J. Hicks). (Manchester).

Conybeare, J.W.E. 1903 *Roman Britain*. (London).

Cook, E.T. 1903 *A Popular Handbook to Greek and Roman Antiquities in the British Museum*. (London).

Cooley, A.E. 2003 *Pompeii*. (London).

Coon, R.H. 1934 *William Warde Fowler: An Oxford Humanist*. (Oxford).

Corder, P. 1932–3 School excavations of Romano-British sites. *Greece & Rome* 2: 80–8.

Cormack, P. 1978 *Heritage in Danger*. (London).

Courbin, P. 1988 *What is Archaeology?* (Chicago).

Couse, G.S. 1990 Collingwood's detective image of the historian and the study of Hadrian's Wall. In Reassessing Collingwood. *History and Theory*. Beiheft 29: 57–77.

Cowan, J.D. 1966 (Richmond). *Archaeol Aeliana*[4] XLIV: 1-4.

Cox, E.W. 1891–2 Notes on the sculptures of the Roman monuments recently found in Chester. *Trans Hist Soc Lancs Cheshire* XLIII–XLIV: 91–102.

Craster, H.H.E. 1920 Francis Haverfield. *English Hist Rev* 35: 63–70.

Crawford, E. 1999 *The Women's Suffrage Movement: a Reference Guide 1866–1928*. (London).

Crawford, O.G.S. 1928 Our debt to Rome? *Antiquity* 2: 173–88.

—— 1953 *Archaeology in the Field*. (London).

—— 1955 *Said and Done*. (London).

Croke, B. 1991 Mommsen in Oxford. *Liverpool Class Monthly* 16.4: 50–7.

—— 1994 Ramsay, Mommsen and the Asia Minor of Acts. *Society for Early Christianity, Newsletter.*

Croone, H.A. 1943 Edward Augustus Freeman, 1823–1892. *History* 28: 78–92.

Crouch, D. 2000 Anglo-Catholicism in Scarborough. The Catholic revival in the Church of England. <http://www.st-martin-hill.freeserve.co.uk/dc2.htm> accessed 1 Nov. 2006.

Crum, W.E. 1924 Hugh Evelyn White. *J Egyptian Archaeol* 10: 331–2.

Cumont, F. 1921 Review of Haverfield 1915. *J Roman Stud* II: 113–14.

Cunliffe, B. 1971 *Roman Bath Discovered* (revised edition 1984, London).

—— 1984 Images of Britannia. *Antiquity* 58: 175–8.

—— 2002 Antiquity and Britain. In Malone and Stoddart 2002: 1112–15.

Curle, A.O. 1941 Sir George Macdonald 1862–1940. *Proc Brit Acad* 27: 433–51.

Curle, J. 1911 *A Roman Frontier Post and its People. The Fort at Newstead in the Parish of Melrose*. (Glasgow).

—— 1939–40 Sir George Macdonald KCB 1862–1940: A memoir. *Proc Soc Antiqs Scotland* LXXIV: 123–32.

Currie, R. 1994 The arts and social sciences, 1914–1939. In Harrison 1994b: 109–38.

Dalton, O.M. 1922 Preface. In Smith 1922.

—— 1929 Sir Hercules Read (1857–1929). *Proc Brit Acad* 15: 518–35.

Daniel, G. 1950 *A Hundred Years of Archaeology*. (London).

—— 1967 *The Origins and Growth of Archaeology*. (Harmondsworth).

—— 1981 *A Short History of Archaeology*. (London).

Davidson, M. 1958 *Memoirs of a Golden Age*. (Oxford).

Davies Pryce, T. and Birley, E. 1935 The first Roman occupation of Scotland. *J Roman Stud* 25: 59–80.

—— 1938 The fate of Agricola's northern conquests. *J Roman Stud* 28: 141–52.

Davis, H.W.C. 1927 Strachan Davidson, James Leigh. In G. Smith (ed.) *Dictionary of National Biography 1912–1921*. (Oxford): 512–13. Revised by R. Smail in Matthew and Harrison 2004 15: 306–7.

Davis, H.W.C. and Weaver, J.R.H. (eds) *Dictionary of National Biography 1912–1921*. (Oxford)

D'E. Firth, J. 1954 *Rendall of Winchester. The Life and Witness of a Teacher*. (Oxford).

Demandt, A. 1990 Theodor Mommsen. In W.W. Briggs and W.M. Calder III (eds) *Classical Scholarship. A Biographical Encyclopaedia*. (New York): 285–309.

Dendy, E.W. 1913 Obituary. Thomas Hodgkin. *Archaeol Aeliana³* IX: 75–88.

Dewey, C.J. 1973 The education of a ruling caste: The Indian Civil Service in the era of competitive examinations. *English Hist Rev* 88: 262–85.

Dickins, G. 1914–15/1915–16 The followers of Praxitiles. *Annual Brit School Athens* XXI: 1–10.

——— 1920 *Hellenistic Sculpture*. (Oxford).

Dobson, B. 1997 Eric Barff Birley, 1906–1995. *Proc Brit Acad* 97: 215–32.

Dodd, P.W. and Woodward, A.M. 1920–2 Excavations at Slack. *Yorkshire Archaeol J* 26: 1–92.

Donagan, A. 1956 The verification of historical theses. *Philosoph Quart* VI: 193–208.

Dowling, L. 1985 Roman decadence and Victorian historiography. *Victorian Stud* 28: 579–607.

Dunbabin, J.P.D. 1994 Finance since 1914. In Harrison 1994b: 639–82.

Dunbabin, T.J. 1955 Sir John Myres. *Proc Brit Acad* 41: 349–65.

Dussen, W.J. van der 1981 *History as a Science. The Philosophy of R.G. Collingwood*. (The Hague).

Dyer, J. (ed.) 1975 *From Antiquary to Archaeologist. A Biography of William Cunnington 1754–1810*. (Aylesbury).

Dyson, S.L. 1981 A Classical Archaeologist's response to the 'new archaeology'. *Bull Am Schools Oriental Res* 242: 7–13.

——— 1989a The rôle of ideology and institutions in shaping classical archaeology in the nineteenth and twentieth centuries. In Christenson 1989: 127–35.

——— 1989b Complacency and crisis in late twentieth classical archaeology. In P. Culham and E. Edmunds (eds) *Classics: a Discipline and Profession in Crisis?* (Lanham): 211–20.

——— 1991 Ancient imperialism and modern nationalities in the study of romanisation in C19th Britain, France and Germany. Abstract of a paper to the 92nd General meeting of the AIA. *Am J Archaeol* 95: 310.

——— 1993 From New Age Archaeology: Archaeological theory and classical archaeology – a 1990s perspective. *Am J Archaeol* 97: 195–206.

——— 2001a Roman archaeologists in the 19th and 20th c. *J Roman Archaeol* 14: 710–13.

——— 2001b Review of Beard 2000. *Am J Archaeol* 105: 715.

——— 2004 *Eugénie Sellers Strong. Portrait of an Archaeologist*. (London).

Earwaker, J.P. 1889 *Recent Discoveries of Roman Remains Found in Repaving the North Wall at Chester*. (Manchester).

——— 1889–91 (Inscriptions from Chester). *Proc Soc Antiqs London*: 204–5.

——— 1891 Roman inscriptions at Chester. *Archaeol Cambrensis* VIII (5): 77–8.

Ebbatson, L. 1994 Context and discourse. RAI membership 1845–1942. In Vyner 1994: 22–74.

Edwards, B.J.N. 2000 *The Romans at Ribchester. Discovery and Exploration*. (Lancaster).

Edwards, C. 1996 *Writing Rome; Textual Approaches to the City*. (Cambridge).

——— 1999 (ed.) *Roman Presences; Perceptions of Rome in European Culture, 1789–1945*. (Cambridge).

——— MS. Resisting Rome?: The Roman empire as anti-model in imperial Britain. Paper delivered at *The Roman Empire: British Empire – Models and*

Perspectives at The British Empire Session of the 64th Anglo-American Conference of Historians, Institute of Historical Research, University of London (June 1995).

Elrington, C.R. (ed.) 1990 *The VCH of England. General Introduction. Supplement 1970–1990.* (London).

Elton, Lord (ed.) 1955 *The First Fifty Years of the Rhodes Trust and the Rhodes Scholarships 1903–1953.* (Oxford).

Elly, T. 1908 *Roman Hayling. A Contribution to the History of Roman Britain.* (London).

Engel, A.J. 1975 The emerging concept of the academic profession at Oxford 1800–1954. In Stone 1975a: 305–52.

―――― 1983 *From Clergyman to Don: The Rise of the Academic Profession in Nineteenth-Century Oxford.* (Oxford).

Es, W.A. van 1983 Introduction. In Brandt and Slofstra 1983: 1–10.

Estyn Evans, E. 1975 Highland landscapes; habitat and heritage. In J.G. Evans, S. Limbrey and H. Cleere (eds) *The Effect of Man on the Landscape: the Highland Zone.* CBA Research Report 11 (London): 1–5.

Evans, A. 1896 On two fibulae of Celtic fabric from Aesica. *Archaeologia* 55: 179–98.

―――― 1897 A Roman villa at Frilford. *Archaeol J* 54: 340–54.

Evans J. 1891 The progress of archaeology. Opening address of the antiquarian section of the Edinburgh meeting. *Archaeol J* 48: 251–62.

―――― 1892 An archaeological survey of Herefordshire. *Archaeologia* 3 (sic): 245–62.

Evans, J. 1943 *Time and Chance: The Story of Arthur Evans and his Forebears.* (London).

―――― 1949 The Royal Archaeological Institute. A retrospect. *Antiqs J* 106: 1–11.

―――― 1956 *A History of the Society of Antiquaries.* (Oxford).

Evelyn White, C.H. 1902 Some recently discovered earthworks, the supposed site of a Roman encampment at Cottenham, Cambs. *J Brit Archaeol Assoc* 7: 93–102; 167–78.

―――― 1904 Earthworks at Cottenham, Camb., the supposed site of a Roman camp or settlement. *Trans Cambridge Huntingdon Archaeol Soc* 1: 55–76; 85.

Evelyn White, H. 1913 Castell Collen fort. *Class Rev* 27: 284–5

―――― 1914 Excavations at Castell Collen, Llandridod Wells. *Archaeol Cambrensis* XIV: 1–58.

Ewing, H. 1999 Pitzhanger Manor. In M. Richardson and M. Stevens (eds) *John Soane. Master of Space and Light.* (London): 142–9.

Faber, G. 1957 *Jowett. A Portrait with Background.* (London).

Farnell, L.R. 1934 *An Oxonian Looks Back.* (Oxford).

Ferguson, N. 1998a *The Pity of War.* (London).

―――― 1998b Battle of the dons of war. *The Times Higher Education Supplement.* October 30: 18–19.

Ferguson, R.S. 1893 An archaeological survey of Cumberland and Westmorland. *Archaeologia* 3: 485–538.

Finkelstein, D. 2002 *The House of Blackwood: Author-Publisher Relations in the Victorian Era.* (Pennsylvania).

Fisher, H.A.L. 1912 Powell, Frederick York. In S. Lee (ed.) *Dictionary of National Biography. Second Supplement III (Neil–Young)*. (Oxford): 129–32. Revised by C. Larrington in Matthew and Harrison 2004 45: 91–4.

—— 1917 *British Universities and the War. A Record and its Meaning*. (London).

—— 1940 *An Unfinished Biography*. (Oxford).

Flecker, H. 1926 *The Letters of James Elroy Flecker to Frank Savery* (with an introduction by Helle Flecker). (London).

Fletcher, C.R.L. 1928 D.G. Hogarth. RGS President 1925–1927. *Geog J* 31: 321–44.

Flinders-Petrie, W. 1931 *Seventy-Years in Archaeology*. (London).

Forbes, U.A. and Burmester, A.C. 1904 *Our Roman Highways*. (London).

Forster, R.H. 1908 The Corbridge Excavations 1907. *J Brit Archaeol Assoc* XIV: 1–18.

—— 1912 The Corbridge excavations 1912. *Archaeol J* 69: 520–5.

Forster, R.H. and Clift, J.N. 1909–11 The forum at Corstopitum. *Proc Soc Antiqs London* XXIII: 291–4.

Forster, R.H. and Knowles, W.H. 1910 Corstopitum. Report on the excavations in 1909. *Archaeol Aeliana³* VI: 205–72.

—— 1911 Corstopitum. Report on the excavations in 1910. *Archaeol Aeliana³* VII: 143–267.

—— 1912 Corstopitum. Report on the excavations in 1911. *Archaeol Aeliana³* VIII: 137–263.

—— 1913 Corstopitum. Report on the excavations in 1912. *Archaeol Aeliana³* IX: 230–80.

—— 1914 Corstopitum. Report on the excavations in 1913. *Archaeol Aeliana³* XI: 279–306.

Foster, J. 1986 *The Lexden Tumulus. A reappraisal of an Iron Age burial from Colchester, Essex*. BAR Brit Ser. 156. (Oxford).

Fox, A. 2000 *Aileen – a Pioneering Archaeologist. The Autobiography of Aileen Fox*. (Trowbridge).

Fox, C. 1933 *The Personality of Britain: Its Influence on Inhabitants and Invader in Prehistoric and Early Historic Times*. (Cardiff).

Fox, E. *et al* 1968 Richmond, Wheeler and Hod Hill. *Antiquity* 42: 292–6.

Fox, G.E. 1889 Roman Norfolk. *Archaeol J* 46: 331–67.

—— 1897 Uriconium. *Archaeol J* 54: 123–73.

—— 1900 Roman Suffolk. *Archaeol J* 57: 89–105.

Fox, G.E. and St John Hope, W.H. 1889–91 On the desirability of the complete and systematic excavation of the site at Silchester. *Proc Soc Antiqs London²* XIII: 85–97.

Fraser, J. 1927 Rhys, John. In Davis and Weaver 1927: 457–8. Revised by M.A. Williams in Matthew and Harrison 2004 46: 623–4.

Freeman, P.W.M. 1989 *From Provincia to Province. The Nature of Roman Imperialism in the Late Republic–Early Empire*. Unpublished PhD thesis, University of Sheffield.

—— 1991 The study of the Roman period in Britain: A comment on Hingley. *Scottish Archaeol Rev* 8: 102–4.

—— 1993 'Romanisation' and Roman material culture. Review of Millett 1990. *J Roman Archaeol* 6: 438–45.

—— 1994 Pompey's eastern settlement; a matter of presentation? In C. Deroux (ed.) *Studies in Latin Literature and Roman History VII*. Collection Latomus 227 (Brussels): 143–79.

—— 1996a British imperialism and the Roman empire. In Webster and Cooper 1996: 19–34.

—— 1996b The annexation of Arabia and imperial grand strategy. In D.L. Kennedy (ed.) *The Roman Army in the East*. J Roman Archaeol Supplementary Series 18: 91–118.

—— 1997 Mommsen to Haverfield; The origins of studies of romanisation in late 19th-c. Britain. In Mattingly 1997: 27–50.

—— 1998 On the annexation of provinces in the Roman empire. *Classics Ireland* 5: 30–47.

—— 2004 Haverfield, Francis John (1860–1919). In Todd 2004: 432–4.

—— in prep. *The First 25 Years of the Liverpool Institute of Archaeology*.

Frere, S.S. 1967/1978/1987 *Britannia: A History of Roman Britain*. (1st edition, 2nd edition, 3rd edition, London).

—— 1988 Roman Britain since Haverfield and Richmond. *Hist Archaeol Rev*: 1–6.

Fulford, M. 1989 Roman and barbarians: the economy of Roman frontier systems. In J.C. Barrett, A.P. Fitzpatrick and L. Macinnes (eds) *Barbarians and Romans in North-West Europe from the Later Republic to Late Antiquity*. BAR Int. Ser. 471. (Oxford) 81–95.

Fulford, M. and Clarke, A. 2002 Victorian excavation methodology: The Society of Antiquaries at Silchester in 1893. *Antiqs J* 82: 285–306.

Furneaux, H. 1922 *Cornelli Taciti: de vita Agricolae*. (2nd edition by J.G.C. Anderson: Oxford).

Gardner, B. 1973 *The Public Schools: an Historical Survey*. (London).

Gardner, P. (with J.L. Myres) 1902a *Classical Archaeology in the Schools* (Oxford: 2nd edition, 1915).

—— 1902b A British Academy of Learning. *Quart Rev* 195: 98–116.

—— 1903 *Oxford at the Cross Roads: A Criticism of the Course of Literae Humaniores in the University*. (London).

—— 1926 *New Chapters in Greek Art*. (Oxford).

—— 1933 *Autobiographica*. (Oxford).

Garnett, A. 1981 Fleure, Herbert John (1877–1969). In E.T. Williams and C.J. Nicholls (eds) *Dictionary of National Biography 1961–1970*. (Oxford): 368–9. Rewritten by P. Gruffudd in Matthew and Harrison 2004 20: 136–7.

Garnons Williams, B.H. 1934–5 The study of Roman Britain in the Sixth Form. *Greece & Rome* 4: 129–38.

Garstang, J. 1900 On some features of Roman military defensive works. *Trans Hist Soc Lancs Cheshire* XVI: 111–26.

—— 1933 Archibald Henry Sayce. *Liverpool Annals Archaeol Anthropol* XX: 195–6.

Gibson, J.P. 1895 Report for 1894 of the Northumberland Excavation Committee. *Archaeol Aeliana* XVII: xxii–xxxii.

—— 1903a Excavations on the line of the Roman Wall in Northumberland. *Archaeol Aeliana* XXIV: 1–12.

—— 1903b On excavations at Great Chesters (Aesica) in 1894, 1895 and 1897. *Archaeol Aeliana* XXIV: 19–64.

Gibson, J.P. and Simpson, F.G. 1911 The milecastle on the Wall of Hadrian at Poltross Burn 1909. *Trans Cumberland Westmorland Antiq Archaeol Soc* XI: 390–461.

Gibson, M. 1988 Joseph Mayer. In Gibson and Wright 1988, 1–27.

Gibson, M. and Wright, S.M. (eds) 1988 *Joseph Mayer of Liverpool 1803–1886*. Society of Antiquaries of London in association with National Museums and Galleries on Merseyside Occasional Papers NS XI. (London).

Gibson, S. 1999 British archaeological institutions in Mandatory Palestine, 1917–1948. *Palestine Explor Quart* 131: 115–43.

Gill, D. 2004 Jones, Henry Stuart (or Stuart-Jones, 1867–1939; Kt. 1932). In Todd 2004: 524–5.

Gomme, L. 1887 *The Gentleman's Magazine Library. Romano-British Remains I and II*. (London).

Gordon, A.E. 1983 *Illustrated Introduction to Latin epigraphy*. (Berkeley).

Gordon, D. 2005 *'My Dear Haverfield'. The Curle Correspondance (1905–1909) – and Letters from and to Sir George Macdonald – with Professor Haverfield, as Contained in the Haverfield Archive in the Ashmolean Library, Oxford*. (Melrose).

Gracie, H.S. 1965 Sir Ian Richmond CBE, MA, Lttd, DLitt, LL.D, FBA, PSA. *Trans Bristol Gloucestershire Archaeol Soc* 85: 230–1.

Graham, A. 1981 In piam veterum memoriam. In A.S. Bell (ed.) *The Scottish Antiquarian Tradition. Essays to Mark the Bicentary of the Society of Antiquaries of Scotland and its Museum, 1780–1980*. (Edinburgh): 212–25.

Graham, M. 1991 Housing development on the fringe of Oxford, 1850–1914. *Oxonensia* 56: 147–66.

Gray, D.H. 1954 J.L. Myres. *J Hellenic Stud* 74: 181–2.

Green, V.H.M. 1957 *Oxford Common Room: A Study of Lincoln College and Mark Pattison*. (London).

Green, V. 1979 *The Commonwealth of Lincoln College 1427–1977*. (Oxford).

Grimes, W.F. 1967 Obituaries. Sir Cyril Fox (1882–1967). *Archaeol Cambrensis* CXVI: 208–10.

Grundy, G.B. 1935 The ancient highways and tracks of Worcestershire and the middle Severn Basin III. *Archaeol J* 92: 98–141.

—— 1945 *Fifty-Five years at Oxford. An Unconventional Autobiography*. (London).

GSW 1912 Arnold William Thomas. In S. Lee (ed.) *Dictionary of National Biography 2nd Supplement vol. Abbey–Eyre*. (Oxford): 60–1. Revised by A.J.A. Morris in Matthew and Harrison 2004 2: 510–11.

Gunn, B. 1949 Sayce, Archibald Henry. In Wickham-Legg 1949: 786–8. Revised by O.R. Gurney in Matthew and Harrison 2004 49: 158–60.

Gunn, H. (ed.) 1924 *The British Empire: A Survey in 12 Volumes – Each Self Contained*. (London).

Gurney, O.R. 1971 Garstang John (1876–1956). In E.T. Williams and H.M. Palmer (eds) *Dictionary of National Biography (1951–1960)*. (Oxford): 395–6. Revised by P.W.M. Freeman in Matthew and Harrison 2004 21: 551–3.

Hall, J.P. 1923 *Caer Llugwy. Excavations of the Roman Fort Between Capel Curig and Bettws-y-Coed*. (edited by F.A. Bruton. Manchester).

Handford, W.T. 1933 *Lancing College. A History of SS Mary and Nicolas Colleges, Lancing 1848–1930*. (London).

Harden, D.B. (ed.) 1956 *Dark Age Britain. Studies Presented to E.T. Leeds*. (London).

Harrison, B. 1994a College Life, 1918–1939. In Harrison 1994b: 81–108.

────── (ed.) 1994b *The History of the University of Oxford. Vol.VIII. The Twentieth Century*. (Oxford).

Harvey, J. 1982 The buildings of Winchester College. In R. Custance (ed.) *Winchester College. Sixth-Centenary Essays*. (Oxford): 177–82.

Haverfield, F. 1883 A Latin inscription from Nicopolis. *J Philol* XII: 292–6.

────── 1887 Roman Dacia. *English Hist Rev* 2: 734–6.

────── 1888a Roman inscriptions in Britain. *Archaeol Rev* II (Sept. 1888–Feb. 1889): 267.

────── 1888b Scholia on Claudian. *J Philol* XVII: 271–3.

────── 1888c Notes from Krain, Croatia and Serbia. *J Philol* XVII: 268–73.

────── 1888d Discovery of Roman coins at Brighton. *Sussex Colls* XXXVI: 244.

────── 1888e Roman remains in Sussex. *Archaeol Rev* I (March–Aug.): 434–40.

────── 1889a Portus Adurni and the River Adur. *The Academy* 20 April.

────── 1889b Roman remains at Scarborough and Chichester. *Archaeol Rev* III (March–July) 1889: 70–2.

────── 1889–91 Provisional account of the Roman inscriptions found at Chester (North Wall). *Proc Soc Antiqs London* XIII: 205–7.

────── 1890 Roman inscriptions in Britain, 1881–1890. *Archaeol J* 47: 229–67.

────── 1891a Roman remains in local museums. *The Antiquary* XXIV: 168–73.

────── 1891b Notes on some museums in Galicia and Transilvania. *Archaeol J* 48: 1–13.

────── 1891c Re-excavated relics. *Class Rev* V: 65.

────── 1892a Epigraphic evidence as to the date of Hadrian's Wall. *Proc Soc Antiqs London* XIV: 44–55.

────── 1892b Roman inscriptions in Britain. *Archaeol J* 49: 176–201.

────── 1892c On a bronze tablet from Colchester. *Proc Soc Antiqs London* XV: 80–95.

────── 1892d The administration of Roman mines. *J Architect Archaeol Hist Soc Chester North Wales* IV: 80–95.

────── 1892e On the site of Portus Adurni and the River Adur. *Proc Soc Antiqs London* XIV: 112–16.

────── 1892f On the site of Portus Adurni and the River Adur. *Sussex Colls* XXXVIII: 217–21 (Reprinted with corrections from the *Proc Soc Antiqs London* XIV: 112–16).

────── 1893a Professor Nettleship. *Class Rev* VII: 369–70.

────── 1893b A walk along the Pfahlgraben. *Proc Soc Antiqs Newcastle* VI: 78–80.

────── 1893c Discoveries of Roman remains in Britain. *Class Rev* VII: 430–1.

────── 1893d Romano-British inscriptions 1892–1893. *Archaeol J* 50: 279–307.

────── 1894a Review of H. Traill's (ed.) *Social England* (1893). *English Hist Rev* 9: 724–6.

————— 1894b Discoveries of Roman remains in Britain II. *Class Rev* VIII: 189–227.

————— 1894c Notes on a visit to the German limes. *Proc Soc Antiqs Newcastle* VI: 246–8.

————— 1894d On the discovery of a fourth inscribed pig of Roman lead in Derbyshire (with J.C. Cox and E. Hubner). *The Antiquary* XXIX: 218–23.

————— 1894e A new theory of the vallum romanum and murus by Prof. Mommsen of Berlin. *Proc Soc Antiqs Newcastle* VI: 223–8.

————— 1895a Notes on hoards of Roman silver coins found in Britain with special reference to the Silchester hoard. In G.E. Fox Excavations on the site of the Roman city at Silchester, Hants, in 1894. *Archaeologia* LIV: 439–94.

————— 1895b Report of the Cumberland Excavation Committee, 1894. *Trans Cumberland Westmorland Antiq Archaeol Soc* XIII: 453–69.

————— 1895–7 The survival of Roman place names. *Trans Woolhope Natural Field Club*: 223–4.

————— 1896a Early British Christianity. *English Hist Rev* 11: 417–30.

————— 1896b Discoveries of Roman remains in Britain III. *Class Rev* XII: 73–4.

————— 1896c The antiquity of place names. *J Architect Archaeol Hist Soc Chester North Wales* VI: 36–41.

————— 1896d *An Archaeological Survey of Herefordshire*. (London).

————— 1897a Report of the Cumberland Excavation Committee, 1895. *Trans Cumberland Westmorland Antiq Archaeol Soc* XIV: 185–97.

————— 1897b Report of the Cumberland Excavation Committee, 1896. *Trans Cumberland Westmorland Antiq Archaeol Soc* XIV: 413–33.

————— 1897c Roman inscriptions from Aesica. *Archaeol Aeliana* XIX: 268–72.

————— 1898a Henry Nettleship. *Biog Jb Alterthumskde* XXII: 79–81.

————— 1898b Report of the Cumberland Excavation Committee, 1897. *Trans Cumberland Westmorland Antiq Archaeol Soc* XV: 172–200.

————— 1898c Discoveries of Roman remains in Britain IV. *Class Rev* XII: 83–4.

————— 1899a Five years excavations on the Roman Wall. *Trans Cumberland Westmorland Antiq Archaeol Soc* XV: 337–44.

————— 1899b On the excavation of a Roman road in Blenheim Park. *Proc Soc Antiqs London* XVII: 333–5.

————— 1899c Report of the Cumberland Excavation Committee for 1898. *Trans Cumberland Westmorland Antiq Archaeol Soc* XV: 345–64.

————— 1899d Some Roman remains in the Upper Thames Valley. *Proc Soc Antiqs London* XVII: 10–16.

————— 1899e On a Greek inscription from Oxfordshire. *Proc Soc Antiqs London* XVIII: 9–10.

————— 1899f Notes on the discovery of a Roman building in Northgate Street. *J Architect Archaeol Hist Soc Chester North Wales* VI: 281–2.

————— 1899g Notes on samian ware. *Trans Cumberland Westmorland Antiq Archaeol Soc* XV: 191–6.

————— 1899h Roman inscribed and sculptured stones preserved at Tullie House, Carlisle. *Trans Cumberland Westmorland Antiq Archaeol Soc* XV: 461–503.

—— 1900 Report of the Cumberland Excavation Committee for 1899. *Trans Cumberland Westmorland Antiq Archaeol Soc* XVI: 80–99.

—— 1901a Report of the Cumberland Excavation Committee for 1900. *Trans Cumberland Westmorland Antiq Archaeol Soc* XVII: 75–92.

—— 1902a Report of the Cumberland Excavation Committee for 1901. *Trans Cumberland Westmorland Antiq Archaeol Soc* II: 384–92.

—— 1902b The Ribchester temple. *Trans Hist Soc Lancs Cheshire* 18: 197–202.

—— 1902c Two hoards of Roman coins found in Somersetshire in 1666. *Archaeol J* 59: 342–5.

—— 1902d Excavations at Chesters in September 1900. *Archaeol Aeliana* IX: 9–21.

—— 1903a *The Manchester Guardian*. November.

—— 1903b Roman Britain in 1902. *The Athenaeum* 7 November: 505.

—— 1903c Report of the Cumberland Excavation Committee for 1902. *Trans Cumberland Westmorland Antiq Archaeol Soc* III: 328–49.

—— 1903d Liskeard, Legio. *Archaeol J* 60: 285–8.

—— 1903e The Aucissa fibulae. *Archaeol J* 60: 236–46.

—— 1903f (Account of a lecture about Roman Yorkshire, delivered to the Annual Meeting of the Royal Archaeological Institute). *Archaeol J* 60: 382–3.

—— 1904a Theodor Mommsen. *English Hist Rev* 19: 80–9.

—— 1904b Theodor Mommsen. *Archaeol Aeliana* XXV: 185–8.

—— 1904c Report of the Cumberland Excavation Committee 1903. *Trans Cumberland Westmorland Antiq Archaeol Soc* IV: 239–49.

—— 1904d On Julius Verus, a Roman governor of Britain. *Proc Soc Antiqs Scotland* XXXVIII: 454–9.

—— 1904e The last days of Silchester. *English Hist Rev* 19: 625–31.

—— 1905 The romanization of Roman Britain. *Proc Brit Acad* II: 185–217.

—— 1906a Notes on the mural problem. *Proc Soc Antiqs Newcastle* II: 304–7.

—— 1906b The Ordnance Survey maps from the point of view of the antiquities on them. *Geog J* XXVII: 165–72; 173–6.

—— 1907a Henry Francis Pelham. *The Athenaeum* 16 February: 197.

—— 1907b Notes on the mural problem. *Proc Soc Antiqs Newcastle³* II: 304–7.

—— 1907c A fragment of arretine ware found at Bicester. *Proc Soc Antiqs London* XXI: 461–2.

—— 1907–08 Henry Francis Pelham 1846–1907. *Proc Brit Acad* VII: 365–70.

—— 1909a *The Provinces of the Roman Empire*. (two volumes; revised edition, London).

—— 1909b Roman Dolaucothy. *Trans Carmarthen Antiqs Soc* II: 14–15.

—— 1909c On the Corbridge excavations of 1908. *Proc Soc Antiqs London* XXII: 521–52.

—— 1910a Ancient imperialism: Introduction: Roman empire. *Class Rev* XXIV: 105–7.

—— 1910b Military aspects of Roman Wales. *Trans Hon Soc Cymmrodorion 1908–1909*: 53–187.

—— 1910c On the Corbridge excavations in 1909. *Proc Soc Antiqs London* XXIII: 213–15.

—— 1910d The Corbridge 'Pottery Shop' and other notes on samian ware (Pan Rock). *Proc Soc Antiqs London* XXIII: 113–21.

—— 1911a An inaugural address delivered before the first annual general meeting of the society 11th May 1911. *J Roman Stud* 1: xi–xx.

—— 1911b Cotton Julius, F. VI. Notes on Reginald Bainbrigg of Appleby, on William Camden and on some Roman inscriptions. *Trans Cumberland Westmorland Antiq Archaeol Soc* NS XI: 343–78.

—— 1911c Roman London. *J Roman Stud* 1: 141–72.

—— 1911d Roman Britain. In H.M. Gwatkin and J.P. Whitley (eds) *The Cambridge Medieval History I. The Christian Roman Empire to the Foundation of the Teutonic Kingdoms*. (Cambridge): 367–81.

—— 1911e Town planning in the Roman world. *Transactions of Town Planning Conference October 1910*: 123–32.

—— 1911f Roman inscriptions at Bitterne and Minster Acres. *Archaeol J* 68: 139–48.

—— 1911g The Brough idol. *Trans Cumberland Westmorland Antiq Archaeol Soc* XI: 296–9.

—— 1911h Report of the 1910 excavations at Corstopitum: Smaller objects. *Archaeol Aeliana* VII: 176–202.

—— 1911i On the Corbridge excavations of 1910. *Proc Soc Antiqs London* XXIII: 478–89.

—— 1911–12 Report on discoveries of Roman remains in Britain in 1912. *Proc Brit Acad 1911–1912*: 409.

—— 1912a/1915/1923 *The Romanization of Roman Britain*. (2nd edition, 3rd edition, 4th edition, Oxford).

—— 1912b Roman history since Mommsen. *Quarterly Review* 217: 323–45.

—— 1912c Roman London. *Class Assoc Proc*: 103–11.

—— 1912d *The Study of Ancient History in Oxford. A Lecture Delivered to Undergraduates Reading for the Literae Humaniores School, May 1912*. (Oxford).

—— 1912e Notes on the Roman coast defences of Britain, especially in Yorkshire. *J Roman Stud* 2: 201–14.

—— 1912f Review of 'Report of the Inspector of Ancient monuments for the year ending March 1911'. *J Roman Stud* 2: 140.

—— 1912g Zur Zeitbestimmung der Sigallatagefässe. *Römisch-germanisches Korrespondenzblatt* V: 29–30.

—— 1913a *The Romano-British site of Corstopitum (Corbridge, Northumbria), an Account of the Excavations During 1906–1912 Conducted by the Committee of the Corbridge Excavation Fund*. (Newcastle).

—— 1913b Review of E. Windisch *Das Keltische Britannien bis zu Kaiser Arthur* (Leipzig, n.d.). *J Roman Stud* 3: 146.

—— 1913c *Ancient Town Planning*. (Oxford).

—— 1913d Ancient Rome and Ireland. *English Hist Rev* 28: 1–12.

—— 1913e Voreda. The Roman fort at Plumpton Wall. *Trans Cumberland Westmorland Antiq Archaeol Soc* XIII: 177–98.

—— 1913f On the excavations at Corbridge in 1912. *Proc Soc Antiqs London* XXV: 146–57.

——— 1914a *Roman Britain in 1913*. British Academy Supplementary Papers II. (London).

——— 1914b Review of J. Déchelette's *Manuel d'archéologie prehistorique celtique et gallo-romaine* (1914). *J Roman Stud* 4: 232–3.

——— 1915a *Roman Britain in 1914*. British Academy Supplementary Papers III. (London).

——— 1915b Review of Cheesman 1914. *Class Rev* XXIX: 218–19.

——— 1915c The ancestry of Albrecht Dürer. *Burlington Magazine* 27: 78.

——— 1915d Catalogue of Roman inscribed and sculptured stones, coins, earthenware etc. discovered in and near the Roman fort at Maryport and preserved at Netherhall. *Trans Cumberland Westmorland Antiq Archaeol Soc* XV: 135–72.

——— 1915e Leonard Cheesman. *J Roman Stud* 5: 147–8.

——— 1916a *Some Roman Conceptions of Empire*. Occasional publication of the Classical Association No.4. (Cambridge).

——— 1916b Matters of public debate. *The Times Literary Supplement* June 29: 29.

——— 1916c Review of J.P. Bushe-Fox's *Excavation at Hengistbury Head, Hampshire* (1915). *Man* XVI: 45–8

——— 1916d Holt. *Archaeol Cambrensis* XV: 222–32.

——— 1916e Tacitus during the late Roman period and the Middle Ages. *J Roman Stud* 6: 196–201.

——— 1917 The first days of Carlisle & comments on the death of Thomas Hodgson. *Trans Cumberland Westmorland Antiq Archaeol Soc* XVII: 235–50 and 263–4.

——— 1918a Roman Leicester. *Archaeol J* 75: 1–46.

——— 1918b Agricola and the Antonine Wall. *Proc Soc Antiqs Scotland* LII: 174–8.

——— 1918c Early Northumbrian Christianity and the altar to the Di Veteres. *Archaeol Aeliana* XV: 22–43.

——— 1918d Centuriation in Roman Britain. *English Hist Rev* 33: 289–96 = Centuriation in Roman Essex. *Trans Essex Archaeol Soc* XV (1919): 115–25.

——— 1919a The character of the Roman empire as seen in west Somerset. *Proc Somerset Archaeol Natural Hist Soc* LXIV: xxiii–xxxvii.

——— 1919b The Roman road in Eskdale. *Trans Cumberland Westmorland Antiq Archaeol Soc NS* XIX: 28–9

——— 1919c The Tullie House fibulae. *Trans Cumberland Westmorland Antiq Archaeol Soc NS* XIX: 1–16.

——— 1920a The provisioning of Roman forts. *Trans Cumberland Westmorland Antiq Archaeol Soc NS* XX: 127–42.

——— 1920b Roman Cirencester. *Archaeologia* 69: 161–209.

——— 1920c The provisioning of Roman forts. *Trans Cumberland Westmorland Antiq Archaeol Soc* XX: 149–50.

——— 1922 *Catalogue of the Roman Inscribed and Sculptured Stones in the Carlisle Museum, Tullie House*. (2nd edition with introduction by R.G. Collingwood. Carlisle).

——— 1924 *The Roman Occupation of Britain* (The six Ford Lectures – revised by G. Macdonald. Oxford).

Haverfield, F.J. and Atkinson, D.A. 1916–17 The first days of Carlisle. *Trans Cumberland Westmorland Antiq Archaeol Soc* XIV: 235–50.

Haverfield, F.J. and Collingwood, R.G. 1914 Report on the exploration of the Roman fort at Ambleside. *Trans Cumberland Westmorland Antiq Archaeol Soc* XV: 337–44.

Haverfield, F.J. and Macdonald, G. 1907 Greek coins at Exeter. *NC* 4th ser. VII: 145–55.

Hawkes, C. 1927 Excavations at Alchester, 1926. *Antiqs J* 7: 146–84.

——— 1982 Mark Reginald Hull. *Essex Archaeol Hist* 14: 1–2 (reprinted from *The Times* 1 December 1976).

Hawkes, J. 1982 *Mortimer Wheeler: Adventurer in Archaeology*. (London).

Hayter, A.G.K. 1921 Excavations at Segontium. *Archaeol Cambrensis* 76: 19–52.

Hayter, W. 1974 *A Double Life*. (London).

Helgeby, S. and Simpson, G. 1995 King Arthur's Round Table and Collingwood's archaeology. *Collingwood Stud* 2: 1–11.

Hellyer, R. 1989 The archaeological and historical maps of the Ordnance Survey. *Cartog J* 26: 111–33.

Henderson, M.I. 1971 Murray, Gilbert. In E.T. Williams and H.M. Palmer (eds) *Dictionary of National Biography 1951–1960*. (Oxford): 757–61. Rewritten by C. Stray in Matthew and Harrison 2004 39: 912–18.

Henig, M. 2004 A house divided: the study of Roman art and the art of Roman Britain. In E. Sauer (ed.) *Archaeology and Ancient History. Breaking down the Boundaries*. (London): 134–50.

Hepple, L.W. 1999 Sir Robert Cotton, Camden's *Britannia*, and the early history of Roman wall studies. *Archaeol Aeliana*[5] XXVII: 1–19.

——— 2002 John Dee, Harleian MS473 and the early recording of Roman inscriptions in Britain. *Britannia* 33: 177–81.

HGR (and all) 1956 Obituary notice. V.E. Nash-Williams (1897–1955). *Archaeol Cambrensis* 105: 150–1.

Hicks, P. 1996 *Neoclassical History and English Culture from Clarendon to Hume*. (London).

Hill, G.F. 1937 Percy Gardner, 1846–1937. *Proc Brit Acad* 28: 459–69.

——— 1945 Ormonde Maddock Dalton, 1866–1945. *Proc Brit Acad* 31: 357–73.

Hingley, R. 1984 Roman Britain: the structure of Roman imperialism and the consequences of imperialism on the development of a peripheral province. In D. Miles (ed.) *The Romano-British Countryside*. BAR Int. Ser. 103. (Oxford): 17–52.

——— 1989 *Rural Settlement in Roman Britain*. (London).

——— 1991 Past, present and future – the study of the Roman period in Britain. *Scottish Archaeol Rev* 8: 90–101.

——— 1993 Attitudes to Roman imperialism. In E. Scott (ed.) *Theoretical Roman Archaeology. First Conference Proceedings*. (Avebury): 23–8.

——— 1994 Britannia: Origin myths and the British empire. In S. Cotham, D. Dungworth, S. Scott and T. Taylor (eds) *Proceedings of the Fourth Theoretical Roman Archaeology Conference*. (Oxford): 11–23.

——— 1996a The legacy of Rome; the rise, decline and fall of the theory of romanisation. In Webster and Cooper 1996: 35–48.

—— 1996b The shared moral purposes of two empires and the origin of Romano-British archaeology. In J.A. Atkinson, I. Banks and J. O'Sullivan (eds) *Nationalism and Archaeology. Scottish Archaeological Forum*. (Glasgow): 135–42.

—— 1997 Resistance and domination: social change in Roman Britain. In Mattingly 1997: 81–102.

—— 1999 The imperial context of Romano-British studies and proposals for a new understanding of social change. In P.P.A. Funari, M. Hall and S. Jones (eds) *Historical Archaeology. Back from the Edge*. (London): 137–50.

—— 2000 *Roman Officers and English Gentlemen. The Imperial Origins of Roman Archaeology*. (London).

—— 2001 (ed.) *Images of Rome. Perceptions of Ancient Rome in Europe and the United States in the Modern Age*. J Roman Archaeol Supplementary Series 44.

—— 2001a Images of Rome. In Hingley 2001: 7–22.

—— 2001b An imperial legacy of the contribution of classical Rome to the character of the English. In Hingley 2001: 145–65.

Hobhouse, C. 1939 Oxford. *As It Was, and It Is Today*. (London).

Hodder, I. 1986 *Reading the Past: Current Approaches to Interpretation in Archaeology*. (Cambridge).

—— 1995 Of mice and men. Collingwood and the development of archaeological thought. In D. Boucher, J. Connelly and T. Madood (eds) *Philosophy, History and Civilization. Interdisciplinary Perspectives on R.G. Collingwood*. (Cardiff): 364–83.

Hodges R. 1989 The British School at Rome. Britain's centre for the visual arts and research in the humanities in Italy. *JACT Review* (2) 6. Autumn: 8–10.

—— 1990 Glyn Daniel, The great divide and the British contribution to Italian archaeology. In E. Henning, R. Whitehouse and J.E. Wilkins (eds) *The Accordia Research Papers* I: 83–94.

—— 1992 An old European. Ralegh Radford at 90. *Current Archaeol* 128: 337–40.

—— 1994 Thomas Ashby's paradise: Walking in the campagna romana. In *Il Lazio di Thomas Ashby (1891–1930)*. (Rome): 33–4.

—— 2000 *Visions of Rome. Thomas Ashby, Archaeologist*. (London).

Hodgkin T. 1883 The Pfahlgraben: an essay towards a description of the barrier of the Roman empire between the Danube and the Rhine. *Archaeol Aeliana* NS² IX: 73–161.

—— 1892 Suggestions for a new county history of Northumberland. *Archaeol Aeliana* XV: 54–63.

—— 1903 Obituary notice of Mr Cadwallader John Bates MA, a VP of the Society. *Archaeol Aeliana* XXIV: 178–83.

Hodgson, G. 1925 *The Life of James Elroy Flecker from Letters and Material Provided by his Mother*. (Oxford).

Hodgson, Mrs T.H. 1898 Notes on the excavations of the line of the Roman wall in Cumberland in 1896 and 1897. *Trans Cumberland Westmorland Antiq Archaeol Soc* XV: 201–10.

———— 1899 Notes on the excavation on the line of the Roman wall in Cumberland in 1898. *Trans Cumberland Westmorland Antiq Archaeol Soc* XV: 365–76.

Hogarth, D.G. 1896 *A Wandering Scholar in The Levant.* (London).

———— (ed.) 1899 *Authority and Archaeology: Sacred and Profane. Essays on the Relation of Monuments to Biblical and Classical Archaeology* (2nd edition, London).

Holder, P. 1982 *The Roman Army in Britain.* (London).

Hopkinson, J.H. 1911 *The Roman Fort at Ribchester.* (2nd edition 1916; 3rd edition 1928 by D. Atkinson. Manchester).

Houlder, E. 2005 Milestone memories. *Pontefract Local History.* <http://www.pontefractus.co.uk/history/milestones.htm> accessed 1 Nov. 2006.

Howorth, H.H. 1898 Old and new methods in writing history, being the opening address of the Historical Section at the Dorchester meeting. *Archaeol J* 55: 122–44.

Hübner, E. 1857 Die römischen Legaten von Britannien. *Rheinisches Museum* 12: 46–87.

———— 1890 Inscriptions from Chester. *J Architect Archaeol Hist Soc Chester North Wales* III: 120–50.

Hudd, A.E. 1912–13 Excavations at Caerwent, Monmouthshire, on the site of the Romano-British city of Venta Silurum in the years 1911–1912. *Archaeologia* 64: 437–52.

Hudson, K. 1981 *A Social History of Archaeology.* (London).

Hughes, H.H. 1935 Robert Carr Bosanquet. *Archaeol Cambrensis* XC: 167.

Hunter, J. 1975 *John Aubrey and the Realm of Learning.* (London).

Hynes, S. 1990 *A War Imagined. The First World War and English Culture.* (London).

Ingamells, J. 1985 *The Wallace Collection. Catalogue of Pictures I. British, German, Italian, Spanish.* (London).

Irving, T.H. 1995 Selection of Vere Gordon Childe's private letters with commentaries. In P. Gathercole, T.H. Irving and G. Melleuish (eds) *Childe and Australia: Archaeology, Politics and Ideas.* (University of Queensland).

Jack, G.H. 1918–20 Memoir. Francis John Haverfield, MA LLD, FSA. *Trans Woolhope Natural Field Club* vols. 1918, 1919 and 1920: 267.

Jackson, W.W. 1915–16 Ingram Bywater 1840–1914. *Proc Brit Acad 1915–1916*: 521–2.

———— 1917 *Ingram Bywater. The Memoir of an Oxford Scholar, 1840–1914.* (Oxford).

James, L. 1995 *The Golden Warrior. The Life and Legend of Lawrence of Arabia* (revised edition, London).

James, S. 2002 Writing the legions: the development and future of Roman military studies in Britain. *Archaeol J* 159: 1–58.

———— 2003 Roman archaeology; crisis and revolution. *Antiquity* 77: 178–84.

James, S. and Millett, M. (eds) 2001 *Britons and Romans: Advancing an Archaeological Agenda.* CBA Research Report 125. (York).

Jenkyns, R. 1980 *The Victorians and Ancient Greece.* (Oxford).

Jobey G. 1990 The Society of Antiquaries of Newcastle upon Tyne. *Archaeol Aeliana⁵* XVIII: 197–216.

Johnson, P. 1998 *R.G. Collingwood: An Introduction*. (Bristol).

Johnson, S. 1989 *Rome and its Empire*. (London).

Johnston, W.M. 1967 *The Formative Years of R.G. Collingwood*. (The Hague).

Jones, D.R. 1988 *The Origins of Civic Universities: Manchester, Leeds and Liverpool*. (London).

Jones, R.F.J. 1987 The archaeologists of Roman Britain. *Bull Inst Archaeol* 24: 84–97.

Kelly, P. 1981 *For Advancement of Learning. The University of Liverpool 1881–1991*. (Liverpool).

Kendle, J.E. 1975 *The Round Table Movement and Imperial Union*. (Toronto).

Kendrick, T.D. 1950 *British Antiquity*. (London).

—— 1971 'In the 1920's'. In G. de G. Sieveking (ed.) *Prehistoric and Roman Studies Commemorating the Opening of the Dept of Prehistoric and Romano-British Antiquities*. (London): 2–8.

Kendrick, T.D. and Hawkes, C.F.C. 1932 *Archaeology in England and Wales, 1914–1931*. (London).

Kennett, W. 1972 *Preservation*. (London)

Kenyon, F.G. 1941 Arthur Hamilton Smith (1860–1941). *Proc Brit Acad*: 393–404.

—— 1952 *The British Academy. The First Fifty Years*. (Oxford).

Keppie, L. 1991 *Understanding Roman Inscriptions*. (London).

—— 1998a *Roman Inscribed and Sculptured Stones in the Hunterian Museum, University of Glasgow*. Britannia Monograph Series No.13. (London).

—— 1998b The Roman inscriptions of Britain. *Britannia* 29: 451–5.

—— 2002 New light on excavations at Bar Hill Roman fort on the Antonine Wall, 1902–05. *Scottish Archaeol J* 24: 21–48.

—— 2003 A walk along the Antonine Wall in 1825; the travel journal of the Rev. John Skinner. *Proc Soc Antiqs Scotland* 133: 205–44.

Keynes, G.L. and Evelyn White, H.G. 1908 Excavation at Earith Bulwarks. *Proc Cambridge Antiq Soc* 12 (NS 6): 257–61.

Knowles, W.H. 1922 Robert H. Forster. *J Brit Archaeol Assoc* XXVIII: 293–5.

Knowles, W.H. and Forster, R.H. 1909 Corstopitum. Report on the excavations in 1908. *Archaeol Aeliana³* V: 305–424.

—— 1915 Corstopitum. Report on the excavations in 1914. *Archaeol Aeliana³* XII: 227–86.

Kuklick, B. 1996 *Puritans in Babylon. The Ancient Near East and American Intellectual Life, 1880–1930*. (Princeton).

Kurtz, D.C. 1985 Beazley and the connoisseurship of Greek vases *Greek vases in the J. Paul Getty Museum* 2: 237–50.

Last, H. 1953 Review of Kenyon 1952. *J Roman Stud* 43: 231–3.

Laurence, R. 1994a *Roman Pompeii. Space and Society*. (London).

—— 1999 Theoretical Roman Archaeology. *Britannia* 30: 387–90.

—— 1994b Modern ideology and the creation of ancient town planning. *European Review of History* 1: 9–18.

Laver P. 1920 The Roman wall of Colchester. *J Brit Archaeol Assoc* XXVI: 22–32.

Lawrence, M.R. 1954 *The Home Letters of T.E. Lawrence and his Brothers*. (Oxford).

Leeds, E.T. 1940 Reginald Allender Smith. *Antiqs J* 20: 291–3.

Levine, J. 2004 The anatomy of history; R.G. Collingwood and Agatha Christie. Reprinted in *Re-enacting the Past: Essays on the Evolution of Modern English Historiography*. (Aldershot): 253–66.

Levine, P. 1986 *The Amateur and the Professional: Antiquarians, Historians, Archaeologists in Victorian England, 1838–1886*. (Cambridge).

Lewis, D. 1975 Bibliographic list. *Annual Brit School Athens* 70: 177–82.

Lewis, H. 1912 Excavations at Prætorium, Castell Collen, 1911. *Archaeol Cambrensis* XII: 183–98 67.

Lewis, P.R. and Jones, G.B. 1969 The Dolaucothi gold mines 1. The surface evidence. *Antiqs J* 59: 244–72.

Lloyd, J.E. 1946 Introduction. In Nash-Williams 1946: 11–23.

Lloyd-Jones, H. 1972 Sir Maurice Bowra 1898–1971. *Proc Brit Acad* 58: 393–408.

Lloyd-Morgan, G. 1996 The early growth of archaeology in Chester: 1849-95. In Chester discovered. The archaeological exploration of an English city. *Proc Somerset Archaeol Natural Hist Soc* 72 (1992/3): 15–32.

Lock, P. 1990 D.G. Hogarth (1862–1927): '...A specialist in the science of archaeology'. *Annual Brit School Athens* 85: 175–200.

Lyell, A.M. 1912 *A Bibliographical List of Descriptions of Roman-British Architectural Remains in Great Britain*. (Cambridge).

Lysons, D. and S. 1806 *Magna Britannia Berkshire*. (Reprinted 1978 with a new Introduction by J. Simmons: Wakefield).

Macdonald, G. 1912 The Corbridge gold find of 1911. *J Roman Stud* 2: 1–20.

—— 1918 Professor Haverfield: A bibliography. *J Roman Stud* 8: 184–8.

—— 1919–20a F. Haverfield 1860–1919. *Proc Brit Acad* 9: 475–91.

—— 1919–20b Anniversary address. *Proc Soc Antiqs Scotland* LIV: 5.

—— 1924 Biographical note. In G. Macdonald (ed.) *The Roman Occupation of Britain*. (Oxford): 15–38.

—— 1927 Haverfield Francis John. In Davies and Weaver 1927: 244–5. Revised by P.W.M. Freeman in Matthew and Harrison 2004 25: 856–7.

—— 1929/1930 Forsuchungen im römischen Britannien 1914–1928. *Bericht der Römische-Germanisches Kommission* 19: 1–85. (Republished in 1930 as *Roman Britain 1914–1928*. The British Academy Supplementary Papers VI).

—— 1935 The dating value of Terra Sigillata. *J Roman Stud* 25: 187–200.

—— 1937 Britanniae statim omissa. *J Roman Stud* 27: 92–8.

—— 1939 Verbum non amplius addam. *J Roman Stud* 29: 5–27.

Macdonald, G. and Park, A. 1906 *The Roman Forts on the Bar Hill*. (Glasgow).

MacGregor, A.G. 1997a The Ashmolean Museum. In Brock and Curthoys 1997: 598–610.

—— 1997b *Ashmolean Museum, Oxford. A Summary Catalogue of the Continental Archaeological Collections*. BAR Int. Ser. 674. (Oxford).

—— 1998 Antiquity inventoried: Museums and 'National Antiquities' in the mid-nineteenth century. In V. Brand (ed.) *The Study of the Past in the Victorian Age*. (Oxford): 125–37.

—— 2001 *The Ashmolean Museum. A Brief History of the Museum and its Collections*. (London).

Mackay, C.H. 1978 *Kelvinside Academy 1878–1978*. (Glasgow).

Mackenzie, Compton 1931 *First Athenian Memoirs*. (London).

Magnus, L. 1932 *Herbert Warren of Magdalen. President and Friend 1853–1930*. (London).

Majeed, J. 1999 Comparativism and references to Rome in British imperial attitudes to India. In C. Edwards (ed.) *Roman Presences. Receptions of Rome in European Culture*. (Cambridge): 88–109.

Malina, J. and Vasicek, Z. 1990 *Archaeology Yesterday and Today: The Development of Archaeology in the Sciences and Humanities*. (Transl. by M. Zvelebil. Cambridge).

Malone, C. and Stoddart, S. (eds) 2002 Celebrating 75 years. *Antiquity* 76

Manley, J. 2002 *AD43. The Roman Invasion of Britain*. (Gloucester).

Mann, J.G. 1953 Sir Charles Reed Peers. *Antiqs J* 34: 149–50.

—— n.d. *The Northern Frontier in Britain from Hadrian to Honorius; Literary and Epigraphic Sources* (n.p.).

Manning, P. and Leeds, E.T. 1920–1 An archaeological survey of Oxfordshire. *Archaeologia* 71: 227–65.

Marchand, S. 1996 *Down from Olympus. Archaeology and Philhellenism in Germany, 1750–1970*. (Princeton).

Marett, R.R. 1934 Lewis Richard Farnell (1856–1934). *Proc Brit Acad* 20: 285–96.

—— 1941 *A Jerseyman at Oxford*. (Oxford).

Margary, I.D. 1962 Roman roads in Britain. Their investigation and literature. *Archaeol J* 119: 92–102.

—— 1973 *Roman Roads in Roman Britain*. (3rd edition, London).

Marsden, B. 1983 *Pioneers of Prehistory, Leaders and Landmarks in English Archaeology (1500–1900)*. (Ormskirk).

Martin, T.S. in prep. *The Neglect of Richard Neville*.

Martin, A.T. and Ashby, T.A. with A.E. Hudd 1901 Excavations at Caerwent... in the years 1899–1900. *Archaeologia* 57: 295–316.

Matheson, P.E. 1911 Review of H.F. Pelham Essays by Henry Francis Pelham (edited by F.J. Haverfield). *J Roman Stud* 1: 130–3.

—— 1927 Warde Fowler William. In Davis and Weaver 1927: 194–5. Revised by M. Lloyd in Matthew and Harrison 2004 20: 600–1.

Matthew, H.C.G. and Harrison, B. (eds) 2004 *The Oxford Dictionary of National Biography* (Oxford)

Mattingly, D.J. (ed.) 1997 *Dialogues in Roman Imperialism. Power, Discourse, and Discrepant Experience in the Roman Empire*. J Roman Archaeol Supplementary Series No.23.

Mawdsley, J. 2000 *Roman Corbridge. An Investigation into the Excavations of 1906–1914*. (Undergraduate dissertation, Dept of Archaeology, University of Liverpool).

Maxfield, V.A. 1982 Mural controversies. In B. Orme (ed.) *Problems and Case Studies in Archaeological Dating*. (Exeter): 57–82.

Maxwell Lyte, H.C. 1918 Rev. E.H. Bates Harbin, Prebendary Wells Cathedral. *Proc Somerset Archaeol Natural Hist Soc* CXIV: 91–5.

May, T. 1904 *Warrington's Roman Remains: the Roman Fortifications ...* (Warrington).

———— 1916 *The Pottery Found at Silchester*. (Reading).

———— 1922 *The Roman Forts of Templeborough, near Rotherham*. (Rotherham).

May, T. and Hope, L.E. 1917 Catalogue of the Roman pottery in the Museum, Tullie House, Carlisle. *Trans Cumberland Westmorland Antiq Archaeol Soc* XVII: 174–97.

McCallum, R.B. 1943 Obituary (Collingwood). *The Oxford Magazine* 4 February: 160–1.

McCallum, R.B., Knox, T.M. and Richmond, I.A. 1943 Robin George Collingwood. *Proc Brit Acad 1943*: 463–85.

McGilchrist, G.R.B. 1919 The Roman road in Eskdale. *Trans Cumberland Westmorland Antiq Archaeol Soc* NS XIX: 17–28.

McIntosh, J. 2004 Wheeler Sir (Robert Eric) Mortimer. In Matthew and Harrison 2004 58: 436–8.

McNeill, W.H. 1977 Arnold Joseph Toynbee (1889–1975). *Proc Brit Acad* 63: 441–70.

Meiggs, R. 1974 Marcus Niebuhr Tod (1878–1974). *Proc Brit Acad 60*: 485–95.

Meltzer, D.J. 1989 A question of relevance. In Christenson 1989: 5–19.

Mendyk, S.A.E. 1989 *'Speculum Britanniae'. Regional Study, Antiquarianism and Science in Britain to 1700*. (Toronto).

Midgley, G. 1996 *University Life in Eighteenth-Century Oxford*. (London).

Millar, F. 2004 Toynbee Arnold Joseph. In Matthew and Harrison 2004 55: 178–84.

Miller, E. 1973 *That Noble Cabinet. A History of the British Museum*. (London).

Miller, S.N. 1925 Review of Haverfield 1924. *English Hist Rev* 40: 262–4.

Millett, M. 1990 *The Romanization of Britain: An Essay in Archaeological Interpretation*. (Cambridge).

Minnen, P. van 1993 A century of papyrology (1892–1992). *Bull Am Soc Papyrologists* 30: 5–18.

Mirzky, J. 1977 *Sir Aurel Stein. Archaeological Explorer*. (Chicago).

Mitchell, S. (ed.) 1988 *Victorian Britain. An Encyclopedia*. (New York).

Momigliano, A. 1966 M.I. Rostovtzeff. In *Studies in Historiography*. (London): 91–104.

———— 1982 Niehbuhr and the agrarian problems of Rome. In A. Momigliano New paths of classicism in the nineteenth century. *History & Theory* 21: 3–15.

———— 1994 Liberal; historian and supporter of the Holy Roman Empire: E.A. Freeman. In G.W. Bowersock and T.J. Cornell (eds) *A.D. Momigliano Studies on Modern Scholarship*. (Berkeley): 197–208.

Mommsen, T. 1886 *The Provinces of the Roman Empire* (two vols., translated by W.P. Dickson, London).

———— 1996 *A History of Rome Under the Emperors* (edited by B. and A. Demandt. Transl. C. Krozjl: London).

Montague, C.E. 1907 *William Thomas Arnold Journalist and Historian* (with Mrs H. Ward). (Manchester).

Moore RW 1939 *The Romans in Britain. A Selection of Latin Texts Edited with a Commentary*. (London; 2nd edition, 3rd edition edited by W.V. Wade 1954).

Mozley, T. 1882 *Reminiscences. Chiefly of Oriel College and the Oxford Movement* (two volumes, London).

MSG 1937 Obituary (Mill Stephenson). *Antiqs J* 27: 449–50.

Muir, R. 1943 *An Autobiography and Some Essays*. (London).

Mulvaney, J. 1994 Another university man gone bad. V. Gordon Childe 1892–1922. In D.R. Harris (ed.) *The Archaeology of V. Gordon Childe. Contemporary Perspectives*. (London): 55–74.

Munro, J.A.R., Anderson, W.C.F., and Milne, J.G. 1896 On the Roman town of Doclea in Montenegro. *Archaeologia* 52: 33–92.

Murray, D. 1896 *An Archaeological Survey of the United Kingdom. The Preservation and Protection of our Monuments*. (Glasgow).

———— 1904 *Museums. Their History and Their Use*. (three volumes, Glasgow).

Murray, G. 1940a H.A.L. Fisher. *Proc Brit Acad* 26: 455–65.

———— 1940b David Samuel Margoliouth. *Proc Brit Acad* 26: 389–97.

———— 1949 Margoliouth, David Samuel. In Wickham-Legg 1949: 597–9. Rewritten by A.F.L. Beeston in Matthew and Harrison 2004 36: 658–61.

Murray, O. 2000 Ancient History, 1872–1914. In Brock and Curthoys 2000: 333–60.

Musty, J. 1986 The origins of the archaeological periodical. *Current Archaeol* 100: 142

Myres, J.L. 1910 *The Value of Ancient History. A Lecture Delivered at Oxford, May 13th, 1910*. (Liverpool).

———— 1915 *The Provision for Historical Studies at Oxford*. (Oxford).

———— 1937 John Knight Fotheringham (1874–1936). *Proc Brit Acad* 28: 551–64.

———— 1939 Sir Henry Stuart Jones (1867–1939). *Proc Brit Acad 1939*: 467–78.

———— 1949 Fotheringham, J.K. In Wickham-Legg 1949: 289–90. Revised by F.R. Stephenson in Matthew and Harrison 2004 20: 539–40.

Myres, J.N.L. 1951 The man and his past. In W.F. Grimes (ed.) *Aspects of Archaeology in Britain and Beyond. Essays Presented to O.G.S. Crawford*. (London): 1–17.

———— 1975 Anniversary Address. *Antiqs J* 55: 1–10.

———— 1979 *Commander J.L. Myres, RNVR. The Blackbeard of the Aegean. The Tenth J.L. Myres Memorial Lecture*. (London).

Nash-Williams, V.E. (Ed.) 1946 *One Hundred Years of Welsh Archaeology 1846–1946*. Cambrian Archaeological Association

Neilson, G. 1912 Obituary notice of J.P. Gibson, FSA. A vice-president of the society. *Archaeol Aeliana³* VIII: 37–45.

Nettleship, H. 1885 *Lectures and Essays on Subjects Connected with Latin Literature and Scholarship*. (Oxford).

Newbold, P. 1913 Excavations at Wall Mile 29/31. Excavations on the Roman Wall at Limestone Bank. *Archaeol Aeliana³* LX: 55–74.

Nockles, P.B. 1997 'Lost causes and …impossible loyalties': the Oxford Movement and the University. In Brock and Curthoys 1997: 195–267.

Oates, D. 1980 Max Mallowan 1904–1978. *Proc Brit Acad* 76: 499–512.

Oliver, Heslop R. 1906 The Roman Wall pilgrimage of June 1906. *J Brit Archaeol Assoc* XII: 269–81.

Ollard, S.L. 1940 The Oxford Architectural and Historical Society and the Oxford Movement. *Oxoniensia* V: 146–60.

O'Luing, S. 1991 *Kuno Meyer: 1858–1919. A Biography*. (Dublin).

Oman, C. 1921 *England Before the Norman Conquest: Being a History of the Celtic, Roman and Anglo-Saxon Periods Down to the Year AD 1066*. (5th edition, London)

—— 1941 *Memories of Victorian Oxford and of Some Early Years*. (London).

Oman, C. 1976 *An Oxford Childhood*. (London).

Oswald, F. 1940 Obituary (Thomas Davies-Pryce). *Trans Thoroton Soc* 44: 123–5.

Oswald, F. and Davies, Pryce T. 1920 *An Introduction to the Study of Terra Sigillata Treated from a Chronological Standpoint*. (London).

Oswald, J. 1920 (Monthly meeting 28 January 1920). *Proc Soc Antiqs Newcastle* IX: 137–8.

Ovenell, R.F. 1986 *The Ashmolean Museum 1683–1894*. (Oxford).

Page W. 1920 Review of G. Macdonald's F. Haverfield 1860–1919. *Antiqs J* 1: 249–51.

Pantin WA 1939 The Oxford Architectural and Historical Society, 1839–1939. *Oxoniensia* IV: 174–94.

Parker, C. 1981 The failure of Liberal radicalism: the racial ideas of E.A. Freeman. *Hist J* XXIV: 825–46.

—— 1990 *The English Historical Tradition Since 1850*. (Edinburgh).

—— 2000 *The English Idea of History from Coleridge to Collingwood*. (Aldershot).

Parry, G. 1995 *The Trophies of Time. English Antiquarianism of the Seventeenth Century*. (Oxford).

Parslow, C. 1998a *Rediscovering Antiquity. Karl Weber and the Excavations of Herculaneum, Pompeii and Stabiae*. (Cambridge).

—— 1998b Review of M. Pagano *I diari di scavo di Pompei, Ercolano e Stabiae di Francesco e Pietro La Vega (1764–1810): Raccolta e studio di documenti inediti*. (Rome 1997). *J Roman Archaeol* 11: 539–41.

Patterson, W.F. (ed.) 1915 *German Culture: The Contribution of the Germans to Knowledge, Literature and Life*. (London).

Pattison, M. 1988 *Memoirs of an Oxford Don*. (edited by V.H.H. Green, London).

Payne, G. 1888 An archaeological survey of Kent. *Archaeologia* 51: 447–68.

Peck, H.T. 1911 *A History of Classical Philology*. (New York).

Peet, T.E. 1928 Angelo Hayter, MA, FSA. *J Egyptian Archaeol* 14: 323–4.

Pelham, H.F. 1897 The Roman frontier system. *Trans Cumberland Westmorland Antiq Archaeol Soc* NS XIV: 170–84. (Reprinted in Pelham 1911: 164–78).

—— 1899 *Reflections on the Study of History and on the Historic Habit of Mind in the Nineteenth Century*. (Liverpool).

—— 1906 The Roman frontier in southern Germany. *Transactions of the Royal Historical Society* XX: 17–47. (Reprinted in Pelham 1911: 179–211).

—— 1911 *Essays by Henry Francis Pelham* (edited by F. Haverfield. Oxford).

Pettigrew, T.J. 1851 On the study of archaeology, and the objects of the British Archaeological Association. *J Brit Archaeol Assoc* VI: 163–77.

Pfeiffer, R. 1976 *History of Classical Scholarship. From 1300 to 1850*. (Oxford).

Philip, I.G. 1997 The Bodleian Library. In Brock and Curthoys 1997: 585–97.

Phillips, E.J. 1977 The classical tradition in the popular sculpture of Roman Britain. In J. Munby and M. Henig (eds) *Roman Life and Art in Britain. A Celebration in Honour of the Eightieth Birthday of Jocelyn Toynbee*. BAR Int. Ser. 41 II. (Oxford): 35–49.

Piggott, S. 1950 *William Stukeley; an Eighteenth Century Antiquary*. (Oxford).

—— 1958 Vere Gordon Childe. *Proc Brit Acad* 1958: 305–12.

—— 1976 *Ruins in the Landscape. Essays in Antiquarianism*. (Edinburgh).

—— 1989 *Ancient Britons and the Antiquarian Imagination: Ideas from the Renaissance to the Regency*. (London).

Pitts, L.F. and St Joseph, J.K. 1985 *Inchtuthil. The Roman Legionary Fortress*. Britannia Monograph Series No. 6. (London).

Platnaeur, M. 1918 *The Life and Reign of the Emperor Lucius Septimus Severus*. (Oxford).

Potter, T. 1986 A Roman province: Britain AD43–410. In I. Longworth and J. Cherry (eds) *Archaeology in Britain Since 1945: New Directions*. (London): 73–118.

—— 1987 The Institute and Roman archaeology: Past, present and future – an outsider's view. *Bull Inst Archaeol* 24: 71–84.

Potter, T. and Johns, C. 1992 *Roman Britain*. (London).

Potter, T. and Stoddart, S.K.F. 2001 A centenary of prehistory and landscape studies the British School at Rome. *Pap Brit School Rome* LXIX: 3–34.

Powell, W.R. 1980 J. Horace Round, the county historian: the Victoria County Histories and the Essex Archaeological Society. *Essex Archaeol Hist* 12: 25–38.

Prout, D. 1898 'The Oxford Society for the Promoting the Study of Gothic Architecture' and 'The Oxford Architectural Society' 1839–1860. *Oxoniensia* 54: 379–91.

Pryce, F.N. 1914 Excavations at Cae Gaer, Llanwig. *Archaeol Cambrensis* XIV: 205–20.

Pryce, F.N. and Davies Pryce, T. 1927 Excavation of the Powysland Club at the Forden Gaer. *Archaeol Cambrensis* LXXXII: 333–54.

—— 1929 The Forden Gaer, Second Interim Report (excavations 1928). *Archaeol Cambrensis* LXXXIV: 100–39.

Pugh, R.B. (ed.) 1970 *VCH. General Introduction*. (London).

Ralegh Radford, C. 1953 Sir Charles Reed Peers (1868–1952). *Proc Brit Acad* 39: 363–8.

Ramsay, G.G. 1909 *The Annals of Tacitus, Books XI–XVI*. (London).

Ramsay, W. 1895 *The Cities and Bishophrics of Phrygia*. (Oxford).

—— 1911 Review of G. Macdonald's *The Roman Wall in Scotland* (Edinburgh 1911). *The Saturday Review* 5 August: 177.

Randall, H.J. 1946 Roman period. In Nash-Williams 1946: 80–104.

Read, C.H. 1906 Anthropology and the universities. *Man* IV: 56–9.

—— 1919–20 Anniversary (Francis John Haverfield). *Proc Soc Antiqs London* XXXII: 1; 164–5.

Reece, R. 1997 Writing Roman Britain. Past indicative, future perfect. *Britannia* 28: 473–8.

—— 2001 Review of Hingley 2000. (London). *Antiquity* 75: 226.

Renfrew, C. 1980 The Great Tradition versus the Great Divide. Archaeology as anthropology. *Am J Archaeol* 84: 287–98.

Reynolds, J.S. 1975 *The Evangelicals at Oxford 1735–1871. A Record of an Unchronicled Movement*. (Oxford).

Reynolds, L.D. and Wilson, N.G. 1974 *Scribes and Scholars. A Guide to the Transmission of Greek and Latin Literature* (2nd edition. Oxford).

Rhys, J. 1884/1908 *Celtic Britain*. (London).

Rhys Roberts, W. 1920 In memoriam Francisci Iohannis Haverfield. *Yorkshire Archaeol J* 25: 349–50.

———— 1922 The connexion of Celtic with Classical Studies. *Trans Hon Soc Cymmodorion 1920–1921*: 137–48.

Richmond, I.A. 1922 Ptolemaic Scotland. *Proc Soc Antiqs Scotland* 56: 288–301.

———— 1925 *Huddersfield in Roman Times*. (Huddersfield).

———— 1926–8 The Roman camps at Cawthorn, near Pickering. First interim summary 1924. *Yorkshire Archaeol J* 28: 332–9.

———— 1941 Sir George Macdonald. *Archaeol Aeliana⁴* XIX: 177–87.

———— 1943a Appreciation of R.G. Collingwood as an archaeologist. In McCallum *et al.* 1943: 476–80.

———— 1943b Robin George Collingwood. *Archaeol Aeliana⁴* XXI: 254–5.

———— 1943c Robin George Collingwood. *Antiqs J* 38: 84–5.

———— 1949 Thomas Ashby. In Wickham Legg 1949: 19. Revised by D. Gill in Matthew and Harrison 2004 2: 625–7.

———— 1950 Hadrian's Wall, 1939–1949. *J Roman Stud* 40: 43–56.

———— 1955/1963/1995 *Roman Britain*. (2nd edition 1963; 3rd edition, reprinted 1995; Harmondsworth).

———— 1956 Frank Gerald Simpson. *Archaeol Aeliana⁴* XXXIV: 219–21.

———— 1957 *The Archaeology of the Roman Empire. A Scheme of Study*. (Oxford).

———— 1959 Sir Edmund Craster. *Archaeol Aeliana* XXXVII: 355–7.

———— 1960 Roman Britain, 1910–1960. *J Roman Stud* 50: 173–91.

———— 1963 Charles Henry Hunter Blair, MA, DLitt, FSA. *Archaeol Aeliana* XLI: 1–4.

———— 1964 Margerie Venables Taylor. *J Roman Stud* 54: 1.

Riddell, R. 2004 Parker, John Henry (1806–1884). In Matthew and Harrison 2004 42: 697–8.

Riden, P. 1979 *An Index of The Reliquary*. (Matlock).

Rivet, A.L.F. 1964 *Town and Country in Roman Britain*. (2nd edition, London).

Rivet, A.L.F. and Smith, C. 1979 *The Place Names of Roman Britain*. (London).

Robertson, A. 1952a and b Obit. (Stueart Napier Miller). *Glasgow Herald* 24 May = *The Times* 5 June.

Robertson, C.G. 1946 Sir Charles Oman (1860–1946). *Proc Brit Acad* 32: 299–306.

Robinson, E.S.G. 1950 George Francis Hill 1867–1948. *Proc Brit Acad* 36: 241–50.

———— 1959 George Francis Hill 1867–1948. In L.G. Wickham Legg and E.T. Williams (eds) *Dictionary of National Biography 1941–1950*. (Oxford): 391–2. Revised by E.S.G. Robinson in Matthew and Harrison 2004 27: 135–6.

Rostovtzeff, M.I. 1924–5 Review of Haverfield 1924. *American Historical Review* 30: 337–9.

Rothblatt, S. 1975 The student sub-culture and the examination system in early nineteenth century Oxford. In Stone 1975a: 247–304.

—— 1997 An Oxonian 'Idea' of a university: J.H. Newman and 'Well-Being'. In Brock and Curthoys 1997: 287–305.

Rudd, N. 1981 *T.E. Page: Schoolmaster Extraordinary*. (Bristol).

Ryan, A. 1979 Transformation 1850–1914. In J. Buxton and P. Williams (eds) *New College, Oxford 1379–1979*. (Oxford): 72–106.

Salway, P. 1981 *Roman Britain*. (Oxford).

Sandys, J.S. 1908 *A Short History of Classical Scholarship*, Volume 3. (Cambridge).

Sayce, A.H. 1923 *Reminiscences*. (London).

—— 1927 David George Hogarth (1862–1927). *Proc Brit Acad 1927*: 379–83.

Scargill, D.I. 1976 The Royal Geographical Society and the foundation of geography at Oxford. *Geog J* 142: 438–61.

Scarth, H.M. 1883 *Roman Britain*. (London).

—— 1887 Britain. A province of the Roman empire as treated in the history of Rome by Theodor Mommsen. *Archaeol J* 44: 351–64.

Schnapp, A. 1993 *The Discovery of the Past*. (Translated by I. Kinnes and G. Vandell, London 1999).

Schneider, F.D. 1952–3 Collingwood and the idea of history. *University of Toronto Quarterly* XXII: 172–83.

Schuchhardt, C.S. 1944 *Aus Leben und Arbeit*. (Berlin).

Schweizer, K.-W. 2004 Stuart, John, Third Earl of Bute. In Matthew and Harrison 2004 53: 173–9.

Scott, E. 1990 In search of Roman Britain: Talking about their generation. Review of Todd 1989. *Antiquity* 44: 953–6.

Scott-Fox, C. 2002 *Cyril Fox. Archaeologist Extraordinary*. (Oxford).

Shanks, C. 1996 *Classical Archaeology of Greece. Experiences of the Discipline*. (London).

Sharpe, H. 1910 *Britain BC as Described in Classical Writings with an Inquiry in to the Portions of the Cassiterides and Thule and an Attempt to Ascertain the Ancient Coast-Line of Kent and East Sussex*. (London).

Shaw, B.D. 1992 Under Russian eyes. *J Roman Stud* 82: 216–28.

Sherwood, J. 1973 *No Golden Journey. A Biography of James Elroy Flecker*. (London).

Shore, A.F. (ed.) 1985 *The School of Archaeology and Oriental Studies, University of Liverpool: Its History and its Collection*. (Private publication, Liverpool).

Simpson, F.G. 1913 Excavations on the line of the Roman Wall in Cumberland during the years 1909–1912. *Trans Cumberland Westmorland Antiq Archaeol Soc* NS XIII: 297–397.

—— 1926–8 The Roman camps at Cawthorn, near Pickering. Preliminary report 1923. *Yorkshire Archaeol J* 28: 25–33.

Simpson, G. 1976 *Watermills and Military Works on Hadrian's Wall. Excavations in Northumberland 1907–1913 by F.G. Simpson*. (Kendal).

—— 1996 Collingwood's philosophy of history. Observations of an archaeologist. *Collingwood Stud* 3: 217–25.

Slofstra, J. 1983 An anthropological approach to the study of romanization processes. In Brandt and Slofstra 1983: 71–104.

Smail, R. 2004 Richard Cornwallis Neville, 4th Baron Braybrooke (1820–1861). In Matthews and Harrison 2004 40 (Original entry by G.C. Boase): 538–9.

Smiles, S. 1994 *The Image of Antiquity. Ancient Britain and the Romantic Imagination*. (New Haven).

Smith, A.H. 1931 Thomas Ashby 1874–1931. *Proc Brit Acad* 17: 515–41.

Smith, R.A. 1922 *Guide to the Antiquities of Roman Britain in the Dept of British and Medieval Antiquities*. (London).

Snodgrass, A. 1985 The new archaeology and the classical archaeologist. *Am J Archaeol* 89: 31–7.

—— 1987 *The Archaeology of Greece*. (Berkeley).

—— 1999 Seperate tables. A story of two traditions within one discipline. In S. Altekamp, M.R. Hofter and M. Krumme (eds) *Posthumanistische klassiche Archäologie. Historizität und Wissenschaftlichkeit von Interessen und Methoden*. (Munich): 105–12.

—— 2002 Antiquity, Wheeler and Classical Archaeology. In Malone and Stoddart 2002: 1102–4.

Social Science Research Council on Acculturation 1954 Acculturation: An explanatory formulation. *American Anthropologist* 58: 249–63.

Sparrow, J. 1967 *Mark Pattison and the Idea of a University. The Clark Lectures 1965*. (Cambridge).

Stallybrass, W.T.S. 1939–40 Oxford in 1914–1918. *Oxford* 6/2 Winter: 31–52.

St George Gray, H. 1925 Obituary. Richard Hensleigh Walters. *Proc Somerset Archaeol Natural Hist Soc* LXXI: 122–3.

Stein, A.M. 1921 *Serindia. Report of Explorations in Central Asia and Westernmost China*. (Oxford).

Stephens, W.H. 1975 The curriculum. In P.H.J.H. Gosden and A.J. Taylor (eds) *Studies in the History of a University 1874–1974*. (Leeds): 247–310.

Stephenson, D. 1980 The early career of J.H. Round: the shaping of a historian. *Essex Archaeol Hist* 12: 1–10.

Stevenson, G.H. 1922 Some reflections on the teaching of Roman history. *J Roman Stud* 12: 192–206.

Stevenson, G.H. and Miller, S.N. 1911–12 Report on the excavation at the Roman fort at Cappuck, Roxburghshire. *Proc Soc Antiqs Scotland* 46: 446–83.

Stevenson, R.B.K. 1981 The museum, its beginning and its development. Pt. 2: The National Museum to 1954. In Bell 1981: 142–211.

Stiebing, W.H. 1993 *Uncovering the Past. The History of Archaeology*. (Oxford).

Stone, L. 1975 The size and composition of the Oxford student body 1500–1909. In Stone 1975a: 3–110.

Stone, L. (ed.) 1975a *The University in Society. Vol. 1. Oxford and Cambridge from the Fourteenth to the Early Nineteenth Century*. (Princeton)

Strachan Davidson, W.L. 1901 Mommsen's Roman Criminal Law. *English Hist Rev* 16: 219–91.

Stray, C. 1992 *The Living Word. W.H.D. Rouse and the Crisis of Classics in Edwardian England*. (Bristol).

—— 1998 *Classics Transformed. Schools, Universities and Society in England 1830–1960*. (Oxford).

Stroud, D. 1984 *Sir John Soane. Architect*. (London).

Stuart Jones, H. 1920 *Fresh Light on Roman Bureaucracy. An Inaugural Lecture*. (Oxford).

—— 1943–4 The foundation and history of the Camden chair. *Oxeniensia* VIII–IX: 169–92.

Stubbings, F.H. 1958 Alan John Bayard Wace (1879–1957). *Proc Brit Acad* 1958: 263–80.

Stürmer, M. 2000 *The German Empire 1871–1919*. (London).

Sweet, R. 2004 *Antiquaries: the Discovery of the Past in Eighteenth-Century Britain*. (London).

Symonds, R. 1986 *Oxford and Empire*. (London).

Taylor M.V. 1917 Woodeaton. J Roman Stud 7: 98-119.

—— 1920 F.J. Haverfield MA, D.Litt, LL.D, FBA, FSA. *J Chester Archaeol Hist Soc* XXIII: 64–71.

—— 1923 *The Roman Villa of North Leigh*. (Oxford).

—— 1939 Romano-British remains. *VCH Oxfordshire*. (London).

—— 1960 The Society for the Promotion of Roman Studies 1910–1960. *J Roman Stud* 50: 129–34.

Thomson, J.A.K. 1957 Gilbert Murray (1866–1957). *Proc Brit Acad* 43: 245–70.

Thomson de Grummond, N. 1996 *An Encyclopedia of the History of Classical Archaeology*. (two volumes; London).

Thornton, P. and Dorey, H. 1992 *A Miscellany of Objects from Sir John Soane's Museum, Consisting of Paintings, Architectural Drawings and Other Curiosities fro the Collection of Sir John Soane*. (Edinburgh).

Todd, M. 1989 *Research on Roman Britain 1960–1989*. Britannia Monograph Series No.11. (London).

—— 1994 A.L.F. Rivet (1915–1993). *Britannia* 25: ix.

—— 2003 The Haverfield Bequest: 1921–2000 and the study of Roman Britain. *Britannia* 34: 35–40.

Todd, R.B. (ed.) 2004 *The Dictionary of British Classicists Vol. 2 (G–N)*; (Bristol)

Tout, T.F. 1913–14 Thomas Hodgkin 1831–1913. *Proc Brit Acad 1913–1914*: 503–7.

Toynbee, A. 1954 *A Study of History*, Vol. X. (Oxford).

—— 1967 *Acquaintances*. (Oxford).

—— 1969 *Reminiscences*. (Oxford).

Toynbee, J.M.C. 1958 Review of Richmond 1957. *J Roman Stud* 48: 202.

Trigger, B.G. 1989 *A History of Archaeological Thought*. (Cambridge).

Turner, F.M. 1981 *The Greek Heritage in Victorian Britain*. (Yale).

—— 1986 British politics and the demise of the Roman republic, 1700–1939. *Hist J* 29: 577–99.

—— 1989 Why the Greeks and not the Romans in Victorian Britain? In G.W. Clarke (ed.) *Rediscovering Hellenism: The Hellenistic Inheritance and the English Imagination*. (Cambridge): 61–82.

Villiers, Lady de 1957 Headington Churches. In *VCH Oxfordshire V: Bullingdon Hundred*. (London): 165–7.

Vincent, E.W. and Hinton, P. 1947 *The University of Birmingham. Its History and Significance*. (Birmingham).

Vyner, B. (ed.) 1994 *Building on the Past. Papers Celebrating 150 Years of the Royal Archaeological Institute*. (London)

Wacher, J. and McWhirr, A. 1982 *Early Roman Occupation at Cirencester.* Cirencester Excavations I. (Cirencester).

Wallace, C. 1994 Donald Atkinson: a neglected Roman archaeologist. *Trans Bristol Gloucester Archaeol Soc* 103: 167–76.

—— 2002 Writing disciplinary history, or why Romano-British archaeology needs a biographical dictionary of its own. *Oxford J Archaeol* 21: 381–92.

Wallace-Hadrill, A. (ed.) 2001 *The British School at Rome. One Hundred Years.* (London).

Walters, H.B. 1899 *Catalogue of the Bronzes, Greek, Roman and Etruscan, in the British Museum.* (London).

—— 1903 *Catalogue of the Terracottas in the Dept of Greek & Roman Antiquities, British Museum.* (London).

—— 1939–40 *The English Antiquarians of the Sixteenth, Seventeenth and Eighteenth Centuries.* (London).

Walters, R.H. 1907 Ham or Hamdon Hill, South Somerset. Discovery of a Roman villa within the line of entrenchments and other finds of interest during 1907. *Proc Somerset Archaeol Natural Hist Soc* 53: 179–82.

Ward, J. 1903 *The Roman Fort at Gellygaer in the County of Glamorgan.* (London).

—— 1911a *The Roman Era in Britain.* (London).

—— 1911b *Romano-British Buildings and Earthworks.* (London).

—— 1916 The fortifications of Roman Caerwent. *Archaeol Cambrensis* 71: 1–36.

Ward, S.G.P. 1957 *A Study of the Administrative Problems in the Peninsula, 1809–1814.* (Oxford).

Ward, W.R. 1958 *Georgian Oxford. University Politics in the Eighteenth Century.* (Oxford).

—— 1997 From the Tractarians to the Executive Commission, 1845–1854. In Brock and Curthoys 1997: 306–38.

Warde Fowler, W. 1903 *An Oxford Correspondence.* (Oxford).

—— 1916 *Essays in Brief for War Time.* (Oxford).

—— 1920 Theodor Mommsen: His life and work. (Oxford): 250-268.

Waterhouse, H. 1986 *The British School at Athens. The First Hundred Years.* (London).

Watkins, W. Thompson 1883 *Roman Lancashire.* (Liverpool).

Weaver, J.C.H. (ed.) 1927 *Dictionary of National Biography 1922–1930.* (Oxford)

Webster, G. 1958 The Roman military advance under Ostorius Scapula. *Archaeol J* 115: 49–98.

—— 1970 The military situations in Britain between AD43 and 71. *Britannia* 1: 179–97.

—— 1980 *The Roman Invasion of Britain.* (London).

—— 1981 *Rome Against Caratacus. The Roman Campaigns in Britain AD48–58.* (London).

Webster, J. and Cooper, N. (eds) 1996 *Roman Imperialism. Post-Colonial Perspectives.* (Leicester).

Welford, R. and Hodgson, R.C. 1913 Cadwallader J. Bates. *Archaeol Aeliana* X: 292–6.

Wellings, Thomas R. 1911 Excavations, Roman Station, Llandridod Wells. *Archaeol Aeliana* XI: 411–20.

Wes, M.A. 1990 *Michael Rostovtzeff, Historian in Exile. Russian Roots in an American Context*. Historia Einzelschriften 65. (Stuttgart).

Westherall, D. 1994 From Canterbury to Winchester: the foundation of the Institute. In Vyner 1994: 8–21.

———— 1998 The growth of archaeological societies. In Brand 1998: 21–34.

Whatley, N. 1964 On the possibility of reconstructing Marathon and other ancient battles. *J Hellenic Stud* 84: 119–39.

Wheeler, R.E.M. 1922 Roman and native in Wales: An imperial frontier problem. *Trans Hon Soc Cymmodorion 1920–1921*: 40–96.

———— 1923 Review of Haverfield 1924. *J Roman Stud* 13: 207–8.

———— 1936 *RCAHM(E) Westmorland*. (London).

———— 1938 Mr Myres on Verulamium. *Antiquity* 12: 210–17.

———— 1939 Review of R.G. Collingwood and J.N.L. Myres' *Roman Britain and the English Settlements*. (Oxford; 2nd edit. 1937). *J Roman Stud* 29: 87–93.

———— 1955 Anniversary Address. *Antiqs J* 35: 153–61.

———— 1956 *Still Digging. Interleaves from an Antiquary's Notebook*. (London).

———— 1961 Review of the *J Roman Stud* 50 (1960) Jubilee Volume. *Antiquity* 35: 157–9.

———— 1965 (Richmond obituary). *Antiqs J* 45: ix–xi.

———— 1966 *Alms for Oblivion. An Antiquary's Scrapbook*. (London).

———— 1968 Review of I.A. Richmond's *Hod Hill Vol.2 Excavations Carried out Between 1951 and 1958* (London 1963). *Antiquity* 42: 149–50.

White, C. 1994 Museums and art galleries. In Harrison 1994b: 485–98.

White, R. and Barker, P. 1998 *Wroxeter. Life and Death of a Roman City*. (Stroud).

White, R.H. 1988 Mayer and British archaeology. In Gibson and Wright 1988: 118–36.

Whiteley, J.J.L. 1997 The University Galleries. In Brock and Curthoys 1997: 611–50.

Who Was Who n.d. Anderson, John George Clark. *Who Was Who 1951–1960*. (London).

Wickert, L. 1959–80 *Theodor Mommsen: eine Biographie*. (four volumes, Frankfurt).

Wickham-Legg, L.G. (ed.) 1949 *Dictionary of National Biography 1931–1940*. (Oxford).

Wiedemann, T. 1997 Mommsen's Roman History: Genesis and influence. <http://www.dur.ac.uk/~dkl0www/histos/1997/wiedemann.html> accessed 1 Nov. 2006.

Wilamowitz-Moellendorff, U. von 1982 *A History of Classical Scholarship*. (Transl. by H. Lloyd-Jones. London).

Wilkes, J.J. 1989 A prospect of Roman Britain. In Todd 1989: 245–50.

———— 2002 Review of Hingley 2000. *Public Archaeology* 2: 126–7.

Williamson, T. 1998 Questions of preservation and destruction. In P. Everson and T. Williamson (eds) *The Archaeology of Landscape: Studies Presented to Christopher Taylor*. (Manchester): 1–24.

Wilmott, T. 2001 *Birdoswald Roman Fort. 1800 Years on Hadrian's Wall*. (Stroud).

Wilson, D. 1987 *Gilbert Murray OM 1866–1957*. (Oxford).

Wilson, J. 1989 *Lawrence of Arabia. The Authorised Biography of T.E. Lawrence*. (London).

Winstanley, D.A. 1940 *Early Victorian Cambridge*. (Cambridge).

Winstone, H.V. 1990 *Woolley of Ur. The Life of Sir Leonard Woolley*. (London).

Winter, J.M. 1994 Oxford and the First World War. In Harrison 1994: 4–25.

Wiseman, T.P. 1981 The first director of the British school. *Pap Brit School Rome* 49: 144–63.

—— 1990 *A Short History of the British School at Rome*. (London).

Woodward, A.M. 1912 Review of Haverfield 1912a. *Archaeol J* 69: 373–4.

—— 1914 The antiquities from Lanuvium in the Museum at Leeds and elsewhere, Pt. 1 – Sculpture. *Pap Brit School Rome* VII: 63–92.

—— 1920 (Obituary). *Annual Bulletin of Historical Literature* 9: 7.

—— 1932–4 The Roman villa at Rudston (E. Yorks.). Interim excavation report. *Yorkshire Archaeol J* 31: 366–76.

Woodward, A.M. and Steer, K.A. 1936–8 The Roman villa at Rudston (E. Yorks.): Third interim report. The excavation of 1935. *Yorkshire Archaeol J* 33: 81–6.

Woodward, L. 1967 The rise of the professional historian in England. In K. Bourne and D.C. Watt (eds) *Studies in International History: Essays Presented to W. Norton Medlicott, Stevenson Professor of International History in the University of London*. (London).

Woolley, C.L. 1907 Corstopitum: Provisional report of the excavations in 1906. *Archaeol Aeliana³* III: 161–86.

—— 1953 *Spadework. Adventures in Archaeology*. (London).

—— 1962 *As I Seem to Remember*. (London).

Wright, R.P. (ed.) 1965 *Roman Inscriptions of Britain*. (Oxford).

York Powell, F. 1893 Review of Haverfield 1892b. *Class Rev* VII: 228–9.

Zouche Hall, R. De 1974 The origins of the Vernacular Architectural Group. *Vernacular Architecture* 5: 3–6.

INDEX

Abbeys 76, 86, 611

Abbotsholme School 384

Abercromby professorship 453

Abergele 414, 448

Aberystwyth 393, 451, 573

Act of Parliament 86

Acton, A. 405, 475

Adel 374, 382, 403

Agenda 1, 4, 12, 20, 44, 49, 131, 219, 228, 253, 254, 277, 336, 346, 433, 487, 506, 532, 535, 581, 583, 587, 624

Aiton, W. 23

Akerman, Rev. J.Y. 63

Alcock, L. 339, 453, 468

Aldershot 292, 624

Alnwick Castle 87

Altenwissenschaft 123, 124, 125, 126, 592

Altertumskunde 132

Ambleside 36, 266, 300, 403, 430, 538

Anatolia 148

Ancient Britons 57, 61, 509, 510, 511, 512, 524

Anderson, J.G.C. 160, 170, 202, 304, 334, 359, 372, 413

Anderson, W.B. 375, 402

Anderson, W.C.F. 298, 304, 318, 328, 333, 334, 343, 359, 371, 372, 373, 375, 377, 398, 402, 410, 413, 429, 430, 435, 436, 437, 440, 465, 466, 470, 476, 590, 621, 622

Anderson College 440

Anglican 25, 26, 50, 75, 98, 99, 103, 108, 109, 114, 126, 526

Anglo-Saxon England 217

Anglo-Saxons 49, 50, 71, 212, 217, 423, 509, 511, 524

Annexation 39

Anthropology 45, 46, 145, 167, 168, 169, 180, 185, 193, 391, 407, 423, 440, 447, 451, 454, 619

Antioch in Pisidia 373

Antiquarianism 5, 43, 44, 45, 49, 53, 54, 55, 56, 57, 58, 61, 62, 63, 64, 65, 69, 73, 76, 80, 91, 92, 93, 94, 122, 163, 204, 294, 337, 407, 423, 476, 506, 564, 586, 593, 594, 597, 601, 610, 617

Antiquarians 31, 36, 43, 48, 49, 55, 56, 58, 59, 62, 64, 66, 70, 73, 79, 91, 92, 93, 94, 95, 133, 136, 140, 158, 213, 218, 224, 226, 237, 248, 252, 256, 273, 274, 276, 296, 341, 342, 358, 390, 418, 420, 422, 433, 439, 444, 449, 470, 471, 473, 489, 508, 593, 594

Antiquaries Journal 83, 93, 395, 399, 546

Antiquity 9, 43, 46, 52, 56, 57, 63, 65, 73, 82, 88, 92, 93, 96, 116, 122, 123, 124, 126, 131, 151, 168, 171, 175, 176, 178, 179, 184, 188, 194, 197, 203, 205, 211, 219, 236, 237, 316, 336, 382, 424, 443, 446, 472, 497, 500, 514, 517, 557, 559, 560, 610, 611, 619

Antonine Wall 61, 65, 78, 227, 251, 258, 260, 261, 320, 345, 413, 421, 452

Appleton, C.A. 207

Appletree 260, 261, 262, 264, 273, 275, 278

Archaeologia 60, 73, 79, 82, 83, 160, 209, 211, 221, 222, 223, 242, 246, 257, 271, 282, 283, 284, 286, 289, 292, 293, 294, 297, 339, 367, 401, 464, 520

Archaeologia Scotica 57

Archaeological Institute of Great Britain and Ireland 82

Archaeological Journal 14, 17, 18, 60, 81, 82, 93, 159, 160, 162, 209, 210, 225, 226, 235, 248, 303, 321, 382, 475, 479

Archaeological Review 63, 64, 74, 80, 157, 160, 162, 209, 210

Armstrong College 38, 42, 276, 284,